Hypercrime

This book presents a new approach towards the interfaces between technology, contemporary crime and regulation. It argues that the conclusion adopted by most criminal justice practitioners and criminologists since the 1990s – that a distinct field of policy and theory referred to as 'cybercrime' has emerged – is flawed on both empirical and theoretical grounds. Not only is this a construction which depends upon a plethora of dubious statistics, it understates the role of State and corporate actors in the production of crimes online. Worse, this 'cybercrime paradigm' offers indirect justification for the increasing acquisition of new powers by governments, so furthering what has elsewhere been characterised as the 'control society'.

Offering a spatial analysis of harms effected by technology, this book situates contemporary crime and its control within longer term historical developments which serve to extend the human body. Characterising the new geometries of social interaction that result in terms of a process referred to as 'hyperspatialisation', the book argues that a concept of hypercrime becomes an equally plausible interpretation of the effect of technologies which 'compress' distance – most obviously the internet or the mobile phone system. Hypercriminalities emerge from a hyperspatial world by way of what McLuhan once called its 'allatonceness' – where the (real) possibilities of ever present, remote harms combine with inflated perceptions of their danger. In such a world not only do credit card frauds, online predators or viruses threaten to harm us, so too do the measures that we create to control them.

Dr Michael McGuire teaches in the Department of Applied Social Studies at London Metropolitan University.

Hypercrime

The new geometry of harm

Michael McGuire

Routledge·Cavendish
Taylor & Francis Group
a GlassHouse book

First published 2007
by Routledge-Cavendish
2 Park Square, Milton Park, Abingdon, Oxon, OX14 4RN

Simultaneously published in the USA and Canada
by Routledge-Cavendish
270 Madison Ave, New York, NY 10016

A GlassHouse book

*Routledge-Cavendish is an imprint of the Taylor & Francis Group, an
informa business*

© 2007 Michael McGuire

Typeset in Times by
RefineCatch Limited, Bungay, Suffolk
Printed and bound in Great Britain by
Biddles Ltd, King's Lynn

British Library Cataloguing in Publication Data
A catalogue record for this book is available from the British Library

Library of Congress Cataloging-in-Publication Data
McGuire, Michael, Dr.
   Hypercrime : the new geometry of harm / by Michael McGuire. –
1st ed.
      p. cm.
   ISBN-13: 978–1–904385–53–0 (pbk.)
   ISBN-10: 1–904385–53–2 (pbk.)
   ISBN-13: 978–1–904385–93–6 (hardback)
   ISBN-10: 1–904385–93–1 (hardback)
   [etc.]
   1. Computer crimes. 2. Cyberspace–Social aspects.
3. Cyberspace–Government policy. 4. Criminology. I. Title.
   HV6773.M384 2007
   3664.16′8–dc22   2007026858

ISBN10: 1–904385–53–2 (pbk)
ISBN10: 1–904385–93–1 (hbk)
eISBN10: 0–203–93952–2 (ebk)

ISBN13: 978–1–904385–53–0 (pbk)
ISBM13: 978–1–904385–93–6 (hbk)
eISBN13: 978–0–203–93952–9 (ebk)

Contents

Acknowledgements

I am grateful to Beverley Brown and Colin Perrin at Routledge-Cavendish for seeing the potential of this book and for continuing to support it through some radical shifts in perspective. Thanks are also due to Simon Hallsworth for more of those conversations during its gestation. Thanks, too, to colleagues at London Metropolitan University – to Brian Hall, for departmental support and to Janet Ransom and Sam Whimster, for reading sections. Thanks to John Jenkins of the Spark Museum for granting permission to use the photograph of the Collins 'wireless' phone on page 69. Special acknowledgements are extended to Michelle Salamon for help with some of the diagrams and to Phil Latham, Joe Fox and John Ronayne at *Industry* for their idiosyncratic insights into the workings of the information technology industry. Finally, thanks to Jenny. She knows why.

Introduction

Crime, 'cybercrime' and hypercrime

In early 1991 filming began on the world's first 'virtual reality' film – the *Lawnmower Man*. The tale of a simple gardener, transformed by 'smart drugs' and virtual reality technology, into a vengeful genius (tagline '*God made him simple. Science made him a god*') did not appeal to the public merely in virtue of offering the first 'virtual sex' – though that no doubt helped. Nor was it just the special effects. Though they were nice. The film contained a subliminal warning: 'Here is a modern Frankenstein' it said, one that was being created under our very noses. And, as usual, it was all the consequence of our meddling with the unknown – this time a hitherto unexplored brave new world called 'cyberspace'. 'There be monsters' was to be inscribed upon its map – a warning to proceed with extreme caution into any world that has such creatures in it.

In January of the same year the Computer Science and Telecommunications Board of the USA issued a report. The opening summary made for some chilling reading:

> We are at risk. Increasingly, America depends on computers. They control power delivery, communications, aviation, and financial services. They are used to store vital information, from medical records to business plans to criminal records. Although we trust them, they are vulnerable – to the effects of poor design and insufficient quality control, to accident, and perhaps most alarmingly, to deliberate attack. The modern thief can steal more with a computer than with a gun. Tomorrow's terrorist may be able to do more damage with a keyboard than with a bomb.
> To date, we have been remarkably lucky.
>
> (CSTB, 1991, p. 7)

Meanwhile, events taking place in the Swiss Alps were apparently about to confirm the worst nightmares of the CSTB. Tim Berners Lee, a British scientist employed at the CERN laboratory near Geneva, had worked out a better way of using the primitive network of computers which then existed. A simple, but universal language of 'hyperlinks' imposed across it would not only ease the accessing of information there but, by extension, increase the number of people using it. There was nothing intrinsically new about the connections themselves since they already existed. Indeed, there was nothing all that different about a computer network either – it was really only the telephone system with some fancier features. But, at a stroke, the accessing and sharing of information between computers across the globe was about to move from the realm of the specialist into the domain of the public – with all the uncertainties that implied.

Elsewhere in 1991, the Central Bank of Nigeria (CBN) issued an announcement. They had become increasingly deluged with complaints and requests for information about what appeared to be a 'new' fraud – one involving the transfer of money to Nigeria in return for new contracts, offshore banking benefits or other rewards. As a result of contacts established over postal and fax communications networks 'millions' of dollars had apparently been transferred and subsequently defrauded (James, 1991; Fagan 1991; Reuter Library Report, 1991). In its statement the CBN protested: 'The bank has no knowledge or record whatsoever of the purported claims or transfers, or even the related alleged contracts' (cited in Mikkelson & Mikkelson, 2003).

In fact the fraud was already a tried and trusted one with recorded variants dating from at least the sixteenth century (Caslon, 2006). But the point was that it *seemed* new and that was enough. The postal network had provided a traditional resource, the fax network a slightly newer one and the reach of the fraudster was about to be extended still further. For them, this new communications network would provide some useful additional opportunities, but was otherwise no more than another kind of day at the office. For the public however, what seemed to be a paradigmatically contemporary crime was about to unfold.

In the years following 1991 there seemed to be little doubt about the correct way to piece together the emergence of a cyberspace, an 'internet', the actions of a few chancers in remote locations and the alarming predictions of the CSTB. A new breed of risk, facilitated by the advent of computers linked globally into this new 'world wide web', had emerged. In turn, the analysis of crime and criminal behaviour had become confronted by the need for a major paradigmatic shift. For in addition to crimes committed in the familiar physical world, a new species – the 'cybercrime' – now seemed to have emerged. Such crime, it seemed, was a direct outcome of our entry in the space where simple people (like the Lawnmower Man) could be transformed into a nightmare of Promethean proportions. Certainly this 'cyberspace' appeared to have some amazing properties. It was not just 'antispatial' (Mitchell, 1995), it seemed to involve whole new forms of experience where the 'virtual' would sit beside and in many cases replace the 'real'. It was, we were told, a 'landscape of rational magic' (Novak, 1992, p. 226), one which offered 'the ultimate fantasies of both individual immortality and collective transcendence' (Jordan, 1999, p. 187). But it was also a place that was; 'rife with ambiguity, paradox and contradiction' (Lyon, 2002, p. 24). For every heaven needs its hell. And so this new space had its inevitable dark side. Cyberspace, we were warned, created 'unprecedented opportunities for crime' (Grabosky & Smith, 2001, p. 29) and 'infinitely new possibilities to the deviant imagination' (Jewkes, 2002, p. 2), one that was likely to lead to the complete 'transform-ation of crime in an information age' (Wall, 2007). Such crime not only posed 'today's greatest threat to consumers' (Symantec, 2006) but, it was argued, '... no area of criminal activity has greater global implications than crime involving technology and computers' (Reno, 1997).

Long before the arrival of the internet proper, in one of the earliest books on computer crime, Donn Parker had argued that computer technologies do not 'appreciably change the number of dishonest people and the opportun-ities for them to act' (Parker, 1976, p. 295). Thus, while there might be 'an arms race between organised crime and law enforcement agencies . . . increas-ing the security of computer systems will prove to be no different in effect from security associated with manual systems of the past' (ibid.). Parker predicted that the use of computers in criminal activities would inevitably increase as computer use widened. But he also suggested that it would be just as likely that adequate security would ultimately contain the problem. The synergising of computers into the internet and the world wide web seemed to force a re-evaluation of Parker's relatively sober discussion. For not only did a distinction have to be made for 'digital' crime (Barrett, 1997) but also for 'virtual crime'. And such a development questioned, 'not only the law as a whole, but criminological theory beyond even criminal law' (Capeller, 2001, pp. 240/1). Without this new paradigm, or the capacity to distinguish between the 'pure' cybercrimes and the 'not so pure' ones (Wall, 2005) it seemed that we were, 'likely to be left with a state of virtual chaos' (Capeller, 2001).

Beyond their task of *identifying* this new form of criminal behaviour, crim-inal justice practitioners and criminologists were also forced to ask what kinds of resources could be used to regulate and control cybercrime. A diffi-cult job, it seemed. Given how the internet had so 'broken down' traditional limitations of the State and policing structures, it seemed possible to inquire whether this cyberspace was a regulable space at all. Yet what an admirable response there was to this call to arms. By 1999 'cybercrime' offences could be prosecuted at the Federal level under at least 40 different criminal statutes (Hatcher *et al.*, 1999), provision supplemented by extensive State legislation (Brenner, 2001) and the US Government was funding the 'war' against cyber-crime to the tune of nearly $110 million annually. Janet Reno's request to raise this budget by a (relatively modest) $37 million was of course to be radically increased in the aftermath of 9/11 (Reno, 2000). With that amount of investment, research and government mobilisation, how could there be any doubt about the reality of cybercrime as a new criminal phenomenon, or the grave seriousness of the threat to society it posed?

But 1991 saw other ways in which computer technologies were being used to dispense harm remotely. At almost around the same time as the US research council issued their report (on 16 January) a massive aerial bombardment against Iraq commenced. Using intelligent missiles, linked by satellite, Baghdad was subjected to the first 'smart bombing'. In cities around the world, people settled down with their dinner to watch this display of faraway pyrotechnics, convinced that such remote technologies were in the process of transforming war forever. The death of over 300 people, mainly civilians, who were incinerated in an air raid shelter at Amiriyah one evening in February was one of a few inconvenient and quickly forgotten sidenotes in this tale of progress. Smart bombs, by and large, never 'missed'. After just 100 hours of ground fighting, Kuwait was liberated, and, on 3 March a ceasefire was declared. A new world order governed by benign warfare where no one 'really' got killed had emerged. 'And the world knew it because of CNN' (Volkmer, 1999, p. 146). For the first time, there was a 24-hour-a-day, live connection to the rest of the world. Slaughtered at a distance, while being watched at a distance, over 200,000 dead Iraqis – among them thousands of children (Daponte, 1993) – had made their own privileged contribution to the newly connected world of 1991.

Elsewhere in the same year, the FBI were holding a series of secret meetings with EU officials to try to persuade them to conform to standards proposed in a new piece of legislation that was in the course of being drafted – the Communications Assistance for Law Enforcement Act or CALEA (Campbell, D., 1999; Walton, 2001, section 6). When it was eventually passed in 1994, US communications companies faced a radically new form of responsibility. Henceforth, any device which facilitated social interaction at a distance was legally required to be designed in such a way that those interactions could also be intercepted by law enforcement agencies. Specifically, terrestrial phone companies, cellular phone services and all other telecom equipment manufacturers were to ensure that the services they offered enabled the government '. . . to intercept . . . all wire and oral communications carried by the carrier . . . concurrently with their transmission' (CALEA, 1994–47, USC sec 103). This was an innocent enough piece of securitization according to the FBI, for such laws were essential 'to preserve law enforcement's ability to conduct lawfully-authorized electronic surveillance while preserving public safety' (AskCALEA, 2006). But this less than comforting reassurance obscured a more fundamental watershed moment. For the first time in history, social interaction itself was to be made subordinate to the needs of the criminal justice system. The fact that the social interactions in question were being conducted *remotely* appeared to make this a 'natural' and obvious necessity, even though remote social interaction had been going on for a lot longer than since the arrival of the internet – or the FBI for that matter. But the FBI didn't have to lean too hard upon the Europeans for them to fall into line. And they were pretty confident that with a lot of shiny new communication toys to play with, the public wouldn't raise too much of a fuss either. After all, as they had pointed out in a 1991 statement before the House Committee on Appropriations:

> In the long term, digital telephone technology will enhance the FBI's ability to collect, share and analyze information. Many of these enhancements will come without any FBI development effort, driven by consumer demand.
>
> (FBI, 1992, cited in Dempsey, 1997)

Meanwhile communications networks were also circulating experiences of events less obviously helpful to these new ruling classes of remote interaction. In early March 1991, during a demonstration of their idiosyncratic approach to crime control, members of the LAPD set about an unemployed construction worker called Rodney King in a darkened Los Angeles suburb. A 50,000-volt Taser stun gun was fired at the unarmed black man, while three officers took turns kicking him and smashing him in the head, neck, kidneys and legs with their truncheons. King suffered 11 fractures in his skull, a crushed cheekbone, a broken ankle, internal injuries, a burn on his chest and some brain damage. Unfortunately for the LAPD however, their dispensings of criminal justice were also being filmed by a member of the public. Within a few hours the video he shot was being viewed across American TV stations. Within a day, it was being watched around the world (*Time*, 25/03/1991).

You would be hard pressed to find a discussion of this wider set of events from 1991 in any text on cybercrime. However in this book I want to argue that it is *only* by adopting this wider perspective that the real order of threat, if any, which has followed from the networking of computers can be appreciated. But to see this we will need to revisit the perceptions that made the ontological muddle of a cyberspace appear so attractive. For the pseudo-distinction between a 'real' space and a 'virtual' space' (cf. Lessig, 1999, p. 10) is a potentially deadly one. Not only does it threaten to mislead us about the true relation between any reconfigurations in criminal behaviours like theft or assault and networked communication, there is a real sense in which appeals to cyberspaces or to uncritical notions of cybercrimes threaten to blur the major reconstitutions of power and control and their effects upon the perception of deviance that are taking place before our very eyes. As one of the most widely published of the contemporary threats which require the dispensation of special powers, the very idea of cybercrime is, I shall argue, deeply implicated in this process.

Cyberspace – as practically every writer on the subject never failed to remind us – was a concept originating in fiction. The project of constructing a criminology upon such a basis might not therefore seem to have been the most sensible of methodological choices. As this book will contest, any transitions in social interaction that can be attributed to the advent of computer networks have been anticipated many times in history. But on no previous occasion has there been any need felt for a theoretical accommodation for schismatic breaks between 'realities' to be made as a result. Rather, as McLuhan (1964) long ago pointed out, each such transition has simply involved an *extension* to the possibilities of the social reality we already inhabit. And with any reordering of social relations comes opportunities for exploiting them that may be not wholly conducive to the public good. So, if it is transitions to social *interaction* which really lie at the core of the (ostensibly) novel forms of criminal behaviour networked computing has brought, it might be better to concentrate attention upon these interactions rather than getting sidetracked by the technology.

None of this need entail denying that there is something of interest and importance going on with the way that crime and criminality is unfolding as a result of computing per se, or networked computers more generally. But it certainly adds nothing to our understanding of this process to mechanically prefix any behaviour that seems to result with the term 'cyber'. If then the idea of a 'cyberspace' is theoretically questionable and the construct of cybercrime empirically suspect, what other approaches to computer-related crime might be of use? There can clearly be no *single* way of dealing with the range of issues raised for criminology by such technologies. But one more obvious stance is suggested if we focus more clearly upon the 'space' in 'cyberspace'. For what does seem significant in all the many and varied reflections upon cyberspace is the way that a certain kind of *experience* of interaction through space is brought to the fore. And such experience relates to the way that computer networks are apparently able to extend the spatial range and character of social interaction. The concept of the network is of course something of a key concept in the social sciences these days (Castells, 1997; van Dijk, 2006) but it would be as mistaken to overplay its significance as it would be to single out computers. Transport and communication technologies have, in senses that will be explored more fully later, always provided 'networked' social interaction. The reason why the network has come so much to the attention of theorists of late seems more to do with their contemporary scale than with their novelty per se. Other concepts of space and interaction, beyond the network, must also therefore be invoked if there is to be anything very new or illuminating in the analysis.

As I will argue then, the result of changes in our experience of space goes beyond a more intimately *connected* social world. We arrive at the state of what MacLuhan once called the 'brand new world of allatonceness' (1967, p. 63), a world where unprecedented forms of continuity in our spatial and temporal experience become the norm. For want of a better word I shall think of this medium of 'allatonceness' as the kind of *hyperspace* which Frederic Jameson associated with our conceptual life in late modernity, something he took to reflect the 'incapacity of our minds, at least at present, to map the great global multinational and decentred communicational network in which we find ourselves caught as individual subjects' (Jameson, 1991, p. 44). But the hyperspace I describe is no mere conceptual gap, but an experiential framework. For not only is every point of interaction within it potentially multiply connected, such exchanges increasingly operate beyond the constraints of 'traditional' space. This then is not the ontological fragmentation suggested by the construct of a cyberspace – a space distinct from 'normal' space. Instead hyperspace is both continuous with and produced out of 'normal' space. It therefore retains all the more limited forms of spatial interaction at its core – while simultaneously extending and complexifying them. This process – one that I will refer to throughout as *hyperspatialisation* – may have come more fully to our attention with recent technologies, most obviously the internet, but it is a process with a long historical period of gestation.

Seeing the effects upon criminal behaviour in terms of hyperspatialisation emphasises what some writers on cybercrime have already suggested (see for example Grabosky, 2001) – that the advent of computers does not produce 'new' crime but simply expands *already extant* deviant possibilities. The expansion is however a significant one, precisely because this process of hyperspatialisation has now reached a crucial juncture. For with it now comes a significant mutation in what Marx thought of as the 'production of subjectivity' (Read, 2002), a transformation of our perceptions and beliefs about the social order and its threats. Some of these perceptions are rooted in real conditions of social change that the hyperspatial produces. But some are not. As the seeming allatonceness of an 'everywhere-crime' permeates these expanded social relations, the feeling grows that nowhere is really safe, that everyone is potentially threatening and that threats may come from anywhere, at anytime. This world of 'catastrophic imagination' as Ericson has recently described it (2007, p. 215) produces its own, unique order of potential harm.

Whilst labels can be as misleading as they are helpful, I shall argue that we might just as well mark this transition in terms of a shift towards *hypercrime* as towards cybercrime. It is a situation of multiple modalities. There are the real harms which emerge from criminal exploitations of increased connectivity and complexified social relations. There are the causal dynamics which typify complex systems that produce chaotic flows of information, able to ripple and grow exponentially from the most insignificant of causes (Hayles, 1991; Shermer 1995). And there are the profound psychological consequences of both of these facts – the parallel inflation in our *fears* and expectations of harm. This then is not hypercrime in the sense of Pinkerton (1995), who used the term to describe what he saw as inexorably rising levels of deviance, a process which threatened the very structure of society. Rather, this is a hypercrime that is spatially rooted and which emerges specifically from the interactive possibilities of a hyperspace. Yet the subtext of Pinkerton's dystopian vision implicitly reflects one underlying psychosis of the hypercrime society. His prediction of an impending collapse of free-market societies, riven by social inequality and permanently expanding crime rates, reflects many current perceptions of an 'everywhere' crime world requiring all pervasive social controls to preserve us from disaster. Like Burrough's 'inter-zone' – that 'composite city where all human potentials are spread out in a vast silent market' (1959) – in hyperspace, everywhere reaches everywhere, and every point within this global lattice has the potential to cause damage.

The role of spatiality in understanding the production and perception of criminal behaviour will accordingly form one of the central theoretical approaches in this book. Whilst, as we will discuss in the following chapter, space has often been invoked (sometimes with brilliant insight) in crimin-ology, it does not always take the *central* explanatory role it merits. Foucault, whose insights upon the relationship between space and crime were ground-breaking enough, was still concerned that the absence of developed spatial analysis represented a major gap in his work. For it was here that his analysis of power, control and with that, deviance, seemed to increasingly centre:

> . . . the longer I continue, the more it seems to me that the formation of discourses and the genealogy of knowledge needs to be analysed . . . in terms of tactics and strategies of power . . . deployed through implant-ations, distributions, demarcations, control of territories and organiza-tions of domains.
>
> (Foucault, 1980, p. 77)

Taking this lead I hope to thereby avoid some of the red herrings that arise from the postulation of *cyber*spaces while acknowledging the affect of spatial experience upon deviance and our perceptions of this.

Harm in hyperspace

The effects of technologies upon our experience of space and time (Innis, 1951), have been variously discussed in terms of 'time-space compression' (Harvey, 1989), 'speed' (Virilio, 1977), 'mobility' (Thrift, 1995) or the 'death of distance' (Cairncross, 1997). Whatever the nuance, there is general agree-ment that a new kind of society, based on information as a commodity, which deploys the network as an organisational metaphor and is dynamically inter-related by 'flows' as a form of economic production and energy (Sassen, 2001; Lash, 2002), is in the process of formation. Whether we locate such a transformation in terms of modernity, radical post-modernity or some other construct is of no major import here. What *is* of interest is the expansionary affect upon social *possibility* produced as a practical outcome of these hyper-spatialisation processes.

For the theorist of 'cybercrime' it has been the possibility of having a credit card cloned or being harassed in a chat room that represent the most obvious negative outcomes of such expansions. But however disturbing such experiences may be, an exclusive focus upon them has tended to divert attention away from more subtle and far-reaching kinds of harm. In particular, one crucial effect of the synergy between 'everywhere' crime in the material and subjective sense involves the transition from Foucault's idea of a disciplinary order to what Deleuze (1992) and more recently Bogard (1996, 2006) describe as the 'society of control'. This concept, only partially developed by Deleuze before his death, has important convergences with views developed by other criminologists and social theorists (Beniger, 1986; Cohen, 1985; Zuboff, 1988; Garland, 2001). Not only does the idea of a control society help clarify the more subtle forms of harm that go with this spatial shift, it can also throw light upon how the term 'crime' is deployed and redeployed as a mode of reinforcing power. For the production of control and control resources becomes, like hyperspatialised crime, an 'everywhere' phenomenon.

The increasingly pervasive range of control mechanisms seem profoundly linked to these mutations in the experience of space and time. Their legitimisation derives much from how we are perceived, how we perceive others and how we seek to quantify and manage the risks which the new modes of spatio-temporal occupation seem to generate. The centrality of spatial explanations is evident in Deleuze's own characterisation of the shift from a disciplinary to a control order. He talks specifically of the 'generalised crisis in relation to all the environments of enclosure – prison, hospital, factory, school and family' (Deleuze, 1992, p. 1), a crisis which amounts to precisely an *opening up* of space into the vistas of a new kind of continuum – a crisis, in other words, of the hyperspatial. The 'rhizomatic' form (Deleuze & Guatarri, 1988), which characterises Deleuze's conceptions of the articulation of control orders, characterises the available pathways. Indeed, as an oppositional metaphor to enclosed space the rhizome is the contemporary topology par excellence – for an indivisible, branching, continuum space is exactly that of the open-ended network. And such a topology certainly presents as many opportunities for control harms as it does for those which result from fraudulent credit card transactions. As we will see, both forms of harm are in fact interrelated – to such an extent indeed that it may be dangerous to attempt to understand one without understanding the other. Controls in this model are, as Deleuze puts it, a 'modulation' (1992, p. 2) where each point is a potential point for the enactment of control. The implications of this rhizomatic fusion of deviance and control results in a geometry of harm that has some novel aspects.

Methods and approaches

An approach purporting to relate a reordering of spatial experience to a reordering of deviant behaviour needs some account of its method. One that follows naturally enough from a 'geometrical' account of harm centres upon quasi-axiomatisation – a set of principles, however qualified, which serve to identify the generalisable ingredients of deviant acts as they move from space into hyperspace. The scheme that will be pursued here, one that takes its lead from Foucault's geography, focuses upon these relations between movement, spatial occupation and transgression. Three basic forms of transgressive occupations – what I will call *incursions* – then serve to map classes of deviant behaviours as they occur and reoccur over different spatial orders:

1   *Simple incursion* – An undesired entry to a space (for example, acts of trespass or surveillance).
2   *Degradative or damaging incursion* – An undesired entry to a space which results in harmful effects towards it (for example, an assault – damage to the space occupied by a body).
3   *Destructive incursion* – An undesired entry to a space which results in its permanent destruction (for example, murder – the permanent destruction of the space of a body).

The cybercrime literature often hints at a recognition of this way of constructing deviance. For example, Wall (2001, p. 3) sets out a concept of 'cybertrespass' – deviant behaviours that involve boundary violations as varied as hacking or website defacement. This concept of incursion acquires a more practical relevance when coupled with a further one – the idea that there can be different *orders* of social space. For example, given spaces such as the 'personal' or the 'propertied', criminal acts from robbery to sexual assault then form classes of damaging incursion to these spaces.

   To supplement this view of deviant actions as negative movements, three further assumptions about criminality will be utilised as methodological principles. The first, which should already be evident, is that a key point of departure for any criminology involves a 'zemiology' (Hillyard *et al.*, 2004), an identification of *harms* and the way that culpability for these may (or may not) be recognised within criminal justice systems. Developing a workable concept of harm has been a task pursued within legal theory, most fully in Joel Feinberg's writings on the subject (1984, 1986, 1988) and in criminology by writers such as Hillyard. Feinberg's concept of harm has substantial continuities with the class of movements set out above in that he considers 'three possible senses of the word "harm": harm as damage, harm as set-back to interests, and harm as wronging' (Stewart, 2002, p. 51). The well-recognised difficulties with this idea of a 'set-back to interests' and more broadly with the concept of harm itself will be discussed in the following chapter. In the meantime, it is worth noting that there are some clear advantages to it as well. There is the fact that the juridical sense of 'crime' is often in limited and self-interested hands, a fact that leaves many outcomes which seem to involve harm to individuals outside of the capacity of law to so judge them. In particular, the effects of hyperspatialisation have very often seemed to outstrip the capacity of legal systems to 'keep up' with certain behaviours eventually deemed to be illegal. The viewing of child pornography stored digitally, an act which remained legal in the UK for some time, is one notorious example. The concept of harm therefore offers a more flexible and politically neutral approach to mapping out the negative affects of hyperspatialisation processes than staying strictly within the bounds of criminal law. And while there may be gaps between perceptions of harm and principles of criminal law there are also key continuities in the recognition of actions seen as harmful (most obviously the destructive incursive movement to body space defined as murder).

A second structuring assumption that follows from this will be that we generally accept *ordering relations* to our sense of what is harmful and that, in spatial terms, these ordering relations relate to spaces of varying importance to us. The ordering of harm – the concept of 'crime seriousness' – is clearly an important construct in justice systems around the world and while, as von Hirsch and Jareborg (1991, pp. 1–2) remind us, 'the jurisprudence of crime seriousness is a topic that has scarcely been touched', the question of how to assess this 'has been gaining importance in recent years, with the increasing influence of desert orientated or "proportionalist" conceptions of sentencing – conceptions which make the severity of punishment depend principally on the gravity of the offence of conviction' (ibid). In what follows there will be no concerted attempt to set out a definitive sense of 'relative gravity' since this is not really what is at stake here. Rather the approach will be to recognise a *primary* space which we wish to legally safeguard from destructive or damaging incursion – the space of the body – and to set out spaces of harm that appear to have an orbit about this. The relative seriousness of harms can then be grounded in this primal space for, as Alistair MacIntyre (1999, p. 8) has pointed out, if 'human identity is primarily, if not only bodily . . . it is by reference to that identity that the continuities of our relationships to others are partly defined'.

The relation of other harms to bodily harm can then be organised around an order of spaces articulated in terms of their *proximity* or distance from the body. For example, most immediate to this ur-space of our body and identity there seems to be a broader region which contains a range of resources that *sustain* the body – resources we frequently like to claim as 'our own'. At the most remote, or 'furthest' proximity from our bodies is the broadest (communal) space at which social life operates – the 'global' social and cultural fabric in which societies of all forms are collectively embedded. This 'secondary' level of social grouping (as defined by Park and Burgess, 1921) complements a more immediate space of sociality – one bounded by 'local' concerns such as the stability of our family, work and sources of sustenance.

An advantage of this conceptual model is that we do not need to consider such spaces in terms of the immediately physical. Since hyperspatialisation processes appear to complexify social spaces, the model allows for consideration of bodily spaces, or property spaces which are extended – as I will term it 'distributed' – in a manner that can, at first, appear abstract. The distributed body, like these other extensions to social spaces, is as much subject to harms and normative concerns as the more spatially delimited versions we are familiar with. Such abstractions have sometimes appeared to strand us within a realm of the 'virtually' criminal (Williams, 2006) ostensibly distinct from physical harms. But though their wider distributions may open them up to more subtle harms, the immediate social spaces of our everyday experience always remain to ground this.

Georg Simmel, whose writings on the continuities between space and social experience will form an important influence throughout what follows, was clear that we should be wary of making any glib association between experience *ordered* by space and experience *caused* by space. Discussing the role of spatial variables such as size, concentration, dispersal, mobility and stability in the conceptualisation of social formations like kingdoms he warned that, 'the necessary spatial involvement of all these constellations . . . runs the danger of being confused with their affective causes' (Simmel, 1997, p. 138). I hope to avoid any such easy association here. Rather it is in the changes to spatial *experience* where the effects upon deviant possibilities and our fears of these will be located. Yet it is also true that causal relations between spatial facts and deviant behaviours have been posited in criminological analyses from the work of the Chicago School through to contemporary thinking on situational crime prevention. So neither will causal associations be totally ruled out.

In what follows then, I will consider criminal behaviour in terms of its extensions across the new spaces of possibility presented by an increasingly hyperspatialised society. Such behaviour and its extensions will be conceptualised in terms of certain fundamental kinds of *movements* through space and hyperspace. The condition of 'hypercrime' which emerges is the product of an inseparable conjunction of material factors produced by the enhanced remote interactivity of contemporary communication and its associated subjective experiences. A new manifold of harm emerges, an essential ingredient of which are, as Deleuze (1992, p. 2) puts it: 'forms of control (that) . . . are inseparable variations, forming a system of varying geometry whose language is digital'.

Outline

The plan and order of this book will correspond to the outline of the above schema. Chapter 1 will set out the main theoretical presumptions of this model, in particular relationships between crime and space and how the concept of hyperspatialisation may impinge here. The idea that deviant acts can be analysed in terms of differing modes of spatial occupation will be explored more fully. Chapter 2 will set out some historical and technological backgrounds to this process of hyperspatialisation and show how the role of contemporary technologies such as the internet or satellite communications form but one part of an ongoing historical reorganisation of spatial experience. Chapter 3 considers how the most immediate proximity we experience – the space delineated by our bodies that I will call, simply, 'proximity 0' – is extended under the hyperspatial, and what kinds of harmful effects may follow from this. Chapter 4 considers the kinds of threat hyperspatialisation may facilitate to the succeeding proximity, that space constituted by what sustains us and which we often think of as the location of our 'property'. Chapter 5 considers the region in which bodies and their properties are embedded – the immediate locality that we think of as a 'familiar', or local space. The chapter will explore whether, as ingredients of this local community such as the family, the experience of friendship places of work and leisure are 'redistributed' by the hyperspatial, they may also become subject to new harms. Chapter 6 extends the analysis to what appears to be the most distant proximity in orbit about the body and to the harms that hyperspatialisation may bring to this 'global' level of political, and civic life. Finally, in Chapter 7 the important question of transitions to control under hyperspatialisation will be considered more closely. Central to the analysis here will be the idea that social spaces are 'shaped' by the actions of control agents and mechanisms such as the CJS, the commercial sphere, or deeper 'invisible' normative presumptions. In this shaping of social space harm may also emerge, for not every shaping distributes the capacity to move freely or invisibly in equal ways. In what follows I hope that by reconsidering the effect of new communications technologies in terms of a few simple principles of spatial experience such as these, some light, however limited, may be thrown upon the new geometries of harm that come with them.

Chapter 1

Crime and space

Space is a practiced place.

(De Certeau, 1984, p. 117)

Human lives are decisively shaped by the spatio-temporal medium in which they move and express themselves culturally. The implications of this have been increasingly emphasised by a number of contemporary social theorists who have drawn upon the seminal work of writers such as Simmel (1997), Inis (1962), McLuhan (1964), Harvey (1989), Lefebvre (1991), Virilio (1977) and others to develop our understanding of the ways in which these influences might operate. Simmel's examinations of the sociology of space attempted to sketch an outline of what he called a 'social geometry' which utilised variables such as distance, proximity, boundary, movement and clustering in order to theoretically ground social interaction. His argument that 'the sensory proximity or distance between people who stand in some relationship to one another' will affect the 'liveliness of sociological interactions' (Simmel, 1997, p. 151) provides a simple example of the way social interaction appears to be necessarily bounded by certain basic spatial constraints. Communication with someone requires their ears or eyes to be within a fixed auditory or visual range; touching someone requires that their bodies be within a 2–3-foot radius; perceiving objects requires that they be presented in space as having a certain shape, a certain degree of tactile resistance, a certain degree of optical transparency and so on. Likewise, to act or do anything at all requires that act to have a duration – the length of time required to complete it. Whilst the role of spatial constraints such as proximity in experiencing phenomena like 'neighbourliness' or 'foreignness' is, as Simmel (1997, p. 138) reminds us, strongly related to 'psychological contents', there are many interactions 'realised in such a way that the spatial form in which this happens justifies special emphasis'.

However one reads the role of spatiality – in psychological or physical terms, as something determining *of* or determined *by* social interaction – clear limitations upon the way societies as a whole are able to construct and articulate themselves seem able to be drawn from an examination of the spatial context in which they are embedded. For our purposes of course the limitations imposed by any social geometry are relevant to the ways that deviant behaviours are shaped. In many ways these determinations seem even more straightforward. It is clear, for example, that a wallet cannot be removed from someone's pocket outside the spatial region determined by the length of the would-be thief's reach. A rape, attack or physical molestation do not seem able to be directed at someone who is too far away to be grabbed or man-handled. Traditional frauds or deceptions have usually required the victim to be within a certain optical and auditory range for their success. And deviant acts, once committed, cannot then be temporally reversed – no matter how many feelings of guilt make the culprit wish that they could.

Deviant behaviour, however subjective its construction, must almost by definition be spatially located since deviant behaviours are always directed *across* space and *between* distinctly located actors. Contemporary statements about the 'negations of space' (Punday, 2000) or 'timeless time' (Castells, 1997, p. 460) need therefore to be understood very carefully – as metaphors about transitions in contemporary spatial and temporal *experience*, not as descriptions of the disappearance of spatial or temporal *constraints* upon those experiences. Castell's claim that 'simplistic notions of (a) systematic co-variance between space and culture' have been 'put to rest' (1997, p. 60) is only credible to the extent that there cannot be absolute or invariant systemacities between these two variables. Whilst a social geometry of deviant behaviours could never be properly axiomatic, it could indicate influences which are structurally formative and therefore prove culturally informative.

Space, time and crime

Lefebvre (1991, p. 2) argued that mathematicians had '. . . appropriated space and time' so that the geometry they produced was merely that of 'an empty area'. But superimposed on this are always:

> Successive stratified and tangled networks . . . paths, roads, railways, telephone links and so on . . . Each network or series or sequence of links – and therefore each space . . . is *produced*, and serves a purpose.
>
> (Lefebvre, 1991, p. 403)

The basis of this spatial production, he argued, lay in social life and in this way Lefebvre's views were partly anticipated by Kant's 'Copernican' revolution in thought. Kant's revolution (Horstmann, 1976) was directed precisely against the idea of a world where the spatio-temporal medium was something inhabited passively, as a form absolutely external to us. Instead, the spatio-temporal relations and orderings we experience are products of fundamental ways in which our cognitive systems impose themselves upon that experience. This makes the experience of space a profoundly social one. As Simmel (1997, p. 138) puts it: 'Kant defines space . . . as the possibility of being together.' The theme is one that has been constantly revisited. For Merleau-Ponty this fact comes down to the ineluctability of our *embodiment* for: 'our body is not primarily *in* space: it is of it' (1962, p. 148) so that we: '. . . grasp external space through our bodily situation' (1964, p. 5). Since embodiment is profoundly 'intercorporeal' it is necessarily a located, social experience. Indeed, even our subjective mental life can be argued to depend upon the positing of some 'generalised other' (Mead, 1934, p. 195), which situates our attitudes within 'interpersonal processes' (Thrift, 1995, p. 17) as much spatial as they are social, a theme further developed by both Garfinkel (1967) and Goffman (1959).

If our nature partly consists in being embodied, spatio-temporally located beings then it is reasonable to suppose that every kind of social interaction, not least deviant ones, must be informed by this fact. Simmel's conception of a social geometry is just one example of a theoretical position that attempts to make some practical uses of this insight. Other social scientists have displayed similar inclinations. Durkheim's work, for example, clearly implied that urban space and its associated forms of organisation may elicit different behavioural patterns than those associated with less concentrated spatial agglomerations such as rural settlements. More recently, anthropologists such as Edward Hall have made more specific attempts to explain how individuals deploy space as an aspect of culture. In particular, his theory of 'proxemics' (cf. Hall, 1966 and 1976) emphasises how our innate sense of distance modifies the way we interact socially. Donald Black (1976) proposed his own version of a 'social geometry' with variables such as the 'horizontal' (which determines the extent of social interactions), or the 'vertical' (which determines the distribution of social resources). (See Bernard (2002) for a critique of Black's views in criminology.)

A key trend in the application of spatial thinking to the explanation of social phenomena – one that will play a central role in the concept of hyper-spatialisation that follows – is the way in which contemporary shifts in the experience of space and time are *reorganising* social relations. A number of writers have pursued this theme. Harold Innis (1962) contrasted face-to-face interaction with an increasing prevalence of remote interaction – an idea taken up by writers such as Calhoun (1992). Innis' ideas were a huge influence upon McLuhan's discussions of the 'global embrace' of communication which are responsible for 'abolishing both space and time as far as our planet is concerned' (McLuhan, 1964, p. 3). In turn, both anticipate the kinds of social reconfigurations referred to by David Harvey in terms of 'time-space' compression, a phenomenon he locates historically in 'the transition from Fordism to flexible accumulation' (Harvey, 1989, p. 284). Giddens (1991) suggested a longer term basis for changes to our experience of time and its measurement, showing how culture was radically altered by the experience of new temporal mechanisms such as clocks and timetables. For Virilio (1986), social interaction has always been a phenomenon shaped by our changing experiences of *speed*, a fact that has been of especial importance in the age of mechanised transport. This theme has been taken up by writers such as Thrift (1996) who talk in terms of the relative *mobilities* of different societies. In turn theorists such as De Certeau (1984), Carey (1989) and Poster (1995) have all made important contributions to our understanding of the way that changing modes of spatial practice are central to the formation of new social relations.

Criminologists have not ignored such ideas. A central trend in explanations of deviance has of course been to consider deviant behaviour in terms of factors *internal* to social actors – maladjustment, psychological or physical malfunction and so on. But *external* contexts have also played an important explanatory role. Variables such as class, gender or social labelling processes are familiar enough resources in this context but appeals to the spatial medium in which such acts are embedded have also been invoked on occasions. The 'cartographic' criminologists (Smith, 1986, p. 3; Hayward, 2004, p. 88) of the nineteenth century such as Quetelet (1842) or Rawson (1839) saw correlations between spatial patterns and offending patterns and some, such as Guerry (1833), worked directly with geographers in the production of their analyses. However, their work was soon sidelined by Lombroso's 'biological turn' in crime analysis and it was not until the rapidly mutating urban environments of the early twentieth century in the USA began to attract the attention of social theorists that spatial explanations became fashionable again. One of the prime justifications for the Chicago School's spatial conceptualisations of deviant activity, in particular their famous 'concentric zones' model, was that it appeared to yield evidence of clear causal patterns. For example, it appeared to legitimise correlations between offending frequencies and specific kinds of urban location. Thus, where urban space was at its most contested, turbulent and unstable (the so-called zone of transition), there was a higher probability of deviance occurring. Their model implied distinct orderings within social space, and associated deviant outcomes with the way the space was occupied (Park *et al.*, 1925; Shaw & McKay, 1942).

The Chicago School model has been heavily criticised, both then and now (Chambliss & Seidman, 1971; Downes & Rock, 2003, p. 75). But while Chicago School theorists never argued that location was an exhaustive factor in explanations of deviance, it was clear that their model was often too specific, thereby limiting its range and application. This meant that it failed to go where its logic suggested it might and to embrace a range of other socially formed spaces, beyond transition zones, that might serve to nurture deviance. For example, corporate spaces, domestic spaces, media spaces and so on all plausibly relate to distinct but under-theorised formations. However, in spite of the many criticisms, one central construct remained influential among theorists and policy makers. This was the idea that certain spatial pre-conditions may affect clustering patterns in deviant behaviour – so-called 'crime hot-spots'. By the 1980s, when developments in statistical modelling techniques coincided with a new period of urban fragmentation, attention turned again to the application of spatial conceptions in crime and crime control. As Cohen noted at the time, a discernible drift within criminology began – one that turned 'away from individuals (and) toward spatial and temporal aspects of crime . . . ecology . . . defensible space' (Cohen, 1985, pp. 146–8).

That trend soon turned into a flood. A variety of work (see for example Sherman *et al.*, 1989, or Nasar and Fisher, 1993) focused increasingly upon the situational as a way of thinking about and dealing with crime. Statistical techniques such as cluster analysis (for example, McGurk *et al.*, 1981), or Log-Linear Analysis (for example, Crowley & Adrian, 1992) helped refine the search for spaces that could be 'controlled' or 'defended' (Newman, 1972). Whilst such spaces were largely mathematical abstract constructions, the search for clustering patterns was expedited by the arrival of tools more rooted in concrete processes, in particular of course GIS or geographical information systems (Harries, 1999; Chainey & Ratcliffe, 2005). The study of spatial influence also went beyond the study of 'hotspots'. For example, the way in which offenders select the sites of their crimes was explained in terms of the purposeful comparison of alternatives by offenders or by their 'routine activities' (Cohen & Felson, 1979).

The influence of such trends has been mixed. On the one hand the drive toward ever greater levels of mathematical rigour creates a pressure for social geometries of deviance in their most literal – that is, rigidly axiomatic – sense. Verma and Lodha's recent (2002) highly formalised spatial analysis of criminal events is one example. Drawing on work such as Brantingham and Brantingham (1978) their 'topological' approach goes beyond the two-dimensional grids of simple cluster analysis so as to locate crime events within multiple spatial, legal and other dimensions where:

> . . . incidents could be seen as the manifestation of movement patterns, routine activities, statutory and administrative laws and socio-economic and demographic characteristics associated with those place-time-law and people dimensions.
>
> (Verma & Lodha, 2002)

Impressive though the resulting models can be, there must again be a certain amount of scepticism about the kinds of 'appropriation' of space by math-ematics which Lefebvre cautioned against. As Hayward counsels, rigidly mathematical 'geographies of crime' centred upon statistical co-variations represent 'nothing less than the deformation of public space, the hollowing out of the urban environment' something which has 'subsequently resulted in the hollowing out of the offender' (Hayward, 2004, p. 101). As far as mainstream criminology is concerned however, there is simply no other theoretical role to be played by spatial concepts. The 'question of space' now largely reduces to ways of regulating it, based upon quantitative patterns which relate offences to locations and times (see Lersch (2004) for a recent example of this view).

By contrast a broader view, able to draw upon these mathematical insights but with a more anthropocentrically centred spatial analytic, seems to offer an equally fruitful line of inquiry. But writers such as Simmel present insights which, though rich, are somewhat fragmentary, lacking the systematicity offered by these more formalised approaches. As a result their conclusions can often seem incomplete – a point Foucault himself concedes: 'Geography acted as support . . . for the passage between a series of factors I tried to relate . . . (but) I either left the question hanging, or established a series of arbitrary connections' (1980, p. 77).

It seems clear then that any use of spatial notions in criminological explanation needs to be at once systematic, but open ended. Equally well, as Simmel showed, a great deal can be illustrated by the use of a few relatively simple but rich spatial concepts. An example of such a concept in Foucault's work was one that Deleuze saw as key to understanding contemporary transitions in spatial experience – one that might, in turn, relate to new geometries of harm. This was the idea of spatial *enclosure* and the degree of permeability of any boundaries. For Foucault, enclosure was fundamental to the disciplinary order he theorised. As seen in environments like the prison and the factory, the role of enclosure was, as Deleuze points out: '. . . (to) concentrate: to distribute in space, to order in time; to compose a productive force within the dimension of space-time whose affect will be greater than the sum of component forces' (1992, p. 1).

Just as crime found rich feeding grounds in the enclosed, narrow spaces of the new urban environments, the parallel punitive response – confinement – deployed enclosed space as a way of *controlling* deviant behaviour. Given this, transitions between different *orders* of enclosure become a useful metaphor for mapping transitions in both deviance and control. In particular, Deleuze suggests that it is the expansion of enclosures into network spaces that provides the underlying dynamic which turns disciplinary societies into control societies. For just as enclosures act to control behaviour in a way similar to molds, the dilution of enclosure and the opening up of space shapes behaviour in a different way. In this more open-ended, dynamic context:

Controls are a *modulation*, like a self deforming cast that will continuously change from one moment to the other, or like a sieve whose mesh will transmute from point to point.

(Deleuze, 1992, p. 2)

Identifying these more subtly qualitative effects of spatiality upon deviance enables us to see beyond a spatial analysis of crime rooted solely in the statistical analysis of crime locations. In particular, the invocation of an opening of enclosures into open-ended networks makes it clearer how distinctions between crime control and crime production are being elided and eroded to produce the hypercrime society theorised in this book. For example, Stan Cohen's earlier vision of social control contained in his metaphor of the 'net' (1985, p. 255) can be specifically distinguished from Deleuze's in terms of the differing spatial articulations of their views. For while Cohen seems to see the contemporary erosion of distinctions between criminality and non-criminality in terms of a 'filling in' of space (the control net *widens* as it simultaneously *narrows* it's meshes), Deleuze's idea centres upon the rhizomatic decentrings of space as an explanation. That is, as control spaces are opened up from enclosures to open networks the traditional social roles that mark out criminal systems (the law breaker and law abider) become harder to distinguish because absolute positions within the rhizome are harder to maintain. Rather than one location indicating a specific social role in virtue of its clear separation from another location, social roles 'bleed' into each other continuously across the modulations of a multiply connected space. Just as the infinite divisibility of space questioned by Zeno's paradox means that the hare and the tortoise can never arrive at the definite location of the finishing line and so complete the race, there is no point on the line between offenders and protectors which can be marked out as a definite point of separation between them. Instead they are 'comingled' into the kinds of hybrids discussed by Latour (1993) and which criminologists have begun to become increasingly interested in (Lippens, 2001; Hallsworth, 2002; Stevens, 2004; Brown, 2006) On this view the meshes of the net do not narrow or widen, they 'transmute' as Deleuze puts it. In turn, as the crude methodologies of deviance control by enclosure are modified by network space, more subtle and continuous approaches for the regulation of individuals arise. For once networked, deviant behaviours can increasingly be controlled *by means of* the network, from any point within it. New mechanisms such as tagging, CCTV. identity cards and the like serve to modulate spatial movement and access in ways that eschew (physical) enclosure by signifying a new regime of control.

At this point it is worth restating an earlier note of caution. It ought not to be concluded that because we have a spatial modelling of deviance we also have a *causal* account of such behaviour. Space must (of course) be *populated* for there to be the kinds of motivations and behaviours which produce criminality. Particularised facts about a society, its hierarchies. its beliefs and norms inevitably continue to play a crucial explanatory role. But neither need the two be completely separate. Psychological causes of behaviour such as motivations and intentions can, as we saw Simmel suggest, have fruitful connections to space if only from their role as a way of 'connecting sensory impulses ... into uniform interpretations' (1997,

p. 138). Social geometries, insofar as they can offer us any insight about the causes of deviant behaviour, are primarily related to constraining effects and their basis in social interaction.

The consensual hallucinations of a 'cyberspace'

One immediate advantage of a clearer focus upon interaction is that it enables us to do without the dubious explanatory resource of a 'cyberspace' to explain crime effected by communication devices. Koppell (2000) nicely summarises the basic conceptual flaw in assuming that, because there are new ways in which social interaction can occur, we are thereby committed to the metaphysical baggage of a new 'space' to facilitate them:

> Ham radio operators have a global network of friends and acquaintances who came together solely through their use of that instrument. Do they exist in 'hamspace'? And why is the manner in which people make first contact so significant? Do pen pals exist in 'penpalspace'? One reason that cyberspace is described as a place is to avoid downgrading it to the status of a mere medium, and perhaps especially to avoid comparisons with television. Those who would distinguish the Internet from television point out that Web denizens are not mere passive recipients of electronic signals. That may be (partly) true. But telephones and the postal system are also communications media that allow two-way communication. We don't regard them as places.
>
> (Koppell, 2000, p. 16)

On this line the social implications of the internet are no more than 'questions of emerging structures of interaction and reorganization of social boundaries that can occur in any medium of communication' (Wynn & Katz, 1997, p. 297). But this sensible and more modest line was, from 1991 onwards, too often overcome by the urge to prefix almost every kind of new social phenomenon with the term 'cyber' – as if this somehow explained it. The temptation in seeing the 'consensual hallucination'[1] of computer interaction at face ontological value – as something like a real place – seems to have had at least two main influences.

One set of influences that were noted earlier were largely cultural, drawing upon films such as the *Lawnmower Man*. The later *Matrix* series was particularly influential here and one continues to see it cited as a way of 'understanding' the significance of computer-mediated interaction (see for example Aas, 2007). Both fed familiar enthusiasms for a 'dematerialised artificial universe' (Aas, 2007, p. 160) now accessible simply by putting on a 'virtual headset'. The compulsion in the idea that here was a 'new' place where we could visit exotic lands, acquire new skills and appearances, engage in messianic acts of creation and destruction and have sex with total strangers (not all of them human) has a familiar pedigree, often associated with technological shifts. The seventeenth-century surge in popularity of fantastical tales about exotic lands, the unknown and the monstrous coincided with the contemporary voyages of exploration, just as the origins of the fascination in the parallel worlds of science fiction date from the point when science was driving the social and industrial transformations of the nineteenth and early twentieth centuries (Todorov, 1975; Law, 1991; Graham, 2002). The appeal of 'cyber-culture' films and articles did not just lie in the satisfying completeness of the hallucinations presented, but the fact that they offered easy and appeal-ing explanations at a time when the social implications of information technology had only just begun to be more widely considered.

The theorists were as bowled over by the enthusiasm as were the general public. Soon a flood of texts arrived attempting to explain 'what cyber-space was'. Some followed Baudrillard (1988, p. 168), seeing with him '. . . (a) passage to a space whose curvature is no longer that of the real, nor of truth'. Others saw it as a 'universal labyrinth' or even an 'exploding crown of neurons' (Levy, 1997, pp. 91 and 236). Such 'techno-hyperbole' (Thrift, 1996, p. 166) was complemented by work like Benedikt (1992b), Heim (1993) or Dodge and Kitchen (2001) which expended a great deal of effort in attempting to map and to philosophically ground these descrip-tive flourishes. A similar enthusiasm appeared to engulf many representatives of the criminal justice system who became increasingly convinced that special forms of legislation and policing were required for 'taming cyber-space' (Moore, 1992). Criminologists tended to agree, offering various degrees of intellectual support for the phenomenon of 'cyberspace crime' (Wall, 2003).

A second influence upon the enthusiastic reception given to concepts of 'cyberspace' was grounded in something of a little more substance. The spread of pre-existing social, economic and communicative networks such as globalisation processes or satellite systems had already seemed to be stretching explanatory boundaries. The sudden, almost magical advent of the internet and large-scale computer networks appeared to have so revolution-ised culture that magical explanations were also required. But though the connectivities offered by computer networks had *accelerated* remote inter-action, this was no more than a manifestation of longer term trends in tele-communications, a prehistory that will be explored more fully in the following chapter. However significant and dramatic the change may have been, no 'cyberspace' was required to explain it, or to understand its consequences. So if the ontological account of this technological shift was wanting, what was of relevance? At this point we need to step back and think about the concept of space in a little more detail.

Conceptions of space

Two broad approaches have dominated our thinking about space. One is to ask what it *is*. And a standard choice is usually presented here. Either space is a 'something' which exists independently of the things which are within it, or it is a 'nothing' which only emerges from the way we consider the relations between objects (Lucas, 1973; Sklar, 1974). On the former (Newtonian) view, space operates as a kind of container, a medium *through* which, and by means of which we move. And as an absolute, against which all else can be measured, it is therefore a medium which would exist whether there was anything in it or not. On the latter (Leibnizian) conception, space is no more than a convenient metaphor which serves as the basis for descriptions of relations between objects. On this view to say that 'I am in space' would analyse into 'I am 10 metres to the east of the large glass building; 1 metre to the north of that post-box; 5 metres to the west of the Liverpool St bus stop' and so on. Sociologists have tended to follow Leibniz in this debate and to hold that space is *not* there independently of the objects which constitute it. Simmel, Foucault and Lefebvre are prominent exemplars of this line but Bourdieu has been among the most committed of contemporary theorists to argue that 'the real is relational' (1998, p. 3). Thus, the dispositions or tastes which locate a social actor in their 'habitus' are nothing other than 'difference, a gap, a distributive feature, in short a relational property existing only in and through its relation with other properties' (ibid, p. 8).

A second question has been to ask what space is *like*. The answer one gets here depends heavily on the specific question one asks. For example, one set of questions has centred upon the overall 'shape' of space – its so-called *topology*. It is of course hard for us to really imagine space as having *any* kind of shape, since in order to be able to imagine such a thing we seem to need to perform the impossible task of 'standing outside' of it. Nonetheless distinctive sets of conceptions have prevailed. The intuitive (or 'Euclidean') view that held sway until the contemporary period was of a 'flat' space, one that possessed three dimensions which stretched evenly (and probably infinitely) in all these three directions. Fundamental conclusions about what space is 'like' and how this affects movement through it then followed. For example, to travel forward through space from some point A would mean (if there were no obstructions) that one would continue to travel forever in that direction. But now suppose space has a different 'shape'. Suppose, for example, it is curled up like a ball. Then, if I started to travel forward from some position on its surface and continued in a straight line, I would eventually return to my point of origin, just as upon the surface of a planet. The huge conceptual shock caused by the new geometries of the nineteenth century which posited these and other, still more radical topologies of space, emphasised that our experience of space is not simply objectively given, but has a cultural component (Toretti, 1978). This does not mean that it stands outside of scientific description, merely that our perceptions may influence the kinds of mathematical theories we choose to describe it. Thus, the way we think about space will affect what we think is possible within it. This means, as Lefebvre put it, that space is:

> Simultaneously a field of *action* (offering its extension to the deployment of projects and practical intentions) and a *basis* of *action* (a set of places whence energies derive and whither energies are directed).
>
> (Lefebvre, 1991, p. 191)

In turn this suggests another formulation of the 'what is space like' question – namely how do we *experience* space – or as Jameson (1991) put it: what is the order of our perceptual habits within space? A short answer, in line with what is being proposed here, is to think of the experiential possibilities a space offers – the way we use it. And just as the new geometries of the nineteenth century forced us to explain our uses of physical space in a different way, so too do changes in the way we use our everyday social space force changes in the 'geometry' which explains that, a point which Simmel was all too aware of.

From space to hyperspace

A recurring theme in discussion of modernity has again been spatial – ideas of dislocation, fragmentation and so on. Marx's seminal observation that many seemingly solid stabilities of life literally evaporated or 'melted' into the air under the new forces of productive change was utilised by Berman (1982) and others as a central metaphor for the rapid shifts and fragmentations of the 'modern'. Likewise the new, 'distinctive experience of space and time' (Frisby, 1985) has been one way of characterising the subsequent economic and cultural shifts associated with 'late' modernity. But the scale and extent to which technology is affecting such experiences may now be at the point of materialising processes previously at the very boundary of physical possibility (cf. Poster, 1995).

Paul Virilio's claim that, 'the reduction of distance has become a strategic reality bearing incalculable economic and political consequences' (1986, p. 133), underlines the potential importance of any such shift. However, it need not be interpreted to imply, as Virilio goes on to say, the 'negation of space' altogether. Harvey (1989) famously theorises the transition in less dramatic terms as 'time-space compression' which he defines as: '. . . processes that so revolutionize the objective qualities of space and time that we are forced to alter . . . how we represent the world to ourselves' (p. 240). But Harvey blurs the material and experiential here. He cannot literally mean that any objective (that is, natural) properties of space and time are altered by culture – such changes can only occur at the level of natural processes. Thus, while modernist spatial logics may be disruptive, '. . . geography continues to matter – as an organising principle and as a constituent of social relations; it cannot be entirely eliminated' (Dodge & Kitchen, 2001, p. 14). The more obvious interpretation of claims about distance reduction in Harvey's idea of time-space compression (something his subsequent discussion goes on to make clear) is that it involves transitions to how we *represent* the world spatially and temporally – not a transition to space or time itself. Or as Lefebvre puts it, changes to 'spatial practice' – the 'particular locations and spatial sets characteristic of each social formation' (1991, p. 33). Harvey charts some key transitions within the experience of space and time along the road between modernity and post-modernity – from the development of perspective in representative art and the advent of maps using scale, and latitude and longitude grids; through to phenomena such as 'instant' gratification and immediate disposability in the fast food industry.

Lefebvre saw a precedence of space over time, arguing that, 'whoever speaks of the world speaks of space and not time' (1976–78, p. 326). By contrast other social theorists – Virilio in particular – have argued that, '. . . what becomes critical . . . is not so much the three dimensions of space, but the fourth dimension of time' (1997, p. 10). But this separation of space from time (or the converse) is unnecessary. As Thrift points out in discussing his own favoured concept of 'mobility', 'mobility takes up both space and time' a fact that is, '. . . one of the elementary insights of a time geography' (1996, p. 285). Certainly, modern physics treats space and time as a composite entity – as a space-time. Consequently, I shall defer to this line and retain the convenience of a 'space-time' in what follows rather than stressing a causal precedence either way. Alterations in our experience of space will therefore be taken to be analytically continuous with those in time.

Most commentators seem to be in agreement about the significance of something like distance compression in spatial and temporal interaction, by way of speed, mobility or related factors. But I will argue that there is more to the process of hyperspatialisation than this. Rather, the hyperspatial forms a *composite* set of processes that have merely been theorised from several different angles. In what follows I will single out at least two further factors which complement time-space compression within the complex of the hyperspatial. The first of these involves what might be called *spatial complexification* – a weaving together of spatial experience in ever more multilayered and multidimensional ways. Two closely related modalities of complexification can be identified:

(i)   *Connection* – a multiplication in the linkages between diverse points within the spatial continuum. In one sense this can be seen in terms of the development of *networks* – something widely recognised in discussions of spatio-temporal compression, whether in terms of transport or communication nets (Mulgan, 1991; van Dijk, 2006). The development of various nets or 'webs' of social interaction (Murdoch, 1995;

Wellman, 1988 and 1999; Law & Hassard, 1999), communication and movement have had a long history, as will be discussed in the following chapter. But the spatial complexifications within hyperspatialisation not only relate to the sheer number of such connections that now exist but also to a new level of *interconnection* – a connection of connections. The 'hyperconnectivity' that results provides for a very different set of experiences that could be provided by just *one* network – even one as diverse as the internet. Instead, multiple network forms now begin to combine and interlock.

(ii) *Hyperposition.* As a result of (i), every location enters into a potential state of *multidimensionality* so that, as Novak (1992, p. 230) puts this: 'every point in a hypermedium has a dimensionality'. This is not just homogeneous connectibility of every point to every other point, but the heterogeneous connectibility which links locations into a multiverse of different *kinds* of network forms. Not only does a simultaneity of social role emerge, but as an inflation in the kinds of possible connection occurs, the representational/informational becomes more deeply integrated within the social-interactive. Thus, while movements within physical space are graduated through successive points orientated along the familiar dimensions of up, down, right, left and so on, hyperpositionality allows for movements that transcend this simple geometry by permitting interaction between psychological, social and informational composites mediated by representations. The key idea of the *hyperlink* – which means that a 'point in a text can . . . open . . . to an animation . . . a frame in an animation can return to a text' (Novak, 1991) becomes translated into the full emotional and perceptual spectrum of the social world.

The central role of representation in providing a sense of connection across many dimensions indicates a rather less discussed ingredient of hyperspatialisation that I wish to single out – what I will call *representational power* – the depth, quality and precision in 'aboutness' now used to model the world. There are clearly different continua at work here. In its most precise form representation relates to the copy or perhaps even the clone – representations formed by Benjamin's process of *technical* reproduction (1969, p. 222). Somewhere towards the other end of this continuum are the more fictive representations – the lie, or the fairy story. Somewhere in the middle are the partial representations of a language, a statistical model or the diagram – non-isomorphic structural correspondences between the representation and the represented (cf. Peirce, 1933; Rorty, 1979; Deleuze & Guattari, 1988; Anderson and Meyer, 2001).

In practical physical terms, the source of the rich representative experiences now offered by informational technology is simple enough. It is founded on nothing more than manipulations of the physical properties of electrical pulses. But at this level such manipulations are of course of little use to us socially. Most of us can no more 'read' a computer machine code, than we could see the individual frames on a film reel or make sense of the dots and dashes in Morse code. Hand in hand with the physical processes that underpin communication and other technologies must therefore go representational *systems* – the ways in which these physical processes are made meaningful and interpretable to us. The coupling of such representation systems with computer technologies has very quickly produced developments which may turn out to be as important as the technology of communication itself. From 'green-screen' experiences of cursors and unintelligible commands, representational power increasingly grants us interfaces with the 'reality repleteness' (Goodman, 1976; Borgmann, 2001, p. 95) of three-dimensional sound, graphics and so on. And as representations model the world and its structures with ever greater precision, a fusion of space with representation begins to occur. Whether one thinks of this in terms of the digital modelling and manipulation of geological or metereological processes, or whether one focuses upon the rich imaginary landscapes of gameworlds (Hartmann, 1996; Sismondo *et al.*, 1999), it is clear that the relation between space and representation has entered a new ball game.

Once 'analogue' forms of representation (Lewis, 1971; Haugeland, 1981; Hayles, 1999; Poster, 2001) were the only resource available – modellings of the world dependent upon the properties of other objects such as wood, oil, ink or sound for their verisimilitudes. The increased sophistication of *digital* representation (representation by way of formal syntaxes) vastly expands its resources. For example, the advent of the computer model (Winsberg, 2003) has greatly extended the capacity of science to represent. Whilst scientific models based purely on language and experiment granted us a significant degree of predictive power and a capacity to interact with nature at the micro-levels (McMullin, 1968), digital representations extend these capacities in ways that confer unprecedented causal (and representational) power.

What this all means is that the mutation of our spatio-temporal experiences into the hyperspatial should be seen at least as much as a *representational* process as anything to do with distance compression or spatial complexification. Representing a space by a map provides a control of that space through constituting it 'as a system of signs' (de Certeau, 1984, p. 128), just as representing a territory by rules, regulations and metric standardisations enables better management of the territory (Mattelart, 1996). But as suggested, enhanced powers of representation also allow for enhanced reality repleteness in our representations of the *non-actual* as well as the actual. It is at this point that talk of representation often becomes confused. Pseudo-distinctions emerge between 'the simulational as well the representational' (Goss, 1995, p. 182) and the virtual is contrasted with the real. In this way, the role of representation is seen to 'threaten . . . the difference between "true" and "false", between "real" and "imaginary" ' (Baudrillard, 1983, p. 3). In the end such talk obscures the fact that enhanced representations in computer models or computer games are as much to do with the *fit* with reality as with any flight to fantasy. 'Better' representation, especially when linked to external devices such as medical probes, cashpoints or missiles, enables us to interact with the immediate world more effectively, not just to experience alternative (or 'virtual') arrangements of that world. And as we will see in a moment, this has major implications for control. For the fusion of space with representation begins to allow those with mastery over representation to begin to be able to determine the space that we inhabit. As Lefebvre reminds us, 'representations of space' are often no more than, '. . . the space of scientists, planners, urbanists, technocratic subdividers and social engineers . . . all of whom identify what is lived and what is perceived with what is conceived' (1991, pp. 31–33).

Three outcomes

At least three significant outcomes follow from our experience of this new composite of speed, distance compression, spatial complexification and enhanced representational power. The first is the development of what has been called variously 'telepresence' (Minsky, 1980) or 'teleaction' – the enhanced possibility of *agency* at a distance (Malpas, 2001; Hannaford, 2001). In our normal experience causation appears to operate very locally. As suggested, within the horizons determined by our bodies we cannot affect things, do things or change things unless they are within a certain range. But spatially compressive technologies such as the telephone, the motor car, and more recently internet and satellite technologies allow us to increasingly change this historic geometric limitation by the 'intrusion of distance' (Giddens, 1991, p. 187).

Consider the case of deep-space probes, or planetary explorers. These might travel many billions of miles, many light years away from earth. Yet given the right representational model and armed with the appropriate communicative technology they become, like any more simple tool, an extension to our bodies and their causal powers. We can directly interact with objects beyond our reach. We can see images of distant planetscapes, 'take walks' across their surface, pick up stones and conduct tests upon them without ever leaving the confines of the immediate spatial regions of our bodies. Work on the technologies of telepresence has therefore been an important strand of research at NASA and other space agencies (see for example Stoker, 1993; Campanella, 2001). But telepresence also has its more prosaic and familiar manifestations. We can alter details of our bank accounts without leaving home. We can order shopping to come to our door without ever going to the supermarket. We can fall in love with someone on another continent (Sveningson, 2002). Telepresence and teleaction, like much else under discussion here, have historical precedents that we will explore in the following chapter. But the full possibilities of remote causation, of doing things at a distance, have only just begun to be explored.

Yet remote causation would be of little use unless it comes with a 'directedness' or precision in its affects. And this directedness depends directly upon the effectiveness of our models or representations. A payment system that transfers money into the wrong account, or a satnav system that represents a final destination that is actually 100 miles away from the intended one, may work to a point – but they are of little use to the remote agent. Sometimes such flaws are obvious enough. But at others – especially where issues of ideology and power intrude – erroneous representation can be less easy to spot. There is not always the pressure to improve certain kinds of model with inadequate 'fit' – for example, a database that misidentifies certain individuals as having high-risk profiles. Only where an inadequate model has more obviously negative effects – one that results in an accident, or a failure to profile a dangerous murderer, for example – can enough social outrage be mustered to force the necessary changes to it. Misrepresentation serves the existing status quo as well as representation.

This takes us to a second outcome of hyperspatial processes that we need to note – one complementary to the advent of full spectrum telecausation. This is the enhanced continuity between control and representation. For those with a better capacity to *manipulate* representations increasingly have power over those who do not – a fact with important consequences for criminality. The enhanced 'fit' between representational models and reality cashed out in terms of *causal power* translates directly into power in the social context. Beniger (1986) defines control as, 'purposive action toward a predetermined goal' (p. 39), but his survey, while superbly broad in its scope, is more concerned with general evolution of control than with its implications for power and deviance that have interested writers such as Deleuze (1992) and Bogard (1996 and 2006). However, the technologies of the telecausal clearly go some way to facilitating greater control. As Mulgan (1991, p. 1) noted, '. . . the first modern global network based on electricity – the British Empire's cable network – was a tool of extensive control, as well as a medium for trade and personal communication'. Much the same can be said about the affects of surveillance technologies, data-profiling technologies and so on. The very etymology of the word 'control' indicates the plausibility and significance of the connection. The term originates in the Latin *contrarotulare* – the act of comparing something 'against the rolls' – the documentation or scrolls (*rotulae*) used to store official records in the Roman bureaucracy (see Beniger, 1986, p. 8). In other words *representational* power – which in this context simply means the extent to which one roll conformed to (or was represented by) another – enabled *control* power, for the representations of economic and other data by means of the rolls within a political entity served as an 'authority' upon which sovereign knowledge and action could be based. It is the fact that representational power now underpins the contemporary order to such an extent that makes the control society thesis a compelling one. Surveillance, or surveillant assemblages (Marx, 1988; Lyon, 1994; Haggerty & Ericson, 2000) which are often cited in this context, are simply a product of this deeper state of affairs. For it is not just an obsession with 'looking' itself which is at play (Lyon, 2006). The right to move and interact spatially is increasingly legitimised by comparison to representations which closely parallel those ancient rolls – DNA databases, the view through a CCTV camera, a risk profile and so on. And in this way deviance increasingly follows from a failure to match a representation *in the correct way*.

Of course representation requires certain stabilities, but one further outcome of the hyperspatial worth noting indicates how, in the case of the ways we are 'represented' to ourselves and to others – our identities – such stabilities can be undermined. The new open vistas of a more connected space create two kinds of issue for the boundaries that determine where we seem to begin and end. For many commentators, what Giddens calls the 'trajectory of the self' (1991, p. 77) appears no longer to be traced as a single line or position but as a series of random breakings and bifurcations or multiple paths. Sherry Turkle in particular has emphasised how, while 'in the past rapid cycling through different identities was not easy to come by' (1995, p. 175) the new possibilities of bodies extended by remote interaction into (for example) multiple online identities (Bruckman, 1996; Taylor, T., 1999) changes this historic fixed point. In this way the new forms of generic social roles noted by Bauman such as the 'stroller', the 'vagabond', the 'tourist' or the 'player' (Slevin, 2000, p. 162) are further supplemented by enhanced opportunities for individual identity experimentation (Fine, 2002). But the deviant outcomes of this do not just centre upon the 'digital personae' which the cybercrime literature has tended to fix upon as the primary vehicles for bodily redistribution. Indeed, the various pseudo-problems about how digital personae can be protected or prosecuted under the law (MacKinnon, 1997) have proved to be somewhat of a red herring. For beyond the disinhibition affects of anonymity (see Suler, 2004) that may promote deviance, wayward identities form another more important source for the production of crime and deviance. This lies as much in the attempts to manage, control and *fix* identity – a point to be discussed later.

As equally important as the extensions to individual identity produced by a hyperspace, are its extensions to *collective* identity – the way that, in connecting dispersed and disparate individuals together, new social unities of purpose and interdependence are facilitated – the *hybrids* alluded to earlier. Simmel's observations about spatiality and society had already indicated the importance of exclusivity and boundaries to social reality – the fact that 'every portion of space possesses a kind of uniqueness' (1997, p. 138). On one level Simmel is restating the philosophical principle of Leibniz' Law – the traditional rule for marking the distinctiveness of objects. According to this law, difference is fixed in virtue of the possession of differing properties, and of course location presents the most basic example of such property, for the nature of physical space usually means that no two objects (of the same kind) can occupy the same spatial points. The experience of hyperspatialisation erodes this certainty, for with the advent of telepresence there also comes what I will call in Chapter 3 the 'distributed' body – bodies that extend through networks in differing ways. Just as the world is distributed through networks to one's doorstep, bringing bad as well as good, so the self becomes 'everywhere' via communications networks. But this is not just a case of what Sheila Brown has described as: 'the body extend(ing) outwards into data; ... disassembled and re-assembled in networks' (2006, p. 231). It is also a case of bodies and their life-worlds increasingly co-mingling across these open spaces into the hybrids that, as we will see, have profound affects upon our sense of crime and our requirements for control.

Psychologies of hyperspatialisation: exhilaration, paranoia and schizophrenia

As suggested, the social effects of the hyperspatial cannot be entirely separated from the psychological ones. These interface with the production and perception of deviance in various ways and I will consider three examples here. Each relate to the psychologies of a world where 'everything is near' and each in a sense therefore also relates to the idea of spatial redistribution – the way location alters from uniqueness to multiplicity. Under the hyperspatial, threats are both always immediate and interconnected in complex ways. As our presence is redistributed outward towards threat, not only does this make us potential victims, it also enhances a certain kind of power – the fact that we can also be potential generators of threat for others. This power, along with others offered by the hyperspatial, brings a form of exhilaration in its wake. The Futurist manifesto written in the early part of the twentieth century, when the hyperspatial was at its early stages, describes another form.

> We declare that the splendor of the world has been enriched by a new beauty: the beauty of speed ... We are on the extreme promontory of the centuries. Time and Space died yesterday. We are already living in the absolute, since we have already created eternal, omnipresent speed.[2]

With speed comes a different kind of exhilaration – what Thrift called 'the sheer joy of bodies in movement' (1996, p. 279). To this we can add still more senses in which the new powers of the hyperspatial offer exhilaration. The pleasure of being able to exert remote influences; the thrill of distributing presence; the pull of inhabiting a new personae and being strong, where one was weak; the stimulations of exerting control over someone, where this was denied before. All of these are not just compelling narcotics. In some cases they can stimulate behaviour we might describe as 'deviant'. The image of the computer nerd, suddenly able to command legions in multi-user games, or to win fair maidens, is a familiar and harmless version of this particular narcosis. But there are other contexts where the exhilarations of the hyperspatial have been argued to promote negative behaviours. The stalker, drawing satisfaction from ensnaring, enticing and tracing their victim's movements with hyperspace technology, or the obscene arousal brought by pushing the button of a missile launcher outline clear potential psychological consequences of the increased capacity to control space from a distance.

There is a price to pay for these powers, for the fracturing of presence that comes with spatial redistributions of the self, or with new hybridisations brings a fracturing in consciousness, that sometimes suggests mass schizophrenia. Deleuze and Guattari made an explicit comparison between the productive systems of the late modern, hyperspatialised world and the production of fractured consciousnesses, pointing out that: 'our society produces schizos the same way it produces Prell schampoo or Ford cars, the only difference being that the schizos are not saleable' (Deleuze & Guattari, 1983, p. 245). The criminological implications of mass schizophrenias are clearly many and varied but they certainly stretch far beyond the actions of lone madmen. The schizophrenic State, dispensing death, injury or control with one part of its consciousness while promising to uphold safety and rights with another, is arguably just as dangerous a production of the hyperspatial as any psychopath. The 'schizoanalytic' method proposed by Deleuze and Guattari (1983) might constitute one way to develop a criminological understanding of the impact upon crime and crime control of the 'redistributions' to social actors of all kinds under the hyperspatial. A more developed analytic of the 'come-down' from exhilaration might offer another.

The tendency to 'hear voices' is one obvious fallout from these social schizophrenias – a fact that should remind us that new *perceptions* of crime are as much a part of extended spatial experience as any new criminal motivations and culpabilities. The very fact that remote action is possible means an uncertainty in interacting with individuals whose motivations may be disguised, unclear or the product of a questionable hybrid. In turn it means that paranoia seems also to be a product of the hyperspatial landscape. In this context, threats of all kinds may be with us everywhere and at all times, so turning the pursuit of (an ever more unattainable) security into a mania that infects the social world as profoundly as any computer virus. As Ericson puts this, 'neighbour is pitted against neighbour in the very act of obtaining security' (2007, p. 215). The normal process of assigning threat to undesirable events now becomes infected with the suspicion that there are not just such events 'everywhere', but such events can *affect* us from anywhere, suspicions that are all too often out of proportion to the actualities. As many have noted (O'Malley, 1998; Hudson, 2003), the governance of justice and security has become: 'underpinned by a new risk mentality that adds a new layer to the more established punitive mentality' (Dupont, 2004, p. 77). But these criminologies of risk are now further augmented by the material uncertainties of a hyperspatialised everywhere threat so that: 'the problem of uncertainty . . . subsumes and replaces the problem as envisaged by risk society theorists of the late twentieth century' (Ericson, 2007, p. 204). Writers such as Garland (1996, 2001), Ericson and Haggerty (1997) and Rose (2000) have all acknowledged the way that the prevention and reduction of uncertainties through techniques of representational power like surveillance, or statistical risk profiling begin to inform and shape every aspect of life. Under the hyperspatial, such uncertainties are multiplied by the sheer number (and kinds) of 'directions' threat may appear from.

A significant ingredient of such fears is that they are not totally irrational or groundless. This is not Baudrillard's hyperreality – 'the product of an irradiating synthesis of combinatory models in a hyperspace . . . sheltered from the imaginary, and from any distinction between the real and the imaginary' (1983, pp. 3/4). The technologies of hyperspatialisation do indeed mean that crime may not just *seem* to be everywhere, but really *can* be committed from anywhere. The subjectivities of a multiply connected world reproduce that familiar saying – 'just because you're paranoid, doesn't mean they're not out to get you' – with a new twist. We are confronted by series of seeming impasses. On the one hand there is a real and material basis to everywhere threat. On the other our perceptions of threat are distorted and magnified. We fear the worst, rather than hoping for the best. In an age when hyperspatialisation offers so many enhanced possibilities of community it is ironic that it also threatens an erosion of trust, so that as our horizons widen, we retreat toward the familiar. As Castells puts this: 'when networks dissolve time and space, people anchor themselves in places and recall their historic memory' (1997, p. 66). Under the hyperspatial then: 'fear becomes part of the communication environment. It cannot be separated from the ecology of communication that connects feelings we have with the messages we receive through . . . information technology' (Altheide, 2002). And this creates a further impasse. Within the open spaces of the network it is only the construction of new walls and gates that seems to offer security from threat. Yet this is always doomed to be a flawed strategic response, for, by their very nature, the open spaces of the network demonstrate the futility of walls.

The manifest failure of the securitisation agenda to offer ultimate security is nowhere demonstrated more clearly than in what is perhaps one of the governing metaphors of hyperspatiality – the threat of the viral. The fear of contagion which so terrified the premodern order, infections that could be transmitted through the invisible medium of 'miasma' (see for example Kinzelbach, 2006) are now reproduced within networks. Just as no posy or handkerchief could ultimately protect the urban dweller from the plague, so too is the redundancy of 'anti-viral' protection revealed daily. Indeed, as we will see later, within the paranoid continuities of hyperspace, anti-virus companies themselves seem as plausible culprits for the release of viruses into communications networks as any disturbed adolescent programmer. Thus the viral and the infective become governing metaphors of social life, both in the practice of interaction and in the psychologies of everyday life. In turn the viral becomes instrumental in the production of criminal hybrids, for we are all as likely to be 'infected' as anyone else. The precise point at which deviant behaviour 'begins and ends' is blurred and, as Hardt and Negri (2004) point out, crime becomes increasingly indistinguishable from other forms of activity. Its everywhereness is universal because 'we are all criminal' so that everyone is under suspicion.

In what follows I will pay more attention to the psychologies of paranoia within hypercrime than to the affects of exhilaration or schizophrenia. But this is only to do with the restrictions of space than because they are any less important. Nor is the omission mine alone, for the effects of all of this upon criminal psychology and perceptions of the criminal have been far less studied than they perhaps ought to have been. However, their origin in new spatial experience is something I shall at least direct slightly more detailed attention towards than normal. It is to the interfaces between crime and space which lie behind this that I now begin to turn more fully.

Crime and space

It has been a near universal assumption within human societies that the occupation of as *much* space as possible is a desirable state of affairs. The result is what Simmel describes as: 'static configurations of space: the boundary and distance, a fixed position and neighbourhood (which) are like continuations of spatial configurations into the structure of humanity' (1997, p. 160). But once a space is occupied, classes of deviant behaviours began to emerge almost automatically. For the question of the boundary then arises again, and transgressions or infringements to its demarcation of space are not generally tolerated. As Simmel puts it:

> . . . where the interests of two elements are directed at the same object, the possibility of their co-existence depends on a border line separating their spheres within the object – whether this be a legal line ending the dispute or a power boundary . . . stating it.
>
> (1997, p. 143)

Inevitably then, boundary infringements have constituted a primary basis for ascriptions of 'right' and 'wrong' behaviours and with that, criminality. And by extending our sense of occupation to more complex social spaces it begins to become clear how Simmel's observation can serve to provide a broad characterisation of unwanted and harmful behaviours. It is perhaps no accident that this association between spatial violation and crime was reinforced by the gradual association of the term 'trespass' with all sorts of unrelated criminal behaviours. 'Thou shalt not trespass' becomes a general injunction against other sorts of boundary infringement. Boundary violation can of course occur in both the constructive and destructive senses. We often tolerate the former (though even here there is contested territory, as anyone who has ever dressed up in drag in an industrial town, or piled up a few bricks and called it art will tell you). The latter we seem, by and large, to reject. The cultural demarcations between transgressive acts that are to be punished and those which are to be celebrated is often a fluid one (Ferrell & Hamm, 1998; Jenks, 2003).

Not only does the idea of a proscribed space and infringements to its boundaries give an outline of how deviance is culturally constructed. The influence of power – in this context the capacity to control movement and access within such spaces – can also be seen. As Foucault put this: 'The spatialising description of discursive realities gives onto the analysis of related effects of power . . .' (1980, p. 71). And so,

> Once knowledge can be analysed in terms of region, domain, implant-ation, displacement and transposition, one is able to capture the process by which knowledge functions as a form of power.
>
> (Foucault, 1980, p. 69)

Spatial occupations and our attitudes towards them can thus become a precursor and ideal type for discussions about the crucial continuum that spans the space between control and harm.

Crime and harm

Sutherland's famous definition of criminology as '. . . the scientific study of *making* laws, *breaking* laws and *reacting* toward the breaking of laws' (Sutherland & Cressey, 1960, p. 3), focused as it is towards existing legal and regulatory structures, has often been found wanting (cf. van Swaaningen, 1999). Perhaps the most obvious (and oft-repeated) critique has been the fact that there are many behaviours which are *not* against the law but which seem to be as equally deserving of the label of criminality. Illegitimate attempts to enforce normative consensus, the sheer novelty of many deviant behaviours which thereby elude legal characterisation, or the crude interventions of power to distort the judgements and consequences of deviance constitute further standard reasons for caution in restricting the study of 'criminalities' to illegalities. Indeed, the very notion of law has sometimes been portrayed as nothing more than an implied violence (Zizek, 1991). For this reason both philosophers of jurisprudence and criminologists have often sought a wider principle than illegality by which deviant behaviour can be characterised. A common solution has been to appeal to some principle of *harm* with one task of criminal justice systems then being recast in terms of 'harm reduction'. Joel Feinberg (1984) provided a broad philosophical argument for this stance while von Hirsch and Jareborg (1991) have sought to test and extend some of Feinberg's principles. Other works such as Dworkin (1994) and Simester & Smith (1996) have examined this from a more legalistic perspective while Tifft (1995), Muncie (2000), Hillyard *et al.* (2004) and Linklater (2006) have considered its broad application within criminology.

A major problem in utilising concepts of harm, or social harm in place of crime lies in providing an adequate definition of the term. Casting the remit of harm too broadly may result in the objection that *any* immoral conduct might be taken as 'harmful' either to oneself or to the society where it occurs (see Devlin, 1965; Dworkin, 1994). But setting its scope too narrowly may then mean that certain kinds of conduct which evade criminal law also evade the harm concept – thereby rendering the appeal to it a waste of time. The concept of harm may also fail by omission. For example, some varieties of immoral behaviour may be seen as so offensive that, even though no identifiable harm results, a widespread normative pressure to criminalise them develops (see Feinberg, 1988). Finally, some harms may be desirable or productive acts – for example, a protest, or action against tyranny that causes damage to property as a result. In such cases much depends upon which social actors have the legitimacy or power to define an action as harmful. But this then threatens to make the application of the term 'harm' as provisional, or as subject to the interests of power, as that of 'crime'.

Hillyard *et al.* (2005) make much of their appeal to harm as a way of going 'beyond' criminology, arguing that the concept 'may be more theoretically coherent and more progressive politically than the current, generally accepted, notion of crime' (p. 15). Yet they then fail to outline the nature of its 'theoretical coherence' by offering any kind of substantive definition of the term. Nor do they appear to make any reference to the considerable body of literature on harm – in particular the work of Feinberg – as a secondary resource for clarifying how they intend to apply the term. The omission is frustrating, particularly since they later concede that a serious objection to the application of harm conceptions in criminology is precisely the fact that it 'appears to be a generalised, amorphous term, covering an enormous range of quite heterogeneous phenomena' (p. 62). One of their responses to such an objection is to appeal to the greater 'ontological reality' of the term in comparison to the term 'crime' – by which they seem to mean a greater weight of international agreement and empirical evidence about the harmful consequences of acts like corporate tax evasion that are missing from 'high-volume' crimes such as failing to pay a TV licence. But this simply re-emphasises the ambiguities in attempting to judge between the relative harmfulness of different acts. For one might point out that the consequences of 'minor' harmful acts such as TV licence payment defaults produce their own amplified social harms, perhaps equal to tax evasion. For example, such acts could also undermine public life by eroding trust and reducing the capacity of publicly owned broadcasting services to function effectively.

They then suggest that rather than attempting to provide unambiguous definitions of harm, it may be best to appeal to cases which establish practice. Thus, specific instances of injurious outcomes such as *physical harms* (for example murders, physical injuries, racial assaults and so on) or what they call *financial/economic* harm (theft, poverty and so on) are invoked. But having left the question of how to define harm hanging, such examples then have the tendency to cross over or to repeat themselves. For example, they go on to set out a category of what they call *emotional* or *psychological* harm (such as the effects of excessive stop-and-search tactics on an ethnic minority) even though this would seem to be adequately contained within a category of bodily harm (unless they are tacitly positing some untheorised variety of mind/body separation). They might respond that some framework is better than none and of course any framework is always open to reflexive revision in the light of further evidence and experience (Rawls, 1971). I shall certainly largely follow the line that we can best begin to understand harm on the basis of *outcomes*, in particular those which, over time, come to be agreed to have the most negative consequences.

Whilst deferring to this pragmatic stance, the approach advocated here also provides for ways in which a more general definition of harm might be essayed, should this be desired. The basis for this goes back to the idea that spatial occupation can be understood in *social* as well as geographical terms. Two useful conclusions follow from such an assumption. First, that there may be distinct regions or boundaries within this social space. Second, that, as suggested earlier, a distinctive region of social space can be associated with the particular set of social possibilities or *capacities* it offers. And this produces an interim lemma: where our occupations of space are affected *negatively* it follows that the specific possibilities of that space for us must be *reduced* in various ways. We arrive, on this line of reasoning, to a view that is closely related to Feinberg's (1984) idea of an association between harm and limitation of *choice*, where the most serious of such limitations relate to what he called our 'welfare interests' – 'the interests a person needs satisfied in order to have any significant capacity to choose and order his or her way of living' (von Hirsch & Jareborg, 1991, p. 8).

If an association between spatial occupation and capacity is accepted, the analytic for actions that induce social harm would then go something like this:

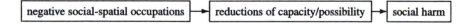

In turn, a provisional taxonomy of harms then begins to take shape. For example, if we think of *embodiment* in terms of spatial occupation then an attack upon the body becomes a harm in the sense that the possibilities of movement that a body grants may be lost. In the case of murder, the possibility of doing anything *at all* is lost. Likewise, where the set of things which are in some sense sustaining to a person – their 'own' things or their property – are affected by negative spatial occupations such as a robbery, a harm is also enacted. An (unwanted) intrusion into or occupation of this space may negatively compromise its possibilities for sustaining the body. For example, it may result in a reduction of the needed (or simply desired) resources it offers. Similar logic can be extended to social spaces of other kinds and the effects of unwanted and negative occupations of them.

In each case it seems that we can relate boundary violation to harm by way of this intervening concept of possibility or capacity reduction. Similarly, if social spaces can be associated with different kinds of capacity, they can be related to the different orders of harm that come from the various capacities which are reduced. Finally, if social spaces are taken to relate to various interests or capacities that form social possibilities for us, it seems clear that this may encompass social spaces which go beyond the immediately 'physical'. In other words, not only can it be used to analyse harms that result from proximal spatial interaction – but also to those which may arise as a result of remote interaction. For if the capacities which characterise social spaces can be redistributed under the hyperspatial it then follows that these too can be subject to damage of varying kinds.

Distance, incursion and harm

A three-point geometry of movements or 'incursions' to these different orders of social space results, one that can be used to identify actions that in the immediate sense are harmful but which in a legal sense may also turn out to be criminal, or at least 'criminalisable'.

(a) **Simple incursion**: Unauthorised or unwanted movement into a space or social space. Capacities need not be reduced under this form of incursion.
(b) **Degradative or damaging incursion**: Unauthorised or unwanted incursions into a space or social space resulting in some level of reduction of the capacities/possibilities it offers.
(c) **Destructive incursion**: Unauthorised or unwanted incursions into a space or social space resulting in a permanent termination of the possibilities/capacities it offers.

Whether (a) can be totally distinguished from (b) is not entirely clear. It may be simply that *some* form of capacity reduction (even if it is only psychological) will always result from an unwanted intrusion. However, it seems useful to distinguish this form of incursion as a way of theorising spatial movements which are not *intended* to cause damage or which result in damage which the subject is unaware of. Such incursions may have special relevance in the context of the hyperspatial where incursions such as hacking or surveillant monitoring raise important questions about the relations between space, harm and criminality.

Coupled with the key spatial notions under discussion in this book – in particular the notion of proximity – various 'clusterings' of harm seem also to emerge, clusterings which appear to bear at least some relation to the groupings of harms and their relative seriousness recognised by criminal justice systems. The relative seriousness of harms cannot of course be a construct which has a foundational logic to it – too many questions of subjective interest are always likely to intervene. But the fact that there appear to be some interesting conjunctions between our 'common-sense' notions about the relative seriousness of harms and spatial orderings given by proximity is certainly worth noting. For, as our value systems become increasingly sensitive to the hyperspatial, any continuities, however provisional, that can offer illumination into how we understand harm may also throw light upon the unfolding perceptions of criminality here.

Spatial orderings of harm

Von Hirsch and Jareborg (1991) try to set out one kind of model for grounding different orders of seriousness in criminal behaviour. In effect they propose what is called an *ordering*. The concept of taxomising phenomena by means of an ordering is a familiar practice in other disciplines – most obviously the mathematical and to an extent, the physical sciences (cf. Davey & Priestley, 2002). The natural numbers, for example, can be ordered by the functions '<' or '>' which results in a pattern where larger numbers occur later in the number series than smaller ones. The utility of this in mathematical operations is obvious enough. Likewise, physical matter may be organised by way of orderings in terms of *mass* – an ordering which produced the indispensable explanatory resource of the periodic table. Ordering functions therefore seem to play an important role in the way we are able to organise our understanding of natural and formal phenomena.

When it comes to the role of ordering functions in the social sciences, however, matters become immediately more tentative and tenuous. Not only has a realm of subjective, value judgement been entered which undermines the veneer of scientific objectivity (cf Whimster, 2007, p. 100ff.), such judgements cannot stand outside the capacities of power and control to shape them. This has not of course prevented social scientists from attempting to utilise orderings on occasions. Quantitative social research, with its resort to ordinal and scale variable levels of measurement, has appeared to offer one kind of basis for the idea but ordering of the social world based purely on quantitative data is always controversial (cf. Fletcher, 1974). The fragile balance within criminology between perceptions of deviance and instances of deviance would appear to make any putative orderings there even more prone to subjective effects.

On the other hand there are certainly common intuitions about the seriousness of criminal behaviours that give the *appearance* of an ordering, whatever their validity. And judgements that there are certain kinds of deviant acts which are 'more serious' than others are of course an important structuring feature of traditional criminal justice structures. Examples appear straightforward and familiar enough. Most societies have seemed likely to regard a murder as a more serious offence than urinating in a garden or to regard offences against private property as more serious than against public property.[3] Such pragmatic agreement seems to be supported by the little research into opinions of crime seriousness there has been done. For example, when asked to rate crime seriousness on a numeric scale respondents often tend to converge in their rank orderings, even across varying social classes (see for example Sparks *et al.*, 1977).

In von Hirsch and Jareborg's (1991) scheme, it is by way of the concept of a 'living standard analysis' that the desired ordering is derived. Drawing upon Amartya Sen's (1987) economic notion and supplementing it with quality-of-life notions such as 'well-being' they define the living standard as 'the means or capabilities for achieving a certain quality of life' (1991, p. 10). And it is standardised because this is what would '*ordinarily* help one to achieve a good life'. That is, one may have an unhappy life because one wishes to be famous, and have failed in this regard. But this would still be consistent with having a good standard of life if one had the means to live comfortably. Harmful action can then be ranked in terms of the degree to which the action affects the living standard. Violent assault is therefore 'more harmful than burglary . . . not because the maimed person's choices have been narrowed more' (as Feinberg's earlier criterion demanded, for example), but because 'the overall quality of his life is more adversely affected' (von Hirsch & Jareborg, 1991, p. 11). Harms then progress 'outward' from this and relate to different orders of legally protected interests – from physical integrity through to material support and amenity, freedom from humiliation, privacy and so on.

Whilst I have no intention of attempting to use such a scheme to produce any definitive ordering to harm, it may at least now be plausible why concepts of proximity might also play a general role within ascriptions of harm. For the *closest* proximity of interest to us seems to be constituted by spaces that we most desire to protect from harm – most obviously the spatial locations of our bodies. The familiar existential condition of embodiment thus becomes translated into a broader role of forming a potential zero point in any scaling of harm. How the seriousness of other harms maps 'outward' from this becomes increasingly controversial, but there seems to be at least some correspondences between the level of capacity removal, our judgements of seriousness and the order of proximity in question. For example, most would probably judge that the theft of their property damages their capacity for living more than vandalism towards a local bus stop.

My consideration of the new extensions to harm will therefore place the body at the orbital centre of this schema of proximities – a 'proximity 0' so to speak. Pursuing this metaphor I will then consider the unfolding of harm towards the series of social spaces which the body inhabits and which it operates through: proximity 1 – a 'property' space of objects, activities and relations where what sustains us and what we own is located; proximity 2 – the basic situation of what Goffman (1963, p. 22) called 'co-presences' where social life is experienced at its most immediate through family, work, friends and other ingredients of local networks. Finally – proximity 3, the conjunction of such local spaces into the global social environment which constitutes the widest communal space we inhabit and which appropriately often seems the most 'distant' from our concerns. As a result, it often seems less important to protect from harm than our bodies, our property or our familiar social world – whether this is justified or not.

Qualifications

A few qualifications are now in order before I can begin to apply the model in a more detailed way. I will consider three for the purposes of clarification. The first relates to whether it offers only a *dynamical* account of the harms that may arise from hyperspatialisation. For in it, harm appears to be theorised in terms of 'active' movement – as (intended) incursion to a social space. Yet it also seems true that harms may arise from someone 'doing nothing' as much as from doing something. For example, a person may stand aside while another is assaulted or robbed. Does the failure to be a good Samaritan then count as harmful? Alternatively, an industrial plant may take no active steps to reduce its carbon emissions, or a State may omit to adequately fund the education of its citizens. Can there be said to have been an overt *incursion* into a social space in such cases? And if not, does the analysis then preclude such omissions being treated as harms? The act of 'nonfeasance', as it is sometimes called (Kortmann, 2001), is legally complex – for it is not always clear whether 'not doing something' is the same as 'failing to act'. There is certainly no compulsion within most legal systems to act to help others, or to force someone to act to prevent harm. Nonetheless, nonfeasance is still consistent with the model, for this is concerned primarily with seeing incursion as a way in which harm is *suffered* rather than as a way of modelling overt attempts to *inflict* harm or the precise culpabilities that go with this. Thus, an agent may be unaware that their actions have led to a harm, or have 'done nothing' in such a way that harm has arisen, but in each case the result will still be an unwanted violation of a social space.

A second issue relates to the intended universality of the claims made. Most obviously, while embodiment is a foundational part of the metric, it should be clear that no one 'universal' body, which shapes the way harms are successively experienced, is meant to be implied. Rather, and as the hyperspatial in fact demands, incursion here is seen as *multidimensional*. So commencing analysis from the fact of an 'embodied state' (Thrift, 1996, p. 14) remains consistent with a variety of subjective experiential overlappings. At the same time it also allows for a great deal of *agreement* on what we judge to be harmful towards bodies and other social spaces – criminal justice systems, as suggested, certainly presume as much.

A third qualification relates to the *way* that harms flow between the differing proximities of social space. Even though the body acts as an orbital centre for our subjective experience and understanding of harm, it is important to be clear that no privileged direction for the *cause* or for the *way* that harm flows between these spaces is thereby intended. For example, actions within global space may well feed back into the harming of individual bodies, or to a local environment, just as an individual's actions may harm the environment. Indeed (as is in fact usually the case), the harmful flows may operate simultaneously across these spaces. Part of the difficulty is that the spaces theorised here are not ontologically distinct but interpenetrate each other continuously. The spaces do not so much connect like the graduated 'slices' of an onion – or even the pieces of a Russian Doll – but form a series of simultaneous 'hyper-positions'. Thus my body is in its space *at the same time* and coextensively as it is within local or global space. Global space is simultaneously composed of multiple bodies and their projects, as well as local spaces and flows of property.

There are obvious consequences for this in how we think of the question of agency. And the presumption throughout will be that agency can be read as having a *collective* as well as an individual basis. In this way, just as a position in one space is simultaneously a position in another, actors characteristic of the different spatialities can *simultaneously* be acting as distinct individuals, while also acting as part of a wider collectivity. In this way the harms which then arise may also (but not always) occur simultaneously over several social spaces. Thus, where a corporation harms global space by marketing faulty foodstuffs it may also harm individual bodies by way of the individual employees who produce them. Likewise, a collective actor like a State may simultaneously violate global or local space by carpet-bombing villages, while the individual actions of the pilots who drop the bombs *also* cause harm to individuals' bodies. The analysis here will avoid these complexities of agency by keeping focused upon the actors constitutive of a particular space and the harms they commit there. Thus if States harm bodies in personal space it will be taken to mean that this occurs through the particularised actors or mechanisms constitutive of that space, whereas if individuals harm States it will be taken to mean that this occurs through the collective actors typical of a global space.

Crucial to understanding the way harm unfolds across these spaces is the way it is understood as a 'limitation of capacity'. But what this means is, as already conceded, open to a degree of interpretation. With destructive incursion, matters are a little clearer in that the removal of (some or all) capacity is absolute. Otherwise 'degrees' of capacity removal must be allowed and a subjective element in then deciding how far capacity must be damaged or removed for an action to be unambiguously 'harmful'. Insofar as any answer could be given to questions about 'how harmful', or 'harmful for who', the provision for *a relatively permanent* outcome seems important. For I may harm your capacity to experience the sunlight by standing in its way and creating shade. But this is not a permanent removal of the capacity and so can easily change very quickly.

But at this point some hand waving is also in order. Whilst it is important to signal an awareness of the philosophical difficulties in deciding *which* degrees of reduction to the capacities offered by social spaces are the harmful ones, it will not be essential in what follows to make a definitive decision on this. For it only needs to be accepted that there are *some* degrees that result in harm to get on with applying the model for its real purpose – as a way of illustrating how the experience of this may be changing as spatial experience is changing. The analysis of hyperspatialisation, and the new geometries of harm that go with this, can therefore proceed without having, in every case, to decide how much of a harm there is or who (or what) was responsible. It is to this wider task that I shall now turn in more detail.

Chapter 2

The making of hypercrime

Either you have stumbled ... onto a network by which X number of Americans are truly communicating while reserving their lies ... for the official government delivery system ... Or are you hallucinating it?

Thomas Pynchon, *The Crying of Lot 49*

The making of hypercrime did not happen overnight – and certainly not in the 15 years since the origins of the internet. The tendency, especially in discussion of cybercrime, to see the advent of deviant behaviours that exploit the technologies of telepresence as 'a significantly new phenomenon, with profound social consequences' (Thomas & Loader, 2000, p. 2) is symptomatic of the dehistoricised overview that obscures their long development. 'Doing things at a distance' (cf. Giddens, 1991) is not something that has emerged from nowhere, or because the American military found out how to link some computers together in the late 1960s. Hyperspatialisation – those transitions in our experience and uses of space and time that facilitate hypercrime – is a process with many historical roots. All that really differs at each stage of its development is 'the *degree* (my italics) to which the friction of space has been overcome to accommodate social interaction' (Harvey, 1989, p. 222). No single technology can be associated with this phenomenon – no matter how quickly it may have served to accelerate such trends. Likewise, technology itself should be seen as only complementary to the social basis for criminal efforts that seek to transcend the limitations of embodiment. As Raymond Williams put this:

... people say 'television altered our world' or 'radio altered the world' or reading further back, 'printing altered the world'. And we usually know, at first, what these statements mean. Evident and widespread social effects have undoubtedly followed the uses of all these inventions. But then ... we have already ... introduced a further category; that of uses. It can then be said that what has altered our world isn't television, or radio, or printing, but the uses made of them, in particular societies.

(1981, p. 226)

To Williams' list we can now of course add the internet. And just as the *use* of any single technology should not be exclusively associated with the making of hypercrime nor should its emergence be exclusively associated with any particular historical epoch. Attempts to transcend space and time have been a feature of almost every culture, irrespective of their level of technological development. And deviant imaginations have always been ready to exploit whatever new opportunities arise from such social developments. As Gabriel Tarde reflected: 'criminals use . . . more intelligently than the police the resources of our civilization' (cited in Deflem, 2002, p. 467). Yet it also seems true that the success of control systems can often be measured in terms of how effectively they are able to transcend spatio-temporal barriers. In his hugely influential *Empire and Communications*, Harold Innis pointed out how the very fact of Empire is 'an indication of the efficiency of communication' (1950, p. 11). In order to better appreciate the origins and historical complexities of the hyperspatial this chapter will outline a broader background to the ways in which these 'resources of civilization' have been exploited than is usual. This will hopefully illustrate more clearly why we should be careful about falling back upon 'cybercrime' as the primary explanatory resource for deviant behaviour that exploits remote technologies. For the substantive archaeology of such behaviours that can be identified suggests a much richer mode of interpretation. I will begin by examining the deeper roots of the hyperspatialisation process itself.

The origins of the hyperspatial

As suggested in the previous chapter, the hyperspatial seems able to be broken down into a number of distinct but complementary components which combine to produce its effects. For example, in addition to more obvious factors such as space-time compression, the role of representation and its powers also appears to play an important part. Castells (2001) seems to make such an association, by explicitly linking symbolic practice with what he terms 'the virtual':

> . . . reality, as experienced has always been virtual because it is always perceived through symbols that frame practice . . . with some meaning that escapes their short semantic definition . . . All realities are communicated through symbols. And in human, interactive communication . . . all symbols are somewhat displaced in relation to their assigned semantic meaning. In a sense, all reality is virtually perceived.
>
> (Castells, 2001, pp. 403–404)

The fact that a representational system abbreviates or omits aspects of reality, or because it is able to represent *non-actual* states of affairs – 'fictions' – does not, as Meinong (1904) argued, mean that we need to grant an existence to non-existent objects. Nor therefore does it license any ontology of the virtual. As perhaps the most flexible of our tools, language not only permits us to abbreviate or compress actual experience, it also allows us to experience the *non-actual*. There is no magic here – for this power comes from the inbuilt semantic and syntactic capacity of language to recombine aspects of the actual into assertions about merely possible or counterfactual situations (Armstrong, 1989). The referential power of language and the concepts it codes are not therefore fixed to their referents (Frege, 1980), just as Saussure pointed out that, 'a linguistic sign is not a link between a thing and a name, but between a concept and a sound pattern' (1983, p. 66). This looseness of reference expands linguistic capacity, but can of course also pose problems with the extent to which we can depend upon language to represent truthfully. Quine's thesis of the 'underdetermination of reference' (1960) presents one well-known summary of this long-standing problem. The underdetermination thesis means that while language serves to represent the world there can never be any decisive *fact* of the matter as to whether the choice of one representational schema performs the role better than another. But this does not mean that the results of our models and representations are thereby simulations, virtualities or some 'mad project of an ideal coextensivity between the map and the territory' (Baudrillard, 1983, p. 2). We would not survive long if this were so. Instead there is a clear measure of success for any representational system purporting to model reality – the extent of causal power to affect that reality it grants to us. By extension, one measure of success of a representational system that purports to model a non-actual situation is the extent to which it enables us to experience realities *alternative* to the actual. There is, in other words, a more interesting idea to take from Castells' oversimplistic equation of linguistic representation with 'the virtual'. This is the idea that by abbreviating, summarizing and even altering aspects of our normal located experiences language – like any representational system – can enable us to 'go beyond' the experiences of time and space presented by the sensory reach of bodies. A feature of a *good* representational system is that it permits the transmission and processing of information not limited to a particular location or time.

Consider, for example, a culture where no linguistic capacity other than what Quine has referred to as 'ostensive definition' was available (Quine, 1978). That is, a culture whose referring terms could only be used to denote objects and experiences which are *immediately* present: 'this food here now', 'that fire there now' and so on. Exchanges of information would be limited to those which involved references to objects within sensory range, at present moments. Such a culture would clearly be a very denuded one, robbed of a large part of the understandings and experiences which we take for granted. It would also be likely to be a much less successful culture in evolutionary terms than those which did possess such representational resources. Fortunately, meaningful discourse does not tend to depend upon ostensive definition alone. Instead language is rich with expressive resources such as tenses, indirect reference or the subjunctive form which means it can 'say more' or go beyond that which can be determined by immediate presence. On the basis of such resources cultures have been able to react, plan and make decisions about states of affairs at distances beyond the sensory reach of their bodies. Behaviours towards objects or events which are not spatially present to subjects are a familiar and essential part of social interaction. Whilst languages may vary in their resources to affect this – Chinese, for example, is notoriously lacking in tenses – language in general has served a central role within culture of making rudimentary forms of 'action over a distance' possible. In this sense it is as much a despatialising technology as any more sophisticated communications device. As McLuhan put this:

> . . . language does for intelligence what the wheel does for the feet and the body. It enables them to move from thing to thing with the greatest ease and speed and ever less involvement. Language extends and amplifies man.
>
> (1964, p. 113)

Language and the hypercriminal – deception and rumour

The encoding of information and its transmission by *language* therefore seems to count as an early, very simple example of a way in which humans have been able to circumvent the limitations of located bodies, in ways that prefigure the hyperspatial. At this point criminality immediately intrudes. For with the advent of such a tool comes the possibility that it might be exploited as a way of gaining an unfair advantage over others. The illicit use of language as a way of deceiving others as to the true state of the world – the phenomenon of deception – is perhaps one of the earliest significant points at which behaviours clearly definable as 'deviant' emerge. And the uneasy continuities between the creative and harmful aspects of deviance that recur repeatedly through the history of crime exist almost from the birth of the lie. For just as criminal innovation has often influenced the development of various technologies, so George Steiner has argued that deception was fundamental to the development of human language itself. More than this, language and the capacities it offers for distorting our experience of reality drives the tensions upon which culture as a whole is based. 'Language' insisted Steiner (1975), 'is the main instrument of man's refusal to accept the world as it is'. Social psychologists have made a similar point – that rumour has played a fundamental role in the evolution of human intelligence and social life (Davis & McLeod, 2003; Dunbar, 2004).

The capacity for deception thus has certain continuities with creativity – a clear sign that, like deviance in general, it may offer benefits as well as harms.

As Nietzsche (1979) pointed out, '. . . what men avoid by excluding the liar is not so much being *defrauded* as it is being *harmed* by means of fraud'. Early examples of self-serving uses of language seem intuitively obvious enough, though precise historical records are at best fragmentary. The curse from the Book of Revelations which declared that, '. . . all liars shall have their part in the lake that burneth with fire and brimstone' (xxi. 8) indicates the level of social disapproval which has always existed against the practice of deception. In oral cultures the use of false reports, whether for the purposes of fraud, robbery or worse, must have been an especial violation of fundamental codes of civility. But as well as anticipating the capacity to acquire illicit benefit through mis-representations of the spatio-temporal, language also prefigures a further aspect of the hypercriminal often seen as 'technologically determined'. Language is also able to *inflate* aspects of the real in ways that stimulate our imagination, and with that our fears. Long before the communicative connectivities of the media existed, networks of linguistic communities generated rumour and tall tales that grew in the telling. The readiness to accept threat is as equally important in forming impressions of hypercriminality as the technologies of telepresence are in facilitating it. And this has always been fuelled by language's capacity to distort spatial experience through exaggeration and implication.

Language can therefore be seen to anticipate several ingredients of the hyperspatialising process. Firstly, in the way that, via its capacity to represent, language obviates the need for immediate presence in acquiring or responding to information. Rudimentary spatial compression occurs. Secondly, by providing a homogenised and universal communication medium it creates a primitive network form which enables limited remote communication through the messaging system of oral transmission. In turn such networks prefigure the hypercriminal by creating a system through which deceptions and rumours – misinformation – may equally flow.

But of course much is also missing from the kinds of capacity offered by hyperspatialisation in its more developed forms. Whilst access to information about remote places and times may be acquired without the requirement to go there, transmission is less immediate or convenient since there always remains the need for presence – the human agent who passes on the information. Likewise, unless the memories of these human transmitters are very good, the representational precision of the message is more likely to be denigrated as transmission reoccurs. Oral traditions tend not to preserve the details of an original event very accurately so that, on its own, language is a defective transmitter over time. Another cultural innovation associated with language was required to improve upon this. In so doing it further increased the power of representation and its significance within the hyperspatialisation process.

Extending the compressive power of language

This crucial development in the loosening of social relations from spatio-temporal determinations was the development of fully *symbolic* communication systems, in the form of writing. George Steiner has argued that one sense of culture itself can be seen in terms of this 'translation and rewording of previous meaning' (1975, p. 31) but this was now a culture in which, according to Harold Innis:

> (humans) . . . were given an artificially extended and verifiable memory of objects and events not present to sight or recollection. Individuals applied their minds to symbols rather than things and went beyond the world of concrete experience into the world of conceptual relations created within an enlarged time and space universe.
>
> (1971, pp. 10–11)

The way in which writing facilitated further transcendence of location is essential to the development of this enlarged universe. For example, Goody and Watt (1968) and Havelock (1963) associated the development of literacy in Ancient Greece with some of the key advances in logical analysis, advances that lie at the foundation of later developments in the representational powers of mathematics and science. Such developments were of course also fundamental to the development of symbolic languages which were to advance computation itself. In terms of hyperspatialisation, the invention of writing had two key effects. Firstly, it further diminished the requirement for presence, since information about spatially distant locations could now be acquired *without* any human transmitter but through artifacts such as scrolls or clay tablets. Secondly, as Innis suggests, by providing for better storage of data it compressed time. Information could now be much more efficiently retained for later transmission than was the case where representational systems were dependent upon human transmitters. Limited forms of interaction between individuals separated by many decades or centuries became possible with the advent of written records. The project of understanding someone's thoughts, or interacting with alternative social formations was facilitated by way of inscriptions on a tomb, notes in a diary or records left by cultures long gone. Whilst this interaction was not yet two-way of course, the communication mechanism that Williams referred to as storage – 'the recording in more or less permanent form, human voices' (Williams 1981, p. 227) – had properly arrived.

Writing and crime

In turn, redistributions in spatial possibility arising from representations that could be stored and reprocessed were implicated in further expansions to deviant possibilities. And the precedent set by language as a resource for deception and fraud was especially enhanced with writing. Previously a person's word had literally been their bond, a verbal contract declared within the presence of others, but writing made this bond transparently and publicly accessible. Yet rather than diminishing the possibilities of fraud, it actively enhanced them. For in *representing* some authority by signatures, seals or other such marks, the scene was set for greater convenience in the illicit copying or reproduction of this authority. Just as with the later case of pin numbers, or ID cards, the attempt to *increase* security by an investment in some unique mark of identification also served to lend any credible forgeries of such a mark an enhanced authority (cf. Lutterbeck *et al.*, 2000). A forgery, invested with the representation of an authority, was much easier to pass off than where authenticity depended upon presence. The forgery and alteration of documents therefore became as much a feature of illicit criminal gain in the ancient world as it is today (Arnau, 1959; Jones, 1990). But moral perceptions about the relationship between authenticity and fakery were not always very clear. When monks at Canterbury were confronted by the accusation that they had altered dates on Papal Bulls to ensure that their primacy should not pass to the seat of York, 'the monks admitted (the documents) were only copies, but nonetheless valid' (Burke, 1991). It has been estimated that one in three documents in circulation in the Middle Ages contained invented dates or other false information (Burke, 1991). Counterfeiting seals of authority, especially royal seals, could be highly profitable, but was also a highly skilled task, requiring literacy and good connections with officials and clerks (Bellamy, 1973). The scale of inventiveness in this prototypical 'white-collar' crime could be impressive. Pike (1873, i, 271–272) reports how, in 1348, a bailiff in Suffolk refused to pay money to a robber posing as a merchant of Ghent who presented him with the royal seal of Queen Philippa of Ghent. The robber returned, this time with a forged letter asking for a larger sum of money which he also refused. An accomplice then showed up posing as a Sheriff's officer with a (forged) writ from the King to the Sheriff of Suffolk. Attached to it was a royal seal (also forged) which required the seizure of goods from the bailiff to the value of the amount that had originally been requested by 'Queen Philippa'. The bailiff, a victim of medieval identity fraud if there ever was one, finally accepted the apparent authenticity of the multiple documents and paid up.

But other kinds of criminal possibilities were also facilitated. Assassinations could now be ordered at a distance, robberies could be planned, sexual assaults threatened. Early forms of 'white-collar' crime emerged as the bureaucracies responsible for the keeping of written records about commerce found ways to distort and thereby exploit such records for profit. In turn, the written objects that conferred these controls over space and time – manuscripts, scrolls and the like – themselves began to acquire a value. Just as the hyper-spatialising powers of contemporary communications services like mobile phones have lent them a value which makes them attractive to thieves, so written communications and documents became objects worth acquiring, illicitly if necessary. In turn the advent of writing enhanced control mechanisms, most obviously in the new capacity to *contrarotulare* or 'compare against the rolls' discussed in the previous chapter – for example, in the keeping of court or financial records. The connections between representational power and control were thereby strengthened and developed. For whoever had control of the records was able to exert power, both in virtue of the knowledge it brought them and also by the capacity to shape and present the version of this knowledge that best suited their interests. Harold Innis has pointed out how the emergence of the professional scribe classes in Egypt and Mesopotamia resulted in a huge expansion of regulatory controls where, 'practically every act of civil life was a matter of law which was recorded and confirmed by the seals of contracting parties and witnesses' (Innis, 1991, p. 35). Likewise in ancient Sumer the association of writing with 'large numbers of legal contracts, deeds of sale and land transfers' (Innis, 1950, p. 30) invokes the role of the authenticated list as a control mechanism.

The power of the written word to affect human culture and to further transcend spatial limitation was greatly developed by a technological shift perhaps as equally profound as contemporary information technology – the invention of printing. The scientific revolution itself (and therefore all the later technologies it stimulated) has often been associated with the advent of printing for, as Postman argues, 'it is no accident that the Age of Reason was co-existent with the growth of a print culture' (1985, p. 53). Whilst, in 1400 the only non-hand-produced visual/paper/ artefacts were those produced by primitive block-printed techniques, by 1500 over 40,000 recorded editions of printed documents were in circulation (Derry & Williams, 1960). Assuming a print run of only around 500 these 40,000-plus recorded titles meant there must have been more than 20 million books in circulation. A flood of information that complexified space and interaction in familiar ways followed. 'At a stroke Europe was covered by a network of a quite new kind and the first modern "medium" established itself, just as quickly as television and data networks have done' (Martin, 2001, p. 132). The new social network form produced provided tighter connections between spatially segregated actors and 'reading communities' where ideas could be published and exchanged. Thus, by the end of the sixteenth century the 200,000 or so titles recorded as available at that time would then have meant that (with a print run of only 1,000) nearly 200 million books would have been in existence (Martin, 2001, p. 138)! This brought immediate improvements to the spatio-temporal limitations of information exchange as better and more accurate storage mechanisms facilitated transmission across wider temporal and spatial intervals. New techniques for taxonomising, ordering and indexing information also improved its universality and accessibility. As Eisenstein (1979) argues, just as with computing technologies, the advent of the printed word provided for a kind of mechanisation of human memory that allowed more time for 'pure' thinking rather than simple rote memorisation.

Inevitably, printing also presented a much more comprehensive set of deviant possibilities than was provided by writing alone. With printing: 'man could now inspire – and conspire' as McLuhan puts it (McLuhan & Fiore, 1967, p. 50). Shorn of the authenticities of presence granted by handwritten documents, mechanised writing provided further ways by which fraud could be practised. For example, in addition to the counterfeiting of coinage (which had always been a problem) paper bills or contracts could now be more easily forged. One common strategy of the late eighteenth century reported in the Newgate Calendar was to obtain an £11 note and then change it into an £80 note by using chemicals to erase the 'leven' in eleven and change it into 'ighty' (NNC, 1818, iv, 232–239). The new crime breach opened up by printing is evident in the fact that, by 1750, over four hundred statutes against forgery were in existence with new ones constantly required to close each new technique which appeared (McLynn, 1989, p. 134). A whole new era in intellectual crime was also facilitated with the possibility of copying books without permission or, as it became known, 'copyright'. Printing also further accelerated the kinds of moral panics and psychoses about unknown threats in ways that anticipate many of the pathological strands discernible within hypercriminality. One theme was a fear of the technology itself – which was often seen as tainted with sickness and infection. A concerned observer from 1795, for example, claimed that excessive reading could cause 'colds, headaches, ... arthritis, hemorrhoids, asthma, ... migraines, epilepsy, hypochondria, and, melancholy' (cited in Murray, 2000, p. 48). In turn a kind of medieval moral panic emerged that sought to construct printing and the act of reading itself as a form of deviant behaviour. But in so doing it anticipated the dilemmas faced by contemporary regulators of the internet – that the power of the printed word threatened to undermine control as much as to enhance it. Thus, early Tudor newsletters were heavily censored along with many other outputs of the new print entrepreneurs – those 'establishments allied to the inventions of Oxford and Cambridge' (Fox, 1998, p. 27). Pope Alexander fretted that:

> It will be necessary to maintain full control over the printers so that they may be prevented from bringing into print writings which are antagonistic to the Catholic faith

while in 1807 the British Parliament were concerned that:

> [G]iving education to the labouring classes of the poor . . . would in effect be found to be prejudicial to their morals and happiness; . . . it would enable them to read seditious pamphlets, vicious books, and publications against Christianity; it would render them insolent.
>
> (both quotes cited in Murray, 2000, pp. 48–49)

The increased capacity of newspapers and pamphlets to link thinkers who shared common views but who were spatially dispersed prefigured the 'extended community effect' of later communicative networks and raised many similar issues about the relationship between control and perceptions of criminality.

The representation of value: spatial complexification and monetary systems

As an instance of a primitive network, reading communities represented an early form of the spatial *complexification* I have argued is as important to the hyperspatial as more familiar constructs like time-space compression. J.R. and W.H. McNeill (2003) traced the growth of a number of other putative networks in history – developments they describe as the 'human web'. They highlight five historical precedents for contemporary networked communication systems. The first they relate to connections established by early hunter-gatherer tribes which were further solidified with the development of agriculture and the closer forms of social interaction that came with settled communities. A second 'metropolitan web' connected the ancient urban centres which spread across Mesopotamia, Egypt, China and so on. The new trading and communication networks they stimulated provided for still tighter, more regular flows of cultural exchange. This metropolitan web was in turn succeeded by a third network described as the *old world web* situated across the bureaucratic empires of the ancient world such as Greece, Rome, India, China and Mexico. From around 1450 this was in turn succeeded by the *cosmopolitan web* which resulted from the developments in navigation. These linked together the 'old' and 'new' worlds and circulated information faster – a process further accelerated by the drift towards urban centres. The *global web* of the last 150 years is then merely a culmination of these longer term trends in the complexification of social space and interaction. It is a process usefully described by van Dijk (2006, p. 23) as a 'thickening' of the network, rather than a 'widening'.

The more tightly connected trading and exchange systems that went with these 'webs' focused economic flows that have played as important a role in diminishing distance as technology itself. By helping to smooth or 'liquidise' various social barriers, historical mechanisms of trade and exchange have always played a crucial role in establishing social connections and then speeding flows across them (Curtin, 1984). Once again representation has been at the centre of this process. The transformation of trade involving commodities with 'manifest', or intrinsic value, to trade involving purely symbolic forms has been central in developing the representational abstractions which foster the multi-dimensional connectibility of the hyperspatial. And a virtuous circle results. The bringing together of otherwise spatially remote societies by the capacity to effect smoother exchange relations both compresses space-time as well as serving to drive the abstraction of these exchange relations still further. As Simmel put it: '. . . economic activity establishes distances, and overcomes them' (1978, p. 75).

As symbolic monetary systems fostered a more developed mercantilism which required constant expansion into new markets, the limitations of purely local economies began to be evaded more effectively. In turn new goods, services and wealth accrued from the strengthening of economies that spread far beyond the local exchange systems. As Harvey put it: '. . . money can be used to command time (our own or that of others and space. Conversely, command of time and space can be converted back into money' (1989, p. 226). But money does not compress time and space in purely abstract terms – it does so by way of real social relations. Citing Marx's dictum: 'economy of time, to this all economy ultimately reduces itself' (Marx, 1976, p. 173), Harvey points out that, 'money measures value, but if we ask ourselves what constitutes value in the first instance, we find it impossible to define value without saying something about how the time of social labour is allocated' (Harvey, 1989, p. 227).

In addition to its compressive powers money, as suggested, also helps *complexify* spatial experience. Its capacity to remove the barriers to exchange arises as much from transcending representational subjectivities as in overcoming spatial distance. By fixing value more universally money quite literally extends the number and varieties of human interaction in previously unimaginable ways. Each further development in the complexity of monetary systems, from the innovation of double-entry book-keeping (Brown, 1968), through to credit systems or futures markets also represents complexifications in social interaction which have enabled humans to further overcome the limitations of the here and now.

But the convenience of systems that offer universal and multiply exchangeable representations of material wealth were bound to come at a price in criminological terms, so many were the new opportunities for illicit gain thereby generated. The enhancement of theft was perhaps the most obvious such outcome. It became a much more efficient and easy task to steal *representations* of value than the objects of value themselves (which could always then be acquired later). In this sense we clearly see how theft from an electronic bank account is little different from theft involving a handful of banknotes or coins. And this increased reliance on representations of value also fostered developments in counterfeiting, for the deviant manipulation of the objects that confer representational value also constituted an irresistible opportunity for gain. By medieval times this problem had become so acute that when, in 1134, Henry I suspected that his own officials had been issuing base coinage he ordered a drastic solution: 'All moneyers in the country should in the 12 days following Christmas lose their right hand and testicles' (MacCall, 1979, p. 149). Abstract representational systems for value also presented easy opportunities for fraud. In particular, the innocence of those who did not always fully understand the way that value could be represented and exchanged in successions of increasingly abstract systems was there to be exploited. And this made them just as easy targets for theft as uninformed individuals engaged in exchanges of values over the internet today. A striking example of such exploitations of innocence within early capitalism was the collapse of the South Sea Company in 1720 and its ruination of many modest investors – an outcome that led to widespread discontent. For it seemed obvious to many that the new knowledge elites of capitalism were exploiting their greater understanding of the financial systems which developed after the foundation of the Bank of England for their own good. Writing in the same year Bernard Mandeville asserted that this 'deep villainy' was not committed by 'poor ignorant rogues' but by 'the better sort of people as to wealth and education . . . great masters in arithmetic (who) . . . lived in reputation and splendour' (1970, p.183, cited in McLynn, 1989, p. 153). The febrile capitalism of Victorian England took these exploitations of innocence to new levels, resulting in a situation where fraudsters 'gleefully collected millions of pounds from hundreds of thousands of investors sublimely ignorant of stock shares and the mysteries of the financial market' (Emsley, 1996, p. 69). The contemporary pattern seen in past experiences is clear again. A new media – money – able to complexify space, then stimulates the growth of a class of deviant behaviours ready to exploit this capacity. Its further abstraction to cope with ever more hyperspatialised forms of exchange and the new opportunities for its illicit acquisition which then arise through information technology is just the latest stage in that long historical process.

Transport networks and speed

The speeding of spatial connection by transportation provides another key instance of early hyperspatiality. As Virilio argues, the 'mass transportation revolution of the nineteenth century' was a mutation affecting 'both public and domestic space to the point where we were left in some doubt as to their very reality' (1997, p. 9). Thus, the command of space enjoyed by the Romans was clearly inseparable from what has been estimated to be around 100,000 miles of road network available to them (Wiseman, 1970). But road and other transport networks were vastly enhanced as agents of the hyperspatial when movement through and across them was speeded up by the new technologies of steam and the internal combustion engine (Beniger, 1986, p. 192). As Harvey pointed out, the development of railways, steam, shipping and the beginnings of automobile travel in the nineteenth century represented an 'incredible . . . long term investment in the conquest of space' (1989, p. 264). The railway network 'eroded . . . remoteness' (Kern, 1983, p. 213) and forced temporal uniformities across space in the need to synchronise clocks and time zones according to the requirements of the rail timetable. What was begun here, now differs not so much in terms of form but in terms of scale as newer transport networks like airlines accelerate and complement the range of geographical connectivities. An equally crucial feature of contemporary hyperspatialisation as communications technology has therefore been the mass circulations of physical bodies across transport networks. John Adams has recently noted how, while in 1950 the average Briton travelled around 5 miles per day, by 2006 the figure was closer to 30 miles (Adams, 2005, p. 2), a figure predicted to double by 2025. But what Adams refers to as 'hypermobility' inevitably brings harms as well as benefits. Cities sprawl and become more dispersed as space is 'consumed'. Problems of social alienation increase, for 'in *hyper*mobile societies old-fashioned geographical communities are replaced by aspatial communities of interest – we spend more of our time, physically, in the midst of strangers' (ibid, p. 2). And in addition to the harms arising from community fragmentation there are many others that might be considered. For example, the continued rise in transport-related injuries, environmental damage from carbon-based fuels, the development of mobility 'haves' and 'have nots', and so on (ibid, p. 5ff.).

Other more traditional kinds of crime that might be related to the hyperspatialising effects of transport have been noted by criminologists. Geographical mobilities by their very nature provide sources and locations for criminal opportunity that have only just begun to be studied in any detail (see for example Paternoster & Tittle, 1988; Newton, 2004). The bandit and the highwayman represent traditional figures who exploited either their own mobilities or those of the transport network as a focus for acquisitive crime (Spraggs, 2001; Brandon, 2004; Hallsworth, 2005). Likewise, the growth in seaborne trade to the UK in the eighteenth century meant that, between 1713 and 1775, there were estimated to be around 20,000 individuals (out of a population of only 8 million or so) who were engaged in full-time smuggling (Cole, 1958). The huge wealth coming into the Port of London alone meant that between 1749 and 1750 nearly £100,000-worth of goods (in eighteenth-century money) were stolen. And nine-tenths of all crime in the Port of London arose from exploitations of opportunity by authorised officials – not professional criminals (McLynn, 1989, pp. 8–9). Deflem (2002) points to research into criminal and legal implications of the railways that was produced as early as 1893 in Germany, while Hanna (1927) and Vold (1946) presented early studies of the role of the car and the aeroplane respectively in stimulating criminal behaviour. Indeed, the mere existence of transport connections generates its own criminalisation process in the form of laws to do with speeding, road safety and so on. And with such infrastructures again comes opportunity. From car radio theft, car jacking or speed racing incidents (see for example Gross, 2007), from airport hi-jackings, passport offences or disorderly behaviour on a plane, transport systems represent a rich field for criminological research as well as feeding and continually reconstructing hypercriminality.

Communication technology and hyperspatialisation
– post and telegraphy

As the growth in texts about cybercrime suggests, hyperspatialisation and its affect upon crime has tended to be most discussed in the context of communication technologies, and especially the internet. But of course networked communications systems again predate the internet by many centuries. One simple example is the development of postal networks. Herodotus described what appeared to have been a remarkably complex postal system at work in the Persian Empire where:

> (for) . . . as many days as there are in the whole journey, so many are the men and horses that stand along the road, each horse and man at the interval of a day's journey; and these are stayed neither by snow nor rain nor heat nor darkness from accomplishing their appointed course with all speed.
>
> (Herodotus, 1924, 4, bk 8, verse 98, p. 96)

Mulgan (1991) indicates how the, '. . . early postal networks of the Persian, Roman, Mongol and Chinese Empires were tools of administration under the direct control of military and political authorities' (p. 1) so serving as useful control mechanisms. The monopoly of communication power by control systems was also maintained under the later, more organised postal networks that developed through the fourteenth and fifteenth centuries. Reserved largely for the sovereign, these postal routes were maintained as tools of political power by hereditary postmasters such as the famous Tassis family who organised complex distribution networks across Europe where, 'each post office along the route was a node for other Tassis services and networks of local carriers' (Arblaster, 2005, p. 22). The nineteenth century saw the biggest developments in the speed, organisation and complexity of the system. The advent of proper addressing methods enabled accurate delivery, while the kinds of transport technologies discussed in the previous section meant that messages arrived quickly enough for something like real-time communication to emerge. The development of mass mailing technologies in the 1880s discussed by Beniger (1986, p. 19) increased the scope and reach of postal systems hugely. For example, the circulation of the first Sears and Roebuck catalogues had risen from 318,000 in 1897 to around 7 million by the 1920s. And while this increased consumer choice, it also fostered what has turned out to be important mechanisms for the control society – databases and direct marketing techniques. Yet though postal systems enhanced the efficiency of message exchange over distance there was still too much of a timelag, and too little in the way of genuine interactivity for it to approach the developed telepresence that full hyperspatialisation seems likely to permit. For a precursor of that we need to look to systems of *tele*graphy – that form of telepresence situated, as the name suggests, in the capacity for 'far' or remote writing.

Whilst sound technologies, such as drums, provided one way of exchanging messages over distance, the visual spectrum was a further obvious resource to be exploited. And just as the vital (acoustic) property of an object used in sound communication was its superior amplification range, visual communication technologies overcame the spatial limitations of our visual systems by extending the distance at which signals could be read. Smoke or fire-based signalling systems which used height or light intensity to be seen from afar were obvious choices. And a mixture of both visual and acoustic signalling systems meant that messages could be exchanged during nighttime as well as daytime periods. Documentary evidence indicates the existence of numerous signalling networks between towns in Mesopotamia over 4,000 years ago, with strong centralised control (Solymar, 1999). But clearly, the effectiveness of their communicative possibilities was limited by the fact that signals would not have possessed a very complex internal semantics. The most complex messages would have been pre-arranged patterns spelling out information such as 'flee', 'the enemy is advancing' and so on. *Alphabetic telegraphy* by contrast was able to utilise proto-linguistic forms of signalling. For example, the Ancient Greek historian Polybius described an ingenious method in use around 300 BC which divided the 24-letter Greek alphabet into five groups. By using two torches, combinations indicating specific letters could be signalled (Polybius, 1925, X, 43). The Romans developed ideas such as these into more sophisticated signalling systems. On Hadrian's Wall, for example, an alphabetic system was used based on two groups of five flags, which allowed them to send messages letter by letter (Donaldson, 1988). Similar systems were still being developed in England as late as the end of the eighteenth century.

This kind of optical signalling reached its fullest development with the work of Claude Chappe and his brother Rene who, for the first time, advanced signalling principles beyond the stage the Romans had reached. A comparatively new kind of spatially compressive technology which had come from the scientific revolutions of the sixteenth century – the telescope – gave them the means to do this. For by using a telescope to read the positions of a T-shaped wooden device which had been rotated to correspond to different letters, clear signals could be sent over much greater ranges. Chappe's system was successfully demonstrated to officials from the French government in early 1793 and subsequently adopted nationally. The world's first telegraph line (a series of signalling stations, each set at distances corresponding to telescope range) was then constructed between Paris and Lille in 1794. It was used successfully as a way of communicating in the ongoing wars against the Prussians and Austrians and adopted enthusiastically by Napoleon who went on to order the construction of a series of lines from Paris to Boulogne and Paris to Milan. Other governments quickly recognised the potential of Chappe's device and followed suit with their own systems. Continuities between the requirements of war and communication stimulated developments in distance compression much as they did with later advances in technology (Winston, 1998; Briggs & Burke, 2002).

Early telecommunication systems and crime

The search and exploitation of opportunities, 'breaches' and weak spots has, by wide agreement among criminologists, been a constant in crime – as much in the immediately physical context as in the hyperspatial (cf. Mayhew *et al.*, 1976; Killias, 2006). As communication systems began to operate over increasingly wide distances weak spots within them inevitably proliferated. The postal system provides several examples. Whilst improving communication, it also offered new ways of acquiring money, of accessing private information as well as creating a new resource for the transportation of illicit material. Royal Mail coaches in England were forced to travel with heavily armed guards (pistols and a blunderbuss) because of the constant attacks by highwaymen (Vale, 1967) while the quasi-heroic figure of the Pony Express rider constantly evading the predations of bandits is a seminal image of hyperspatialised telecommunication crime (McCormick, 2001). In Thomas Pynchon's *Crying of Lot 49* the evolution of the W.A.S.T.E. system – the 'underground' mailing system descended from the Tassis families' original monopoly – becomes its own metaphor for deviance.

Criminal exploitations of the telegraphic system followed almost as quickly as it was developed. Uniquely, we have a historical record of one example of this. A practical application for Chappe's optical telegraphic system was financial – he had the idea that it might serve to transmit information about shifts in the Stock Market. Others soon had a similar idea, though not as part of any organised system of financial news but for their own personal gain. Telegraph operators at one station were bribed by the Blancs – two brothers who worked in banking – to include deliberate errors in the signals. These preset 'errors' were actually a kind of steganography (a code hidden within other codes) that could be read by the Blancs to provide them with advance information about movements on the Paris Stock Market. What to anyone else looked like simple mistakes in the transmission process, were in fact the equivalent of coded information, information that served to provide illicit profit. The Blancs were able to exploit this for over two years, until their ruse was finally discovered in 1836. They admitted to their system but argued (quite reasonably) that it was not technically illegal since the acquisition of financial information for gain was how Stock Markets were supposed to operate. Since no appropriate legal clause could be found to prosecute them they were acquitted with costs only and the brother who survived longest went on to become one of the richest men in Europe. The 'Bordeaux Affaire', as it became known, quickly persuaded French deputies to criminalise any further attempts to use these new distance technologies for personal gain, by voting for a State monopoly in telegraphic communication (Solymar, 1999, p. 39).

The Victorian internet

By the 1830s a chain of optical telegraph towers stretched across Europe, a literal 'mechanical' internet clanking and grinding out a proto-hyperspace just as early machines were mass producing textiles, steel or consumer goods. However, this stretching of spatial limitation was about to be further accelerated by way of *electronic* telegraphy. What was to result was so complete in its global reach that its development has sometimes been referred to as the 'Victorian Internet' (Standage, 1998). This new type of telegraphy can, as before, be divided into two basic groups: wire and wire*less* telegraphy. Each marks an important distinction in the way hyperspaces may be implemented – routed through specific physical infrastructure such as cables, or as invisible, all-pervasive fields within space.

As an instance of the former, wire telegraphy requires the physical medium of a cable in order to connect locations together. Through this, electric currents must be sent steadily enough and with sufficient precision to enable a magnetic needle or pointer to turn at the receiving end. Meaningful signals can then be attached to different frequencies of needle pointings. Once discovered, the basic principles here were quickly developed – in England by Cooke and Wheatstone and most famously in the USA by Samuel Morse and his partner, Alfred Vail. Though there was initial scepticism, the spread of the new technology so quickly outpaced optical telegraphy that, only six years later – by 1852 – there were something like 23,000 miles of telegraph lines stretching across the USA and nearly 3,000 miles in the UK (Hugill, 1999). By then Prussia had around 1,500 miles and the technology had spread as far afield as Chile and Australia. Though still separated into individual networks, their merging into 'super-network' form was inevitable. In Europe the Austro-German telegraph union of 1850 integrated the Austrian telegraph system with various German states and other European countries quickly followed suit. By the mid-1860s, when a cable had finally been successfully laid between Europe and the USA, transatlantic communication was established for the first time. At a banquet for Morse in 1868, he was celebrated for having 'annihilated both space and time in the transmission of intelligence' (cited in Standage, 1998, p. 87).

Simple though the technology may have been compared to the contemporary internet, many basic principles of telepresence were already in place. The business world, for example, was quick to spot that the possibility of 'tele-conferencing' was now possible, as George B. Prescott reported in 1860:

In accordance with a previous arrangement, the *employés* of the American

Telegraph Company's lines between Boston and Calais, Maine, held a meeting by telegraph, after the business of the line was concluded for the day, to take action upon the resignation of Asa F. Woodman, Esq., Superintendent. Thirty-three offices were represented, scattered over a circuit of seven hundred miles . . . Each speaker wrote with his key what he had to say, and all the offices upon the line received his remarks at the same moment, thus annihilating space and time, and bringing the different parties, in effect, as near to each other as though they were in the same room, although actually separated by hundreds of miles.

(Prescott, 1860, pp. 350–352)

Deviance and control on the Victorian internet

For those smart enough to take advantage of the more pervasive compressed social relations that came with electronic telegraphy, potentially larger profits awaited. The author Alexander Dumas in his novel *The Count of Monte Cristo* was quick to outline its scope as an aid to fraud. Published in 1844/5 – at the very beginning of the electric telegraph era – the book relates how, as part of his revenge upon Dangars, the man who helped imprison him falsely for treason, the Count bribes a telegraph operator to send false messages to Paris. As a result, Dangars begins his slide into the financial ruin that ultimately completes the Count's vengeance.

But Dumas' literary imagination had already been anticipated by the practical deviant mind. Once again the acquisition of financial knowledge 'ahead of normal time' was the aim, with access to betting results in advance of their publication the target on this occasion. Previously, results from races could take up to a day to be transmitted from one part of a country to another. In England this meant that they were not usually published until the next day. From the very earliest days of the telegraph attempts were made to take advantage of its capacity to 'accelerate' time by placing bets with advance knowledge of who had won a particular race. In the 1840s a clear way in which telegraphy could be used to exploit this time/space lag was demonstrated. The case involved a man who entered the telegraph office at Shoreditch Station in east London. The man told the guards that he had 'left his luggage and shawl in the care of a friend' and sent a telegraph requesting his friend to forward these items on the next train. The reply duly came back: 'your luggage and tartan will be safe by the next train'. All very innocent. In reality the man's accomplice was positioned at a station near the Epsom race-course on Derby day. And the term 'tartan', far from being a passing reference to the man's shawl, was actually part of a code the men had developed to refer to the colours of winning horses! Rules were very quickly introduced to prohibit the transmission of such information, though this did not prevent individuals from continuing to try different versions of the ruse (Standage, 1998, p. 102).

While the telegraph provided a new resource for the hyperspatialisation of crime other, older technologies of time and space were implicated in two other streams that fed into constructions of hypercriminality. As with contemporary remote communication systems this involved a mixture of enhanced control and greater levels of fear. The rise of cheap, mass distributed newspapers and literature – in particular the 'penny dreadful' publications with their lurid tales of violence, horror and gentlemen thieves – did not just spread public disquiet about crime, they were also seen as *causes* of crime (Sutter, 2003). The Pure Literature Society – direct ancestors of contemporary moral guardians of communication culture – called for such publications to be banned, pointing to reports about:

> ... the harm done by the 'penny dreadfuls' ... (the) ... magistrates (who) have before them boys who, having read a number of 'dreadfuls' followed the examples set forth in such publications, and robbed their employers.
>
> (Harmsworth, 1893, cited in Sutter, 2003, p. 167)

And at precisely the same time as the popular media were disseminating fear of the new allatonceness of crime with their tales of 'penny dreadful' crazed youth and Victorian serial killers, remote communication had also begun to offer enhanced resources for its policing. One case sets the scene. Fiddler Dick, a famous pickpocket of the 1840s, had developed a strategy of robbing people at railway stations and making his getaway by train. Since the train was, at that point, the fastest of ways in which anything – including information – could travel, Fiddler Dick invariably escaped the long arm of the law. His reach was seemingly universal and everyone who travelled was potentially under threat. However, on 28 August 1844 he and his criminal companion, Oliver Martin, made a new kind of mistake when they chose to commit a robbery. For this time they made their escape on the London–Slough train – one of the very few routes which now had a telegraph line running alongside it. The police in London were able to cable their colleagues in Slough, and Fiddler Dick and Martin were promptly arrested upon disembarking. The extensive coverage of the story in the news media of the time impressed many, especially those in government, who had been sceptical about the possibilities of the telegraph (Standage, 1998, p. 51).

A second example of the potential boost to law-enforcement agencies and control mechanisms that came with the onset of an increasingly 'joined-up' society came the following year, with the arrest of one John Tawell. The offence again involved Slough, where Tawell had murdered his mistress. Police there were able to send a description of him by telegraph to Paddington. Tawell was intercepted as he tried to leave the train in London and was subsequently hanged. Hyperspatiality clearly had as much to offer law-enforcement agencies as the deviantly inclined – a fact that developers of the telegraph were not slow in picking up. A series of advertising posters used to promote the London–Slough telegraph trumpeted the fact that: 'by its powerful agency murderers have been apprehended (and) thieves detected' (cited in Standage, 1998, p. 52). Londoners for a while referred to telegraph wires as 'them cords that hung John Tawell' (Solymar, 1999, p. 56). In 1910 its control capacities were even more spectacularly demonstrated in one of the most famous 'transcendings' of the old spatio-temporal order by policing systems. This was the (seemingly impossible) apprehension of the murderer Dr Crippen who, having killed his wife had fled, mistress in tow, to the USA by transatlantic steamer. Leaving nothing to chance, Crippen made sure that his mistress was disguised as a man. But his caution came to nothing in the face of the reach of the new technology. The police in London sent a telegraph on to the USA where Crippen was picked up as soon as the boat docked and brought straight back to the UK amid great publicity. As *The Times* triumphantly reported: 'Escape no longer lies across the ocean' (cited in Solymar, 1999, p. 149).

In fact, as suggested earlier, the possibilities for using communications systems for control purposes were implicit from the very outset. Espionage networks are widely recorded in the ancient world and have played key political roles ever since (Dvornik, 1974; Austin & Rankov, 1995; Singh, 2000). And while signalling technologies have always been crucial for military success, the advent of instantaneous remote communication changed the nature of armed conflict forever. General Sherman, who made successful use of the new electronic telegraph to coordinate supplies in his march upon Georgia commented that, 'The value of the telegraph cannot be exaggerated' (Greeley, 2002). Just as the later internet was to issue from the military, so the telegraph facilitated the growth of spatial occupation and domination by the emerging brokers of the corporate-industrial state.

Other branches of the widening control network quickly followed this lead. In the early 1880s the Chicago Fire Department was contracted to build fire alarm boxes employing telegraphic signals. These were located throughout the city, and were meant to help citizens report fires much more quickly. Meanwhile in 1880, the Chicago Police Department also began using call boxes on the streets, a technology not introduced in the UK until the 1920/30s (MPS, 2007). The boxes vastly improved official communication among the police as well as control. Patrolmen were obliged to make hourly 'duty calls', a requirement that not only improved coordination but enabled their stricter supervision. Citizens could also report crimes, though they needed to obtain keys to the boxes which, since they were selectively distributed, meant that relatively few crime reports were made (Thale, 2004).

Representation, code and control in telegraphy

The capacity to *observe* interactions across the new telegraphic networks was, as with optical telegraphy, fairly straightforward. In security terms the proliferation of 'nodes' in the communicative flow of representations created a serious multiplication of weak spots, available for deviant exploitation. The bribery, or co-opting of the telegraph operators who were required for the system to function was a tactic that had already been explored in the Blanc brothers' scam discussed earlier. But operators were also at risk from the use of physical threat or force. The security implications of this were clear enough. As the *Quarterly Review* pointed out in 1853:

> . . . the clerks of telegraph companies are sworn to secrecy but we often write things that it would be intolerable to see strangers read before our eyes. This is a grievous fault in the telegraph and must be remedied by some means or another.
>
> (cited in Standage, 1998, p. 105)

The obvious solution was a technical one – to enhance the representational power of the communications elite. For by *coding* messages the influence of the telegraph operator would be reduced and, it seemed, the security of messaging enhanced.

The problem was that different codes were in use within different national telegraph systems. To avert this problem of control the International Telegraph Union, formed from a meeting of 22 countries in 1865, sought to harmonise coding procedures. It conceded that it would be necessary to allow others aside from governments – most obviously the commercial world – to share some of the control granted by the representational power of code. A huge expansion in the use of the telegraph was the result (Stewart, 1929; Kieve, 1973). In 1872 the Western Union telegraph introduced a 'secure' code enabling sums of up to $100 to be transferred between towns. By 1877 up to $2.5 million was being transferred on an annual basis, a staggering transformation of financial practice. For companies such as Western Union this soon became their main business, superseding the communications side altogether. But this wholesale movement of money into the emerging hyperspace of social interaction also began to present a flow of wealth that would be hard to resist for the criminal.

Meanwhile this new 'open access' to the benefits of coding provoked precisely the kinds of control tensions between service providers and users familiar to users of contemporary hyperspatialising technologies such as broadband or mobile phones. Since the cost of sending a telegraph depended upon the *length* of the message, users came to parallel conclusions to those employing contemporary messaging systems – make savings by *shortening* their length through coded words and phrases. The response of the telegraph companies also paralleled contemporary providers of services such as text messaging or broadband to any such ingenuities – impose new kinds of restrictions in order to maintain profits (see for example Richardson, 2001; Ward, 2001). But almost as soon as some new set of restrictions was imposed, new message codes were developed that evaded them. For example, some tried to get around costs measured in terms of the number of words used by simply using 'extra-long' words which, with appropriate code books, could be unpacked into an original message. The telegraph companies responded to this by restricting word length to a maximum of 15 letters in length. In turn new code books quickly emerged which conformed to this restriction but which still resulted in a saving on the cost of sending. By 1885, telegraph companies had been forced to respond to new ways of evading this ruling by bringing down the permitted word length to ten letters and requiring each word to be a genuine word in specified languages (including Latin!). By 1894 a dictionary of 'permitted' words was published by the International Telegraph Union (ITU), containing around 250,000 words of between five and ten letters. Any telegram which did not use such a word would then be subject to charges at the (higher) cipher rate (Standage, 1998, p. 112). But so many complaints flooded in about the words chosen that the ITU was forced to start again. The scheme never reached completion, partly due to the complexities of printing so many code books, but mainly because the telegraph's role as the primary vehicle of communicative hyperspatialisation was about to draw to its close.

Another way in which control of the telegraph network was subverted by utilising its services at reduced costs was to 'piggyback' messages across it without permission. Just as computers can be hijacked or, as we will see in a moment, telephone calls had for free, there were some ingenious precedents for this in the earlier telegraph networks. One story of this relates to a kind of 'informal' telegraph underground set up by one Irving Vermilya in the early twentieth century. Vermilya's system was able to 'steal' power from the telegraph lines in order to fuel his private communicative network which connected a group of around 40 friends together. Vermilya relates how:

> In the course of time, this line grew considerably, as my many friends can vouch for. Fellows, it was some line. After three or four years, it had grown to be six miles long, and had forty-two different fellows and girls on it. It stretched from one end of the city to the other. It even ran under ground for a distance of two and a half miles.
>
> (Vermilya, 1917)

Eventually the power requirements of Vermilya's 'private' telegraph network had grown so strong that in order to boost the transmission signal he and his friends needed to run a line off the main overhead cables. The operation was both precarious and elaborate. It required climbing a telegraph pole, excavating a hole into it, concealing the wire under putty, running it downward and hiding the feed wire within the ground. The operation was nonetheless a great success as Vermilya reports:

It would have taken a greater detective than Sherlock Holmes to ever dig that tap up, or discover it. The fact is proven by the knowledge that we had the juice coming from this source for two years.

(Vermilya, 1917)

The control capacities of owners of the telegraph network to prevent such 'guerrilla' communication were clearly a great deal less than those who dominate contemporary hyperspatial technologies. Whilst his story was never circulated widely at the time Vermilya and others like him symbolised the coming control conflicts and the new forms of struggles to label behaviours as 'deviant' that did not conform to the mores of network ownership.

Connecting space further – the telephone

The speed at which the telegraph was accepted and spread was matched only by its rapid demise. At precisely the point of its greatest global reach a new network, far more developed in its capacity to deliver telepresence, accelerated the process of hyperspatialisation still further. In turn, this 'remote speaking' or *telephone* network began to further the possibilities for and perceptions of deviance. Within two or three years of Morse's death in 1872, work to perfect the 'harmonic' telegraph – a device capable of transmitting sound at different pitches (not least the human voice) – was well underway. Whoever the 'true' inventor of the telephone can be said to be – Elisha Gray, Antonio Meucci or Alexander Graham Bell (Bruce, 1990; Coe, 1995) it was Bell who, in 1876, filed for the patent for this harmonic telegraph.

The full significance of this new invention was not initially appreciated. Even Bell appeared, at first, to share the view of the financiers – that the telephone was no more than a slightly more sophisticated form of telegraph. The public were quicker to grasp the key possibility of the new technology: '... direct communication by speech ... without the intervention of a third person' as an advert for the new Bell Telephone Company put it (Casson, 1910). Within two years of its patent there were 10,000 Bell telephones in use in the USA. This number gradually increased to around 266,000 in use by 1893 and around two million by the turn of the century (US Bureau of Census, 1975, pp. 783–784). As Fischer (1997) points out, the telephone companies continued to assume that its uses for remote interaction would conform closely to those of the telegraph rather than as a form of increased community and sociability. Thus the 1909 AT & T annual report reasoned that 'the public had to be educated to the necessity and advantage of the telephone ...' (AT & T, 1909, p. 28) in particular '... its practical uses in common with the telegraph' (ibid, p. 27).

Fischer (1997) analyses a series of advertisements for telephone companies between 1909 and the 1940s which show how this 'sociability' use of the telephone grew and was actively promoted as the telephone companies gradually cottoned on to the way the public wanted to use it. For example, prior to World War I, the ratio of advertisements stressing social uses of the telephone over those relating to business or other uses was around 1:10. By the 1940s it was around 1:1. The original view – that telephone lines permitted 'transmission of large numbers of communications of the most trivial kind', a fact that required tactics such as time limits on calls to reduce 'purely idle gossip' (cited in Fischer, 1997, p. 287) had by the 1930s been transformed into adverts which declared that 'Friends who are Linked by Telephone Have Good Times!' or 'Friendship's Path Often Follows the Trail of the Telephone Wire'. And, in a direct invocation of the potentials of telepresence, adverts which commanded users to 'Voice-visit with Friends in Nearby Cities!' (all ads cited in Fischer, 1997, p. 282/3). Remote social networking had arrived in earnest. Inevitably, so had the potential to exploit this for personal gain.

Early telephone crime

Once again the role of deviant behaviour in exploiting the new technology was also central to its development. Bell's acquisition of the patent has itself been regarded by many as less than morally upright (Evenson, 2000) and over 600 lawsuits were taken out against it – including five at the US Supreme Court (Huurdeman, 2003, p. 177). But many other variations of questionable behaviour in the way telephone technology developed followed soon enough. One famous example relates to the contribution of Alvin Strowger. In 1891, Strowger found a way of evading the requirement for a human operator when connecting phone lines by patenting a form of automatic switching. This eventually became the basis for the multiple connectibility which made telephone systems properly 'multiple-user'. The 'Strowger Switch', as it became known, could connect one line to any of 100 lines by using relays and sliders and was still in use over 100 years later in some places (Hill, 1953; Hugill, 1999). But it appears that Strowger, originally a funeral parlour director, may have been inspired to get his patent in first (others were inevitably working on similar ideas) because of attempts by a rival funeral parlour to exploit the spatial connectivities of the telephone for private profit. As with the telegraph, all calls at that point had to be routed via a central operator, making their integrity crucial. However, in Strowger's case, it seems that the local operator was in fact the partner of the owner of this rival funeral parlour. Strowger became convinced that she was intercepting inquiries about local funeral services and redirecting them to her husband's parlour, so to combat these illicit spatial manipulations he developed the automated switching system which secured his place in the halls of telecommunications fame.

Recorded history of early telephone crime tends to be rather thin on the ground for it seemed at first that the arrival of the telephone might serve to actually reduce crime. As Pool notes, 'in their most enthusiatic statements commentators sometimes forecast that the telephone would so tip the balance between "hunters" and "hunted" that the problem of ordinary crime would be virtually solved' (Pool, 1983, p. 95). The naivity of this view is clear enough – especially given that the period when telephone use began to spread coincided with prohibition in the USA. As a result, associations with its role in the furtherance of bootlegging and mob activity were increasingly made. One outraged commentator of 1907 described telephone companies as 'allies of the criminal Pool rooms' in an article for the *Cosmopolitan* magazine and accused the New York Telephone Company of profiting by at least a million dollars a year (around 2% of its total revenues) from the telephones installed in pool halls which were 'used for gambling purposes and for nothing else' (cited in Pool, 1983, p. 97). Other sources anticipate the internet porn panic in the associations they made with the telephone and the spread of vice. One obvious use was for summoning prostitutes – the very origin of the term 'call-girl' derives from the new possibilities of ordering sex remotely which the telephone created.

Fears of 'telephone crime' sometimes specifically invoked its enhanced capacity for telepresence. For example, there were several predictions that telephones would allow burglars to call somebody to ascertain if they were at home, thereby stimulating a new kind of crime wave (see Telephony, 1907). A boom in 'telephone confidence men', able to defraud people remotely over the telephone, was also predicted, along with a new 'hi-tech' crime – cheating the telephone company of its services (Pool, 1983). However, it is interesting to note that unlike the advent of computers and 'cybercrime' there was never felt to be any need to record 'crimes by telephone' distinctly. And this means that a lot of what can be determined about telephone-related crimes must be inferred from a patchwork of information, educated guesswork and painstaking archival research. For example, though details are sparse, other 'remote' crimes, such as the first obscene calls or stalking and threatening calls, were also presumably in existence – as equally facilitated by the anonymity offered by the telephone as anything provided by the internet.

The telegraph had already indicated some ways in which anonymity could be used for sophisticated frauds. But as with any new technology more mundane opportunities of this kind also open up. A classic instance of this sting noted earlier, one which has recurred again and again in the history of the hyperspatial, is to exploit the lack of public understanding of its technologies and cultures. The sheer novelty of telephone technology – a device enabling voices to be 'heard' from great distances – was a further gift to anyone willing to exploit the failings of ignorance. The example of one Frederick Collins and his 'wireless' telephone provides such a case. In 1903 Collins founded the Collins Wireless Telephone Company which claimed to sell a device that could make telephone calls without wires. Collins was, in effect, trying to market and to sell a mobile phone 60 or 70 years in advance of its inception. He even authored a number of articles and pamphlets on the subject including 'Wireless Telegraphy' (1905) and the 'Manual of Wireless Telephony and

THE SEATTLE SUNDAY TIMES
Sept. 5, 1909.

FOR AUTOMOBILES

The Collins Wireless 'Phone Will Eliminate Many of the Troubles
Experienced While Motoring at a Distance
from a Garage.

MESSAGE FROM AN AUTOMOBILE.

Telegraphy' (1909). Amongst his many dubious claims was that his pseudo-mobile phone would enable car drivers to 'call for assistance' while on the road.

But Collins' tall tales could not withstand proper scrutiny for long. A number of his associates were arrested and charged with selling fraudulent stock and in 1909 Collins himself was charged with giving a misleading demonstration of his wireless telephone at the Electrical Show in Madison Square Garden, New York (Jenkins, 2007). He was sentenced to spend three years in jail in Atlanta for his efforts.

Telephone crime: two issues of control

The extent to which the telephone network offered resources for control and the extent to which it offered resources for subverting control is as contentious an issue as it has proved to be with later communication technologies like the internet. The development of wiretapping offers an illustration of the former, the development of the so-called 'phone-phreaking' underground an instance of the latter.

As we saw with the hijacking of telegraphic technologies, attempts to use telephone systems for free represented nothing new. But the so-called 'phone-phreaking' movement of the 1960s onwards, which had similar aims, took such subversions to a new, much more organised level. Though it has now become a founding information society morality tale of the capacity of simple human intellect to 'outwit' complex technology, phone phreaking was actually a fairly low-tech approach at the beginning. Techniques were directed at the automated dialling systems which, in the USA, had become widespread by the 1960s. Here, the 2600Hz (frequency) tone was used to signal that a line had become available and was ready for reuse. If somebody could *recreate* this tone during a call that had already been paid for (in particular toll-free numbers) the line would reset itself ready for a new number to be inputted. This call could then be had for free. One of the locations where such techniques were first (illicitly) experimented with was, ironically enough, at MIT – a leading centre for research and development in computing. This deviant experimentation by MIT students was made a great deal easier when an engineer working for Bell Telephones published a dry article intended for telephone engineers in an obscure technical journal. Unfortunately for Bell (and the engineer), the article happened to contain comprehensive details of the frequencies used on their phone systems. Bell were less than happy when the article started to be widely circulated across college campuses (Rosenblaum, 1971). Students at MIT, with their unique access to many of the early computers, soon found ways to combine this information with available resources and to thereby mimic the tones used by phone companies for long-distance telephone calls. They could then literally take a free 'piggy-back' ride across the telephone lines. Just as with so many of the security issues in more advanced information technology systems, the weakest point was often with the providers themselves.

Within a few years the so-called 'blue box' device, which utilised a tone generator to reproduce the 2600Hz frequency, was developed and with this, phone-tones could be mimicked fairly easily. As with Vermilya's underground 'telegraphic' network, a kind of community began to emerge around the practice of 'phone phreaking' as it became popularly known. Like the hackers which succeeded them, the phone-phreaker community seemed at first to be driven as much by the thrill of subverting control of a technology as it was by getting something for free. Some techniques of subversion were more exotic than others – for example, one popular legend grew up that it was possible to mimic the required frequencies (and so be connected) by simply whistling, though the evidence for this has been disputed (see Schall *et al.*, 2002). Another popular phreaker legend relates to the free toy whistles given away in the Cap'n Crunch cereal popular in the US at the time, whistles that happened to precisely mimic AT & T's 2600Hz tone. One John Draper, the purported discoverer of this serendipitous coincidence, became known, inevitably, as Cap'n'Crunch and acquired his own kind of celebrity status in the phreaking community. Having found his vocation, he was reluctant to give it up and was even apparently able to provide seminars on how to hack phone systems while serving a prison sentence for his cereal-related deviance. Upon release, he was arrested again but eventually his skills brought him respectability within the nascent IT industry where he continues to make appearances at conferences (Schall *et al.*, 2002, p. 65; Draper, 2003). More involved technologies for obtaining free calls sprang up and soon there were a variety of devices in circulation. In addition to the blue box, there was the 'red box' which could be used to replicate the tones used in call boxes in order to obtain free calls, or the 'black box' which could be attached to a phone so that free calls could be made *to* that number (AOH, 2007).

The advent of digital exchange networks made subversions of the telephone increasingly difficult but phreaking continues to occur, often in more organised, overtly criminal forms. And linked to newer techniques such as the reprogramming of telephone company switches it continues to pose problems. For example, one estimate of the losses caused by phone fraud in 1998 placed it between $4 billion and $8 billion annually (Judson, 2000, p. 67). One example from the mid-1990s was of a group calling themselves the 'Phonemasters', who not only managed to steal tens of thousands of phone card numbers from AT & T but found and called private White House telephone lines and were even able to examine high-security FBI computers (Hopper & Stenger, 1999). Phreaking techniques have also been adopted for deviant purposes in other contexts – some of them refreshingly unorthodox. In 1996, for example, 25 per cent of Borneo's public pay phones mysteriously disappeared. Eventually it emerged that the handsets had been stolen by local fishermen so that they could use them, phreaker-style, to emit a high-pitched sound which attracted fish (Katz, 1999).

These (relatively minor) subversions of the phreakers were long preceded by control uses of the telephone. By 1910 the activities of the NYPD had come to the attention of the State legislature when it discovered that the police had developed the capacity to tap just about any line of the New York Telephone Company. Then, as now, the police were more than happy to use this capacity to excess. In 1916 the *New York Times* revealed that the police were enthusiastically eavesdropping on the conversations of most visitors to New York reporting that, '. . . the trunk lines of hotels were tapped and the conversations of all hotel guests listened to' (cited by Diffie and Landau 1998, p. 155). At first the federal government appeared to prefer to avoid confronting the regulatory issues raised by telephone monitoring and so left such decisions to States. But the legality of wiretapping and its status as a potential harm could not be ignored forever. The arrest, in 1928, of Roy Olmstead, who was running a $2-million-a-year bootlegging operation, forced such issues into the light of day. Olmstead's arrest was directly linked to evidence obtained by means of telephone wiretaps installed by federal agents, though no warrant had ever been obtained for them. Olmstead appealed and in *Olmstead v. United States* the Supreme Court ruled that the evidence obtained from tapping Olmstead's phone calls was permissible. They argued that the Fourth Amendment, which had originally been invoked, had not been compromised since it only protected 'tangible' things. Since conversations are 'intangible', tapped conversations did not constitute search and seizure and so were permissible. Only one of the Supreme Court judges raised any doubts. In a lucid anticipation of issues to come Judge Louis Brandeis argued that:

> Whenever a telephone is tapped, the privacy of the persons at both ends of the lines is invaded ... as a means of espionage, writs of assistance and general warrants are but puny instruments of tyranny and oppression when compared with wiretapping.
>
> (Brandeis, 1928)

In spite of the Judge's prescient observations, the trend in favour of the government's right to listen to anything it wanted to had been clearly established.

Supreme Court cases in 1967 reinforced such powers by rendering wiretapping a judicially legitimised search and seizure behaviour. The resulting wiretap law was supposed to allow wiretapping by law enforcement agencies only as a last resort and of course 'innocent' US citizens were meant to be exempt from this. Though it seems clear that the FBI and numerous other government agencies continued to engage in spying incursions, the decision by the Bush government in 2005 to engage in widespread domestic wiretapping of American citizens without the use of *any* kind of warrant removed this last constraint. At the same time it also emerged that widespread surveillance of US citizen's financial records had been taking place. By then the contribution of fear of terrorism to a developing sense of hypercriminality enabled Bush to more or less ignore the muted calls for his impeachment (Davis, T., 2006) and to press ahead, not only citing extraordinary circumstances but the ambiguous constitutional claim that the executive was not compelled to comply with other branches of government in such circumstances (cf. Gore, 2006). A later Senate Judiciary Committee approved a programme on a party-line vote that would allow the National Security Agency to eavesdrop without a warrant on the international phone calls and e-mails of everyone in the United States (Lichtblau & Zernike, 2006).

In the UK, the advent of the telephone provoked little in the way of debate over its uses as a control mechanism. There is, after all, no historic right to privacy in the UK. Like the CALEA legislation in the USA discussed earlier, the Regulation of Investigatory Powers (2000) required providers of communications to permit a 'reasonable interception capability' though telephone taps for national security purposes had to be authorised by the Home Secretary, the Scottish First Minister or the Foreign Secretary. However, the Home Secretary *could* permit other public authorities to access 'communications data' without a warrant. Such data might include not only a message's source and destination but also its type – for example, the location of a particular mobile phone location or sites visited online. The process is (nominally) overseen by the so-called Interception of Communications Commissioner – a rather shadowy figure who has kept a low profile since his appointment. Of the 1145 warrants for interceptions issued in 2001 under RIPA the commissioner noted 'a significant number of errors and breaches'. However, he decided no action need be taken because 'none of the breaches or errors were deliberate'. The Investigatory Powers Tribunal itself operates in secret and rarely upholds cases of illegal wiretapping. Some 563 local and other public authorities in the UK now have powers to tap phones or read e-mails and over 400,000 requests to copy phone bills or internet logs were made in 2006 (Campbell, 2007).

The advent of computing

The previous sections have suggested just how long-drawn out the gestation of the various technologies and social practices of the hyperspatial have been. But of course it is the advent of computers which has focused minds most clearly on these processes and which has spawned the idea that there is something 'different' in criminal behaviours that result – the phenomenon of 'cybercrime'.

In hyperspatial terms the computer was for a long time no more than an isolated counting machine. Cumbersome early devices like the Colossus machine at the University of Manchester were experimental curiosities and even with the development of smaller machines using transistor technology access to advanced computation remained very limited (Ceruzzi, 2000; Rojas & Hashagen, 2000). At least two more factors were required for the computer to have any serious role in the development of hypercriminal behaviours. First, they needed to be linked together to form networks similar to the telegraph or the telephone. Second, their use needed to extend beyond restricted governmental or corporate ends towards *personalised* access, so as to create a viable 'social web' open to deviant exploitation. The development of 'personal' computers such as the Altair 8800, the Apple, the BBC Micro or the Commodore 64 was instrumental in this widening of access. But it still took the role of 'big government' – that is, the military – to make the decisive breakthrough. In response to the Russians' development of a hugely important hyperspatial technology – the first Earth-orbiting satellite, Sputnik, the US Advanced Research Projects Agency (ARPA) was created. With little sense of the broader consequences ARPA went on to create one of the first functioning computer networks by linking together universities, government facilities and military sites (Abbate, 1999). 'Packet-switching' technology, a functioning manifestation of hyperpositionality, enabled information to be exchanged by *more* than one route through a network and played an important role in making networks function efficiently. This small network developed from its first centre at UCLA with the gradual acquisition of new nodes through the 1970s and 1980s until 1990 when it was split by the National Science Foundation into the NSFnet, able to operate at much higher speeds. With this came significant implications for global power which once again manifested the connections that Innis had made between 'Empire' and technology. Just as Britain's command over the infrastructures of the telegraph network sealed its role as a major world power, the 'global telecommunications hegemony' (Hugill, 1999, p. 236) of the USA that replaced this was achieved through the 'submarine telephone cables installed by Bell and through Intelsat' (ibid). And though the arrival of fiberoptics and cheaper satellite technology appeared as if it might undermine this hegemony, at a stroke the advent of the internet seemed to have restored it. At this point however the computer network was still little more than a glorified (in fact more limited) telephone system. For a form of the hyperspatial to emerge which was able to complexify space more fully a different way of *thinking* about connectibility was required.

Hyperlinks, hypertext and the populating of hyperspace

Whilst it was technically possible for more than one user to engage in conversation, social interaction via telephones remained a largely two-way interchange. But what makes hyperspatial interaction so different, as suggested in the previous chapter, is not just that it has a multi-*user* aspect but that it also has a multi-*dimensional* aspect. That is, it does not just simultaneously connect user to multiple user. It enables these users to interact with *representations* – for example, databases, graphic or visual material and so on. In so doing it permits the kinds of connections to be made between users and representations which go beyond logic of texts, by means of the logic of content. In the medium of the hyperspatial any *concept* and its representation can, in principle, be connected to any other kind of concept. The logic of the *hypertext* or of the *hyperlink* vastly complexifies social interaction and our access to information (cf. Landow, 2006).

As the new HTTP and HTML languages were imposed upon the (already extant) physical structure of the internet to create the 'world-wide web' (Calliau *et al.*, 2000) documents could be connected together by hyperlinks – addresses contained within them which, upon clicking, linked immediately to whatever document was contained at that address. Important though this was in technical terms, many of the *fundamental* concepts of hypertext –

multiple hyperlinked documents – could already be said to be in place. For example, Joyces' *Finnegans Wake* had arguably anticipated the basic form of this in its complex compressions of word and meaning and in the metalinkings between concepts enabled by its prose form. Its publication in 1939 was soon followed by a further manifestation of the hyperlink concept in a seminal essay called 'As We May Think' by Vannevar Bush. In it, Bush described the idea of the 'memex' – a device which would be able to link every kind of knowledge by using complex connections between microfilm, projectors and viewers. Though the memex was more of a sketch rather than a serious engineering proposition, Bush outlined a form of dynamic information retrieval and connection that should sound very familiar to the users of the current internet:

> Wholly new forms of encyclopedias will appear, ready-made with a mesh of associative trails running through them, ready to be dropped into the memex and there amplified. The lawyer has at his touch the associated opinions and decisions of his whole experience, and of the experience of friends and authorities . . . The physician, puzzled by its patient's reactions, strikes the trail established in studying an earlier similar case, and runs rapidly through analogous case histories . . . The chemist, struggling with the synthesis of an organic compound, has all the chemical literature before him in his laboratory. . . . There is a new profession of trail blazers, those who find delight in the task of establishing useful trails through the enormous mass of the common record.
>
> (Bush, 1945)

The possibility for deviant uses of the memex did not seem to have occurred to Bush, though of course there is as much use in being able to call upon the 'wisdom' of criminals as of scientists. Especially when the same medium also facilitates the criminal act itself.

It was not until around 1964, when a maverick thinker called Theodor Nelson instigated what he called 'Project Xanadu', that Bush's insight began to find something like a concrete realisation. Nelson's aim, several years ahead of both the ArpaNet and Berners-Lee's hypertext language, was to create a kind of 'universal library' – in effect a hypertext resource – that made it possible to link every document to each other – a process he called 'transclusion'. But this was a much more sophisticated kind of connection than the kinds of hyperlinks available on the current internet. Instead of the selected links to whole documents, every document would be able to contain *any part* of any other document (Wolf, 1995; Nelson, 2007). Though Xanadu was never realised in full, it was probably a closer approximation to what full hyperspatiality might ultimately offer than what is provided by the current internet. As Umberto Eco forecasted, 'We may conceive of hypertexts which are unlimited and infinite. Every user can add something . . . (to) . . . implement a sort of jazz-like unending story' (Eco, 1996).

Making hyperspace invisible

The development of the hyperlink was a crucial manifestation of one requirement for networked remote interaction to become more fully 'hyper-spatial'. It was one stage in a long process of gestation that, as we saw, has had as much to do with non-technological *social* innovations, such as language or economic flows, as it has with developments in transport or advanced communication systems. But a turning point has now certainly been reached, one where hyperspatial experiences are beginning to be integrated into every form of social interaction.

The seamlessness of such experience has been greatly facilitated by the advent of invisible 'always-on' and all-pervasive communications networks. Again, the basic form of these has been around for longer than might be imagined. In 1887 Hertz had provided a concrete demonstration of what had seemed to be a purely theoretical idea, one first suggested by the founder of electromagnetic theory, James Maxwell. Hertz showed how electromagnetic energy could be spread *invisibly* through space and could thereby form physical connections between spatially dispersed locations. Hertz thought his discovery to be interesting but of 'no use' (Susskind, 1995). Marconi thought differently and so helped transform this 'merely interesting' observation into the practical realities of the wireless telegraph, patented in 1897 (with a US version patented by Tesla). Within just three years – by 1900 – the first 'wire-less radio transmission' had been made across the Atlantic. In turn radar, satellite and optical/laser communication technologies gradually augmented the range of technologies able to connect points in space 'invisibly'. The most recent examples of this invisible communications network, the mobile phone and wi-fi-based internet computing systems, have furthered the seamlessness of telepresence, creating the possibility of hyperspatial connectivity becoming as all-pervasive an experience as breathing.

The process of *convergence* – of different technologies fusing into indistinguishable all-powerful tools – further adds to the possibility of all-pervasive access. Thus, as the mobile phone becomes ever more like a computer, and a computer ever more like a communication device, the differences between such technologies become ever more irrelevant (Kim, 2005; CSTS, 2007). What are sometimes called 'embedded systems' make the seamlessness of interactivity across distance ever more pronounced. The increasing presence of information technology in more and more everyday items, from refrigerators to clothing, begins to make social life spatially multi-dimensional at every level of interaction. Further technologies on the way – most obviously faster computers, or the much-mooted integration of technology with biology – will put the 'presence' in telepresence into full-blown bodily experiences, as our sensory mechanisms are connected into an all-pervasive multidimensional synopticon.

Hypercrime and computers

The complex of behaviours, possibilities and perceptions referred to here as 'hypercrime' has, as the previous sections have indicated, been a long time coming. It hasn't always involved computers. But it certainly involves them now. The first recorded 'computer crime' took place, according to some sources, in 1958 (Parker, 1976; Bequai, 1987) though there was no recorded federal prosecution of any computer-related offence until 1966. By 1967 computers in the US Strategic Air Command headquarters had been tapped and military data accessed. By 1976, when the first real text on computer crime was published – Donn Parker's *Crime By Computer* – there had been, according to him, only 374 recorded cases. Many of these were scarcely worthy of the title of computer crime, since they related to offences such as the theft of the computer itself. Moreover most had been directed at isolated computers, rather than networked ones. Given that there were around 150,000 computers then in circulation, Parker concluded that this level of offending *could* be taken to imply that 'computer abuse is minimal and under control' (1976, p. 15). However, Parker also noted anecdotal evidence to suggest that many such crimes were simply not being reported. The fog surrounding the true level and significance of crime by computer seems to have been there from the beginning, and it has hardly lifted since.

It was of course only with the emergence of computer *networks* that this technology began to make a significant contribution to contemporary crime. The phone phreakers had provided one kind of template for deviant exploitations of a communications network, and their example was only furthered in the context of networked computers with the advent of the *Bulletin Board System* (BBS). In particular 'underground' communities, similar in spirit to those spawned by the phreakers, began to exploit this new communicative resource to interact and exchange information in new ways, some of it ostensibly 'deviant' (Zetter, 2005). For example, via forums called *elite boards*, early hackers could swap notes on new techniques as well as distributing pirated software. Pornography also made its inevitable entrance and was stored and exchanged via Bulletin Boards from very early on (cf. BBS Archives, 1995; BBS Corner, 2006).

However, the numbers using Bulletin Boards remained fairly small and deviant activity there remained mostly marginal. But in 1984, in a seminal research paper, Fred Cohen introduced a new term to the public – the computer 'virus' (Cohen, 1984). Not only did he define the term, he demonstrated a working example of a virus. Self-reproducing programs which could copy themselves had already been produced – for example, the Animal program which infected mainframe UNIVAC systems and, on PCs, the so-called 'Elk Cloner' virus which was used to infect an Apple II computer in 1982 (Lemos, 2003). Both were limited in their reach – the Elk Cloner, for example, could only be spread by floppy disk and so for it to spread it had to be actively copied from one disk drive to another. And this suggested what was to become the only real safeguard for avoiding the threat of hypercrime – the extent to which isolation from connection could be attained. The new pathologies of the viral did not just signify a neat technical feat but a condition of hyperspace itself. Within it, harmful infections could arise at any time, from any direction, and could spread extremely rapidly. As Cohen pointed out:

> Absolute protection can be easily attained by absolute isolationism, but that is usually an unacceptable solution . . . (thus) the most important ongoing research involves the effect of viruses on computer networks. Of primary interest is determining how quickly a virus could spread to a large percentage of the computers in the world.
>
> (Cohen, 1984)

By 1988 the 'Morris Worm' had become the first viral threat to operate fully in the wild and to spread itself across the nascent internet (Schmidt & Darby, 2001). With the advent of the 'viral' the 'allatonceness' which characterises the hyperspatial was now realised as a form of all-pervasive danger across computer networks. In tandem, computer crime began its transformation from isolated, low-key incidents of fraud or tampering into part of the stream of spatially transcending behaviours which culminate in hypercriminality. How more precisely I shall now begin to map out.

Chapter 3

Proximity 0: Body space

> Variety and possibility belong to the very structure of the human organism.
> (Wiener, 1954, p. 51)

If harm can be modelled in terms of spatial incursion then one space above all stands out as a source of undesirable incursions. This is the space so proximal to us that it constitutes the primary location of our being – the space where our bodies are *located* at any given moment. But there seem to be significant variations in judging the culpabilities related to harming bodies. Most societies have accepted the right to harm bodies in self-defence while other forms of killing such as suicide or euthanasia have often counted as immoral, especially in Christian contexts (Donnelly, 1990; Larson *et al.*, 1998). Bodies of 'uncertain status' – for example, those belonging to the foetus or the terminally ill – have raised their own set of moral ambiguities (McMahon, 2002), while harming behaviours in the pursuit of beauty or status such as dieting, plastic surgery, or body piercing have been tolerated or censured on different grounds at different times (Pitts, 2003).

In spite of this, there also appears to be one common principle which holds for most societies, most of the time: the more proximal the body, the less acceptable any damage towards it. Both emotional and geographical factors count in such weightings. Aside from one's own (highly proximal) body, the bodies of loved ones, relatives, or fellow citizens count as 'more' proximal in varying degrees – and therefore more worthy of protection. Temporal proximity also plays a role in the intensity of our concerns. For example, if someone is told that they will be attacked in the future they will probably be less concerned than if an attack is about to or is already taking place. After all, there may yet be some way of avoiding this. And if someone has already *been* attacked then, while scars may remain, the attack is at least over. Whilst not absolute, it is upon such relatively simple geometries of distance that many of our judgements of the seriousness of any bodily harm seem to rest upon.

Whatever the ambiguities, the hypothesis that destructive or damaging incursions into body spaces is regarded as among the most serious of actions is certainly supported by the way such actions are handled in almost every kind of criminal justice system. Take, for example, levels of punitive retribution. In 2006, 68 countries in the world punished murder by way of the death penalty (Amnesty, 2006) while in just about every other national context the penalty of life imprisonment was reserved as the maximum penalty. Similarly, the average sentence length for murder in the USA in 1995 was around 266 months (230 in the UK), compared to 88 months for robbery (40 in the UK), 43 months for burglary (14 in the UK) and 23 months for motor vehicle theft (8 in the UK) (US DOJ, 1998).

The hyperspatialisation of bodily harm: bodies and distributed bodies

We can now begin to turn to the key question that will occupy the rest of this book. How more precisely do the new experiential geometries of hyperspatialisation shape and change deviant behaviours and the responses to them? There appears to be an obvious difficulty when it comes to considering the effect of this process upon our bodies. The immediate physicality of a bodyspace would seem to diminish the ways in which the 'action at a distance' implicit within hyperspatiality can promote incursions which lead to destruction or damage. The capacity to inflict damage or destruction to a body seems ineluctably associated with the requirement for proximity. Furthermore what Foucault called 'histories destruction of the body' (1977, p. 148) is a theme that has been taken up enthusiastically, and often literally by many commentators on information technology. The view that bodies simply 'disappear' during computer-mediated interactions (Kroker, A. & M., 1987; Redhead, 1995; Lyon, 1994, 2001) has become an influential one, entailing that interactions in 'cyberspace' occur between nothing more than 'disembodied subjectivities' (Featherstone & Burrows, 1995, p. 12).

If one takes this 'disappearing body' thesis seriously, then any criminology of the body as it is articulated over remote interaction would seem to be a non-starter. The theoretical intractabilities of a 'virtual self' (Agger, 2004) or its 'cyberbody' seems to lead us nowhere other than, in the words of Lacan, towards an 'ontology of farts – virtual gas' (1994). So a difficult choice appears to be on offer. Either we must reject this view and maintain a commitment to 'traditional' physical bodies which is unable to account for the novelty of harm as it is reshaped under the hyperspatial. Or we are left with two distinct kinds of entity, locked into the kind of substance dualism that characterised Cartesian distinctions between mind and body, with all its problems of explaining how interaction and causal harmony between two such things can ever occur. The result for any considered stand on the *ethics* of harm towards bodies appears fatal. Positions such as Pierre Levy's (2000), which sees cyberspace not just as a new ontological space but as the latest stage in what he calls 'hominization', threaten an ethical perspective upon network interaction that is, as Frohmann (2000) has argued, 'stripped of any serious moral dimension'.

Some have tried to square the circle by blurring the choices. For example, though Argyle and Shields (1996) argued that the body 'cannot be escaped' (p. 58) in computer-mediated interaction, they also appeared to suggest that such interaction seemed 'to separate us from each other in a physical sense' (p. 60). As a result, the body 'remains' – though only in virtue of 'memory traces ... (that) allow us to experience with our physical selves and all the other multiple layers that do not require us to be in the flesh' (p. 96). What these 'multiple levels' of disembodied experience actually amount to are rather vague. Traces of physical-like expressions in online interaction – 'emoticons' such as a smiley face, or the use of explanatory conventions like <frowns> during responses – are one suggestion. These 'lead us back to our-selves, back to our bodies to try to understand what it is a person is trying to say' (ibid, p. 67). But there is of course no need to 'lead us back' anywhere. Our bodies are already there *having* the experience. Appeals to memory begin to look suspiciously like fudges or just another in the long line of question-able mechanisms that have been proposed for dualistic interactions between distinct substances, with Descartes' appeal to the pineal gland (Descartes, 1984) among the most notorious. At any rate memory, as a profoundly brain-dependant resource, would hardly be adequate as a basis for explaining the *absence* of a body.

But there is perhaps an intermediate position. Shorn of the metaphysical baggage of a 'cyberspace' we can focus upon what actually *happens* to the body as its experience of spatio-temporal interaction changes. Merleau-Ponty's insistence that: '. . . we are in the world through our body, and . . . we perceive the world with our body' (1962, p. 206) need not mean that 'the inexhaustible richness of reality repleteness' (Goodman, 1976, cited in Borgman, 2001, p. 95; Dreyfus, 2001, p. 59) offered by bodily experience cannot be extended and reshaped by *new* experiences such as interaction at distance. There is, after all, nothing unusual about being changed by experience.

If we turn again to Minsky's (1980) concept of telepresence one sense of what this might mean is presented. In this context no 'extra' traces are required since immediate sensory experience remains rooted to its immediate physical basis. We talk on the telephone and we hear with our ears. We watch satellite footage and experience this with our normal visual apparatus. Such sensory experience is perfectly able to accommodate other more psychological aspects of remote interaction by way of their 'supervenience' (as this is sometimes called) upon embodiment (cf. Kim, 1993; Stalnaker, 1996). In this way any dilemmas about the distinction between a virtual and a physical body turn out to be nothing more than a version of the standard philosophical dilemma about the extent to which mental events are distinct from physical events. Since mental events are *realised* by (physical) brain events (the question goes), how can they be distinct? Yet they surely must be distinct since mental events *cause* things in a way that appears distinct from physical events. It is my intention to open the door that causes me to open it, not merely a particular firing of neurons. But in supervening upon neuronal firings (without being reducible to them) the mental event remains both distinct *and* wedded to a (physical) body. In the same way, a remote interaction, such as the lifting of a glass in a virtual world, is experienced through and by the body while also retaining a certain causal autonomy from it. Thus, just as the supervenience relation allows for identity between mental and physical events without that amounting to reduction, so our experiences of the hyperspatial are founded upon the physical without that entailing an exhaustive reduction to the physical.

Having secured continuity then, where more precisely is the difference? Norbert Wiener, writing long before the advent of contemporary networked computing, suggests a general outline: '. . . where a man's word goes and where his power of perception goes, to that point his control and, to an extent, his physical existence is extended' (1954, p. 13). In other words, Wiener invokes an idea proposed earlier. This is the view that, just as the specific capacities available to us are formative ingredients of a social space, their various *extensions* can be seen to augment that space. McLuhan, writing 10 years later (though still before the advent of networked computing), takes up this theme in his account of the '3,000 years of technological extensions to our bodies' (McLuhan, 1964, p. 5). On this view the so-called virtual body is nothing more unusual than the latest version of what happens with *any* technology – a physical body, enabled to do things that it could not do previously. All that makes the hyperspatial stand out to the extent that it does is the *totality* of capacity extensions that it seems to offer and the multiple modalities of their experience.

Rather therefore than there being any fission between the body and some new category (virtual or otherwise), the body and its capacities to interact are simply extended, or as I shall prefer to say *distributed*, across wider and more connected regions of possibility. These distributions need not just be sensory. Important psychological ingredients, such as one's feelings of identity, also shape the sense of multiple location, when manifested at the point of social interaction through interfaces like a mobile phone number or an e-mail address. The bodily 'assemblage' that results, to use a currently fashionable term (Deleuze & Guattari, 1988), is again hardly a very new idea. Its major historical source lies in Leibniz's theory of the *monad* – complex particulars formed by collections (that is, assemblages) of properties (Leibniz, 1965), an idea reconsidered by Gabriel Tarde (1999). Sheila Brown has recently drawn upon Tarde in discussing Latour's concept of an 'actant' – 'simultaneously informational and organic entities, technology co-extensive with the human sensorium or self/personhood' (Brown, 2006, p. 230). Brown also invokes Latour's concept of the *hybrid* in this context (ibid, p. 228), though she seems to see hybrids in terms of technological/organic fusions, rather than the broader forms of social unities theorised here (see Latour (1993) for a relevant discussion). But even 'techno-organic' fusions are hardly very new – the walking stick/human hybrid might represent one venerable example. It is not even clear that technology is essential to the bodily assemblage. For example, at a time when the telephone and the telegraph had begun to remodulate our sense of 'where we are', William James (1890, 1950) had presciently outlined a similar view of networked bodies – the self as a material sum collectively located in a variety of social constituents – the body itself, but also its property, its family, its clothes – its social location as a whole, for, '. . . properly speaking, a man has as many social selves as there are individuals who recognize him' (James, 1950, p. 294; see also Belk, 1988). More recently Boulter and Grusin have described this phenomenon of distribution in terms of what they call 'remediation':

> . . . to say that the self is expressed in its email affiliation is not to say that the self is disembodied but that it is embedded in a particular media form . . . the same is true of all the mediated expressions of the networked self; the self that participates in a video conference is embodied as a video and audio image; the self that surfs the web is embodied in its IP address, its web browser and its plug ins.
>
> (Boulter & Grusin, 2006, p. 5)

However one nuances the idea, it seems clear that there is a viable position here for understanding remote interaction which eschews the needless mysteries of aetherised cyber-bodies. Physicality is retained while simultaneously being enhanced by an increase in its capacities. In terms of communication, one way in which the body can be seen as redistributed is by focusing upon the multiple nodes of social interaction which open up to it. All remain rooted to a sensory centre, while simultaneously functioning beyond its location, as follows:

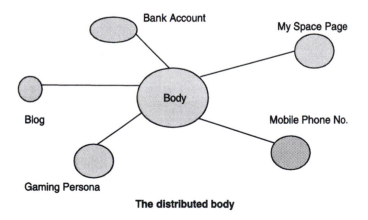

The distributed body

The spectra of possibilities at each node clearly operate at different levels of social complexity. Some are relatively denuded, while others approach the vibrancies of a fuller sensorium of reality repleteness. But overall the result is simply a further kind of unity or assemblage, one that continues to express the 'variety and possibility (that) belong to the very structure of the human organism' (Wiener, 1954, p. 1) while extending these varieties and possibilities spatially further. Such extended unities have been noted in many ways and in many other contexts. For example, Canny and Paulos (2001) noted instances from transport technologies: 'motorcycle racers whose lives depend upon their ability to become one with the machine' or bus drivers' 'extraordinary sense of the extended body' as they 'pass within inches of a parked vehicle without contact' or cab drivers who 'use the extended body to bump and jostle and compete for territory' (p. 279). What Michael refers to as the 'hyperhybridisation' of human being with car (1998) submerges and obscures each within the other (cf. also Urry, 1999, p. 10) in ways noted in different contexts by Hayles (1995).

With these redistributions of bodily experience and agency comes the possibility of a redistribution of harms to the body and the necessity for thinking more deeply about what this might mean. McLuhan was very clear about one set of negative consequences of bodily extension, noting how a kind of inverse process of 'amputation' (1964, p. 42) follows with every augmentation. For example, the wheel might extend the foot, but in using the wheel (be it chariot or car) we at the same time *amputate* the foot by creating conditions for its redundancy. The extension of the central nervous system by communication technologies similarly threatens it with potential 'amputations'. It may, for example, become numbed and deadened to novelty, or it may be impaired with 'overstimulations', overstimulations which directly correlate with the kinds of manias sensitive to perceptions of hypercriminality.

In what follows, I will largely restrict my attention to more obvious classes of criminal harms which might result from the hyperspatial, though this theme of 'amputation by extension' will always be kept in mind as a background factor. Two key instances of bodily harm will be distinguished. First, *absolute* or central bodily harms, where the physical body itself is damaged or destroyed through influences that may be attributable to hyperspatiality. Second, *partial* (or peripheral) bodily harms, where the damage or destruction is more centred upon the nodes of the redistributed body. It is the former class which more obviously retain their traditional judicial gravities, since any incursions which threaten the basic capacity of the body to continue are more likely to violate our most basic normative assumptions. The latter class of potential incursions, though largely unprotected by legal sanction may, in context of the hyperspatial, also be viewed as harmful if the body's capacity to interact in spatially extended ways is somehow reduced. For instance, there may be psychological damage which limits or affects the quality of this experience. Or there may be limitations and restrictions placed upon the ways the body is able to *access* hyperspatial interactions. Removal of physical access is one straightforward example of this; limitations placed upon the identity requirements needed to interact legitimately constitutes a more subtle instance of access restriction.

The hyperspatialisation of bodily destruction – some trends and examples

There is no better way to consider the sheer spatial immediacies of killing than by means of the methods in which it is typically carried out. In the UK in 2003/4, the methods used to effect the 833 recorded killings there broke down as follows:

Method of killing	% of homicides involving this method in 2003/4
Sharp instrument	28
Hitting and kicking	17
Shooting	9
Asphyxiation/strangulation	8
Blunt instrument	8
Burning	3
Drowning	3
Other/not known	24

Source: Povey, 2005

The figures indicate that in (at least) 60% of cases some form of clear proximal physical contact between murderer and victim was at work involving fists, knives and so on. The use of a blunt or sharp instrument, of fists, or of strangling someone are actions where the distance is close up and deadly. Even the figures for shooting involved a degree of proximity since they also include the use of the weapon as a blunt instrument. Proximity entered killing during this period in another important way too. The British Crime Survey for the same year indicated that around 40% of male victims and 63% of female victims *knew* or were personally acquainted with the main suspect (BCS, 2003/4). The conclusion seems obvious enough. If we are to suppose that hyperspatialisation is having a significant effect upon killing then 'killing at a distance' ought to be increasing. But killing in the UK context continues to be predominantly articulated in terms of spatial and social proximities of various kinds.

In principle, remote killing has of course been possible ever since humans were able to hurl stones from slings or fire arrows from a safe distance. Indeed from the Winchester Rifle through to the Star Wars program, weapons capable of dispensing death at a distance have often been an innovatory force in the very development of technologies of hyperspatialisation (Virilio, 1997). How then is our indubitable capacity for dispensing death at a distance manifesting itself in the contemporary context? Geographical variations within killing methods provide one kind of illustration. For example, if we compare the methods of killing in the US with those in the UK there seems to be a far higher likelihood of distance, rather proximity playing a part:

Method of killing	% of homicides involving this method in 2001
Firearms	70
Knives	14
Hands, fists, feet	7
Blunt objects	5
Other (e.g. poison, explosives)	4

Source: FBI, 2001

In the 60 years before the US Civil War only 14 of the homicides in New York City involved guns. But since then, homicide in the USA has become notoriously associated with the use of firearms (Cook & Ludwig, 2000). Given the leading role of the US in the general application and development of distance technologies – from the telegraph and the telephone to the internet – there are obvious temptations to see some sort of correlation between these facts. But there are also special circumstances to do with gun ownership and control which intervene in the US context, and it would in any case be foolish to assume that distance is involved in homicide simply *because* a gun has been used. After all, a shooting at close range does not seem to count as any more of a 'remote' killing than a knife thrown from the same distance.

To avoid such complications, suppose then that we discount gun-related deaths as an *unambiguous* class of distance killings. One obvious class of distance technologies – which might include bombs, artillery, missiles and other such weapons – remain to be considered. It is at this point that it becomes hard not to conclude that the hyperspatial has indeed had a significant affect upon the character of killing. Whilst figures for civilian and military deaths in the twentieth century vary according to source, most agree that a figure of 100 million plus is at the lower end of estimates (Clodfelter, 2002; White, 2005). Compared to the estimated 20 million or so who died this way in the nineteenth century – itself a near doubling of the previous century (Sorokin, 1957; Clodfelter, 2002) – this near 500% rise in killing rates seems, in a very large part, to be attributable to an increased variety and sophistication of distance-killing technologies. It is striking then that contemporary discussions of distance killing – slanted, inevitably in terms of the affects of the internet – rarely take their departure from this stark fact.

Instead discussions of causality are almost entirely situated in the context of the enhanced social *connectivity* which hyperspatialisation brings. A variety of factors are usually cited which appear to link increased connectivity to enhanced levels and threats of killing:

(i)   Increased victim availability.
(ii) Increased invisibility/anonymity for potential killers.
(iii) Increased modes of access to potential victims.
(iv) Increased levels of temptation (for example, because of (i) & (ii)).

That is, the wider transport or communication connectivity hyperspatialisation facilitates seems to provide for greater victim availability. And the advantages of the stranger it brings provide for motivation. Add in exhilarations such as being able to modify personal identity during a 'hunt' for victims and a lethal cocktail of influences seems to have been produced, one which feeds an (understandable) popular assumption that the possibilities of telepresence directly increase the danger of encountering 'killers on the web' (Berry-Dee & Morris, 2006) or 'crazy psychopaths . . . and unsavory stalkers destroying innocent people's lives . . . (and threatening) . . . your safety and well-being' (Andert & Burleson, 2005). And it is easy to be misled, even with official figures. For example, looking again at UK data, there seems at first to be some evidence that the increased exposure to strangers brought about by the internet might indeed have increased the threat of murder. Between 1993 and 2003 a rise of around 20% in killings by a 'stranger' was recorded in the UK, with 24% of victims unacquainted with their murderer in 1994 (roughly commensurate with the beginning of wider internet use) compared to 44% in 2002/3 (Povey, 2005). But can this 20% rise really be directly related to enhanced hyperspatialities? Closer scrutiny of the figures indicates why we should be cautious. To begin with, since the Home Office category of stranger killing included cases where there was 'insufficient information', many of the incidents making up this 20% cannot be unambiguously associated with killing caused remotely. It is also clear that the 2002/3 figures were artificially boosted by the killings attributed to Doctor Harold Shipman (172 in total). Since the Home Office category of 'stranger killing' includes those killings conducted in a 'commercial, business or professional relationship, where the suspect killed a customer or client in the course of carrying out their occupation' (Povey, 2005, p. 3), the Shipman killings would then come under the 'stranger' category. Yet the administering of fatal doses of drugs (his preferred method) is usually a very close up and proximate form of murder and, as a doctor, Shipman was no stranger to his patients. With the 'Shipman effect' removed, stranger killing shows only an 8% rise since 1993 (to 32%).

What is also clear is that even this figure offers no distinction between spatially *proximate* or spatially *remote* stranger killings. Once this crucial fact is taken more clearly into account some predictably traditional trends emerge. One relates to gender. Males were far more likely to be killed by a stranger than females (37% compared to 21%). Furthermore many of these killings, though *committed* by a stranger, had nothing to do with distance but the crude brutalities of (spatially proximate) violence. For example, quarrels, being beaten up on the street, as a result of attempted theft and so on. In other words, stranger killing (what seems to be the best available category for analysing anonymous forms of threat) is hardly ever related to communications-based 'cyber killing' but to typical social factors such as the male exposure to violence, or the loss of temper. Figures for the US support this conclusion. In 2000, the number of females shot and killed by a husband or intimate acquaintance was nearly four times that committed by male strangers using all types of weapons (Violence Policy Center, 2002). Finally, even where remote communication technologies can be implicated in the course of a murder it is still the case, as the following examples will emphasise, that matters must culminate in a spatially proximate denouement. Remote death effected by means of communication networks is therefore all but non-existent unless, as we will see later, very particular forms of agency and highly specialised agents are at work.

Killing me softly

In spite of the apparent lack of any real evidential base, apocryphal tales, rumours and myths about 'cyberkilling' continue to abound. One typical 'self-help' text about the dangers of online interaction, the alarmingly titled 'Web Psychos, Stalkers and Pranksters', provides a sample warning:

> Worried about the psychos taking over the web? You should be. They're waiting for you. What do they want? Some enjoy watching you struggle helplessly as they harass and stalk you. Others want to abuse you in other ways, to feed their own dark desires . . . Then there are the really danger-ous ones, those who want to take over your life completely . . . to rule you . . . own you . . . become you.
>
> (Banks, 1997, sleeve notes)

These suggestions of an always present and dangerous hypercriminality wait-ing online is one which the cybercrime literature has unfortunately done little to correct. Detailed analysis about the measurable effects of computer net-works or other hyperspatial technologies upon killing has been largely con-spicuous by its absence. Even where a more critical stance is offered there remains a tendency to substitute assumption for fact. For example, Jewkes' (2006) discussion of individuals portrayed in the media as having been 'killed by the internet', while signposting the moral panics inherent in the reporting of such cases, still manages to conclude that they 'provide a snapshot of internet-related crimes that have *resulted* (my emphasis) in the abduction, torture or death of individuals in countries around the world' (ibid, p. 4). Though conceding that 'there is nothing inherently sinister in the technology itself' Jewkes, like many others, gets it wrong by blurring the crucial issue of agency. Many things may be 'related', or involved in killing, but more is required to be able to say that they *result* in killing. And much more still is required to be able to infer that a distinct species of crime thereby emerges – no one would conclude that because a bicycle was used to ride to a scene of crime an instance of 'bicycle crime' had occurred. The crucial issue that is almost always left unanalysed is the *extent* to which the internet, as opposed to many other mechanisms that may be used along the way, contributes decisively towards the killing itself. As we will see in discussing some of the cases Jewkes highlights, as well as other examples, it is almost always the case that the effects are far more subtle than portrayed. And they are rarely, if ever, decisive.

One example of the complex routings and interactions through hyperspace that result in destructive spatial incursion can be seen in the case of Amy Lynn Boyer, a 20-year-old dental assistant and college student from Nashua, New Hampshire in the USA. Unbeknownst to her Amy had been stalked since school by one Liam Youens who had become obsessed with her, but appeared to have little hope of transforming this obsession into a physical encounter. Instead, Youens resorted to using some of the resources of the hyperspatial to pursue his goals. He set up a website (amyboyer.com) where he detailed fantasies of how he intended to kill her, fantasies which he was to ultimately carry out (Boston Phoenix, 2000). On the website Youens declared: 'I have always lusted for the death of Amy . . . I'll lay in wait across the street further down at 4 p.m. . . . When she gets in I'll drive up to her car blocking her in, window to window I'll shoot her with my Glock.' But though the website certainly provided evidence of Youens' intentions, it is clear that nothing there actually *facilitated* the killing. The internet, insofar as it contributed to the killing at all, appears to simply have put Youens in touch with the commercial source which provided him with the information that was to prove deadly. Youens was able to use search facilities provided by a Florida company called Docusearch.com which he used to trace the victim's birth date, Social Security number, home and work addresses. Yet the resources provided by his online activities had to be supplemented by an extensive use of proximal space which involved him driving around, waiting outside Amy's office and so on. Finally, in October 1999 he carried out the threat detailed on the amyboyer.com website before then turning his gun on himself. The tool used to kill her, along with five other firearms he possessed, were not acquired through the internet, but legally purchased from Wal-Mart, gun shows and old-fashioned newspaper ads.

The 'murder.com' headlines which the killing attracted (Boston Phoenix, 2000) are therefore better seen in the light of an afternote to the murder. For it was here that a more telling set of connections between online communication, agency and culpability is revealed. Amy's parents launched an action against the company Docusearch (who had made a profit of $109 from selling the information to Youens) and in 2003 the New Hampshire State Supreme Court ruled that information brokers can be held responsible when the data they sell puts people at risk of criminal misconduct (EPIC, 2003). But loopholes in the legislation (brought about by intense lobbying from the data-marketing industry) undermined the possibility of holding companies like Docusearch responsible for their reckless management of personal information. Data merchants, financial institutions and private detectives continued to have the right to exchange Social Security numbers among themselves or allow local governments to sell personal records which contain Social Security numbers (Greene, 2000).

The Amy Boyer case thus offers a mixed and complex picture of the way hyperspatialised culpabilities operate in instances of criminal murder. To say that this was a cyber killing or that Amy had been 'killed by the internet' appears to implicate the technology directly in what Youens did. But this grossly distorts what happened. If there *were* any other agency than Youens' own intentions then there seems just as much justification here for holding the commercial motivations of Docusearch to account. But clearly 'commercially facilitated murder' reads less well than 'internet murder'. Finally it is important to emphasise again that all the events that led to Amy Boyer's murder did not result from any encounter on the internet, but from an encounter that first took place in *proximate* physical space – the school where Youens first saw her.

A further case often prefaced with the 'cyberkilling' tag was Israel's 'first internet murder' (Herschmann, 2001). But upon closer examination this again turns out to be another example of the tangled sets of cause-and-effect relations usually at work in such tales. And again the judgement that it was a cyberkilling seems to have had more to do with the demonisation of remote technology than with any unambiguous causal correlation. Its characterisation as an 'internet murder' seems to have depended almost entirely upon factors to do with social connectivity, on this occasion an initial contact over the internet between 16-year-old Ofir Rahum and a '20-year-old American' whom he met in the Israeli chat-facility Rotter.net. The contact (which again might have as easily been initiated by a newspaper advertisement, or through any number of other media) was brought into spatial proximity when a meeting was arranged in Jerusalem. But the meeting was a foil for a more sinister purpose. After a second meeting had been set up Rahum was then apparently kidnapped, driven to somewhere near the Palestinian town of Ramallah where he was shot 15 times and his body left in the trunk of the car. Tragic though these events were, the internecine politics of Israeli/Palestinian relations clearly had at least as much to do with the murder as the internet. And if the charge of 'murder by remote technology' is to be applied, then, as we will shortly see, there are many other killings in the Middle East that more credibly fit that particular bill.

The more one looks, the more these widely circulated instances of 'cyber-killing' appear to vanish into the smoke of a 'cyberspace'. Take Dr Mike Godwin, 'inventor of a method of psychological and geographic profiling which is revolutionizing the way police track and capture serial killers' (Amazon, 2004). His case story 'Cybermurder.com: Bound for Death' (Godwin, 2005) reveals 'the dark and secretive world of cyberspace', a place where Sharon Lopatka died, strangled by loner Charles Glass (in his trailer). But about the sum total of the internet's contribution to what ultimately ensued was an initial contact. In fact Lopatka had travelled to meet Glass (voluntarily), had been engaged in erotic strangulation (consensually) and had then died (accidentally). Glass, who panicked and tried to conceal the body, was never convicted of 'cybermurder' – nor even of old-fashioned murder, merely involuntary manslaughter.

There is of course a relatively straightforward way of testing this idea that the volume of killing has been in any way increased 'by the internet' – to just *look* at one simple (and readily available) metric – the overall homicide rate. For example, by using the USA as a key indicator it is clear that the trend in homicide between 1992 and 2000 (precisely the period when the internet spread and gained its purportedly deadly influence) was actually downward. In 1992 there were an estimated 23,760 murders in the US (a rate of 9.8% per 100,000 population) compared to 16,204 in 2002 (a rate of 5.6%) (USDOJ, 2004). The trend in the UK, though indicating a slight rise remained at a much lower rate than in the USA and figures here also included statistics for manslaughter and infanticide. Detailed analysis of these UK figures suggests that the rises here were also disproportionately associated with young men (rather than the clichéd internet victim figure of the stalked female). More-over rather than communication technology playing the central role in their deaths there are equally strong arguments to suggest an association with the influence of *economic* factors – in particular the recession of the 1980s and early 1990s (see Dorling (2005) for one such argument).

It is clear from this kind of (easily accessible) evidence that, if there has been any growth in killing that exploits time-space compression then technologies such as the internet, deployed by lone 'web psychos', are not the primary culprits. However, there is another kind of agent (possibly psychopathic, but certainly not a loner) which does seem able to exploit the capacities of such technology with far greater levels of 'success'. I will return to this point shortly.

Killing symbioses

Communication systems – be they smoke signals or postal networks – have always been a way of bringing together individuals who might never have met in proximal space. When such connections are enhanced by technologies with greater interactivity there is almost a statistical inevitability that individuals with the kind of interests that might otherwise have lain dormant will be brought together. The mutual reinforcement of their shared interests that results may create forms of social or psychological interdependence that form classes of entity of particular interest within hyperspaces – the *symbiont*, as well as the *hybrid*. Whilst hybrids invoke the idea of fusions of separate entities or objects into a new individuality (however incongruous), symbioses suggest individualities which remain distinct but which operate interdependently and in harmony. And in just the same way that there is no necessarily technological aspect to hybrid fusions, symbiont life can also be realised in purely social (that is, non-technic) ways. Rather than Haraway's cyborg (1991), or the human/technic hybrid discussed by Brown (2006), I suggest a wider, socially rooted basis for the symbiont, something especially facilitated by hyperspatialisation.

Symbioses in nature – the animal that eats another's parasites, for example – are usually mutually beneficial. Human examples, like the biological and social interdependencies between a mother and a child, are also accepted as 'normal' and reciprocally supportive. But there are other examples of individuals brought together by telepresence where there are reinforcements and sharings of more questionable needs – needs that test our sense of the deviant and its regulation at profound levels. Some of these symbioses – particularly those of a sexual nature – can, as we have already seen, become deadly. The 'issue' in symbiosis then is again not the internet, or any other communication technology, but those forms of interdependency that we wish to sanction and those that we do not.

A symbiosis is particularly fragile where it has been partly imagined. In the context of remote communication this may lead to intimacies and sharings of information which are inappropriate or self-destructive. For example, Larry Froistad, a computer programmer from San Diego, was eventually jailed for forty years after having confessed to murdering his daughter in a fire while chatting online at Moderation Management, a support group for problem drinkers. Froistad's symbiosis with the group's interdependencies may not have been entirely delusionary for, while some members contacted the police after his confession, many did not. Indeed the fact that Froistad was reported led many of those who held their counsel to criticise the informants as 'betraying a confidence' (CNN 01/05/1998).

Symbiosis only becomes deadly where there are shared interests in bodily incursions that are damaging or destructive. Such interdependence can have a number of forms, but one obvious and more prosaic variety comes with the material connection between somebody who wishes to sell their services for killing and someone who wishes to purchase such services – the hired killer. Again, there have always been individuals prepared to offer such services, but encounters with them have usually required the kinds of social contacts that few of us (fortunately) possess. The extent to which the telegraph or the telephone facilitated such encounters is not known with any precision but, as suggested in the previous chapter, there seems little reason to doubt that they were as instrumental in this context as they were in other crimes. Yet the few well-published cases where contacts of this kind have been established via the internet have gathered more alarmist headlines. But far from helping such transactions the internet seems rather to have hindered them, for most have been highly unsuccessful. The flaw is obvious enough. Killing symbioses played out within a public arena are almost always likely to be noticed by someone.

One case from 2000 is typical. A man from England who had become obsessed with a Texan woman whom he had met online (only to discover she was already married) then set up a website which offered £100,000 for her murder. His jealousy was further aroused when the woman sent photographs of herself and her husband on their wedding day in order to persuade him that she was telling the truth. In response he set up a further website using these photographs with the (now reduced) price of £25,000 for their 'termination'. This reduction in the premium does not perhaps suggest an entirely serious proposal. Nonetheless, the site claimed that payment would be dispatched once photographic evidence had been received of the couple's murder and included details of their home address and telephone number. Though nothing ever actually happened, the case was seized upon by the media and widely reported as a 'contract cyberkilling'. The individual concerned was intercepted long before any suitable 'client' appeared and, while he protested that the websites were nothing more than 'a joke', he was eventually convicted on two counts of making threats to kill (Sheriff, 2000).

Potential symbioses like these, though exotic enough, are as nothing to more dramatic cases which have fed the public imagination. Here the symbiosis – an interest in killing and *being killed* – is even more clearly steeped in interdependencies which appear morally unacceptable. The case of Armin Meiwes, the so-called 'internet cannibal' who met his symbiont over the internet and then ate parts of him, fascinates us, not *because* of the role of the internet, such as it was, but because we simply cannot imagine the utility in such a symbiosis. It is the details that drive the fascination further. The willing response of Bernd Juergen Brandes to Miewes' advertisement for young men, available for 'slaughter and consumption'. The sex, followed by their attempts to eat Brandes' (fried) penis and his subsequent killing and partial consumption by Miewes make no sense to us except as a category of the fantastic in its most monstrous form. But to resort to the internet as the *explanation* for such behaviour merely reflects an inability to understand its complex foundations in human behaviour and psychology. Miewe's initial conviction – eight years for manslaughter (based on the apparent consent of the victim) – was inevitably overturned when the public's fascination with the case forced a retrial. A new sentence of life imprisonment for murder and 'disturbing the peace of the dead' was the outcome (Naughton, 2006).

The chance of individuals such as Meiwes or Brandes ever meeting in narrower spatial proximities is of course small, but certainly not impossible. Nor would it depend exclusively upon the internet, for a mobile phone, a dating agency or any other social mechanism might just as well have contributed. The point which must again be stressed is that we do not generally regard other mechanisms for interaction as dangerous or culpable. If we did, most of the ways in which social interaction forms and develops would simply come to an end. That there is an inherent *risk* in new experiences or encounters is not something that can be legislated for – even if this was what was really wanted. But hypercrime, as we see once again, originates as much in the minds of its audience as in the means provided to perpetrators.

Collective killing in hyperspace

The idea that telepresence may not just promote the killing of individuals, but of whole groups of individuals, has been a foundational psychosis within the 'cyberspace is dangerous' mindset. Inevitably it is the figure of the 'terrorist', that contemporary monster *par excellence* which has been the most productive in the perceptions of everywhere-crime which breeds such impressions. The scenarios are, by now, familiar enough. Key electronic installations such as an air traffic control system are taken over, and planes redirected in such a way as to cause mass death; control systems for large dams, nuclear power stations or chemical works are hacked into, resulting in massive flooding of large population areas, nuclear holocaust or biological meltdown (Arquilla & Ronfeldt, 1993; Gordon & Ford, 2003; Verton, 2003). Or computer systems in hospitals are sent into chaos, and missiles 'captured' by infiltration of their guidance systems. And so on. All seem, prima facie at any rate, to constitute very serious ways in which the hyperspatial might be utilised by motivated individuals to inflict mass casualties. As the National Strategy for Securing Cyberspace Report put it: 'Cyber attacks can burst onto the Nation's networks with little or no warning and spread so fast that many victims never have a chance to hear the alarms' (DHS, 2003).

One response to these perceptions of threat was the insertion of provisions relating to 'cybermurder' during the passage of the US Homeland Security Bill. Life sentences were reserved for those deliberately transmitting a program, information, code or command that impairs the performance of a computer or modifies its data without authorisation, 'if the offender knowingly or recklessly causes or attempts to cause death' (Findlaw, 2002). But the provisions were subject to wide criticism by many legal professionals in the US, not least for the numerous ambiguities of language which appeared to make it difficult to direct charges appropriately. In particular the term 'recklessly' seemed applicable to almost *any* attempt to hack into a system, not just those with murderous intent (Poulsen, 2002). The result, it was argued, would be that these provisions would simply end up serving as a leverage for plea-bargaining with many teenage hackers preferring to take a lesser sentence than to be threatened by the possibility of the life sentence contained in the Bill.

Deeper questions about the effectiveness of the concept of 'cybermurder' arise from terrorist mass killings when some of the provisions it has provoked are considered. Not only is the psychology of the hypercriminal often at work here, so too are more traditional factors like power and manipulation. For example, the 8,591 locations identified as 'potential sites for terrorist attacks' in Indiana (30% more than New York and twice as many as California) seem to have had as much to do with the interests of what has been increasingly called the 'security-industrial complex' (cf. Mills, 2004) as with any credible terrorist strategy. The $130bn-worth of Federal funding available to provide protection against apparent terrorist and cyberterrorist threats, together with an inclination to 'reward' Republican politicians who had taken a strong (that is, supportive of the Bush administration) line on the 'war on terror' were also plausible influences (*Observer*, 10/09/06).

Aside from definition, there is another, rather more pragmatic problem with the idea that mass killing is likely to result from terrorist infiltrations of computer networks. This is the inescapable fact that *nothing* like a cybermurder in the form of terrorist mass killing has yet been proved definitively to have occurred (Weimann, 2004). Yet the very fact that there has NOT been such an attack has also been reason enough to suppose that there might be. There are, after all, unknown unknowns. Shea (2003, p. 9), in a report for Congress, conceded that 'Since there has never been an attack on domestic critical infrastructure industrial control systems which caused intentional damage, even in cases where hackers have successfully broken into these systems, industry representatives believe the cyber-threat to be low'. Nonetheless, '. . . an attack on a chemical or liquid natural gas plant facility's control systems might lead to . . . widespread physical damage' (ibid, p. 11). Many commentators have begun to agree that the danger of mass killing presented by 'cyberterrorists' is at best a low-risk threat, at worst a questionable control construction (Green, 2002; Schneier, 2003; Weimann, 2006; Yar, 2006). To find examples of mass killing which do make use of remote technologies it is necessary to look elsewhere.

The deadly power of representation

> 'I play the Terminator, but you guys are the real terminator.'
>
> (Arnold Schwarzenegger, July 2004,
> Camp Victory, Baghdad Airport Road)

As we have seen, one way in which the hyperspatial is produced and experienced is in terms of enhanced representational power. Sometimes representation permits us to explore counterfactual contexts – alternative permutations of the actual. But there are many other occasions where this is decidedly NOT representation in terms of simulations which have 'no relation to any reality whatsoever' or which are their 'own pure simulacrum' (Baudrillard, 1994, p. 6). In many contexts representations go beyond their role as control mechanisms to form tools that provide significant additional resources for killing. The supposed threat from enhanced social connectivity is as nothing compared to efficiencies of digital representations, causally linked to physical environments, in dispensing death.

The briefest perusal of eBay or other online shopping sites brings up a range of devices with the kind of representational power that, were they to be deployed by a serial killer, or (god forbid) a paedophile would cause universal outrage. But though lone killers do not yet seem to have made much use of devices like the video and cellular spyphones, infinity transmitters, night vision optics, invisible earpieces, listen-through-wall devices, GPS tracking devices or photoblockers that were available from a specialist site during one online search (Cornerspyshop, 2006), there certainly *are* scenarios where these tools have been extensively utilised for the purposes of killing. But in each case, for (only slightly) different reasons, objections have been muted. One context is where this representational power is directed towards the taking of life considered to be of 'less value' than human life. The advent of remote, 'pay-per-view hunting' in the USA complemented the already extensive use of sensing and representational technology deployed by humans who kill animals for sport. Hunters who were 'too busy' to actually make it into the open air and do the work required for a live shooting were able to take advantage of the site 'live-shot.com' set up by a Texan entrepreneur (site now defunct). With a 'hunting' session costing from around $1,500, internet shooting was not cheap. But for the comfort of killing from the armchair, many thought it worth the price. Hunters could log on at a prescheduled time to watch a feeding station on their computer screen. When the animal they ordered approached food that had been laid out, the net 'hunter' was able to use his mouse to aim and with a click, the rifle could be fired remotely. Sanity seems to have (mostly) prevailed here and a raft of legislation followed to ban internet hunting in the US (Humane Society of USA, 2006). But given that the physical location of the hunter is ultimately irrelevant, pay-per-view hunting seems more than likely to crop up within other, less easily managed jurisdictions.

However, the growth in representational power implicit within hyperspatialisation finds its most complete and potent demonstration upon the battlefield. Early representational technologies here amounted to little more than the sight on a rifle, or the acuteness of a soldier's aim. But troops are now increasingly linked by computer command and control systems, moving together as '... prostheses of the machines ... internal elements of the complex mechanical and electronic apparatus' (Hardt & Negri, 2004, p. 44). Enemy forces can be better targeted and more effectively hit as a result of the telecausal properties of computer models and distance weapons. And, having overcome distance, the process of killing need not also be limited by weather conditions or other adverse factors such as fog, fallout or nightfall. Armed with night vision, remote sensing devices and bodysuits an enemy continues to exist visibly and transparently as bodies available for killing. And now the abstractions within representation become especially deadly. For as the capacity to dispense death at distance becomes more precise, the human body begins to vanish from the scene. Instead, 'clinical' airstrikes or high-velocity rifles surgically remove opposition – wherever it is perceived to exist, battle-field, built-up area (or both). Computer-controlled 'smart' bombs are dis-pensed, bereft of the culpabilities of agency, ignorant of the existence of bodies. Once again the psychologies of a cyberspace are partly implicated in the requisite socialisation which permits this. The close correlation between the virtual as a device for producing 'unrealities' and the resulting disassoci-ation between representations of killing and the results of killing is perhaps no accident. Tales of US soldiers in Iraq training on computer games, then playing computer games before, after (and some times during) raids, are symptomatic (Wright, 2004; Vargas, 2006). As Hardt and Negri put this:

> . . . war becomes virtual from the technological point of view and body-less from the military point of view: the bodies of US soldiers are kept free of risk, the enemy combatants are killed efficiently and invisibly.
>
> (2004, p. 45)

The conclusion appears to be inescapable. These refinements to represen-tational power mean that the most effective killers who emerge under hyper-spatialisation are not the psychopathic loners of the popular imagination, but highly organised collectivities such as the State. Nor even are these the 'rogue' states normally supposed to threaten collective space. Rather, it is the advanced, 'rational' democratic governments, who have so far acquired the most complete levels of representational power and which have con-sequently had the greatest success in inflicting mass killing. Implicated with them is the realm of commerce, which supplies and manufactures much of the technology that makes this all possible. In this way the pursuit of new markets becomes as great an influence upon the growth of distance killing as any number of disturbed loners armed with a web camera.

Voluntary death

The former all constitute a few examples of the ways destructive incursions which result in *involuntary* death are being dispensed under hyperspatialisa-tion. Expansions in communication have also been held responsible for negative effects upon voluntary death. The apparent phenomenon of the 'internet suicide' has been widely discussed within populist and academic sources (Baume *et al.*, 1997; Alao *et al.*, 1999; Thompson, 1999; Whitehouse, 2005) though this too is rarely grounded in proper evidence or analysis. One problem with evaluation here is the mixed moral perceptions of the act. Judgements about the status of self-killing have always been highly culturally relative (Szasz, 1999; Minois, 2001) and even the supposed divine prohibition against it in Christianity is, as Schopenhauer forcefully pointed out (1892, p. 41), lacking in biblical support.

Despite the inconsistencies, fundamental prejudices against suicide remain in most Western contexts and this seems to have fuelled a great deal of the misrepresentation of the real level of threat posed by 'internet suicide'. The dread of symbiosis features as a subliminal theme, centred upon the way that hyperspatialisation has enabled what should be a lonely and tragic act to develop its own forms of community and support. Instead, the charge goes, networks can be accessed that increase the likelihood of suicide occurring, especially among the vulnerable – and in particular young people. In the willingness to accept this, the deeper facts tend to get ignored.

Symbiosis is often perceived in the development of so-called 'suicide' websites which are argued to provide new levels of expertise and technical support for the act and have provoked a rash of 'stop pro-suicide' websites in response.[1] But if such information is to be found it is usually within unmoderated newsgroups rather than 'suicide websites' per se. And even here sentiments are rarely unambiguously in favour of suicide. Whilst it is true that postings on such newsgroups can provide information about ways to kill oneself more effectively or efficiently, they also serve as discussion forums, ways of exchanging ideas and feelings about an act that many subscribers there (already) see as something inevitable for them. Little rigorous research has been carried out on the potentially positive effects of such newsgroups and the emotional and community support that may *prevent* as much as cause suicide. The level of such support offered there can actually be surprising. A survey of one newsgroup conducted over a period of three months indicated that out of a sample of 1000 messages, 64% offered supportive or under-standing comments, 42% directly counselled against self-harm, while less than 8% contained statements that might be construed as directly supporting suicide (McGuire, 2006).

Not only is it therefore unclear whether such newsgroups are (unambiguously) promoting self-killing, it is even less clear whether they have had any noticeable affect upon the level of suicide itself. In 1993, prior to the development of wide internet access, the suicide rate (per 100,000) among 15–24-year-olds in the USA stood at 13.5%. By 2002 this rate had *fallen* – to 9.9%. Amongst 25–34-year-olds the rate stood at 15.1% in 1993, again falling to around 12.6% by 2002 (Kochanek *et al.*, 2004). Both of these age groups seem more likely to have been keener users of the internet than older groups over this period and yet no discernible rise in the suicide rate among them emerges as a result of their exposure. The UK displayed a similar trend with the suicide rate among young men down by nearly 7% since the mid-1990s (NSPS, 2006).

The moral panic here then seems to relate not so much to any measurable increase in suicide but to more overtly symbiotic factors such as its open discussion, or the sharing of methods for effecting it. In particular, by enabling an especially stark kind of symbiosis – the increased opportunity to commit suicide with others – hyperspatialisation seems to transgress against the assumption that suicide should be an isolated experience. The comfort in not having to die alone is obvious enough, though there may be something in the argument that being with other similarly minded individuals may strengthen resolve, making a last-minute change of mind much less likely. But examples of communal suicides are not uncommon and have by no means always been associated with the hyperspatial (Brown *et al.*, 1997). It is in the Far East however where the trend has appeared to be the strongest – most obviously in Japan and Korea where the phenomenon of communal suicide, faciliated by the internet, has received a great deal of (global) press coverage (see among many others Haines, 2004b; McCurry, 2004; BBC, 02/02/06; CNN, 11/02/05; Owen, 2006). Prima facie, numbers here do appear to be on the increase. According to figures from the Japanese National Police Agency (Leyden, 2006), since they began to collect data on this in 2003, deaths resulting from online suicide pacts have broken down as follows: 2003 – 34 deaths, 2004 – 55 deaths, 2005 – 91 deaths. In other words, the number of communal deaths 'facilitated by the internet' *seems* to have nearly trebled. With no other context the rise appears alarming. When seen in light of the fact that more than 34,000 Japanese took their own lives in 2003 (Curtin, 2004) a slightly different perception emerges. For taking this into account, the proportion of so-called internet suicides constituted less than 0.1% of the total, meaning that suicide pacts make up an extremely small proportion of Japan's suicides. Given also that figures such as the above have only been collected for three years (and by what method and under what categorisation is not clear) it would be foolish to deduce any significant long-term trends from them. In Korea, where the suicide rate appears to have doubled between 1985 and 2002 (from 10.2 to 18.7 per 100,000) suicide websites have again been singled out as 'the cause' (Sang-Hun, 2007). The dramatic economic growth of South Korea over the same period and the resulting social pressures to succeed are largely ignored as factors, though there seems to be no less evidence for this as a potential cause.

In spite of the obvious difficulties in trying to prove a definitive internet/ suicide link new control mechanisms continue to emerge to 'manage' the threat. Numerous self-appointed web-guardians have taken up their (self-appointed) task of 'regulating' suicide websites. One group – WiredSafety – reported how they had come across suicide websites in Japan and had taken 'appropriate' action. In the words of Parry Aftab, their executive director – 'when children and the Internet are concerned . . . no one knows more . . .

than Parry Aftab' (Wired Safety, 2006) – 'We report them to local law
enforcement . . . or the ISP to have them take down the sites. But they just
pop up someplace else' (Huus, 2003). Quite how the linguistic expertise of
American family groups stretches to the monitoring of Japanese websites, or
indeed upon what form of invitation they do so, remains unclear.

Hyperspatialisation and its accidents: indirect killing effects

In a now famous argument, Paul Virilio suggested that there is a sense in which
every technology brings about the conditions for indirect or unintended killing
– its own particular form of 'accident':

> . . . no technical object can be developed without in turn generating 'its'
> specific accident: ship=ship wreck, train=train wreck, plane=plane
> crash, etc. The accident is thus the hidden face of technical progress.
>
> (Virilio, 1999, pp. 92–3)

But it is also true that the fear of accidents threatened by new technologies
often outstrips the actualities of their deadly potential. For example, early
forms of distance compression by new transport technologies were initially
regarded with levels of caution which seem comical to us today. Under the
notorious 'Red Flag' Act in the UK, horseless vehicles – that is, cars – were
not permitted to drive faster than four miles an hour and required someone
to walk ahead of the vehicle, carrying a red flag, to warn other road users
(Setright, 2004). Such trepidations were gradually submerged as other competing psychologies of desire (for exhilaration, for convenience and so on)
took precedence. This triumph was of course greatly expedited by the new
commercial conglomerates of transport ready and eager to profit from the
mass acceptance of the automobile, or the aircraft. At this point, as with
smoking, a kind of inverse form of rationality took over, one that sublimated
or ignored the more genuine risks of transport technologies, while substitut-
ing other, less harmful ones in their place. Consider, for example, the recent
death rate in Europe resulting from car usage.

In the USA the comparative rate was, at the upper end of this range, standing at 14.75 in 2003 (USDOT, 2004). Yet for the period 1999 to 2001, the
comparable homicide rate was 1.6% (per 100,000 population) in the EU and
5.6% in the USA (Barclay *et al.*, 2003). Thus, while the specific accidents of
transport technology offer a far higher level of danger than other technologies it is other darker, more intangible threats, such as hi-jacking, which
assume greater precedence within the social imaginary.

Similarly inconsistent attitudes can be seen towards communication technologies. Take, for example, the physical networks or infrastructures it
requires. In order to send and receive signals from mobile phones, to

Road deaths: EU comparison, 2003	
	Rate per 100,000 population
United Kingdom	6.1
Netherlands	6.3
Sweden	5.9
Denmark	8.0
Finland	7.3
Germany	8.0
Ireland	8.4
Austria	11.5
Italy	10.5
France	10.2
Spain	12.8
Belgium	14.5
Greece	14.6
Portugal	14.8

Source: ONS, 2006b

exchange information across the internet, or to power up the hardware that drives all this a vast physical system of wires, power grids, aerials and so on is required. Such infrastructures are less obvious to the eye than those for transport, yet are equally active ingredients of the physical environment around us, whether in the form of visible factors such as masts or wires or invisible factors such as wavelengths at the high end of the energy spectrum – radio, electromagnetic and so on. 'Electrosensitivity', a condition purportedly arising from exposure to the electrical frequencies emitted from this infrastructure, has often been mooted as one damaging outcome of it. Sufferers report a variety of symptoms from ear pain, headaches, nausea, depression and skin rashes. Cancers have also been reported (ES-UK, 2005).

Not surprisingly, almost every company likely to profit from such technology is quick to scoff at the idea of any serious threat. The scientific evidence is, as yet, certainly ambiguous so that only Sweden officially recognises electrosensitivity as an illness, with well-organised support groups which attempt to collate information and examples of harm (FEB, 2006). But certain evidence suggests that the threat may extend more widely than this more sensitive group. In their 1999 Study (NIEHS, 1999), the US National Institute of Environmental Health Sciences were profoundly sceptical about any definitive correlation, but they did accept that research which suggested a link between childhood leukaemia and electromagnetic radiation '. . . cannot be dismissed as random or negative findings'. Indeed, they estimated that there might be around 2.5–5% of leukaemia cases per 100,000 arising in this way.

Together with other prominent bodies such as the International Agency for Research on Cancer (IARC), they have accepted that magnetic fields are a possible carcinogen. Their conclusions have been supported by other independent research (see for example Ahlbom *et al.*, 2000; Greenland *et al.*, 2000).

Brain tumours have been rising at about 1.7% per year over the last 25 years in the UK (ONS, 2006) though recent research in five European countries (Schoemaker, 2005) appeared to suggest little evidence of any link to mobile phone use. But this research has been criticised on various grounds. For example, the UK pressure group Powerwatch pointed out that the study only considered acoustic neuroma, a rare (about 6% of brain tumours) and slow-growing, benign tumour. They also pointed out that the report *did* find a 1.8-fold increased risk of acoustic neuromas developing in the side of the head where the mobile phone handset was usually held (Powerwatch, 2005). An equally telling indication of the risk landscape here can be seen in the apparent refusal of some insurance underwriters to offer 'product liability cover' to mobile phone manufacturers against possible damage to users' health (Ryle, 1999). Meanwhile, in 2000, parents were advised by the UK Department of Health that they should not let children use mobile devices 'excessively' in case of possible health risks (Schaefer, 2000). The difficulty in making clear judgements is typified by the ambiguous media responses to a recent report from the UK Health Protection Agency (HPA, 2005) which reviewed the literature but conducted no new research. The *Guardian* (4/11/05) asserted that it found: 'no scientific evidence that exposure to electrical appliances causes illness', while the *Sunday Times* (11/9/05) interpreted it to mean that 'electrical fields can make you sick'.

That infrastructures of the hyperspatial, transport or otherwise, can produce specific (and fatal) accidents, seems plausible enough. Less plausible are reports that network technology – in particular the immersion experiences associated with online gaming – can create forms of 'over-exposure' which are fatal. In 2003, for example, a Hong Kong computer game enthusiast was supposedly found slumped dead at a terminal by a policeman in a game centre after playing the online game Diablo II for many hours. His death in Hong Kong's Yuen Long district came eight months after a 17-year-old game centre employee was also found dead after apparently playing Diablo II through the night. Warnings were immediately posted in cyber cafés around Hong Kong advising customers not to spend 'too long' playing games uninterrupted (*The Age*, 13/01/03). Later in 2003 it was reported that a 24-year-old South Korean man had been found dead at an internet café in Kwangju, 160 miles south-west of Seoul, after using the computer non-stop for most of the weekend without eating or sleeping (Gluck, 2002). In fact the precise circumstances of the deaths were vague and seem just as likely to have resulted from some prior physical condition.

Hyperspatial death – folk devils and guilty parties

To ask how killing and death has been affected by hyperspatialisatisation processes raises the inevitable problem of where to draw the line. For example, ought early compressive technology such as the Winchester rifle or radar be included within the remit of a 'hyperspatially' assisted killing? If however one keeps focused solely upon the role of information technology, some clear patterns do seem to emerge. Far from it presenting some dark and murky (virtual) reality where 'web psychos' lurk to ply their loathsome trades, the familiar monopolies of violence seem to have been extended in much the same way as bodies, or indeed social life in general, have been extended. And one of the clearest manifestations of this fact lies in the uneven distribution of the capacity to inflict death. Whilst the increased efficiencies in targeted killing provided by 'intelligent' weapons and the pervasive technologies of representation may be ignored, they cannot ultimately be denied. Web psychos there may be, but if we could measure our nightmares in terms of simple quantity, they would not be among the worst the hyperspatial has to offer.

Damaging incursion – violence towards the body

In considering the effects of hyperspatiality upon damaging incursions, or *violence* towards bodies, two broad categories frame the basic possibilities: physical violence – violence to the actual body itself, and psychological violence – violence to the general mental well-being of a subject. The distributed body appears especially susceptible to the latter given the special connection between our psychological life and the ways in which we tend to experience the hyperspatial at present. I will consider these psychological harms in a moment, but I shall begin by considering examples of violence to the body that hyperspace might seem to promote, with the issue of sexual abuse prominent here.

Sexual abuse in hyperspace

Just as the advent of the telephone was considered to have promoted prostitution and to have created the call-girl, the internet has been perceived to have furthered various forms of sexual abuse. I will now consider three such charges which have been specifically directed toward the internet.

(1) The internet provides opportunities for meeting individuals and subsequently sexually abusing them

The phenomenon of 'grooming' – the enticement and entrapment of individuals (often, but by no means always children) for the purpose of sex presents a clear context where the internet seems to promote circumstances which lead to sexual abuse. As a result it has received wide and dramatic coverage. But as even Interpol point out, the covert predator is 'the exception rather than the rule' (Interpol, 2007) and predation is more usually a proximate rather than a remote interaction located at places 'where children frequent, a play park or swimming pool for example', one which can take 'many months, even years, and often begins with the process of grooming the parents of the child' (ibid).

Whilst there have been numerous cases where the internet played a role of establishing an initial contact (see for example BBC, 13/12/01), some form of proximal interaction – a physical meeting – is usually required for there to be abuse. Where remote interaction is more clearly part of the abusive behaviour, it tends to be more psychological than physical. One striking case of this involved a man who was able to 'take control' of his victims' computers by planting viruses on them which caused strange and disturbing malfunctions. For example, disc drive drawers would open and close on their own, random text would appear on the screen or the monitor would turn itself off and back on again (Cowan, 2006). Such apparent control was clearly an unnerving experience for the victims and seemed to have enabled him to persuade several of them to comply with his main aim – the acquisition of explicit sexual images. He was eventually jailed for 10 years and, though the details are not entirely clear, it appears that he may have also been involved in a separate case of (proximate) sexual abuse of a 14-year-old girl. Other cases entail a more tenuous involvement of remote interaction in the sexual abuse. For example, another story of 'internet rape' appears, upon closer inspection, to have largely involved the sharing of online rape fantasies. Three men who had never met in proximate space had online discussions centred upon (often violent) plans for raping young girls. The police were not aware of any of this until one of the men apparently became disturbed by the tone of the conversation and informed them of what was said – a further example of the dangers in assuming that remote interaction fosters genuine symbiosis. The men were convicted of a conspiracy to rape (the first time in the UK this arose solely as a result of online exchanges) even though they protested that they never had the intention of enacting their fantasies (Howe, 2007).

Though the specific culpabilities of communication technologies in such cases are, as seen, often extremely diverse (often involving no more than an initial contact), concerns raised by them have stimulated a wave of legislation around the world. In the UK, for example, the 2003 Sexual Offences Act made it an offence to arrange a meeting with a child, for oneself or someone else, if there is any intention of sexual abuse (even though meetings with such intentions presumably took place before the advent of the internet). In the USA, bills to ban or restrict access to social networking sites have been introduced in States such as Georgia, while the proposed Deleting Online Predators Act (DOPA) threatens to totally prohibit schools and libraries from providing any sort of access to chatrooms, or social networking websites by minors. The Bill has been opposed by the American Library Association who pointed out that libraries were already compelled to block content 'harmful to minors', and that the legislation was so broad and heavy-handed it would damage students' access to distance-learning materials along with their use of e-mail, wikis and blogs (*Library Journal*, 28/07/2007).

Though it is undoubtedly true that communication tools can serve as a way for meeting potential sexual victims, does the level of threat from remote interaction really equate to the level of public fear about it, or justify ham-fisted legislation like DOPA? A large problem in deciding is the poor quality of data about rape – especially in the UK, where the capacity of resources like British Crime Survey to measure sexual abuse effectively has been widely questioned. One problem is definition. For example, the narrower definition of rape based on the amended Sexual Offences Act was argued to have pro-duced an apparent *fall* in prevalence rates from 61,000 (based on earlier data) to 47,000 after it was passed in 2000 (Myhill and Allen, 2002). Another difficulty is the way that variations in measurement tools may also produce wide divergences – for example, the US National Crime Victimisation Study of 1992 produced findings that were four times higher than previously once the wording of the questions had been altered (Greenfield, 1997).

But certain inferences about the relation between communications tech-nologies and sexual offences can be drawn, in spite of these methodological problems. One relates again to *who* is committing the rape. The category of stranger rapes – which again seems to provide the best available measure for covert predators who operate over the internet – *declined* in the UK for the under-20-year-old-group between 1987 and 2000 by around 6–7%. As suggested earlier, it was not the anonymous internet stalker who was most likely to represent the real threat, but the partner or proximal acquaintance – with around 85% of rapes in the UK in 2004 committed by familiar indi-viduals (Kelly *et al.*, 2005, p. 15). Fifty-four per cent of these rapes were by intimate acquaintances and a large proportion of rape statistics involve repeat assaults by the same perpetrator. It is also important to note that stranger rapes are the ones *most likely* to be reported, with sexual assaults by partners, family members or other acquaintances likely to be under-recorded as a result (ibid, p. 20).

It seems clear then that the internet alone cannot be definitively associated with any rise in the prevalence of rape. Nor can it be claimed that threats from remote or anonymous attackers have risen. Those inclined to rape may have acquired an additional tool, and in certain limited instances additional resources for exerting psychological control and intimidation. However, it is by no means clear this has made perpetrators any *more* deadly than they already were.

(2) The internet provides new opportunities for procuring or 'trafficking' in potential sexual victims

The UN Population Fund has estimated that anything between 700,000–1,000,000 women may be trafficked across international borders annually (UNFPA, 2006). Communication and transport technologies have a multi-faceted role in the growth of these kinds of harms. The growth in budget airline networks offers one kind of resource (see for example Jeeves, 2005), the use of the internet as a resource for exchanging information about the buying or selling of sexual victims, female or male, in communicating is another (Hughes, 2003). Often discussed in this context are the forums where males discuss and swap pointers about where they can obtain sexual services from women (the notorious worldsexguide.org is one prime example). But while some of the women under discussion may have been abducted, such forums cannot in themselves be held responsible for this – though of course the charge that they *promote* prostitution might be argued to have an indirect effect upon such practices. But as with suicide it is also not implausible that such sites enable 'clients' to discuss their sexual activities in an open, public forum rather than conducting them invisibly or furtively. In fact such forums may even provide a way of circulating information about potential abductees and of enforcing certain moral 'norms' about behaviour towards women who sell sexual services (cf. Monto, 2004). Similar reflections apply to the various 'bride forums' discussed earlier where men can select women for relationships. A very small number may be implicated in trafficking (though no reliable data for this exists) but others may simply be part of the online sexual economy, serving as fronts for sexual services such as escorts, massage, or more symbiotic extremes of sexual preference. Some may even result in legitimate and genuinely fulfilling relationships for both parties. The rise in trafficking is a complex social phenomenon and hyperspatiality, where any causal association with this can be discerned, seems more likely to be implicated in terms of its transport technologies than its communication technologies, much less the internet.

(3) The internet provides a way in which sexual abuse and violence to physical bodies is instigated for remote entertainment

Perhaps the most most plausibly 'remote' threat from remote technology in terms of sexual abuse is where it enables an abuse to take place at a distance. The interface between the sale of sex and women online is complex and while live porn sites created by women themselves have been argued to constitute 'identity projects that appropriate cultural expectations of sexuality' (DeVoss, 2002, p. 75), others may involve coercion or worse. One example, investigated by Donna Hughes (2000), was the live bondage sex show which an American pornographer, resident in Phnom Penh, added to his internet site. The 'Rape Camp' was advertised as a 'pay-to-view' service where customers could relay requests for torture and sexual abuse for fees at around US$15 for 10 minutes, US$40 for 30 minutes or $75 per hour (Deutsche Presse-Agentur, 14/10/1999). The man commented:

> It might promote violence against women in the United States, but I say, 'Good.' I hate those bitches. They're out of line and that's one of the reasons I want to do this . . . I'm going through a divorce right now. . . . I hate American women.

He was eventually arrested by Cambodian authorities but rather than facing a possible five-year sentence for violations of laws relating to human trafficking and sexual exploitation, American consular officials intervened and he was deported without charge instead. As Hughes (2000) points out, 'None of the women were interviewed. No information about their well-being, experiences or wishes was included in the news stories!'

Whilst sites like the Rape Camp seem to be rare, there are many others which like to trade on fantasies about the actualities of rape. For example, one search conducted in 2006 for 'rape websites' brought up 9,650,000 hits (Google 03/2006). Though most were porn sites containing *simulated* rape the content was frequently disturbing and offensive on a number of different levels – not least in terms of race as well as gender, for example. One site offered 'the largest archive of the most violent rape content EVER PRODUCED' and included special 'ethnic sections'. The site related how 'Asian women are famous for their beauty, their obedience and their submissive nature. They are the perfect victims' or (in the 'Violent Russians' section) how 'Russian women are some of the most beautiful in the world, especially when they are begging for mercy after being gang-raped by strangers in the street!'

Susan Dwyer (2006) argued that the enactment of such sexual fantasies which the online experience contributes towards is not 'just' a matter of fantasy. Rather it, 'concretises sexual fantasies, providing enduring and substantive representations of what might otherwise exist "just" in someones heads' (p. 82). Whilst followers of the BDSM scene usually stress the enjoyment of simulation and the mutually supportive aspect of the practice (Williams, D., 2006), it is not always clear that everyone in possession of these 'concretised representations' of violent fantasy will be willing (or able) to reproduce them in such supportive environments (France, 1984).

It is at this point that many commentators begin to worry about the influence of the representational power offered under hyperspatialisation and its capacity to turn fantasy into too close an approximation to actuality. And certain cases appear to offer a degree of support to these concerns. One fantasist who crossed the line, not as a rapist himself, but as someone who used the identity of an in-law to play out rape fantasies, was arrested in New Jersey in 2002. The man had engaged in online discussions posing as a housewife who wished to be raped. But he then crossed the invisible line into actuality and gave out the address and personal details of a female in-law as the housewife who was having these fantasies. Predictably enough, she very soon began to notice men waiting in cars outside her home. The man was eventually arrested after he gave out the address of a former neighbour during an online rape fantasy chat (Hopkins, 2005). He was sentenced to 10 years in prison under a new and very extensive State law, which made it an offence to use the Internet to lure or entice someone to a location with the purpose of committing a crime. But the readiness of politicians to press for new legislation here was also criticised as an overreaction since the case could apparently have been handled under existing legislation (Lomas, 2005).

Even where a real and agreed sexual symbiosis is in operation harmful outcomes can occur if the boundaries of its restricted context are violated. Sometimes this can be through intent, but occasionally by way of bizarre misunderstanding. In 2003, for example, a San Diego man broke into a woman's apartment believing she was part of a game he had played out online. Only when he asked for her chatroom name did he realise he had broken into the wrong apartment and the 'fantasy attack' ceased. Though he did manage to get charges of attempted rape dropped, he was forced to admit to burglary and received a one-year jail sentence (Haines, 2004).

'Happy slapping'

A peculiar example of the interface between violence and the representations of violence ostensibly promoted by communicative technology has been the (apparent) phenomenon of 'happy slapping' noted in the UK from around mid-2004 onwards. Here an unprovoked assault upon an individual takes place which is then filmed or photographed on a mobile phone to be played and replayed later. Perpetrators of such assaults, where it was possible to identify them at all, often seemed to view them as purely ludic. One informant described it as: 'slapping someone round the face while playing lethal bizzle pow pow in the background . . . fucking hilarious especially when it is total surprise' (Mr W, *Urban Dictionary*, 2007). However, the true extent of the phenomenon, or its precise association with hyperspatialisation is hard to assess. There certainly seem to be potential motivations in the *possibility* of the violence being viewed, either as a way of gaining a dubious peer celebrity, or for voyeurism of the kind that will be discussed shortly. But whether this goes beyond anything other than a digital extension of masculine bravado is not clear. Nonetheless the 'happy slapping' phenomenon was soon reported to have stimulated a rash of attacks (for example Jenkins, 2005), with Saunders (2005) reporting over 500 stories in the UK media and calls from teacher groups for parents: 'not to buy their children video-enabled devices as they "lead" to happy slapping' (p. 5). Numerous websites where footage of attacks was available were reported to have emerged but closer inspection of many such sites indicated that they simply traded on the brief notoriety of the term and were mainly focused upon sales of other items such as DVD players, shareware, games and audio files. Links to such sites appeared to be highly ephemeral and were gone almost as soon as they had appeared (see iFilm (2007) for examples still extant in 2007). The growth of user-generated content sites such as YouTube has in any case provided a much broader outlet for such footage together with the inevitable calls by politicians and the media for the removal of violent videos from them (see for example *Daily Mail*, 20/10/2006). There are no specific penalties for happy slapping since these are subsumed within existing legislation for assault. In the end the happy slapping phenomenon appears to have been a typical production of the hyper-criminal, incorporating the instantaneousness of remote culture and a real form of violence used as a temporary commodity of stimulation, both furthered by our eagerness to *believe* in it as something new. The vicious attack in London in 2004 which resulted in the death of the victim and which was filmed on mobile phones by the youths who perpetrated it was widely reported as a 'happy-slapping killing' (*Guardian*, 15/12/05). But the extent to which mobile phones provoked the attack or were simply an ingredient of an already present amoral viciousness, culturally informed by telepresence, simply cannot be determined with any clarity.

Psychological violence in hyperspace

Sexual violence to the body can of course often be closely continuous with psychological violence. Though psychological violence was, for a long time, barely acknowledged, by 1943, in *Bourhill v. Young* [1943] A.C. 92, 103 Lord Macmillan indicated how there could be legal recognition of '. . . injury . . . without direct physical contact' so demonstrating that '. . . the distinction between mental shock and bodily injury was never a scientific one' (HOP, 1997). Hyperspatialisation would seem to especially enhance the possibilities of propagating this kind of violence. The attacker can dispense harm at a distance, they can often do so under a cloak of anonymity (whether real or not) and they can direct attacks in very precise ways.

Harassment, stalking and bullying

Stalking individuals by way of remote communications or, to use the inevitable terminology, 'cyberstalking', has been one of the more widely discussed forms of 'new' harms that hyperspatialisation has been associated with (Greenberg, 1997; Ellison & Akdeniz, 1998; Ellison, 2001; Ogilvie, 2000; Jones, 2003; Yar, 2006). As a form of intrusion into personal space, network connectivities would have appeared to increase access to stalking. But the idea that 'characteristics peculiar to the internet ... make the medium particularly attractive to the stalker and harasser' (Ellison, 2001, p. 143) cannot imply any *necessary* connection between computer networks and this kind of harmful behaviour. The phenomenon of 'hate mail', for example, has been around for as long as there have been messages delivered, by post or other means. And almost as soon as it was invented the telephone provided all the kinds of ingredients for this offence that are supposedly 'characteristic' of the internet – enhanced connection, anonymity, disinhibition, the chance to play with identity, and an immediacy of presence which produces misplaced feelings of intimacy.

When it happens, being stalked by someone using communication tools is clearly a disturbing experience. However, whether 'cyberstalking' is distinct from stalking in general is questionable given that a more precise examination of many purported 'cyberstalking' cases reveals a complex interweaving of proximate and remote interactions. One stalker, for example, who was jailed for five months in the UK after sending obscene text messages and e-mails to his victim and posting personal details of her on internet prostitution sites, had originally met her through mutual friends (BBC, 20/05/03). In another case a female executive who fired a newspaper photographer for downloading pornography began to receive subscriptions to *Playboy*, porn spam mails and a call from a fish company to: 'discuss her order to stock a five-acre lake with fish' (Radcliff, 2000). However upsetting, it is not clear that offensive behaviour spread over such a variety of media is automatically 'cyberstalking' any more than the receipt of hate mail is.

Aside from these definitional problems (when does 'stalking' become 'cyberstalking'?), deciding upon the actual level of the problem depends heavily on which source is consulted. In a much-quoted report from 1999, the US Attorney General spoke of 'potentially ... hundreds of thousands of recent cyberstalking incidents in the United States' (USDOJ, 1999), a figure supported to some extent by Yar (2006, p. 123) who cites the British Crime Survey for 2003 which indicated that around 1.2 million women and nearly 900,000 men had been stalked in the previous year. Yet by contrast the pressure group Working to Halt Online Abuse (WHOA), who record details of cases where victims of stalking approach them directly, found a steady decline between 2000 and 2004, from 353 reported cases down to 196 (WHOA, 2006). While this appeared to be followed by a rise in 2005 to 443 cases, it is still clearly a much lower level of stalking than the previous figures. And on closer examination it seems that these high-end sums may be either speculative or misleading. For example, the Attorney General's figure is actually based on general statistics for stalking. The inference then made – that there *may* be similar levels of 'cyberstalking' – is an approach which the report itself concedes is a '... "back of the envelope" calculation (which) is inherently uncertain and speculative' (Attorney General, 1999). Further, much of the specific evidence from law enforcement agencies cited in the report is methodologically questionable and, as the report concedes, 'anecdotal' (ibid).

Meanwhile, the BCS figures cited above include no specific reference to stalking across the internet, nor do they offer any longitudinal evidence of a *rise* in stalking offences. And of the 8% of women who claimed they had been stalked (Walby & Allen, 2004, p. 17) almost all said that this had happened by mail or telephone, or by spatially proximate methods such as loitering outside the victim's home. It is also worth again noting that the report showed (p. 61) that around 93% of aggravated stalkings (those which were accompanied by at least some level of violence) involved an intimate or known person – 22% of them former partners. The WHOA statistics indicated slightly lower levels of familiarity – though these statistics were of course specifically related to online stalking and even here, there were still around 50% respondents who had met the stalker offline.

Clearly, while the use of computers in stalking incidents does occur, the idea that this is a *distinct* species of stalking, one that needs to be distinguished by the 'cyber' prefix, simply fails to take into account the kind of hard evidence that is available. The use of hyperspatial interaction in stalking offences is one of a range of techniques the stalker uses and even then, rarely the most common. And if we are to talk about 'cyberstalking' why restrict this to the pursuit of an individual by another individual? The phenomenon of corporate cyberstalking – where a company pursues, persecutes or harasses an individual by technology – has been put forward as a phenomenon worthy of consideration (Bocij, 2002) though, needless to say, it has received nothing like the same level of discussion.

Similar questions arise with bullying which, with the addition of that inevitable prefix, now becomes 'cyberbullying'. Once again it is hard to separate fact from fiction here given the quality of much of the data. Research published in 2006 by the Anti-bullying Alliance in the UK (Smith *et al.*, 2006) suggested that up to one in five children may have been bullied via the internet or mobile phones. But these findings, which received the inevitably alarmist coverage (see for example BBC, 27/07/06), were based on a very small sample of only 92 children – and were based *only* in London, not throughout the UK. The 'one in five of *all* children' claim is thus highly misleading. By contrast a report by MSN (MSN, 2006) found a far lower level of cyberbullying indicating that only 5% of children in the London area said that they had been 'cyberbullied' – not 25%. The MSN report had a wider regional breakdown and claimed to be able to offer authoritative insights into cyberbullying in Scotland, Wales, the North, the Midlands and the South of the UK, as well as in London. But given that the (total) sample was again small – this time numbering only 518 subjects – it is hard to see how, when filtered by region, the numbers would have been sufficient to sustain such generalised assertions.

Though remote technology may play some role in spreading bullying it might just as well be argued to play a role in *preventing* it. A range of 'technical' services offered by mobile phone operators such as Intelligent SMS Centre (iSMSC) are available for children who get bullying texts. These can log the mobile number of the sender with their mobile operator and further messages from that number can then be stopped before it reaches the child's phone. Some websites also offer free SMS services, allowing text messages to be sent to phones anonymously via the net (which somewhat undermines the initiative). Any increased stress young people may suffer as a result of bullying by internet or mobile phone can also be balanced by the range of support websites that now exist. For example, groups such as the Anti-Bullying Alliance (Anti-Bullying Alliance, 2007) or StopText Bully.com (StopText Bully.com, 2007). This kind of support was certainly *not* available to bullied children of previous generations. Finally it cannot also be overlooked that the mobile phone now serves as much as a source of *security* to young people as a source of threat. One piece of research indicated that up to 80% of young adults say having a phone makes them feel safer, not more threatened when they are out and about (Mobile Life Youth Report, 2006). This research also indicated that most 11- to 17-year-olds (nearly 70%) continued to regard traditional playground bullying as a far worse problem than the menace of 'cyberbullying'. There is little doubt that young adults have taken advantage of possibilities such as texting as one their main communicative forms. And of course where this is used to send threats or insults it is not only upsetting, but frightening. But it is also clear that for young people themselves the benefits far outweigh the kinds of harms that government-funded campaigns set out to find.

Remote harassment has also found a new extension in the recent phenomenon of 'bluejacking' or 'toothing' involving the Bluetooth technology which enables mobile phones, computers and personal digital assistants to be interconnected by a short-range wireless connection. In this way, anyone who has switched on their Bluetooth technology becomes 'visible' to others who also possess it, since Bluetooth-enabled devices can search for other devices within their short range. Messages or pictures, often offensive, can then be forwarded in ways that have proved to be a nuisance or harassment to the recipient (*Register*, 5/11/2003).

Hate crime

Connectivity itself is neutral. As Raymond Williams (1981) reminded us earlier, it is the way it is *used* that is important. So, one of the central and positive aspects of networked communication – the fact that anyone can use it to air their views or to access the views of others – means that opportunities for those whose views are offensive or hurtful to others are also presented. Similar problems which were encountered during the development of print publishing now confront publishing on the internet – the potential spread of 'hate' sites where abuse on the grounds of race, sexuality and so on can be freely circulated. Since such views have always existed, the question is how far the apparently increased opportunities for their expression have increased harm as a result.

The problem of 'hate' or 'bias' crime is also one that has been increasingly legislated for. In the US, civil rights statutes such as the 'Conspiracy Against Rights' (USDOJ, 2007b), which makes it illegal for two or more people to conspire to injure, threaten or intimidate someone in the exercise of any right provided by the US Constitution have played their part. In addition, federal law offers increased sentences if a defendant can be shown to have selected a victim because of their ethnicity, gender, religion, disability, sexual orientation and so on. Prosecution is most likely to be achieved where violence has been threatened (Yar, 2006, p. 103). As Leets (2001) points out, the US has been rather more permissive in its attitude towards hate speech online than other countries such as Germany, Canada or Sweden where national laws allow for hate-site developers to be prosecuted and their sites taken down. In the UK, the 1965 Race Relations Act has been extended in various ways – for example, in 1998 an offence of racially aggravated assault was defined. In response, some (for example Jacobs & Potter, 1998) have argued that such legislation is a waste of time and that these laws breach not only free speech traditions but, 'exacerbate rather than ameliorate social schisms and conflicts' (p. 144).

There seems little doubt that, in terms of the *volume* of content available, remote communications networks – in particular the internet – have increased the amount of hate speech circulating. One of the first hate websites (with white-supremacist content) seems to have appeared in 1995 and it is unclear how many now exist, though one estimate from 2005 put the figure in excess of 4,000. Software which scanned over 2 million messages exchanged between 2003 and 2004 found that 32% contained anti-Semitic content and over 20% anti-Islamic sentiments (Palti, 2005). Many of the sites – such as the KuKlux-Klan sites in the US – are unrepentant in the presentation of their views. For example, the Imperial Klans of America state on their website that:

> The IKA hates: Muds, spics, kikes and niggers. This is our God given right! . . . The Klan always has to back up what we say with facts, while the media says they have a right to lie and are protected Alien Jew Owners from the international Jewish banking cartel who run Satan's world and system. We come in the name of THE LORD God JESUS CHRIST, Amen.

> (IKA, 2007)

Other racist sites like to present themselves in more media-friendly terms. One of the largest sites, Stormfront, coordinates and links a variety of racist groups across different jurisdictions such as France, Serbia, Russia, South Africa, NZ and Australia (Stormfront, 2006). The site appears to cover a range of 'neutral' issues such as culture, poetry, philosophy and health. Sections on 'fitness' and 'preparedness' (which includes details on sniper training) are less innocuous and most of its forums are full of predictably virulent racist views. The British National Party site (BNP, 2006) has also sought to include a variety of sophisticated media aids and techniques to blur the boundaries between its hate-based messages and those of legitimate media sources. The shift towards hybridisation that network connectivity fosters makes this kind of mixing of media legitimacies much easier to present. Hatred can of course also arise from specific incidents as well as from more generalised prejudice – something the temporal immediacies of the web are especially suited for circulating. In the wake of the July 2005 bombings in London a number of websites were set up, some to affirm solidarity in the face of the attacks, but many others to incite race hatred under the guise of 'revenge' (Muir, 2005).

Of course, as with other negative outcomes such as bullying, it is easy to overlook the positive, oppositional processes enhanced connectivity also produces. Thus, while hate sites appear to gain increased exposure and circulation, so do sites that promote awareness and exposure of racist activity. A variety of online support groups exist – in the UK, for example, the Unite Against Facism site (UAF, 2006) provides information and assistance against far right groups. In the USA sites such as Biashelp (Biashelp, 2006) provide information that helps challenge some of the user-friendly mythologies put about by the more media-savvy racist groups. In opposition to sites which expose the activities of racists, sites used by the right to distribute identities and addresses of anti-racist campaigners have also unfortunately (but probably inevitably) emerged. For example, the site 'Redwatch' in the UK which claims to be 'your way of hitting back!' (Redwatch, 2006) has been linked with a rise in knife attacks on anti-right activists on their doorstep, resulting in calls in the House of Commons for the site to be closed down. Yet curiously, the Home Office appears to have been less capable in the pursuit of racist sites than it has been in filtering out 'child-porn' sites – claiming that this is 'too difficult' because of the overseas hosting of the sites (BBC, 21/06/06).

Voyeurism: indirect experiences of killing and violence

In Michael Powell's great film study of voyeurism *Peeping Tom* (1960), the killer adds to the thrill of the kill by placing a camera and a mirror on the end of a spike. In this way the victim is not only impaled, but is able to watch themselves die – a scene that is simultaneously recorded so that their final expressions of terror are then available to be played and replayed at will. The disturbing nature of the plot echoes many of the uneasy aspects of contemporary representation that seems to go with the hyperspatialisation process – a complex of seeing, re-seeing and being seen. Debord related the obsessions with viewing in contemporary life to a new form of hegemony – that of spectacle, which:

> . . . is not a mere decoration added to the real world. It is the very heart of this real society's unreality. In all of its particular manifestations – news, propaganda, advertising, entertainment – the spectacle represents the dominant *model* of life.
>
> (Debord, 1994, I, 6)

For Debord, spectacle (which we can read in terms of the representational power that helps sustain hyperspatiality) 'is not a collection of images, it is a social relation between people that is mediated by images' (1994, I, 4). For others, the contemporary process of watching and rewatching may be best associated with psychoanalytic compulsions. David Lyon has recently invoked Freudian and Lacanian concepts of 'scopophilia' in this context – the love of looking – an idea he sees as a more general explanation for his thesis of the 'surveillance' society:

> Scopophilia and in particular the voyeur gaze seem to have become culturally central in late or postmodern times which helps explain why companies and governments seem to have so little trouble selling and installing surveillance technologies.
>
> (Lyon, 2006, p. 51)

Whilst acknowledging the 'aesthetic' aspects of looking, the examples of violent images that pervade hyperspace perhaps need some broader account. It is not just that such technologies make representations of violence something more easily and more widely accessible. And contra Lyon, it is often not *just* the 'pleasure of looking' that drives this. The possibilities of voyeuristic forms of *participation* and the way this is enhanced via telepresence also seem to play a part. We end up neither with the panopticon – the few looking at the many, nor even the synopticon (Mathieson, 1992) – the many looking at the few. More often it can feel like the multitude participating in the brutalisation of the multitude.

Cultures often demonstrate a deep-rooted penchant for secondhand participations in violence, one that, as Bataille emphasised, is as much connected to our basic erotic drives as to any kind of 'surveillance fetishism'. This is a '. . . fear and at the same time a fascination for the violence of the "other side of things". . . . And in the world of discontinuity, there is "fundamental violence" in the erotic act' (Schinkel, 2004, p. 25). Thus, images of military victories against enemies on ceremonial columns, arches and the like marked one early way in which those who were not present could exult in the violence enacted. 'Live' enactments of violence for general entertainment such as gladiatorial contests very quickly accelerated this participatory voyeurism to new levels. Though heavily sanitised, early (photographic) technologies of hyperspatialisation enhanced the immediacy and vividness of the public's experience of war. More luridly enjoyable images were supplied by the growth in crime photography itself. Bertillon's photographs of Parisian crime in the nineteenth century were widely popular (Parry & Bertillon, 2000) and anticipated the popularity of similar photographic explorations of deviance and its consequences in work such as Hannigan's for the *Daily News* in the 1920s (notably his photographs smuggled out of executions). The work of the New York photographer Weegee continued this tradition (see Keller, 2005). Other resources that provided for indirect titillation – most obviously the 'respectable science' involved with medical photography – were often as gruesome as anything resulting from crime or war (see for example Burns, 1998).

The increasing availability of images of violence provided by hyperspatial technologies like photography have posed political as well as moral problems of a kind that will be explored more in Chapter 6. Whilst Fenton's early photographs of the Crimean War did not display violence, the US Civil War was covered more graphically. An exhibition of Matthew Brady's photographs of the Battle of Antietam in 1862 drew viewers directly *into* the spectacle, provoking the *New York Times* to look a little closer, commenting that: '. . . these pictures have a terrible distinctness. By the aid of the magnifying glass, the very features of the slain may be distinguished' (*New York Times*, 20/10/1862). Images from both world wars tended to be more restricted but by the Vietnam conflict new problems of image control emerged owing to the proliferation of unattached war photographers. For many, the wars in Vietnam and the Gulf War marked new departure points for the connection between representation, voyeurism and politics (Arnett, 1997; Neuman, 1997; McCleneghan, 2002). In terms of political culture this meant a vastly increased awareness of news management and a resulting focus upon 'appropriate' images. But with increased visual proximity also came a kind of moral distance. For the public, the experience of war and the death that went with it began to approach something akin to a video/computer game. With cameras attached to missiles, television viewers around the world could literally 'take a ride' to the target. Supplemented by the advent of 24-hour news coverage on CNN a feeling of distanced unreality was created (cf. Der Derian, 2002) which inevitably began to displace the criminalities of physical violence with the thrill of participatory spectacle – a process that many would argue culminated in the obscenities of Abu Ghraib (Mirzoeff, 2005).

The sheer variety of ways in which physical violence is being re-articulated as spectacle under hyperspatialisation processes is sometimes stunning. In a hyper-connected spatial medium remote experiences of death continue to be enhanced by the newer possibilities of instant recording and communication devices now available. This 'omni-perception' (Lyon, 2001, p. 147) allows for 'multidirectional and multiple information flows' (Wall, 2006, p. 345) that transform us all from minimal to maximal witnesses, where the experience of some natural or manmade disaster is simultaneously the possibility of its transformation into data ready to be more or less instantaneously broadcasted. We all become familiar with images of earthquake or flood victims, of the dead laid out beside crashed trains. We have all heard and seen murder victims sending photographs or text messages of their last moments and the panicked calls of the 9/11 victims as they faced their end. News agencies now regularly solicit such material as the role of the journalist becomes another hybrid of the hyperspatial – the journalist-citizen.

A whole industry of websites have sprung up, more a result than a cause of this process, whose function appears to be to log and archive death in its most horrible form – with sites such as Ogrish.com (Ogrish, 2005) making images of car-crash victims, suicides and worse more available than ever before. Violence voyeurism had a significant addition in 2005 with the arrival of 'nowthatswhatIcallfuckedup.com' – a forum which introduced itself as follows:

> "America isn't easy. America is advanced citizenship. You've gotta want it bad, cause it's gonna put up a fight."

The 'advanced citizenship' on offer here amounted to the 'right' to view violence from the war in Iraq in some of its most extreme forms. The material, often sent in by soldiers serving at the front, was mostly horrific and footnoted with pumped-up comments such as 'USA!!' or 'Don't Mess with the Best!!' In a sign of the hybrid moral continuities of the hyperspatial, the same source contained links to porn sites, photographs of soldiers' wives, graphic sexual imagery of female soldiers (supposedly) serving in Iraq and so on (Starr, 2005). The US government made overtures to block the site almost immediately, aware that photos of mutilated Iraqis taken by soldiers with their digital cameras was hardly going to present the best spin on their 'Operation Enduring Freedom'. By late 2005 the site had been taken down for 'unspecified' reasons and its operator arrested (Ellsworth, 2005).

Humorous sites that hybridise death and violence with entertainment have also emerged to continue older traditions of guignol. The site Deadbodyguy.com made a minor web celebrity out of Chuck Lamb who specialised in posing as bodies which had died from a variety of grotesque causes, crumpled at the foot of stairs, electrocuted in a bath, hanging from a room fan and so on. In a symptomatic fusion of media availabilities and the contemporary quest for celebrity, Land's stated ambition was to appear as a corpse in a TV film or drama of some kind – any kind.

Legitimate and illegitimate voyeurisms

The State, with its privileged access to representational resources, has been as keen to use communicative technologies to sanitise its violence as insurgent groups have been to use them for advertising it. The neutralisation of the brutal realities of the death penalty by their transformation into a form of public service information available (for free!) upon the web is a significant example of this. The punitive-entertainment hybrid that emerges (cf. Hallsworth, 1996) has obvious continuities with other cruelties for pleasure that permeate social life, such as popularity shows or celebrity torture shows (Presdee, 2000; Hallsworth, 2006). It also has clear continuities with a commodification process (cf. Christie, 2004) which 'achieves its ultimate fulfillment in the spectacle' (Debord, 1994, pp. 2, 36).

In the USA, States which continue to enact the death penalty have often a sizeable electronic presence where spectators become voyeurs, while being reassured that they are 'learning' or 'being educated' about the criminal justice system and the death penalty. One can view photographs of the accused on death row; examine the length of their sentences; see details of the crimes they were sentenced for and read the last words they utter before they are dispatched. In some cases it is even possible to scrutinise menus for the last meals requested by condemned prisoners or, more bizarrely still, to take a 'virtual' tour of the cells in which condemned prisoners are held. 'Useful background facts' are provided to emphasise the 'fun' educational aspects of execution – comparative data about prisoners executed in a particular State over time, details of the ethnic breakdown of prisoners and so on.

Of the 38 States which enacted legislation to reintroduce the death penalty after its suspension in the 1960s, Texas has executed the highest number of prisoners (372 since 1976), while Florida has executed around 60 individuals (Death Penalty Information Center, 2006). Both of these 'high execution' States pay particular attention to the way that their killing is represented and broadcasted. The Criminal Justice Department of Texas devotes a large proportion of its website (TDCJ, 2007) to 'death penalty information' – with handy biographical details of offenders on death row, breakdowns of the electrocutions carried out, historical information about execution in Texas going back to 1923 and a 'death row factsheet' including cost breakdowns on items such as the drugs used for lethal injection ($86.08 in August 2006). Florida offers the virtual death row cell 'tour' or a visit to the dubiously titled section 'Florida Corrections – Centuries of Progress' which provides an overview of the:

> ... history of corrections in Florida (which) is as colorful and diverse as the thousands of inmates who have passed through its doors since 1821 – by turns brutal, funny and heartbreaking, but above all, informative.
>
> (FDC, 2005)

Virginia, second in the execution league tables (97 killings since 1976), appears to be a little more coy on its Department of Corrections website (VDC, 2006). Death row statistics are available but are hidden inside a more comprehensive 'facts and figures' section. A 'High Security Virtual Cell Tour' is available, though not overtly linked to death row detainees. However, should you need to brighten up your office space the 'Correctional Enterprises' section of the site is there to help you. Here you can purchase a range of office materials like the 'Extreme Comfort Chair' (really) while a visit to the site's 'Design Center' will enable you to 'exchange ideas about design – aesthetic and functional' in order to create an office space that is 'a warm comfortable place to spend time'!! This cross-fertilisation of punishment-entertainment hybrids with design centre sensibilities is disturbingly bizarre. One positive (sounding) argument that has been advanced about the vicarious pleasure to be had in examining photographs and facts about death row prisoners is that it helps them 'get their case across'. But the extent to which there is any correlation between a presence on a website and corrections to injustices is not clear. It is hard to shake the impression that the punitive-entertainment hybrid is simply extended, with the many 'pro-death' sentence websites which then spring up in response to any sign of remission or pardon for the condemned adding further scenes to the sideshow (Pro-death Penalty, 2006; see also Sheeres, 2001).

There appears to be an inverse rationale at work for those with lesser capacities to inflict killing in mass terms, though an entertainment hybrid is also still present. The spectacles here use hyperspatial resources as advertisements that both promote their willingness to inflict violence as well as serving to recruit new martyrs. In the wake of the jihadism that flowed from the Iraq and Afghanistan invasions and the Palestine conflict, a monstrous double of the USA's manipulation of hyperspace seems to have developed (Manning, 2006). The use of brutal spectacle as an advertisement (and warning) of intent of course goes back to the heads impaled on London Bridge and beyond. The violent exploitation of extended space by Islamic fundamentalists is continuous with this but also with a perfectly rational political strategy – the circumvention of the representational control exerted by Western governments, and the cooperation of their media in this project. Within the Islamic world itself the dissemination of 'promo' videos for suicide operations, from Palestine and Chechenya to London, has now become a norm. Circulating film of a martyr's last moments has not only provided status and support for their family in the community, it also acts as a further kind of incentive for 'immortality'. The narcotic of participatory voyeurism thus combines a complex set of motivations and justifications.

As Western powers have sought to supplement their spatial domination with a broader occupation of hyperspace that will be considered in more detail in Chapter 6, attempts to filter and close down access to such footage at every point of entry are made. At the same time a political continuity between the jihadis who practise violence and those who simply *circulate* violent images (often for the purpose of legitimate journalism) has been firmly planted in the minds of the public. The Arabic station Al-Jazeera, continually portrayed by the USA as 'supporting terror', has been widely harried and excluded from news reporting (see for example Lettice, 2003). Indeed, the Bush administration even contemplated complementing their spatial wars by an attack upon representation itself – the bombing of Al-Jazeera's head-quarters in Qatar. The fact that this was not just a neutral State, but a key US ally in the region appears to have made little difference to their thinking (Plunkett, 2005). By late 2006 over 80 journalists had been killed in Iraq alone – a higher total than any other previous conflict, higher even than the total for all of World War II (CPJ, 2006). Forty-four of these were directly murdered, the rest killed 'in crossfire', with the US contributing to 14 of these deaths. Amongst them was the ITN journalist Terry Lloyd, found by a British court in October 2006 to have been 'unlawfully killed by US Forces' (ITN, 13/10/06).

How far States have the power to close down representation absolutely becomes increasingly unclear in the context of the citizen-journalist hybrid. Pictures and videos of many supressed incidents could continue to be accessed on sites such as 'www.threeworldwars.com', while footage of beheadings has even resurfaced upon websites for many extreme right groups as 'proof' of their belief in the New World Order and other 'liberal' conspiracies. Yet while digital footage taken by soldiers helped circulate awareness of atrocities carried out at the Abu Ghraib prison (BBC, 08/05/04), and murders by serving military in the region, Americans on the domestic front were rarely permitted to see images of the violence on their news. Even the sight of coffins of their own dead soldiers returning from the conflict was, notoriously, felt to be 'too upsetting' for them to view (Zoroya, 2003).

Violence as leisure in hyperspace

The participatory voyeurism of violence can now be further extended by participation within specific representations of it. A leisure-violence hybrid that complements the punitive versions just considered permits endlessly repeated experiences of killings, mutilations and assaults. The deaths inflicted in gaming scenarios, like many other kinds of interaction in hyperspace, appear to be a trivial matter at first. After all, they are 'just' games. But online, multi-player acts of slaughter, whether 'only' representational or not, cannot help but raise questions about the effect this has upon our broader normative attitudes towards death.

As an illustration, consider the bodycount arising from a single computer game – the game Doom II, for example. Clearly there are many copies of Doom in circulation – one source put sales at over 2.9 million by 2006 (JA, 2007) and each game owner is likely to have played it from anywhere between 20 to 2,000 times – in some cases no doubt even more. So we can make the highly conservative assumption that one million copies of this game have been played to completion. Given that the game constitutes some 30 levels, each populated with, say, 50 monsters, playing the game through to its completion would result in the deaths of 1,500 creatures. If we then multiply this by the million times (at least) it has been played, we arrive at a bodycount of more than a billion. It is staggering to then reflect that in this *one* game representations of more deaths than have occurred in every war in human history are circulated and experienced.

Why would such reflections be of any interest to criminologists? One obvious point of reference would arise if there were overtly criminal outcomes of gaming. Though it seems highly unlikely that violence against representations in gaming could ever be judged a criminal harm, one kind of precedent has in fact been set by legislators in Germany. After a violent school shooting, criminal justice officials in Bavaria and Lower Saxony proposed that a new offence which punishes 'cruel violence toward humans, or human looking characters inside games' should be created (Johnson, 2006). The potential pitfalls of such legislation are obvious enough. How 'human-looking' does a representation have to be before it is illegitimate to slaughter it? And would the mass slaughter of non-human-looking representations continue to be acceptable? And what kinds of moral implications might there be of this?

Whilst the move to criminalise violence against representations is a space to be watched with interest there are other outcomes of interest to criminologists here. These seem to depend more heavily upon an issue considered briefly earlier – the extent to which there may be measurable psychological or behavioural effects which result from computer use, in particular violent gaming. Specific associations were made in many populist sources between playing the game Doom and the perpetrators of the school shootings at Columbine – for example, Grossman (1999, p. 77) argued that 'their killing spree resembled something out of a typical Doom scenario'. Critical questions about the effects of gaming can also be found in, among many others, Provenzo (1991) and Herz (1997). But similar associations were made in the 1950s, this time between exposure to comics and violent behaviour. Psychologists such as Frederic Wertham circulated his thesis of the 'seduction of the innocent' (Wertham, 1954) and the US Congress for one took him at his word. In the Senate report on comic books and juvenile delinquency it was concluded that such texts:

> Offer short courses in murder, mayhem, robbery, rape, cannibalism, carnage, necrophilia, sex, sadism, masochism, and virtually every other form of crime, degeneracy, bestiality, and horror.
>
> (US Congress, 1955–6, Section III)

The result was the Comics Code Authority which was supposed to regulate the kind of content available to young people in comic books (Nyberg, 1998; McCloud, 2000). The later 1980s craze for 'Dungeons and Dragons', a role-playing game which set the tone for many of the subsequent computer gaming scenarios, was also associated with a range of negative effects upon teenagers – in particular suicide (Dear, 1984). Others saw suicide as just one of many negative effects Dungeon and Dragons games were likely to provoke, warning of the 'deadly explosions to come' (Brooke, 1985).

Beyond psychological harm: capacity reduction and the distributed body

It may also be possible to argue that, under these transitions to spatial experience, psychological damage is merely the *start* of the ways in which a broader experience of embodiment contributes to a broader experience of harm. Such an outcome would clearly pose further problems for a criminology centred purely on legalities rather than harms. Indeed, the 'posthuman' discussed by Hayles (1995) or the technosocial hybrids identified by Latour (1993) and more recently outlined by Brown (2006) may raise difficulties for the notion of harm itself. For what sense can be made of the idea that a harm has occurred when it has involved neither a physical nor a psychological aspect of the body? Returning again to the idea of bodily redistribution as an enhancement of capacity, something like a viable class of extended bodily harms seems to emerge which may not be restricted to mental damage alone. For by pointing out reductions to these enhanced capacities it may then be possible to avoid the dualist impasse of saying that, 'if it is not the physical body which is harmed, then it must be the mind'. As we saw, the enhanced capacity of a distributed body can manifest itself in numerous ways – most obviously its capacity to interact in telecausal ways. Where this, or related capacities are impaired, something like an idea of harm to our distributed bodies may then be sustainable.

One apocryphal (though misleading) tale of hyperspatialisation which has often been seen as an instance of this broader class of harm concerns the purported 'virtual rape' that took place in the very early text-based multi-user domain (or MUD) called LamdaMOO. This much discussed case (Dibbell, 1993; MacKinnon, 1997; Lessig, 1999; Williams, 2001) centred on the actions of a comic book villain persona calling itself 'Mr Bungle'. The creators of Mr Bungle (for it was a collective effort) developed a programming sub-routine which was able to gain control of the way users responded to text interactions. They were thereby able to make it appear that the personae of these users were engaging in a variety of sexual behaviours, a number of them verging on the perverse. The citizens of Lamda-Moo were suitably outraged, claiming that Mr Bungle had, in effect, carried out a form of cyber or virtual rape. As such he ought to be subject to strictures, regulation and punitive action of the kind we normally associate with a 'real' rape enacted by a 'real' person.

The keenness on the part of many commentators, as well the inhabitants of Lamda Moo, to normatively construct the attack as a rape again has much to do with the artifice of a cyberspace that goes with the story. The supposed absence of the body then poses the pseudo-problem of how a 'rape' could have occurred – thereby shifting the tale into a modern metaphysical mystery story. One solution, to consider the idea of harm to a 'persona' used in an online interaction, simply defers the problem for it then becomes unclear as to what is distinctive about a 'persona' being harmed as opposed to somebody's mental life. Another solution (Williams, 2001) has been to read the Bungle attack 'performatively' – as a textual expression of repressed violence towards women. But this also postpones the question of harm – this time deferring it away from the body towards semantic considerations. Whilst performativity may provide evidence of underlying social *structures* of harm, this is not of course criminal, nor even obviously harmful 'in itself'. And even if performativity re-enacts some original harm, this is a harm originally experienced by human bodies – nothing virtual.

Once the cyberspace ingredient of this tale is jettisoned the interpretation becomes a lot clearer, if perhaps a little less thrilling from the science fictive point of view. The bodies engaged in each of the interactions remained physical bodies, albeit ones redistributed spatially. The harms of the experience, if there were any, were thus had by those bodies. It is hard then not to conclude that it was the *psychological violence* experienced by the victims that is the primary concern. Certainly, Dibbell reported that at least one of the women who suffered the attack experienced it in terms of a psychological experience akin to those of physical rape victims (Dibbell, 1993). Fears about re-entering the environment or of panic seem also to be evidence of psychological damage rather than anything more exotic. We have no problems in accepting psychological sexual violence in the contexts of other remote communications, whether that be through harassment, obscene phone calls, oppressive speech and so on. To describe an obscene phone call as 'telephone rape' (Hott, 1983) seems no different than what happened in this online context and if this does not require any elaboration about the kind of 'body' involved it is hard to see why the Bungle case, or others like it, would be different or to require a segmentation of local judicial and moral requirements 'in cyberspace' away from 'normal ones' – even where 'code' is involved (MacKinnon, 1997, p. 224; Lessig, 1999, pp. 74–78).

By drawing upon the idea of capacity reduction or removal, a more distinct sense in which personae, or other aspects of the distributed body can be harmed may emerge, a sense that does not obviously simply reduce to psychological damage. How this plays out is not yet clear, though one obvious suggestion would be the way that electronic identity is increasingly used to grant or deprive individuals of capacity in extended and remote contexts. Another more basic suggestion might relate to the way that any capacity to utilize the distributed body effectively will clearly be affected by a removal of the technology that facilitates this. This has been a common punishment handed out to hackers (Painter, 2001; Smith, 2004), though the multiplicity of ways in which access to hyperspatial interaction can be realised would appear to make this an extremely difficult kind of sanction. The specific affects of such deprivation upon the user are not usually considered, though mobile phone deprivation has been shown to create anxiety in certain contexts (Park, 2005). There is a clear enough sense in which some of the limbs of the distributed body are literally 'amputated' by such a punishment, in a reversal of the process described by McLuhan (1964). But of course damage need not be permanent since access can usually be re-attained, though aspects of the distributed body may still have been harmed by loss of personae or other identic privileges of moving through the space. Such a view might enable us to see those without any access to such technology in the first place as being more than 'information poor' (van Dijk, 2006). They might actually be seen as 'disabled' in the sense of being deprived of a full use of their distributed bodies.

Harm to our distributed bodies, if it is to be distinct from psychological harm, needs to be clearly related to a practical or functional loss of some kind. Capacity reduction appears to present one viable sense of this, however limited. But there is another key problem in conceiving of genuine harm in this context – the absence of something that, within narrower experiences of embodiment, we take for granted – the sense of any real *risk* in the experience of harm. The sense of fear and threat that normally compels us to preserve our physical bodies at almost any cost often vanishes where our distributed bodies are involved. As Dreyfus puts it, '. . . avoid(ing) extremely risky situations is precisely why remotely controlled planet exploring vehicles . . . were developed in the first place' so that 'as embodied human beings we must constantly be ready for dangerous surprises' (2001, p. 59). Paramount here of course is the possibility of death which provides such an ultimate kind of authenticity that if reincarnation can come with the acquisition of a new password, or a restart button, the harm in dying online seems questionable. This 'reincarnation' problem appears to undermine many kinds of bodily extension as being worthy of criminological interest so that it may be that only where a capacity reduction is complete, or final enough that we will be able to say that a genuine harm has occurred. Or perhaps, under the hyperspatial, the demand for allatonceness will become so pervasive that even temporary loss of the capacity to interact remotely will acquire its own distinctive sense of damage.

Harming the cyborg's body

Conceiving of harm to the body in terms of damage to its extended presence has much to do with Simmel's 'problem of the boundary' and related issues of its 'territoriality' – where we want to say that a body begins or ends. One final sense of bodily harm under the hyperspatial that I will consider before closing also relates to boundaries, but this time in the context of hybridisation. The gradual fusion of our bodies with technology that has been so widely discussed raises one set of interesting questions here. As 'theorized and fabricated hybrids of machine and organism' we are, in Donna Haraway's ever more prescient observation, '. . . cyborgs. The cyborg is our ontology' (Haraway, 1991, p. 150). And as heart pacemakers, dialysis machines, artificial limbs and other technologies, medical or otherwise, inter-face with our flesh it becomes harder to treat her observation as no more than a provocative invocation of the science fictive (Klugman, 2001). Further technic fusions, such as the implants of radio transmitters beneath the skin, or use of micro-electrodes to remotely control the flight of a pigeon (Highfield, 2007) seem likely to press further problems about the nature of bodies. Two questions of criminological interest arise at this point. First, whether this process of hybridisation is in *itself* desirable or harmful. Or is there something inherently criminal in this process? This first question can be dismissed fairly quickly. Integrating the body with technology is a choice that was made long ago, from the addition of wooden legs to the use of a glass eye. Since the desire to preserve the body is usually so high among us all, we can probably all assume that, where a fusion of the machinic with a body extends its life there is unlikely to be much normative resistance to it. However, the extent to which patients in vegetative states are conscious, or should be kept alive by machines, has created wide ethical controversies (cf. Singer, 1996).

A second criminological question here – how this process of hybridisation is managed, owned and regulated – raises more pressing issues. One obvious problem is the way that in fusing our bodies with the machinic we run the risk of gaining control in more limited spatial contexts but losing it in wider ones. Whilst we may regain the use of a limb or extend our lifespan there also appears to be an enhanced possibility of being externally or remotely affected in our newly machinic form. We can already be tracked and monitored by our cyborg 'exoskeltons' – the mobile phones and similar devices we carry around with us. Transmitters on our clothing or beneath our skin would seem to extend this possibility further. Establishing a careful outline of rights and criminalities would seem to be essential if the shift towards the cyborg body is one that is to be conducted with rights and standards attached to other areas of the social world.

And there is an even more extreme class of potential harms here – ones which, at this point in history, enter more obviously into the realms of science fiction. In Gibson's *Neuromancer* the 'Black Ice' – caused by a feedback loop in the brain linked to the web – is described, a process resulting in the brain burning up and the ultimate death of the victim. As parts of the body become increasingly machinic we can certainly imagine the possibility of remote death being effected by such a process, even if the details are as yet vague. Pacemakers may be remotely turned off, electronic limbs incapacitated. In turn, if our bodies become continuous with machines, might not the reverse also be increasingly possible? That is – might machines become more body-like? At a time when professors of robotics are happy to fantasise about their simulations of humanity, or methods for downloading minds to machines (Moravec, 2000) the phenomenon of the automated agent – the so-called 'bot' – presses its own questions about bodily harm. Such issues have only just begun to tap at the outer reaches of criminology (even though as we will see in the next chapter certain kinds of bot are already implicated in financial crimes). Whether there could be a point when a criminology of robot bodies and the harms they may endure becomes a field of study is at present still only a 'fascinating' question. But in hyperspace, with its hybrids and symbionts, it is now an intelligible question.

Chapter 4

Proximity 1: Property space

Economic activity establishes distances and overcomes them.

(Simmel, 1978, p. 75)

Self-interest dictates our concern in preventing destructive or damaging incursions to the spaces occupied by our bodies. But bodies cannot be sustained without resources. They must be embedded within a further region of possibility or capacity which provides for their various needs – from biological survival to aesthetic fulfilment. The broader space which provides this is felt to be so highly personal to us and to provide so many possibilities that it has often been seen to constitute the things 'possessed' or owned by us. Levels of crimes against this region are among the highest in most societies, or at least the most highly reported (Newman, 1999). And for many, preventing harm or violation to the kinds of objects and values constitutive of this space has often seemed to be of almost equal importance as preventing harms to their bodies.

It is not surprising then that the seemingly inexorable rise in acquisitional crime brought about by the internet has been a rich source upon which different strands of the cybercrime industry has fed. Tales of shadowy hackers waiting to take over identities; of Russian gangsters draining bank accounts dry or of organised credit card fraudsters acquiring pin numbers through covert surveillance networks have all fed into a febrile atmosphere of danger to property. Telecausal threats to what we own are an important influence upon perceptions of hypercriminality, requiring 'tough action', and the ceding of further special powers to policing, security and legislative agencies. The phenomenon of 'cybertheft' – defined as the 'different types of acquisitive harm that take place within cyberspace' (Wall, 2001, p. 4) – thereby emerges seemingly ready formed. But it would again be mistaken to attempt to understand what is happening to acquisitive crime by an exclusive focus upon computers. Just as other spatially compressive technologies such as the automobile or the telephone have contributed to the new geometries of theft, so too have changes within social interaction – particularly in the social meanings of value and exchange articulated through global economies. But differences there are and they will be mapped here in a two-tier way: differences in the *kinds* of things which are stolen and differences in the *way* things are stolen. This chapter will attempt to explore some of the influences upon theft in a world where telecausality, enhanced social connectivity and precisifications of representational power seem to transform it into another viral form of everywhere-crime, something possible *at* anytime, *from* anyplace.

Hyperspace and illicit acquisition

What kinds of variable might be of relevance in considering the spatial extension of theft? Utilising standard conceptualisations of criminal acts such as Brantingham and Brantingham's (1991) would require detailed variable sets involving place, time, law, offender and more. By contrast Cohen and Felson's 'routine activities' theory (1979) is based on just three necessary conditions – the offender, the target for the offence, and the guardian (or absence thereof). Though this greater simplicity is appealing there would appear to be a fundamental problem in any straightforward application of routine activities theory to remote theft. The theory largely dealt with proximal instances of crime and, as Felson later conceded, 'specifically excluded threats from a distance' (2000, p. 162). Some criminologists have seen, in the (apparent) failure of routine activities theory to apply to crime online, a reason to support their belief that cybercrime is 'novel' (Yar, 2005). But such an inference is both invalid and misleading. It is invalid because it is clear that *all* that could be inferred from any failing within routine activity theory to be applicable to crime online (even assuming this to be true) is the inadequacy of routine activities theory – not some categorical distinction in the nature of crime itself. And it is misleading because, by continuing to insist that cybercrime is a novel form of criminal activity, the central issue is again blurred – the fact that it is the spatial modifications to social interaction which count – not the advent of the internet per se.

In fact the variables deployed in routine activities theory seem perfectly adequate to examine the broad features of remote theft, even if the theory remains wanting in other ways. For example, the seeming mystery raised in the cybercrime literature that: 'bags of money do not travel . . . along telephone lines' (Grabosky *et al.*, 2002, p. 15) signals the relevance of clarifying the nature of targets here – the *kinds* of objects available to be stolen in hyperspatial contexts. At whatever distance a theft occurs there must always be *some* target – or it could not be theft in the first place. The question then simply becomes what kinds of target these might be and how, if at all, the hyperspatialisation process has affected them. In turn a second variable utilised in routine activities theory – how any target is protected – also retains its relevance. For at whatever distance a property space is accessed there is always the issue of *how* this occurs – guardian or no guardian. Again, if there is anything distinctive about theft under hyperspatialisation we might also expect certain changes in the conditions here.

The analysis which follows will therefore be based upon combinations and associations between these two fundamental variables:

(i) *Target* – The kinds of objects which possess a value sufficient to be worthy of theft.

(ii) *Access* – The methods utilised for acquiring such objects (without the permission of their owners).

Of course the offender and their motivations also remain as relevant to explaining *why* a crime occurs in extended space as they do in more immediate contexts and there is much to say about this. But since it does not seem obvious that the motivations to profit illicitly *change* very much because of the spatialities involved (need or greed seem to operate pretty much identically, near or far), I will keep my focus upon the above two variables in order to generate the examples and comparisons relevant to considering how theft is being extended.

Routine activities theory argued that the suitability of a target for theft could be summed up by the acronym 'VIVA' – its value, inertia, visibility and access (Felson, 2000). But while such acronyms make for nice PowerPoint presentations, they are often unnecessarily complex. For example, it follows clearly enough that theft will tend to relate only to objects which are *capable* of being appropriated. As Lessig pointed out: 'there are no special laws about the theft of skyscrapers' (1999, p. 123), so that referring to an object's 'inertia' is not especially informative. Visibility too seems to be a largely superfluous factor once the question of access has been considered, since visible targets must be a subset of the easily accessible targets. For if they are visible *without* being easily accessible (the Crown Jewels, for example) their attraction as a target usually declines. However, the first factor in the VIVA acronym – value – does seem something that is useful to consider in more detail, not least because it directs us beyond technology fetishism as a basis for understanding the hyperspatialisation of theft and back towards its roots in social practice. Central to any transitions in what counts as a target is surely the way that value itself may be transformed. It is to this question of value under hyperspatialisation and its affects upon the character of targets that I will turn first.

Value and the market

In order for a target to have value, it must be infused with forms of social significance that either make it an end in itself, or which allow it to be exchanged for goods and items held to be desirable within a market. Hyperspatialisation appears to be heavily implicated within a key movement in the contemporary formation of such significances: 'the shift in the location of value from the tangible to the intangible' (Wall, 2006, p. 356). But the transformation of (commodity) objects by way of their increasing abstraction is no more mysterious than the redistribution of bodies considered in the previous chapter. Intangibilities and abstractions in theft-worthy objects enabling them to 'travel down telephone lines' long precede the advent of the internet. Certainly, the widespread conclusion that contemporary economies have shifted decisively towards 'information' production – what Hardt and Negri call 'immaterial labour', 'labour that produces immaterial products such as information, knowledges, ideas, images, relationships and effects' (2004, p. 65) – is a clear sign that the business of practical economics has not had to make any special provisions for a 'cyberspace'. For economies are in fact *already* hyperspatial, not just in their capacity for maintaining exchange relations between 'tangible' objects (such as bags of money) or more abstract ones (such as digital cash), but in their readiness to continually adapt to changes in value which transcend location. Central to such continuities is the existence and functioning of a market, and criminologists have noted the importance of markets in the practice of theft in various ways. For example, Sutton *et al.* (2001) argued that theft of a target might be regulated by *controlling* its market, while Clarke (1999) discussed how a target's *disposability* within a market can make it of interest to criminals.

Early trading systems often involved barter goods such as horses which possessed high intrinsic value but low levels of liquidity, or convertibility (cf. Davies, 1996, p. 43). As the development of trading networks began to hyperspatialise markets (see MacNeill & MacNeill, 2003), more convenient systems of exchange were developed involving objects *without* obvious intrinsic use values. For example, the cowry shell, found mainly in the Maldives, became a widely used unit of exchange across Africa, Oceania and the Middle East. No 'cowry space' needed to be conceptualised for meaningful exchanges to occur, for the cowry shell economy was fully integrated with the shifting realities of a physical market and the social influences upon changes in value. The fact that a woman could be exchanged for two cowry shells in eighteenth century Uganda, but by 1860 up to 1,000 were required (Davies, 1996, p. 36) may be attributable to cowry shell inflation or to improvements in the status of women, but either way its exchange value remained determined by the realities of a material social base. A more universal quasi-abstracted exchange unit than cowry shells was of course gold. Not only did this possess certain intrinsically desirable properties such as longevity, rarity and decorative appeal (Sutherland, 1959), it also possessed features which compress space in ways that the cowry shell could not. For example, it can be weighed, and tested for quality, both features which enhance its universal convertibility, further freeing value from particularised tastes or preferences.

This kind of interrelationship between exchange systems and the hyperspatialisation process was suggested in Chapter 2, and was something that was especially manifested in the further abstraction of value through money. It seems clear enough how monetary systems functioned to alter spatial experience since not only did they 'lubricate exchange' (Harvey, 1989, p. 100), they acted as unambiguously precise symbolic representations of quantity. These symbolic quantities could serve as stand-ins for physical objects while permitting 'remote' forms of trading to be conducted with accuracy and convenience. Trading mechanisms based on pure representation such as paper bills were superior to piles of gold, with their bulk and openness to disputes about weight or quality. Exchanges based on representational networks, representations equated with and transformable into real physical things, were therefore in operation long before the advent of electronic markets. This is the 'power of money to bridge distance' noted by Simmel, one that 'enables the owner and his possession to exist . . . far apart' (1978, p. 333). In so doing it ultimately 'abolishes . . . distance . . . and unites in one act the distance and proximity of what is to be exchanged' (ibid, p. 128).

The convenience of money anticipated still more sophisticated economies, where multiple abstract or symbolic forms circulate and are exchanged. These forms may possess value in virtue of something specific that they represent, but more often because there is simply a social consensus that representation itself has value. The development of late capitalist economies has therefore merely accelerated long extant social arrangements so that '. . . capital has become not merely mobile, but hypermobile' (Warf & Purcell, 2001, p. 225). Money itself becomes subjected to further levels of abstract representation, perhaps most familiarly as 'plastic cash' – the credit and debit card systems we now take as normal and commonplace. Beyond this lie representational systems of even greater complexity and abstraction such as currency trading markets, government bonds, corporate shareholdings and the like. But at no point are there any discontinuities in value – no fracture between a cyberspace economy or a physical economy. All exchanges work together in an embedded system finely tuned to desire production and acquisition – all of it held together by our trust in the flow and meaning of the value of representations. At its most abstract, as in a futures market, conventions of material exchange all but vanish in the literal 'nothingness' of exchanges based only on our hopes and expectations (Parameswaran, 2003). As with fear or risk, under a regime of allatonceness value not only *accelerates* time, time and 'future-time' become commodities which have positive (or negative) values.

The fact that abstract representations have causal power which allows them to be connected and converted into desirable commodities, services or experiences produces a mutual trust that numbers can stand for or be equivalent to other (physical) things. And in this way the hyperspatialities of exchange systems *function* and function to produce exchange values that are measurable and accepted as universal. As Simmel puts this: 'The technical form of economic transactions produces a realm of values that is more or less completely detached from the subjective personal substructure' and this economic process, '. . . disregards the fact that values are its material, its specific character is to deal with the equality of values. In much the same way, geometry has its aim the determination of the relationship between the size of the objects without referring to the substances for which these relationships are valid' (Simmel, 1978, p. 80).

It is this guarantee of equality of exchange, irrespective of location or proximity that underpins hyperspatial value. The entrance of networked computers into the picture alters little that is fundamental here because distance transactions have long been key to this process. Equally well, many processes of illegal acquisition have also long been shaped by their capacity to manipulate distance. So just as there are no mysteries about the gradual abstraction of value, neither are there any about the gradual abstraction of theft. Both represent logical extensions of processes which have always been implicit in the process of trading.

Hyperspatialised economies and globalisation

The nature and shape of the new information economies of the world have been widely discussed. As ever, Marx's discussions of modern shifts in the economic base form a rich source for conceptualisation here, anticipating as they do many aspects of the hyperspatialisation of the modern economy – in particular its abstractive powers where the 'solidities' of spatial location and immediate physicality are increasingly 'melted'. In place of traditional locatively determined trading, built on material production and national sovereignties, speed, fluidity and spatial dispersal mark the character of such transactions. Harvey shows how, for Marx, capital must increasingly, 'strive to tear down every spatial barrier to . . . exchange, and conquer the whole earth for its market', to 'annihilate this space with time, to turn over capital in the "twinkling of an eye" ' (Harvey, 1999, p. 377). The phenomenon of globalisation – the connecting together of national economies into a global network – is the logical outcome, one that commentators almost always associate with '. . . information, communication, and media technologies that . . . instantaneously connect people across vast geographies . . . (and) growing levels of worldwide migration' (Suárez-Orozco et al., 2004, p. 14).

Globalisation has been argued to redefine social-spatial experience into what Bauman (1998) calls a 'post-geography'. Within this, spatial and socio-economic processes merge to form various important feedback loops. Changes and expansions within the market provoke changes to communications technology which then exert reciprocal effects upon trade and business. Transport technologies extend and restructure trade which then requires transport systems to adapt to its needs. Economic and political interventions in turn shape and become shaped by these global feedback loops, deterritorialising and reterritorialising financial flows. To attempt to understand the ways in which this increasingly interconnected and interdependent global economy furthers new opportunities for thieves by an exclusive focus upon the use of computers, or even information technology in general, risks missing much. The fact that personal computing makes such crime easier (cf. Wall, 2007) plays a part, but not the decisive one. Instead it is clear that illegal acquisition in the contemporary context makes use of *all* of the resources of the hyperspatial economy and its globalised nature. Theft itself becomes increasingly 'connected' – as much by its organisational structures as by its deployments of transport or communication networks.

The transformations of value just discussed – from physical trading items into abstracted monies – represent one kind of influence upon connected theft. The greater availability and faster circulation of wealth generated by these global trading flows represent another. For such flows present a new and obvious pot of riches to dip into. In the UK alone, internet sales more than doubled from £19 billion to £39.5 billion between 2002 and 2003, while the value of internet purchases rose from £18.7 billion to £39.9 billion over the same period (ONS, 2003). This close association between available wealth and the exponential growth in transport and communication technologies which help circulate it within networked trading systems act together to produce multiple 'points of entry' – another generation of the 'breaches' recently described by Killias (2006) that have facilitated crime waves throughout history. This signals again that it is the opportunities for theft which are at least as important as any particular technology (cf. Mayhew *et al.*, 1976). Complementing opportunities for access provided by increased flows of wealth across global networks are other social factors. Our new expectations have a particular role to play here. We now demand the right to retrieve money from ATMs whenever we desire, to shop remotely, access credit and so on. But such convenience comes at a price – the exposure of our more widely distributed property to new incursions and predations.

The complex continuities between opportunity and value as theft is hyperspatialised clearly require much in the way of further research and analysis. An economy and the ways in which it may be exploited deviantly remind us that we must see an economy as Simmel did, in terms of 'a particular form of behaviour' and that the wealth it produces lies not in 'exchanging *values* but in the *exchange* of values' (1978, p. 80). Any transformation in theft that arises from the hyperspatial may be as much to do with this as with the peculiarities of networked computing.

Hyperspatialised money and liquid targets

In representing value at ever higher levels of liquidity and abstraction, money becomes increasingly indistinguishable from the processes of immaterial production – something, in fact, close to information itself. But this greater and more universalised convertibility always remains consistent with Simmel's conception of the fundamental role of money – one associated with 'the spatial distance between the individual and his position' (ibid, pp. 332–333).

It also makes it a purer representation of the *capacities* provided to the body by hyperspatialisation. Its role as: 'the purest example of the tool' (Simmel, 1978, p. 210) is further reproduced and strengthened – an: 'outcome of the drive to perfect money as a frictionless, costless and instantaneously adjustable "lubricant" of exchange while preserving (its) quality . . . as a measure of value' (Harvey, 1999, p. 251). As a target for theft, money itself becomes an increasingly flexible and convertible form of value. In this form its acquisition is both easier and more desirable.

The transformation of money into an increasingly hyperspatialised target for theft appears to encompass everything from the wider use of credit cards to the advent of so-called 'e-money' (Solomon, 1997; Cohen, 2003). Whilst credit and debit cards are now well-established liquid targets, does e-money also fit this bill? A problem with seeing something like e-money as a genuinely 'new' kind of target for theft is that, as with the concept of cybercrime itself, it is very easy to get beguiled by the 'e' in 'e-money'. Instead, many claim that 'in the end, the internet e-money that exists is not a new type of money at all' (Krueger, 2005). A basis for such misunderstanding is to forget how its value is socially determined. The requirement for trust in any successful development of 'e-money' is just as crucial as it was with less fluid varieties. As Hayek (1976) noted, somebody armed with just a photocopier and a personal computer will not in general be trusted to 'pay the bearer' the agreed value of any symbolic representation as much as social actors with larger resources, such as states, usually are. But problems with trust and confidence have regularly undermined attempts to create viable e-money – Beenz.com, founded in 1998, folded only two years later, while systems such as Mondex, Visa Cash, or Canada's Exact card only ever reached trial stage and are now largely defunct (Böhle *et al.*, 1999). In much the same way 'e-gold' systems like GoldMoney, OSGold or E-Bullion (see for example E-Gold, 2006) have had mixed success so far (Dibbell, 2002). However, such instabilities are not the only reason why these systems do not really represent 'new' or alternative targets for theft under the hyperspatial. More familiar online payment systems like Paypal have been successful precisely because they are tied more effectively into the global trading network. But as soon as this happens an 'alternative' currency simply *manifests* this network and can no longer be differentiated from it. As Krueger (2005) puts it, 'Payments exhibit strong network effects. Therefore, any new instrument that is meant to be more than just a niche product has to be firmly connected with the payment backbone: the bank-based retail and wholesale payment system.' What all supposedly alternative money systems do (if they work) is to provide another way into the network and this perhaps tells us something about the character of theft under the hyperspatial. Where values are increasingly distributed across networks the significance of *access* into the network often becomes greater than the significance of particular targets themselves.

Much the same can be said for another way in which contemporary money is adapting itself – the so-called 'electronic purses' – cards and similar items which have values and which can be topped up. While systems like Mondex, mentioned above, did not catch on, 'purses' of available credits which can be converted into specific *functions* such as transport appear to have had greater success (van Hove, 2000). If proposals for turning contactless payment systems such as London's Oyster card into a more complete form of electronic payment like Hong Kong's Octopus card (Goff, 2006) go through, their value as targets will accordingly increase. But this will again be because they are convertible into other values and so, in effect, manifest the global financial network which guarantees this. Much the same line of reflection applies to proposals to turn mobile phones into contactless payment systems (Hammersley, 2004; Grinsven, 2007) – a process particularly suited to countries which lack a developed banking network such as Kenya (Rice, 2007). The cumulative result of all this is profoundly hyperspatial – a bizarre hybridisation blurring the boundaries between communication companies, banks and credit card companies. And the more people who sign up to such systems the more value accrues across the network – the so-called 'network externality effect' (see Liebowitz & Margolis, 2007). Money is a paradigm case of this, but so too are classic objects of hyperspatialisation such as fax machines or mobile phones. To the thief, provided the target remains convertible, all this just means is more ways in which value can be illicitly acquired. In a context where targets merge into a network of inter-convertible values, access at any point to this becomes an all-important determinant of illicit gain.

Further targets – services and social values

Certain targets for theft exhibit little change in the face of these spatial transitions – in particular those objects which retain intrinsic value or which can be easily exchanged. Thus 'standard' objects such as jewellery, wallets or I-pods continue to be targets for 'standard' opportunistic theft, as presumably they always will be. However, even in these traditional contexts hyperspatial connectivity seems to have *some* affect upon the prevalence of theft – most obviously in its expansion of the marketplace through the new online points of distribution and exchange such as eBay where goods may be laundered or resold more easily (see for example Steiner, 2003; Haines, 2004).

The increased value in 'services' that come with economic shifts away from the production of physical commodities presents targets with a more obviously hyperspatial character (cf. Bell, 1973; Gershuny, 1978; Schelp, 1981). It seems natural to locate services within network models of trading, where value is situated within social interaction – or at least the *representations* of such interaction like tickets for transport or for sporting events. These become items which can be bought, sold, stolen or forged. But thefts involving representations of services may sometimes be supplemented by the theft of services themselves. Of course there are certain practical problems here –

many services such as counselling or financial advice cannot easily be 'stolen'. But there are other instances which are more amenable to theft – for example, obtaining social security payments fraudulently or tampering with utility meters. The theft of this form of service also has its historical traditions – the illicit tapping of water from aqueducts was apparently a major problem in the Roman Empire (Blackman & Hodge, 2001). The phenomenon becomes more prominent in a context where services increasingly underpin social interaction, and therefore value. For access to hyperspatiality usually involves some kind of charge – mobile phone bills, television licences or fees for a broadband connection – so that the temptation to get this for free is obvious enough. The theft of these 'access' services has also had a long history. As we saw in Chapter 2, telegraph services were sometimes taken for free and the acquisition of unpaid telephone calls spawned its own underground culture. But the low-key form of service theft practiced by the phone phreakers has now become a developed criminal industry. One estimate from CFCA (the Communications Fraud Control Association) in 2006 (CFCA, 2006) estimated that communications theft stood at around at the $55 billion mark.

The advent of wi-fi and its furthering of invisible networks has created its own permutation of service theft – wi-fi hijacking. In 2005, in one of the first cases of this kind in the UK, a West London man was given a 12-month conditional discharge and fined £500 because he had apparently 'piggybacked' onto the wireless broadband network of a local resident by sitting outside in his car and logging on (Wakefield, 2005). Difficult spatial and legal questions were raised here – not least, the nature of the offence. Rather than prosecuting him under the Computer Misuse Act – for 'gaining unauthorized access' to a computer network – the Communications Act was used and the man prosecuted for 'dishonestly obtaining an electronic communications service'. A youth in Singapore was handed an 18-month suspended sentence and 80 hours of community service in 2007 for a similar offence (Thompson, 2007). As wi-fi networks spread and become more invisibly pervasive such occupations may become harder to control and more ambiguous as 'theft'. Some reports have even suggested that people may leave wi-fi networks open deliberately, so they can claim that any downloading of child pornography was done 'by someone else' (Wakefield, 2005).

In addition to the service itself, the hardware required to provide access also presents an attractive target for theft – especially if this is easily disposable. Just as new objects which gave access to spatial compression such as automobiles generated earlier forms of criminal interest, the theft of computers and other electronic goods inevitably began to climb steadily from the 1980s onwards. Research by the UK Department of Trade and Industry found a 60% increase in computer-related theft between 1994 and 1996 (Whitehead & Grey, 1998, p. 11). In the 1990s, theft of access tools was increasingly supplemented by further technologies of the hyperspatial – mobile phones,

Blackberries and so on. Further mini-crime waves followed, with mobile phone theft particularly associated with street robberies and harmful effects on young people. Figures vary, with the UK Home Office suggesting around 700,000 annual thefts of mobiles in 2002, while private research sources put the figure closer to around 1.3 million (Leyden, 2002).

Information as a target for theft

An enhancement in the value of information per se – from data to celebrity gossip – is paradigmatic of the increasing fusion of immaterial production with desirable commodities. Predictably, an increase in the desirability of information as a target for theft has also followed (cf. Newman and Clarke, 2003, ch. 3). However, it is important, when discussing information as a potential target, to be clear as to what exactly the term refers to. For example, mathematical theories of information (see for example Shannon and Weaver, 1949) are of limited use in understanding information theft since, as suggested, what is crucial to its forming a viable target is that it *represents something of value* in a social system – the particular string of binary digits that represents a bank balance, a round-the-world e-ticket, a shopping transaction and so on. However, one feature of the mathematical theory does carry across. Information must represent *correctly* for it to possess value or else it is of course merely misinformation – and there is no value in stealing data about driving licences or bank accounts if this is out of date, or incorrect. In this sense theft of money itself often now counts as a form of information theft, since money stored and transferred online simply represents correct information about available values. And this value holds true even where the information never leaves its abstract representational context. Thus as money stolen online is transferred into further online accounts it retains its status as information by continuing to accurately represent a convertible value.

Keeping focused upon the role of the social world in providing information with value helps clarify many of the misconceptions about theft when it is directed at what seem to be targets of 'pure' information such as the magical swords within online gaming scenarios, or 'digital' real estate. There are no puzzles about the value of 'virtual' objects as targets for theft and no difficulties about cyberspace/real space connections they imply. Like all targets they represent investments of social meaning and social time which have resulted in an accretion of value (Zelizer, 1997). The fact that there is not (yet) a thriving global trade in the theft of magic swords does not therefore have anything to do with their 'virtuality'. It is simply evidence that not enough people have invested enough social meaning and time in contexts where they grant such things a value. As a result such objects have (at present) low convertibility and therefore a low level of attraction to thieves.

Where such 'pure' information *is* perceived to have value, individuals may be prepared to go to extraordinary lengths to get hold of it. The story of the Chinese man who murdered a fellow game player because of a dispute over a 'dragon sabre' in the Legends of Mir 3 game (BBC, 31/03/05) is not some weird cyberspace story of misplaced faith in imaginary objects, but one of the oldest templates for criminal behaviour in the book. For here was an object with an exchange value meaningful to social actors, something which led to the desire to illicitly acquire it, a desire which, as so often before, then provoked violence. A useful comparison might be made with other kinds of object which have a value obvious to very few people, yet which can still be worth stealing. A piece of art or a collectible object might only be recognised as valuable by a handful of people in the world and passed by as worthless by the rest of us. But because we are *told* that these possess value by experts, it is accepted that they (really do) possess value. If enough people say that an informational object such as a magic sword possesses value then, even for those of us with no interest in online gaming, it may come to be accepted that it has. At that point not only does its value increase, so too does its attraction as a target.

The 'Linden Dollar' currency used in the online world Second Life is a recent example of the growing acceptance in the value of information as traded in narrow online gaming scenarios and its convertible continuities with the wider world. There can already be value involving exchanges of services in such context or limited resources such as (so-called) virtual real-estate. But there is nothing really very virtual about any of this. The fact that the Joint Economic Committee of the US Congress has been discussing questions of taxation in relation to what are, effectively, as much trading centres as worlds, is a sure indication of the seriousness with which economic activity in these supposedly 'autonomous' worlds has begun to be regarded (Foley, 2006). Economists have begun to apply theoretical constructs such as the utility function to these emerging trading systems (cf. Castranova, 2003, 2005) and to treat them as real economies, subject to all the considerations of the wider global system of which they are ultimately a part.

In the hyperspatial order, information increasingly extends its multifaceted social form. With that, its value as a target for theft becomes more multi-faceted. As with money, convertibility is central to this – even if conversion into further information is all that occurs. And as information is increasingly contained within databases, and identification and other key indicators of social role are themselves transformed into information, its value as a target for theft further rises. The 'information economy' and its effect upon theft presents no special mysteries for, like hyperspatialisation itself, it is ultimately a profoundly social fact.

To summarise then – the table below provides some instances of the sort of transitions to targets for theft which have been noted here:

Location	Type of object	Example
Proximal space	Physical resource	Oil, gold
	Physical object/commodity	Shoes, DVD player
	Physical service	Ticket
	Abstract/physical trading item	Money
	Abstract resource	Digital real estate
	Abstract object/commodity	Digital music file
Hyperspace	Abstract service	Communication supply
(extended space)	Information (i)	Company data
	Information (ii)	Identification data
	Etc.	

If it is possible to summarise the affect of hyperspatialisation upon targets for theft in any very simple way, it would seem to lie in how there is an increasing reduction in differentiations between them and an increased distribution of their value within networks. In such a context access to and protection of networks then becomes one of the central issues in the understanding of theft. It is to this question of access and its protection that I will now turn.

Hyperspatialised theft – how to access a property space

Techniques for the defence of property have varied in their historical sophistications. One apocryphal tale from India records how, under the Emperor of Annam, precious jewels or other valuables were placed inside large blocks of wood which were then sealed. The blocks were placed on small islands or alternatively, sunk beneath the waters of pools within the inner courts of the palace. Within these waters the royal 'guardian angels' lay in waiting – crocodiles kept on starvation rations so that they were always hungry. Opportunist theft was clearly not the wisest of options in such a context (Schlage's History of Locks, 2007). For most of us of course such elaborate techniques of property protection are out of the question. But no matter how sophisticated the protection we are able to place around our property, theft involves techniques which continually evolve to get around them.

MacIntosh (1971) outlined a persuasive case for associating changes in the techniques of access with changes to the socio-economic background. Her analysis related specifically to processes of urbanisation and industrialisation, processes which brought about important changes in the 'technique of thieving and changes in the social organization of thieving' (1971, p. 116). MacIntosh emphasised the constant interplay between owner and thief in securing and preventing access as, 'owners adopt more effective protection techniques and so force the thief to change his procedures' (ibid). Questions of access have featured in the work of recent criminologists in various ways. For example, in terms of the defensibility of spaces (Newman, 1972) or, as noted earlier, the role of guardians discussed in routine activities theory (Cohen & Felson, 1979). But it is also clear that such questions apply as much across extended proximities as they do within immediate space. Indeed, questions of access, as noted in the previous section, seem to assume even greater significance in this context. The concept of *trespass*, proposed by David Wall (2001) as a way of thinking about certain forms of computer crime, is an acknowledgement of the key role of access to spaces in this context.

In general then, there seems to be overall agreement that a crucial ingredient of theft relates to the ways of finding a 'way in' to the spaces which manifest an individual's property in whatever form that takes, abstract or physical. Thus, by understanding the fundamental strategies of access, a better understanding of how they might be adapted under hyperspatialisation may also be had. At least four broad templates for attaining an unwanted incursion into a property space seem to be available.

(i) Access by open door   The most obvious and straightforward way in which access to an individual's property can be had is where there *is* no protection at all in place for it. The absence – not just of a competent guardian, but of any guardian at all – is often too tempting a form of access to resist. The examples are familiar enough. Leaving a front door open, losing a wallet in the street, forgetting to lock a bicycle. Of course it does not follow that where property is undefended it will *automatically* be stolen – wallets may be returned to owners and front doors that have been left open may not result in an intrusion. Nonetheless, where the 'open-door' form of access is available it will invariably be exploited by those to whom illicit acquisition poses no special moral problems. In one sense, attaining an 'open door' to property summarises the aim of all other methods.

(ii) Access by force   Assuming that some form of protection does exist – even if this is as minimal as a trouser pocket – a further way of accessing property-space is then required. One that requires little in the way of guile or intellect is the deployment of force. There seem to be two ways in which force can be used to acquire access to a target. One is the use of *direct* force – force applied to the owner of the target themselves. For example, brute physical strength or the use of weapons might act to eliminate the possessor or to so physically disable them that 'open access' is then gained. Alternatively, the owner may simply be forced to provide access by the use of *threat* of violence. The use of force in theft is usually legally defined as robbery, as, for example, in the 1968 Theft Act, Section 8 which states that: 'A person is guilty of robbery if he steals, and . . . in order to do so, he uses force on any person or puts or seeks to put any person in fear of being then and there subjected to force.' For our purposes, the use of *psychological* force to obtain access to a target via threats

like blackmail will also be included within this strategy. Force also offers access to property in a more basic way – by its application to the systems or structures meant to protect the property. For example, a door, window, safe and so on may all be subject to force.

(iii) Access by fraud or deception   Access to property spaces can also be had by the use of deception. It is clearly a much more effective and economical way of acquiring access to a property if the owner can be persuaded to 'open the door' willingly. But since nobody but the foolish or the eternally optimistic is likely to provide willing access to their possessions to unsolicited parties, the would-be thief must find other ways of achieving this. Techniques of deception or fraud then come into play. The history of fraud is rich in the ingenuity of such approaches. For example:

(i)   The victim is persuaded to provide access to their property for some ostensibly legitimate use – as a donation to a non-existent charity perhaps.
(ii)   The victim is persuaded to provide access to their property in order to acquire ostensibly legitimate items – non-existent or low-quality goods, for example.
(iii) The victim is distracted in some way.

(iv) Access by key   Access to property can also be attained by *replicating* the kind of access the owner might use. This approach comes into its own where more sophisticated techniques of protection are used by the owner in order to provide security. An obvious example of such a protective measure is a lock/key. Where the owner of a property is the sole possessor of the key to the lock, then there is no problem. But if someone else is able to either obtain access to the key or to replicate the key itself then they will in turn replicate the means of access.

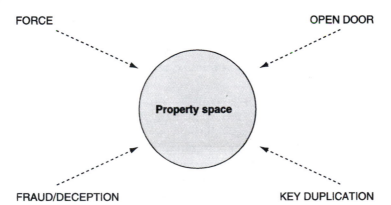

How these four 'master' ways pictured above for obtaining illicit access to a property space might be extended across space will now be considered in more detail.

Open doors in hyperspace

Whilst the exploitation of an open door cannot in honesty be termed a 'strategy' for theft, since it depends upon the naivety, forgetfulness or plain stupidity of a victim, unguarded property spaces provide a tempting resource that thieves, especially the opportunistic ones, find hard to resist. A small but significant level of theft occurs this way. For example, at least 10% of thefts from vehicles in the UK in 1999 involved access achieved by way of an unlocked door (Kinshott, 2001). The figure was even higher for access to buildings with around 20–25% of burglaries in the UK between 1998 and 2000 resulting from access through an open door or window (Budd, 2001). Hyperspatialisation provides several novel ways in which access to a property space can be 'left open'. Very often the problem will relate to a technical misunderstanding of the new forms of access on the part of the owner. Standage (1998) reports how users of the new telegraph system were frequently unable to understand that physical objects, including money, could not be sent 'down the wires'. Telepresence extends the apparent conceptual problems here with many failing to grasp the security implications of leaving remote access points to property wide open. For example, many of us will have opened internet banking accounts on public access terminals and then failed to close them down or left behind cards in ATMs. Unprotected data left on a lap-top or a mobile presents another open point of access should it be left unattended (see for example Compton, 2003), while one survey found that one in four residential wireless routers had no security protection, meaning that their wi-fi connection offered a literal 'open door' to personal financial details (Jacques, 2007).

Force as a strategy for hyperspatialised theft

Assuming that property is protected, other strategies must be put into play if access is to be attained. The use of force to gain access to property is extremely common in spatially proximate contexts. For example, nearly 70% of burglaries of detached properties in the UK between 1998 and 2000 involved force applied to either the doors or windows, or to a person who answered the door (Budd, 2001). But the strategy of force – an obvious enough option in proximate space – appears at first to be more problematic where this is applied remotely, across networked spaces. The idea of a 'cyberspace' and its implication that bodies disappear during communicative interaction would appear to significantly reduce opportunities for the use of force. If however continuities between embodiment in both its immediate and distributed senses are accepted, several options for the use of force then remain.

An obvious approach is to deploy force in an *immediate* physical context to gain access to property that is distributed remotely or electronically. Thus, access to an internet banking account might be had by the simple threat of physical violence ('give me the account number or I will kill you', 'give me your pin code or I will beat you up' – and so on). Crude force is less easily applied towards physical access points into hyperspace. For example, no amount of physical force applied to a personal computer will provide access to banking details. There are however certain senses in which force can be remodulated to act in ways more specific to the technology. For example, situations where a secure system is breached as a result of a flooding of its protections by multiple log-on attempts (the so-called 'denial of service' attack) might be taken to represent a kind of forcible attack on that system (cf. Todd, 2000; McDowell, 2004; Mirkovic *et al.*, 2005). Certainly, as a result of such attacks property may be forcibly acquired, or protections for other kinds of target diminished.

Overall though, force – at least in its crudest form – appears likely to be an increasingly less successful method of attaining access to extended property spaces than alternative methods. This seems especially true where significantly large illicit acquisitions are being sought. For even if a physical body has been forced to provide access to remotely distributed property, the increasing presence of electronic safeguards often serves to prevent large-scale withdrawals. A credit limit is one obvious instance of this, but there are other more sophisticated protections. So the use of force to gain access to hyperspatialised property is almost always best directed at distributed bodies. Such force usually involves threat – either in the form of direct emotional or psychological pressure upon an individual, or towards the infrastructures that permit property to be remotely exchanged.

Extortion: extensions to force

A widening of network structures produces a widening in points of access to the network – the 'nodes' such as phone numbers, pin machines or websites. In turn these become targets for extortions. Indeed, since access to hyperspace *itself* now has value the threat that access might be forcibly closed down or compromised can also serve as a mechanism for extortion. Victims can vary from companies who specialise in providing internet services, to companies whose business depends heavily upon their network presence. In either case a loss of functionality spells potential financial disaster and the application or threat of force to this infrastructure can accordingly result in a capacity to gain access to the victim's property. Grabosky *et al.* (2002) cite a report from the Sunday Times suggesting that even by 1993–95 some £42 million had been extorted from various financial institutions which had been persuaded that their computer systems had been crashed. The threats made to the owner of the 'Million Dollar Home page' in 2006 is a more recent example. By the simple ruse of offering advertising space on a web page for $1 a pixel the owner made his million, attracting a great deal of publicity along the way. Unfortunately this also attracted threats to close the site down unless a ransom of up to $50,000 was paid (BBC, 06/01/06; Sanders, 2006). An alternative, slightly more sophisticated trend in system extortion that emerged around the same time involved a process where important files were encoded on a user's machine and payment then demanded for software that could decode them again (Websense, 23/05/05).

Blackmail and threats

Force can also be exerted in more overtly emotional or psychological terms by the use of blackmail, or other kinds of threats. For example, threats may be made that sensitive information will be released in order to intimidate a victim into handing over money. One such case came with reports in 2003 of office workers in the UK who had been indiscriminately targeted by a blackmail/extortion threat. Claims were made by e-mail that a worker's computer could be taken over and – unless a fee was paid – the PC would be attacked. The attack was said to involve wiping important files or, more deviously still, downloading compromising child pornography images on to the machine. An ingenious part of the scam was the fact that it was targeted at low-level employees who were initially too scared to report it in case they were not believed. And because the amounts demanded were (at first) small, payment was often made (CNN, 29/12/03; Best, 2004).

Grabosky *et al.* (2002, p. 38) also report instances of people cruising chatrooms to acquire personal information which can then be used to extort money from individuals. For example, husbands cheating on wives on the internet might be threatened with the prospect of having e-mails or other kinds of communications forwarded to their partners. A variant, deployed against institutions, is to threaten to disclose information about failures in the company which might be embarrassing. One example here is where details of accounts, credit card numbers or similar have been acquired. In 2000, Barclaycard was forced to close down its online banking activities after their security was breached and details of customer credit cards made available. An IT consultant was arrested after allegedly threatening to reveal details of these breaches unless £25 million was received (McCarthy, 2001). Yet another variant of this access strategy is to threaten the release of embarrassing disclosures about company practices or policies (cf. Killoran, 2003; Nakishima, 2007).

Deception as a strategy for theft in hyperspace

As telepresence is enhanced, developments in remote interaction have provided a whole new set of tools for fraud as an access strategy. Though, as discussed in Chapter 2, disguise and the subversion of identification are age-old strategies they are now reinvented as a new craft form – often, as we will see, with the unwitting assistance of those who are meant to be the experts at using identity to protect property. Natural greed and the temptations that lie in acquiring something for nothing are temptations which provide an opening that fraudsters know all too well how to exploit. The problem of ignorance discussed earlier – the lack of a proper understanding of the way a new technology or social process works – also figures in easing access. A victim's belief that there can be profit from a new technological development, coupled with the willingness to defer to others more 'skilled' in its use, results in a vulnerability that may provide rich pickings for anyone willing to exploit it. As we saw in Chapter 2, the early histories of financial networks, telephone and telegraph networks were full of tales of the naïve who saw investment or profit opportunities in the new technology, only for their ignorance to result in losses through fraud.

It is important to be clear that this material exploitation of lack of technical awareness need not only relate to low-level person-to-person fraud. The process of hyperspatialisation has often been witness to the willingness of 'respectable' industries and businesses to profit by exploiting gaps in the knowledge or understanding of citizens. The resulting losses may involve damage to public, rather than private property, for example, an undermining of public basic services or resources. But the collective harms that result may be every bit as significant in the long term as the defrauding of a single individual's bank account. An example from within the development of transport networks gives us one flavour of the general idea here.

During the mid-twentieth century, in order to maximise profits from the developing automobile industry, General Motors engaged upon what appeared to be a deliberate policy of removing street-cars and other public transportation systems from US cities to make way for their own products. To effect this deception, they formed the National City Lines (NCL) company in 1936. NCL immediately began an aggressive policy of purchasing local street-car firms, a policy which quickly resulted in the acquisition of over 100 companies across 45 cities in the USA. They then embarked upon (what appeared to be) a suicidal process of destroying their business – either by motorising street-cars, or removing them from city centres altogether. By 1950 the number of street-cars across the USA had fallen from 73,000 to just 18,000. But of course NCL's policy, far from being suicidal, was firmly in the interests of their owners, General Motors. A clear sign of the underlying intent here was the willingness of other interested companies to collude in NCL's destruction of public transportation. Thus over $9 million were contributed to the company by Firestone (the tyre company) and Standard Oil – both of whom also had a great deal to gain from the development of an automobile industry. In 1949, the companies concerned were found guilty of 'conspiracy to monopolize the local transportation field'. But their penalty amounted to nothing more than a $5,000 fine, while seven executives found individually guilty were fined the risible sum of one dollar each (Hyslop, 2002). Meanwhile the scene had been set for the huge rise in automobile use in the 1950s, a rise which was to do so much to harm city space, life and environment across America. Indeed, the resulting destruction of communal life, the depopulation of urban centres and the inexorable spread of dis-located suburbias arguably had as much to do with the rise in crime rates across the USA in subsequent years as any of the more familiar factors that are cited. Practically under their noses, the US public had effectively been the victims of a giant confidence trick which traded in their urban public trans-port networks for the ambiguous benefits of a 'self-mobility' technology – the automobile.

Online fraud

Deceptions of the kind just outlined are arguably just as pernicious an exploitation of ignorance about hyperspatiality as any credit card scam, though one would have to look long and hard in the cybercrime literature to find any recognition of this. Instead attention is almost exclusively focused on the well-publicised forms of remote theft that appear to have emerged (as if by magic) with the internet. As suggested, the claims to novelty here are often disingenuous, since many of the techniques involved are tried and tested methods of fraud. As ever in criminal history, like follows like, so that the rise in online fraud has simply tracked the rise in online tradings of value – pro-ducing an almost 'natural' statistical outcome. This does not make losses incurred in this way any less distressing, nor does it reduce the need for adequate protections to be in place. But it should remind us that simple rises in volume do not automatically equate to evidence of new or distinct forms of deviance. Especially when it appears that many of the claims about the relentless rise in online fraud – most obviously those involving identification – are either false, or worse – conspicuously misleading. As we will see, over a period where we have been repeatedly warned of the 'rising tide of internet fraud' (Rusch, 2005) and how card and identity crime are 'out of control' (Moores, 2006), a 'critical national and global threat' which is 'growing exponentially' (Gordon et al., 2003), annual figures for credit card fraud have often fallen, rather than risen.

Nonetheless it remains true that the techniques of deception make for a better strategy than force in illicitly exploiting communicative networks like the internet. The result is a large number of well-documented online scams which exploit remoteness and gullibility simultaneously. Funds transfer scams have been among the most widely discussed with the 419 or 'Nigerian' Fraud, discussed in the Introduction, counting as one of the founding legends of the cybercrime industry (Smith, R. et al., 1999). The 419 scam exploits greed by mailing persuasive-sounding pleas in return for some promised reward (which never arrives) but which serves to deliver valuable account details to the fraudsters. Laundering and reshipping frauds also exploit the naivety of net-users by persuading them to act as fronts for the receipt of stolen goods or money without their knowledge (cf. FBI, 2003). The online sale of fake goods or services such as university degrees (Berlant, 2003) also exploits both greed and naivety as a way of making easy money (see also FTC, 2003).

Key duplication

A final technique for accessing property spaces that I will consider here involves exploitation of one of the central features of the hyperspatial process – its enhancement of representational power. On this occasion what is being represented is the owners' *own* mode of access to their property – most often via some form of key protection. Should a thief be able to acquire an adequate representation of this 'key' they will, in effect, be able to reproduce the same kinds of powers of entry as the owner. Duplication need not be exact – a paper-clip used to open a lock may be as adequate a representation as the original key. The test of adequacy for the duplication is its functional, or causal equivalence – that is, it must reproduce the access to property that its owner possesses. 'Duplicating' key access by simply stealing the original key is the most simple way of doing this and provides a highly viable way of accessing property. For example, over the period 1998–2001 keys were used in 85% of incidents of vehicle theft in the UK. Some keys were obtained through burglary (37%) but at least 18% of cases where they were used involved the 'open door problem' – the owner having left the keys in the car (Levesley *et al.*, 2004).

As the technology of keys has changed so have techniques of duplication. Under the hyperspatial this has meant a gradual shift from the task of duplicating *physical* structures of keys, towards a reproduction of the more subtle forms of key access that have been developed. One such transition has involved mathematisation – the transforming of key technology from a lining up of physical levers and bolts in some correct sequence into the lining up of correct sequences of numbers or algorithms. The combination lock or safety deposit box, which required the right set or numbers to be entered in the right sequence to attain access, set the scene for their transformation into fully hyperspatialised key forms (cf. Phillips, 2005). That is, into the pure numeric sequences used to protect access to information stored remotely, be it of financial, political or some other value. The use of such 'numeric' keys and the art of deciphering them is the concern of cryptography – a representational technique that has become indispensable to the use of information technology and remote interaction (cf. Schneier, 1996).

Key technology has now taken a further turn, one with deep significance for the contemporary control society. A battery of techniques and guarantees from birthdates, addresses, and other ways in which an individual can be *identified* have begun to effect the transformation of the body itself into a form of key (Schneier, 1999; Nanaveti *et al.*, 2002; Smith, R., 2007). The supposed advantage of biometric 'signatures' such as fingerprints, voice prints, retinal patterns, DNA fingerprints and so on over the traditional signature is that they represent keys that 'cannot' be duplicated. But this assumption, as we will see, is a contentious one. Also contentious is the balance that needs to be struck between biometric keys as a form of protection – in the present context for property – and biometric keys as a form of power. As we shall discuss in subsequent chapters, biometric techniques are equally available to control systems as ways of enforcing their monopolies upon representation and its legitimacy. As such they can become as much a tool for the limitation of our movements as they are for the protection of our property.

Identification as a key

As the use of identification related keys for accessing property or other restricted spaces has grown, so too have the confusions surrounding them. Such confusions distort the real facts about the contemporary uses of identification in protecting access to commodities perceived to have value. Amongst the most common and insidious confusion is the perception that it is an identity *itself* rather than an identification key that can be 'stolen'. This idea produces a driving myth of the hypercrime society – the idea that everywhere crime now so proliferates that even 'identity itself' becomes a subject for theft. In turn the requirement to find ever more 'infallible' ways of securing the use of identification as a key generates a project to simplify and fix identity which flies in the face of the wider distributions and complexities of hyperspatialisation (Taylor, 1992; Glass, 1993; Turkle, 1995; Joinson, 2003; Kalouche, 2005). As a result, the opposite of what is intended is produced – an inflation in criminal opportunities for exploiting these simplifications. At least three criminogenically fertile outcomes of this misguided project to simplify identity can be singled out:

(i)   Easier and more varied ways of duplicating legitimacy. By attempting to use simple and universal keys to compress identity into identification a set of vastly enhanced (but also simplified) targets for key duplication are presented to the criminal.

(ii) Improved viability of access to value networks. Once an identification key has been acquired, the uses of it to attain access is less likely to be challenged than with traditional keys, because of assumptions about their greater infallibility, and hence legitimacy.

(iii) The creation of an identity economy. The potential profits to be had in developing identification keys, or techniques for their 'protection' leads, in turn, to an associated industry – an 'identity economy' which trades in such things. As this economy develops it presents another set of potential breaches to be exploited. In particular the simplified set of identification protocols it trades in become targets for illicit acquisition, so leading back to (i).

Though the hypercrime mindset requires us to acknowledge the (so-called) identity thief as responsible for 'one of the fastest growing crimes of the twenty-first century' (van der Meulen, 2006, p. 5) it is plausible that the generation of new honeypots created by this proliferation of identification keys presents a threat to the security of our property that may be equally serious. And it is a threat further compounded by the failures of our new 'guardians of identity' to guard identity very effectively. But before I turn to some examples of this, it will be useful to clarify the relationship between identification and identity a little more.

Identification and identity

Criminologists and social scientists like to complicate discussions of identity by distinguishing its different 'aspects' – for example, purported differences between our social and legal identities (Finch, 2007). But is a letter signed by my doctor something that relates to my social or legal identity? Is my visual appearance part of a legal or a social identity? Does a biometric profile grant us social or legal rights? The real distinction of interest here is between identity itself and its complement identifiability or better, *identification* – the process by which identity is epistemically established (Marx, 2001).

Identity is a much more elusive concept than identification in that it relates to *all* the properties that make us what we are. As we saw in the opening chapter, the (philosophical) question of identity has traditionally been dealt with in terms of Leibniz's Law (Black, 1962; Hacking, 1975). Here, identity relates to *every property* (metaphysical, personal, social or otherwise) possessed by an individual or object. But though Leibniz's Law provides a general underpinning for our common-sense notions of identity it is clearly an unusable principle when it comes to contemporary requirements for identification. Instead, identification is about the selection of some 'privileged' or definitive *subset* of properties, convenient for bureaucratic purposes, which are considered sufficient to determine identity. It is the requirements of identification that give the appearance that there are different 'forms' of identity, since as Gary Marx (2001) puts this, 'there are different degrees of identifiability' – that is, more or less rich subsets of properties (signature, DNA sample, etc.) used for identification. But of course the term 'identification theft' has a much less dramatic ring than 'identity theft'. It is therefore less likely to fuel the kinds of perceptions of hypercriminality required for the ceding of special powers to commercial, or governmental agencies. In turn the term 'fraud' has a less emotive pull than 'theft'.

Nonetheless, many criminologists have insisted that a viable distinction between identity theft and identity fraud *can* be maintained. For example, Finch suggests it holds in virtue of the fact that:

> Identity fraud involves the impersonation of another person for a

particular purpose after which the person reverts to their own identity, while identity theft is characterized by the abandonment of one identity in favour of another.

(2007, p. 34)

But this (somewhat confusing) distinction appears to distort the conceptual realities of identity in exactly the same way as official senses of it have done. Identity cannot be 'abandoned' any more than it can be 'reverted' to. It consists of all the properties that make us what we are. What *can* be altered is the way we are identified – either to ourselves, to others, or simply for the purposes of legal authentication. Thus we can change our hairstyle, or we can change our address but this does not alter our identity, only ever how we are identified. Since no one can ever be 'permanently deprived' of their identity the very construct of identity theft is therefore fundamentally flawed. But individuals *can* be defrauded by properties or features used to identify them being used illicitly. In general then I will prefer the term *identification fraud* to describe the range of activities where keys based upon identification are used for illicit access into property spaces. We shall shortly consider how much of a threat such fraud seems to present, but first we need to consider some of the ways in which identification keys may now be acquired.

Methods of identification fraud

The term 'identity theft' is not only misleading in virtue of its being a conceptual red herring, it also obscures the wide range of strategies whereby identification keys can be used for the purposes of illicit acquisition. There seem to be at least three broad species of such techniques:

(a) Creation (of a new identification key).
(b) Alteration (of an existing identification key).
(c) Theft (of an existing identification key).

Not only is theft therefore just *one* of three ways for utilising an identification key in illicit acquisition, it is far from clear that it is the most serious or widely practised of available methods. I will now consider some of these approaches more closely, commencing with some more 'low-tech' ways in which identification frauds can be effected before moving to techniques that seem to more obviously exploit technologies.

Creating and altering identification

One can *create* an identification, either by creating a key that duplicates an existing one, or by creating a new key altogether. In a context where identification keys become highly trusted authentications of the right to access property or information, creating such keys then provides a lucrative resource for opening up access to loans, credit and so on, a fact which then holds equally for the alteration of an *existing* identification. In addition, the creation of new identification can offer less long-term complications than attempting to steal a pre-existing one. There is, for example, the major advantage that no one is likely to complain about the illicit use of their identification. Sometimes the names of real individuals may be used, though these will usually be individuals without any major interest in the use of their identification as a key – that is, the dead or the newly born. Amongst techniques here can be included:

- Counterfeiting proof of identity documents such as a driving licence, or a utility bill which provides proof of address. The quality of widely available duplication technologies is now extremely high, with the result that very convincing-looking documents can be produced. And forging these kinds of documents can be a relatively straightforward affair since at least some of them, especially utility bills, have no especial 'fraud-busting features'. The UK alone issued over 6 million new passports in 2004 (*Times*, 11/07/06) and nearly 7 million driving licences (DVLA, 2005). Factoring in other proof of identity documents (such as utility bills) that are regularly issued to over 24 million households in the UK (Census, 2001) as well as the myriad forms of financial documentation, it is clear that there is a pool of hundreds of millions of forgeable documents circulating *every year*. And this is just in the UK. Thus the 3,000 recorded fraudulent applications for passports and driving licences in 2001 is probably just the tip of a very large iceberg (CIFAS, 2004).
- Acquiring birth/death certificates as a basis for creating a network of interdependent identifications. This so-called 'Jackal scam', named after the film in which it featured, is among the best-known ways of acquiring identic keys (BBC, 15/09/03). Identity may be further built up and reinforced by acquiring a whole range of documents which confirm each other. Thus, one might start with a birth certificate and then use that to obtain a social security number, a bank account and so on. CIFAS describe this as the 'fastest growing identity theft crime' with around 70,000 families in the UK discovering that details of a deceased family member had been used to open accounts such as credit cards and loans – a rate of increase of around 60% a year (CIFAS, 2004). If these figures are accurate they represent a far greater growth rate than frauds arising from the *theft* of keys.
- A related technique is to use banking programmes to set up *new* card accounts as guarantees of identity. In turn these also assist in building up the network of identification keys which provide legitimacy. This kind of fraud again appears to be growing at a far greater rate than frauds involving the theft of keys, with one estimate claiming a 51% rise in 2005 – especially in new credit card accounts (Javelin, 2006).

An intermediate step between the creation of an identification key and the stealing of someone else's is where existing identifications are altered for reuse. For example, credit card numbers or other proof of identity documents can be slightly amended in small but significant ways – such as a slight misspelling of the surname (Wang *et al.*, 2004). There have even been cases recorded where credit cards can be 'ironed' to alter names (Dolu, 2004).

Stealing identification keys (I) – scavenging

While the creation or alteration of identification keys seems to be a very common, if not *the* most common method of identification fraud, it is the theft of such keys that is usually presented as the most serious kind of threat. But rather than it depending upon the kind of sophisticated, manipulations of technology which are meant to be the mark of the 'identity thief', stealing identification keys, as we will now see, very often involves quick and easy 'low-tech' methods, rooted in long-established criminal traditions.

Bin raiding or 'dumpster diving' for details of identification such as pin or account numbers has been an obvious and well-discussed tactic here (see CIFAS, 2005; Thompson, 2005; USDOJ, 2007) as has the acquisition of diaries, or other sources where such data might be kept. The observation of keys in use, in restaurants or retail environments is another easy way to scavenge for data, while the amount of information relating to identification circulating in postal networks presents an obvious temptation for exploitations. Figures in the UK indicated that up to 34,000 passports had been 'lost' in the post between 2001 and 2006, including 700 misplaced in the first year of the expensive new 'secure delivery service' (Rodrick, 2006).

Stealing identification keys (II) – manipulating guardians

Where gates and guards exist to protect a restricted space an obvious strategy for gaining access is to 'persuade' the guards to open the gates. The investment in sophisticated protection of identification keys amounts to nothing if those who manage them can be persuaded – wittingly or unwittingly – to hand over the information they guard. While attention tends to focus on 'low-ranking guards' such as banking or security staff, consideration also needs to be given to guardians in more executive positions, a point I will be considering more in a moment. There can be no definitive catalogue of ways in which guardians can be co-opted or deceived into handing over identification key data – imagination and the powers of persuasion seem to be the only limitations here. One more recent tactic has been to target 'clusters' of guardians. In 2005/6, for example, employees in the Bradford/Leeds area of the UK (where a number of call centres for major banking institutions such as the Abbey, HSBC, Direct Line are based) were reported to have been approached by individuals hanging around nearby in order to acquire details of accounts. Over the same period figures published by the banking payments association APACS indicated that fraud in the areas surrounding these centres rose by 16%, even though it fell everywhere else in the country (*Guardian*, 01/04/06). Meanwhile in Glasgow – another centre where personal data is processed – police reported that 1 in 10 call centres had either been infiltrated by fraudsters, or had staff members who had been 'won-over' by threats of violence or the offering of bribes (*Computer Weekly*, 27/10/06). The 'offshoring' of call centres to locations such as India provides for a further variation of this tactic. Given that offshored workers usually earn less than their Western counterparts, reports which emerged in 2005 of staff in Indian call centres offering personal details such as passport data, passwords and addresses for sale (BBC, 23/06/05) are predictable enough. Further research in 2006 by ITN and Channel 4 indicated substantial evidence of the trading of identification key data in India (Channel 4, 05/10/06).

Stealing identification keys (III) – utilising technology

As identification keys are fixed in ever more technologically determined ways it is inevitable that technology itself will increasingly be exploited to acquire them. While these strategies tend to attract the most attention in the media (no doubt partly because they seem to confirm the existence of the 'cyber-crime' threat) the theft of identification keys by technological means still retains many structural parallels with older techniques.

For example, so called *phishing* (or sometimes *pharming*) involves a degree of 'cultivation' of an owner of an identification key that involves old-fashioned psychology as much as technology. This fraud involves placing a 'bait' such as fake websites or personal e-mails intended to give the impression that they come from a legitimate enterprise (Ollman, 2005; Richardson, 2005). Once directed to a bogus website where a victim may be asked to update personal information or similar, passwords and credit card numbers can then be obtained. The new procedures to permit new third party payments online enacted by the National Westminster Bank in 2003 provoked a wave of such attacks – by creating an official communication which could be duplicated in order to exploit customers' trust (Leyden, 2003). Another variant of this strategy were e-mails circulated to eBay users offering 'great tips for successful Christmas selling' which directed them to the site 'ebaychristmas.net' where they were asked to enter account details (McMillan, 2005). Fake websites set up to receive donations for disasters such as the 2005 Tsunami in South East Asia or Hurricane Katrina have been a particularly cynical phishing strategy (cf. Leyden, 2005b).

As with most cybercrime 'statistics' the situation for all varieties of phishing is presented in terms of an inexorable upward trend. But the actualities here tend to depend upon which set of figures is consulted. For example, Symantec's biannual Internet Threat Report said that more than 157,000 unique phishing messages were sent during the first six months of 2006 – representing an 81% rise in phishing messages (Symantec, 2006). Other figures to May 2005 suggested the significantly lower figure of a 28% annual rise, representing around 2.4 million Americans falling victim and financial losses of about $929 million (Musgrove, 2005). There certainly seems little doubt that phishing is an attractive option for thieves, at least in the short term. Yet the fact that it is often almost impossible to tell the difference between a fake and a real website means that it is gullibility, rather than technology per se, which remains as valid a basis for explaining it as technology.

Copying the numeric codes contained on credit and debit cards by 'cloning' (or sometimes 'skimming') has also been an inevitable development in the techniques of key duplication. Where security details are all contained on the card's magnetic strip theft has been a relatively straightforward process. For with the strip duplicated only a signature which (roughly) matches that on the card is required for the transaction to go through. Copying can take place at various access points to the network such as point of sale in restaurants or retail outlets but most obviously at ATMs where devices as various as hidden cameras, copying devices which resemble the card slot and even complete fake ATMs have been used to gather or copy the key data (BBC, 09/04/04; Sachdave, 2006; Cardwatch, 2007). The *keylogging* strategy, a more recent variant of access by duplication, captures an identification key by acquiring data about how a keyboard is being used (most obviously the passwords and pin numbers entered to accounts). This can be done with increasing ease by the planting of a disguised 'trojan' keylogging program on an individual's computer. Keylogging software is readily available and simple versions of it can be downloaded from many sites. Planting a keylogging program remotely is not complicated and can be done by concealing them within e-mails, downloads or other material accessed from the web. Home computers, with their often low levels of security, seem especially vulnerable here, with one report suggesting that keylogging attacks grew from around 3,753 in 2004 to 6,191 in 2005 (Verisign, 2005).

By introducing a second level of protection (in addition to numeric data on magnetic strips) the 'chip and pin' form of card security – where a pin number, checked against a chip contained in the card rather than a signature, is used to verify that the card is genuine – seems to have made card cloning/copying a more complex process. But still not an impossible one. Indeed, it has arguably deepened the problem, for a major problem of chip and pin is that it has widened the number of locations where individuals use their cards and their security codes in conjunction. Previously this might only have been an ATM, but now pins are displayed during transactions in supermarkets, restaurants, clothing shops and so on – making it much easier for the vital security details to be observed or filmed. The lack of vigilance at point of sale by sales assistants, convinced that secure transactions are occurring, exacerbates the problem further (Radford, 2005).

It seems only a matter of time before thieves recalibrate their techniques to exploit chip and pin protection. The rise in 'Card not Present' fraud, or cards used fraudulently abroad, where chip and pin security is absent (APACS, 2007) is one way around. Another possible technique, demonstrated by researchers at Cambridge, was to extend the 'copying' concept, this time by copying chip and pin terminals rather than cards. By replacing certain internal components of the terminal it was possible to render every feature of the chip and pin transaction under the control of the fraudster. The researchers demonstrated how they could even make a terminal play the Tetris computer game if they so desired! (Vijayan, 2007). Other techniques such as 'intercepting' the chip and pin process in use were also demonstrated by the team. Chip and pin is therefore likely to be no more than another step in what Donn Parker (1976) once called the 'arms race' in technology crime (see also Ekblom, 2000; Newman & Clarke, 2003, p. 147). The real danger for property lies in the belief that it is somehow 'more secure' than every other form of key which has been invented to protect it.

The 'theft' of identity: critical reflections (I) – problems with data

A perfect example of the cycle which produces enhanced control in response to a seemingly enhanced need for securitisation can be seen in the way that the misnomer of 'identity theft' has been constructed and circulated to a credulous public. Considering that it scarcely existed a few years ago, its apparent transformation into the 'growth crime of the 21st century' (Lemos, 2006) has certainly been staggering. The US Federal Trade Commission claimed to have received 161,819 reports of ID theft in 2002, up from 86,198 the year before and 31,117 in 2000, with losses reaching around $343 million. In 2004 the FBI claimed that 'studies show that more than 10 million Americans were victimized by identity crime in the space of one year, with estimated losses exceeding 50 billion dollars' (FBI, 2004). The UK government website set up to 'help and inform' individuals about identity theft argued that: '. . . it is estimated that more than 100,000 people are affected by identity theft in the UK each year, costing the British economy over £1.3 billion annually' (Home Office, 2004b). Given the continual flow of these and similar figures it is hard *not* to feel intimated. But how do the figures for identity theft stand up to more detailed scrutiny?

On the one hand, as we have just seen, there are serious problems with the very concept of the 'theft' of an identity. But questions equally arise from the fact that, as with so much of the data that purports to measure 'cybercrime', a great deal of the evidence about identification fraud arises from private or governmental sources which have clear vested interests in the promotion of fears about identification security. The emerging 'identity economy' to be examined in the following section provides an increasingly lucrative source of profit to the private sector and resulting questions about the reliability of its data. Likewise, arguments like the one repeatedly advanced by the UK government in their case for the introduction of identity cards – that they will 'protect us' from identity theft – raise parallel questions about the status of government statistics (Ahmed, 2002; HOC Home Affairs Committee, 2004; Home Office, 2006).

Let us first consider volume – the number of people who are supposed to have been affected by identification fraud. Upon closer examination it quickly becomes clear that the numbers you get depend upon whom you ask. For example, one recent 'survey' by the insurance company Chubb (Chubb, 2005), which happens to sell a number of policies that 'protect against identity theft', claimed to have shown that around 20% of Americans were affected by identity theft every year. The figure is equivalent to nearly 60 million individuals – far in excess of the FBI claim there were *10 million* Americans affected annually (see Bergstein (2005) for other problems with the Chubb survey). But the FBI figure also appears to be open to some difficult questions. Not only does this much cited statistic actually arise from a 2003 report by the company Synovate, rather than the FBI, the research was never even *commissioned* by the FBI, but by the Federal Trade Commission. As a private market research company, Synovate have profited from other commissions to 'research identity theft' (see for example First Data, 2005) which raises further questions about their commitment to objectivity. Either way, by 2005 the widely circulated 10 million figure had been quietly downgraded by Synovate by at least one million – giving a revised figure closer to 9 million of Americans affected by identification fraud. As one might imagine, this revised figure did not received anything like the same levels of press coverage. Instead one continues to see the 10 million figure cycled and recycled in the media and other sources as an indication of the 'seriousness' of the issue. But even the lower, 9 million figure, has some problems. As Cate (2005) suggests, the revised figure is also questionable since it includes misuse of *existing* credit cards. Subtracting that, it then turns out that fraudsters had opened *new* accounts or committed similar misdeeds in the names of just 3.2 million Americans in the previous year – a significant drop from the original 10 million.

Figures for the crime are also clearly boosted by public misunderstandings of the concept when questioned in surveys. Many individuals, if the question is put to them, willingly accept that they have been the victims of 'identity theft' while failing to understand what that term means. Thus, they will often include instances of straightforward account fraud here – distorting the figures further. When the broad and vague notion of 'identity theft' is narrowed down to its real form – the use of identification keys – there is a great deal of evidence to suggest that many frauds involving identification are actually *falling* – not rising out of control. Citing the 2005 Nilson report on credit card fraud in the USA (Nilson, 2005), Cate points out 'From 1992 to 2004 . . . the cost of credit card fraud had fallen by more than two-thirds from $.157 to $.047 per $100 in credit card sales. Fraudulent charges are lower as a percentage of credit card use in the United States than anywhere else in the world' (2005, p. 6). We will come back to this point shortly.

The 'theft' of identity: critical reflections (II) – the identity economy

The use of identification within the growing immaterial economy produces a new commodity to be traded in – the identification key. Such keys increasingly generate their own forms of economic activity and profit which throws a second kind of critical light upon the 'problem of identity theft' – its role in bolstering this burgeoning identity economy.

One manifestation lies in the sale of products and services which help you 'protect' your identity. Take, for example, the Identity Theft Resource Centre. Its plethora of dubious statistics – ('. . . victims now spend an average of 600 hours recovering from this crime, often over a period of years. Three years ago the average was 175 hours of time, representing an increase of about 247%') – includes a predictable recycling of the FBI/FTC figures above. As well as helping protect you against the 'nation's fastest growing crime', the Centre is extremely keen to offer you its resources for speaking engagements (ITRC, 2004). It is at least a non-profit organisation. But enter 'identity theft' into any search engine and a host of promotional offers from credit reference agencies and other interested parties spring up, all offering 'peace of mind' and protection against the 'nation's fastest growing crime'. For a small fee of course.

The trade in personal information further fuels the identity economy. Even in 1999 one estimate suggested that the average US citizen may have been profiled on over 100 different databases (Shapiro, 1999, p. 259) – a figure presumably much higher by 2006. Estimating the level of profits is hard because the personal information industry is less than forthcoming about what it gets up to. But one indication of the kinds of profits industry figures imagine are available can be had by considering the (projected) profits for direct marketing companies (heavily dependent upon the acquisition of personal datafiles) – nearly $2.7 trillion dollars by 2005 (Direct Marketing Today, 2001).

One especially shady branch of the economy lies with credit reference agencies such as Experian, Equifax and Transunion who already make a lot of money out of personal information by selling credit reports to lenders or other such sources. But they may also profit by selling so-called 'header' information (details such as names, addresses, phone numbers, dates of birth and, in the US, Social Security numbers) from credit reports to credit lenders who are interested in mailing out credit offers to consumers. In the US, credit bureaus are supposed to be legally forbidden from selling on credit report information for *non*-credit purposes. But they *can* collect data available in public records, such as drivers' licence information or information about buying habits and sell this on to businesses offering non-credit products or to government agencies. In 2004, for example, drivers in North Carolina who received traffic violation tickets were surprised to find letters from local attorneys arriving very quickly afterwards. The decision to centralise county court records in North Carolina had turned out to be commercial gold for a company called SpeedingTicket.net who struck a deal with the State to pay it 10 to 30 cents for each record that it downloaded. Everyone (but the offender) profits. The State now collects around $1.7 million annually from such data sales while SpeedingTicket.net is able to then charge lawyers between 50 cents and a dollar to relay the data. In turn the lawyers obtain a list of addresses for a marketing mail-out. Like many other similar traders in personal information SpeedingTicket.net has expanded quickly and now also operates in Florida, Washington, New Jersey and numerous other States (Bergstein, 2004).

The commercial sector has developed a variety of seemingly innocuous ways of acquiring personal information. Product warranty cards, store loyalty cards and even so called 'consumer satisfaction' surveys are often fronts for the acquisition of information, information which can then be legally traded-on – say to insurance companies – with no knowledge on the part of the individual whose identity has become a commodity to be bought or sold. In the US many stores now routinely request data such as a address or zipcode when a purchase has been made – even if the transaction has not involved the use of a credit card.

One destination for all this personal data is to assist with ever more precise forms of telemarketing. In 2003, for example, Dunhill International Lists were offering lists of personal information organised around the following categories (among many others):

> *Affluent America*: '. . . the most comprehensive database of million-aires, multi-millionaires and billionaires and their wealthiest neighbors available anywhere. . . .'

> *Sub-Prime Auto Loan Applicants*: '. . . These individuals are in dire need of credit . . . They could not qualify for a conventional loan and therefore financed an automobile with a sub-prime auto lender.'

> *Opinion Molders Database*: 'Effective Mailing Lists to Reach "Influentials" in Media, Government, Business, Religion, Education, Medicine, Environment and more!'

> (EPIC, 2004)

Specialised 'information brokers' – companies such as Choicepoint – can offer in-depth dossiers about individuals which are up to 30 pages in length or more and contain details about assets, licences, bankruptcies, business affiliations and criminal offences. In this repackaged form they are often able to end up selling back information to an original vendor – frequently government departments. There are also more overtly questionable ways in which they use data – with Choicepoint under particular focus here. One set of questions has arisen around the way its data may have been used to influence voting – most crucially in the controversial 2000 US election which was won by George Bush on the narrowest of margins in Florida. Back in 1998 the Florida state government had signed a contract worth around $4 million with a company called Database Technologies, which later merged into Choicepoint. Very soon after the election questions began to be raised about Choicepoint's role in the result. Data it held, which was widely used in the election to certify the right to vote, appeared to be suspect in key ways. For example, some voters were listed as criminals for alleged offences said to have been committed several years *in the future* while others who had been convicted of a felony in a different State but had their rights restored by said State, were still listed as 'not eligible to vote'. Other individuals were listed as criminals purely because of a name coincidence even though other data (such as date of birth) showed that the criminal record did *not* apply to the individual in question (cf. Palast, 2002).

Maybe all this amounted to nothing more than shoddy information keeping on the part of Choicepoint rather than criminal behaviour (itself a kind of indictment, given that data storage is meant to be its business). But residents in Pennsylvania – where Choicepoint was fined $1.375 million by the State for illegally selling on customers' data obtained from driving records – might be one group who would question their noble intentions (PID, 2000). Either way, by 2006, Choicepoint was back in the election business – again in suspicious circumstances. In the wake of 9/11 the company had (for reasons never fully explained) been employed by the FBI to collect information on voters in Venezuela, Brazil and Mexico. And in the Mexican election of 2006 there were disturbing echoes of the Florida election when voters in left-leaning districts of Mexico found their names had 'disappeared' from voting registers. The right of centre candidate (and strong American supporter) Felipe Calderón won the election with a mere 402,000 votes while 820,000 ballot papers were returned blank. Protesting its innocence, Choicepoint said that it had returned or destroyed its Mexican files when it learned that collecting voter information happened to violate Mexican law (Palast, 2006). In 2005, Choicepoint generated earnings of more than $1 billion, an increase of 15% from the previous year (Choicepoint, 2005a).

The identity economy: who guards the guardians?

Given that the identity economy generates 'immaterial' banks of data on billions of individuals, a pressing question in dealing with identification-based crime arises – who guards the guardians? In particular, does their competence in managing the valuable information they store justify the large profits they are generating from using it? Given the available evidence, the short answer appears to be that they are not. Take the information brokers Choicepoint again. In early 2005 the *Wall Street Journal* reported a major security breach at the company which resulted in data on millions of individuals being downloaded for use by individuals unknown (*Wall Street Journal*, 03/05/05). The company strenuously denied this number, though it did concede that there had been a breach. However it claimed that 'only' around 145,000 records had been stolen and in a less than complete statement of guilt purred:

> We take fraud seriously. We have provided benefits to potentially affected consumers that no other information company has done before and that several companies have since emulated.
>
> (Choicepoint, 2005b)

In fact it later transpired that, far from there being any security breach, Choicepoint may actually not only have sold the data (including addresses, phone numbers and social security numbers) for fees of $100 to $200, but that the people they sold this to may have been involved in frauds involving identity! (EPIC, 2005).

Soon after, another of these information brokers – Lexisnexis – conceded that it too had had large amounts of confidential data breached and stolen over a two-year period. Meanwhile in February 2005 information was stolen from more than 2.2 million MasterCard and 3.4 million Visa accounts in the US, when a company processing credit card transactions was broken into by a hacker. Over a short four-week period from April to May 2005 it was estimated that there were security breaches involving sensitive personal information belonging to over 2 million people. And the list goes on (and on). In April, for example, HSBC was forced to send out warning letters to around 200,000 customers using the General Motors GM Mastercard, whose details had been 'compromised' (BBC, 15/04/05). Note that these cases occurred over just a *four-week* period and relate only to disclosed information breaches – there may have been many more than these. They also of course relate only to data stolen in the USA, not anywhere else in the world (Sahadi, 2005).

Out of 56 million incidents the worst offenders in terms of individuals affected were financial institutions – with 46,531,750 people affected (12%), and governmental institutions – with 4,002,100 affected. In one of the biggest and most recent examples of this kind, personal information belonging to over 26 million US military veterans was lost or compromised when a laptop containing these details was stolen in early 2006 (CNN, 23/05/06). Yet the authorities waited over two weeks before releasing any details to the public or even to the potential victims. The laptop was apparently 'returned' in September and the impression given that things had returned to normal. But no indication of what had happened to the lap top between May and September, or who had used it, was given. A recent update on figures for data breaches suggest that the number of records containing sensitive personal information which have been improperly accessed due to the incompetence of identity guardians has now exceeded 100 million (PRC, 2007).

Identity theft – the making of a modern mythology

Updated figures published by the UK government in 2006 (Home Office, 2006b) appeared to show that identity theft had risen from the previous estimate of £1.3 billion in 2002 and was now costing the UK economy around £1.7 billion. The figure was slavishly recycled in predictable sources (cf. *Sunday Times*, 01/12/06) and even those which might have been expected to interrogate the evidence more critically (cf. Fildes, 2006). The figure, as the government graciously conceded, was only a 'best estimate'. Actually it was far worse than that. It was based on back-of-the-envelope calculations – voodoo statistics of the very worst kind – and has been widely criticised as a result (see for example Gilligan, 2005). As with their earlier (2002) report, the government's updated figures simply added data from sources which were *not there* on previous estimates, making no attempt to compensate for this in percentage or any other terms. On these grounds alone a 'rise' from £1.3 billion to £1.7 billion is not too surprising. But many of the additional figures were also suspect. For example, the annual cost of money laundering (£395 million) was somehow included even though the Home Office accepted that this figure was 'for illustrative purposes' only and that 'no figures are currently available on the proportion of money laundering that relies on identity fraud' (Home Office, 2006b). Likewise, a figure of £372 million was included for telecommunications fraud – even though this was a *total* figure, much of it having absolutely nothing to do with identification at all. Thrown into the pot too were the estimated costs of various *enforcement* measures such as the '. . . estimated cost of . . . activity required to help prevent abuse of the driving licence in identity crime' or the '. . . *approximate* cost to Immigration and Nationality Directorate of undertaking enforcement activity against individuals who *may* be involved in some form of identity theft or identity fraud, *potentially* involving document abuse' (Home Office, 2006b, my emphasis).

In spite of the earlier caveats any definition of identity theft was conspicuously still lacking. Not only did this mean that almost any kind of fraud using identification (and as we have just seen, plenty that did not) was treated as 'identity theft', there was also no coherent way of comparing between what different agencies were calling 'identity fraud'. Even figures from more credible sources were presented in a highly misleading way. For example, figures drawn from the UK payment service APACS were used to suggest that £505 million had been lost to identity theft in 2004. But now consider the figures which were *actually* produced by APACS:

Type of fraud/theft	2005	2004	2003
Fraud on stolen or lost cards	£89.0m (-22%)	£114.5m	£112.4m
Counterfeit (skimmed/cloned) card fraud	£96.8m (-25%)	£129.7m	£110.6m
Card ID theft – fraudulent applications	£12.4m (-5%)	£13.1m	£15.3m
Card ID theft – account takeover	£18.1m (-24%)	£23.8m	£14.9m
Card-not-present fraud (phone/internet/mail)	£183.2m (+21%)	£150.8m	£122.1m
TOTAL	£439.4m (-13%)	£504.8m	£420.4m

Source: APACS, 2006

As the above table indicates the picture of fraud is far more complex than was suggested in these simplified government figures. APACS themselves complained that the government had included their *total* figure for fraud for 2004 rather than bothering to distinguish those specific instances involving thefts of identification keys. Even more importantly the figures indicate a conclusion suggested earlier. Far from identity theft constituting an inexorably rising threat, the APACS figure not only showed that fraud then *declined* to £439 million in 2005, but that almost all kinds of fraud involving cards have declined by 13% since 2003. Only one – the 'card not present fraud' – was rising, a figure at least partly attributable to an accompanying rise in online shopping or other transactions over the internet during this period.

Nor was the gradual decline in card fraud found by APACS an isolated finding. Research for the FTC conducted by Javelin and Better Business Bureau (BBB, 2005) also showed that card fraud was falling, a point noted in the research by Cate (2005) mentioned earlier. It was also far more likely to be committed *offline* than online. Even more importantly, it was *proximity*, not remoteness that appeared to be the problem – as the following table clearly indicates:

How was personal data obtained	%
Lost/stolen wallet, card or chequebook	30
By relative/friend	15
By an employee with access to data	10
Office transaction	9
Stolen mail	8
Spyware	6
Taken from rubbish	4

Source: BBB, 2005

Far from such fraud being attributable to remotely located identity thieves, in nearly 70% of cases it was either our *own* fault, someone close to us such as a family member or an untrustworthy employee who was to blame. Computers were only involved in around 11.6% of known-cause identity fraud in 2004, with even less involving a specific theft of identification (BBB, 2005).

Fraud arising from access to property obtained by identification keys is clearly a problem – but then so is the theft of wallets, or fraudulent tax returns. That there has been a growth in the phenomenon is not because it represents 'one of the most serious threats facing us today', but because, under hyperspatialisation, more property is being circulated and accessed in immaterial forms and more is being protected by identification keys, often by incompetent guardians. In a context where Identity Fraud Task Forces are set up or Identity Fraud Tsars proposed as public relations exercises (White House, 2006; BBC, 06/10/07) where identity cards turn out to be bigger threats to the security of our identity than what they were supposed to protect us against; and where ostensibly independent advice bureaus such as the 'National Fraud Center' are really private enterprises run by the same LexisNexis company which both profits from identity as well as managing to consistently compromise its security (LexisNexis, 2007), it is little wonder that there are reasons to be sceptical about identity theft. As one of the major modern mythologies which sustain and feed hypercriminality, its social constructions may ultimately be more insidious than the frauds supposed to give rise to it.

Intellectual property: target and access

An important example of the unfolding interplay between targets for theft and access to them can be found with 'intellectual property'. As traditionally defined this relates to 'creations of the mind' such as inventions, literary and artistic works (cf. Schecter & Thomas, 2003). But as with many of the abstracted forms of property that form targets of theft, intellectual property can also be seen as a form of information. Its representations can be more elusive in terms of their functionality and the value that accrues since this is often purely aesthetic – a piece of music or an idea. However, where these also acquire commodity value then the value of intellectual property goes beyond individual tastes as a target for theft.

One key enhancement to representational power discussed earlier has played a central role here. This is the advent of mechanical reproduction and the increasingly more refined capacity under hyperspatialisation to produce nearly identical representations of an original – the process of 'copying' things. The development of printing preceded the technical (and cultural) developments of the late nineteenth and early twentieth century famously discussed by Benjamin (1969), so facilitating the possibility of mass copying long before this was furthered by the new technologies of photography, gramophone records or film.

The possibility of increasingly precise representation means that the production of a copy may become all but indistinguishable from the theft of an original. Indeed, any original object to an extent 'disappears' into its copies. It is perhaps therefore in this context that we find the closest realisation of something like an 'identity' theft. This is not the straightforward theft of a painting or a book which falls within the category of 'old-fashioned' theft. It is something else that is stolen here – the *template* or basic pattern underlying the painting, or the book which is used to produce (potentially unlimited) duplicates of the artefact.

Attempts to restrict ownership of and access to ideas and creations have their oldest origins in the existence of marks or signs which indicate their unique and authentic origins. The classical world frequently marked pottery with symbols such as bears and lions or even the maker's name, and there seems to have been evidence of such behaviour in numerous other locations from pre-colonial Nigeria to China (cf. Azmi *et al.*, 1997). In turn the regulatory structures of Copyright Law, Trademark Law and Patent Law were developed as ways of offering more sophisticated protection for ideas in modernity (cf. Koepsell, 2000).

This process arrived at one very contemporary obstacle with the question of how 'software' – the programs which drove information technology – could be protected against theft by duplication. As a mathematical algorithm software seemed to represent a *natural* process – something open to anyone to discover and use – not a thing that could 'belong' exclusively to anyone. But the legal process eventually managed to turn this into a commodity when a Supreme Court ruling of 1981 ordered that because software 'did something' it could be patented. A flow of patent applications soon turned into a flood and by 2003 IBM had become the largest recipient of patents with around 3,400 issued and a holding of more than 40,000 worldwide (Choate, 2005).

File wars

Books, images, sounds and indeed almost any cultural artefact which can be digitally copied may now be the subjects of theft by reproduction without permission (see for example Bollag, 2004). But perhaps most emblematic in the nexus of issues to do with property rights, creative freedoms and the politics of information are the questions that have arisen around the copying of music. Even in the pre-digital period copying albums was not allowed, though there were often 'bootleg' copies of performances that were circulated and sold – sometimes with the approval of the artist. Yet the music industry managed to survive 'problems' with illegal overseas pressings and the active 'home-taping' industry that accompanied the advent of the tape cassette (Yar, 2007). With the arrival of networked computing, what began as a low-key swapping and sharing of music on bulletin boards has grown into a global form of exchange of intellectual property. The resulting 'file wars' between owners and downloaders have taken many twists and turns. The development of 'peer-to-peer' sites where users could literally 'share' their music meant that by 2001, around 26 million people were using Napster – the most well known of these sites (BBC, 20/07/01). But after a series of legal responses by the recording industry, by 2006 the game appeared to be up. In mid-2005 a US Supreme Court decision had ruled decisively against the idea that file-sharing sites merely 'connect' users and were, instead, fully liable for the actions of file sharers. Soon afterwards Grokster, one of the last P2P sites up and running, finally folded in the face of the ruling and agreed to suspend downloading from its site as well as paying around $50 million in damages (BBC, 08/11/05).

The aftermath: darknets and the new digital underground?

However, matters were not to be quite so simple. Indeed, the film industry was also to be drawn into the problem as films and television programmes were increasingly swapped and traded by way of the new *BitTorrent* software which allowed a number of people to download portions of a file simultaneously from differing sites thereby speeding the download process. In turn BitTorrent-related sites began to be pursued by actions launched by the MPAA. Between late 2003 and 2006 the International Federation of the Phonographic Industry (IFPI) had taken out around 16,000 civil lawsuits against individuals in the US, with 3,590 choosing to settle (BBC, 28/03/06). Around 4,000 actions have been pursued in Europe (ibid). Compared to the huge numbers of downloadings of film and music files such figures were clearly very small. Yet on the face of it, it seemed that even this symbolic gesture had sufficed to have finished off music piracy for good.

In fact one of the key principles of a hyperspace – connectivity – had been overlooked. One response from the downloading community which exploited this was to create an ingenious new kind of 'sub-network' – so-called hubs or darknets (see Lascia, 2005). In principle these are 'private' networks where connections only take place between trusted individuals. They are usually small, sometimes with fewer than 10 users each. Actually the term 'darknet' can refer to any private communication hub, but it is most often used in reference to file-sharing networks (Biddle *et al.*, 2002). Pursuing such networks is much harder for the content police, provided the hub is kept properly private. Not that this has deterred the music and film corporations from trying. Undercover agents from the industry now attempt to infiltrate such hubs and to acquire evidence that files are being shared. Raids against residences from Texas to New York were conducted in 2004 against users of the so-called Underground Network after an undercover FBI agent had downloaded copies of films not yet released (Krim, 2004b). But with over 7,000 members the Underground Network clearly did not possess anything like the covert nature of some of these hubs.

Underlying all of these actions, initiatives, prosecutions and incursions into multiple social space by those seeking to protect content are further profound questions about the control society culture which it both reflects and manifests. In previous generations a group of friends who borrowed each other's records, or who taped something to play at home were never likely to be pursued by the FBI, monitored by remote technologies or to be raided by squads of police in the small hours and have their bedrooms turned over (Malik, 2005). But in hyperspace, the continuities and hybridisations between criminality and what would once have been 'normal' behaviour erode our sense of where these boundaries can now be drawn. Copying a file no longer signifies a desire to keep up with one's favourite band, or to follow a TV serial which cannot be viewed any other way, but of an involvement in organised crime – perhaps even support for international terrorist networks such as Al Qaeda (AACP, 2002). In such a context it is little wonder that powerful corporations such as Sony see no problem in placing surveillance software within their products which do not just damage hardware, but open up systems to attack by viruses. Thus, lawsuits were issued against Sony in 2005 after it was found to be using what was called a 'root kit', a copy-protection kit that concealed itself deep within Windows software (Ward, 2005) – a process that impaired the performance of the computer in many cases. By making unauthorised changes to a machine Sony opened itself up to prosecution under various legislations such as the UK Computer Misuse Act, though of course the UK, or the US government never chose to see any problem here. Instead, it was only private actions by groups such as the Electronic Frontier Foundation which eventually forced Sony to admit what it had done and to settle for damages it had caused to private users (EFF, 2007).

The price paid for these file wars appears to have been high, in terms of all the new controls, the assaults on privacy and the emotional and psychological damage done. Yet for all this, the triumphs of the industry in controlling the 'problem' may still be less than they like to publicise. Recent research appears to show that after an initial decline in downloading in the face of the legal onslaught, downloads had begun to rise again from 2004/5 (Bachmann, 2006). And it was not students or lawless teenagers who were doing the downloading, but middle-aged professionals, ready to use hyperspace in the way they felt appropriate. Meanwhile the market for legal music downloads is projected to grow from 2% to 36% of profits by 2011, generating over 4 billion euros of revenue for the industry – in spite of all their hardships (Jennings et al., 2006). The unresolved tensions between theft, property rights and control continue to be problematised by the process of hyper-spatialisation and there seems little indication that they will play themselves out anytime soon in the future.

Chapter 5

Proximity 2: Local space

Fellowship is heaven, and lack of fellowship is hell; fellowship is life, and lack of fellowship is death; and the deeds that ye do upon the earth, it is for fellowship's sake ye do them.

(William Morris, 1888, ch. 4)

Multiply picnics.

(Henry Ward Beecher, cited in Putnam, 2000)

Bodies do not exist in isolation. The things they possess are not had alone. There is a social context – an immediate external environment which underpins their continuities. Within the most local and familiar version of such space we find our regular places of shelter – the 'home' (in whatever form that takes) – which serves to preserve the body against the environment and to protect it from threats. It is here that we conduct the activities that provide for its sustenance – working to generate food and other commodities or to acquire them through trade. And it is here that we conduct the key relationships of our life with family, friends or neighbours. Such environments have most often been spoken of in terms of the idea of 'community' (Poplin, 1979; Bauman, 2001), though the term is a heavily contested one. What does seem plausible however is that the social geometries of community have important continuities with spatial location – close proximities turn social actors into familiar faces, distant proximities into strangers.

Whatever it is called, this immediate space of sociation has often been felt to be under pressure as a result of increased hyperspatiality. The stretching and contracting forces imposed upon social interaction have, in the case of local, communal space, provoked varying perceptions of its likely fate. Putnam's (2000), which invoked the Henry Ward Beecher quote of a century ago as a wake-up call to community, represents the pessimistic line. He argues that the 'social capital' generated by participation in immediate social networks such as parent–teacher associations, sports clubs or even family gatherings is in decline in the face of manifestations of the hyperspatial, in particular television. Television, he argues: 'increases aggressiveness . . . reduces school achievement, and . . . is statistically associated with "psycho-social malfunctioning".' Worse still, other communication technologies 'may . . . be undermining our connections with one another and with our commu-nities' (Putnam, 1996). Such perceptions have inevitably now been extended to the internet where the argument that 'computer networks isolate us from one another, rather than bringing us together' (Stoll, 1995) is the latest vari-ation of this charge. Others (for example Rheingold, 1993; Meyrowitz & Maguire, 1993) have been much more enthusiastic about the prospects for community it brings, most especially in the view that, 'the application of communication technology creates new social spaces' (Cutler, 1995, p. 24). Whether the role of such technologies can be implicated in the ultimate kind of harm a community can undergo – its destruction – or not, there are many other less dramatic threats that might be associated it. Harms to or inside the home, local environmental pollution, monopolistic practices at the super-market or discrimination within the workplace have all been singled out as contemporary instances of the potential damage posed to local social life. The question for this chapter is then the extent to which this is true, and how far hyperspatialisation may be implicated in any such harms.

Local environments

A purely spatial sense of a 'local' environment seems clear enough at first. It is that proximity at which social life is conducted in ways most familiar and regular to us. But for Heidegger this proximity also required a more active ingredient, a 'making' and a 'building' within space that he called 'dwelling':

> Man's relation to locations, and through locations to spaces, inheres in his dwelling. The relationship between man and space is none other than dwelling, (and) . . . building, by virtue of constructing locations, is a founding and joining of spaces.
>
> (Heidegger, 1971, II)

It is through such active familiarity with a space that we turn it into a 'place', somewhere that we are connected to in ways that differ from other spaces. As Castells has put it:

> The overwhelming majority of people, in advanced and traditional soci-eties alike, live in places, and so they perceive their space as place-based. *A place is a locale whose form, function and meaning are self-contained within the boundaries of physical contiguity.*
>
> (Castells, 1996, p. 423, emphasis in the original)

But is this move from space to place, with its transformations of mere immediacy into something of social significance, preserved in any meaningful sense under hyperspatialisation? Or has place now become, as Giddens puts it, 'phantasmagoric' (1990, pp. 17–19)? And if it has, are the results of such transformations something *worth* preserving from harm?

As suggested, liberal applications of the term 'community' have been a standard option for fleshing out an understanding of local spaces which go beyond the construct of simple proximity. Whilst this term is hardly any more transparent than the idea of the 'local' as far as matters of criminal justice are concerned it has, as Squires (1999) pointed out, now become a given to frame concepts of local crime control in terms of an appeal to these ideas of community or neighbourhood. Whether notions such as 'community safety' have enhanced our understandings of crime within local space or simply provided for the production of community folk demons like 'feral youth' is a deep question (cf. Fremeux, 2005). At its worst, as Lacey and Zedner (1995) warned, the use of 'community' in crime control risks becoming a way of isolating an 'us' from some imagined 'them'.

In addition to such ideological presumptions, notions of community are plagued by conceptual opacities. Suppose, for example, Tonnies' (1955) much discussed formulation of community is pursued. The distinction between an immediate (local) space and the broader (global) spaces in which localities are nested could then be seen in terms of a distinction between two different kinds of communal association – a *gemeinschaft* and a *gessellschaft*. That is, a distinction between social groupings based on a 'feeling of togetherness' and informal personal contact and social groupings sustained by more instrumental goals – associations such as a business collectivity, for example. It is far from clear how usefully this distinction carries across into the contemporary context. For example, Tonnies thought that the city was more like an *association* between individuals than any more intimate grouping and was therefore 'typical of Gesellschaft in general' (1955, p. 266). But given the cumulative effects of globalisation and hyperspatialisation it seems just as plausible to view cities (even large ones like London) as much more like 'local' phenomena – places which have a greater day-to-day immediacy for us (should we live there) than other more distant locations. Likewise, the social forms of contemporary work – impersonal groupings directed towards purely functional goals – ought also to count as an instance of *gessellshaft*. But it might equally be argued (as indeed will be the case here) that work is not just life '. . . distorted into factory routine' (Tonnies, 1955, p. 270), but one of our most immediate and local of experiences. Our places of work often constitute familiar environments for us and can be the source of many of our most personal social relations. Like Putnam and so many contemporary theorists of community (Davies, 1998; Bauman, 2001; Agamben, 2003; Katz *et al.*, 2004), Tonnies was also unsure about its fate, though his doubts arguably had as much to do with the rigidities of his distinction as with any real decline.

Central to the problem of definition here are the qualifications resulting from the historical and geographical instabilities of a local region. It seems unarguable that processes of spatio-temporal compression and spatial complexification have had a large part to play in this – with the result that the region of experiences counted as 'local' by individuals has tended to co-vary with the ranges of what counts as 'proximal' to them. Thus, locality was a much more spatially delimited region a hundred or even fifty years ago than today (Braudel, 1981). Less comprehensive transport systems, for example, meant that people spent more time close to their family, or working close to where they were born. In the same way more restricted communication networks shaped a keener sense of the 'strangeness' of the world outside immediate experience.

The influence of mobilities directs us back to the 'compulsion to proximity' (Boden and Molotch, 1994) as a basis for defining locality – by way of the collecting of bodies together within what Habermas calls 'social spaces that are small enough to be familiar' (1987, p. 395). Whilst the connection would need careful handling for it to work in any detailed way, some relation between proximity and familiarity does appear to resonate with certain necessary factors that go with the idea of a locality. Above all, proximity generates spatial *regularity* – which in turn generates familiarity. If any passage to space B must always involve a 'starting from' or a 'passing through' space A because of its immediate proximity, certain natural consequences seem to follow for our attitudes towards A. To pass through a space often enough suffices to form an association with that space, just as actions repeated enough times generate forms of temporal regularity which appear 'stable'. If, as was argued earlier, social space is a production of experience, then regularity in experience seems to produce spaces of familiarity. As Heidegger acknowledged, 'the spaces through which we go daily are provided for by locations' so that 'to say that mortals *are* is to say that *in dwelling* they persist through spaces by virtue of their stay among things and locations' (1971, II).

Though he was less interested in the idea, Tonnies acknowledged the role of spatial immediacy in his conception of community, pointing out that neighbourhood, '. . . is essentially based on proximity of habitation' so that 'proximity of dwellings . . . necessitate many contacts of human beings' (1955, p. 49). Such a concept seems to go beyond more emotive ideas of 'community' for by emphasising the role of temporal and spatial proximities it seems possible to avoid what John Dewey called the dangers of the 'eulogistic' senses attached to community – the sense in social philosophy that 'is almost always uppermost' (Dewey, 1944, p. 7). In this way the '. . . "warm circle" . . . that naïve immersion in human togetherness . . . nowadays available increasingly only in dreams' as Bauman puts it (2001, p. 10), may be evaded. Concepts of spatial proximity, like temporal regularity, may also provide a basis with sufficient flexibility for imagining the ways in which local space undergoes continuous historical transformation. In what follows then, it will be this combination between regularity, proximity and familiarity that is taken to preserve our experience of the 'local' as it is redistributed across the hyperspatial.

Local spaces: their features and their value

If it is accepted that there *can* be a clear enough sense of a locality for there to be some form of value that we place upon it, the idea that localities are worthy of preservation from harm can also be investigated. It then becomes essential to have some grip on what features of a local space might generate normative and criminological issues. Presumably proximity must translate into something more than what Poplin (1979, p. 8) calls 'geographical integrity', just as 'frequency' must go beyond simple repetition if they are to generate social formations worthy of legal or normative protection.

What does seem plausible is that proximity and frequency give us a sense of an *investment* in social ties and the spaces or activities of which they are a part. Simple daily reinforcements of emotional attachments go a long way towards explaining why we care for our families more than strangers, or why we tend to support our friends more than our work colleagues and our work colleagues more than someone we happen to pass on the street. The role of frequency in the transformation of space to 'place' perhaps has as much psychological significance as attachments acquired through building (see for example Canter, 1977; Sennett, 1989; Gieryn, 2000). Thus, through these basic geometries of frequency, nearness and limitation, a kind of topography of localities, however provisional, begins to emerge. In turn such geometries generate their own sets of resources for grounding notions of harm as localities are extended across wider spaces of interaction.

So what more specific features of proximal and frequent social interaction might be singled out as constitutive of a 'locality'? At the centre of regularly inhabited proximal space is surely the place that is often called 'the home'. Tonnies (1955, p. 42) recognised ties of kinship as part of his tripartite sense of *gemeinshaft* but kinship or 'family' is again only a sufficient, not a necessary condition for a home. Simmel (1997) noted how the bonds that tie any group communally are likely to be stronger if they have a 'home' or a physical centre of activity and he specifically contrasts this with more mobile forms of life. But everyone, even those who continue to lead some version of nomadic life, will have a familiar location or locations, places where they feel comfortable, where they sleep or raise children (Khazanov, 1984; Casimir & Rao, 1992). Given that this place will usually be where we spend a great deal of our time, frequency again plays a part in our sense of the domestic. As Wise (2000) put this, 'Identity is grounded in habit; the repetition of action and thought establishes home', while Lyotard argues that, 'the temporal regime of the domus is rhythmic' (1991, p. 191), so that, 'the domus is the space-time of . . . reiteration (ibid, p. 193).

As a 'rhythmic' centre of our life we like to invest in this place-that-is-home by building. Something important of ourselves will then be expended in these locations – most obviously the labour we are prepared to exert in order to make this privileged region of space more amenable to our tastes. Whether such actions involve a simple reordering of the space, such as the moving of a tree trunk to sit upon, or a more sophisticated process such as choosing a paint scheme, they mark out this part of space as *symbolically closer* to us than other parts of space (cf. Wilson, 1988; Mack, 1993; Ciaraad, 1999). Such symbolic investments can also contribute to our sense of the domestic as this becomes more spatially extended and distributed. In turn, harm or damage can then arise to any distribution or concentration of this kind.

As also suggested, a further place in which we invest regular time is our place of work. Again, there are historically broad or historically narrow interpretations of this concept (Auster, 1996; Sennett, 2000; Castree *et al.*, 2003). For most of us 'work' now reduces to the place we go for part of our week in order to receive a fixed sum of money in return for performing a fixed range of tasks. But there are clearly broader interpretations of the concept than this (Joyce, 1987; Pahl, 1988). In its most minimal sense, work is an activity closely associated with the production of resources that ensure survival. And such activity automatically implies a range of places *where we must go* to acquire or produce such resources. In this sense the 'workplaces' of hunter-gatherer tribes might centre on their favourite hunting sites, places where they gather certain berries or collect water. In turn, a sense of ownership *of* and identification *with* the places where this labour is conducted emerges. Such identifications have of course been argued to have been loosened under the delocating tendencies of wage-based capitalist economies. Here, as Marx taught us: 'the object produced by labour, its product, now stands opposed to it as an alien being, as a power independent of the producer' (Marx, 1964, p. 122). Marx is equally clear about the detrimental effect this shift has upon community for '. . . what is true of man's relationship to his work, to the product of his work and to himself, is also true of his relationship to other men. . . . Each man is alienated from others . . . each of the others is likewise alienated from human life' (ibid, p. 129). Thus even the effects of early hyperspatialisation upon the workplace seemed to bring a loosening of the continuities between the spaces where we acquire sustenance and our feelings of ownership towards them. But even if we are not now always *aware* of the space and activities that constitute worklike practices, there seems no doubt that harm – whether damage or destruction – can occur to them.

While work activity spaces have usually been coextensive with sustenance gathering spaces in traditional social contexts, this changes under the experience of modernity. At first this means an increased differentiation between productive practice and consumptive practices (Amin, 1994; Slater, 1997) as the local stream or the bramble patch are replaced by specialised locations for the acquisition of goods and commodities. But as the economies of late modernity produce ever more seamlessly connected 'flows of capital' (Castells, 1996, p. 412) hybridisation – as in other contexts – begins to undermine distinct enclosure between work and consumption space. Thus the 'worker-student' discussed by Deleuze is complemented by the phenomenon of the workplace-supermarket, the workplace-coffeeshop or even the work-place-home (with a crèche attached). Such hybridisations further blur our perceptions of value so that at the very point when supermarkets become finely tuned palaces of desire-satisfaction they also become alien to us – something we do not or cannot own. Being 'lost in the supermarket', as the Clash once put this, not only signifies the inauthenticity of the efforts of supermarket chains to associate themselves with ideas of community and locality that I will consider later, but dehumanised and divested of their communal origins, an inability to appreciate the harms that can arise to our spaces of sustenance gathering is produced. Only with the very recent development of legislation and literature in relation to issues as various consumer fraud, food-related crime or harmful practices in the fashion and clothing industries has this begun to change (see for example Breslow, 1995; Norrgard & Norrgard, 1998; Walters, 2006).

The hybridisation of social roles and functions which spatial complexifica-tion brings also means that sustenance gathering becomes increasingly sub-sumed within the remit of 'leisure' activities. The widespread prediction that capitalist societies would gradually increase the amount of leisure available to individuals has proven to be less than accurate (cf. Schor, 1991) but there is still a misplaced assumption that such societies have 'more leisure' than earl-ier societies (cf. Thomas, 1964). These perceptions of leisure richness are now partially sustained and managed by an increased circulation of hybrids which strive to make all kinds of social practices, even work or shopping, into 'leisure-experiences'. The subsumption of leisure into consumption also threatens to obscure its relation to cultural production. There has been a strong connec-tion between non-work activities and the realm of cultural activity in most societies. Non-work provides periods of time for 'non productive expend-itures' (Bataille, 1991/2). Songs can be sung, tall tales spun, social intercourse fostered in disengagements of the rational mind through dancing, decoration and so on. Contemporary forms of non-work – going on holiday, visiting cafés and nightclubs or engaging in hobbies and pastimes – appear to many to be 'less cultural' than visits to theatres or art galleries (Russell, 1996; Rojek, 2000). But whatever one's judgement about the relative value of high or low cultural leisure forms, all such activities require particular spaces where they are experienced. And such spaces, whether they be specialised constructions like a dance hall, or informal random gathering points like a public square, can be subject to behaviours that damage or destroy them. Because leisure has seemed either trivial, or a luxury, legislation to protect it, as Collins (1993) indicates, has often been lacking. What interest there has been from criminal justice systems has largely related to interventions based on moral concerns and the perception that certain dances, forms of music, sexual behaviours and so on are 'corrupting' and therefore in need of regulation (see, among many others, Foucault, 1990; Thornton, 1996; Jenks, 2003; Lopes, 2005). In the contemporary context the risk-aversion psychoses of hypercriminality have tended to shift legal interventions in leisure away from morality towards safety legislation (Sunstein, 2004; HSE, 2007).

Finally, local spaces can also be said to provide a key location for the simple act of 'sociation' itself. The group of friends we gather around us form regular points of contact that constitute a key ingredient of local networks (Fischer, 1982). We are likely to suffer if they are harmed, or to be harmed if we are deprived of friendship. And all such elements of human contact, familial, work-based or simple friendship constitute elements of an environment that we recognise and feel familiar with. Damage to the social elements of this space can be harmful to us, just as damage to the local environment itself can be.

The hyperspatialisation of locality

How more precisely then, if at all, have these ingredients of local life been redistributed by the effects of telepresence or spatial complexification? As in earlier discussions of local space, it is the notion of community that has tended to serve as the metaphor for locality in the cyberspace literature, with the example of 'online' or 'virtual' communities held up as paradigmatic of the relevant reorganisations (Rheingold, 1993; Kollock & Smith 1999; Preece, 2000). But the ongoing extensions to local space have deeper roots than computer chatroom interactions alone (Morley, 2000). We saw, for example, in Chapter 2 how the telephone became increasingly marketed in terms of its beneficial effects upon friendship. And long-distance relationships have also been sustained by the kind of transport available – witness, for example, the 'social nodes' found around transport links (Schaefer & Sclar, 1980), or what Urry calls the 'production of new scapes that structure the flows of people and goods along particular routes, especially motorways (producing) a rewarping of time and space by advanced transportation' (Urry, 1999, p. 8). The effects upon settlement seen in budget airline destinations represent the latest example of this phenomenon.

The rearticulation of presence again provides one important departure point for understanding processes of change here. But in the context of locality do these rearticulations of presence pose their own kind of problem – of 'understanding how social functions are sustained within spaces devoid of physicality' (Williams, 2006, p. 48)? Whilst it is obviously tempting to see online communities in terms of something like Tonnies' 'gemeinshaft of mind' it is not clear that this alone suffices to secure a sense of an extended local space, much less to motivate sufficient social concern for the creation of legislation to protect it. Rheingold – one of the more enthusiastic utopians about the role of the internet in redistributions to community – has recently revised many of his more sweeping opinions about its role in this process. Instead he now concedes that, 'questions about the social impact of digital media must be part of a broader debate that encompasses many communications tools and more than the past five years of history' (Rheingold, 2006, p. 21). So the task of identifying the way in which locality and community operate across extended communication networks need not be too centred upon the internet itself. Nor need it be bogged down in ontological dilemmas about 'non-physicality'. As with the body, community *remains* physically rooted while also finding new spatial redistributions at differing proximities.

Here Rheingold's (1993) formulation – that a form of community emerges when, 'enough people carry on . . . public discussions long enough' (p. 5) – does still hold water. For it is a further reminder that it is investments in time and energy, realised through simple geometries of spatial and temporal frequency, which remain as important to extended forms of community as they are to more proximal ones. Networked computers play only a secondary role in these more fundamental social processes. And as the work of social network theorists such as Wellmann (1988, for example) reminds us, communities have always functioned perfectly well in the face of spatial dispersal and remote interaction. The huge amount of geographical mobility in societies from neolithic through to medieval times was sustained via trading links, kinship structures and early forms of long-distance communication. In this sense 'communities are far flung social networks and not local neighbourhood solidarities' (Wellmann, 1999, p. xiii).

But while spatially extended communities are founded upon more than technology and have, in a sense, always been with us, attention to the influence of technology in their redistributions certainly merits attention. Take, for example, the way that an experience of communal life familiar to us in proximal space – that of our *front door* or access point – is maintained and extended. Just as any entry into the public realm of a local space regularly comes through a front door, so entry to hyperspatial relations will often come through access points which appear to divide private from public spatiality. Within transport technologies, access points are represented by structures such as train stations, airports or the motorway slip-road. With information technology these may become the mobile phone or the home computer. But such access points not only provide transitions to a community beyond the immediately personal. They can also become imbued with familiarity and belonging – a fact that may explain attempts to personalise them in various ways. In local space the colour of the front door or the way it is decorated signifies and celebrates the transition from the external to the inner space of the home. Likewise stuffed toys on a computer monitor, a particular screen-saver, 'amusing' mobile ringtones and the like not only represent forms of personal expression but also emotional investments in the access point. And as a form of building and marking our space, they already 'domesticate' the access point in ways that signify a 'living-there' which is more than transitory. As Heidegger puts it, 'building is not merely a means and a way toward dwelling – to build is in itself already to dwell' (1971). In this way, the 'creation of a fixed point in the universe . . . (is what) the domestication of space consists in' (Askegaard, 1991, p. 12).

Access points in hyperspace can thereby signify a fundamental extension to local space – that involving our 'base' or 'home'. Everyone, whether they are aware of it or not, has something like these extended 'bases' in hyperspace, places where they spend most time or which they visit most. An obvious example is a person's mail account – their literal 'personal address' distributed across extended space – the door that others come to knock upon when trying to make contact. In 2006 when asked why they had gone online the highest number of users (91%) said that it was to check their e-mails (Pew Internet Project, 2006). An equivalent figure (91%) said their reason for logging on was to use a search engine to 'find information' (ibid). This sense of launching ourselves into hyperspace to do something, or to connect with the wider community closely parallels the way that we engage in social life in more proximal communities.

A specific attempt to evoke the familiar and to personalise access points like e-mail and search engines has been the creation of 'portals' by service providers such as Yahoo or Google. Personalisation remains a buzzword in the formation of net experience with such sites competing to evoke a sense of belonging to a greater community (BBC, 20/05/05). There are a range of familiar services such as news, weather, stocks, recipes, e-mail and blogs available at a glance. There may be other features such as 'digital secretaries', access to chat or dating sites and even scope for personal photographs or biographies – all aiming to capture enough of a sense of the personal, a local familiarity that encourages users to make this their regular point of access. The development of personalised locales seems likely to remain central to the distribution of content on the net and hence to our experience of hyperspatialisation. In February 2006 Yahoo had around 115 million unique visitors – still significantly higher than Google's 92 million, though the growth in its rate of visitors was slowing – a 5% rise between February 2005 and February 2006 compared to a 21% rise for Google over the same period (Walker, 2006).

However, personalisation only works as a true reproduction of the domestic into hyperspace where there is some form of shaping or building of the space, since: 'because it produces things as locations, building is closer to the nature of spaces and to the origin of the nature of "space" than any geometry and mathematics. . . . In this way . . . do genuine buildings give form to dwelling in its presencing and house this presence' (Heidegger, 1971). Cheung (2006) discusses the 'home on the web' that is constituted by building various presentations of self, while the broader 'domestification' of information technology is something that has begun to attract broader theoretical attention (see for example Kraut *et al.*, 2006). As with access points in immediate space, there are not only differing degrees of personalisation (see Lupton, 1995) but also differing levels and *kinds* of usage occur here. For example, there is evidence that women use e-mail more than men as a home-base by which they can 'sustain or invigorate their personal relationships' (Boneva & Kraut, 2002, p. 397). The growth of portals has therefore arguably been surpassed by other kinds of entry into hyperspace which appear to offer still greater scope for personalisation and building. Prominent among these are the social networking sites, which not only trade heavily on the idea of gaining access to something like a local network but also allow for more complex ways for the building of a space where the self can dwell and be presented within community.

The success of such sites can be measured in the rise of visitors to them. Over the 2005/6 period Myspace saw a 318% rise in its usage (Walker, 2006) – far higher than that for Yahoo or Google. Chatrooms, news groups, usenet and bulletin boards, the natural precursors of the social networking site, continue to maintain a presence online for those unwilling to be absorbed into the newer sites. The circles of familiarity developed over long periods mean that many have survived, in spite of their (these days) relatively unsophisticated interfaces. Rather like the unfashionable café or pub frequented by an older generation, their very lack of visitors can give them a 'cosiness' redolent of domesticity. Multiplayer online game scenarios represent more complex potentials for the regularity of experience that builds familiarity. From early (often purely text-based) environments through to highly complex MMOGs (massively multiplayer online games) such as 'World of Warcraft', users can modify their experiences of the spaces extensively, especially in the form of rooms or 'private' spaces.

An alternative trend is the gradual redistribution of immediate domestic space *itself* rather than the creation of new representations of it. The wealth of detail about their immediate domestic experience individuals are willing to make available remotely serves to reconstruct the space of the familiar in broader ways. Thus we find, 'millions of people . . . (with) homepages with personal information about themselves and their interests often featuring their families friends and even their pets' (Cheung, 2006, p. 30). And this extension of bases or 'homes' under hyperspatialisation also relates to the traditional role and representation of the home as a place of refuge and support. A number of studies have found that support is a key reason why individuals repeatedly visit certain sites (Korenman & Wyatt, 1996; Mickelson, 1997; Ridings & Gefen, 2004). Such sites act both as 'quiet points' which may offer maternal, paternal (and even sisterly/brotherly) forms of advice. Whole local communities can also be redistributed hyperspatially with the mixed success of attempts to create 'wired communities' (cf. Schuler, 1996) counting as one example (Carroll & Rossen, 1996; Graham & Marvin, 1996; Dohoney-Farina, 1999). More recent examples of a similar idea have included the 'urban digital network' provider – for example, Cityspace.com, which delivers 'local information and digital services in public spaces' through wireless networks, digital transport networks and on-street information terminals. These registered a rate of growth of around 185% over the 2005/6 period (Walker, 2006).

Regular *activities* constitutive of local space – such as work, gathering sustenance or leisure – can also be spread wider in straightforwardly physical terms. On one level global industry as a whole spreads labour across scattered locations, so that the factory situated at the bottom of the road becomes a business spread across many continents (Castells, 1997, p. 216ff.; Hodson 1998). In addition, there is also the phenomenon of the redistribution of work by and through telepresence itself. Many of us already spend large sections of our working lives interacting with remote locations, answering e-mails, researching online and so on. US figures from the onset of IT in the office indicated the trend – a rise of around 20% in the amount of time spent using computers at work between 1995 and 1999 (NSF, 2000). In the same way the rise of home/work hybrids such as the 'home' or 'teleworker' also redistributes labour away from its traditional local spatial clustering pattern. Of the three million or so individuals engaged in teleworking in the UK in 2005 (a rise of nearly a million since 1997) most of these carried out their work via computers (ONS, 2005, p. 417). In turn teleconferencing, broader geographical relationships with suppliers and producers, the repetition of online experience by visits to spreadsheets, office intranets, use of e-mail and so on all contribute to the sense of hyperspatialisation to work practices (cf. Garton & Wellman, 1995).

The rise of online shopping discussed in Chapter 4 constitutes one among many examples of the redistributions to sustenance gathering and consumption. There are many more. One less obvious instance involves the many tasks required to simply maintain our redistributed forms of life, tasks which require constant interfacing with remote technologies: filling in online forms to gain access to our bank account; the clearing of spam from our inboxes – which on one estimate took an average of 7.9 seconds per message (O'Neil, 2003), responding to telephone messages or texts; ensuring virus controls are up to date; maintaining passports and other documentation – and so on. All represent activities that sustain and preserve our extended presences and so, logically, might be included under the rubric of 'work' activities. Examples of such sustaining practices apply even within fully representational environments like online gaming experiences. Here the gathering of experience points, engaging in quests and similar tasks or the renewing of passwords and profiles represent extensions to working life. In turn, the blurring of work activity with leisure, social and cultural forms entails aspects of duration and frequency which also foster feelings of an extended 'local' familiarity.

Whether it be online gaming environments, travel sites, cookery spots or even our favourite porn sites, proximity – retranslated as the temporal frequencies spent in remote interaction – initiates a sense of ownership and familiarity within us that can often match that engendered by more tangible locations. And all this is of course purely within the context of the internet. Other technologies and contexts which there is not time to examine fully here also play their part. Increased transport links may serve to extend a community of friends over greater distance, just as the telephone helps maintain extended family connections – even where the family members are on different continents.

Local and glocal

Though distance is supposed to have met its 'death' with the advent of global communications networks (Cairncross, 1997) the effect of this upon local life often appears contradictory. As Brown and Duguid (2002) point out, 'downtowns grow denser (and) . . . consumption remains surprisingly local' (p. 5), while 'local problems and local skills . . . develop robust regions, not around distant hubs but around local knowledge' (ibid, p. 15). The complications of the local/global continuum in hyperspatial relations are one of the many problematic dualities of social structure there such as 'homogeneity and heterogeneity, integration and differentiation, unity and fragmentation' (van Dijk, 2006, p. 171). The complexification of social relations produced by compressive technologies seems to take us directly towards global levels of interaction while at the same time making those global relations feel more 'local'. McLuhan's famous proposition that: '. . . electrically contracted, the globe is no more than a village' (1964, p. 5) often seems to pose far more questions than it answers.

One way of resolving this apparent contradiction between the simultaneity of global and local experiences has been to deny locality altogether and to simply assert that globalisation is the winning hand. On this view the diversities and differences arising from local identity are submerged within the homogeneities of global capitalism becoming, as we saw Giddens put this, 'phantasmagoric' (1990). Alternatively the local is posited against the global 'as a site of resistance and liberation' to the 'dehumanising' forces of global change (Dirlik, 1996, p. 22). But there is another possible response, one that resolves the contradiction by seeing a possible synthesis in proximities, rather than an opposition between them. This view sees localisation as a process which is not only simultaneous with, but *consistent* with globalisation (Featherstone, 1996; Wellman & Gulia, 1999). Such arguments frequently draw upon Roland Robertson's concept of 'glocalisation' (1992, pp. 173–174) – the 'simultaneous process of universalising and particularising tendencies of the global valorisation of particular identities' (ibid, p. 130). For example, one now familiar way of promoting countries as 'global' travel destinations is to emphasise their 'local' characteristics, whether that be red phone boxes and warm beer to represent the UK or exotic temples and tiger safaris for India. The role of commodification in the formation of such marketing clichés indicates that we should be careful in assuming precise equalities between the local and the global under hyperspatialisation. As Robertson warns, 'the local is not best seen . . . as a counterpoint to the global' (ibid, p. 130). If the local is to continue to matter at all it must be in terms of the role it plays as a constituent of this composite process of glocalisation. In this sense the glocal, like the hyperspatial in general, is a simultaneous enhancing of both local and global experience, one where each affects the other without completely cancelling the other out. We do not in other words need to regard 'the global and the local as dichotomies separated in space and time, rather it would seem that the processes of globalisation and localisation are inextricably bound together at the present phase' (Featherstone, 1996, p. 47).

From the criminological point of view the distinction only really continues to matter if there are distinctive harms that can be attached to each of these proximities. The rest of this chapter and the one that follows will attempt to set out *how* they are distinct in these more specific terms.

Violating local spaces

One could argue that the very formation of settled community and its buildings represent a precaution against the fear of external harm – the sense of 'architecture as a defence against the terror of space' (Harries, 1982, p. 58). The landscapes of contemporary community often seem to be blighted in a way that enacts a specific version of this psychological and material dread. In this sense the hypercrime society is but the latest instance of the fusion of subjective and actual harm produced by the experience of living in proximity to others. Local spaces increasingly face what Zukin has called the 'institutionalisation of urban fear' by processes such as the 'privatisation and militarization of public space making streets, parks and shops more secure, but less free' (1995, p. 38). A distortion of local life occurs which alters the very way that its inhabitants perceive and respond to it. The warm and safe familiarities of the local are transposed into the:

> Safe neighbourhood, visualised as armed gatekeepers controlling the entry; . . . a paring down of public areas to defensible enclaves with selective access; the criminalisation of residual difference; . . . it is in the cognitive frame of this evolution that the new notion of 'community' is formed.
>
> (Bauman, 2001, p. 115)

The sense of 'everywhere-crime' that the hyperspatial appears to present to us is perhaps at its most subversive within the space of the locally familiar.

The rise in 'anti-social' legislation, private policing or control of transient or 'illegitimate' street populations creates new continuities between the market and fears of crime in the form of 'domestic security'. Here:

> Neighbour is pitted against neighbour in the perpetual search for signs of anti social behaviour and in the use of private policing services and surveillance technologies aimed at displacing troublesome people onto someone else's territory.
>
> (Ericson, 2007, p. 202)

'Community safety' becomes a euphemism for the paranoid community with danger potentially around every familiar corner. But what, if any, is the real order of threat from hyperspatiality to local life, and how might our sense of this be better organised?

Even though the legislation against anti-social behaviour has indicated a readiness to develop some kind of legal framework for the protection of local life, it has tended to have a very limited agenda and to be largely directed against familiar groups of folk devils. And while our existences may vitally depend upon properly functioning commonalities (for example, the shared labour that provides resources for the whole community) by and large violations to our body, or the more immediate proximities of a family will worry us a great deal more than seemingly abstract threats to localities – especially where this is not our *own* locality. Labour violations to foreign workers are likely to attract far lower levels of outrage than the introduction of congestion charges in a local town centre.

A version of Simmel's boundary problem also affects our sense of how local space can be harmed, further undermining attempts to build a coherent legal framework here. Demarcations of this space are inevitably far more ambiguous than the points at which our bodies, or what we own, begin and end. This is not only because such a space is fragmented and spread across a greater variety of concerns and activities. Since this is first and foremost a *shared*, communal space it is one formed from multiple, and even contradictory interests.

For all these reasons (and more) the sharing of contemporary local space has frequently been associated with a sense of diminished responsibility – the assumption, either that someone else ought to sort out the problems, or that there is simply nothing that can be done about them. Renewing neighbourhoods and communities through shifts in decision-making and funding processes has been one form of response (cf. Duncan & Thomas, 2000). The concept of 'regeneration' itself has been another panacea (Couch *et al.*, 2003), though it has also been argued to be as much a matter of population management as a source of real change (cf. O'Neil, 1995; Taylor, 2000). In what follows I will ignore such problems and assume that this local space is something of value in *both* its proximal and more remote forms and can therefore be subject to harms by destruction or degradation. The question which then follows is whether hyperspatialisation has made such potential harms any worse, or any different.

Harms to our homes – technology and family life

One regular theme in recent discussions about changes within local space has related to their effects upon the very cornerstone of life there – the family. Lyotard's conclusion that, '. . . domesticity is over and probably it never existed except as a dream . . .' (1991, p. 201) is reflected in the many problems supposedly faced by the home and family discussed by commentators. Not only was Durkheim's 'conjugal' family and its traditional kinship ties swept away by modernity (Lamanna, 2001), the more integrated 'nuclear' family which succeeded it is also now supposed to be in decline (cf. Wright & Jagger, 1999). Hyperspatial technologies such as television, telephones and the internet (cf. Nie *et al.*, 2002) are centrally implicated in this, their apparent culpability manifested in several kinds of damaging effects. For example, there is an increased separation between family members and the decline of communal interaction in customs such as the family meal, or conversation in the evening. Couples spend less time together and more time attending to mobile phones, e-mails and so on; children spend long hours alone in their bedrooms, gaming or watching television. As a result communication within the family breaks down and its role as a bonding force in community life is increasingly diminished (Popenoe, 1993). It is hard to assess these concerns objectively, since evidence for any direct correlation between the advent of such technologies and the damage to families they are meant to cause is often ambiguous. For example, studies such as Winn (2002), while pointing to certain negative affects, in no way suggest that this results in a 'destruction' of family life.

But no matter how ambiguous the empirical research, the willingness to find damage in hyperspatial technologies has been taken to various extremes. In the 1950s, for example, a widespread panic grew up around the idea that subliminal messages in TV programmes were influencing cognitive systems (cf. Dixon, 1971). Recent studies continue to warn of the effects of television in similarly dramatic terms – one 2004 study, for example, argued that 'too much' television can 'rewire' a developing child's brain (*Washington Times*, 05/04/04). The report conceded that it did not establish a link between content and effects upon developing brains, but pointed to the fast cuts and edits in children's programming as the danger. Makers of educational TV programmes were quick to challenge some of these findings (ibid), but the received view of television as something detrimental to the brain and to social skills continues to hold. Instead of providing an intellectual resource, television is just another part of the 'speeded-up electronic media (which) has no order or meaning and is not to be taken seriously' (Postman, 1985, p. 99).

The readiness to find threats towards domestic life in such technologies has now of course been extended to computers. But again what facts about their threat can be established tend to be misinterpreted or simply inflated. In August 2006, for example, the *New York Times* carried a report which appeared to suggest that intimacy between couples was on the decline 'because lap-tops are used in bed' (Hafner, 2006). The report went on to cite evidence from a study by sociologists at Duke University which, it claimed, indicated that too much computer use was shrinking access to friends and confidants. As a more detailed scrutiny of the published research indicated, no such conclusions were supported so that less than a week later, the newspaper was forced to print a retraction. The Duke University report had NOT found any association between excessive computer use and a decline in conjugal relations or shrinking circles of confidants, merely that, in general, Americans tended to now have smaller circles of confidants than previously (*New York Times*, 31/08/06). Whilst there is scepticism among many psychologists as to whether technology addiction can be measured in any meaningful way (see for example Wallace, 1999; McKenna & Bargh, 2000), an increasing number of 'self-help sites' such as www.internetaddiction.com (slogan: 'Families that play together stay together') continue to promulgate the idea that the overuse of remote access technologies is 'destroying' family life.

A particular area of concern now centres increasingly on the threat remote access and telepresence experiences pose towards children, both in and beyond the home (see among many others: Affonso, 1999; Strasburger & Donnerstein, 1999; Cordes & Miller, 2000; Cho & Choen, 2005). Sexuality, especially children's own sexual natures has figured as a constant theme in discussions here. Some fears are rooted in understandable enough concerns – the potential actions of groomers hunting for child victims online considered in Chapter 3 are clearly of concern to everyone. Other issues, such as children's increased exposure to pornography online are less 'obviously' harmful. For the precise level of danger from such exposures again often depends upon which source you choose to consult. One widely cited study claimed to have shown that 42% of internet users aged between 10 and 17 'had seen online pornography' over a 12-month period. Sixty-six per cent of these said they did not want to view the images and had not sought them out (*USA Today*, 02/05/07). Given the contemporary level of access children, especially teenagers, have to the internet and given the amount of sexual imagery available there, the figure actually seems rather low. This single-minded focus upon the internet also diverts attention away from the many other sources where children can now view sexualised imagery. 'Lad mags' such as *Loaded* or *FHM* – as easily accessible as any pornographic website – represent one kind of source. But perhaps more socially pervasive is the role of advertising, where sexualised images far more accessible than what is available via the internet bombard young people on billboards, in magazines and so on (cf. Bell, 2007). Surveys such as the above also fail to paint an accurate picture in virtue of their inevitable lack of any real comparative historical metric for 'exposure to sexual images'. We simply do not know precisely what percentage of teenage boys in say, the 1950s, looked at erotic imagery, flicked through copies of *Health and Efficiency*, or peered through holes in girls' shower rooms. That there may now be different *expectations* of sex seems undeniable, that it may be affected by an availability of more diverse and explicit sexual imagery is possible, but whether this is inherently a 'bad thing' is questionable. And whether what is happening is ultimately any different from the regular historical swings in attitudes towards sex (liberal to conservative and back again) is also open to dispute. Whether any such change can be specifically attributed to the affect of technology is even less clear. More sober reflections such as these have of course made little or no difference to the determination to find 'a problem', so that copious funding for projects such as the recent 'EU Kids Online' initiative (EU Kids, 2007) continues to be made available in the attempt to prove it.

Rather less discussed has been the effect upon children and family life of more subtle harms facilitated by hyperspatialisation – in particular the enhanced control mechanisms it offers. Whereas children's experiences of technology in earlier generations were largely mediated by parental recourse to the on–off button, parents now have recourse to a staggering array of control and surveillance devices. The tracking of children's movements in both immediate and remote space can now be effected by listening devices, GPS tracking devices and a burgeoning industry of 'net-nanny'-type software. As Haggerty (2003, p. 205) reports, even teddy bears may now come with cameras hidden inside them. As well as the ubiquitous monitoring of their access to remote interaction, children's movement around proximate space is also increasingly under scrutiny through radio transmitter technologies such as RFID. Keeping track of a child's movements to and from school may (just about) be understandable on the grounds of safety. But the slow creep towards total surveillance of children, even as they move around *within* schools, creates a more uneasy feeling. In one case from Sutter County Los Angeles, where this extended to the placing of radio frequency readers *inside* children's bathrooms (without the permission of parents) such obsessive monitoring becomes slightly sinister (Lucas, 2005). After all, under other circumstances observing children in toilets with cameras might be regarded as suspicious, or even criminal behaviour. But when 'responsible' control agents such as parents, school authorities or theme parks such as Legoland (Sullivan, 2004) behave like this, it is somehow assumed to be a 'natural' and perfectly legitimate form of voyeurism. And so we arrive at the bizarre situation where companies selling sophisticated covert spy devices get to form commercial alliances with suppliers of fancy dress costumes for children. In 2006 'Trackershack', a company specialising in surveillance technologies such as spyphones, bugging devices and miniature cameras, collaborated with the Angels Fancy Dress shop in central London to create Halloween costumes which can spy on children (BBC, 23/10/06). Just like the marketing of the kit for DNA samples reported by Ericson (2007, p. 194) which suggests that it could be 'cross-sold' with baby cards and birthday cards (for greater profits), this coupling of childhood with advanced techniques of security results in one of the more disturbing hybrids of the hyperspatial.

While all of this may be well intended enough, there is a plausible danger that it can end up having harmful effects upon family life at least as serious as exposure to online pornography. Not only does it create questionable imbalances in the distributions of authority between parent and child. There are also questions about the false sense of security surveillance and tracking technology engenders. For how useful would an RFID tag hidden in items of clothing likely to be should the child lose the clothing? And if a child were to encounter a real paedophile is it really likely that bugged clothing would protect them? How far therefore does the very resort to a pervasive securitisation of children's life actually make both children and parents feel *less* secure?

A number of recent studies have noted how adult anxieties may actually be inducing psychological trauma in children (see for example Barrett *et al.*, 1996) or at the very least, radically undermining the richness of childhood experience (Children's Society, 2007). Such anxieties now extend in particular to limitations placed upon the creativity and self-expression of children in the use of new technologies. Brian Simpson has recently noted that an ironic effect of the concerns about children 'going online' may actually be to curb their traditional freedoms to express themselves in different play situations, for the '. . . internet may serve positive aims in terms of . . . identity experimentation or even as a form of recreational play' while 'the need for children to experiment with roles, including adult ones is a long established tradition in children's play culture'. However, '. . . the manner in which laws . . . are used to construct the problems of identity deception on the internet also denies the way children use the internet' (Simpson, 2005, p. 129).

Harms to our homes – the invasion of domestic space

The respatialisations of remote technology also present a new range of incursive threats to the home. Just as with individual human bodies, homes and households have become subject to increasing scrutiny and cataloguing for commercial purposes (Turow, 2006). Beniger (1986) traced the origins of many of these techniques which were rooted in the older remote communications networks. From the advent of mail order catalogues in the 1870s and the creation of tele-marketing in the 1920s, through to today's data-profiling of households by postcodes or other identification tags, the home is now locked into a 'networked multilogue between marketers, consumers and products' (Elmer, 2004, p. 55). More coercive techniques such as 'cold-calling' not only intrude upon privacy, they can become oppressive. According to the Direct Marketers Association's (DMA) own figures, nuisance call bureaus in the UK now receive around 155,000 calls a month (*Guardian*, 28/01/06). The level of intrusions here can also be seen in figures from the 'self-regulation' mechanism set up by the DMA – the Telephone Preference Service (TPS) – where people can sign up to indicate that they do not wish to be cold-called. Registrations here rose from 6 million in 2004 to 11 million by 2005, with around 100,000 new registrants every month (ibid). But in hyperspace there is always a way around such obstacles. For example, as call centres are increasingly 'off shored' to places like India such regulations may be impossible to enforce, making cold-calling harder, not easier to constrain.

A variety of instabilities to the well-being of the home – in both its immediate and distributed forms – can be argued to result. Constant marketing intrusions sometimes force families to change numbers, or to restrict access to the household's presence within communication networks. And where a number *has* been made to become ex-directory an ironic outcome is often the exclusion of family or friends rather than the nuisance caller. Other kinds of pressures from such incursions have, on occasions, resulted in irreparable damage to it. The death of Richard Cullen provides one tragic but all too typical example of such an outcome. The events that led to Cullen's ultimate suicide began with a loan of £4,000, eventually transformed into a debt of £130,000 as a result of the constant credit card and loan offers which then followed (Ronson, 2005). A program called Mosaic, used by credit card and credit reference companies to profile homes by postcode (also used apparently by both Labour and Tory parties) had identified the Cullen family as a Mosaic Group B11: 'Happy Families: Families Making Good.' A B11 profile contains useful advice (to the marketing companies) such as: 'likely to be interested in adverts for financial products . . . keen to take advantage of easy credit'. So in spite of Cullen's mounting debts, companies like Barclaycard not only permitted him to have three *separate* cards, they also loaned him a further £6,000 – a sum later increased to £13,000. The blasé attitudes of those responsible further emphasise the basic disrespect for family life represented by these incessant incursions into their domestic space. In 2003, the CEO of Barclays was called before a House of Commons select committee to explain why, given that the base interest rate had gone down to 3.5%, Barclaycard was now charging 17.9% on its credit cards. 'I don't borrow on creditcards' he retorted, 'it is too expensive' (Ronson, 2005). By January 2006, UK spending on credit cards had risen by £733 million – the highest rise for over a year. By March 2006 total UK consumer debt on credit cards stood at around £57 *billion*, nearly £1,000 for every man, woman and child in the UK (*Times*, 01/03/06). Yet compared to the more sensationalist issues of sex or technology addiction there has been little discussion of the ways in which this manifestation of remote interaction can harm family life. There have been even fewer studies to measure it.

As the redistribution of the home from immediate space into the hyper-spatial proceeds apace, many of the basic courtesies surrounding entry to domestic space seem to be increasingly compromised. Compromised by its exposure within hyperspace, traditional ideas of a home as a 'castle' or a refuge become increasingly unsustainable as unwanted incursion becomes a 'norm' there. One example of this are the many programs now able to effect-ively pass uninvited through our extended 'front doors' and to take up resi-dence at will. Figures for early 2006 suggested that there may be as many as 21 online spies attached to every Windows PC in the UK – the highest figure in Europe (Webroot, 2005). And while we hear a great deal about the dele-terious affects of junkmail or spyware on business, the real victims are the millions with PCs at home which lack the kinds of protections afforded to governmental and corporate modes of access. Nor is this only a question of intrusion, for this 'malware' often ends up impairing, or denying a house-hold's access to remote communications altogether (CDT, 2003). 'Domestic security' is forced towards a new level of control within hyperspace by incorporating new kinds of filter to block these invasions. And this constant need for the extended home to keep the external world at bay may then, ironically, result as much in isolation within the network as connection.

Sustenance gathering harms – work and shopping

As the way we work is transformed by time-space compression, earlier forms of abuse like child-labour may have been halted, but new ones constantly emerge to take their place. Indeed, contemporary globalisation, especially in the rapid growth of the new economic giants like China, has arguably even begun to lead to the reintroduction of these older forms of workplace harm. As the sweatshop spreads, rights previously taken for granted are dispensed with in many locations. A copious literature on globalisation and work within the information economy has reviewed many of these potential abuses (see for example Lee, 1997; Cigno *et al.*, 2002; Silver, 2007). In turn influential commentaries such as Castells' (1996) eulogy to the network society have been criticised for downplaying harms to the workplace that come with its economic shifts. Both Castells and similar theorists stand accused of peddling what amounts to a '. . . right-wing celebration of contemporary capitalism' (Jessop, 2003, p. 2).

With hyperspatialisation the pre-existing power asymmetries between workers and employers have acquired a new dimension, one that will also be examined in the following chapter. One of its more obvious manifestations can be seen in the hierarchicalisation of spatial access in the workplace – a phenomenon manifested in everything from entry swipe cards with different levels of privilege, to the inflation in monitoring. Increasingly such controls extend beyond the workplace by means of the startling expansion of employ-ers' influence over their employees' private lives (cf. Zuboff, 1988; PRC,

2006). In the context of work, the movement from the logics of enclosure to those of modulation noted by Deleuze mark the transition from direct regulation by a supervisor or line manager via crude temporal controls like 'clocking in', towards new and subtle workplace coercions. There is, for example, the use of variable wages, 'a modulation of each salary, in states of perpetual metastability' (Deleuze, 1992, p. 2) where 'the brashest rivalry' is presented as, 'a healthy form of emulation, an excellent motivational force that opposes individuals against one another . . . dividing each within' (ibid). The logic of the continuum is seen again, blending worker identity into hybrids such as the 'worker-student' locked into perpetual training – control posing as the possibility of self-advancement.

As a result, work begins to extend continuously into the minds, attitudes and private lives of the workforce. This is not just about the subtle requirement for 24-hour working *availability* – the tendency for '. . . immaterial labour to blur the distinction between work time and non-work time, extending the working day indefinitely to fill all of life' (Hardt & Negri, 2004, p. 66). It also relates to rights employers have often acquired to regulate lifestyles that have nothing to do with work. Thus, it is increasingly common to find practices such as workplace drug-testing; enforced psychological examinations; polygraph 'lie-detector tests' and even genetic testing enacted in the workplace. Even by 1997 the American Civil Liberties Union had found that between 6 and 10% of employers were conducting some form of genetic testing. In a survey of over 1,000 employees, nearly 22% reported that they had suffered from 'genetic discrimination' – disproportionate treatment as a result of constituting 'perceived risks' (ACLU, 2000). The US Department of Labor itself conceded that this now constitutes 'a serious workplace issue' (DOL, 1997). And as working presences are distributed across working (and non-working) spaces more widely, improved data manipulation and enhanced monitoring expose them to perpetual forms of recording and interpretation. As Gary Marx reports:

> A Bank of America vice-president, commenting upon the 200 criteria used to assess workers in his credit-card division proudly states, 'I measure everything that moves'. He also measures a lot that doesn't move.
>
> (Marx, 1999)

I will return to the effects of the hyperspatial in the territorialisation of control over working life in a moment. First, I want to consider some more basic effects it might have upon work, effects which seem to threaten it with damage or complete destruction.

Destructions and degradations of work

Amongst all the harms (short of serious physical harm or death) that can be suffered at work, a destruction of the right or capacity to work is about the most serious. Destruction may arise through work being taken away, or by the loss of the capacity to work altogether, through injury or death, for example (cf. Castells, 1997, p. 217). Information technology has often been centrally implicated in such destructive processes (Rifkin, 1996; Castells, 1997). The paradigmatic instance of the struggle against workplace technologisation was of course provided by the Luddites in their attacks against the new machinery they saw as responsible for removing their capacity to sustain themselves and their families (see Sale, 1995). The very fact that the term 'Luddite' has come to be synonymous with anyone who *resists* technology indicates the extent to which the 'inevitable' pressure for development triumphed over arguments which supported protecting working life in the face of change (cf. Robins & Webster, 1999, pp. 39–42).

At least two factors associated with hyperspatiality and its technologies might seem to promote various negative effects upon work:

(i)   Restructuring in the places of work.
(ii) Restructuring in the nature and types of work.

The wholesale devastation of the newspaper print industries in the 1980s provides an example of both trends. Within the space of a decade or so, an industry which had retained working practices similar to those of the nineteenth century was utterly transformed. In the UK the 'place of work' for the newsprint trade was removed from its traditional Fleet Street home and forcibly relocated, decimating the workforce along the way (Bain, 1998). A central justification was the 'inevitability' of technological change. The well-planned scheme by Rupert Murdoch's News International Corporation to relocate print workers to Wapping, in London's Docklands, resulted in the summary dismissal of any worker who voted to strike in protest and a bitter industrial dispute that lasted for over a year. After 1,262 arrests, mass picketing of the new printing plant and disturbing scenes of violence between police and strikers, the print unions were eventually broken and industrial relations in the UK changed forever (BBC, 15/02/86). The advent to fully hyperspatialised print methods where journalists could submit copy from anywhere in the world and have typeset instantaneously was attained – but at a significant and predictable cost to a traditional working community and the well-being of their families.

Other well-documented labour trends resulting from the advent of a 'networked society' also seem to have been of mixed benefit to workers. The practice of offshoring – relocating whole business processes from one global location to another – has clearly only been made possible by significant spatial compression (Palen, 2003; Doh, 2005; Blinder, 2006). It certainly seems clear that the huge rise in the labour flexibility required by 'liquid' economies has not always worked out to the best advantage of workers (Kelly, 2000) – with some even arguing that it may, on occasions, result in a return to effective forms of slavery (Bales, 2004). At their best it is clear that 'flexible' work patterns can permit greater individual control and freedom within working life. But in practice the rise of part-time, flexible working over the past 20 years has, as Castells suggests, produced a 'disposable labour force that can be automated and/or hired/fired/offshored depending upon market conditions' (1997, p. 295). These effects have inevitably tended to impose themselves more negatively upon marginalised groups in the workplace such as women (Seron & Ferris, 1995; Carnoy, 2000; Perrons et al., 2006) though some have even argued that there are also negative consequences for business (Bivens, 2005).

Shifts towards information technology-driven forms of labour required by the immaterial economy have also resulted in the rise of new forms of workplace injury, both mental and physical. From repetitive strain injuries or RSI, back and eye problems through to the threat of various cancers the information society, as discussed in Chapter 3, has brought with it a range of 'specific accidents'. In the USA, workplace strain injuries have been estimated to affect about one million US workers each year (NAS, 2001) while in the UK the number of people with RSI has increased by more than 50,000 over the three years to 2005 (CSP, 2005). Meanwhile the use of mobile phones, as much as for work as for leisure, was estimated to be the cause of around 3.8 million RSI injuries per year (Grenville, 2006). Psychological effects can be partly seen in the growth in stress-related illnesses, a change that appears to be directly related to the 'disappearance of distance' between work and home. In 2004 one survey measured the cost to the US economy at around $300 million – a cost ultimately borne as much by employers as workers. And health costs resulting from stressed employees can be 46% higher, or an average of $600 more per person, than for other employees (Schwartz, 2004). In the UK around 9.5 million working days were lost in 2005/6 through musculoskeletal disorders directly related to their work, with an estimated average of 17.3 days off work per worker over that 12-month period (Jones et al., 2006). This equates to an annual loss of 0.41 days per worker.

Concerns about the physical and mental effects of hyperspatialisation in the extended workplace are paralleled by concerns about its effects upon the general quality of life there. At the core of these worries is the relation between networked information technology and fears of 'dehumanisation' – for example, the rise of the so-called 'battery worker'. Whilst the production line worker of mid-capitalism was afforded few rights and often seemed to be no more than a 'Taylorist' unit of production (Littler, 1982; Braverman, 1999) there was at least a coherent labour movement which sought to redress such harms. The remodulation of work under the demands of globalised economies has not just seen the erosion of many such traditional protections for workers (Wallach & Sforza, 1999; Kelly, G., 2000; Breining-Kaufman, 2007), it has also brought an apparent decline in union membership and power (cf. Gospel & Wood, 2003; Slaughter, 2007). As a result there has been less concern and less pressure to address potential workplace harms – especially in archetypical locations for 'information'-based labour such as call centres. Here hours tend to be long, breaks few and the pressure to achieve targets high. A 2004 report by the UK Health and Safety Executive found that: 'the risk of mental health problems is higher for call handlers and job-related well-being is lower compared to benchmark groups of employees in other occupation' (HSE, 2004, p. 8). This was a general problem for those who worked in the larger (battery) call centres (employing 50 and over) and for workers in the telecommunications and IT business sector in general (ibid). As a disembodied presence whose function is relentless information production, the call centre worker may also be subject to harms other than 'new Taylorism'. Many of them – especially those located in spatially remote or foreign call centres – are further dehumanised as 'alien others' and subjected to abuse or racial insults that would be unacceptable in other contexts (Ahmed, 2006; Campbell, 2006).

The emergence of the 'battery' worker under hyperspatialisation now appears to have taken a decisive turn with the extension of technologies previously applied only to the control of animals to human bodies in the workplace. The radio frequency identification chip (RFID), a transmitter that can be linked to databases for product or livestock control has begun to be used to track workers' movements in a variety of work contexts – in some cases chips have even been inserted below the skin (Waters, 2006). This is not just a way of degrading workers' humanities, or ignoring their rights – it signifies a striking manifestation of the new class of 'control' harms in operation. Whilst such controls, as we have already seen, can now be seen in many areas of social life, their articulation within the workplace is worth considering in a little more detail.

The hyperspatialisation of workplace control

The 'disappearance of disappearance' noted by Haggerty and Ericson (2000) does not just imply, as Gary Marx has put it, that 'genuine anonymity appears to be less common than in the past' (2006, p. 100). In the context of work it raises a key question about workers' rights – whether they have the *same* kinds of right to invisibility as do their bosses. The answer seems clearly not. The expansion of worker surveillance has begun to be widely documented (Aiello, 1993; Ball, 2001; Hartman, 2001). But it is not always seen as being a problem in itself. Instead focus has tended to centre more upon the advent of the internet in the workplace – a development almost immediately portrayed in terms of a kind of free-for-all for employees to cruise questionable websites or to spend excessive time on personal e-mails. The promulgation of such perceptions led, in a by now familiar pattern, to the necessity of imposing new controls – in this case those involving enhanced monitoring of an employee's forms of hyperspatial access.

In the UK legal protections against such monitoring are highly fragmented with statutes such as the Data Protection Act offering certain rights, while the later Regulation of Investigatory Powers Act (or RIPA – see Chapter 7) somewhat complicates matters (Findlay & McKinlay, 2003). In 2000, the TUC outlined a five-point set of guidelines for surveillance in the workplace which attempted to balance rights with employee responsibilities in the workplace. It suggested staff should be told how and why their e-mail, phone calls or internet use were being monitored and to require consent to be given (TUC, 2000). In 2003 the new UK 'Information Commissioner' published the third part of the Employment Practices Data Protection Code *Monitoring at Work* (ICO, 2006), which set out conditions for monitoring in more detail. This complemented codes at the European level where the ILO (International Labour Organization) and the Council of Europe have set out guidelines relating to data protection in the workplace (EC, 2002).

However, all of these were only guidelines and were not legally binding. By contrast employer rights to (legally) monitor workers were secured with RIPA. Though employers are still required to comply with the Data Protection Act and to inform employees if they are monitored electronically, a wider variety of reasons for monitoring can now occur – computer viruses, to monitor how staff deal with customers, or to ensure workers are not using the internet to access offensive material. And while the Human Rights Act is supposed to prevent covert monitoring, even here there can be exceptions. For example, employers can monitor communications covertly for reasons of 'national security', to detect unauthorised use or 'to ascertain whether business standards and procedures are being complied with and establishing the existence of facts' (Pinsent-Masons, 2005). In some cases, covert monitoring of performance has also taken place and, though challenged legally, been upheld by courts (see McGowan v Scottish Water in *Amicus*, 2005, p. 8).

In the US, an employer's right to monitor electronic information is underpinned by the Electronic Communications Act of 1986 which only permits monitoring related to protecting the business. It is supposed to cease if the content is purely personal, does not violate laws, or threaten the business in any way (Olzak, 2006). But monitoring of e-mails – often resulting in disciplinary actions – has been widespread. One study found that nearly two-thirds of all US companies discipline employees for abuse of e-mail or internet connections, with up to 27% having dismissed employees for this (AMA, 2001 – see also Privacy International (PI, 2004) for a summary of workplace surveillance rights in various national contexts). In 2000, for example, Dow Chemical Company fired 50 US employees and threatened 200 others with suspension after they claimed to have found 'offensive' material in their e-mails. More than 7,000 employees had their e-mails opened. The Fourth Amendment is also meant to act as a partial constraint upon government officials, employers and law enforcement officers along with recent legislation such as the Notice of Electronic Monitoring Act of 2000. But workplace agreements on privacy and monitoring are largely discretionary and employees can be dismissed for reasons relating to monitoring, however thin, provided sufficient notice is given. Even keeping a blog can be grounds for dismissal, with well-publicised cases of this such as Delta Airline's sacking of Ellen Simonetti, one of their flight attendants, after she posted pictures of herself in uniform on her blog (Negroni, 2004; Simonetti, 2007).

Abuse by staff

A central justification for employee snooping has been the perception that staff are likely to 'abuse' the privilege of hyperspatial access by importing private behaviours into the workplace. The blindingly obvious asymmetry in attitudes here – the perception that the increased export of work time into private time does NOT, by contrast, pose any special problems – is striking. Even where 'work–life' imbalances are recognised, it is often the employee who takes the blame rather than the employer (for example, because they 'opt' for career over spare time) (Hansen, 2002).

The quantity of statistics available purporting to show the *negative* effects of net use at work is therefore predictable (cf. Leyden, 2006 for one example). So too is the fact that many of these statistics tend to have been gathered within the private sector. Even then, the picture which emerges is not one that completely fits the received perception of workers constantly surfing the internet for personal reasons. For example, one survey of over 350 employees by the Chartered Institute of Personnel and Development found that staff were much more likely to be reprimanded for excessive e-mail writing (CIPD, 2005). Other studies found that only 15% of organisations reported cases of downloading pornography while no more than 13% had dished out penalties for excessive web surfing (AMA, 2003).

Another received conclusion here, that firms 'lose money' as a result of these activities, is also worthy of more detailed scrutiny. A number of surveys have purported to show that abuses of communication technology in the workplace cost UK business 'millions' of pounds per year in lost productivity (Jackson, 2005). By contrast a study by The Radicati Group, 'Enterprise Wireless Email Market Trends', 2003–2007', suggested that access to e-mail might actually *increase* productivity with the finding that employees using wireless e-mail will have put in an extra 55 minutes of work per day (Visser, 2003). The obsession with internal threats from employees in the face of what would seem to be a greater risk to the successful functioning of a business – the many external threats to network integrity and safety – was starkly revealed in a 2006 survey for the UK Department of Industry. This indicated that 63% of all UK companies and 89% of large firms had an 'acceptable usage' policy relating to the use of internet by staff – a far higher percentage than the number of firms which had policies relating to the security of their internal information in place! (DTI, 2006).

As if all this were not enough, other factors related to network dynamics with their sudden and chaotic flows of data might also give workers reason to be careful about the use of e-mail in the workplace. A number of apocryphal tales of e-mails that come back to haunt the sender have emerged, some leading to disciplinary proceedings. For example, e-mails from a female employee detailing her boyfriend's sexual prowess and from a bank employee inviting colleagues to her birthday party in a highly pretentious manner (Vasagar and Topham, 2000; Ballinger, 2006; Button, 2006) were circulated to millions of readers around the world within hours. Very occasionally the network appears to deliver a roundabout form of just deserts. An e-mail sent by a well-paid legal executive asking his secretary to pay a £4 dry cleaning bill for some ketchup which had been accidentally spilt on his trousers was also copied and recopied and quickly recycled across hyperspace (Mikkelson, D & Mikkelson, P., 2005). His subsequent resignation was another telling manifestation of the folk justice of a wired world.

Shopping and harms

As has already been noted, shopping and sustenance acquisition has been increasingly affected by hyperspatialisation – most obviously by being conducted remotely. In the USA, retail e-sales increased at an average annual growth rate of 26.4% between 2000 and 2004, compared with 3.9% for total retail sales. Of course direct commodity acquisition was still the primary form, with e-sales still constituting only 2% of total retail sales (US Bureau of Census, 2004). This balance seems likely to shift fairly quickly – 71% of individuals surveyed in 2006 said that they had gone online to buy something (Pew Internet Project, 2006). On the plus side, this developing shift in retail habits may enable a 'magnification' for small businesses, giving them access and entry to markets that were previously closed to them (Lapham, 1997). But it is also likely to grant greater control to retailers – for example, in the use of high technology to monitor the supply and movement of food and other goods. It also means that, as consumers of goods, we are ourselves likely to be monitored to ever higher degrees of precision by retailers. Thus, it is not just the way that increased flows of goods and payments across networks enhance the opportunities for theft which ought to be of interest to criminologists here. The greater technological control of food and commodity supply brings in its wake other more subtle harms that may affect local spaces, though these are almost always outside of the remit of the criminal justice system.

Degradations to local trading relations

In promoting a general increase in both the number and *varieties* of social connectivities, hyperspatialisation has an inevitable effect upon the relations between suppliers and consumers of products. In particular, many kinds of symbiotic and hybrid trading practices open up or are extended, some of which may be argued to degrade or to damage accepted ethical standards. One long-established trading symbiosis of this kind has been the exploitation of human bodies or body parts as commodities. But the activities of Burke and Hare and the other 'traditional' body snatchers (Ross and Ross, 1979; Schultz, 2005) appear minor when compared to the economy of human body exchange (alive or dead) now enacted across contemporary trading networks.

We saw in Chapter 3 how the phenomenon of 'internet brides' or female trafficking represented one form of a more connected trading in human bodies – on this occasion live ones. Apparent attempts to sell babies online add a further permutation. One case from 2000 was centred in Shanghai when advertisements for the babies were spotted on eBay's Eachnet site, the US online auction house's Chinese website. Baby boys were being advertised at 28,000 yuan (US$3,453), while girls were available for around half the price at 13,000 yuan (US$1,603). Aside from the predictable gender inequalities – even within the baby market – obvious and major ethical questions arise about the existence of any such trade. The seller claimed that all the babies, which were to come from Henan Province, would be available within 100 days of birth. According to Chinese authorities, no deals were actually struck on this occasion, though there were a number of hits to the site and messages of enquiry were left (*China Daily*, 20/10/05). Whilst nothing concrete seems to have emerged from this story, other cases – for example, the British couple who acquired twins through an internet site run by a Californian child broker (Carvel *et al.*, 2001) – are an indication that, however low key, forms of child or baby trading which exploit the global market now exist.

The market in body parts is more extensive and brazen, and global trading networks vastly extend the opportunities for realising symbioses between purchasers and willing vendors. Such symbioses are often not just exploitative but patently criminogenic. In 1998, for example, Chinese authorities were accused of harvesting body parts from prisoners about to be executed – one source indicated that even their skin had been sold on to the cosmetics industry for beauty products (Cobain & Luck, 2005). Such practices have been strenuously denied by Chinese authorities though several doctors have come forward to provide evidence of the trade (Siddle, 2001). Canadian officials also began an investigation into citizens who had visited countries such as China, India and the Philippines, having paid over $100,000 for the trip, yet had no paperwork to explain why (Siddle, 2001). In the US more than 16,800 families appear to have been represented in lawsuits claiming loved ones' body parts were stolen for profit over the last 15 years. Some reports suggest that sales of organs have topped $6 million (*USA Today*, 28/04/06). These are harvested for medical research or transplanted and stolen and recycled from cadavers (see Harrison, 1999; Cheney, 2006). In 2006, a criminal conspiracy between owners of a funeral home and a company called Biomedical Tissue Services Ltd resulted in charges being brought in the US. The group were charged with looting bones and body parts from over 1,000 corpses (among them the former BBC presenter Alistair Cooke) and selling them on for medical transplants (Bone, 2006). But there are willing donors too. In 1999, in a notorious internet legend, a human kidney was put up for sale on eBay. Bidding had reached around $5.7 million before eBay put a stop to the auction because it contravened their rules outlawing the sale of body parts. In fact selling one's own organs is illegal under federal law, counting as felony punishable by up to five years in prison or a $50,000 fine. Global trading networks linking those who sell their body parts due to poverty, to service those who can afford this luxury, raise profound questions about the new global inequalities of hyperspace (Lloyd-Roberts, 2001). At the same time there are also some who have argued that a global trade in human organs and body parts ought not only to be legal but, since it represents a beneficial outcome of enhanced trading connectivities, should actually be encouraged (Jefferies, 1998; James, 2002).

This particular symbiosis is of course just one of the many questionable demand/supply chains which may be activated by enhanced connectivity. Shopping under the hyperspatial allows for a wide range of needs and wants to be satisfied – often at the very boundary of what is legally acceptable. For example, over 1,100 stun guns were sold to New Yorkers through eBay from September 2003 to August 2005. A 900,000-volt Taser stun gun and a $400 'Air Taser' that delivers a 50,000-volt were available, even though the State banned such weapons (*North Country Gazette*, 11/10/05) Meanwhile an International Fund for Animal Welfare probe found 9,000 live animals or products for sale in one week on trading sites such as eBay.live. A gorilla was up for sale in London and a Siberian tiger and four baby chimps on US websites (IFAW, 2005). Animal body parts traded included hawksbill turtle shells and shahtoosh shawls made from the endangered Tibetan antelope. DNA testing kits (*Register*, 18/08/06), rare and prescription drugs (Keizer, 2005; Thompson, 2006) or prescribed fireworks (MacDonald & Carpenter, 2006) were just a few of the many other varieties of goods traded at the boundary of legality and illegality between 2003 and 2006.

Incursive harms in trading – loyalty and respect

Works such as Beniger (1986) have traced the growth of the 'mass feedback technologies' – technologies which have had their own particular part to play in the development of hyperspatialisation and its associated cultures of control. Methods of monitoring attitudes and opinions of consumers have become an indispensable tool of the retail world. From magazine question-naires to customer databases the growth of what has also been called con-sumer intelligence (Elmer, 2004) has refined the capacity of 'desire-machines' (Deleuze & Guattari, 1977, 1983) to function ever more sensitively. But this is not just simple incursion into local spaces of consumption; important issues relating to the extent to which the behaviour of bodies should be influenced are also raised. Exploitation by advertising is monitored in the UK by the Advertising Standards Authority (ASA, 2007) – which contains a variety of adjudications on the extent to which behaviour can be manipulated. But codes of practice here are still largely voluntary.

Other behaviours of retail outlets in this regard might be argued to touch upon something which would also seem to be a crucial measure of the quality of local life – the degree of 'respect' exhibited within a community for other social actors there. It is an issue that has begun to receive the attention of the criminal justice system, especially in the UK under the much trumpeted New Labour programme of 'respect' for the community and the drive to punish 'anti-social' behaviour (Home Office, 2004c). A broader appreciation of the way that respect could function as a regulatory force within the community – such as that advocated in Sennett (2004) – widens attention beyond standard folk demons like beggars or young people towards the actions of certain retailers and their treatment of customers. Given retailers' own willingness to highlight their respect for and partici-pation within community, it seems appropriate to consider the extent to which they meet such standards. It soon becomes clear that the effects of hyperspatialisation upon their practices often result in actions which directly contradict such claims.

One mark of disrespect has been the increased assumption by stores that it is acceptable to ask for personal details at point of sale. These have no bearing on the sale itself but of course provide the store with additional marketing resources. In the USA in particular the assumption that a purchase means a handover of other details has reached endemic proportions. Informal research conducted for this book indicated that over 70% of stores in the USA (especially stores in malls) were now asking for personal details such as home telephone numbers or zip codes when conducting purchases by credit cards – even though these were irrelevant to the security of the purchase. Marketing schemes designed to 'reward' loyalty and 'punish' the disloyal (by way of increased costs or other discriminations), 'involve surveillance of con-sumers in the name of trust . . . activities (which) actively encourage new forms of consumer anxiety under the rubric of customer satisfaction' (Turow, 2006, p. 280). And as those 'disloyal' customers who cannot afford to enrol become ways of 'managing the customer roster, rewarding some, getting rid of others' (ibid, p. 204) new forms of discrimination and exclusion divide local communities. But the major retailers have convinced themselves that they can 'persuade' you to be loyal to them. Hence the explosion in marketing literature with titles like 'The 22 Major Factors that will Shape the Future of Company Loyalty'; 'Inside the Mind of the Loyal Client'; or the authoritative sounding 'Twelve Laws of Loyalty' (Wisemarketer, 2006).

The ubiquitous 'Store Loyalty Card' is a prime mechanism within these strategies. As almost everyone is probably now aware (itself a symptom of the pervasiveness of the strategy) loyalty cards purport to offer reductions on one's shopping bill in return for which a consumer provides 'basic' personal information, such as postcodes and addresses. In the UK most cards fall under the data-sharing Nectar scheme and are permitted, under the Data Protection Act, to be used to collect personal information and data on shopping habits provided (voluntarily) by Nectar collectors when they sign up. Members of the scheme can then choose whether or not to provide additional information – such as how many people there are in their household, or how many cars they own. Once signed up, the card is used to collect points, while details of the date, location and points earned – though not what was actually bought – is retained in Nectar's extensive databases.

Stores love to enhance the 'cosiness' of their relationship with their targets/customers by an uneasy mixing of metaphors of 'community' and 'privilege' in the marketing of these cards. For example, signing up to the Tesco clubcard in 2006 provided the lucky customer/target with 'exclusive' access to the Tesco Food Club; The Tesco Baby & Toddler Club; The Tesco Wine Club and even the Tesco Healthy Living Club (Tesco, 2006). Tesco sought to further promote its image of 'responsible and giving members of the community' by offering vouchers which could be exchanged by schools for ICT equipment. The scheme was heavily criticised in a report by the Consumers Association which suggested that nearly £250,000 of shopping was required to provide a computer that would cost only around £1,000. And not only would the administration of the scheme be likely to divert teachers' time away from teaching, so many vouchers were required to get a computer that it was an unrealistic target for many schools – especially in deprived areas, where parents would be likely to be able to afford much less for food (Smithers, 2001). Tesco's director of corporate affairs Lucy Neville-Rolfe responded (less than sympathetically) that the scheme, 'beat standing in the playground on a wet Saturday trying to sell cakes for a few pence'. In spite of the scheme's 'triumph' in winning the 'Nestlé Social Commitment' (*sic*) prize at the Food and Industry Awards of 2000 its real value seems to have declined substantially. In 1998 and 1999, the value of computer equipment passed on to schools represented around 1.14% of the company's UK profits. By 2004 the ratio had fallen to 0.52% though Tesco apparently continued to see this as '. . . a scheme that basically offers something for nothing' (Pratley, 2005). When loyalty marketing and voucher schemes culminate in the use of school children as a way of promoting brand awareness, legitimate questions arise about the extent to which the relentless evocation of 'community' by supermarkets really involves very much 'respect' for the notion of respect. With such questions in mind, schemes such as Tesco's new 10-step 'Community Action' plan which aims to 'put community at the heart of how we run our business' (Tesco, 2007), merit more critical attention.

Research by the UK Consumer Association's magazine *Which* raises further questions about the use of loyalty cards. They estimated that, in 2000, the average annual grocery spend was around £2,900 which, given the standard supermarket reward of 1%, would provide customers with a grand annual return of just £29 for all their efforts. Lucky customers who had collected 4,500 points on their Boots Advantage card – equivalent to £900-worth of toothpaste and shampoo – could look forward to 'a visit to a leisure centre' as a reward for their loyalty (Addley, 2000). In turn, various studies which compared shopping at stores with loyalty cards to those without, found there was often little real difference in cost (Gordon, 1999; Vanderlippe, 2002).

But while the customer ends up with returns from loyalty schemes that are often small to insignificant, the stores themselves acquire the very useful immaterial commodity of customer information. And though the information gathered is not supposed to be sold on or shared with companies outside the scheme, it *can* be used to target Nectar collectors with 'special offers'. The supermarket company Sainsbury's also uses the scheme to collect more detailed information on the products customers buy, information it uses for marketing purposes (Levey, 2003; Buckley, 2004), while in 2005 Safeway's card policy openly stated that:

> We may share information with affiliated companies or third parties as necessary to fulfill your on-line grocery order or other requests for service, and as necessary to obtain payment for products and services we may offer.
>
> (Bosworth, 2005)

As with all the new information reservoirs, once such data is available, it becomes a resource waiting to be used and traded. And confidential customer information gathered by cards or similar schemes has also been passed for the purpose of more overt forms of control. In one notorious incident, a housewife in North Wales was mistakenly arrested after Tesco staff claimed to have seen her steal a blouse on CCTV and passed on details of her private address to police. The woman had gone to the store in order to buy flowers for her recently deceased mother and while doing so had apparently placed her scarf in her handbag. However, because it had a similar colour to blouses on sale there, staff monitoring the CCTV system immediately assumed it had been stolen. A few days later police arrived at her house and arrested her – having tracked her down through the (personal) details logged under her store loyalty card. She was eventually offered some flowers and a goodwill gesture of £750 by the supermarket – not too much of a dent in its annual profits of £1.6 billion (Bellis, 2004).

However questionable these examples of the increasing capacity of stores to invade property and private spaces, they are as nothing to the bigger projects underway. In these, monitoring not only occurs at the level of *voluntary* passing on of information. Increasingly stores are seeking to improve their profit margins by what Tesco has misleadingly dubbed 'the next stage of bar-coding' – the wholesale implanting of radio-transmitters, RFID or 'spychips' into products themselves (cf. Albrecht & McIntyre, 2006). But RFID or 'Radio Frequency Identification' is certainly NOT the 'next stage of bar-coding'. For unlike RFID, bar-codes do not provide unique identification for a product, nor can they be used to track objects from a distance. By associating unique markers with every individual product, RFID devices (unlike bar-codes) enable supermarket retailers to make precise correlations between the purchase of particular items and specific individuals. And because they are very small devices the RFID technology can be concealed within packaging, or can even be printed over, making detection almost impossible. Radio frequency technology makes in-store surveillance easy, giving stores the potential to follow shoppers around, monitor their activities and even photograph them as they browse or take up items from the shelves. Though enthusiastic supporters of RFID like Tesco and Walmart claim that RFID is used merely to improve customer service, several instances of in-store surveillance of customers (usually without their permission) have been recorded (cf. Jha, 2003; CASPIAN, 2005). Nor is their claim that tags are 'turned off' once customers leave the store consistent with the evidence. For example, customers at the Metro chain in Germany picketed their stores when they found that RFID tags had not just been concealed in products from IBM, Gillette and Procter & Gamble which were on sale there, but also in their store loyalty cards. More seriously, the tags had *not* 'deactivated' after customers had left the store, opening up a range of new surveillance potentials to commerce (Zetter, 2004).

The question of interpersonal 'respect' within community is clearly central to how effectively that community functions. But for all the UK government's commitment to making this central to community crime control, examples such as these may lead one to wonder if its policing is always being directed at the right actors. Especially when the prosecution of anti-social behaviour often appears to be partial and erratic. Thus a recent attempt by one concerned local community member to enforce an ASBO against Tesco for noise pollution (*East Anglian Daily Times*, 08/04/05) – seemingly a clear violation of community order and well-being – came to nothing when Tesco used its greater legal resources to draw out the case into a long appeal. If there is to be a viable notion of respect *within* the community, in both its proximate and remote forms, it can surely only function where the requirement for respect applies equally, to all members of that community.

Consumption and environmental harms

As the increased interest in 'green crimes' underlines (Davidson, 1981; Edwards *et al.*, 1996; Situ & Emmons, 1999; Walters, 2005; Varady *et al.*, 2007) perceptions that a functioning community must also be a sustainable one have grown in recent years. It is not clear however whether hyperspatialisation produces outcomes that are always consistent with this goal.

Problems of local environmental pollution emanating from the infrastructures of hyperspatialisation such as mobile phone masts were already considered in Chapter 3. In turn environmental harms at the local level are frequently (though not always) connected with damage that occurs at the global level. But it seems clear that there is also environmental damage which can be specifically associated with communal life. For example, there may be a blighting of property prices or the gradual degradation of an area through depopulation and a rundown in local services. Or there may be a hollowing out of local economies, as a result of the actions of commerce – an issue which provoked the UK's Competion Commission to launch an ongoing investigation into the state of local grocery markets (Competition Commission, 2007). In this section I will consider this idea in terms of the themes developed in the previous section by considering some of the environmental effects of large supermarkets and other retailers upon local spaces.

One potentially negative outcome of hyperspatiality here lies in the effects of distance shrinking upon food production and distribution. As food retailers adopt the logic of the hybrid and become banks, clothing stores, entertainment centres and coffee shops they not only devour whole swathes of local and regional economies, they pose increasing risks to the quality of that space as a whole. As one recent report into the effect of food retailers upon local life put it: 'big supermarkets don't usually make good neighbours. There are often significant social and economic impacts associated with (their) opening' (FOE, 2005, p. 7).

One form of damage generated by the streamlining of food distribution and production by database and tracking technologies comes from supply lorries, constantly required to respond to micro-variations in movements of products on shelves. A near-24-hour delivery process results which brings noise and toxic pollution to many previously peaceful neighbourhoods (see for example Woods, 2005). Further costs to the environment from transporting such goods across the new global food networks are also now increasingly recognised. A 2005 report for DEFRA (Smith *et al.*, 2005) noted that, since 1978, the annual amount of food moved in the UK by HGVs has increased by 23%, while the average distance for each trip has increased by over 50%. As a result they estimated that of the 19 million tonnes of carbon dioxide produced by food transport in 2002, 10 million tonnes were emitted in the UK representing 1.8% of the total annual UK CO_2 emissions. Meanwhile, though airfreighted food accounted for only 1% of food tonne kilometres and 0.1%

of vehicle kilometres, it produced 11% of the food transport CO_2 equivalent emissions. It was also the fastest growing method of food transportation. Likewise, the distances involved in transporting food around town centres were estimated to have increased by 27% since 1992, mainly because of an increase in shopping for food by car. The change away from frequent visits to local stores towards more widely spaced (weekly or twice-weekly) visits to large edge or out-of-town supermarkets has clearly had a great deal to do with this.

Information pollution: vandalism and littering

Whilst the kinds of problem just outlined seem likely to offer serious levels of long-term harm to communities, greater attention has tended to fix upon more obvious forms of damage such as vandalism. 'Vandalism' is however a loose term which lumps together a wide variety of behaviours. For example, graffiti and tagging are often treated as being on a par with purely 'destructive' forms of vandalism like damaging street furniture. But this 'creative vandalism' has also been seen as an important cultural form of deviance, something that can even enhance communal life (cf. Ferrell, 2005).

As our local space is extended and redistributed, destruction or damage towards it proliferates in much the same way as vandals operate in more proximal space. Home websites, blogs, company or political sites, advertising pages and so on have all proved to be tempting targets for the wantonly destructive. Sometimes such attacks also have a creative, or political edge – in 2003, for example, the UK Labour Party website was defaced when a picture of US President George Bush carrying a dog with Tony Blair's head superimposed on it appeared (BBC, 16/06/03). At other times attacks on websites or gaming environments appear more related to traditional pleasures of sheer destruction or exhibitionism.

The Wikipedia has been an emblematic target for combinations of both creative and destructive vandalism. As a 'user-generated' resource, editing 'Wikis' (as its entries are known) is relatively easy, with much depending upon the altruism of its (mostly unpaid) contributors. And as one of the most visited of non-profit sites it inevitably attracts a lot of attention. Obvious targets such as entries for George Bush or Islam are regularly defaced – sometimes crudely, at other times with more humour. Defacements range from the obsessive (changing statistics and numerical data), the surreal (scrambling text on the entry for 'dyslexia'), to the plain childish (entries such as 'my teacher is gay'). The ultimate affect of this compulsive vandalism upon the Wikipedia's capacity to offer its unique 'democratic' editing style (about as 'communal' as communal gets) is as yet unclear (cf. Kleeman, 2007). Vandalism can equally extend into more personal communal spaces such as a personal website, a blog or a social networking page where a great deal of time and energy may have been invested. Thus there are now numerous accounts of pages on Myspace, Facebook and so on having false photos inserted or content defaced in other ways (Kleeman, 2007). Calls for a code of conduct for blogging have also arisen after the line between vandalism and psychological threat has been crossed with the insertion of random death threats into some blogs (BBC, 28/03/07). Meanwhile Williams' (2004) study of web vandalism suggested negative effects on the distributed community may parallel those in proximal space – for example, the creation of 'crime hotspots'. Here, 'avoidance behaviour, similar to that occurring in the offline world, may create hotspots of deviance within the online arena' (Williams, 2004, p. 20). Whatever the motivations for vandalism online, Zone-H, a site that records defacements of websites, now has a very large archive of examples (Zone-H, 2007). And other forms of vandalism and littering begin to emerge as communities extend into more hyperspatial forms. The problems of spam – unwanted mail which clogs up e-mail boxes – have attracted legislation, though it is unclear how far this has reduced the flow (Wall, 2005). Blog-spamming, the '. . . digital equivalent of flyposting' which posts links to commercial sites, is a new variant which disrupts personal and public space, with one estimate suggesting that around 94% of comments to blogs now contain some form of spam (Pollitt, 2007). The proliferation of pop-up or banner advertisements which users are increasingly confronted with online, represents another extension to the littering of public space in its extended sense (McWilliams, 2003; BBC, 21/02/05).

The commodification of community

By pressing the question of what has happened to the idea of local space under hyperspatialisation, the inevitable fate of the (ambiguous) notion of community also arises. As we have seen, two assumptions guide standard thinking in this regard. First, that 'more community' is always and unquestionably a good thing. Second, as was noted at the beginning of this chapter, that community tends to be undermined or even destroyed by contemporary life and especially the hyperspatial technologies that go with this. Computers, as Stoll put it, 'isolate us from each other' (1995). Even Howard Rheingold, previously an 'optimist' (perhaps even a utopian) with regard to the effects of the internet upon community, has been more guarded recently. In particular he worries that there might be something in the criticism that remote communication is playing a role in the 'commodification of community' (cf. Rheingold, 2006) – a transformation of social relations into commodity forms for the ultimate purpose of generating capital, informational or otherwise. The purchase of Myspace by Rupert Murdoch's News International for a cost of around $580 million (Rosenbush, 2005), or the $1.6 billion purchase of YouTube a year later by Google (Markoff, 2006), is not just a sign of inflation in the social networking 'product' but an indication of the significance that corporations now see in the saleability of community.

But 'community commodification' might also be seen in the actions and perceptions of many users of these sites themselves. The limited ethnographic research into the use of these sites has tended to stress their positive social functions (Boyd, 2003, 2006). But it is clearly all too easy to begin to place a quantitative rather than qualitative value upon friendship and community when one measures popularity simply by the amount or number of networks one is connected into. 'You don't exist' is often now the judgement of those who lack access to such networks (Bigge, 2006; Cassidy, 2006). As discussed in the previous chapter, there is increasing evidence to suggest that those who do not possess an appropriate form of access to hyperspace such as a mobile phone, may find themselves socially excluded or shunned in various ways (Context, 2006). Such attitudes cannot be entirely disassociated with the ways 'community' is constructed by such technologies and within such sites. Having a list of 'contacts' on a mobile phone, or being able to generate 'friends' lists (which link to further friends lists) not only creates (to the outsider) an intimidating (though ultimately unrealistic) impression of endless and boundless community. It also sets in motion a concretisation of social difference marked by 'levels of popularities' and reinforces ideas of 'more is better' in networks. In so doing it not only arguably divides, but actually threatens to undermine a key aspect of human connection – time. The fact that friendships and communities can be acquired by simply posting pictures of someone, rather than by negotiation, problem-solving and genuine investment in energy, may be harder to appreciate. Of course, a dystopia of commodified friends, relations and family may prove to be as unrealistic as Rheingold's original vision of utopian online community. But what does seem true is that community always remains something 'to be found', in both its immediate and remote senses. To forget this as community spreads through hyperspace may be to threaten it with harms far more insidious than the kinds which have been considered here.

Chapter 6

Proximity 3: Global space

> Would you really feel any pity if one of those dots stopped moving forever?
> If I offered you twenty thousand pounds for every dot that stopped, would
> you really, old man, tell me to keep my money, or would you calculate how
> many dots you could afford to spare?
>
> (Harry Lime, from *The Third Man*, 1949)

Of all orders of social possibility, perhaps the broadest that can be subject to
harm is that constituted by the overriding political, cultural and power structures which inform our world. As with local space, the character of this
broader region and the possible harms that attach to it derive from collective
experience and its roots in communal life. Unlike that space, communality
here is expressed in terms of the most all-encompassing descriptions of social
practices that humans engage in, not just those determined by their immediate communal concerns. Violations to this region and the collective actors
which shape it seem therefore even further removed from personal levels of
concern, though, ironically, their effects can be wholly destructive – not just
for individuals, or even local communities – but for human life itself. The
possibilities for control here are, accordingly, also total. It is no surprise
then that attempts to secure control of this social space have been such an
historical source of contest and conflict.

Given all of this, it should be even less surprising that hyperspatialisation is
transforming such struggles. According to Hardt and Negri:

> Network power, a new form of sovereignty is now emerging and it
> includes as its primary elements, or nodes, the dominant nation states,
> along with supranational institutions, major capitalist corporations and
> other powers.
>
> (2004, p. xii)

The material resources of hyperspatialisation appear to be heavily implicated in these pervasive 'netscapes of power' (Winseck, 2002) and to have

significantly enhanced the capacity of certain global actors to exert control over others (Jordan, 1999; Held, 2002; Beck, 2006). More optimistically, it has also been held that these enhancements and centralisations of control may be balanced and even undermined by new social formations emerging from an extended spatial order (Grimes & Wharf, 1997; Downing, 2001; Himanen, 2001). This chapter will focus upon some of the harms associated with this unfolding process.

There are clearly many examples that could be selected for consideration. What Castells has referred to as the 'globalisation of crime' (1997, p. 259) might incorporate everything from money laundering, transnational corporate frauds to people trafficking. But conceiving of globally based crime in terms of these 'crimes of globalisation' (Barak, 2001) tells only part of the story. For the purpose of this chapter the rights, or – to use a much abused word – our 'freedoms' to *use* this space in basic ways will serve as the framework for considering harm here. The capture and inversion of these terms by the neo-conservative right (Lakoff, 2006) sometimes makes it hard to appreciate the many ways in which the freedom and right to experience global space (in its broadest senses) can now be undermined. Traditional concepts of freedom – such as freedom of assembly and association; of movement; of expression and thought and so on have been radically affected by hyperspatialisation and the capacities for control it offers. Worse, restrictions upon these freedoms are more easily sold to global audiences in the context of the apparent 'everywhere-threats' of the hyperspatial. In turn, other, newer kinds of freedoms brought by its reshapings of spatial experience threaten to disappear before we have barely become aware of them.

One expression of the spatial conflicts manifesting within global space will be of particular interest – the extent to which our interpersonal rights to visibility and invisibility should be balanced. Even more fundamental than this right to experience global space as visibly (or invisibly) as the new normativities of the hyperspatial permit is the right to *occupy* this space. In part this involves the general issue of global mobilities, but it can also be seen as the right of global collectivities to life and to quality of life – the very capacity to occupy space at all. One threat to this right comes from near permanent extensions to the global state of war. Another arises in the increasing social divisions between certain global collectivities over others. In both cases, remote interaction seems to be heavily implicated.

Global spaces – some conceptions

One obvious approach to thinking more clearly about a global space as the 'broadest' of social spaces is to contrast its more extensive form of communality with the narrower formations discussed in the previous chapter. In addition to the kinds of community/society, *gesellshaft/gemeinshaft* distinctions discussed there one might follow Park, Burgess and Cooley and make a distinction between a local community and the wider, more impersonal formations of the global in terms of the distinction between *primary* groups – 'those characterised by intimate face-to-face association and co-operation' (Cooley, 1909, p. 15) and *secondary* groups – those which substitute ' "secondary", for direct, face-to-face, "primary" relations'. For Park and Burgess indirect social relations of this kind were closely associated with the hyperspatial, springing variously from, '. . . modern methods of urban transportation and communication – the electric railway, the automobile, the telephone, and the radio' (Park & Burgess, 1921, p. 24). More ambitiously, one might follow social network theorists and try to produce some 'graph' of relations that could represent sets of connections distinct from purely local ones in virtue of their quantity, spread, or some other such measure (White *et al.*, 1976; Scott, 2000). But couched in such abstract terms, something crucial about this global space seems to be left missing – the fact that it is as much formed by a process of struggle and negotiation, as it is from variables such as size or mode of connection. The wars of position and manoeuvre discussed by Gramsci (1988, VII, I) seem integral in forming global space, since for him 'strategy (is) inherently spatial' (Jessop, 2005, p. 15). Any properly *social* sense of global space cannot therefore avoid incorporating questions relating to the way positions are balanced within it. For upon this, fundamental questions of justice hang.

Historical precedents for something which might be called a 'global-space' might include concepts such as the 'polis' or city which formed the centre of life across the Greek world (see for example Aristotle, 1998, 2, 8–9), its importance inscribed in the plethora of terms such as 'politics' which derive from it and which underpin many of our basic ideas about social organisation. Or attention might centre upon Hobbesian ideas of the Leviathan, that 'artificiall man' (Hobbes, 1950, p. 103) which represents another sense of human collective organisation at its widest. But it is also clear that important differences remain between these earlier ideas and the way in which a global space is now perceived. First, there was a lack of cartographic and physical detail about the full *spatial* extent of the globe. Second, and following from the first, there was a lack of awareness of the full range of human *societies* that occupied this space. Preferring the term *globality* (cf. Albrow, 1996), Martin Shaw has emphasised this point – social relations only become properly global when 'they are significantly and systematically informed by an *awareness* of the common framework of worldwide human society' (Shaw, 2000, p. 12, my emphasis). Third, and also inseparable from the previous two points, was the fact that the kind of communicative infrastructure which makes a truly 'global' awareness of totalised cultural interconnectivity possible at all was not present.

Such reflections emphasise how important it is to form a conception of globality that incorporates considerations of more than simply the economic sphere. For the character of global-space is at least as much dependent upon the connectivities of interaction and opinion provided by communication networks as it is upon trading. Habermas' discussions of the 'public sphere' outlined how the administrative power of states and governing bureaucracies are in constant tension with the realm of public debate fostered by the development of contemporary media forms from the coffeehouse to the newspaper, with the internet serving as but the latest of this long line of communicative tensions (Carey, 1989; Calhoun, 1992; Kellner, 1997; Volkmer, 2007). Habermas has been one of the strongest advocates of the idea that adequate communication structures are foundational to his conception of a global space – as the span of a 'civil' society. The notion of civil society implies a spatially accretive logic – a 'site of social congregation ... active precisely at those moments when, and in those locales where people have gathered' (Breslow, 1997, p. 239). In so doing, it forms that 'space across which the state, the public sphere and the private sphere meet' (ibid). Whether 'civility' – the mutually respectful conduct required for social interaction to function effectively – follows automatically from this social/spatial accretion is a moot point. The 'withering away' of civil society described by some commentators (Hardt, 1995), does not automatically imply a 'post-civil' stage, because this is 'too reactive to do justice to this new paradigm of social relations ... mobility, speed and flexibility are the qualities which characterise this separate plane of rule' (ibid, pp. 40–41). The double-edged role of communication in this is all too evident. Within the global level of human association defined by Hardt and Negri (2001) as Empire, communication brings 'society entirely and globally' (p. 347) under its regime. On the other hand, for the buzzing connections of the 'multitude', it offers about the only resource which could extend the possibility of a challenge to current conditions of Empire (ibid).

Whilst the concept of global space seems able to accommodate the role of communicative and economic spheres as well as transport structures, physical geographies and political organisation, in order to avoid having to spell out *every* kind of significant ingredient within it, I will restrict myself to two basic social geometric notions in defining its basic character. First, I will view it as a *totality* of local spaces, a summation of existing forms of community and the individuals and their actions who make them up. In turn this will amount to a simple limit condition – a boundary upon social possibility which is relative to specific sets of material historical circumstances. The specific *kinds* of capacities and powers it confers then serve to distinguish it as a space from others that have been analysed here. For example, whereas the capacities conferred by a local space relate to particular sets of communal activities possible within that immediate region (socialising with friends, working, relaxing at home), global space offers extended social relations that go far beyond the local. And by acquiring a 'global' perspective we can begin to see beyond the narrow boundaries of our immediate communities and to transform our perspectives and all the spaces we inhabit accordingly.

The extent to which global perspectives are relative to specific temporal-spatial localities – the historical and material conditions of particular societies – is clear enough. In many cases, the global space of a society might be almost precisely commensurate with its local space. But for us, the space of 'globality' now fully encompasses the physical space of the globe itself. Indeed, it now also needs to be thought of as extending beyond even these boundaries. For, satellite and other remote technologies have begun to extend human presence and interaction far beyond the surface of the earth. Thus, the use of 'extra-terrestrial' space to control events on the globe's surface (through satellite and GPS technologies, for example) is now commonplace. In turn, the militarisation of this more remote space now becomes an inevitable material fact. The new US National Space Policy of 2006 noted that: 'those who effectively utilize space will enjoy added prosperity and security and will hold a substantial advantage over those who do not' (USNSP, 2006, pp. 1–2). To this end its central policy proposal was to, 'enable unhindered U.S. operations in and through space to defend our interests there' (ibid). This proposal to reduce US space vulnerabilities is, in effect, a proposal for a 'space control' (Logsden, 2006), one that manifests a more extensive geographical territorialisation of global space than ever before.

The realisation that our contemporary global space actually now extends *beyond* the globe itself is a further reminder that we should not get too bogged down in associations between the term global and the physical limits (or shape) of the earth. Rather, it emphasises again the social basis to any such space and the way, in turn, in which this impinges upon our perceptions of boundaries. As Simmel famously put this: '. . . a boundary is not a spatial fact with sociological consequences, but a sociological fact that forms itself spatially' (1997, p. 142) Once formed however, 'it produces strong repercussions on the consciousness of the relationship of the parties' (ibid). The organisational capacity of a community able to command space is one more sign that the realities of power here are manifested in forms of control that transcend a terroritorialised space – however far across the globe this now stretches. Rather than becoming fixated on geographical notions to understand the character of global space, it is perhaps to the global actors who *exert* such controls that we should therefore look.

Traditional global actors: harm and culpability

As the constituents of a *collective* space it seems plausible that global actors need also to be understood collectively – though as the parts upon which these various social wholes depend, micro-individuals continue to figure foundationally here. But granting a role to social collectivities is of course to be landed with well-known difficulties of agency that not only infect criminology or jurisprudence, but also social science as a whole. For if an agent is collective, how then to collectively ascribe agency – let alone guilt or blame?

One solution is purely ontological – to treat the collective as an individual like any other and one therefore capable of purposive collective action. Simmel's idea of a 'collective individuality' (1971) represents one version of this solution. Other approaches try more directly to show how responsibility for some harm *could* be shared by a group – even though not every member of it may have been actively responsible for the harm. Feinberg (1968) formulated some useful distinctions which addressed this. He argued that in distributing collective responsibility, there are really two cases of interest: cases where members of a collective *contribute* to harm but at different levels (collective but distributive fault), and cases where every member of a collective shares the *same* fault (collective and non-distributive fault). He claims that it is only the latter that can be properly said to be an instance of 'group liability'. For many however the very idea of collective responsibility is not just conceptually opaque, but morally unpalatable. As H.D. Lewis put this: 'value . . . belongs to the individual and it is the individual who is the sole bearer of moral responsibility . . . collective responsibility is . . . barbarous' (Lewis, 1948, pp. 3–6).

Given the conceptual difficulties in setting out a working notion of collective responsibility, the legal position on this has inevitably been ambiguous. Whilst cases for corporate liability on manslaughter or environmental damage charges have been pursued in cases such as the Bhopal disaster of 1984 or the *Exxon Valdez* oilspill of 1989 they have rarely been made to apply to the company as a whole (see Donaldson, 1982; French, 1984; Slapper & Tombs, 1999; Wells, 2001). Not only is it obviously impossible for a company to be 'jailed', large fines may simply end up hurting employees innocent of any offence. Attempting to assign collective culpability to States has proved equally problematic. The genocides in Nazi Germany and more recently in Rwanda provoked questions of group guilt that were never satisfactorily dealt with by the courts. Whilst many argued that the German people were collectively responsible for Nazi crimes, the only real legal aftermath – the Nuremburg trials themselves – only ever directed charges at specific individuals within the regime (see Jaspers, 1961; Arendt, 1987). More recently, the ICC Statute of July 1998, which defines the procedures and the substantive law of the proposed International Criminal Court, clearly limits the scope of its powers to individuals stating, in article 25(1), that: '. . . the Court shall have jurisdiction over natural persons . . .' (ICC, 1998).

By contrast the charge of institutional racism famously levelled at the Metropolitan Police during the Macpherson report into the death of Stephen Lawrence essayed a kind of (quasi-legal) basis for collective responsibility, one centred on consequences. This was the idea that organisations could, through their cumulative omissions and failures, produce culpable outcomes not solely attributable to single individuals. On this line the Metropolitan Police Force was guilty of racism 'as an institution' by way of its: '. . . collective failure . . . to provide an appropriate and professional service to people because of their colour, culture, or ethnic origin' (Macpherson, 1999, 6.34). Collective culpability here does not require any overall group 'consciousness' or agency, because it emerges at the individual level – from the (often unwitting) behaviours of an organisation's members.

I intend to evade the many philosophical complexities in discussing how culpabilities can be attached to collective agents by simply accepting that legal systems *do* now recognise certain forms of collective guilt, even though the concept is clearly in need of much refinement. Given such an assumption, some fairly obvious collective actors quickly become apparent when the question of culpabilities for harm within global space is raised. Perhaps most obvious is the State, or 'nation-state' – that '. . . contingent, destructible association of human beings inhabiting an identified territory . . . joined in being subjects of a ruler or government' (Oakeshott, 1990, p. 228). See Poulantzas (1978) for a less conservative perspective on this concept.

It would seem equally impossible to discount key representatives of commerce like multinational companies as global actors. Of course in purely spatial terms, firms always begin as local rather than global entities. Not only do they thereby operate purely *within* state boundaries, their capacity to act is, at first, usually subordinate to that of States. But the clear reciprocal relationship between hyperspatialisation and the development of multinational commerce has increasingly enabled many companies to operate beyond local or State boundaries so that, as Robert Reich has emphasised: '. . . in the past firms had a clear nationality, but . . . in recent years fundamental changes in the organization of work have made the nationality of multinationals irrelevant. They have become stateless "global webs" ' (Jones, G., 2006, p. 5).

The global reach of corporations seems indubitable. In 2000, the majority (51) of the world's 100 largest economic entities were corporations rather than states, with the sales of US corporations such as General Motors, Walmart and Exxon Mobile outstripping the GDP of countries like Denmark, Saudi Arabia or New Zealand (Anderson & Cavanagh, 2000). Like States and indeed most varieties of agent (global or otherwise), corporations act to preserve and further their interests and in so doing can bring about harms to others. Transnational fraud or damage to environments are obvious examples but there is an equally important class of such harms which involves the physical bodies that constitute and maintain business organisations. From the machine tool operator to the delivery boy, the software designer to the marketing assistant, the basis of any corporation lies in the collective productive activities of its employees. And just as social actors *external* to the organisation can be harmed by its actions so too can its own human base – whether by accident, or design.

The gradual growth in awareness among workforces that they too were collective agents and could act together to *prevent* such harms takes us to a foundational example of a third kind of global actor, one that we will consider more in the next section. Groups such as workers, or their unions, have often acted in ways distinct from States or commerce and seem therefore to be worthy of distinct consideration. These 'non-state' actors, as they are inevitably often now referred to (see for example Underhill *et al.*, 2000), have ebbed and flowed in terms of their historical effects and significance. Most often the concept of such agents has been associated with the phenomenon of shared group 'identities' – a communal sense of belonging which stands outside of the unifying metaphor of the State. Tribes, or religions, would count as obvious instances of collectives which existed long before there were any States against which to contrast them.

The emergence of collectivities based around class consciousness marked a new stage in the formation of such identities, one that responded in particular to the concentrations of control within global space that came with advanced capitalism. In so doing, class-based collectivities like unions or other emancipatory political movements provided a structure beyond simple biological or cultural determinants around which 'non-state' global agents could find common identities. The term 'identity politics' (cf. Calhoun, 1994) has sometimes been used to refer to the emancipatory activities of non-state actors – most especially those organised around characteristics such as gender, ethnicity, sexual preference and so on. Castells distinguishes between a 'resistance identity' and a 'project identity' (1997, p. 8) in this context and argues that project identity is particularly significant in that this produces *subjects* and such subjects form 'the main potential source of social change in the network society' (ibid, p. 67).

Clearly there are many different ways of taxonomising collectivities in global space that are discontinuous with States or business but I shall simply treat *all* of the above as a 'third' kind of actor within global space. However, caution is still required, for while many kinds of project – such as environmentalism – seem clearly 'emancipatory' it would be much too simplistic to assume that these are the only kinds of interests humans organise collectively around. We will consider this point in more detail in a moment.

Hyperspatialising global spaces and their actors

David Held (Held *et al.*, 1999) suggests that the effects of globalisation result in a 'shared social space' (p. 1), a fact he specifically associates with transformations in the *spatial* organisation of the social world. He highlights at least three types of change of this kind, changes which sound very familiar in the context of what has been said about the hyperspatial. Globalisation, according to Held, involves: 'the *stretching* of social, political and economic activities across frontiers, regions and continents' (ibid); the *intensification* of various flows such as trade, finance, migration or culture and the *speeding up* of global interactions and processes. Giddens also appears to see the 'inherently globalising' character of modernity in terms close to the hyperspatial defining it as an '. . . intensification of worldwide social relations which link distant localities in such a way that local happenings are shaped by events occurring many miles away and vice versa' (1990, p. 64).

Yet in spite of such obvious continuities, hyperspatialisation is not 'just' globalisation, though globalisation is arguably very much an instance of the former. For example, as we have seen, hyperspatialisation is a much longer term process than globalisation – one that has been underway almost ever since humans first sought to extend the spatial limitations imposed by their bodies. Nor is it a process likely to come to an end should a fully globalised 'world political and economic system' ever be created. The reach of remote interaction already stretches far beyond the confines of the globe and is likely to continue to extend. Finally, it also seems clear that the cultural consequences of hyperspatialisation are likely to be wider than any purely economic or political outcomes of a joined-up world. Moral, epistemic, and even metaphysical consequences that we can barely imagine may yet also count among the longer term effects of the hyperspatial.

One undoubted beneficiary of these spatial reorganisations has been the corporation, a fact not only witnessed by the frequently superior capacity to create wealth than State but in their increased *cultural* influence over global space. As Deleuze put this:

> . . . the factory has given way to the corporation. The family, the school, the army, the factory are no longer the distinct analogical spaces that converge towards an owner – state or private power – but coded figures – deformable and transformable – of a single corporation that now has only stockholders. Even art has left the spaces of enclosure in order to enter into the open circuits of the bank.
>
> (1992, p. 3)

The 'smooth space' which this corporate culture seeks to promote furthers the capacity of firms to operate invisibly and beyond territorial boundaries (real or imagined) so that: '. . . the world is now a single field within which capitalism can operate' (Waters, 1995, p, 57). With it comes the cultural penetrations of the firm – viral marketing as taste, debt as membership, promotion as popularity and corporations which have souls – 'the most terrifying news in the world' as Deleuze put it (1992, p. 4). Supranational institutions linked to the interests and cultures of business organisations – whether IMF or the World Bank – extend the influence of corporate culture in hyperspace still further, while the covert rise of private equity conglomerates such as Blackstone remove even the constraints of the shareholder from the dominations of the profit motive (Macalister, 2007).

By contrast, the effects of hyperspatialisation have often been seen to have had a negative influence upon the State. Castells, for example, has argued that 'State control over space and time is increasingly bypassed by global flows of capital, goods, services, technology, communication and information' (1997, p. 243), a view which has found favour with a number of theorists of globalisation (see for example Ohmae, 1995). Similar views were put forward by many of the early theorists of cyberspace who saw, in addition to emerging forms of transnationalism, an emerging set of 'cyberspatial' realities which would stand outside of the reach of both state and commerce. In his famous 'Declaration of Independence of Cyberspace' (1996) John Perry Barlow addressed the 'Governments of the Industrial World' – those 'weary giants of flesh and steel' – to affirm:

> I declare the global social space we are building to be naturally independent of the tyrannies you seek to impose on us. You have no moral right to rule us nor do you possess any methods of enforcement we have true reason to fear.
>
> (Barlow, 1996)

The fact that 'state policies are everywhere more and more orientated toward facilitating, if not directly governing, the shape of information industrialism' (Ross, 2006, p. 381), has led to the charge that Barlow's manifesto was no more than a form of 'pure self-indulgence' (ibid, p. 383). And as Lawrence Lessig reminded us, the grubby reality we actually see within remote interaction is 'control . . . coded by commerce, with the backing of government' (Lessig, 1999, p. x). So rather than there being any fragmentation of the State in the face of increased transnational flows of wealth or communication, it has been able to call upon a variety of resources and tactics to maintain its status.

The smooth spaces of the network and their 'deterritorialisations' (Deleuze & Guattari, 1972) are one important example. As the State begins to be able to link information continuously, from database to database, from medical record to criminal record, from credit rating to library book loans, a form of State power emerges which is arguably more enhanced than it has ever been. And by co-operation or collusion with the corporation, whether internally, or by way of supranational institutions such as the European Union, or the IMF, the State seeks to further extend its influence, and thereby its lifespan. Whether these efforts amount to nothing more than a temporary stay of grace remains to be seen, though there must be suspicions that the State may have traded in short-term gains for a longer term decline. In surrendering so much of its *raison d'être* to the cultures of commerce and the new supranational order of Empire, States may yet have limited themselves in ways that signal their ultimate demise.

The transformations wrought to these traditional global actors by hyperspatialisation are as nothing to the changes it has brought to the 'non-state', identity-based collectives. Bauman (2001) invokes Jock Young's memorable phrase: 'just as community collapses, identity is invented' (Young, 1999, p. 164), and describes these changes as a:

... transition from emancipatory politics to a politics of self-actualisation in a reflexively ordered environment, where that reflexivity links self and body to systems of global scope.

(Baumann, 2001, p. 214)

For Castells by contrast, this shift relates to a dialectics of social evolution where 'resistance confronts domination, empowerment reacts against power-lessness and alternative projects challenge the logic embedded in the new global order' (1997, p. 69). And the ranks of these traditional groupings, from social pressure groups to ethnic collectives like the Kurds or the Palestinians, have been further augmented by others especially facilitated by hyperspatiali-sation processes. These more recent collective actors have founded their pro-ject identities upon specific causes such as prisoner conditions and treatment (Amnesty), or environmental abuse (Greenpeace) (see for example Cohen & Rai, 2000; Hamel et al., 2001).

As signalled in the previous section, it would be misleading to assert that this third species of global actor can be exclusively identified with projects that are 'emancipatory'. Indeed some may have little in the way of a defined project at all. 'Young people', for example, clearly have a collective role to play on the global stage (just as increasingly, 'old people' do) though their emancipatory projects can only ever be very fragmented and general. Likewise, as Castells reminds us, many social movements may be as conservative as they are emancipatory – with Christian fundamentalists, orthodox Islamicist groups or extreme nationalists representing obvious examples. Of course it might be said that such collectives seek a kind of 'emancipation' for their own projects, however intolerant they might be to others. But at this point the attempt to define global actors in terms of emancipatory goals threatens to become unnecessarily subjective. For this reason, in what follows I shall adhere to a simpler line – it is in the drive to create (or conserve) spatial continuity by some project of identity that this third species of global actor emerges, one conducted in the face of a multiplicity of other (potentially competing) projects. Note that overtly criminal collectives are also accom-modated by this conception – by way of the distinctively 'criminal projects' that unify them and which they seek to maintain in the face of opposition. Though their projects are limited ones – an accumulation of wealth or influ-ence for selfish ends – they also serve to collectively 'unify' actors, in much the same way as other more respectable projects can do. Seen in this way their goals are not so different from the projects of traditional global actors like States and in particular corporations – as others have already pointed out (see for example Lea, 2002; Ruggiero, 2004) – especially given their increasing organisation by way of various global networks.

This chaotic variety of non-state groupings has recently been characterised in terms of the concept of the 'multitude' (Hardt & Negri, 2004, p. 97ff.). This is not what used to be seen as the 'mob', an easily manipulated mass driven by irrational social forces. For, while the multitude may consist in a fragmented and often contradictory set of collective projects, it also possesses a certain degree of organisation. To use the language of contemporary physics, the multitude is a self-organising, emergent phenomenon – a firm of social patterning that may present an appearance of chaos – but this is in fact 'deterministic' chaos, driven by dynamic and thermodynamic laws (Prigogine, 1984). And this says much about the involvement of hyperspatial technologies in the growth and coordination of the multitude. The multiple nodes and pathways within a hyperspace create optimal conditions for phenomena associated with states of dynamic equilibria to form. But the 'strange attractors' which count as structures in deterministic chaos are realised here in remote communication and mobility, spatial complexifications which promote the unity and purpose of the multitude(s). The 'swarm intelligence' strategy (Bonabeau et al., 1999) which mirrors the collective problem-solving capabilities exhibited by termites or bees becomes increasingly available to such groups by way of the enhanced network structures of the hyperspatial – with the internet just one (albeit obvious) instance of this.

Anarchy in IT: hacking, identity groups and the web

In addition to the transformations exerted upon global collectivities both old and new, hyperspatialisation might also be argued to have promoted 'cultures' (Taylor, 1999; Cere, 2007) or 'communities' (Levy, 1984; Poulsen, 2005a) specific to its technologies. It says a lot about the continuities between hyperspatialisation and hypercrime that such groupings, celebrated as 'pioneers' of the computer age in early works such as Levy (1984) and Turkle (1984), have so quickly been associated with deviance and criminality. The arcane knowledge and distinctive skillsets that appeared to go with the new priesthoods of information technology certainly gave the impression that this new subculture constituted part of a 'technopower elite' (Jordan, 1999, p. 135). The apparent continuities between such knowledge and the emergence of new forms of 'viral' threat with its 'assertive, alien presence, its intrusive otherness' (Dibbell, 1996), merely served to confirm such suspicions.

The political background of the 1960s and the DIY culture of the 1970s encouraged the perception that a new 'underground' had emerged. And there was an obvious enough target to resist, one situated in the assumptions and presumptions of the corporate computer industry itself (Ceruzzi, 2000). But the ludic, puzzle-solving characteristics of the 'geek' or nerd culture that centred upon ostensibly lone projects of technical skill and DIY bravado spawned its own variety of fragmented, highly individualistic collectives; first the phreakers, then the hackers, the crackers and every other kind of information technology group which specialised in 'feat(s) imbued with innovation, style and technical virtuosity' (Levy, 1984, p. 23). More overtly political varieties of hacker, dubbed somewhat inevitably as 'hacktivists' (Taylor and Jordan, 2004), extended their specialised knowledge into direct digital action against those perceived to be undermining the original 'freedom and purity' of the internet. As discussed in Chapter 2, this has turned out to be somewhat of a compromised rebellion. The large number of former hackers who have ended up taking the dollar and working for the security firms is one example of what Taylor describes as 'the enervating pitfalls that face those who seek to redirect the corporate control of technological progress to more human ends' (2000, p. 55). Whilst hacker culture may have drifted into the 'microserfery' (Coupland, 1995) that Taylor fears, it is perhaps in some of the ongoing legacies of struggle that the long-term significance of its cultures may be revealed. The practical techniques, the styles of resistance, the websites, discussion groups and other, more underground meeting points, are all resources which have become available to other identity groups as they seek to perpetuate their projects within the totalising control landscapes of hyperspace.

The increased public perception of hackers as an isolated elite, single-handedly responsible for the dissemination of viral threats meant that their celebration as folk-heroes was always likely to be succeeded by a process of demonisation and a hacker 'crackdown'. A variety of influences seem to have figured in this transformation. Media representations played one (predictable) kind of role. As Taylor (1999) reports, when inane films like *Wargames* (1983) were shown to the US Senate as a way of 'educating politicians about hacking', it was clear that reality principles were not going to play any great part in the shaping of political perceptions here. And in the wake of the post 9/11 security manias, the emergence of the concept of 'cyber-terrorism' furthered the idea that anyone caught using a computer in ways that did not strictly conform to proscribed norms might be a threat. The gradual increase in the use of hacking techniques by criminals sealed their negative image.

As the hacker becomes, with the rest of us, a potential subject of mass criminalisation, it is unclear whether their brief ascendancy as a focus for discussions of the 'culture' of information technology has now passed. But however it turns out, some of the techniques they pioneered for using subverting network control are worth considering briefly before beginning to focus upon the new global criminalities in more detail. The hacking techniques and specific feats of technical expertise I will leave to one side as obvious enough. Instead I will focus upon two more subtle templates they offer for ways in which resistance to control in hyperspace might be marshalled.

Arming for struggle in hyperspace (I): communicative power

Networked interaction offers new forms of coordination in resisting the control potentials of extended space. In particular networks have been argued to produce massing and swarming potentials where, 'innumerable independent forces seem to strike from all directions at a particular point' (Hardt & Negri, 2004, p. 91). The concept of *communicative power*, developed in Habermas' later work, offers one useful metaphor for manifestations of swarming in less overtly conflictual contexts.

Habermas (1996) argued that: 'all political power derives from the *communicative power* of citizens' (p. 17). As Flynn (2004) points out, Habermas' concept owes much to Hannah Arendt's (1958) idea that power always emerges in collective action, something which contemporary communication networks, with their capacities for coordinated telepresence, seem ideally placed to direct. But the translation is not entirely straightforward. For Habermas, communicative power also requires communicative rationality and as such, 'it can issue only from structures of undamaged intersubjectivity found in non-distorted communication' (1996, p. 148). The connectivities of the hyperspatial – especially the internet – do not always seem best placed to provide 'non-distorted' communication but this need not mean that communicative power cannot function according to other, less enlightenment-based senses of rationality. There may be no obviously identifiable meta-narratives which coordinate action across hyperspace, but this does not mean that action remains uncoordinated. Communicative power, once hyperspatialised, might well shape social space outside of the direction of the traditional agendas of globalisation.

A much discussed example of the way in which communicative capacity facilitates the interaction of identity groups has been seen in the coordination of action and protest. Events such as the World Trade Organization meetings in Genoa and Seattle, or the International Monetary Fund's meeting in Washington, D.C. served as early instances of the way the internet could be used to direct protest (Tabb, 2000; Garcelon, 2006). Being able to reach hundreds of thousands – even millions – of individuals with a single e-mail was an obvious and major improvement upon more traditional methods such as posters or leaflets for coordinating action (Townsend, 2002). There was also (at first) the advantage that protest could be organised more covertly, and so could manifest itself in directions that might otherwise be blocked by security forces. Such tactics quickly went mainstream and were adopted in protests at Republican and Democrat National conventions between 2000 and 2001 (*Between the Lines*, 2007), which were all coordinated online. Even fringe US politicians like Howard Dean found themselves able to move to the centre through carefully coordinated uses of communication – to the extent that Dean was at one point described as having been 'invented by the internet' (Wolf, 2004). Republicans were equally receptive to the implications of communicative power and made extensive use of it – particularly in the flood of coordinated telephone calls cited as one of the key reasons for Bush's re-election in 2004, in spite of growing misgivings among the American electorate (Balz & Allen, 2004). More recently, protest against the war in Iraq has been another channel which has both focused and coordinated networked action through sites such as the United for Peace and Justice (UFPJ) site in the USA (Boyd, A., 2003, UFPJ, 2007) and the Stop the War Coalition in the UK (Stop the War, 2007). Together with sites like the Independent Media Center (IMC, 2007) they provide a more organised set of locations for the exercise of communicative power than was available in the mid- to late 1990s, and can offer a truly global coverage of the struggle for human rights or other issues.

It is of course as easy to overestimate the effect of communicative power through 'net-activism', digital undergrounds (Cere, 2007) or nodal politics (Lebkowsky, 1997) as it is to underestimate it. There is often a tendency to see it as a panacea, or for it to be a way in which the old left or right simply attempt to reinvent themselves. On the other hand the swarm formations enabled by complex communicative networks clearly serve to disseminate more fragmented and disparate forms of protest outside of centralised political ideologies. The characterisation of the UK anarchist group Reclaim the Streets as a 'disorganisation' (Reclaim the Streets, 2003), nicely summarises the potentialities in the agency of a multitude, as opposed to formal, hierachically structured bodies of opposition. But a politics (and criminology) of the multitude is at least, in part, a politics and criminology of desire (Deleuze & Guatarri, 1983; Goodchild, 1996), one which implies a potential loss of control that is as frightening to the old (or new) left as it is to the right.

The naivety of thinking that, by simply 'showing up', communicative power can effect change can be seen in attitudes towards the so-called 'flashmob' which has sometimes been seen as a direct manifestation of the political possibilities of swarming. Coordinated by mobile phones or notices posted on websites, a flashmob can suddenly assemble in a particular location, often for no other reason than to confuse the public. Flashmobs seem to have started in the US but quickly spread to a number of different cities where they have usually engaged in absurd or surrealist acts of various kinds. For example, in Rome in 2003, mobbers turned up at a bookshop and began asking for non-existent books. In the US, at a Toys-R-Us store in New York, a mob gathered to stare at an animatronic dinosaur before falling to their knees moaning and cowering every time the dinosaur let out one of its preprogrammed roars (Kornblum, 2003). In the UK mobs have gathered at commuter stations such as Liverpool Street in order to suddenly and silently start dancing in unison to music on headphones (David, 2005).

The flashmob strategy has on occasions been applied in more overtly political ways. In Russia, for example, groups wearing grinning plastic Vladimir Putin masks flashmobbed St Petersburg city centre (Putin's home town) in protest at the Russian presidential election of 2003. And on this occasion there were arrests, with around 15 mobbers detained for causing a disturbance and disrupting traffic near the Nevskiy Prospekt (*St Petersburg Times*,

31/05/05). Overall however the consensus seems to be that, while flash-mobbing has important continuities with the kinds of networked protest forms seen above, its role is mainly apolitical (Rheingold, 2002; Nicholson, 2005). Indeed, many now argue that the phenomenon is all but over – not least 'Bill' (now revealed as Bill Wasik), the self-proclaimed inventor of the flashmob who recently declared that, 'the flash mob, which dates back only to June 2003, had almost entirely died out by that same winter, despite its having spread during those few months to all the world's continents save Antarctica' (Wasik, 2006). Indeed, Wasik suggests that its real message may simply have been to challenge the very concept of swarming itself and the readiness of people to exhibit herd instincts and blindly follow the 'latest' scene or trend. As he points out: '. . . its very form (pointless aggregation and then dispersal), (was) intended as a metaphor for the hollow hipster culture that spawned it' (ibid). The rush by the corporate/advertising world to use flashmobbing perhaps underlines Wasik's point – especially in the recent Ford/Sony 'Flash Concerts' ('sudden' unannounced appearances by groups, circulated by e-mail and mobile) to promote their new Ford Fusion line. This supposed 'new take on the underground "flash mob" phenomenon' (Ford Motors, 2006) was, according to Ford, 'all about challenging people to break free from their reality TV shows and office cubes, and inviting them to come out and play with us' (ibid). Whilst the obituary of flashmobbing is perhaps a little premature (reports of them continued well into 2006 – see for example MacCormack, 2006) their embrace by corporate America is hardly likely to forward Rheingold's view that they represent 'the next social revolution' (2002). At the same time the decentred network swarming potential partly manifested by the flashmob seems unlikely to have run its course. Hyperspatialisation may yet foster broader, more complete productions of its potential.

The pluralisations of journalism and reportage via the growth of blogs – personal postings on the web that reflect upon just about every conceivable topic – have also enhanced communicative power. As well as providing sites for expression and the circulation of ideas, they can also be coordinated in order to express a political point. The 'global bloggers' day organised by the Committee to Protect Bloggers in order to protest against the imprisonment of two Iranian bloggers (Twist, 2005) represents one instance of their potential for communicative coordination. Inevitably other less 'disinterested' collectivities have also sought to exploit the potential of the blog. For example, 'Lonelygirl15' whose confessional videos on YouTube attracted a wide following, was ultimately revealed to be the commercially inspired creation of filmmakers developing ideas for a script (Heffernan & Zeller, 2006). And more blatant attempts to use such personalised spaces for spreading control messages have also appeared. In late 2006, for example, the US government began uploading anti-drug videos on to the YouTube site – resulting in the somewhat surreal scenario of government anti-drug propaganda rubbing shoulders with clips of how to grow and produce marijuana

(CNN, 19/09/06). Naturally business has been equally aware of the potential here (cf. Scoble, 2006). In the United States, there were more than 5,000 corporate bloggers posting commentary for internal and outside readers and 89% of corporations reported that they are either blogging or plan to blog (Flynn, 2006).

Arming for struggle in hyperspace (II): representational power

A great deal of discussion in social science has been centred on the semiotics of misrepresentation and the tendencies of our representational systems to create reality, rather than to model it. The 'indefinite referral of signifier to signified' (Derrida, 1978, p. 25) can be a useful gap to exploit for the powerful, as Marx noted. But it is also clear that a monopoly of representations which approximate reality can be as productive a resource for power as the former, if not more so. As Norbert Wiener put this, 'to live effectively is to live with adequate information' (Wiener, 1954, p. 17). And, extending Wiener's point – to live *without* adequate information is to live in the shadow of those with access to it. We have already seen a variety of instances of how representational power enhances the capacity of control elites – the capacity to more effectively aim missiles and annihilate enemies; the capacity to profile suspect populations; the capacity to increase profit by more effective targeting of consumers and so on. Access to more and better forms of information accordingly signifies a defining struggle within global space under hyperspatialisation.

For some, the seeming expansions in the availability of information are producing a new pluralisation and socialisation of politics. This is not just 'teledemocracy' (cf. Becker & Slaton, 2000), the way that '... citizens and social organizations are able to directly determine at a distance ... what goes on at the political heart of the system' (van Dijk, 2006, p. 102), but also the idea of an open government, transparently producing information for general consumption. Political elites certainly like to circulate the impression that they are in favour of this kind of democratic pluralism and have the technological means to deliver it. Hence the drive by politicians to advertise their 'e-government' credentials through the placing of 'open' information like government statistics and reports on the internet. In the UK the willingness (and capacity) of government to 'share' data has been questioned by a number of critics (see for example Cross, 2007). And a series of costly mishaps in the delivery of 'e-government' has seriously undermined public confidence in its credibility. As Margatts (2003) suggests, blunders in the delivery of online government services such as the computerisation of the Child Support Agency had cost UK taxpayers well over £1 billion by 2003 alone. In the US, claims by politicians to be able to deliver electronic voting have been shown to be similarly expensive and error-prone. Its introduction for the Presidential election of 2004, far from solving the problems in reading ballot papers associated with the controversial election of Bush in 2000, seemed merely to have exacerbated them (Keating, 2004; Schneier, 2004). By 2007 Florida – the State most associated with voting irregularities – had announced plans to return to paper voting, at a projected cost of $32 million. Asked what would happen to the electronic voting machines upon which millions of dollars had already been spent the new State Governor Charlie Crist merely commented: 'The price of freedom is not cheap' (Goodnough & Drew, 2007).

The proliferation of 'user-generated content' also serves to increase the amount of representations/information in circulation. But this is not *just* about being able to view amusing videoclips of pets. As discussed in Chapter 5 such content can offer useful information that enables consumers to make better choices about where to sit on planes, to shop ethically, or to vote tactically (Toynbee, 2001; Biever, 2005). Information points specifically deal- ing with the rights of remote interaction are an important development here. The Electronic Frontier Foundation, for example, founded (in 1990) to 'fight measures that threaten basic human rights . . . (in) . . . the vast wealth of digital information, innovation, and technology that resides online' (EFF, 2005), has a variety of useful online resources. It coordinates and pursues a range of issues connected to digital media rights and provides a forum for enabling lawyers and others interested in digital freedoms to defend cases where these are perceived to be under threat. If control of global space depends, ultimately, upon adequate representation – upon information rather than disinformation – illegitimate uses of it may ultimately be treated as a criminal act as serious as any of the more traditional varieties. But for this to happen hyperspatialisation must generate a genuine increase in the flow of representations which actually do represent.

The hyperspatialisation of global harms

Too close a focus on the effects of transitions in spatial experience upon contemporary global crime raises a danger of being drawn into generalities which bear no relation to *actual* crime committed at the global level. Thus, Findlay (1999), who argued that '. . . time-space compression, which is global- isation, has enhanced material crime relations', was also charged with having '. . . nothing to say about global markets for weapons, drugs, or shady finan- cial products . . . (and failing to) . . . spell out how the collapse of time and space makes the running of transnational syndicates or networks easier' (Lechner, 2000). On the other hand, by compiling endless lists of criminal activities such as transnational financial crime, or illicit flows of drugs across international borders (cf. Van Schendel & Abraham, 2005) there is the risk of overlooking the new spatial pressures upon borders and boundaries that underlie and explain these global processes. If hyperspatialisation does, as it seems to, have an effect on global harm, explanations ought somehow to centre itself upon this fact.

To avoid this impasse I intend to simplify my focus on harm at the global level by way of the theme outlined at the start of this chapter – how the spatial struggles for control within global space, in all its many forms, may reproduce themselves as harm. In fact, since global actors have been partly defined in terms of the way they seek to realise and promote their own 'projects', specific forms of harm fall naturally enough out of this theme. For read in terms of the spatial analytic proposed here, the pursuit of projects by global actors amounts to the capacity they acquire to stably occupy, or to move relatively freely through global space. In so doing, the capacity of other groups to do the same may inevitably be either damaged or destroyed.

For example, destruction of one State by another is an incursion/occupation within global space which permanently limits the capacity of another State to maintain its own project and seems therefore to count as an unambiguous 'global harm'. An aggressive project by one firm to limit the capacity of another to continue trading also seems to count as an instance of such a harm – either for the latter firm, or for the projects of collectives such as the firm's workers, or the local population where it is based. Indeed (as we would hope), this kind of analysis seems to equally apply to the specifically 'criminal' projects of globalisation. For example, the project of trading in drugs globally, or of trafficking people across borders can also be seen as a species of struggles centred upon uninhibited movement through global space. And such acts seem 'clearly' harmful because of the way that they disproportionately impinge upon the projects and identities of other groups. For example, the negative affects of a drugs trade upon a particular social class or ethnic group, the damage to the moral health of a local community, and the destruction to the bodies within that community.

Whilst the basic topography of harmful relations between global actors has been little changed by the advent of hyperspatiality, the way that harm can be dispensed between them does seem partly altered. Obvious examples might include the way in which organised criminal groups can now damage a corporation by an incursive attack upon their database management system or a collective organised around a project of resistance might impair against a State's capacity to act by means of a denial of service attack centring on its airline infrastructures. Similarly such groups might now also succeed in inflicting damage upon a business collective by publishing material on a website which exposes activities it had sought to conceal. In the same way a State might now seek to damage a commercial collective by restricting their capacity to trade globally, or a commercial collective might seek to damage a State by selling arms to some group engaged in conflict against that State.

In the discussion that follows, I will avoid having to consider every kind of harm arising from these new struggles for spatial control, by considering such control struggles in their most simple and primal of forms. On the one hand this is war itself and, as we will see, it is striking how this primal battle for spatial dominance now seems to infuse the character of so many other harmful struggles in global space. For example, we can often see the mindset and character of war in many of the ongoing struggles for commercial advantage, or in the conflicts between identity groups as they seek to establish their own projects over others. In the broadest sense I will consider here, war becomes a new and fundamental kind of struggle for spatial dominance – the extent to which one group can enforce the visibility of others within global space while maintaining its own invisibility from them. Insofar as a struggle to occupy global space is taken to be 'more harmful' than another, it will again be on simple quantitative grounds. Thus, the more projects which an occupation or incursion results in damaging, the more harmful the project which sponsors this will be taken to be. Whilst this is by no means a complete or fully satisfactory rationale, it will at least suffice to facilitate the comparisons required here.

Spatial control: war and cyberterror – destructive incursion at the global level

The practice of war has always had intimate continuities with processes of technological change. As McLuhan once put this: 'every new technology necessitates a new war' (1997, p. 98). Given its role as one of the primary sources of harm within global space and every other, it will be useful to consider what, if any, changes to the practice of war have arisen from hyper-spatialisation. For van Creveld (1991) the transformation was obvious enough – a decline in von Clauswitz's 'conventional' war involving government, governed and armed forces and an increase in 'low-intensity' conflicts not always conducted between States. Hardt and Negri take this kind of analysis still further, arguing that states of war have begun to permeate social relations in ways that resonates strongly with concepts of hypercriminality. They claim that war becomes 'a permanent social relation . . . the primary organising principle of society' (Hardt & Negri, 2004, p. 12), something that Agamben (2005) argued has been unfolding since at least the 1930s.

It has of course always been possible for civilian populations to feel the affects of war in an immediate way, but the twentieth century developed technologies which refined its destructive effects to new levels. Enhanced remote killing techniques, as we saw earlier, produced the aerial bombardment of cities and the threat of a mutually assured destruction by atomic missiles. For the first time in history, World War II produced more civilian deaths than military ones (Clodfelter, 2002), a trend maintained in conflicts such as the Vietnam and the Iraq wars. Even by 1967, Lewin's *Report from The Iron Mountain* had noted that: '. . . readiness for war characterises contemporary social systems more broadly than their economic and political structures which it subsumes' (cited in McLuhan, 1997, p. 116).

But the experience of war as something that must be permanently prepared for is more fully hyperspatialised when its limits 'are rendered indeterminate, both spatially and temporally' (Hardt & Negri, 2004, p. 14). In this context it begins to operate across and within boundaries indiscriminately, becoming as much a war against concepts or practices – the war on drugs, the war on digital piracy, the war on terror and so on – as against spatially proximate clusters of defined enemies. Instead enemies are potentially everywhere and we arrive, as Ericson has recently put this, at 'the blur of a war on everything' (2007, p. 41). The hybrid of the citizen-criminal is further mutated into the citizen-enemy, the enemy 'within' who potentially stands on every corner. In this climate 'war has become virtually indistinguishable from police activity' (Hardt & Negri, 2004, p. 14), a matter of security rather than defence, something which requires '. . . actively and constantly shaping the environment through military and/or police activity' (ibid, p. 20). Traditional concepts of the justifications and conduct of conflict are lost – in particular that of the 'just' war (cf. Neff, 2005) – for states of everywhere wars are not about righting wrongs but the need to prevent threat by any means necessary. One result is that 'justice does not belong to the modern concept of war' (Hardt & Negri, 2004, p. 15).

The manipulation of space has, as Gramsci noted, long been a feature of war within modernity. As a master strategist of war Napoleon was well aware of this, pointing out simply that: 'strategy is the art of making use of time and space' (cited in MacLuhan, 1997, p. 107). His pioneering use of the telegraph network discussed in Chapter 2 was one example of this insight put to practical use. Even more pragmatic was his order that troops should march on the same side of the road, to better focus the speed and movement of his armies (Chandler, 1964). This combination of spatial management and technology in conflicts has now extended more fully into the hyperspatial for, 'all wars today tend to be netwars' (Hardt & Negri, 2004, p. 55).

The use of technology to compress time and space for strategic advantage has of course been a tactic used ever since the first spears or arrows were launched at a safe distance, without the need to engage face to face. But the project of fully automated, remote war conducted without the need to commit ground troops now makes control and domination of immediate physical spaces something increasingly secured by control and domination of extended space. Satellite imaging, pilotless drones or 'robotic' warriors (Cahlink, 2004; Defencetech, 2004) and the shift to battlefield command decisions deferred to computers (USJFCOM, 2006; Wood, 2007) creates a hyperspatialised control net finely tuned for the delivery of lethal or destructive action where human agency is increasingly secondary. The variety of representational powers deployed create '. . . a surveillant assemblage that aims to seamlessly connect sensors, fighters and decision makers' (Haggerty, 2006, p. 254).

Inevitably the effects upon violence and destruction are significant. Under the subliminal logic of war as information management, space becomes an abstract representation of coordinates and positions where killing is replaced by 'deletion' and the 'backspacing' of individual bodies. The reach of the 'cyberterrorist' remains limited when compared to these capacities for lethal spatial control. But as hypercrime transforms criminal into combatant, some semblance of parity is necessary for the resulting war on cyberterror to be credible. Thus, even though in 2003 Congress concurred that there had never been a serious attack by computer upon critical infrastructures, a report for Symantec in the same year (Gordon & Ford, 2003) had concluded that: 'computers and, in particular, the Internet, played a key role in the execution of the September 11th attacks' (p. 4). This 'key role' amounted to no more than the fact that some airline tickets had been booked online, e-mails had been exchanged and some internet searches had been conducted. Indeed, in various briefings the FBI was clear that, despite rumours to the contrary, no 'secret codes inside emails' had been used by the attackers (Conway, 2002). The internet was simply one convenient tool among others that they used – telephones, postal communications (and of course flight training schools). If the internet can be said to have played a 'key role' in the attack then so could almost any other of the tools used – for the taxis that took the attackers to the airport, or the restaurants that sustained them also played their part. But once again 'cyberterrorism' makes for a better soundbite than 'taxi terrorism', 'flying school terrorism' or even 'restaurant terrorism'.

The gap between perceptions and realities here has been played out in terms that frequently approach the absurd. Thus, we find strategic analyses highlighting the possibility of attacks directed at the production of breakfast cereal (Collin, 1996); stories of men arrested for buying 'too many mobile phones' (CBS 15/08/06); individuals thrown off planes for 'speaking Arabic' or wearing the 'wrong' kinds of t-shirt (Haines, 2006; Hampson, 2006; Dunn, 2006); a man questioned under the Anti-Terrorism Act because he had played a Clash song in a taxi (Campbell, 2006) and priests removed from a US Airways flight because they were praying (MSNBC 21/11/06). One plane was even diverted because a women was suffering from severe flatulence (BBC, 06/12/06). While there may well be a 'geometry of terrorism' (Black, 2004) where the reduction of distance plays a role in the capacity of smaller collectives to strike at larger collectives, we should not forget that it is the larger collectives who have (so far) been far better at exploiting it.

War (II): destructive incursions by network – 'cyberwar'?

The hyperspace of networked communication has often been predicted to threaten something even worse than so-called 'cyberterrorism' – full-blown 'cyberwar' itself. Indeed, 'cyberwar' has been proposed as the 'perfect terrorist weapon' (Bodisch, 2002). Accordingly the US think tank The Rand Corporation has argued that cyberwar is not just 'imminent' – but is already underway (Arquilla & Ronfeldt, 1993, 1996), a position partly endorsed within the academic literature (see for example Haggerty, 2006, p. 252). Not surprisingly the military have been especially keen to agree and to highlight the 'dangers' of cyberwar. In 2004, for example, the chief of the Australian Defence Forces announced to a conference on Asia-Pacific security in Sydney that more than 30 countries had 'advanced and aggressive' programmes for waging war by computer. He argued that, 'cyberattacks (would) provide both state and non-state adversaries with new options' – options likely to pose serious threats in the future (Bickers, 2001).

Even where something like a 'cyberwar' can be said to occur, the point at which the actions of individually motivated hackers begin and some State which is backing them ends is rarely clear. One supposed example occurred after the accidental bombing of the Chinese Embassy in Belgrade, when Chinese hacktivists posted messages such as, 'We won't stop attacking until the war stops!' on US government websites (Messmer, 1999). A 'Middle Eastern' cyberwar was also widely reported to have broken out in 2000 when sites run by the group Hezbollah were hit by Israeli 'hackers' in response to a kidnapping of Israeli soldiers. Hezbollah's site was shut down several times while nearly 250 successful attacks against sites for the Israeli Army, Foreign Ministry and Parliament (among others) were apparently made (Gentile, 2000; Trendle, 2002; Denning, 2002). But any impression that this was a conflict attributable only to 'hackers' was put to rest when, in 2002, the Israeli Defence Force was implicated in closing down Palnet, the main Palestinian ISP, rendering internet use in the West Bank all but impossible (Conway, 2002, p. 440).

The fingerprints of government are all too evident in 'cyberwars' once one looks a little deeper. In 2001, Chinese and American hackers purportedly declared another trans-Pacific 'cyberwar' following a collision between a US spy plane and a Chinese fighter (Delio, 2001). After China took the plane and detained the crew, US hackers claimed to have attacked 40–50 Chinese websites, either defacing them with messages about the 'cowardice' of the Chinese government, or taking over the vulnerable ones completely. In response a Chinese hacker group calling itself the Honker ('red user') Union of China threatened retaliation in order, as they stated on their website, to 'defend state sovereignty . . . and deflate anti-Chinese arrogance' (Ward, 2001b). Many Chinese news organisations said on their websites that the idea of 'May Day war' had been widely discussed in newsgroups in China. The attacks sponsored by the Honker Union seem to have been extremely well directed, with one report suggesting that the White House itself was brought down by a Chinese hack-attack for a few hours (Anderson, 2001a). Given the level of governmental control over web activity in China it seems highly unlikely that they would not have given at least some tacit approval to the attacks. In 2007, a shutdown of much of the communication infrastructures in Estonia by a denial of service of attack involving nearly a million computers may also have been sponsored by the Russian government in response to a dispute over the removal of wargraves by Estonia (Halpin, 2007). Meanwhile the US military appears to have an extensive program for using the internet or other communications technology in warfare. For example, the CNA division (Computer Network Attack) – a sub-group of the US Joint Task Force–Computer Network Operations (JTF–CNO or just the CNO) – is rumoured to be developing a range of weapons that use computer networks as methods of attack (Maney, 2003).

In spite of the hype, security experts have been highly sceptical about just how much of a 'cyberwar' many of the incidents which are regularly cited really constitute. As one commented, many were more like 'kids doing graffiti on the subways . . . in real cyberwars, the motivation would be not media hype but true cyber-terrorism. In a real cyberwar, guys won't quit after five days because the press stops covering it' (Delio, 2001). Instead of an apocalyptic information system meltdown, much of what seemed to really have emerged were forms of minor vandalism largely directed against 'unpatched and vulnerable Windows and Linux servers . . . Any ten year old could have defaced these Web sites' (Linux Security, 2001). Wars of information certainly exist – examples can arguably be found in contexts as diverse as the control of the media in Stalinist Russia, attempts by tobacco companies to obscure the dangers of smoking (Glanz, 2000), or the project by conservatives in the USA to remove 'liberal' academics from universities (cf. Jacobson, 2004). But they involve far more than an attack upon a website. And they are rarely solely attributable to the actions of 'a few hackers'.

Netwar and protest

The use of the terms 'cyberwar' or 'cyberterrorist' often obscures more mundane realities of protest or attempts by relatively marginalised identity collectives to get their message across. Thus guerrilla-based conflicts such as the ongoing struggle in Sri Lanka have often been associated with grander narratives of network incursion. In 1998, for example, in what was cited as the 'first known attack by terrorists against a country's computer systems' (AP, 05/06/98) Tamil guerrillas flooded Sri Lankan embassies with up to 800 e-mails a day over a two-week period. Some messages stated specifically that: 'We are the Internet Black Tigers and we're doing this to disrupt your communications' but other than this there was little evidence of anything that could really be called 'terrorism'. Nonetheless, its initial characterisation as the 'first cyberterrorist attack' continues to turn up in various sources, governmental and academic (Wilson, 2003) – even though it was again probably little more than an exploitation of a few poor security patches. Claims by the Sri Lankan government that the Tamil Tigers have engaged in a globally organised network of identity theft to fund their 'terrorist activities' are a new spin on the 'cyberwar' theme (BBC, 24/04/07).

Paradigmatic forms of hyperspatial incursion have arisen where certain groups have felt themselves to be under threat. In particular, the perception on the part of many Muslims that Western nations, most obviously the USA, are attempting to impose or reinforce their own global hegemony has stimulated protest and attempts at information control via communication systems. A group calling themselves 'GForce Pakistan' have again been widely referenced as having engaged in cyberterrorism/cyberwar – even on occasions 'cyber-jihad' (Anderson, 2001b). However, the group appeared to have been mainly protesting against the conflict in Kashmir, and their actions were often little more than hacks on to Indian websites in order to leave offensive messages expressing their protest. Aside from a few 'ultimatums' issued and some expression of support for Osama Bin Laden posted online, they seem to have achieved little else. Nonetheless, one finds reports in the literature of GForce being involved in a 'mideast-cyberwar' (Denning, 2002, p. 6). Their threat to Western interests seems hardly to have been decisive when the worst that could be recorded of their actions was that '. . . some of their defacements included photos and professional quality graphics' (!!) (ibid). In Mexico another much discussed protest that (partly) utilised the internet was in support of the Zapatista uprising of the late 1990s by the self-styled Electronic Disturbance Theater (EDT), an influential force in web 'sit-ins' against various sites (Rolfe, 2005). But the 'cyberwar' or even 'cyberterrorism' label seems even more inappropriate here. Instead, the protest seems to have been better characterised as, 'a struggle against the odds by challenging the containment efforts of the Mexican government' (Froehling, 1999).

Other hyperspatialisations of conflict in global space have resulted in challenges to corporate as well as State interests. Companies such as Walmart, Exxon, Tesco or McDonald's perceived to be extending their spatial reach with morally unacceptable policies increasingly face challenges which utilise hyperspatialisation. Most obviously the communicative power provided by tools such as websites or blogs. In response, companies have frequently appealed to the criminal justice system on the grounds of defamation but the claim made that websites which post arguments against corporate activities make them 'hate websites' (Hale, 2002), seems to be stretching matters somewhat.

Companies are increasingly likely to respond by deploying these new communicative resources themselves – often in the form of rival websites. For example, the oil company Exxon dedicated a section of its website to rebut claims made on the 'StopEsso' website (Stopesso.org) which, it claimed, presented 'a highly misleading view of our company, our views and our actions' (Exxon-Mobil, 2005). Following the damage done to McDonald's in the wake of films such as 'Supersize Me' (2004), companies have even resorted to producing their 'own' news stories in response. The highly critical film, *Wal-Mart: The High Cost of Low Price* (2005) was countered with a 10-page press release by Wal-Mart which described it as a 'propaganda video'. A film, *Why Wal-Mart Works and Why That Makes Some People Crazy* (not funded 'in any way at all' by Wal-Mart) also followed (cf. Garafoli, 2005; Pitzke, 2005). Displaying their commitment to balance, neither film was then offered for sale in Wal-Mart outlets. The balance in hyperspace between good and bad publicity and the gain or loss in global influence which results can be a subtle matter of choice.

Wars between identities

It is an almost inevitable consequence of spatial transformations which promote multiplications of identity that tensions between these identities will also be promoted. And this multiplication produces novel extensions to war. As McLuhan put it: '. . . when our identity is in danger we feel certain we have a mandate for war' (McLuhan & Fiore, 1997, p. 97). These generalised wars of identity, coupled with the technology of the hyperspatial, need not mean overt violence or a resort to weaponry (though neither is ruled out). It can also express itself in the uberpresent sense of a necessity to 'stand out or be assimilated'. As suggested in the previous chapter, the lack of some kind of presence in hyperspace – something that promotes our individual or collective significance – increasingly signals a new form of death – media obscurity (Bigge, 2006; Cassidy, 2006). 'Celebrity culture' becomes a euphemism for the trench warfare of endless self-promotion as Myspace, Facebook and the homepage promote a droning, low-intensity conflict between cults of a million, million selves, where survival involves simply 'not being voted out'. In a real sense such wars, simultaneously individual and collective, form the new sound of the multitude at war with itself.

Other less self-indulgently rooted conflicts between identities derive from deeper differences in belief and come with a greater likelihood of overt acts of damage or destruction. A typical example is the conflict between groups who hold that abortion is acceptable and those who reject this. Both have been eager to use remote communication to promote and extend the reach of their views. Sites like wechooselife.net or armyofgod.com promote an aggressively anti-abortion line, with gruesome photographs which they claim depict aborted foetuses scattered among liberal helpings of biblical pronouncements. They offer links to promotional sites for individuals like Paul Hill, executed for shooting a doctor and his bodyguard at an abortion clinic in Pensacola in July 1994. On his (still extant) site Hill argues from beyond the grave that his killing 'would uphold the truths of the gospel at the precise point of Satan's current attack (the abortionist's knife)' (see Knapp, 2001). Countering these are a range of 'pro-choice' sites such as www.abortionrights.org.uk or www.naral.org. This enhanced capacity to coordinate and publish their beliefs can feed group identity by promoting a sense of their collective project. Unfortunately it may also contribute to the certainty that their views are irrefutably correct and that they therefore have the 'right' to enter into conflict to defend it. Up to seven abortion workers were shot dead in Florida in the late 1990s by such groups and though Hill has now been executed himself, his website continues to argue that, 'if you believe that abortion is lethal force you should uphold the force needed to stop it' (Army of God, 2007). In much the same way a host of other identity groups centred on race, national identity, religion, morality and more now use the new communication networks to transform their collective projects into struggles of position and continuity within global space.

Business and governance – old symbiosis or new spatial tensions?

The idea of a symbiotic dependence between the interests of States and commerce has been widely explored in views such as Poulantzas (1969). For example, the colonialism of the nineteenth century, which vastly globalised (Western) State power, was usually a direct outcome of the commercial activities of chartered trading companies such as the British and Dutch East India Companies, the French West India Company and so on (Chaudhuri, 1965; Carlos & Nicholas, 1996; Armitage, 2000). This '. . . unspoken possibility of adversity for business . . . as an all-pervasive constraint on government authority' (Lindblom, 1977, p. 178) continues to exert its force. But while collusion in control is the more predictable arrangement between States and commerce, hyperspatialisation has sometimes produced tensions in this relationship – with the right to monopolise remote interaction producing a new site for potential conflict.

The practice of war again provides a fruitful source for examining this. And here we increasingly find strange hybrids of States that behave like businesses, and businesses that behave like feudal lords, a hybridisation seen perhaps most starkly in the way in which war now becomes pervaded by business logics, and business logics by war. Of course ever since the arms business became a globalised industry (Krause, 1995), there have been economic pay-offs for commerce in the perpetuation of war. Translated into the contemporary context it is sometimes hard to see where the marketing ends and the killing begins. Such themes were played out at conventions held in London between 2003 and 2005 for Europe's largest arms fair, the Defence Systems and Equipment International, where a wide selection of high-tech material for conducting war was available. Against the usual background of the ambience of a trade fair – flashy audio-visual presentations and pumping music – delegates (many of them ostentatiously decked out in military insignia of dubious regimes) were able to browse and select a variety of murderous remote killing devices. Protecting delegates of the 2005 fair against 'protestors' cost the UK taxpayer around £4 million (they were apparently unable to protect themselves, in spite of the plethora of control technologies available for sale). But not one of the sizeable police contingent assigned to guard the event were apparently able to spot the stall for TAR Ideal Concepts Ltd of Tel Aviv. Offered for sale in their brochures, *Riot Control, Homeland Security* and *Company Profile*, were stun guns and stun batons – weapons all banned in the UK (Thomas, 2005). The presence of Israeli companies in this global defence market is no accident. Naomi Klein has recently pointed out how the practice and expertise of hyperspatialised war has now transformed Israel's economy with increased exports of devices such as unmanned drones, electro-sensitive barrier technology, biometrics, surveillance products and air passenger profiling and prisoner interrogation systems. Together these represented around $1.2 billion of its $3.4 billion worth of defence exports (Klein, 2007) in 2006/7, now making Israel the fourth largest arms exporter in the world – ahead of the UK.

The irony of an (apparently legitimate) sale of items within a jurisdiction where they are meant to be illegal is only one among many raised by State–commerce hybrids in the context of war. Another is the way that a conflict may be commercially sponsored by a country's industries even when the political masters are officially opposed to it. The contradictions in New Labour's 'ethical foreign policy' – which apparently permitted it to continue to trade in arms to oppressive regimes in East Timor – have been a widely criticised example (see for example Pilger, 1999). Another permutation is for weapons to be sold by the commercial part of the hybrid which end up being used to kill soldiers from the State part – the so-called 'boomerang' effect. In 2003, for example, arms were traded by the US to over half of the regimes in the developing world (13 out of 25) defined as undemocratic in a Human Rights report published by the US State Department itself. Over $2.7 billion worth of arms were transferred to these countries under the Foreign Military Sales and Commercial Sales programs (Berrigan *et al.*, 2005). And of the last *seven* conflicts where US soldiers have been engaged militarily, from the ongoing wars in Iraq and Afghanistan through to Yugoslavia (1998), Haiti (1994), Somalia (1992) and Panama (1989), their opponents deployed military hardware manufactured by US businesses against them (Berrigan *et al.*, 2005; Glanz, 2006).

Examples of profiteering in the conflict in Iraq provide an even starker instance of dubious collusion between State and corporate sectors in global space. Between 2002 and 2004 Exxon-Mobil's revenues rose by nearly $100 billion to around $300 billion – resulting in some of the largest company profits in history (Exxon-Mobil, 2004). To many it seemed hard not to attribute at least some of this increase to defence contracts arising from the war. Meanwhile the company Halliburton (which notoriously included Vice-President Cheney as one its former employees) appeared to be writing its own rules in the wake of the conflict. Their performance in carrying out the RIO-2 contract to restore Iraq's southern oilfields was openly criticised in a series of US congressional reports (cf. Waxman, 2006) which concluded that it had been 'overwhelmingly negative', while defence contract auditors challenged $45 million of costs as unreasonable or unsupported. Many other companies awarded contracts in Iraq appeared to have followed Hallburton's lead in skimming off costs with the result that, according to one senior CPA adviser, the Iraq occupation turned into a 'free-fraud zone' (Regan, 2005).

One the one hand then, the new global state of 'Empire' described by Hardt and Negri (2001) appears to be a plausible analysis of the developing relations between State and corporations in global space. On the other hand tensions also arise – especially between States and foreign commercial collectives. A particular source of contention has been where a country has sought to use its intelligence-gathering powers against foreign businesses in direct competition with its own. For example, just at the time when communications technologies were widening and complexifying spatial experience in the late 1990s, the European Parliament began to conduct a series of investigations into allegations that the United States had been using a satellite surveillance network for industrial espionage (BBC, 05/07/00). France had already begun its own inquiry here, complaining that the highly secret Echelon system which can intercept millions of telephone, fax and e-mail messages every day (Campbell, 2000) was increasingly being used to pass on information to American companies, in order to give them a commercial advantage over their European rivals (Furnell, 2002). The report which eventually emerged established that, in spite of official denials on both sides, Echelon did at least exist. Originally set up to monitor communications during the cold war it had become clear that the network was also being used for the monitoring of private or commercial messages. The report ultimately backed away from specific accusations that the Americans were using the network to gain unfair economic advantage. But unofficial suspicions remained and part of the rumoured network, the Bad Aibling station near Munich, was closed in 2001.

In 2006/7, it further emerged that the US had been systematically monitoring private financial transactions conducted both by European businesses and citizens. On this occasion however there appeared to be evidence of disturbing levels of collusion between the USA and European commerce. The European Commission and its data protection office accused the Belgium-based company SWIFT (Society for Worldwide Interbank Financial Telecommunication) of supplying the US Treasury and the CIA with names, account numbers and sums involved in various transactions and also pointed the finger at the European Central Bank and other financial institutions which it said had done nothing to prevent the information abuse (Traynor, 2007). In spite of protests by SWIFT and its members that they had been threatened with subpoenas by the USA, the Commission concluded that they had all broken European data protection laws through their 'hidden, systematic, massive and long-term transfer of personal data to the United States Treasury in a confidential, non-transparent and systematic manner' (Ballard, 2006).

'Normal' commercial rivalries may also cause tensions with States in the governance of global space. As far back as the telegraph, industries engaged in the production of hyperspatial technologies have been especially vigorous in exploiting their monopolies in ways perceived to be contrary to 'market principles'. One example of this dynamic can be seen in responses to the activities of Microsoft following their initial failure to spot the commercial potential of search engines. In their attempt to retrospectively 'fix' this problem, and win back some of the ground that companies such as Netscape had gained, Microsoft's tactic was to bundle its own search engine – Internet Explorer – as a part of operating systems like Windows 98. Because of Microsoft's dominant market share, users were then more or less compelled to acquire Internet Explorer whenever they acquired a new PC. In so doing, Microsoft not only laid itself open to the criticism that rival commercial search engines – and Netscape in particular – had been put at an automatic disadvantage. With full portal control, users could also be endlessly redirected to Microsoft-related products and services. A variety of legal actions were launched in the US against this blatant attempt to enforce a commercial monopoly, most significantly threats to break up the company by the Department of Justice. But after several years of inconclusive skirmishing actions were ultimately withdrawn, leaving Microsoft to effectively dominate access to hyperspace by networked computers – at least so far as US jurisdiction was concerned. (See *Washington Post*, 2002–2005 for a detailed account of these extended legal battles.)

Matters did not progress quite so smoothly for Microsoft in Europe, where a record anti-trust fine of 497 million euros ($640 million) was imposed upon the company in 2004 by the EU (COMP/C-3/37.792 Microsoft) for failing to allow its software to run with media players such as Apple's Quicktime. The ruling required Microsoft both to provide technical details to server software makers and to offer a version of Windows without Media Player (McCullagh & Kawamoto, 2004). In January 2005 Microsoft said that it would comply with this (Vise, 2005), but not only did the company drag its feet over implementing the requirements, the launch of the new operating system Vista threatened to provoke a further set of actions. ECIS, the lobbying body which represents IBM, Nokia Corp., Sun Microsystems Inc., RealNetworks Inc. and Oracle Corp. as well as Linux operating system businesses such as Red Hat Inc. complained that many features of Vista violated the ruling. In particular the new XAML language it uses was seen as 'a plot to replace HTML and to help Windows applications dominate the Internet' (Sutherland, 2007).

Public v private hyperspaces

New conflicts with commerce have emerged as State and local administrators attempt to open up wider access to the hyperspatial by providing free wi-fi interchanges. Previously the privilege of the well-heeled few, initiatives to improve access have emerged in several public contexts. One programme, pursued by the city of Philadelphia, aimed to provide wi-fi coverage over an area of 135 square miles by attaching wireless antennae to lampposts, an idea cities such as New York, Taipei, Calgary in Canada and Leiden in Holland have sought to emulate. In the UK, London boroughs like Westminster have plans to extend wi-fi access to all residents (Shifrin, 2006) with plans for the City of London as a whole also underway (Tanner, 2006). But the various cable and communications companies (keen to maintain their monopolies) have been less than happy with these moves to help citizens benefit from the knowledge economy. In response to the moves in Philadelphia, companies like Verizon and Comcast lobbied and backed a bill in the State of Pennsylvania which effectively blocked the provision of municipal wi-fi networks by requiring States to offer the right to run the network to the incumbent provider (Lake, 2005). As the idea of public wi-fi has become increasingly popular the corporate stance has shifted its tone, emphasising its commitment to the forging of 'public/private' partnerships – in reality a way of running a two-tier service. In other words, basic access for the less well-off, 'special services' for the fee-paying subscriber. The award of the San Francisco municipal wi-fi contract to Google and Earthlink in 2006 underlined exactly this kind of problem, with the free (Google-run) network likely to run at a much slower speed than the paid-for (Earthlink) version (Orlowski, 2006).

The battle to control full spectrum access to hyperspace is likely to develop along a number of fronts. And the commercial world appears to be capable of being more than vindictive if it does not get its own way. In Louisiana, for example, the provision of a free municipal wi-fi service in New Orleans set up in the wake of Hurricane Katrina appeared to upset BellSouth, the local network provider. BellSouth retaliated by closing down a Louisiana call centre (at a cost of around 1,300 local jobs) and withdrew an offer to donate a damaged building for housing the New Orleans Police Department, though the provider of course denied that there was any connection here (Krim, 2005). Meanwhile, BellSouth has been one of the prime movers in the attempt to impose 'web-charging' – something that would fundamentally change how people use the internet. The idea, also favoured by other network providers such as AT & T, is that access would again be 'prioritised', this time according to the 'space used' on the network – with those who pay, again likely to get faster and better quality forms of access. In response, a collection of lobbying groups, from consumer protection organisations to large search engine and content providers like Yahoo and Google, have been pressing legislators to retain what is termed 'network neutrality' (Stern, 2006). Whereas earlier networks such as the telephone did *not* prioritise between interactions across them, the argument that certain content (such as film streaming) 'takes up more network space' than others, threatens to allow hardware providers to affect and to shape content for the first time. At present the question of net neutrality is largely one that will affect American users of the internet, since the European Commission is committed to the concept of equal access (Warner, 2006). But without legislation, network neutrality in Europe depends upon its 'tacit acceptance' by the former European telecom monopolies like BT or Deutsche Telekom. Even if some form of network neutrality *were* to be given legislative protection in either the USA or Europe, the issue of equitable uses of hyperspace is likely to continue to resurface in other contexts, with the advent of Web 3.0 or developments in newer higher speed networks just some of the ways in which this spatial conflict is likely to continue to resurface.

Hyperspace and the representation of presence: visibility and invisibility

Harms generated by struggles for spatial control can also be seen in more subtle conflicts which centre upon presence in all its increasingly redistributed forms. The role of surveillance technology in marking presence is a topic that been well discussed in the literature (see Norris & Armstrong, 1999; Lyon, 2001; Haggerty & Ericson, 2006; Marx, 2006, among many others). In fact such discussions signal the importance of a deeper issue here – how the visibility and invisibility of presence within space is now managed, and by whom. As diverse identity collectives seek to distribute their presences more extensively within global space, it is surely no accident that, simultaneous with these wholesale redistributions of presence, identity itself starts to become an issue around which criminality is constructed. The issue does not so much relate to the *having* of an identity, but to the having of the *right kind* of identity. And as we saw in Chapter 4, this effectively translates into the having of legitimate *identification*. In terms of the hyperspatial, identification is not just used to mark static presence but, by way of the traces it leaves in transactions, databases, interactions and so on, to mark its distributions. Asymmetric rights of access to these traces and variations in the requirement for identifiability increasingly demonstrate how invisibility becomes a privilege in one context, a crime in another (see Marx (2001) for some typical rationales which support the need for visibility and others which justify the right to invisibility).

It is interesting to note how invisibility has often been associated with deviance. In the *Republic*, Plato tells the story of the Ring of Gyges which has the power to confer invisibility but which, as a consequence, corrupts the user absolutely. In the story, a peasant in the service of the King of Lydia who finds the ring seduces the King's wife and then assassinates him before seizing power for himself. Plato is clear about the potential relation between invisibility and deviance arguing that: 'if you could imagine anyone obtaining the power of becoming invisible and never doing any wrong . . . he would be thought . . . to be a most wretched idiot'. Thus, invisibility appears to lend itself naturally to deviance for, 'wherever anyone thinks he can be safely unjust, there he is unjust' (1998, II). In H. G. Wells' *Invisible Man*, a similar association between deviance and invisibility is made repeatedly. The mere possession of the power of invisibility is enough to not just tempt the main protagonist towards minor acts of deviance – but towards the point, ultimately, of murderous insanity.

Control of visibility – read as unambiguous identifiability – thus becomes not just a priority, but a control obsession. We find no clear precedent for this in earlier regulatory systems, and where it did occur it was more often a retrospective control – to mark where some criminal act had already been committed. For example, amputation, branding or tattooing were common practices by which criminal identities were made universally visible (cf. Burrus, 2003). The transition towards fully transparent systems of identification seems to have begun with modernity itself. Identity shifted from the status of privilege to that of a requirement as the passport, once issued by a sovereign as a mark of 'favour', began to be granted by the Secretary of State from 1794 (Torpey, 2000). And other more extensive proposals for fixing identity were also proposed. In his *Principles of Penal Law* Bentham argued that the only way for States to keep track of citizens was to have everyone tattooed at birth, so that, as Fichte put it, '. . . each citizen shall be at all times and places . . . recognised as this or that person' (cited in Caplan, 2001, p. 49). Bentham's proposal for total visibility may have been technically unrealisable at the time, but newer scientific techniques involving biometrics along with proposals to genetically screen all citizens at birth (Ashbourn, 2000; Caplan & Torpey, 2001; Nanaveti *et al.*, 2002; HGC, 2005; Smith, 2007) seem to make State control of identity ever more practically feasible.

In turn, the redistribution of our bodies and its hybridisations with technology provides for an even wider, 'extra-biological' set of traces that can be collected. The way that the body now 'extends outward into data' (Brown, 2006, p. 231) was examined in Chapter 3 and can be seen in traces as various as online purchases, use of e-mail, bank accounts, or a person's participation within an online community. No matter how disguised, or routed throughout different servers, exchanges and access points, remote access leaves a trace.

The 'having of presence' within databases, commercial, security, insurance, health or otherwise is not just something now expected of us by State or corporate agents. It also becomes a social norm, something we all expect of each other. For example, whereas the possession of a mobile phone was still a novelty in the mid-1990s, within less than 10 years a failure to possess one had begun to attract increasing levels of social disapproval (Bautsch *et al.*, 2001; Geser, 2004). One recent ethnographic survey indicated that individuals increasingly tend to shun members of their peer groups who do not possess a mobile phone (Context, 2006). And while there may not (yet) be a legal requirement to possess mobile communication devices, a variety of other social pressures such as the disappearance of public telephone booths, the requirement to supply mobile phone numbers in many transactions or to provide availability for job interviews, are making it something which is increasingly impossible to avoid. The association of deviance for those who do not conform to the requirements of visibility begins to take many forms.

One of the starkest instances of the drive towards complete visibility was the proposed US project for TIA – or 'total information awareness'. Advanced (inevitably) in the wake of 9/11, the project aimed to use a combination of techniques from data-mining through to biometric controls as a way of providing information to the State about almost every kind of recordable citizen activity, no matter how trivial (Safire, 2002). High-level meetings between Admiral John Poindexter, one of the developers of TIA and the data-management company Acxiom relating to data storage and collection methods, suggested the collusion between State and private sectors in shaping this new landscape of visibility (EPIC, 2005b). Funding for the project was withdrawn in 2003 – even though the Defense Advanced Research Projects Agency (DARPA) had changed its name to the more sound-bite-friendly 'Terrorism Information Awareness' programme because the name might have 'created in some minds the impression that TIA was a system to be used for developing dossiers on U.S. citizens' (Singel, 2003). But despite the demise of TIA there are plenty of other programmes for citizen visibility that continue to emerge. For example, the amount of data collected by the TIDE initiative (Terrorist Identities Datamart Environment) – which, for the first time, combined information on foreigners and US citizens into a single database – quadrupled between 2003 and 2007. Yet about 50% of the time a name was triggered on the TIDE watch list, it seems to have involved a misidentification. Even Catherine Stevens, the wife of Senator Ted Stevens of Alaska, was apparently frequently delayed at airports while airlines checked with TIDE to ascertain whether she was in fact Cat Stevens – the singer now known as Yusuf Islam, who has been denied entry to America for 'unspecified reasons' (DeYoung, 2007).

The irony is that, in an age where control of information increasingly brings control of space, visibility need not even be total for control to be maintained. As the Prince of Darkness himself put it in response to Faust's questioning, 'Omniscient? No, not I . . . but well-informed' (cited in Whitaker, 2006, p. 166). Within the continuum of hypercriminality and the citizen criminal hybrids it generates, the mantra that goes, 'if you have committed no crime you have no reason to hide' gets subtly translated to, 'if you have a reason to hide, you've committed a crime'. The basic flaw in this reasoning is rarely appreciated. For the inference:

'if not p then not q'

is NOT logically equivalent to

'if q then p'

as any logician worth their salt will point out. Yet the inference that deviance *can* be read simply from an unwillingness to be visible becomes a guiding rationale of control – even though it is an invalid one. During the 'terror' which followed the French Revolution, Robespierre put the argument like this: 'I say that anyone who trembles at this moment is guilty; for innocence never fears public scrutiny' (cited in Zizek, 2007). As we now know, the 'terror' which motivated Robespierre's warning had nothing to do with any potential insurrection by citizens against the French State, but was a terror waged by the French State *against* its citizens. We might wonder if much has changed.

The transformation of global harm

This chapter has (by necessity) focused upon a very small subset of examples issuing from the spatial conflicts global actors may engage in, conflicts which create various orders of damage to both the space and its actors. Though most forms of harm within global space can be modelled in these spatial terms there are, as conceded, many other instances plausibly associated with hyperspatialisation that have not been discussed in detail here. These do not just relate to overtly criminal behaviours such as the transnational actions of criminal gangs but to other forms of damage – in particular, the emergence of a global underclass, marginalised economically and excluded from the advantages of the hyperspatial itself.

Enhancements in remote interaction certainly seem to directly correlate with an increased concentration of economic advantage in global spatial clusterings. Technology plays an increasing role in shaping the flow and generation of wealth in highly striated ways. Thus investment and capital flows are increasingly determined by the speed of computing and the way that accompanying financial networks are locked into privileged economies. Indeed, the asymmetric capacity to utilise spatial technologies can even extend to the manipulation of the natural world, so producing outcomes which have their own unique taint of criminality. For example, the growth in the representational power of information technology means that bio-tech companies are now able to contemplate the development of so-called 'genetic use restriction technology' (GURT) which makes crops produce sterile seeds. At a stroke, the dynamics of global agriculture might change, forcing millions of poor farmers into a new order of economic dependence. For while such seeds might be resilient to certain diseases, farmers would no longer be able to hold any back for re-sowing the next year and would instead be compelled to purchase them from the bio-tech companies (Lean, 2006). Elsewhere the drive to hyperspatialise economies such as China and India produces a range of cultural and economic degradations from rural peasants in Tibet, to urban slum dwellers in Mumbai (cf. Mehta & Shepherd, 2006).

The relationship between struggles for control over movement and occupation within global space and harm is nowhere clearer than in the tendentious issue of global mobility. The emergence of a global mobile elite – skilled or valued individuals able to move across borders in ways beyond mobility underclasses (Sklair, 2001) – can be seen in a variety of contexts, from work and migration through to the globalisation of tourism (Urry, 2001; Pickering & Weber, 2006). It is clear that all of these mobilities are as much related to new forms of legitimacy in movement as to the simple fact that air travel is often beyond the economic capabilities of the very poor. I will be looking at the regulatory character of these technologies more fully in the next chapter, but we can conclude this chapter by reflecting again on some of the barriers that are currently going up throughout global space. The impression often given is that such barriers have always been there, and that space has always been divided in this way. This is, to say the least, somewhat disingenuous. As Bauman has put this: 'it is only when the border posts are being dug and the . . . guns are aimed at trespassers that the myths of borders antiquities are spun' (Bauman, 2001, p. 17). The translation of physical borders into the hyperspatial – borders that serve to limit various orders of social capacity to do with property, the personal or the local – merely extends this process. And as the hypercrime mindset also pervades global space, mobility becomes suspect at every level of movement – requiring what Bowling and Weber describe as punitive 'migration policing' (2004). But the 'other' is not only located across an ocean or in a dark corner of the globe – it is here, outside the walls of the gated community under the gaze of the CCTV camera.

The irony of all this is that such restriction may not only harm those who are prevented from travelling. There is evidence that the global economy itself may also be damaged. For example, one study found that worldwide GNP could be more than doubled if there were no immigration controls on the labour market (Hamilton & Whalley, 1984) while only a 3% increase in immigration quotas could boost world GNP by 0.6% (Walmsley & Winters, 2002). But the logics of the new strategies of 'access' or 'area denial' (cf. Krepinevich et al., 2003) are not always rational – their end is merely to occupy space. Within global space the harms which result take on, by definition, their most pervasive and widely threatening form.

Chapter 7

Shaping space

The regulatory ecologies of hyperspace

> The geometrical properties of space are not independent, but they are determined by matter.
>
> (Einstein, 1920, XXXII, p. 1)

Adequate regulation is obviously essential if the potential advantages of capacities like telepresence are not to be subverted for selfish gain. Yet temptations to exploit control are always likely to arise where there are both plausible rationales for its necessity and new sets of resources for its implementation. Predictably enough, such temptations appear to have been irresistible so far. An obvious question then arises; are the growing quantity and variety of regulatory mechanisms directed at hyperspatial interaction helping to maximise its positive benefits or are they also creating new sets of harms in their wake?

In this chapter, instances of some of the more obvious regulatory influences upon such experience will be explored. The analysis will again be primarily centred upon the production of these within communication networks though, as before, this will be taken to serve as a kind of shorthand for what is unfolding within the other kinds of network which complexify spatial experience. Preconceptions about the role of a 'cyberspace' have, as elsewhere, had their effect upon perceptions of this process. Perhaps the most obvious of these has been the conclusion that special problems for regulatory systems are now posed, requiring unique approaches and measures. We are told, for example, that 'cyberspace is resistant to regulation by any particular sovereign' (Williams, 2006, p. 145) so that 'the jurisdictional and substantive quandaries raised by border-crossing electronic communications' need to solved by 'conceiving of cyberspace as a distinct "place" . . . by recognizing a legally significant border between cyberspace and the "real world" ' (Johnson & Post, 1996). The apparent result is that 'our current crime control model cannot deal effectively with cybercrime' (Brenner, 2007, p. 14). Problems raised by hyperspatialisation, for example, the issue of transjurisdictionality – how national laws can function across international boundaries – have clearly raised important questions. But demarcating a 'legally significant border' between reality and virtual reality is certainly not how criminal justice systems have elected to deal with them. Nor should criminologists. Just as our experience of space across narrow and extended contexts remains ontologically continuous, albeit altered, so too does the application of the law and the readiness of policing systems to enforce it.

In what follows I intend to view regulation as a dynamic, rather than a static force in the ordering of spatial experience, in particular as something that has an active function in the *shaping* of social space. Though the ideal of perfect regulation is to create a smooth space of connected control, as Deleuze and Guattari point out: 'the forces at work within space continually striate it' (1988, p. 500). Not only should we therefore '. . . never believe that a smooth space will suffice to save us' (ibid.), we should pay special attention to the striations in space regulation produces. For however well intentioned they may be, it is in these shapings of space that the real traces of the regulatory order are to be found, for better or for worse.

Whatever the illusions about the 'place' that was cyberspace (Hunter, 2003), any idea that remote interaction was unregulable has been widely shown to have been an absurdity (Lessig, 1999; Biegel, 2001) – not least by the steady flow of legal initiatives which have followed the development of the internet. Indeed, far from posing problems for regulation and control, hyperspatialisation seems to have significantly enhanced its potential resources. Worse than this, the spectre of 'joined-up' criminality, of the 'hypercriminal', that the allatonceness of remote interaction raises has set a process of legislative panic into motion that challenges many rights and protections previously taken for granted. In addition to law, what Ericson (2007) has called *counter-law* (following Foucault, 1977, p. 221), begins to seep into civic life eroding many of our traditional protections. As regulation moves from enclosure into an increasingly networked and open-ended phenomenon, much enhanced control capacities become available – resulting appropriately enough in what Bogard (1996) has referred to as 'hypercontrol'. But to emphasise any single factor – computer code, policing or law – in the context of these increasingly pervasive regulatory formations is to miss the wood for the trees. In order to counter any such temptation, I will posit a regulatory *landscape* to situate complex interactions between these different orders of control. The pressure of counter-law, where it seems that 'the legal order must be broken to save the social order' (Ericson, 2007, p. 26) emphasises how visualising such a landscape in terms of mechanical lists of laws, old or new, is simply inadequate. Rather it is only in the cumulative *shape* of the space in which these legal productions are embedded that the real intent and the extent to which they are effective can be grasped. The underlying question for this chapter will therefore be: how does the contemporary control order attempt to shape the hyperspatial?

Codes, rules and representations

A tempting and obvious way of considering the role of regulation in the 'information age' has been to fix upon computer systems and the formal languages that constitute their 'architectures'. If one has been seduced by the cyberspace idea – that a *distinct* space of interaction somehow results from these formal codings – the assumption that this space is then a technologically determined one follows naturally enough. Lessig (1999) which, on a superficial reading might appear to have endorsed such a form of technological determinism, in fact made it clear that other kinds of regulatory constraints governing interactions across the internet must also figure. Constraints such as the market (or commerce), social norms and the law itself exert a distinct force, but are:

> ... plainly interdependent. Each can support or oppose the others. Technologies can undermine norms or laws; they can also support them. Some constraints make others possible, others make some impossible. ... Norms constrain through the stigma a community imposes; markets constrain through the price that they exact; architectures constrain through the physical borders they impose and law constrains through the punishment it threatens ... the same model determines the regulation of behaviour in cyberspace.
>
> (Lessig, 1999, p. 88)

Whilst there is much here that is plausible enough, criticisms about detail have been raised. Not only is the nature of each constraint a little vague, the key question of *how* they interrelate to produce their regulatory landscape is left open-ended. As Wall (2005) put this: 'Lessig's underconceptualisation of the four constraints ... threatens to oversimplify the relation between them (which he) tends to portray in functional, rather than relational terms' (p. 324). This compartmentalised functionality perhaps reflects an assumption derived from the American constitutional model – that separation between legislative, judicial, commercial or other regulatory functions is more than an ideal, or a purely conceptual construct. Missing too is any real sense of the *disproportionate* effects of some constraints upon others, disproportionalities which signal a crucial regulatory force about which Lessig's model has little to say – the subliminal effects of power. For the production and practice of law is no more a neutral process than the 'market' is an invisible hand functioning to bring about perfect balances between supply and demand. Both are manifestations of social orders where power and control are implicit, if not overt constraints. Prices can be fixed and firms will operate in their own interests, just as a conservative judge will legislate differently from a liberal one.

The relationship of law to government is also left hanging – States get no mention as distinct constraining forces upon regulation within Lessig's model, perhaps again due to an assumption that the judicial function really does operate independently of State influence. In a State where Supreme Court judges are transparently political appointees this is a surprising oversight. In the wake of the erosions of an independent judiciary by the Bush government it begins to appear simply naive. As Ericson points out, 'extraordinary circumstances' declared by governments can be all too easily used to bypass the judicial function transforming it into an 'instrument of suspicion, discriminatory practices ... denial of rights and exclusion' (2007, p. 209). And as Agamben (2005) has suggested, suspension of the law for the convenience of sovereign power – the *iustitium* of the Roman Senate in the face of an external threat – is increasingly a norm, not an exception within the contemporary order.

Yet while the complex interrelations between regulatory constraints cannot be overlooked, nor should more simple and general ways of interpreting them be ignored. Viewing constraints upon remote interaction in terms of purely technological architectures may be simplistic, but architecture can also serve as a broader metaphor for space-shaping practice, one with its roots in a variety of more informal social 'codes'. Seen in these more general terms, code can offer an alternative strategy for modelling regulatory practice within the hyperspatial. To appreciate how, we need to return to the notion of representation. Though the code which structures the architectures of information technology is based on formal symbolic languages, such languages are not *isolated* symbol systems but are locked into complex levels of representational practice. As a formal symbol system, a computer language must represent physical machine states in ways that facilitate computation but is also coordinated with higher order representations which are meaningful to us. For it is of course largely by means of such higher order representations (words, pictures, sounds) that we are able to interact with computers at all (Cummins, 1989; Mitchell, 2002). As McLuhan and Fiore put it, 'the hand that filled the parchment built the city' (1967, p. 48) and code, as one among our many representational practices, is ultimately owned by us, rather than functioning as some independent abstract force. Analysis of formal languages – from Frege and Church's early insights (see for example Church, 1941; Frege, 1967) or the great work by Alan Turing (1936) through to more recent work on 'deviant' or fuzzy logics (Haack, 1996) – has been essential to the successful practical development of information technology. So far as I know, however, there has been little discussion of the 'sociology' of such languages – partly because they are normally supposed to be independent of any taint of the social. Yet every formal computer language, whether it be Fortran, ASCII, C+ or higher order authoring softwares such as Photoshop, are as much *cultural* artefacts as any chisel or opera. As such they serve as much to reveal the presumptions and prejudices of the societies that created them as they do to facilitate computation. This does not make them purely subjective or culturally relative constructions. Part of the key to understanding the representational power I have alluded to throughout is that formal or informal representations can be as equally to do with *making* things work as they are with *obscuring* the way things work.

So codes, even in their most restricted form as formal machine languages, are already social in virtue of the fact that they function as representations made meaningful to us, but which also make tools as various as a DVD reader or a car transmission system *function* under our control. In so doing they also echo the way regulation as a whole shapes a social landscape. For a formal code to 'work' in the context of computation it must produce non-random outputs – which is really to say that it instantiates an *algorithm* – the rule-governed processes which are at the heart of computation. Algorithms, as formally understood, are rule-governed procedures directed at some task which, given an initial state, terminate in a defined end-state. But the class of rule-governed procedures need not be limited to purely *formal* algorithms. In a looser sense algorithms can be seen as a kind of 'recipe' – a set of steps which, if followed correctly, produce a desired outcome. Following the recipe to make a chocolate cake is, in this sense, not so different from computing a function though it can have different 'solutions' – just as the social algorithm for taking the Underground from Oxford Street to Leicester Square can be achieved by more than one set of rules.

The important point here is that the concept of a rule-governed process bridges the apparent divide between formal and informal shapings of practice, between regulation rooted in a mathematical architecture and that in a social architecture (Winch, 1958; Bloor, 1997). This does not mean that social life simply *reduces* to the operation of rules. It is obvious, for example, that we could never be 100% sure about precisely which rule was in operation during any social process. As Wittgenstein puts this: '. . . not only rules, but also examples are needed for establishing a practice. Our rules leave loopholes open, and the practice has to speak for itself' (1972, 21e, p. 139). But in speaking for itself, a practice always suggests the possibility of *some* constraint, however open-ended, that underlies it. It is in these constraining possibilities that the shapings of the social space which govern movement there are revealed.

Regulatory geometries and rule-based ecologies

Regulatory practice therefore 'produces' social space in a sense, just as (conversely) differing 'curvatures' within social space provide evidence of differing regulatory formations. Wall's critique of Lessig's modalities of constraint seems to have something of this in mind – particularly in his suggestion that each constraint be seen as 'spaces or sub-architectures' so that 'legal spaces are quite different to social spaces, which are different from market spaces' (Wall, 2005, p. 325). Lessig's modalities then become, '. . . different types of spaces each with their own architectures (which) . . . enable us to demonstrate the complexity of the relationship between law and social action' (ibid, pp. 324–325). But having introduced this potential association between regulatory practice and spatiality, Wall then rather leaves the idea hanging. It is clear that he sees rules as something implicit within these spaces in that he *equates* them with the (undefined) notion of a 'sub-architecture'. But the failure to develop this idea adequately leaves it unclear how a shift to 'legal' or 'market' space does any better than Lessig's model in linking together the functioning of diverse regulatory forms. Wall's claim that legal spaces are 'quite different' from market spaces just as both in turn differ from 'social spaces' further complicates matters unnecessarily. It is not really clear that these spaces are distinct at all – a legal space is every bit as much a 'social space' as is a market space. As suggested, there are conceivably different *orders* of social space – this book has theorised them in terms of relative proximities. And it is also seems plausible that regulation operates more or less formally across these different social spaces (being sent to bed early by one's parents represents an informal form of control within local/domestic space while that exerted over global space by the International Criminal Court is a formal one). Given that regulation is not separate from these spaces, the question then is how the complex interactions between competing influences of rules at differing levels of formality act together to shape social space. And what this ultimately comes down to is the extent to which one rule is subject to *exceptions* in the face of another rule. I will return to this important qualification shortly.

This notion of spaces shaped by rules takes us naturally back to the concept of a 'regulatory geometry'. This need not be axiomatic for, as Wittgenstein decisively showed (1953, pp. 185–243), any social practice may be consistent with descriptions of more than rule. Indeed, as Dreyfus (2006) points out, caution is required in assuming that rules are *consciously* being followed at all. Instead, social action is shaped only by rule-like *influences* – what Dreyfus calls 'copings'. For example, a chess master can be, '. . . *sensitive* to the rules of the game even if he is not following the rules consciously or unconsciously. Even if he can't remember the rules, they nonetheless govern his coping by determining what looks permissible' (Dreyfus, 2005, p. 9). In the same way, Bourdieu explains how his (less than elegant) concept of a 'structuring structure' can function within: 'Systems of durable, transposable dispositions . . . which generate and organise practices and representations that can be objectively adapted to their outcomes without presupposing a conscious aiming at ends or an express mastery of the operations necessary in order to attain them' (1990, p. 53). Such dispositions centre upon 'the schemes of the habitus, . . . (which) . . . function below the level of consciousness and language' (1984, p. 466), and in this way 'the habitus, the product of history, produces individual and collective practices, and hence history, in accordance with the schemas engendered by history' (1977, p. 82).

It is here that the concept of 'degrees of exception' can enter to explain the way a wide variety of rules interact to produce their overall effects. Rules which admit of limited degrees of exception impose little choice upon what we ought not to do (we cannot will boiling water not to scald us, however much we want it not to, just as we cannot easily delete our tax records, as much as we would like to). But other rules allow for greater exceptions, presenting us with contexts where we can more easily *choose* not to respect a constraint. Thus, the rule governing incursions to property expressed by a 'Trespassers Will Be Prosecuted' sign can easily be ignored.

The useful metaphor of a *landscape* introduced earlier provides an easier way of picturing the complex interweavings of regulatory practice generated by laws and constraints of varying degrees of exception. It is only taken as whole that the shape of a landscape can be understood, something manifested in the overall limits upon our capacities to move and behave that result. Just as natural features such as a marsh, a desert or a mountain range may restrict movement through a space, so might social norms like an incest taboo, a belief in a divine command or a gender structure shape our social movements by limiting the range of actions available to us, without ever definitively ruling them out. The distinction between *natural* law (*jus naturale*) – which derives from natural processes or which relates to 'self-evident' truths about the social world (such as equality), and *positive* law – which relates to regulatory structures developed by humans to regulate their world, invokes something of the differences here, though the fit is by no means precise (George, 1992).

But the metaphor of a landscape needs a further ingredient for it to serve as a way of conceptualising this totality of regulatory influence. For blockages and barriers like a mountain range (or a 'Keep Out' sign) allow only for *static* or preventative regulation. But behaviour is of course shaped by reactive, as well as preventative formations. The mere presence of a law does not shape movement on its own since laws, like 'Keep Out' signs, can be ignored. A reactive feature, such as a policing response is also required for the regulation to function. For example, an electric fence may have a sign that partially shapes movement by warning what *would* happen if it *were* touched. The shock that we receive should we ignore the sign and touch the fence then adds reactivity to precaution in shaping behaviour. One approach to theorising these more dynamic or responsive ingredients of the social world has been to appeal to *biological* concepts, in particular the capacities of systems to 'self-regulate' by instantaneous internal adjustments. Durkheim, for example, famously saw social order in terms of homeostatic feedback loops where a society as a whole acts as 'a regulative force [which] must play the same role for moral needs which the organism plays for physical needs' (1952, p. 248).

Parsons' structural functionalist model also explained regulation (especially in its more reactive form) in terms of dynamic responses or self-adjustments. For example, in the case of deviance:

> ... there have developed in our type of social system ... mechanisms which, within limits, are capable of forestalling and reversing the deep-lying tendencies for deviance to get into the vicious circle phase which puts it beyond the control of ordinary approval-disapproval and reward-punishment sanctions.
>
> (Parsons, 1951, pp. 319–320)

The Chicago School famously extended biological analogies by treating social landscapes, most obviously the city, as a set of interrelated dynamic processes which resembled an *ecology*. Thus:

> The structural growth of community takes place in successional sequence not unlike the successional stages in the development of the plant formation. Certain specialized forms of utilities or uses do not appear ... until a certain stage of development has been reached, just as the beech or pine forest is preceeded by successional dominance of other plant species.
>
> (McKenzie, 1924, p. 297)

Their kind of ecological model was of course more focused on the way that factors within social spaces interact to produce deviance, rather than regulation. And the ecological analogy was directed at a specific site of social interaction (the city) rather than sets of social practices as a whole. But there seems no reason why the idea of an ecology cannot also be used to model regulation more generally. Indeed social *practices* – like regulation – might even offer a more productive locus for the application of ecological concepts than fixed empirical contexts like cities. Indeed, many of the criticisms the ecological model received were based precisely on the fact that what worked for Chicago failed to apply to many other kinds of city or social space.

If such intuitions are plausible, the concept of *regulatory ecology* emerges, a landscape where the 'geological or tectonic' effects of deep-shaping regulatory mechanisms combine with more immediate or transient regulatory forms (cf. Hosein *et al.* (2002) for an approximation to this idea). In these more naturalistic terms, reactive elements in a landscape become its 'dynamic' regulatory forms – the bee that stings when bothered or the bramble that pricks when it is disturbed. The full effects upon individuals of this interplay between the reactive components of a regulatory landscape and its more static components are of course much more complex than can be described here. But, in the absence of exhaustive formal quantifications of these interrelations such a metaphor does at least allow us to picture some ways in they might be played out. A regulatory landscape is thus the dynamic and striated system of the distortions within social space, one that manifests itself in the capacities for movement available to social actors of different orders. How far the regulatory ecologies of the hyperspatial simply perpetuate those of more proximally based forms of human life will now be considered.

Regulation in space and hyperspace: computers and exceptionlessness rules

The widespread deference to the view that 'technology is a more effective regulator of cyberspace than laws, norms or markets' (Williams, 2006, p. 147) is justified in various ways. For example, there is the apparent ability of technology '. . . to alter behaviours, its ability to be shaped, its rapid adapatability, its ex ante approach, its wide reaching scope, its sensitivity towards criminal and sub-criminal activity and its less visible approach to social control' (ibid). But the underlying rationale for seeing technology as the more 'natural', or effective regulator of remote interaction actually hangs on the more basic point just identified – the degree of exception any rule appears to possess. Thus, 'technological rules' – those instantiated in a computer architecture – appear to be privileged and different because they involve the kind of rule which admits of *no* exception when following it. In so doing such rules appear to remove the component of choice associated with 'human' forms of regulation. To be blocked from entering a website by a piece of code is to be filtered out by the merciless constraint of programming, a regulatory logic seemingly incompatible with the variety of constraints realised by 'Keep Out' signs, laws, or a policeman on the corner. But there are at least three flaws in this line of reasoning.

First, it assumes that there really *are* such things as 'exceptionless rules' – at least outside of purely abstract contexts. Whilst valid inferences in logic appear to follow rules necessarily (that is, without exception), this is only because the rules are part of an abstract system which is isolated from particular content and where every term and operation has been constructed in accordance with strict principles of proof. Yet even here there have been questions about how 'necessary' or exceptionless the rules of logical form really are (cf. Margolis, 1995). Debates about the exceptionlessness of mathematical rules have been even more contentious (cf. Dummett, 1959; Wright, 1984). And when it comes, not just to the rules of computational systems, but to computational systems embedded in physical machines, the assumption that some system of exceptionless rules is thereby manifested is even more tenuous. Computation itself has been demonstrated to be a process that can be realised in systems (like distributed networks) where formal rules play little part in the production of representations (Horgan & Tienson, 1989; Aizawa, 1994). Moreover computation may not just be open to exception because of fallibility in *social* terms (for example, in virtue of bugs in programming) but because natural processes at work in a computer may also subvert its smooth functioning. Thus, exceptionlessness may fail as much through a random fluctuation in an electron's path, as through an error in engineering.

A second problem for the faith in the relative exceptionlessness of computationally embedded rules compared to socially embedded varieties is the indubitable fact that code is something that can, and has been transgressed against during numerous instances of system hacks. Whilst it is true that the skills required to do this are arcane or in the hands of a privileged knowledge elite so, it might be argued, is knowledge and application of the law. We do not regard the law as a totally distinct species of regulation, or as something less impervious to subversions or transgressions because it is arcane, or in the hands of a privileged knowledge elite of barristers and judges. In a direct and obvious way techniques such as hacking subvert code in ways which prove that, as Wittgenstein long ago argued, rules are not just 'there' to be broken – they are, by our very conception of them, consistent with more than one way through the front door.

The claim that speed of response – the 'rapid adaptability' mentioned by Williams above – differentiates computational rules from socially embedded ones can also be questioned. Just as the instantaneousness of a negative social response to some act, or the immediacy of a bee sting do not set them apart from other natural phenomena, the speed of computer architectures proves no categorial distinction from other regulatory forms. Like bees, electric fences, or disapproving glances, computer architectures function as one part of an overall system which shapes social space.

The point again is that while regulation may function with varying degrees of exception and varying degrees of immediacy across telecommunication or transport networks, all of them are ultimately species of *social* network. Each is therefore connected to regulatory systems governing these other social networks and is formed by the presumptions and norms present there. As Greenleaf pointed out:

> Architecture is not neutral, but embodies choices and values, it reflects the interests of the codewriters and its legitimacy as regulation can and should sometimes be questioned.
>
> (1998, p. 594)

As the variety of ways in which hyperspace can be accessed becomes wider and more integrated with the social world, perceptions of fundamental differences between 'regulation in a technical context' and 'regulation in a social context' seem likely to diminish. In the long run, the apparent exceptionlessness of rules governing computer interaction will seem no more special than the regulatory technology of a door, or a fence, or a road sign. The real question of interest will, as usual, consist in who owns or shapes their ecology.

Regulatory ecology and rule diagrammatics

An obvious approach towards modelling the combined effects of these regulatory forces is *diagrammatically*. Foucault specifically invoked the diagram as a way of mapping regulation – with his construct of the panopticon serving as a:

> *Diagram* of a mechanism of power reduced to its ideal form; its functioning, abstracted from any obstacle, resistance or friction . . . represented as a pure architectural and optical system.
>
> (Foucault, 1977, p. 205)

In turn, Deleuze saw how this device could be generalised to produce an explanatory resource that was capable of charting a:

> Map of relations between forces, a map of destiny, or intensity . . . which acts as a non-unifying immanent cause which is coextensive with the whole social field.
>
> (Deleuze, 1988, pp. 36–37)

The utility of the diagram in representing functional relations is witnessed in the way it is reproduced across many disciplines as a methodological resource. The functional map of an engineering diagram, the spatial map of a geographical location, or the map of a 'phase space' used by physicists to model the dynamic possibilities of a system, all clarify and map key relations between forces in different contexts, in much the same way Deleuze describes. In criminology, diagrams have also been utilised for various purposes – most obviously in the representation of 'crime hotspots' of the kind discussed earlier or for the Chicago School's model of relations within an urban ecology. But diagrams can also map more abstract relations of interest to criminologists. Foucault's diagram of the panopticon represents one example. Elmer's diagram of personal information flows and their ownership which allows us to 'trace the everyday data economy in which habits, routines rhythms and flows are digitised for the purposes of control' (2004, p. 47), represents another.

This at any rate is how I intend to make sense of such relations as they are extended in hyperspace. Whilst there are many metrics which might serve to compose such a diagram I aim to keep matters as transparent as possible by utilising just three coordinate scales in the subsequent analysis. First, and following the reflections of the previous section, it will be useful to consider a scale which locates the relative *formality* and *informality* of any regulatory formation within the landscape, thereby situating them with respect to the important idea of the 'degree of exception' it (ostensibly) admits. Thus, at one end of this scale would stand the rules which admit of *few* exceptions (mathematical algorithms such as computer code being one example). At the opposite end might be located more informal constraints with multiple exceptions such as a request, or a set of guidelines.

A second coordinate frame will relate to the *visibility* of control functions. Visibility is a crucial determinant of how 'natural' a regulatory form seems and this is important because not only can this affect how legitimate we perceive it to be, but also how easy it is to subvert it. Technology may be a more effective regulator of online interaction because of 'its less visible approach to social control' (Williams, 2006, p. 147) but this raises profound questions about its social acceptance. As discussed in the previous chapter, these more 'dispersed, pervasive, fluid, and invisible' controls (Simon, 2005, p. 1) are increasingly a factor in the shaping of the hyperspace we inhabit. More invisible modes of control such as RFID transmitters or a credit profile can then be contrasted with overt or *transparent* ways of shaping space – the law counting as a notable example – with all the perceived legitimacy this position on the scale then brings.

By combining these two coordinate scales a basic and primitive diagram for mapping a regulatory ecology then emerges:

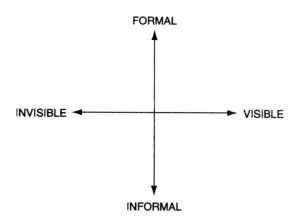

Though primitive, the diagram not only serves to map most of the regulatory constraints so far discussed but, as desired, to render some of their inter-relationships more transparent. Indeed, rather than seeing them as *distinct* forces it becomes clearer how they act together to form a continuous land-scape of control. For example, the diagram below indicates how a technical architecture or code shapes the landscape in terms of a form of control which blends formality and invisibility. In this way it constrains movement within hyperspace in a manner that admits of few exceptions and in (largely) imperceptible ways.

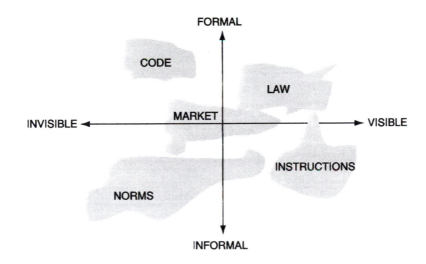

But as the diagram also suggests, while the invisibility of formal architecture may be greater than that possessed by the law, it is perhaps of a lesser order than many (more informal) social norms – even though their effects are just as visible in resulting social behaviour. The norm that once required women to be skilled in needlework was coded nowhere, nor written down in any form, but was evident enough in its particular limitation on certain forms of female social expression. By contrast the market can be seen to shape movement within social space in more mixed ways, constraining action both visibly and invisibly, with constraining functions that have formal and informal aspects. Thus, rules governing sales of shares may be very formal and open to public scrutiny, while deals done behind closed doors may be largely invisible and operate highly informally, through the logic of the nod and the wink. By contrast a set of instructions (say, for assembling a piece of furniture) will usually have a more formal character and (since they need to be accessible), tend to be visible. Of course none of these constraints operate according to precisely defined territories but rather overlap irregularly. In particular, the way they have been depicted above is only suggestive and is certainly not intended to serve as any definitive territorialisation of their functions.

A third possible scale that will also be utilised in the analysis to follow might relate to the temporal dimension and the *reactivity* of a constraint – the degree to which it is more or less immediately responsive to transgressions. And by adding this third scale we then move from a two- to a three-dimensional model of regulatory forces of the kind seen here:

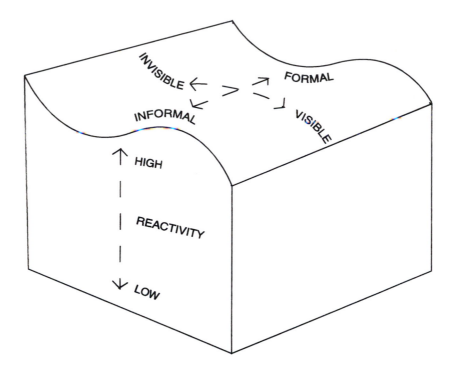

At the highly reactive end of such a coordinate scale might be placed a response such as the shock administered by an electric fence, in contrast to more long-drawn-out responses – for example, a wait for execution on death row – which stand at the other. In turn the diagram might situate a mechanism like the police within a more immediately visible part of this regulatory space than something like a 'force field'. At the same time the constraining power might operate more covertly than an electric fence (should the police be in 'plain clothes' or undercover).

In discussing a regulatory ecology for hyperspace I will therefore restrict analysis to the space produced by forces under these varying scales of formality, visibility and reactivity. And even though the effects of each will be discussed separately, the assumption will always be that they (and others not discussed) generate controls in coordinated and cumulative ways.

Borders, psychological boundaries and nomadic space

What partly defines a hyperspace is the new routings it seems to offer through space, routings seemingly able to bypass many of the constraints of traditional boundaries. This takes us back to a supposed difficulty for regulation produced by advanced forms of remote communication – the problem of *transjurisdictionality*. That is, the way in which the reach of legal and policing structures based on national boundaries may now be subverted by criminal behaviour operating across and beyond these political divisions of social space. Yet while borders and boundaries which base their legitimacy upon natural features, or traditional ethnic divisions may have become harder to sustain, the idea that what results are unregulable, or even unregulated spaces was, as we have seen, suspect from the outset. And as it has become clear that the supposed problems of regulating the internet created by a 'borderless world' of cyberspace were nothing other than rhetorical dead-ends (cf. Goldsmith & Wu, 2006), an inverse conclusion about contemporary jurisdiction arises.

For what also seems plausible is that cross-border control by States and other control elites may actually have become *easier* rather than harder. Indeed, rather than dissolutions to distinct jurisdictions serving to obstruct or block control, such dissolution can serve to further its reach. As we will see in the sections to follow, beyond the traditionally enclosed territories of a State, a more unified, smoother space of jurisdiction begins to emerge, one that goes beyond political boundaries in far more comprehensive ways than previously.

But while political and control elites are finding ways to deal with violations to jurisdiction caused by violations to geographical boundaries, this is not to say that other problems do not also arise. One relates to an observation made by Simmel about the underlying origin of boundaries – for these are 'in a deeper sense ... still only the crystallisation, or spatial expression of ... psychological limitation processes which alone are real' (1997, p. 142). And in this way: 'it is neither countries, nor plots of land, neither urban districts nor rural districts which bound each other to each other, rather it is their inhabitants or proprietors who exercise this reciprocal effect' (ibid). Thus while the temporary irritations of a few cross-border anomalies of jurisdiction may be tidied up, other more psychological forms of social fall out may still be present. In particular, this world of interconnected mobilities appears to threaten the historical security provided by boundaries formed from natural features such as mountain ranges and their subsequent reifications into political borders. Not only can threats enter more easily through an 'open' space, nomadism itself – that form of social life most suited to 'unbounded' and (literally) 'unsettled' space – appears to make an unwanted reappearance into history. This is not just about new forms of deviant migrations – though as the public pressure to police them more coercively suggests, that seems bad enough to us. Nomadism also presents a more perplexing threat, for migrants (like settlers) at least possess a logic which is comprehensible to us. Migrants see connections between *places*, something expressed in the way that, as Deleuze and Guattari put it, 'migrants go from one *place* to another' (1988, p. 385). By contrast, the logic of the nomad is dangerously different, for they, 'just go from one place to the other as a consequence and material necessity:

since the beginning, places are considered by them as stages in their way'
(ibid). In other words, the testing of borders by hyperspatiality, with all its
remote mobile communication tools, its global travel networks and cross-
border flows transcends simple problems of jurisdiction and points to a
deeper kind of dread – the fear of spatial anarchy. And this has inevitable and
profound consequences for the kinds of regulatory systems we now
construct.

For Deleuze, the failure to recognise the influence of the open spaces of
nomadism represents no less a problem than a failure of historical understanding itself:

> History is always written from the sedentary point of view and in the
> name of a unitary State apparatus, at least a possible one, even when
> the topic is nomads. What is lacking is a Nomadology, the opposite of a
> history.
>
> (1988, p. 23)

As hyperspatialisation begins to re-problematise this project, our original
sublimation of nomadic life into the projects of enclosure produce various
forms of compensation. One response reflects Florian Znaniecki's claim
about 'social' sublimation – the idea that it produces 'psychological conform-
ism' (1925, p. 169). Here it manifests itself as the general acceptance that
there really is a 'problem of the border' in the regulatory context, requiring
that we 'really do' need more regulation to cope with it. Another possible
response is more disturbing. For, as Freud later argued:

> After sublimation, the erotic component no longer has the power to bind
> the whole of the destructiveness that was combined with it, and this is
> released in the form of an inclination to aggression and destruction.
>
> (1991, p. 475)

In this sense, it may also be possible to see the new violent geopolitics of
spatial control, of military interventions, and aggressive monitoring of space
as reactions to boundary violations in the geographic sense. Either way,
as our original sublimation of nomadic life is challenged by the influences of
time-space compression and the open space of the network, legal transjuris-
dictionalities may be among the least of the problems which result.

Transjurisdictionality and borders in agency

As Simmel counselled, the social-psychological basis to boundary formation
cannot therefore be overlooked if we are to understand our responses to the
violation of boundaries. In turn, erosions to other 'more natural' boundaries
produced by hyperspatialisation may generate their own kinds of problems of

transjurisdictionality. Given the discussions of previous chapters an obvious instance of this would seem to lie in the way that, by their spatial redistribution, erosions to the legal culpabilities determined by bodily boundaries may be produced. For if, in the redistribution of bodies, *agency* also becomes redistributed where then is jurisdiction to be directed towards? This has been a far less discussed 'problem of transjurisdictionality' in the geographic sense, but there seems to be at least two contexts where it might make sense.

(i) Dissolutions to agency by location

The direction of a jurisdiction usually requires a culpable body with some definitive location. But there seem to be several ways in which hyperspatialisation might intervene to blur this. An instance relates back to geographic factors – most obviously in terms of where the offence was held to have occurred. For example, in 2005, an attempt was made by a Saudi citizen to sue the *Wall Street Journal* in London for libel. However, under a landmark ruling by the House of Lords, it was decided that publishers on the internet could not be sued in the UK *unless* there had been 'substantial publication' in the UK (Gibb, 2006). Since it was judged that very few people had read the article in the UK, sufficient ambiguity about the location of the offence remained for the culpable body (in this case the *Wall Street Journal*) to avoid any prosecution.

Agency may also be blurred by even more pronounced forms of distribution across the network itself. One example can be seen in a series of puzzles which have arisen over whether to hold an ISP, a website or an individual accountable for actions deemed to be criminal. Various rulings have attempted to clarify this, though ambiguities remain. In the 1991 case of *Cubby v CompuServe* for example, CompuServe were sued because of a defamatory message that had appeared in a local newsgroup (Halberstam, 1999). The court ruled in their favour when they argued that the posting had been carried out by a third party who had been employed to edit information on the newsgroup and that their position was therefore similar to a newspaper vendor – someone without control over the content of the newspapers they sell. But on another occasion, in the similar case of *Stratton Oakmont v Prodigy* in 1995, the ruling was that agency was distributed in another way. Though Prodigy had been careful to employ individuals who would remove any defamatory material from the local newsgroup it ran they were still found to be the publishers of this statement (EFF, 1995). Since Prodigy had specifically advertised itself as a 'family orientated computer network', it was held to have 'assumed responsibility' and as an agent, to therefore be culpable for the content it provided.

(ii) The dissolution of agency by automation

A second permutation of boundary dissolutions to bodies that may cause problems for jurisdiction can be seen in the rise of so-called 'bot-nets' – networks of computers, usually infiltrated by malware which makes them open to remote control (Schneier, 2006; Wall, 2007, p. 130ff.). One potential difficulty is that, since bot-nets are an outcome of a *sum* of network activity, any location for agency disappears further into its connections. Of course, there is, further down the chain, some person or persons responsible for setting up the bot-net – the bot 'herder' as they are sometimes known – and court and policing responses actions have been accordingly directed at them. In 2005, for example, a net of around 100,000 bot computers was stopped by the arrest of three men in Holland for running it (Lemos, 2005). But longer term, one can envisage reasons why, as automated crime networks become more common, this strategy might become more difficult. One problem is that disguising bot-nets, already easy because of their network context, may become still easier. For example, the use of peer-to-peer software not only disguises the net itself, but can make the herders harder to find. In turn an increased use of encryption to mask the net (and therefore the herder) from detection software is also predicted – indeed, many in the computer industry argue that such techniques are already widely in use (Evers, 2005). As automated processes become more common and the herders disappear further and further into the background, it is possible that identifiable chains of human command may become so distant that definitive individual culpability becomes almost imperceptible. One solution – increased levels of legislative pressure applied to ISPs and other providers to take responsibility for bot-nets (Mimoso, 2005) – may simply compound difficulties. As ISPs find ways to evade legal comebacks, locating the chains of culpability required to establish agency is likely to become even more obscure. And there is a final problem relating to automation itself. For what happens where a 'rogue' or out-of-control bot-net that has been set up for legal or innocent purposes (as an experiment, for example) does not behave in ways originally intended? In particular, who (or what) is to be held guilty if it damages an essential system, or causes a crash which results in fatalities, especially if a court of law can find no definitive evidence of original intent for this to happen?

Temporal boundaries and jurisdiction

Problems for regulation can arise as much as from the destabilisation of certain temporal borders as from the spatial ones. In turn, what might be called, following Virilio (1986), the 'dromology' of regulation – the speed at which reactive mechanisms can be marshalled and deployed within a social space – then becomes a central question. The dilemma seems to operate in at least two ways. One relates to the speed in which *available* mechanisms for regulation and control may be outstripped and their temporal boundaries thereby subverted. The pace of a bot-net which outstrips the response speed of control architectures provides one example, with some attacks lasting less than four seconds (Espiner, 2006b).

A second example of the problem for the temporal boundaries of regulation relates to the production of new control mechanisms. The 'perpetual present' of the hyperspatial which is so '. . . outrageously puffed up by all the commotion of our communication technologies' (Virilio, 1997, p. 137) – what Walter Benjamin called 'now-time' – can produce ethical and political disjunctions between technology, social opinion and praxis with the exponential increases in networked interaction simply adding the most recent complication (cf. Berleur & Brunnstein, 1996; Hamelink, 2000). The temporal 'shrinking' of evolution via genetic manipulation, the outpacing of natural ecologies through technical ones or even the enhanced availability of pornography in the face of every attempt to restrain it, all represent instances of regulatory dilemmas raised for control in the face of speeded up time. Either its responses are simply outpaced, doomed always to lag behind, or its responses are too quick. Made insecure by the inadequacy of their dromological inefficiencies, regulatory systems literally 'shit themselves' – producing waste in the form of a host of ill-considered, poorly conceived and ineffective responses (cf. Bataille, 1991). The moral panics of hypercriminality and the (seeming) incapacity of jurisdiction and policing to cope may then serve to transform the states of exception described by Agamben (2005) into a 'diarrhoeatic' flow of control. Like the child on the roller-coaster or the condemned man on the scaffold, regulatory systems open their bowels in the face of a dromological logic which outstrips them, excreting law in panic (or pleasure?) as the limits to what can be ultimately be controlled are sensed. A desire to 'bury' the evidence is another kind of response. The finding by IT security firm Defcom in 2003 (*Observer*, 27/04/03) that over two-thirds of organisations did not report computer attacks is typical. In the same way as shame in *excessive* legal excretion is sometimes covered by 'burying' it away from public scrutiny, so the failure to excrete *enough* control can be a source of shame.

These more subtle problems of jurisdiction are not much discussed. But however the range of boundary issues posed by hyperspatialisation are spun, it would be wrong to think that it is only criminal behaviours which benefit. It is important to be clear how security and regulatory systems are equally extended so that, as will now be considered, *advantages* as well as disadvantages accrue to them as a result. I shall therefore now move to examine in more detail the ingredients of the regulatory ecology being constructed within hyperspace, commencing with what is usually considered to be the most fundamental of regulatory forms – the visible and formal mechanism of the law.

Formal and visible (I): regulation of movement and the legislative landscape

Aside from Johnson and Post's (1996) and Lessig's well-reported contributions, numerous authors (see for example, Loader, 1997; Koepsall, 2000; Biegel, 2001; Spinello, 2003) have reflected upon the changes that new communications systems – most obviously the internet – appear to have forced upon the formal and visible regulatory mechanism of the law. Whilst analysis here has too often centred on the pseudo-issue of how to legislate for the 'virtual' or for 'cyberspace (Mnookin, 1996; Huber, 1997; MacKinnon, 1997; Drucker & Gumpert, 1999; Williams, 2006), others have paid closer attention to the way that law, like other regulatory mechanisms, becomes 'distributed' across space in new ways (Brenner, 2004). By and large, law has proved itself to be amenable to the regulation of a hyperspace. As to whether the laws directed at remote interaction are as balanced or 'lawful' as they are in the case of proximate interaction is another question. As we will now see, the answer often appears to be that they are not.

Legislation governing networked communication – and in particular computer-based interaction – has been a predictably haphazard affair in the UK. The history of laws governing telegraph, telephone or older hyperspatial networks has always been piecemeal – reactive measures rather than the product of any overall vision, many of them centred on moral controls (Katsh, 1989; Lloyd & Mellor, 2003). In the case of online environments the story has followed this general pattern, though as the hyperspatial has appeared to increasingly produce the 'hypercriminal', important differences have also emerged. What was at first adaptation has tended to become over-production and a concern with preserving or extending existing structures at the expense of other rights (cf. Akdeniz *et al.*, 2000). Together with the USA. the UK and other European countries have responded to the (apparent) temporal and spatial subversions of the dromology of law by producing legislative mechanisms which attempt to keep hyperspatial interaction firmly within the remit of the State or commercial governance. Thus, as the following (selective) table of legislations suggests, while some attention has been paid to rights of interaction such as privacy and free speech, the balance has been very much towards the maintaining and extending of control.

	Law	Sample scope/provision
1984	Telecommunications Act	Prohibited the sending of obscene material over public telephone networks.
1988	Criminal Justice Act	Made possession of indecent photographs or 'pseudo-photographs' of children an offence.

(continued overleaf)

	Law	Sample scope/provision
	Copyright Designs and Patents Act	Storage in any electronic medium without the consent of the author or the relevant rights holder made to constitute an infringement of the primary right of copying.
1990	The Computer Misuse Act	The first specific UK legislation directed at 'unauthorised' computer uses such as intrusion into systems, or their use in criminal acts.
1994	Criminal Justice and Public Order Act	Further restrictions on the creation or possession of child pornography.
1998	Data Protection Act	Protection of rights over data storage.
2000	Regulation of Investigatory Powers (RIP) Act	Created NTAC (The National Technical Assistance Centre), able to monitor internet traffic for various (unspecified) reasons. Other rights of monitoring set out.
2001	Anti-Terrorism, Crime and Security Act	Strengthened surveillance laws – especially in relation to the internet.
2005	Identity Cards Bill	Enforced requirement to possess an electronic identity governed by a centralised database of biometric information.
2006	Police and Justice Act	Doubled sentence for hacking from 5 to 10 years. Banned 'hacking tools'.

Of all of these legal initiatives it is really only the 1998 Data Protection Act that can be said to have offered any significant new 'rights' to individuals in the context of remote interaction. Otherwise, almost every other piece of legislation listed here has extended the capacities of UK control systems in various ways – even where (such as in the protection of children online or the introduction of identity cards) the law has been ostensibly related to enhanced public safety.

The haphazard introduction of the Computer Misuse Act, for a long time the key piece of legislation governing online behaviour in the UK, is emblematic here. The legislation itself was only enacted after an acquittal by the House of Lords of two hackers who had been prosecuted unsuccessfully under the 1981 Forgery and Communications Act – a process that ended up costing over £2m in legal aid. Equally culpable, it might be argued, were British Telecom for having so underestimated the requirement for network security that the hack (a relatively simple one) took place at all (Higney, 2006). Though the Act quickly became out of date with the development of communication technologies – not least the internet itself – the Home Office was continuing to protest its adequacy as late as 2004, arguing that it only needed basic amendment to deal with specific issues such as denial of service attacks (see Home Office, 2004d).

But the 'light touch' in improving the gaps in the Computer Misuse Act argued for by the All Party Internet Group (APIG, 2004), was not manifested in its less than transparently named successor, The Police and Justice Bill (PAJB). Instead, a range of draconian new sentences were made available – in particular a large increase in the length of prison sentences for hacking offences. Aside from its failure to set out legislation for the 'information age' in ways that represented a broader public interest, the Bill also manifested clear signs of a failure to comprehend even the basic security requirements of the IT industry. Its new offence of 'making, supplying or obtaining articles for use in computer misuse' was criticised for being so poorly worded that it would make the use of just about any kind of tool required to bypass security measures in order to repair system faults (such as password recovery software) a potentially illegal act (LibertyCentral, 2006). Crucial clauses in the Bill meant to deal with the omissions of the Computer Misuse Act – for example, those relating to denial of service attacks or spyware – also hung on highly ambiguous definitions and ran to less than a couple of pages long. In comparison, clauses relating to the return of child porn images ran to seven and a half pages (cf. Spyblog, 2006). By general agreement the amendments to the Computer Misuse Act seen in the PAJB represent a patched-up revision and a serious failure to think through hyperspatial regulation in a joined-up way (cf. Thompson, 2006).

Meanwhile the (2000) Regulation of Investigatory Powers (RIP) Act, which created the National Technical Assistance Centre (NTAC), in order to intercept 'information of interest' to policing agencies was attacked as little more than a 'snooper's charter' by a number of civil liberties groups (Wakefield, 2002). The so-called 'Investigatory Powers Tribunal', created to act as a court of appeal for anyone believing that investigating officers had unlawfully intercepted their communications when collecting evidence, was also widely criticised, not least for the poor level of resources it was given (BBC, 18/04/01). As Akdeniz et al. (2001, p. 19) point out, the 'structure remains complex, with several different commissioners covering activities which may in fact all be part of the same operation'. Worse, 'the quality of their review process fails to inspire confidence' (ibid). The fact that the act hybridises the role of ISPs, transforming them into a branch of law enforcement agencies, was less discussed, though the providers and companies themselves were far from happy. A particular complaint related to the lack of clarity about who was to bear the costs of installing the black boxes intended to allow police interception of communications which the Act required (Loney, 2002). ISPs were also concerned that the 2001 Anti-Crime and Terrorism Act further transformed them into policing agencies with its requirement that they retain net-data for up to six years. Even the police themselves conceded that the proposal might actually be in breach of the Human Rights Act (Fenwick, 2002; BBC, 28/01/03).

The legislative traditions of the USA are presumably one influence on what appears to be an even greater readiness to regulate remote interaction by way of legal mechanisms. This volume of legislative flow is of course further enhanced by the different jurisdictions at State and Federal levels. The result is a complex set of legal provisions for remote interaction. For this reason it is impossible to summarise every kind of legal response to the new demands of networked communication within the USA. However, the following table again provides some sense of the ways in which control has taken precedence over the protection of rights in the legislative process here.

	Law	Scope/provision
1986	Computer Fraud and Abuse Act	Directed at unauthorised entry to computer systems.
1994	Communications Assistance for Law Enforcement Act (CALEA)	Made it easier for law enforcement to wiretap digital telephone networks. CALEA forced telephone companies to redesign their network architectures to make wiretapping easier.
	Computer Fraud and Abuse Act	*Amendment.* (Safeguarded classified government information as well as certain financial information stored digitally, while also creating offences for malicious damage of computer systems and trafficking in stolen computer passwords.)
1996	Computer Fraud and Abuse Act	Further amendment.
1997	The No-Electronic Theft Act (NET Act)	Tightened restrictions on the reproduction and dissemination of copyrighted intellectual property such as software, music and movies.
1998	Digital Millennium Copyright Act (DMCA)	Prohibited the circumvention of copyright protection systems.
	Child Online Protection Act (COPA)	Directed at protection of minors and aimed to prevent any individual from making any communication, commercial or otherwise, that includes material 'harmful' to minors. *COPA was blocked by the US courts several times and in 2004 the Supreme Court ruled that it had 'potential for extraordinary harm and a serious chill upon protected speech'.*
	The Protection of Children from Sexual Predators Act	Included internet-specific provisions for reporting child pornography to authorities.
1999	Anticybersquatting Consumer Protection Act	

2000	Notice of Electronic Monitoring Act	Directed regulation of workplace monitoring.
	Child Internet Protection Act (CIPA)	Required libraries and schools to use 'technology protection measures' on every computer connected to the internet.
2001	Computer Fraud and Abuse Act	Amendment.
	Patriot Act	Enabled the government to monitor an individual's web surfing records, use roving wiretaps to monitor phone calls made by individuals 'proximate' to the primary person being tapped, access Internet Service Provider records, and to monitor the private records of people involved in legitimate protests.
2002	Homeland Security Act – (section 225: 'The Cyber Security Enhancement Act')	Established a National Infrastructure Protection Center. Broadened surveillance powers of Patriot Act – e.g., ISPs required to disclose private information to government agents, not just law enforcement officials.
2003	CAN-SPAM Act	Attempted to regulate unsolicited mails (spam).
2005	Real ID Act	Requires creation of a national database linking all ID records of US citizens together.
2006	Deleting Online Predators Act (DOPA)	Proposes restricting the accessing of social networking sites and chatrooms by minors.

The earliest of the acts listed here, the 1986 Computer Fraud and Abuse Act, set the tone for what was to follow, becoming a key tool in the 'hacker crackdown' which took place in the late 1980s and early 1990s (Sterling, 1994). Likewise the CALEA Act of 1994, as discussed in the introduction to this book, was a fundamental step in making remote interaction subject to the needs of control first and to those of rights second. Other legislation such as the Patriot Act of 2001, the Real ID Act of 2005 and the Deleting Online Predators Act (DOPA) of 2006 continue to demonstrate that the rights of citizens to interact remotely have been restricted as much as protected by US legislation.

But the USA has also been a key centre in resisting the imposition of controls upon remote interaction. Just as draconian new laws for the monitoring of identity in the USA were coming online, well-organised campaigning groups such as the EFF or Privacy International were using the new communicative resources to oppose them. The EFF's recent strategy of focusing upon corporate actors who support such control measures represents a new twist in this tale. The action launched against AT & T for 'violating the law and the privacy of its customers by collaborating with the National Security Agency (NSA) in its massive, illegal program to wiretap and data-mine Americans' communications' (EFF, 2007b) sets a new tone in the unfolding struggle to ensure that the regulatory ecology of hyperspace works in the interests of the many, rather than the few.

Given the supposed 'problem' of transjurisdictionality raised by the internet one would expect there to have been concerted attempts to attain harmony when it comes to legislation at the international level. The fact that international cooperation has been so far been less than comprehensive, is perhaps a further indication that the problem for legal capacity may not be quite so pressing as we are regularly led to believe. Indeed, it might also suggest that States are ultimately less than willing to 'share' hyperspace in any other way than that which directly extends their own control powers. Whilst Europe has managed to attain a fair degree of (predictable) harmony on laws dealing with mobility and cross-border migration (Geddes, 2000), there are important aspects to do with remote interaction – such as e-commerce – where agreement has been less obvious (see, for example, the controversies centred around the European Union Directive on the patentability of computer-implemented inventions in AEL (2006) and EU (2006)).

About the only really successful attempt at harmonising communications control policy at the European and International level has been the European Convention on Cybercrime. As well as issues such as illegal access and interception, data interference, computer-related forgery and fraud, child pornography and offences related to copyright, the Convention also covers law enforcement issues, as well as regulations concerning the storage of data, the search and seizure of computer data and the real-time collection and interception of transmissions (COE, 2001). Nonetheless, the treaty has faced various strands of opposition. Some argued that it offered businesses more protection than individuals, while digital rights groups focused on threats such as enhanced surveillance capacity, and the possibility that the laws in one country could be used against citizens of another (EFF, 2006). The tensions in 'sharing' hyperspace – even for control purposes – are indicated by the international reluctance to sign up to the Convention, so that it was not ratified by the US Senate until 2006, for example (Gross, 2006). Other proposed international agreements such as the Hague Convention on Jurisdiction and Foreign Judgment remain in legislative limbo at present with no final settlement in sight, even though negotiation of the Convention began back in 1992 (CPTech, 2005).

Formal and visible (II) – networked policing, uberpresent security

Legal structures continue at least to form a *visible* and *formal* influence upon the way our experience of this extended social space is being shaped, in spite of certain trends towards subterfuge. By contrast the reactive/dynamic components of the regulatory landscape increasingly operate in less visible ways.

The development of policing mechanisms has had a close association with the unfolding of modernity and therefore with hyperspatiality itself, most obviously in the concern with spatio-temporal management. In particular, their task of locating and identifying the location of transgressors or 'managing' the environment by scrutinising 'matter out of place' forms an obvious manifestation of the move towards comprehensive securitised spaces (Ericson, 2007, p. 28). As a result, the accelerations in spatial complexification and compression within late modernity seems to have had an especially focused effect upon the practice and scope of policing. Extensive discussions about the effect of communication and mobility technology upon police practice in the literature (cf. Manning, 1992; Deflem, 2002; Newburn, 2003) reflect growing perceptions of the importance of this fact. In turn, as its capacity for spatio-temporal management is enhanced with an increased availability of databases, profiling and surveillance technologies, policing is directed at the assessment of risks and threats to security (Garland, 1996; Ericson & Haggerty, 1997). In the context of a culture of 'allatonceness' and its global hybridisations, policing is transformed into an inverse reflection of threat itself, becoming an everywhere-present and everywhere-necessary phenomenon which regulates across *external* political borders and *internal* bodily borders.

An important outcome of these spatial dispersals is a gradual seeping of policing functions into other social bodies and structures – what has been termed 'multilateralization' (Bayley & Shearing, 2001) or 'nodal governance' (Johnston & Shearing, 2003). Taking his cue from these characterisations, Dupont (2004) makes an explicit parallel between policing and networked interaction, arguing that 'networks are increasingly becoming a key element in the governance of security' (p. 87). As our experience of threat moves from the criminal to the hypercriminal, policing moves beyond its location within the State apparatus to hybridise with many other kinds of social institution from education through to the workplace so that 'security pervades . . . every aspect of modern life' (Dupont, 2004, p. 77). Dupont identifies at least four levels of this enhanced policing and security network from local security provisions involving agents such as residential groups or local businesses; networks involving 'institutional bureaucratic projects or the pooling of resources across government agencies' (ibid, p. 80); international networks which link national police forces or privatised security agencies; and finally 'informational networks' – the communicative structures which link policing agents in one country with those in others.

But the networking of policing can be argued to go even further. With increased hybridisation there is a bleeding of *different* networks into one another, so that all kinds of social actors – ordinary citizens as well as police officers – become active nodes in the global policing network. Whether through the testimony of silent witnesses such as mobile phone cameras or CCTV, the RFID tagging of children or the increased numbers of non-service personnel engaged in police work, a 'civilianisation' of policing occurs (Forst, 2000, p. 19) as it pervades everyday life in new and unprecedented ways. But while such developments again evoke 'totalised' control systems there are also serious questions as to how *effective* or even how complete the networking of policing has so far been, in spite of the hyperbole surrounding it. Some question the extent to which there has been a genuine break with the past (Jones & Newburn, 2002), while others wonder about the weakening effect that pluralisations of policing may have had upon traditional policing/government relations (Loader, 2000). And in spite of the much heralded developments in 'knowledge' or 'evidence'-based policing (Sherman, 1998; Dean & Gottshalk, 2007) it is not clear that any general improvement in police performance has resulted. For example, the enhanced representational power provided by a combining of databases, profile recognition technologies and so on ought, in terms of everyday policing at least, to have made street operations more 'intelligence led' with a clearer focus on targets. Instead, old-fashioned techniques of 'officer intuition' or the 'matter out of place' principle have continued to prevail (Hallsworth & McGuire, 2003, 2005; Baker & Vasquez, 2007). Elsewhere there is an increasingly irrational deployment of resources away from measurable or overt threats, towards attempts to enforce laws and directives that are more to do with the manias of hypercrime or control. The obsessive monitoring of potential online predators, or the interception of the communications of innocent citizens count as one obvious instance here.

One good example of the haphazard and uneven adaption of existing police structures to the new demands of the hyperspatial can be seen in the sorry tale of the UK's first and much trumpeted specialised 'cybercop' unit. The National Hi-Tech Crime Unit was set up in 2001 to replace the operations of the previous Computer Crime Unit. But there were immediate and numerous criticisms of this body. Some were based on its poor resourcing – with around only 40 officers for the whole of the UK and funding of just £25 million (spread over a three-year period) (Ward, 2001; Wearden, 2004). Other criticisms focused on the overly cosy relationships between the NHTCU and the private sector. Furthermore, given the supposed spread and complexity of the 'cyber' threat the unit appeared to be woefully short of adequate or objective data about computer crime, and less than prolific at producing its own, tending to rely on private sector figures rather than independent research. During the research for this book, the unit could offer nothing other than a rather vague-sounding 'business survey' of computer crime which, despite numerous requests, never actually materialised. The inadequate support offered by government to the NHTCU and the conceptual confusions over what form of policing 'crimes by computer' actually required, speeded its ultimate demise. When it was finally 'disappeared' – barely five years after its creation – suspicions that the policing of cybercrime in the UK was more of a public relations exercise than a serious policy were inevitably fed.

Though the cybercrime trope seemed to be a useful fear to raise in the public mind when pressing the case for control mechanisms such as the identity card, the termination of the NHTCU was a stark practical reminder of the real extent to which the UK government had prioritised 'hi-tech' crime over other concerns.

The creation of SOCA (the Serious Organised Crimes Agency) by the New Labour government in 2006 signalled the effective termination of NHTCU operations, though its demise was dressed up as an 'amalgamation' into the new agency. As one legal commentator on IT law and policing provision pointed out: 'It is surprising and a little disappointing that the NHTCU isn't even mentioned in the publicity material for SOCA. While SOCA's manifesto includes combating frauds that use the internet, we really can't say whether SOCA will be more effective than the NHTCU' (Robertson, 2006). A de facto reduction in the resources devoted exclusively to the policing of the internet seemed hard to dispute. For example, the SOCA Board indicated that only 10 per cent of SOCA's effort would be directed at fraud – even though this includes phishing, a problem apparently so serious that in the very year SOCA was created, government sources had warned of an 8,000% increase in its prevalence (BBC, 13/12/06).

More seriously, the disappearance of the UK's only specialised policing agency for computer crime threatened a variety of potential operational lacunae. Since fraud by a motivated individual would fall outside of SOCA's remit to deal with organised crime, whose responsibility would it now become? Even though it was the lone hacker and fraudster who had been presented as the new folk devil of 'cyberspace', no policing provision apparently now existed to deal with them other than the traditional resource – less well-equipped and informed local police services. The Home Office's chaotic handling of what data the NHTCU had built up further indicates how poorly the transition had been thought out. When questioned about what had happened to the NHTCU's database of evidence – presumably an invaluable resource in the 'fight against hi-tech crime' – the best response the Home Office could offer was that the contents of the NHTCU website had been 'saved onto a disk' (Lettice, 2006)!! Whilst it is arguable how important the few recorded successes of the NHTCU were in controlling computer crime (cf. Leyden, 2005) what is certainly true is that no specialised unit at the national level in the UK now remains to deal with it. And while SOCA is supposed to have become the new 'centre of excellence' for dealing with computer crime, confidence in its competence in dealing with the new mobilities and security requirements of information was not enhanced when it turned out that half of its officers had been issued with the wrong photographs on their ID cards, and that someone had forgotten to issue them with enough squad cars (*Sunday Mirror*, 30/04/06). Moreover, if SOCA was meant to be an enhancement to *police* capacity in the fight against high-tech crime, government claims that it was 'not a police force' raised other questions about process and accountability (Harfield, 2006).

Provision for computer crime in regional UK police forces such as the West Midlands Police Hi-Tech Crime team or the Metropolitan Police continues to exist, though its resourcing remains questionable. According to the Metropolitan Police's website they offer '. . . a centre of excellence in regard to computer and cybercrime committed under the Computer Misuse Act 1990' (Metropolitan Police, 2006) but the '. . . computer forensic duty officer' and 'advice to officers on issues of computer evidence retrieval' (ibid) this seems to amount to does not suggest an especially high level of sophistication in the 'fight against hi-tech crime'. It also remains unclear how national provision for IT security via bodies such as UNIRAS (the Unified Incident Reporting and Alert Scheme), or NISCC (National Infrastructure Security Co-ordination Centre) (NISCC, 2006) is coordinated with SOCA or with these local levels of IT policing.

It is hard not to conclude from all this that, in spite of its claims, the UK government's response towards policing under hyperspatialisation is either shambolic, a public relations exercise, or that the level of threat is not quite so severe as we are regularly led to believe it is. Yet the willingness of the New Labour government to make political capital from the paranoias of hyper-crime has been clear enough, manifesting itself in a constant stream of 'new' initiatives – all directed towards populist targets which require little real investment. Take, for example, the creation in 2005 (supposedly as part of SOCA) of the Centre for Child Protection – a new policing structure meant to 'protect children from internet paedophiles' (BBC, 01/04/05). The Centre was set up to target individuals who distribute child porn images or who are involved in pursuing children online – the so-called 'grooming' that was considered in Chapter 3. Open 24 hours a day, the Centre would enable individuals to report 'suspicious' online activities, such as inappropriate behaviour on chat sites. The UK government made much of how this and other services it offered, like management of the national database of child abuse images, would be a 'major step towards cleaning up the internet'. It was far less forthcoming about the fact that the Centre would not be receiving any further funding than what had been previously apportioned, via the National Hi-Tech Crime Squad – around £6 million per year. Vague promises about extra funding coming from the private sector did not bolster confidence that this was any more than another form of symbolic governance. Nor, when it finally became operational in April 2006 as CEOP (the Child Exploitation and Online Protection Centre) was it clear how exactly its work was going to add to, or be any different from similar pre-existing bodies such as (among many others) the Internet Task Force for Child Protection on the Internet (ITF, 2001), the Internet Watch Foundation or the Virtual Global Taskforce (see below).

The United States, by comparison, has been far readier to create specialist policing agencies for the 'fight against cybercrime'. Its self-proclaimed 'war on terror' led to predictable though still dramatic rises in investment here, especially in new agencies meant to protect US information networks from attack by criminals. At the State level most police forces now possess some kind of 'cybercrime' unit, while Federal-level internet policing has become a highly centralised operation. Informal provisions like the FBI's Internet Fraud Complaint Center was augmented by more specialised approaches such as the formation of the FBI Cyber Division in 2002. In 2003 the US Department of Homeland Security (DHS) created a new unit, called the National Cyber Security Division (NCSD), as a division of the Infrastructure Protection Directorate to tackle net security (Olsen, 2003). As in the UK, reviews of this provision have been mixed – not least in a highly critical DHS internal report of July 2004 (Krim, 2004). Two previous cybersecurity heads had resigned in 2003 over internal difficulties and the credibility of the new initiative was hardly improved when its director, Amit Yoran, resigned after just one year in the post. Yoran had apparently expressed private frustrations with colleagues over what he considered a lack of attention paid to computer security issues within the agency (Lemos, 2004). Less than six months later Roy Liscouski, the Department of Homeland Security's assistant secretary for infrastructure protection, also resigned without issuing any statement (Mark, 2005).

Supplementing specific government provisions such as the NCSD are a range of semi-privatised 'cyber watchdogs' – often partnerships between the public and private sectors. An important example is the United States Computer Emergency Readiness Team (US-CERT) which issues warnings about potential security problems for networks (US-CERT, 2006). But the body has been criticised by many in the industry for slow responses or ineffective advice (Broersma, 2005), with its tendency to collude with commercial software companies against open source software an especial bone of contention. In their Cyber Security Bulletin of 2005, for example, US-CERT claimed that out of 5,198 reported vulnerabilities, 2,328 were found in Unix/ Linux systems while only 812 had occurred in Windows operating systems! (US-CERT, 2005). The hugely disproportionate nature of this finding suggested some undue influence from Microsoft, especially given the reputation among IT professionals for the greater reliability of Linux. Critics of the report pointed out how problems with the browser Firefox were specifically categorised in terms of Unix/Linux operating system flaws, even though Firefox also runs with Windows platforms. The statistics were also criticised by the organisation Common Vulnerabilities and Exposures (CVE), which maintains a common vulnerability database. It pointed out that the report failed to offer any credible evaluation of the relative security of the platforms because of methodological problems – figures had been collected from different sources with different vulnerability collection criteria (Espiner, 2006).

At the international level, visible and reactive mechanisms for the regulation of hyperspace are largely maintained by traditional policing agencies such as Interpol though its main role appears to be one of facilitation – for example, setting up a series of 'working parties' from among its members on information technology crime (Interpol, 2007). Otherwise it is the online predator issue which seems to have had the most effect upon international cooperation, with agencies such as the Virtual Global Taskforce harmonising operations between various national forces (VGT, 2007). But its significance as a properly 'global' policing mechanism is hard to measure precisely. For example, even one of its great 'success stories' from 2006, when a groomer was arrested after arranging to meet a 14-year-old girl, hardly involved any great detective work or the mobilisation of international resources. The man was arrested because the force had been tipped off by the girl (Lewis, 2006) – resulting in a job that might have been just as easily carried out by local police as any specialised 'virtual' or even global taskforce.

Overall then, the development in hyperspatialised policing, though it contains a great deal that reflects the foregrounding of control tendencies, also reflects the human element in complexifications of social space. The transition towards 'network' forms of policing noted by Dupont and others is not a seamlessly efficient progress, but an uneven one, retaining as much in the way of traditional policing provision as it does the 'hi-tech' variety. The disjunction between what Brodeur (1983, 2000) has called 'high and low' policing – one between old-style law enforcement and an all-encompassing form of policing which is 'absorbent . . . hoarding all encompassing intelligence' and which 'conflated legislative judiciary and executive . . . powers' (Brodeur & Leman-Langlois, 2006, p. 171) seems to have become more pronounced. However, its effectiveness – something which governmental sources repeatedly insist is essential to our security – is less clear. Thus, we should perhaps not so much fear Big Brother in the context of the new global forms of policing, but 'Big bungler, driven mad by too much power and too much speed' (ibid, p. 196).

Formal invisible control (I): filtration

In addition to *visible* policing functions, dynamic or reactive control mechanisms can also operate through purely technical means, hence *invisibly*. For the increasingly seamless interweavings between interactions in hyperspace with those of our proximate life make the control of movement across transport or communication networks appear to be as much a 'natural' as a social process. And, as representations of identity – identifications – are transformed into legitimising mechanisms or keys, this control becomes easier. Thus, it is a feature of a control society that it is: 'a society . . . marked by the use of the password, while the disciplinary society was marked by the watchword' (Deleuze, 1992, p. 3). An important outcome of this was discussed in the previous chapter. In a context where space is criss-crossed by invisible barriers and filtration points, the capacity to become 'invisible' and to move smoothly through such filtration points increasingly becomes a mark of distinction and a source of power.

In functioning as controls upon access and movement through the hyper-spatial, formal representations and their technical hardware reproduce traditional spatial forms such as doors, walls or bridges. In so doing they not only serve to causally constrain movement, but to psychologically frame our expectations towards this. We have already considered Simmel's discussions of the psychological effects of borders, and the effect of doors and entrances upon our attitudes towards spatial division is one that Simmel also explored with great acuity. As he put it: '. . . the door represents how separating and connecting are only two sides of the same act' (1997, p. 172) so that, 'the door becomes the image of the boundary point . . . not in the dead geometric form of a separating wall but rather as the possibility of a permanent interchange' (ibid, p. 173). This dual nature of the barrier is of course fundamental to the 'allatonceness' of the hyperspatial experience. In emancipatory terms a door represents the possibility of 'at any moment stepping out of this location into freedom' (ibid, p. 174), a promise which has a great deal to do with the exhilarations of connectedness. For with every connection offered there is the ever-present possibility of its being one that leads towards new experience, new knowledge or new relationships. At the same time the existence of access points, even those created through formal representations, also creates the possibility of movement through them becoming subject to control.

Most immediately, filters at *physical* doorways such as airport security gates, or entrances to corporate offices proliferate with the aid of information technology. Tools such as RFID chips within passports or the kinds of fingerprinting and biometric technologies now under use in the US-VISIT scheme allow more in-depth scrutiny and filtering at official border-crossing points (Ackleson, 2005; EPIC, 2006). At 'illegitimate' points of entry like the (highly) permeable US/Mexico border, the use of unmanned aerial vehicles, cameras, sensors, satellites and radar coverage within the new US Secure Border Initiative (SBI) also shift proximal physical borders firmly into the realm of hyperspatial control (DHS, 2006; Koslowski, 2006). At remote, or computer-mediated access points such as websites or portals, filtration is even more pronounced. A number of States which regulate their proximal spatial boundaries very tightly – in particular China – have been accused of 'seeking to assert information sovereignty over the Internet' (Villeneuve, 2006) though controls upon the internet seem almost as prevalent in the Western context. And the extent to which 'democratic' institutions and businesses are willing to collude with States such as China in the censorship and pursuit of citizens perceived to be using hyperspace 'illicitly' make any claims of moral superiority here difficult to sustain.

Filtration of content operates over a variety of access points – not just at international gateways, but *within* States – at schools, businesses or public libraries, for example. Intentions vary, from preventing access to content perceived to be obscene through to the prevention of online gambling. As is typical of invisible control mechanisms, accountability and transparency is very low with the result that States and commerce exert disproportionate levels of control – often with little awareness of this on the part of the public. Filtration may work by a simple list-based process (lists of addresses of sites which are blocked) or by software which scans sites for 'banned' keywords in order to block access if they are detected. As Villeneuve (2006) points out, the results are often crude and lead to two basic problems – over-blocking and under-blocking. Thus, '. . . not only do filtering technologies often block access to content that is unrelated to banned topics, they often do not block access to all content intended to be blocked' (ibid). Efficiency however, is not the only name of this particular game.

China's control architecture for access and movement within hyperspaces uses techniques so similar in principle to the barrier technologies once used to keep the 'barbarians' out that it has been dubbed 'the Red Firewall' or the 'Great Firewall' (Hermida, 2002; Doherty, 2003). Cybercafés offered a physical point of control with many simply being closed down by the authorities, or forced to install monitoring software (*Guardian*, 15/02/05; RSF, 2006). Other techniques have centred upon blocking of online communication itself (Opennet Initiative, 2004). One way this has been done is by promoting the use of 'Chinese specific portals' such as Xinhua.com which only allow certain things 'in' or 'out'. In this way most external content can be filtered to block politically sensitive comments, images or information. To make matters more secure any kind of software that might be used to get around these blocks has also been subject to State control – a process much facilitated by the willingness of Western companies such as Google and Alta-Vista to censor undesirable websites and pages (CNN, 26/01/06). The earlier readiness of media companies like News International's Star TV to remove BBC news from its network (Murphy, 1994) set a dubious moral precedent for the acceptance of censorship in the interests of commercial advantage. In a more serious abnegation of responsibility for human rights, Yahoo were accused by Reporters Without Frontiers of providing the Chinese government with information that helped to identify and convict two Chinese citizens who had posted critical comments about corruption and human rights abuses. The writer Li Zhi was jailed for eight years and Shi Tao for ten years (Rosenberg, 2005; MaCartney, 2006). As a result, the actions of Yahoo, Google, Microsoft and other Western IT companies have been widely questioned – not least in the US House of Representatives where they were accused of having acquired great wealth and power but 'little social responsibility' (*Wired*, 15/02/06).

Less pervasive but more subtle forms of filtering have been monitored in supposedly more 'democratic' contexts such as India, USA, Australia and Canada (Opennet Initiative, 2004b; RSF, 2006). But the collusions between State and private sectors in such contexts, together with cultural prejudices about the rights conferred by 'business imperatives', not only make such control appear seamless, but normal. For example, commercial filtering software databases like Smartfilter (see Secure Computing, 2007) are usually compiled without any public input, resulting in a situation where, as Villeneuve puts it, 'U.S. corporations are in a position to determine what millions of citizens can and cannot view on the Internet' (2006). Nonetheless, some instances of filtering are clumsy and obvious enough. For example, a week or so before the 2004 US election, the net-monitoring firm Netcraft announced that all attempts to view the George Bush election site from outside the US were being blocked (BBC, 24/10/04). Why the blocking occurred was not clear. An innocent explanation might simply have been that the Bush camp decided that it was unnecessary to keep the site open to overseas visitors with the date so close to the election. The more cynically minded might have pointed out that the action succeeded in blocking out numerous US overseas voters, many of them potential Democrats. To the cynical, the timing certainly seemed rather odd.

Following the unprecedented wave of securitisation in the wake of 9/11, something like 36 websites and over 600 public databases were also shut down. Even a report by the (State-funded) Rand Corporation was critical of the move, arguing that most of the proscribed sites posed little security risk (Baker *et al.*, 2004). Indeed, details about potential targets like airports and power plants were readily available elsewhere – textbooks, non-government sites, trade journals or maps.

Formal invisible control (II): footprints, hunting and traces

Movement within hyperspace can be shaped by straightforward blocking, but it may also be influenced by the extent to which it can be 'followed' – a direct result of the increased capacity of remote technologies to track movements through extended space. Of course, passage through proximal physical spaces has always resulted in certain traces that remain, whether in the form of a broken blade of grass or the discarded shard of pottery found in an archaeological survey. Extended into hyperspace, such traces become even more permanent and visible indicators of where we go and what we do, forming representations that can be both accessed and monitored for the purpose of control.

On the other hand, the novelty of tracking technologies should not be too exaggerated. The hunting of prey has almost always been a social practice made more efficient by extensions to human capacity. The Ancient Greek word for hunting – 'kynegeia' – deriving directly from their word for dog (*kynos*), signals how spatial limitations on senses were transcended in the drive to improve the effectiveness of our tracking abilities. Traditional techniques of hunting such as *stalking* (surreptitiously following traces of prey, or prey itself), *baiting* (using decoys or lures to attract prey) or *trapping* (using devices such as snares, or pits to capture prey), form a rich resource for contemporary criminologists to study (Lee & DeVore, 1968; Bettinger, 1991), especially those interested in techniques of deviance and control online. Continuities in attitudes towards prey as well as structural equivalences of hunting techniques recur in striking ways as spatial experience is extended.

The capacity to track is of course extremely useful in the pursuit of legitimate policing, detection or punitive functions. But tracking in extended space often has no such clear purpose – hunting and tracing increasingly occurs simply because it *can*. Sometimes the goal is to understand our habits, thereby extending control into desire regulation. For desire, like everything else, also now leaves its own traces within hyperspace. As we saw in Chapter 3, direct marketing agencies and other such bodies seek to follow these desire trails with ever greater efficiency by gathering information about purchasing patterns, responses to advertisements or willingness to take up offers (see Elmer, 2004, p. 64). With our movements having generated a 'desire profile' our thoughts and needs can then be better moulded for the purpose of profit (and most assuredly *not* for customer service).

Though certain resources like call-tracing technologies were in use long before the advent of the internet, these have been vastly supplemented by new capacities – most obviously the 'keylogging' software discussed in Chapter 4 which can record everything we do when interfacing remotely by keyboard. A variant of this are the 'cookies' – small programs placed on our hard disks, usually without our knowing about it (Bennett, 2001). Ostensibly there to grant easier access and recognition to regular users of sites, cookies are often employed in a more overtly regulatory fashion, leaving messages about where we visit, how often we do so and so on. In 2006 it emerged that a number of US government websites – for example the Air Force or the Treasury Department – were using cookies to track visitors' actions even though this was supposed to be against Federal Law. And though most cookies should be temporary it was found that many of these were not set to expire until 2016 at the earliest! (McCullagh & Broache, 2006). The new science of computer forensics extends these processes of tracking to their ultimate end. In hyperspace, it seems increasingly true that nothing is ever really 'deleted', so that a forensic analysis of a hard disk is often able to join together activities and communications long thought to have been sent to the trash can (Casey, 2000; CFW, 2007).

Techniques of contemporary detection and tracking are further facilitated by radio, satellite and television technologies such as RFID, GPS or CCTV. In turn these imaging forms of tracking are complemented by more 'static' impressions of our movements stored in data-traces – credit ratings, medical records and so on (Clarke, R., 1988; Cubitt, 1998; Marx, G.T., 2006). Again the relative asymmetries of visibility here say everything about the real order of control within contemporary regulatory ecologies. Whilst our telephone numbers are recorded and required by control agents such as telecommunications companies, or State policing bodies, there is no 'right of reply' here. Caller ID, portrayed as a security benefit to the user, has also been turned in yet another telemarketing tool (EPIC, 2007), though whenever we attempt to use it to obtain the numbers from corporate nuisance callers these are nearly always now logged as 'caller unknown'. Yet if users attempt to protect themselves by putting a block on their own caller ID, many firms will now simply refuse to accept the call (Ferguson, 2004).

Invisible informal – regulation by format

Another 'invisible' mode of control in the emerging regulatory ecology of hyperspace operates in more informal ways. Its control effects are again related to technology but also involve more social factors like the operation of the market and the role of ownership. The role of the private sector is at its most complex and pervasive here. The early stages of almost every technology of hyperspatialisation were at least as much a story of the *shaping* of interactive spaces as it was the interaction itself. And for those who were quickest off the mark, whether it was Alexander Graham Bell or Bill Gates, there were huge opportunities to mould the new spatial possibilities as they wanted, with little initial opposition. As a result the original developers of such technologies were able to shape the kind of hyperspace that was available at its most fundamental level, by way of their choices on such matters as interfaces, functionalities and so on. Just as often, the shape of this space was often down to 'unintended' factors like the choice of particular graphic, or set of access commands.

The twists and turns of commercial Darwinism resulted in a gradual centralisation of interface technologies for hyperspace into the hands of companies such as AT & T – a script which repeated itself within the development of information technology proper. The format of the early Unix or 'MS-DOS' interfaces served to regulate behaviour very simply. For only those able to utilise the impenetrable text-based commands used in DOS could take advantage of the remote interactive resources such as Gopher or FTP which were then available (Moschovitis *et al.*, 1999, p. 161). The advent of 'graphical user' interfaces, based on icons and click-and-drag techniques, and 'easy' web browsers like Mosaic, or Netscape Navigator widened access (Wolf, 1994). Ironically, it also began to centre control in the hands of the few who owned the formats.

The *deflations* in possibility within networked communication forced by commerce and its stranglehood on formats can be dramatic. 'Surfing' through hyperspace, by way of the internet or mobile phones, may indeed 'everywhere have replaced the older sports' as Deleuze put it (1992). But this does not always result in the freedoms that the term suggests. Instead we 'amputate' our sense of choice or independence by deferring to devices such as search engines to narrow down the options for us. A shaping of space results – some of it unintended, some of it a direct outcome of commercial imperatives, and the deliberate manipulation of our movements.

Features such as Microsoft's smart-tags, or Google's 'autolink' facility began to direct movements across the internet in ways desired by the companies who had paid for links to them to be highlighted, arousing a great deal of protest as a result (Lettice, 2001; BBC, 22/02/05). But of course Google's own search system works by reinforcing the likelihood of 'popular' sites being returned high on the return list, thereby marginalising smaller businesses or sites of interest by placing them lower down on the search list. And our own behaviour then reinforces this. For example, one analysis indicated that the top result on a search usually gets around 42% of follow-on 'click-throughs', the second around 11.2%, while the 10th item on the list only gets around 3% (Arthur, 2006). In turn, the phenomenon of 'googlebombing' – using the quantitative basis to Google's search mechanism to send people to particular sites – has emerged. The 2004 US election campaigns featured a number of examples of this, with rival parties manipulating the Google search algorithm by flooding the web with references to opposition candidates and links to unfavourable articles. In this way a search for a rival politician would be more than likely to link to opinions which showed them in a negative light (Zeller, 2006). A similar technique managed for a long time to link the search term 'miserable failure' to George Bush's website until Google finally intervened to prevent this (Cohen, 2007).

The issue of format control is just one example of how acquiring 'useful' information may not only become a privilege, but a mark of a 'hyperspatial control elite'. Just as in proximal physical spaces, the hi-jacking of a genuine market by alliances and oligopolies can itself shape space to produce very restricted options for movement. In the context of the internet this seems likely to become even more pronounced should the 'net-neutality' discussed in the previous chapter be lost and cable providers allowed to create two-tier services by charging for the use of their hardware. Such skewings of movement may even reduce the capacity of the much vaunted next stage of the internet – Web 3.0, or the 'semantic' web – to deliver choice. Instead of 3.0 delivering searches that operate with greater 'intelligence' it may be equally likely that this process will also be subverted for commercial ends. The regulatory question then becomes how 'intelligent' is an intelligent search? For if intelligence itself can be transformed into species of commercial control, the regulatory landscape that emerges with Web 3.0 may be infinitely more limiting and dangerous than anything now presented.

Visible/invisible informal shaping – statutory control and self-regulation

To many of the early net-utopians self-regulation was not just an ideal – it seemed to be the likeliest way in which remote interaction would ultimately be shaped (cf. Johnson & Post, 1997; Price & Verhulst, 2000; ILPF, 2007). Williams' recent argument that '. . . only in instances where deviant activities exceed the capacities of internal regulation should terrestrial bodies become involved' (2006, pp. 148–149), reflects the durability of this view. But it has not been clear how realistic, nor even how desirable a proposition self-regulation really is. As we shall see, it is an ideal which, in practice, has often led to the kinds of oligopolies, dictatorships and regulatory brutalities that match anything proximal spaces have had to offer. Alternatively, it simply disguises a deference to more institutionalised control systems.

Whilst 'self-regulation' appears to involve a more informal species of regulatory patterning, formal methods are clearly not ruled out. For example, the use of code to control behaviour in 'self-regulating' online worlds is obvious and widespread. Regulatory invisibility is again the result, but invisibility also arises from more undefined and subliminal norms which play a powerful role in these environments. Given the potential variety in the methods for attaining 'self-regulation' I will therefore consider it in terms of one simple measure – the degree of 'autonomy' which is aspired to, or which appears to be presented. In this way self-regulation might be viewed in terms of a continuum which runs from the lesser autonomy of bodies seen at (i) through to the (ostensibly) full self-regulation seen at (v).

(i)   Quasi-independent advisory or watchdog bodies without policing powers but with important connections to pre-existing centres of power.
(ii)   Codes of conduct.
(iii) Individually based forms of regulations such as web filters, parental controls or similar.
(iv)   Self-appointed web 'guardians'.
(v)   Regulatory practices within autonomous hyperspatial communities.

Limited self-regulation

A foundational example of the first level of informal regulation are private bodies, usually with strong links to government, whose task it is to enforce certain standards upon networks of different kinds. Internet Service providers or 'ISPs' are one obvious instance of this with respect to the internet. They perform various regulatory functions such as content filtering, along with statutory surveillance roles imposed by legislation like the UK Regulation of Investigatory Powers Act. The influence of State legislation of this kind upon (purportedly) autonomous bodies raises serious questions about the real extent of the 'self' in self-regulation (cf. Cannataci and Bonnici, 2003). Older networks tend to be governed by bodies with less regulatory power. In the UK, for example, the body Ofcom has a wide regulatory brief, which covers television, radio, telecommunications and wireless communications services. As stated under the Communications Act of 2003 its job is to:

(a) ... further the interests of citizens in relation to communications matters; and, (b) to further the interests of consumers in relevant markets, where appropriate by promoting competition.

(Ofcom, 2006)

This task covers everything from 'maintaining plurality in the provision of broadcasting' or 'applying adequate protection for audiences against offensive or harmful material' through to the more vague function of '. . . ensuring the optimal use of the electro-magnetic spectrum' (ibid). The multiplicity of their regulatory functions and the lack of powers they possess for enforcing them has raised questions about the effectiveness of such bodies (cf. Gibbons, 1998). The Federal Communications Commission (FCC), which has a similar role in the USA, is an older established body dating back as far as the early radio industries. Its remit – 'regulating interstate and international communications by radio, television, wire, satellite and cable' (FCC, 2006) – has been similarly controversial at times. And as with Ofcom, questions have been raised as to how independent of the industry it is meant to regulate it really is. In 2004, for example, when it appointed a new 'Consumer Advisory Committee' – supposed to act as a counterweight to continual industry lobbying – 'consumers of telecommunication services' were apparently not what the FCC had in mind for its members. Instead, more than a third of the available 35 seats were given to representatives from interested parties such as AT & T, BellSouth, and the National Association of Broadcasters (Pearlstein, 2004). Its accountability to the public is just as ambiguous, consisting as it does of five commissioners all directly appointed by the President (Havick, 1983; Hilliard, 1991).

Focusing upon the internet proper, a confusingly large number of different supervisory groups intervene to shape interaction across it, from groups such as IAB (Internet Architecture Board), through to the Worldwide Web consortium which takes care of new web standards. Most prominent is the group ICANN (Internet Corporation for Assigned Names and Numbers) whose function is to decide how to assign 'domain names' (such as 'google.com' or 'bbc.co.uk'). In one sense then, ICANN operates almost as a kind of land registry body, distributing space accordingly. Absolute uniqueness is required for the addressing system to work, so that no two distinct individuals or locations can use the exact same domain name. But with such responsibility automatically comes a great deal of influence in 'shaping' the World Wide

Web, and by extension, our experience of hyperspace (Schiavetta & Komaitis, 2003; ICANN, 2007).

Not surprisingly, given such fundamental control potential, ICANN is widely regarded with suspicion (Froomkin, 2000; PFIR, 2000). The ongoing reorganisation of the World Wide Web naming system has foregrounded some of the basic tensions here. One common complaint is the fact that ICANN is not just *based* in the USA but is, effectively, an arm of the US Department of Commerce which was instrumental in setting it up. The suspicion that US State and commercial interests come first in the policies of ICANN is never far away in the minds of many internet users. Equally controversial is the issue of its accountability. Despite initial promises that it would have a board of directors, some of whom would be elected from its 'membership', by 2006 no elected members yet existed. In addition, it had been decided that only five out of the nine existing directors should be elected after all, allowing the remaining four (already self-selected) directors to stay on at will. Questions have also been raised about suspect 'arrangements' between the private sector and ICANN. In 2005, for example, in the face of heavy competition, the US company Verisign's control of the .net registry (the fourth largest on the web) was extended until 2011. Under an original deal brokered by the US government, Verisign had also held control over the .com, .org and .net domains. In 1999 it made a tactical decision to relinquish the .org and .net domains in return for being allowed to hold on to .com. Given this privilege, the fact that the company was not just allowed to then bid again for .net but was ultimately granted rights over it caused understandable resentment. The .net address is a lucrative pot, handling around $700 billion annually in internet commerce (around 30% of the total). In addition, the annual fee of $6 required from retailers if they wish to maintain the .net registration in the master registry brings in around $30 million a year (McGuire, D., 2005).

This quasi-feudal monopoly over internet governance, by a body with almost zero accountability and which is firmly under US and (by extension) Western domination has inevitably provoked calls for change. As part of this response, sites such as Icannwatch which monitor and evaluate the actions of ICANN have emerged (Icannwatch, 2007) and countries outside of the US and Europe have attempted to wrest some of the regulatory power of ICANN away. For example, at the World Summit for Internet Governance at Tunis in 2005 a motion was put forward by countries like Brazil, China and others which argued that domain name control should be ceded to the UN (Poulsen, 2005b). The motion was seen off by the decision of European governments to defer to the existing American structure (a decision they presumably felt best served their own long-term interests). In response, the US government appeared to make a small concession to the increasing flood of complaints about ICANN by promising to grant it 'full autonomy' by 2009. However, all this so far seems to amount to is that ICANN will no longer need to report to the US government every six months (Gow and Wray, 2006).

Purity police – the IWF and unaccountable regulatory practice

A second species of quasi-independent bodies shaping communication networks are various unelected 'semi-advisory' bodies. Such groups often purport to represent the public interest on specific issues – though again, usually without any hint of genuine democratic governance or accountability. One notorious example from the UK is the Internet Watch foundation (IWF). The IWF was founded in 1996 as a 'partnership' between government, police forces and internet service providers. It likes to project the image of pluralist involvement by characterising itself as a 'service' that enables web users to report content that they see as potentially harmful. However, the list of sponsors for the IWF's pages in 2005 – which included MSN, BP, 02, Nokia, MacCaffee, AOL, NTL, Tiscali and Virgin Mobile among others – hardly suggest that the public are centrally involved in its workings (IWF, 2005). One of the IWF's favourite strategies in attempting to justify its existence is to resort to questionable statistics. For example, one of its early claims was that, as a direct result of its efforts, the amount of 'harmful content' hosted by British websites had fallen from 18% to 1% of the total (cf. IPPR, 2004, p. 3). A reasonable question, one might ask was how this 'harmful content' had been defined and measured. Since no effective definition of 'harmful content' had been produced in nearly 100 years of previous broadcasting industries the idea that a clear and transparent formulation of this for internet content had suddenly emerged was, at the very least, surprising. Unfortunately the IWF has never seen fit to share the details of its semantic breakthrough with the British public.

Perhaps aware of the spuriousness of the idea that there could be any precise measurement of the harmful content it has 'reduced', the IWF regularly resorts to handy folk devils such as the 'internet paedophile' to bolster its legitimacy. It is clear, given the evidence of earlier chapters, that child pornography is hardly the *only* harmful kind of content one is likely to encounter on the web, but it is apparently about the only sort which the IWF chooses to recognise. If the body were nothing more than a quango with the symbolic function of making the industry look like it is 'being responsible', then the IWF's role in shaping remote interaction might be of less concern. But the levels of control the IWF has attempted to exert over parts of the UK internet mean that its actions must be regarded with more suspicion (cf. Akdeniz, 1998). Such suspicions have, after all, been raised by members of the IWF itself. In an earlier attempt to present itself as an autonomous body 'working for net freedom' the IWF managed to recruit Malcolm Hutty, head of the Campaign Against Censorship of the Internet in Great Britain, to its

Board. But the partnership did not last for long. In 2002, Hutty resigned from the body because it was 'not prepared to listen to criticism' of their plans to increase efforts to censor perfectly legal material (Grossman, 2002). The IWF had already lost ISP representative Clive Feather and deputy chief executive Ruth Dixon over similar complaints.

In spite of widespread internal and external criticisms the IWF has made no attempt to offer checks and balances in its attempts to censor online content. Instead, with the backing of the Blair government, the IWF increasingly took upon itself the role of instructing ISPs to remove material considered to be offensive. In the first five years of its existence it managed to remove nearly 30,000 items from the internet – even though nearly 95% of the material would not have been subject to actions in UK courts (Evans, 2002). The justifications for such actions took a further turn for the worse in 2004 when the IWF began to cooperate with British Telecom (BT) in the introduction of its new filtering software called 'Cleanfeed'. The websites which Cleanfeed quietly blocks access to have not been subject to any *independent* assessment or evaluation – they come from a list compiled and provided by the Internet Watch Foundation. Such a relationship not only radically changes how telecommunications companies interact with the UK public, they significantly enhance the IWF's (unelected) powers to decide upon what may or may not be seen. The dramatic, and apparently instantaneous success of Cleanfeed in filtering 'harmful' content appeared to undermine the complaints of civil liberties campaigners about the role of the IWF, but closer inspection of their statistics raise troubling questions. Following the launch of Cleanfeed in 2004 BT claimed that, between 21 June and 13 July, the software had indicated around 230,000 attempts to access child porn – nearly 20,000 attempts PER DAY! These figures rapidly became facts, as hyperspace worked its influence and they were immediately networked and reported around the world. Shock and outrage was duly expressed in sources as geographically dispersed as the *Washington Post* and Australia ABC (ABC, 2004; *Washington Post*, 20/07/04). But, as several commentators pointed out, 230,000 in 22 days is 10,454 a day, *not* 20,000 (Docherty, 2004). The trade body for Internet Service providers, the ISPA, investigated these claims and expressed its own concerns about possible misrepresentations. For example, was Cleanfeed measuring the number of 'hits' (attempts to download individual files from illegal websites) or 'visits' (number of attempts to visit the website)? Likewise if Cleanfeed was using URLs of images, this would also impact on the statistics since a database containing URLs of images rather than the pages holding them would cause several 'hits'. Furthermore since Cleanfeed returns a 'not found' error, people visiting the sites may have assumed an error and so retried at least once – potentially increasing the statistics by a factor of at least 2! (Richardson, 2004).

BT rejected these criticisms and so the Cleanfeed filtering operation continues. By 2006 it was reporting a new figure of 35,000 attempted attempts to access child pornography per day (Richardson, 2006). The idea that, in the space of two years, there had been a *threefold* rise (from the original 10,000) in the number of individuals daily attempting to access child pornography in the UK seems faintly implausible – especially given the vastly increased likelihood of prosecution. But of course no independent scrutiny of these statistics was available – so that it was only by comparison with the IWF's own data (which was of course the basis for BT's filtering operation in the first place) that such claims could be made. Suspicions that the figures might be inflated by other kinds of sites being filtered were raised by critics who pointed out that, since the 'not found' message is all that is returned upon attempting to visit a blocked site (by accident or design), there is no way of knowing precisely what *is* being blocked. There is no line of accountability if a site is entered mistakenly, no clear way for a site to get itself removed from 'the list', and no guarantee that sites cannot be added silently – perhaps even at government behest (Thompson, B., 2004).

In the USA, though there is less readiness to legislate in the case of free speech, the spread of self-appointed purity police has a far wider base, drawing from the varies agendas of religious organisations, parents' groups, the private sector and so on. Groups such as the CyberAngels – 'the world's oldest and largest internet safety organisation' – claim to intervene wherever necessary (CyberAngels, 2007), while other sites such as the Network Abuse Clearinghouse (NAC, 2007) have, like the IWF, set themselves up as a place where abuse or abusive users can be reported. The NAC denies that blacklists are kept and, as it concedes, 'listing a domain in the abuse.net database does *not* imply that the domain has ever done anything abusive' (ibid). But the NAC is far less forthcoming about the kinds of checks it makes about domains which have been misidentified, or what redress is made when this occurs. Other 'family'-based moral guardians such as Family Watchdog ('Awareness is your Best Defence') offer filtering assistance. Part of this involves a search engine which not only allows people to check on sex offenders in their area, but to receive e-mail or mobile phone updates on any 'breaking' news about abusers (Family Watchdog, 2007).

Questions do not just arise about the unaccountable regulatory powers of such sites, but also their readiness to link the 'helpful' service they offer with (often unrelated) commercial promotion. Indeed, many such services appear almost to be little more than entertainment industry hybrids that feed off hypercrime paranoias. One example, the 'Cybercriminals Most Wanted' website (CCMW, 2007), allows one to enter the thrill of the chase by seeing who is the 'most wanted cyberfugitive of the week'. These vicarious excitements are supplemented by listings for the 'most wanted terrorist', the 'most wanted hijacker' or the (slightly less dramatic) 'most wanted for questioning'. The site also provides searches where various 'cybercrime professionals' offer their expert services (at a price) – from forensic specialists in Alabama and private investigators from Michigan through to expert witnesses from Oklahoma or internet attorneys in Austria.

Crude commercial exploitation of parents' (understandable) fears about dangers to their children online is widespread. In 2005, for example, the site Safesurf (Safesurf.com) which likes to style itself as 'the original internet rating system', also contained sponsored links to sales of designer sunglasses, concert tickets, night vision goggles and long-range rifle-sighting devices. The McGruff Crime Dog site, based on a familiar figure to American children, was also mixing its messages with liberal doses of commercial sponsorship. Its site offered 'McGruff® products . . . (that) will make a positive difference in the communities that you live in and that your business or organization serves' – in particular the 12-page Internet Safety guide available for $2.50 (McGruff, 2006). Also available for the same price was the 'McGruff® Safe Kids Total Identification System' which helps you fingerprint your child in a 'fun, educational and non-threatening way' – with reductions down to $1.75 for orders over 50.

Online community regulation – public executions and wizard dictators

Whilst the idea that self-regulation would serve as the governing regulatory form online appears to have been misplaced, a frequent theme in discussions of net regulation are the parallel subcultural spaces, such as gaming environments which, in developing their own 'regulatory orders', have seemed to present, 'an exercise in legal anthropology, a chance to examine a legal order separate from our own' (Mnookin, 1996, p. 247). But whatever the novelty of their interior controls, it is increasingly clear that such communities are firmly subordinate to the regulatory ecologies of the wider world, no matter how many times the term 'virtual' is applied to them.

It is equally clear that the regulation of such environments does not result in any kind of anarchist's utopia. For the creation of such communities seems to bring with it an inevitable desire for anarchy – a desire on the part of some to disrupt or destroy interactions there. Whether such disruptive behaviour originates in more broadly based appetites for destructive interaction or in the character of hyperspatial interaction itself – with all its availability of extended identities – is unclear. Either way, the emergence of some form of anti-social behaviour seems almost always inevitable (Collins, 1992; Donath, 1998). Regulatory responses can be equally irrational and far more savage.

The earlier story of the Lamda MOO community and its 'rapist' Mr Bungle was one of the earliest and best-documented accounts of what happens when an online community seeks to regulate behaviour and to shape its social space (Dibbell, 1993; MacKinnon, 1997). As suggested earlier, the deviant actions of the Bungle persona seem best judged in terms of psychological harm, though the Lamda MOO group itself was less inclined to be so broad-minded. The result of their joint deliberations on the Bungle crime was a retribution that was swift and deadly – the public execution and effective extinction of the character. Studies that have examined the way regulation emerges in such contexts (cf. Barzilai-Nahon & Neumann, 2005; Williams, 2006) seem to confirm this tendency. Online communities, far from personifying the liberal 'feel-good' love-in represented by early groupings such as the WELL, seem better characterised in terms of control tendencies that verge towards the pathological. Tyranny, autocracy and the willingness to destroy or punish through humiliation emerge as common and accepted regulatory forms.

Rule within such communities is almost always through some form of elite – either the techno-priest governors who set up and maintain the environment and whose word is final, or members who have simply been around long enough to discipline the 'newbie'. Mnookin (1996) discusses the rule of the 'wizards' in Lamda MOO – the technicians who coded and maintained this online environment. They had originally declared that the world should be a 'democracy', with members voting to make decisions about its direction and the wizards implementing them. However, after only a few years of this experiment an announcement was made – the wizards now intended to take full control, declaring, 'we will no longer attempt to justify every action we take' (Mnookin, 1996, p, 287). As Mnookin points out, since this option had always been available (in principle), 'the memo . . . was like a coup d'etat by a group that had always held the reins of power' (ibid). Even where some semblence of 'regulated pluralism' (Slevin, 2000, p. 215) does occur, it often turns into the rule of the mob. For example, Williams' (2006) study of the Cyberworlds environment indicated evidence of monopolistic domination by 'world owners', before a shift to 'forms of vigilante justice, peer pressure and ostracism' or 'modes of public ridicule . . . intended to humiliate the virtual offender' (pp. 114–115). Any concept of 'virtual' law for such environments is therefore rarely likely to be democratic, but a law made for the many, by the few.

More recent and sophisticated environments such as the widely hyped Second Life demonstrate the increasingly blurred boundaries between the 'bracketed' controls of online spaces and external regulatory contexts. As discussed in Chapter 3, an important continuity of this kind are the financial exchange mechanisms which allow for transfers of capital between the wider economy and the Second Life version – all inevitably subordinated to the wider structures of banking and commercial control. Regulations upon intellectual copyright are particularly severe. For example, even anyone wishing to set up something as innocent as a Second Life 'fan-site' must comply with long lists of rules and regulations:

Required Trademark and Copyright Information. You must include the following information on your website: 'Second Life® and Linden Lab® are trademarks or registered trademarks of Linden Research, Inc. All rights reserved. No infringement is intended.'

(Second Life, 2007a)

And while Second Life role players may be convinced that they are immersed in an autonomous alternative reality, the owners of Second Life have developed a keen sense of the legal requirements of the broader hyper-spatial regulatory order their 'world' is continuous with. For example, they insist upon:

Compliance with Laws. You may not use our name, logos or other marks or intellectual property in any manner, or in connection with any enterprise or purpose, that is in violation of applicable laws.

(ibid)

It is also clear that no matter how developed the alternative identity which has been acquired, even the tiniest hint of interest from the criminal justice system is likely to puncture the identic bubble. For personal data can be released, where it is:

... reasonably necessary to fulfill your service request, to third-party fulfillment houses, customer support, billing and credit verification services, and the like; to comply with tax and other applicable law; as otherwise expressly permitted by this Agreement or as otherwise authorized by you; to law enforcement or other appropriate third parties in connection with criminal investigations and other investigations of fraud; or as otherwise necessary to protect Linden Lab, its agents and other users of the Service.

(Second Life, 2007b)

In particular:

Linden Lab can (and you authorize Linden Lab to) disclose any information about you to private entities, law enforcement agencies or government officials, as Linden Lab, in its sole discretion, believes necessary or appropriate to investigate or resolve possible problems or inquiries, or as otherwise required by law.

(ibid)

Scrutinising such legal niceties (and there are many more), one might wonder whatever happened to the fantasy in fantasy environments. As the external world increasingly punctures the illusory bubble of 'autonomous worlds' with sponsored advertisements, shopping opportunities or band promotions it is clear that Second Life is ultimately little more than a glorified super-market where customers get to wear fancy dress and use fake names while having the occasional phone sex. In such a context the idea that:

> the online environment is so different . . . in terms of physicality, demo-graphics, geography and sociality that any form of external regulation would fail to recognise the minutiae that distinguish them
>
> (Williams, 2006, p. 124)

seems more implausible than ever.

The regulatory ecology of the hyperspace we increasingly inhabit then is not the product of code, of fantasy, or any other individual constraint, but of the collective rules that we make and build. And its shape, in both narrow and extended spatial contexts, re-instantiates all the usual social constants of control and hierarchy – whether the social actors concerned are pretending to be blue fluffy rabbits, using their credit cards, or crossing a border. Hyper-space, whatever else it turns out to be, is shaped in our own image.

End space

Afterword

Well I'm not braggin' babe so don't put me down
But I've got the fastest set of wheels in town
When something comes up to me he don't even try
Cause if I had a set of wings man I know she could fly
She's my little deuce coupe
You don't know what I got.

The exhilarations of mobility celebrated in the driving songs of the 1950s and
1960s are revealing on any number of levels. Modernity's mission to subjugate
the tyrannies of spatio-temporal location had been further advanced by an
'automobile age' which now offered new capacities to compress space and
time to the multitude. But we also certainly did not know what we got. For
with such freedoms came costs, in the form of the pollutions, the road deaths,
the diminishings of public transport, the destructions of city centres and the
compromise to community which have also now been associated with the
widening of access to 'automobility'. Just as the Futurist's celebration of
speed and machinery presaged the techno-carnage of two world wars, the
new transport networks opened their own Pandora's box of harms. And so,
as we have learned to be more wary of the exhilarations to be had in 'annihilating space and time', we are less confident about the latest of our bodily
extensions – the global networks of interaction and information now under
construction. For if you can connect to everyone – then everyone can connect
to you. There is no safety behind locked doors and no security in security.
Where opportunity lies, crime (naturally) follows – but who, or what, or even
how is the criminal is more problematic than ever before. That spatial manipulations can bring harm in their wake is not in doubt. As this was once put –
'eliminating distance kills' (Rene Char, cited in Virilio, 1997, p. 22). But in
what way is not always obvious. For if deviance and criminality, like everything else within the network can now be a hybrid – how do we *know* who it
is safe to be connected to and who it is not? As the new geometries of
interaction provided by the mobile phone, the fax machine, the chat room or

even the budget airline allow criminality to be produced from anywhere, at any time, a clear head is required in responding to Nils Christie's (2004) question – how much crime do we *want*? But annihilating space and time is, unfortunately, just as likely to produce what Jock Young has recently referred to as 'vertigo' (2007).

The story of cybercrime has been one representation of this ongoing transition, and it has seemed a good story to many – politicians, policing and security agencies, banking officials, insurance companies, data brokers and software protection companies – with criminologists, like just about everyone else, happy to come along for the ride. This book has argued that such a story is a radically incomplete one. In its selective technological fetishisations, the cybercrime story has both dehistoricised and distorted a process with profound social roots and with implications far wider than can be captured by a few tales from the internet, however satisfyingly complete they may appear to be.

Whilst there are no doubt many other narratives around which this process and its affects upon crime and our perceptions of crime could be arranged I have argued that we can find one good, or at least better, story by looking to the reorganisations of spatial experience which underlie the internet and similar conduits for remote interaction. I have grouped these reorganisations together as 'hyperspatial' – processes that originate in ancient aspirations within human culture to extend the reach of bodies. And I have argued that the recent acceleration in the technical means for 'acting at a distance' has simply refocused and redirected these historical trends, albeit with greater levels of precision and affect. But in offering the fullest expression yet to the emancipatory potentials of remote interaction, contemporary hyperspatiality has significant effects upon the material possibilities for crime. Like other stages on its way, an 'amputative' effect also arises, for in the rich possibilities of remote interaction are to be found a tangled set of collective psychoses.

In a nutshell, the idea explored in this book is that the hyperspatial *produces* the hypercriminal. But the real and material affects upon the practice, skills and techniques of crime and their new materialisation, like other social experiences, as an everywhere phenomenon also means that hypercriminality is no mere collective fantasy. Its hyperreality is no 'desert of the real' (Baudrillard, 1983, p. 2). It is a product, both of social interaction and social imagination – dispensed globally, dispersed instantaneously. The character of its harms will not be captured by a mechanical churning out of 'crimes which (in some way or another) involve computers' – for in hyperspace, the continuum between the normal and the pathological seems to demand a different kind of attention than within proximate space.

Allatonceness – living in the hyperspatial

At their most fundamental level, the implications of the 'hyperspatial' for crime relate to the advantages and disadvantages conferred by an experience of transcendence, specifically the transcendence of location, in both its corporeal and coordinate senses. Geometry offers us one sense of what this might mean. For any geometry is, in part, defined by the space which it describes and such descriptions come down to the set of motions which are possible within that space. On this line, a space is transcended where certain motions occur which are outside of what is standardly possible – that is, where the 'boundaries' of the space are transgressed in some way. Just as in a two-dimensional space vertical movements would be nothing less than an inconceivable magic, or in a three-dimensional (Euclidean) space the meeting of parallel lines an impossible contradiction, the process of adding dimensions or extra properties to a space (such as its curvature) permits connections and movements that would appear otherwise impossible. For any space then, there is its *hyperspace*, the higher order space in which it is embedded and which is defined by a set of motions otherwise impossible within its lower order counterpart (cf. Valente, 2004).

There is no need to get bogged down in mathematical geometry, or bedazzled by revisionary metaphysics to find a more grounded sociological utility in this idea. For 'space' we can substitute 'social space' and for motions we can substitute the social possibilities or capacities conferred by a particular social space. Transcendence in this context then simply relates to ways of acquiring or extending social possibility and interaction. For McLuhan, as we have seen, such extensions related primarily to extensions of the body. But it is clear that we can think more broadly than this. Community, political life, property and many other ingredients of social experience may also be extended, bringing in their wake new ways of interacting or simply acting deviantly. This transcendence of the spatial limitation of bodies and its effect upon social interaction is certainly more than an interesting theoretical idea. The evidence for it is all around us, through we quickly forget to notice it, so natural do the extensions come to appear to be. In one sense a technology is ever only noticeable because, as this was once put, 'it doesn't work yet' (Adams, 1999). Whether as carriage or car, abacus or computer, a hyperspace (in its social sense) is formed *out of* our actions while simultaneously becoming *part* of them.

This higher order sphere of interaction is therefore more than the conceptual lacuna identified by Fredric Jameson (1991) as a 'hyperspace', for it consists in real and identifiable sets of experiences. There is time-space compression – the reorganisation of distance discussed by writers such as Innis or Harvey. Complementary to this are the enhanced mobilities of movement and transmission that come with *speed* which makes compression possible. In turn space is experienced as something *complexified* as previously disconnected locations form new composites and integrations. The network can only be a partial metaphor for this process, however useful. Not only because spatial complexification involves many varieties of connection beyond those provided by transport or communication but because part of what makes space 'hyperspatial' is a 'networking of networks'. And this also produces a hyperlinking of meanings, mediated by representation which extends our reach still further – not just *through* space but into multi-faceted ways of interacting through and with information. This fourth ingredient of the hyperspatial has featured less prominently in other discussions of the way spatial experience is being transformed, but it is clear that enhanced capacities of representation are as essential in enabling us to experience these new interactions as the telegraph cable was in its day. One way this is seen is in the dependence of telepresence upon the computer models used to exert effects in places where bodies cannot go – the very far, or the very small. Another way it is seen is in high-definition representations of *alternative* spaces – the so-called 'virtual' worlds so beloved of theorists on cyberspace or cybercrime. But the virtual is no separate or ontologically isolated experience – it is continuous with every other experience within a hyperspace. And just as there is no virtual reality in the sense of a reality distinct from any other, nor does virtual crime subsist as an independent category. There are representations, connected to other representations, connected to our proximal or to our remote experiences. Being a victim of crime at any point in this chain of connections is as real an experience as any other kind there has ever been.

Boundaries: crime and hypercrime, control and hypercontrol

The everywhere present, everywhere connected space that emerges from this complex fusion of processes was likened by McLuhan, in a slightly different context, to a purely 'acoustic' space, one where connectivities are not discrete, but continuous and all pervasive. For, as he pointed out, we always say, 'Music shall *fill the air* . . . never music shall fill *a particular segment* of the air' (1967, p. 112). Within a hyperspace, the imaginary of a social order which disciplines by enclosure is as redundant as the belief that music is located 'somewhere'. Within hyperspace all social roles have the capacity to bleed into and submerge each other like a sound wave 'fills' the air.

Simmel's problem of the boundary thereby resurfaces as a key point of departure in the analysis of contemporary crime, just as it does for understanding the hyperspatialisation of social life in general. The deterritorialisations and reterritorialisations of a hyperspace geometry produce various forms of redistribution – a smearing outward of enclosed spaces such as the body, property or community. In turn this produces re-evaluations of where we are, where our property is, where local life and the State might be situated. And in so doing it also forces us to think again about where *harm* is, and where it might come from. Some effects, in criminal terms, are clearly fairly negligible. Street robberies, sexual assaults, damage to property or drunken disorder continue to exploit the possibilities available within proximal space much as they ever did. But other effects are more pronounced.

Property crime – most obviously in its 'psychologised' form as fraud – has also appeared to have acquired a new prominence. In fact, as something long sensitive to the effects of distance compression, property (at least in its monetary form) adapts quickly to hyperspace, forming dense and abstract flows that greatly multiply the possibilities for illicit acquisition. And as value is abstracted into more comprehensive network forms, theft now becomes as much about access *to* the network where value is, as it does about acquiring specific targets. The failure of both financial and justice systems to appreciate some of these subtleties means that many attempts to manage or prevent online financial crime actually worsen matters. Responses to the apparent threats posed by the 'theft' of an identity are one example. For, as property is increasingly protected by keys based on identification, the more such keys that circulate. Hence, the more ways into this network of value that open up. Misreadings of the transitions to property crime parallel the way that threats to the body in hyperspace have also been overstated. Sexual exploitations – most obviously those involving children – while always of concern, are in no way proportionate to the level of responses being enacted. Nor have there been any significant rises in the murder rate, or inflations to suicide that can be attributed to remote communications – unless one focuses upon the uses to which States and other control agents have put these technologies.

Elsewhere, as landscapes of local and global space are extended, misjudgements of the boundary problem also generate apparent threats which divert attention away from more insidious harms. The dread of spatial anarchy as long submerged cultures of nomadism are revitalised by mobility, produce spatial controls that create new kinds of global underclasses. In addition to the new asymmetries in economic and global mobility, imbalances in visibility and its policing exert a divisive affect upon all of us. And as local space becomes continuous with the global sphere of interaction, questions of respect take on more profound forms than the misdemeanours of feral youth. As commerce attempts to exert its own form of control over the consumer body with technologies of distance such as RFID or loyalty cards, the community itself is 'disrespected' by an upsurge in extended forms of anti-social behaviours. Intrusions by marketing or by spyware stake out new kinds of questions about anti-social behaviour and its criminalities, just as the 'commodification' of communities by remote social-networking where friendship is measured by quantity, rather than quality, force us to re-evaluate the whole issue of local harms.

It is also clear that a hyperspace produces boundary violations that we are less sure how to judge. A more connected world produces enhanced *symbiosis* – conjunctions of interests or goals which, for reasons of spatial or social distance, were previously closed or unattainable. *Hybridisation* takes this process still further, creating not just harmonies within social interaction but new fusions of them. These new formations of the hybrid and the symbiont, which extend beyond machinic/biological assemblages into the very heart of social interaction, produce more subtle effects upon criminality and the way that we choose to construct this. And so we wonder. Is it acceptable to sexually assault someone if they wish to be assaulted? Is it permissible to commit suicide *en masse* – as a social act? Could it ever be legitimate to eat someone if they wish to be eaten? And in our fixations upon the overtly 'monstrous' hybridisations, do we miss other, more deadly combinations that the hyperspatial brings in its wake – the citizen-criminal, the retail-jail, the modified-foodstuff, or the soldier-policeman? What is clear is that trying to reclaim certainty in terms of vacuous constructs like the 'cyberthief', the 'cyberterrorist', or the 'cyberstalker' is not going to be of very much long-term help.

It has also become an increasingly important consequence of hyperspatialisation that for every resource granted to control, there is a constant need for extra ones to supplement them. In this way the control society goes beyond the risk society, for attempts to 'manage the future' through statistical models or to 'defend space' by suspect profiling are absorbed, then superseded by the demands of spatial and temporal allatonceness. Of course some clear disadvantages for traditional acts of crime arise in the face of these new control capacities. The dark spaces for robbery become scanscapes, subject to remote intervention. And physical or sexual violence now leaves traces that can be tracked as easily as any offensive e-mail, as DNA continues to bear the witness of its code within an ever present temporality of possible detection.

Not every capacity for control is as welcome. Nor do these negative unfoldings of control involve only technologies of the database, the RFID chip, or the identity card. They can equally be seen in the insurance or direct marketing profiles, or even the votes on the reality show. And for every security advantage brought by enhanced control there is also a price to pay. For a smoothing of space which helps catch the criminal results in a smoothing of space for everyone else. As increasingly hybridised productions ourselves, we all become subject to the criminal gaze in this smooth space. The Leviathan finds itself in the network, constantly evaluating the potentials for boundary violation without fully understanding what boundaries now are.

Whither cybercrime? Wherefore hypercrime?

The thesis of cybercrime – or cyber crime if you like to split hairs (Smith *et al.*, 2004, p. 5) – is arguably another production of the hypercriminal itself. Its resulting obsessions with panics about financial crime or online predators mean that it has had little to say about State or corporate crimes involving the internet and even less about the increasing continuities between control, technology and irrational fear that are a product of a hypercrime society. It is hard not to feel that its utility as a tool for criminological inquiry is thereby compromised. So if its story is as incomplete or perhaps even as misleading as I have been suggesting, is the cybercrime agenda likely to just wither and die? The answer, for the time being at any rate, seems to be clearly not. For as both a vehicle of and legitimator for contemporary control there are plenty of vested interests in keeping it alive. The money spent by governments in developing their cybercrime programmes, and its usefulness as a justification for the productions of controls like identity cards is one influence. The need for the cybercrime industry to continue to sell its products for identity security, viral protection and surveillance is another. The rich pot of international funding available for research which 'explains' online child pornography, or which 'analyses' identity theft offer the academic their own reasons for perpetuating the story. All combine to lend it a kind of de facto existence.

It is important to re-emphasize that what has been suggested here is NOT an argument against the fact that computers or the internet are used in crime and will continue to be used whenever opportunity knocks. And if the study of 'cybercrime', 'cyber crime' or 'Cybercrime' amounts to the descriptive task of identifying the annual number and variety of crimes carried out by computer, then there will certainly be work enough to go around. Painting by numbers is one way to represent the world, though it does not of course ultimately tell us very much about what that world really looks like. On the whole though I suspect that in the long term, in spite of the vested interests here, the cybercrime agenda is not one that can be sustained indefinitely. Central to its problem – one that we have seen throughout – is the dismal failure to sort out the issues of *agency* in crime, from the *tools* of crime. As Douglas Adams once succinctly put this:

> Newsreaders still feel it is worth a special and rather worrying mention if, for instance, a crime was planned by people 'over the Internet.' They don't bother to mention when criminals use the telephone or the M4, or discuss their dastardly plans 'over a cup of tea,' though each of these was new and controversial in their day.
>
> (Adams, 1999)

Just as 'telephone crime', 'motorway crime' or 'cup-of-tea crime' never got off the drawing board as organising metaphors for deviance, cybercrime's brief ascendancy looks increasingly inappropriate – or worse, just dated.

So what if, as I have suggested, we do think more broadly than this and invoke spatial interaction, extension and social possibility in the context of contemporary deviance? What if we use the language of hyperspace or even hypercrime? Surely, it might be said, such considerations of space should be left to the mathematicians – or at least to the situational crime control crowd? Lyotard points out one reason why such a conclusion would be wrong:

> . . . it is hard to believe that what has been discussed between scientists and philosophers for a century must be of no interest to the . . . ideology of communication. The problems out of which emerged non-Euclidean geometry . . . and non Newtonian physics are also those which gave rise to the theories of communication and information.
>
> (Lyotard, 1991, p. 116)

In other words, not only are communication technologies fundamentally associated with producing the changes in the way we experience space, the way we *conceive* of space affects the communications technologies we produce and more importantly, the uses we put them to. Yet in a world where large proportions of budgets for crime control are directed at spatial management what would 'work' about a 'post-Euclidean' criminology? In particular, what would it look like? In this book I have only been able to deal with a painfully small class of consequences for harm which might arise from the geometries of a hyperspace. The 'magical' appearance of the internet and the pervasiveness of the cybercrime story has not only meant that it is the internet which has figured most prominently in the discussion here – often to the exclusion of the rich range of hyperspatialisating technologies and modes of representation now open to us. It has also meant that a great deal of the analysis has (necessarily) centred upon forms of interaction and experience conducted at a *distance*.

It should be clear by now however that our new experiences of space incorporate the very *near* as much as the very distant. Remote interaction applies equally here and has also been vastly aided by the technologies of representation and their capacity to model and to permit interaction with very small objects. In other words a more developed treatment of hyperspace and its effects upon deviant behaviour would need to see the continuum of the hyperspatial extending in a *single* medium of allatonceness. That is, one that analyses deviance conducted very 'close up' (in the manipulations of the molecular, the chemical, the atomic or the subatomic level) as much as that conducted from 'very far'. There are clearly huge implications for the practice of crime and perhaps even more for crime control which follow from our increased access to micro-spatial interaction. The manipulation of 'near-space' for harmful and destructive ends in the detonations at Nagasaki and Hiroshima puts the threat of harm arising from 'cyberterrorism' firmly into perspective, just as the implications of enhanced control over chemical and biological information seem far greater than the problems of card cloning. Yet the modification of genetic codes, the effects of narcotics (legal and illegal), the damage to the environment by chemical spillages, the theft of genetic information or its applications for control purposes are issues which have only just begun to be seen in terms of legalities and harms. And the prospect of our enhanced genetic understanding being used to produce biological hybrids which complement the more intangible social ones considered here is surely not an issue that ought to be left to the judgements of ethics committees alone. There are important consequences for the unfolding of crime and criminal justice here which are at least as significant as the illicit use of pin numbers.

It is clear, even from the brief signposting of threats from remote interaction at the very near, that many other issues arising from hyperspatiality would need to be dealt with before any serious account of the hypercriminality that goes with it could be constructed. But whatever criminology we ultimately choose to deal with transformations to the legal and the illegal, the normal and the deviant under these new regimes of spatial experience, it is clear that it should be one kept as free as possible from the vertigo of space-time annihilation. In a connected world, where consciousness and the social imaginary are themselves redistributed, the threat of madness is as much a danger of the network as credit card fraud. Marshall McLuhan – never mentioned in the cybercrime literature, even though almost everything he said is of fundamental relevance to the unfolding of 'crime by computer' – sums up the situation for crime control and our understanding of crime in the face of the hyperspatial like this:

> As our senses have gone outside us, Big Brother goes inside. So, unless aware of this dynamic, we shall at once move into a phase of panic terrors, exactly befitting a small world of tribal drums, total interdependence, and superimposed co-existence. [. . .] Terror is the normal state of any oral society, for in it everything affects everything all the time.
>
> (McLuhan, 1962, p. 32)

In our new 'oral' society, connected by networks that compress and complexify social space the tribal drums can beat very loud. Here, every latest 'personality' on YouTube, every latest e-mail rumour, every phishing attack, every virus or every online notification of a paedophile living nearby, provides us with experiences of a directness only paralleled in contexts where information travelled orally. But to see computers, the internet or mobile phones as what is *central* in this process is to fail (spectacularly) to see the wood for the trees. As Deleuze reminds us:

> Even technology makes the mistake of considering tools in isolation: tools exist only in relation to the interminglings they make possible or that make them possible . . . a society is defined by its amalgamations, not by its tools.
>
> (1988, p. 90)

The amalgamations and interminglings of the hyperspatial have only just begun to be explored within criminology and in the social sciences in general. But we can be sure that whatever is ultimately inferred from them we should be careful, as ever, to sort out the real harms from the phoney ones. All that is mingled may not turn out to be gold – but this does not mean that it will hurt us. Nor of course, is there any guarantee that it will not.

Notes

1 Crime and space

1   William Gibson, who notoriously coined the term 'cyberspace' in his *Neuromancer* (1984), used this phrase to describe it.
2   Originally published in *Le Figaro*, 20/02/1909. Reprinted in full in Ferrier *et al.* (1988).
3   There is nothing fixed here of course. It is *logically* possible that there could be normative systems where assault is relatively praiseworthy and library book theft a capital offence. The pragmatic point is that this does not seem to be a world where such conceptions are in operation.

3 Proximity 0: Body space

1   You can, for example, sign a petition to 'stop' suicide websites at http://www.thepetitionsite.com/takeaction/123299342?ltl=1155224223.

Bibliography

AACP 2002 *Proving the Connection: Links Between Intellectual Property Theft and Organised Crime*, Alliance against Counterfeiting and Piracy, London: AACP.

Aas, K. 2007 'Beyond the "desert of the real": crime control in a virtual(ised) reality' in Jewkes, Y. (ed.) *Crime Online*, Collumpton: Willan 160–178.

Abbate, J. 1999 *Inventing the Internet*, MIT Press.

ABC News 2004 'BT Child Porn Filter Stopping 23,000 Per Day', see: http://www.abc.net.au/news/newsitems/200407/s1158220.htm (viewed October 2004).

Ackleson, J. 2005 'Border Security Technologies: Local and Regional Implications', *Review of Policy Research*, 22(2), 137–155.

ACLU 2000 *Genetic Discrimination in the Workplace*, Factsheet (31/12/00).

Adams, D. 1999 'How to Stop Worrying and Love the Internet', *Sunday Times* 29/08/99, available at: http://www.douglasadams.com/dna/19990901-00-a.html (viewed March 2007).

Adams, J. 2005 'Hypermobility: a challenge to governance' in Lyall, C. and Tait, J. (eds) *New Modes of Governance: Developing an Integrated Policy Approach to Science, Technology, Risk and the Environment*, Aldershot: Ashgate.

Addley, E. 2000 'Card Tricks', *Guardian* 101/05/00, see: http://www.guardian.co.uk/Archive/Article/0,4273,4016830,00.html.

Affonso, B. 1999 'Is the Internet affecting the social skills of our children?' Retrieved March 10, 2004, from http://www.sierrasource.com/cep612/internet.html (viewed March 2007).

Agamben, G. 2003 *The Coming Community*, University of Minnesota Press.

—— 2005 *State of Exception*, University of Chicago Press.

The Age 13/01/03 'Terminal Gaming', see: http://www.theage.com.au/articles/2003/01/13/1041990220891.html.

Agger, B. 2004 *The Virtual Self*, Oxford: Blackwell.

Ahlbom, A. (*et al.*) 2000 'A pooled analysis of magnetic fields and childhood leukaemia,' *British Journal of Cancer*, 83(5), 692–698.

Ahmed, K. 2002 'Rebellion over plans for ID card', *Guardian* 30/06/02, see: http://observer.guardian.co.uk/libertywatch/story/0,,746744,00.html.

Ahmed, Z. 2006 'Abuse rattles Indian call centre staff', BBC 22/02/06, see: http://news.bbc.co.uk/1/hi/business/4738804.stm (viewed March 2007).

Ahrens, F. 2004 'MPAA to Sue Over Movie File Sharing', *Washington Post* 05/11/04, see: http://www.washingtonpost.com/wp-dyn/articles/A25784-2004Nov4.html.

Aiello, J.R. 1993 'Computer-based work monitoring: electronic surveillance and its effects', *Journal of Applied Social Psychology*, 23(7), 499–507.

Aizawa, K. 1994 'Representations without Rules, Connectionism and the Syntactic Argument', *Synthese*, 101, 465–492.

Akdeniz, Y. 1998 'Who watches the Watchmen II: Accountability & Effective Self-regulation in the Information Age', *Cyber-Rights & Cyber-Liberties (UK) Report*, available at: http://www.cyber-rights.org/watchmen-ii.htm.

Akdeniz, Y., Walker, C. and Wall, D. (eds) 2000 *The Internet, Law & Society*, Longman.

Akdeniz, Y., Taylor, N. and Walker, C. 2001 'Regulation of Investigatory Powers Act 2000 (1): Bigbrother.gov.uk: State surveillance in the age of information and rights', *Criminal Law Review* (February), 73–90.

Alao, A., Yolles, J. and Armenta, W. 1999 'Cybersuicide: The Internet and Suicide', *American Journal of Psychiatry*, 156: 1836–1837.

Albrecht, K. and McIntyre, L. 2006 *Spychips: How Major Corporations and Government Plan to Track Your Every Move with RFID*, Nelson Current.

Albrow, M. 1996 *The Global Age*, Cambridge: Polity Press.

Altheide, D. L. 2002 *Creating Fear: News and the Construction of Crisis*, New York: Aldine de Gruyter.

AMA 2001 'Annual Survey on Workplace Monitoring and Surveillance', *American Management Association*, 18 April.

—— 2003 'E-Mail Rules, Policies and Practices Survey', *American Management Association* (in conjunction with the ePolicy Institute, and Clearswift).

Amazon 2004 Book Description: 'Tracker: Hunting Down Serial Killers' by Godwin, M., available at: http://www.amazon.com/exec/obidos/ASIN/1560256346/oasisinstitut-20.

Amicus 2005 'Privacy At Work', *Amicus Guide*, June, see: http://www.amicustheunion.org/pdf/PrivacyatWork.pdf (viewed March 2007).

Amin, A. 1994 *Post-Fordism: A Reader*, Oxford: Blackwell.

Amnesty 2006 'Facts and Figures on the Death Penalty', see: http://web.amnesty.org/pages/deathpenalty-facts-eng.

Anderson, B. 1991 *Imagined Communities: Reflection on the Origin and Spread of Nationalism*, London: Verso.

Anderson, K. 2001a 'Whitehouse website attacked', BBC 05/05/01, see: http://news.bbc.co.uk/1/hi/world/americas/1313753.stm (viewed March 2007).

—— 2001b 'Hacktivists take sides in war', BBC 23/10/01, http://news.bbc.co.uk/1/hi/world/americas/1614927.stm.

Anderson, M. and Meyer, B. (eds) 2001 *Thinking with Diagrams*, Dordrecht: Kluwer.

Anderson, S. and Cavanagh, J. 2000 'Top 200 – The Rise of Corporate Global Power', *Institute for Policy Studies*, available at: http://www.ips-dc.org/downloads/Top_200.pdf.

Andert, S. and Burleson, D. 2005 *Web Stalkers: Protect Yourself from Internet Criminals and Psychopaths*, Rampart TechPress (Sleevenotes see: http://www.rampant-books.com/book_2004_2_stalkers.htm).

Anti-Bullying Alliance 2007 Homepage, see: http://www.anti-bullyingalliance.org.uk/Page.asp.

AOH 2007 'Phreaking Boxes', *Art of Hacking*, see: http://artofhacking.com/tucops/phreak/boxes/index.htm.

AP 05/06/1998 'First Cyber-terrorist Action Reported'.

APACS 2006 'UK Card Fraud Losses in 2005 Fall by £65m', Press Release 06/02/06, see: http://www.apacs.org.uk/media_centre/press/06_03_07.html.

—— 2007 'Fraud Abroad Drives Up Card Fraud Losses', Press Release 03/10/07, see: www.apacs.org.uk/media-centre/press/03.10.07.html.

APIG 2004 'Revision of the Computer Misuse Act: Report of an Inquiry by the All Party Internet Group', House of Commons, June, available at: http://www.apig.org.uk/archive/activities-2004/computer-misuse-inquiry/CMAReportFinalVersion1.pdf.

Aquinas, T. 2006 *Summa Theologica*, ed. Gilby, T., Cambridge University Press.

Arblaster, P. 2005 'Posts, Newsletters, Newspapers: England in a European System of Communications', *Media History*, 11(1–2), 21–36.

Arendt, H. 1958 *The Human Condition*, University of Chicago Press.

—— 1987 'Collective Responsibility', in *Amor Mundi*, ed. Bernaver, J.W. Dordrecht: Martinus Nijhoff Publishers, p. 50ff.

Argyle, K. and Shields, R. 1996 'Is there a Body in the Net?' in Shields, R. (ed.) *Cultures of Internet*, London: Sage.

Aristotle, 1984 'Nicomachean Ethics', in *The Complete Works of Aristotle, The Revised Oxford Translation*, vol. 2, ed. Jonathan Barnes, Princeton University Press.

Aristotle 1998 *Politics* (trans E. Barker), Oxford University Press.

Armitage, D. 2000 *The Ideological Origins of the British Empire*, Cambridge University Press.

Armstrong, D.M. 1989 *A Combinatorial Theory of Possibility*, Cambridge University Press.

Army of God 2007 'Paul Hill Website', see: http://www.armyofgod.com/Paulhillindex.html.

Arnau, F. 1959 *The Art of The Faker: 3,000 Years of Deception*, Boston: Little Brown.

Arnett, P. 1997 'Vietnam and War Reporting', *Media Studies Journal*, pp. 33–38.

Arquilla, J. and Ronfeldt, D. 1993 'Cyberwar is Coming!' *Comparative Strategy*, 12(2), 141–165.

—— 1996 The Advent of Netwar, *Rand Monograph*.

Arthur, C. 2006 'Top of the Heap', *Guardian* 31/08/06, see: http://technology.guardian.co.uk/weekly/story/0,,1861112,00.html.

Arvidsson, A. 2006 ' "Quality Singles": Internet Dating and the Work of Fantasy', *New Media & Society*, 8(4), 671–690.

ASA 2007 'Advertising Standards Authority Website', see: http://www.asa.org.uk/asa/.

Ashbourn, J. 2000 *Biometrics: Advanced Identity Verification: The Complete Guide*, Springer.

AskCALEA 2006 CALEA homepage, see: http://www.askcalea.net/.

Askegaard, S. 1991 'Towards a semiotic structure of cultural identity'. *Marketing Semiotics*, Series F(62), Nyt Nordisk Forlag Arnold Busck A/S, Copenhagen, 11–29.

AT & T 1909 *Annual Report*, available at: http://www.porticus.org/bell/att/historical_financial.htm.

Attorney General 1999 'Cyberstalking: A New Challenge for Law Enforcement and Industry', www.cybercrime.gov.

Auster, C. 1996 *Sociology of Work: Concepts and Cases*, Thousand Oaks, CA: Pine Forge Press.

Austin, N.J. and Rankov, N.B. 1995 *Exploratio: Military and Political Intelligence in the Roman World From the Second Punic War to the Battle of Adrianople*, London: Routledge.

Azmi, I., Maniatis, S. and Sodipo, B. 1997 'Distinctive Signs and Early Markets' in A. Firth, *The Prehistory and Development of Intellectual Property Systems*, London: Sweet and Maxwell.

Bachmann, M. 2006 'Lesson Spurned? Reactions of Online Music Pirates to Legal Prosecutions by the RIAA', Conference Presentation, American Society of Criminology, Los Angeles, November.

Bain, P. 1998 'The 1986–87 News International dispute', *Historical Studies in Industrial Relations*, 5, 73–105.

Baker, A. and Vasquez, E. 2007 'Number of People Stopped by New York Police Soars', *New York Times* 03/02/07, see: http://www.nytimes.com/2007/02/03/ nyregion/ 03frisk.html?_r=1&oref=slogin.

Baker, J. C. *et al.* 2004 'Mapping the Risks: Assessing the Homeland Security Implications of Publicly Available Geospatial Information', Rand Corporation (MG-142-NGA).

Baker, K. 1999 'Taming the Wild, Wild Web', *Business Week* 04/10/99, see: http:// www.businessweek.com/1999/99_40/b3649021.htm.

Bales, K. 2004 *Disposable People: New Slavery in the Global Economy*, Berkeley: University of California Press.

Ball, K.S. 2001 'Situating Workplace Surveillance: Ethics and Computer-based Performance Monitoring', *Ethics and Information Technology*, 3 (3), 209–221.

Ballard, M. 2006 'Hands Off our Bank Data, Europe Tells US', *Register* 23/11/06, see: http://www.theregister.co.uk/2006/11/23/ec_swift_ruling/.

Ballinger, L. 2006 'Embarrassed City Girl Apologies as Party Email Goes Around the Globe', *Daily Mail* 25/08/06, see: http://www.dailymail.co.uk/pages/live/ articles/news/news.html?in_article_id = 402244&in_page_id = 1770&in_page_id = 1770 &expand = true.

Balz, D. and Allen, M. 2004 'Four More Years Attributed to Rove's Strategy', *Washington Post* 07/11/04, see: http://www.washingtonpost.com/ac2/wp-dyn/ A31003-2004Nov6?language=printer.

Banks, M. 1997 *Web Psychos, Stalkers and Pranksters*, Coriolis Group.

Barak, G. (ed.) 1991 *Crimes by the Capitalist State: An Introduction to State Criminality*, Albany: State University of New York Press.

—— 2001 'Crime and Crime Control in an Age of Globalization: A Theoretical Dissection', *Critical Criminology*, 10 (1), 57–72.

Barclay, G. *et al.* 2003 'International Comparisons of Criminal Justice Statistics 2001', Issue 12/03, *Research, Development & Statistics Directorate*, Home Office, see: http://www.csdp.org/research/hosb1203.pdf.

Barker, F. 1984 *The Tremulous Private Body: Essays in Subjection*, London : Methuen.

Barlow, J. 1996 'A Cyberspace Independence Declaration', available at: http://www. eff.org/Misc/Publications/John_Perry_Barlow/barlow_0296.declaration.txt.

Barrett, N. 1997 *Digital Crime: Policing the Cybernation*, Kogan Page.

Barrett, P.M., Rapee, R.M., Dadds, M.M. and Ryan, S.M. 1996 'Family Enhancement of Cognitive Style in Anxious and Aggressive Children', *Journal of Abnormal Child Psychology*, 24, 187–203.

Barzilai-Nahon, K. and Neumann, S. 2005 'Bounded in Cyberspace: An Empirical Model of Self-regulation in Virtual Communities', System Sciences, HICSS '05,

Proceedings of the 38th Annual Hawaii International Conference, p. 192b, available at: http://ieeexplore.ieee.org/search/wrapper.jsp?arnumber =1385627#.

Bataille, G. 1991/2 *The Accursed Share*, I–III, trans. Hurley, R., MIT Press.

Baudrillard, J. 1983 *Simulations*, New York: Semiotext(e).

—— 1988 'Simulacra and Simulations' in *Jean Baudrillard, Selected Writings*, Poster, M. (ed.), Stanford: Stanford University Press, pp. 166–184.

—— 1994 *Simulacra and Simulation*, Trans. Sheila Faria Glaser, Ann Arbor: University of Michigan.

—— 1998 *The Consumer Society: Myths and Structures*, Sage.

Bauman, Z. 1998 *Globalization: The Human Consequences*. New York: Columbia University Press.

—— 2001 *Community: Seeking Safety in an Insecure World*, Cambridge: Polity Press.

Baume, P., Cantor, C.H. and Rolfe, A. 1997 'Cybersuicide: The Role of Interactive Suicide Notes on the Internet', *Crisis: The Journal of Crisis Intervention & Suicide Prevention*, 18 (2), 73–79.

Bautsch, H. *et al.* 2001 'An Investigation of Mobile Phone Use: A Socio-technical Approach', *Department of Industrial Engineering*, University of Wisconsin, see: http://www.cae.wisc.edu/~granger/IE449/IE449_0108.pdf.

Bayley, D.H. and Shearing, C.D. 2001 *The New Structure of Policing: Description, Conceptualization, and Research Agenda*, Washington, DC: National Institute of Justice.

BBB 2005 'Javelin Identity Fraud Survey Report', produced for Federal Trade Commission by Better Business Bureau in conjunction with Javelin Strategy & Research, see: http://www.bbb.org/alerts/article.asp?ID=565 or http://www.javelinstrategy.com/research?all=true.

BBC 15/02/86 '1986: Printers and Police Clash in Wapping', see: http://news.bbc.co.uk/onthisday/hi/dates/stories/february/15/newsid_3455000/3455083.stm.

BBC 05/07/00 'European Parliament Investigates US Industrial Espionage', see http://news.bbc.co.uk/1/hi/world/europe/820821.stm.

BBC 18/04/01 'Cybercops Arrest Online Liberty', see: http://news.bbc.co.uk/1/hi/sci/tech/1283127.stm.

BBC 20/07/01 'Napster Use Slumps 65%', see: http://news.bbc.co.uk/1/hi/business/1449127.stm.

BBC 13/12/01 'Man Faces "Internet" Rape Charge', see: http://news.bbc.co.uk/1/hi/scotland/1489150.stm.

BBC 28/01/03 'MPs Urge Changes to Net Snooping Laws', see: http://news.bbc.co.uk/1/hi/technology/2702889.stm.

BBC 20/05/03 'Stalker had Sophisticated Cyber Plan', see: http://news.bbc.co.uk/1/hi/uk/3040623.stm.

BBC 16/06/03 'Labour Website Hacked', see: http://news.bbc.co.uk/1/hi/uk_politics/2993550.stm.

BBC 15/09/03 'Has the Jackal Passport Scam Had its Day?', see http://news.bbc.co.uk/1/hi/magazine/3098104.stm.

BBC 10/03/04 'US Bars Backdoor Pop-up Adverts', see http://news.bbc.co.uk/1/hi/technology/3551356.stm.

BBC 09/04/04 'Camera Recovered from Cashpoint', see: http://news.bbc.co.uk/1/hi/england/tees/3614047.stm.

BBC 08/05/04 'US Powerless to Halt Iraq Net Images', see: http://news.bbc.co.uk/1/hi/world/americas/3695897.stm.

BBC 12/10/04 'Nine die in Japan "Suicide Pacts" ', see: http://news.bbc.co.uk/1/hi/world/asia-pacific/3735372.stm.

BBC 27/10/04 'Bush Website Blocked Outside US', see: http://news.bbc.co.uk/1/hi/technology/3958665.stm.

BBC 16/02/05 'US "Using Spying Drones on Iran" ', see: http://news.bbc.co.uk/1/hi/world/middle_east/4269835.stm.

BBC 21/02/05 ' "Most Annoying Ads" Pop Up Again', see: http://news.bbc.co.uk/1/hi/business/4284449.stm.

BBC 22/02/05 'Google's Toolbar Sparks Concern', see: http://news.bbc.co.uk/1/hi/technology/4287539.stm.

BBC 17/03/05 'UK Police Foil Massive Bank Theft' see: http://news.bbc.co.uk/1/hi/uk/4356661.stm.

BBC 31/03/05 ' "Game Theft" Led to Fatal Attack', see: http://news.bbc.co.uk/1/hi/technology/4397159.stm.

BBC 01/04/05 'Centre to Tackle Net Paedophiles', http://news.bbc.co.uk/1/hi/uk_politics/4399183.stm.

BBC 15/04/05 'Security Scare Hits HSBC's Cards', see: http://news.bbc.co.uk/1/hi/business/4444477.stm.

BBC 20/05/05 'Google Offers Personalised Pages', see: http://news.bbc.co.uk/1/hi/business/4565379.stm.

BBC 23/06/05 'Indian Call Centre Fraud Probe', see: http://news.bbc.co.uk/1/hi/uk/4121934.stm.

BBC 08/11/05 'Grokster Quits File-sharing Fight', see: http://news.bbc.co.uk/1/hi/technology/4416484.stm.

BBC 06/01/06 'The Million Dollar Student', see http://news.bbc.co.uk/1/hi/magazine/4585026.stm.

BBC 02/02/06 'Web Suicide Pacts Surge in Japan', see: http://news.bbc.co.uk/1/hi/world/asia-pacific/4695864.stm.

BBC 10/02/06 'Spyware Warriors Call for Action', see http://news.bbc.co.uk/1/hi/technology/4696532.stm.

BBC 20/03/06 'European Phishing Gangs Targeted', see: http://news.bbc.co.uk/1/hi/technology/4825072.stm.

BBC 28/03/06 'BitTorrent Search Site Hits Back', see http://news.bbc.co.uk/1/hi/technology/4853674.stm.

BBC 21/06/06 'Action Urged on Far-right Website', see: http://news.bbc.co.uk/1/hi/uk_politics/5102836.stm.

BBC 27/07/06 'Government Acts on Cyberbullies', see: http://news.bbc.co.uk/1/hi/education/5210886.stm.

BBC 27/07/06 'More Than 95% of E-mail is "Junk" ', see: http://news.bbc.co.uk/1/hi/technology/5219554.stm.

BBC 23/10/06 'Costumes Track Trick or Treaters', see: http://news.bbc.co.uk/1/hi/england/london/6078076.stm.

BBC 6/12/06 'Flatulence Leads US Jet to Divert', see: http://news.bbc.co.uk/1/hi/world/americas/6213644.stm.

BBC 13/12/06 'Online Banking Fraud "up 8,000%" ', http://news.bbc.co.uk/1/hi/uk_politics/6177555.stm.

BBC 28/03/07 'Call for Blogging Code of Conduct', see: http://news.bbc.co.uk/1/hi/technology/6502643.stm.

BBC 24/04/07 'Motorists Hit by Card Clone Scam', see: http://news.bbc.co.uk/1/hi/uk/6578595.stm.

BBC 06/10/07 'MPs Call for Identity Fraud Tsar', see: http://news.bbc.co.uk/1/hi/business/7031137.stm.

BBS Archives, 1995 Archive File Area, see: http://archives.thebbs.org/.

BBS Corner 2006 Home Page, see: http://www.dmine.com/bbscorner.

Beck, U. 2006 *Power in the Global Age: A New Global Political Economy*, Cambridge: Polity Press.

Becker, T. and Slaton, C. 2000 *The Future of Teledemocracy*, Westport, CT: Praeger.

Belk, R.W. 1988 'Possessions and the Extended Self,' *Journal of Consumer Research*, 15 (2), 139–168.

Bell, D. 1973 *The Coming of Post Industrial Society*, New York: Basic Books.

Bell, R. 2007 'Love in the Time of Phone Porn', *Guardian* 30/01/2007, see: http://education.guardian.co.uk/egweekly/story/0,,2001171,00.html.

Bellamy, E. 1888 *Looking Backwards 2000–1887*, Houghton Mifflin.

Bellamy, J. 1973 *Crime and Public Order in Britain in the Late Middle Ages*, London: Routledge & Kegan Paul.

Bellis, D. 2004 'I'm Angry I Can't Sue for Arrest Nightmare', *IcNetwork*, 17/05/04 http://icnorthwales.icnetwork.co.uk/news/regionalnews/tm_objectid=14248256&method=full&siteid=50142&headline=i-m-angry-i-can-t-sue-for-arrest-nightmare-lynn-pierce-name_page.html.

Benedikt, M. (ed.) 1992 *Cyberspace, First Steps*, MIT Press.

—— 1992(b) 'Cyberspace, Some Proposals' in Benedikt, M. (ed.) *Cyberspace, First Steps*, pp. 119–224.

Beniger, J. 1986 *The Control Revolution: The Technological and Economic Origins of the Information Society*, Cambridge, MA: Harvard University Press.

—— 1987 'Personalisation of the Mass Media and the Growth of Pseudo Community', *Communication Research*, 14(3), 352–371.

Benjamin, W. 1969 'The Work of Art in the Age of Mechanical Reproduction' reprinted in *Illuminations*, New York: Schocken Books.

—— 1994 'Writing, Time, and Task', in P. Osborne and A. Benjamin (eds), *Walter Benjamin's Philosophy*, London: Routledge.

Bennett, C.J. 2001 'Cookies, Web Bugs, Webcams and Cue Cats: Patterns of Surveillance on the World Wide Web', *Ethics and Information Technology*, 3 (3), 195–208(14).

Bequai, A. 1987 *Technocrimes: The Computerisation of Crime and Terrorism*, DC Heath & Company.

Bergstein, B. 2004 'Database Technology Helps Lawyers Scoop Up Clients', *USA Today* 28/03/04, available at: http://www.usatoday.com/tech/news/2004-03-28-database-chasers_x.htm.

—— 2005 'Beware the Numbers Hype About ID Theft', *USA Today* 13/11/05, see: http://www.usatoday.com/tech/news/techinnovations/2005-11-13-id-theft-numbers_x.htm.

Berlant, M. 2003 'Government Investigates Online Sale of Fake Diplomas', *The Daily Aztec* (San Diego State U.) 12/02/03, see: http://www.uwire.com/content/topnews021203002.html.

Berleur, J. and Brunnstein, K., (eds) 1996 *Ethics of Computing: Codes, Spaces for Discussion and Law*, London: Chapman & Hall.

Berman, M. 1982 *All That Is Solid Melts Into Air: The Experience Of Modernity*, Verso.

Bernard, T. 2002 'Donald Black's Influence in Criminology', *Contemporary Sociology*, 31 (6), 650–652.

Berrigan, F., Hartung, W. and Heffel, L. 2005 'U.S. Weapons at War 2005: Promoting Freedom or Fueling Conflict?', Arms Trade Resource Center, World Policy Institute, available at: www.worldpolicy.org/projects/arms/reports/wawjune2005.html.

Berry-Dee, C. and Morris, P. 2006 *Killers on the Web: True Stories of Internet Cannibals, Murderers and Sex Criminals*, John Blake Publishing.

Best, J. 2004 'Criminal Gangs Blackmail Web Users with Porn Threat', ZDNet 22/07/04, see: http://news.zdnet.co.uk/security/0,1000000189,39161410,00.htm.

Bettinger, R.L. 1991 *Hunter-gatherers: Archaeological and Evolutionary Theory*, New York: Plenum Press.

Between the Lines 2007 'Global Social Justice Movement; Archives', see: http://www.wpkn.org/wpkn/news/gopconvention.html.

Biashelp 2006 Bias Help website, see: http://www.biashelp.org/.

Bickers, C. 2001 'Cyberwar: Combat on The Web', *Far Eastern Economic Review*, 16 (8).

Biddle, P. *et al.* 2002 'The Darknet and the Future of Content Distribution', ACM Workshop on Digital Rights Management presentation paper, available at: http://www.bearcave.com/misl/misl_tech/msdrm/darknet.htm.

Biegel, S. 2001 *Beyond Our Control? Confronting the Limits of Our Legal System in the Age of Cyberspace*, MIT Press.

Biever, C. 2005 'Voters Empowered by Internet Swap Shop', *New Scientist* 30/04/05, see: http://www.newscientist.com/article.ns?id=dn7330.

Bigge, R. 2006 'The Cost of (Anti-)social Networks: Identity, Agency and Neo-luddites', *First Monday*, 11 (12), see: http://firstmonday.org/issues/issue11_12/bigge/index.html.

Bivens, L. 2005 'Truth and Consequences of Offshoring', *Economic Policy Institute Briefing*, 155, see: http://www.epinet.org/content.cfm/bp155.

Black, D. 1976 *The Behavior of Law*, Academic Press Inc.

—— 2004 'The Geometry of Terrorism', *Sociological Theory*, 22 (1), 14–25.

Black, J. 1999 'Losing Ground Bit by Bit: Information Rich, Information Poor', BBC 1/11/99, see: http://news.bbc.co.uk/1/hi/special_report/1999/10/99/information_rich_information_poor/472621.stm.

Black, M. 1962 'The Identity of Indiscernibles', *Mind*, 61, 153–164.

Blackman, D.R. and Hodge, A.T. (eds) 2001 *Frontinus' Legacy: Essays on Frontinus' De Aquis Urbis Romae*, Ann Arbor: The University of Michigan Press.

Blinder, A. 2006 'Offshoring: The Next Industrial Revolution?', *Foreign Affairs*, 85 (2), 113–128.

Bloor, D. 1997 *Wittgenstein: Rules and Institutions*, London: Routledge.

Blythman, J. 2004 *Shopped: The Shocking Power of British Supermarkets*, Fourth Estate.

BNP 2006 British National Party website at: http://www.bnp.org.uk/.

Bocij, P. 2002 'Corporate Cyberstalking: An Invitation to Build Theory', *First Monday*, 7 (11) see: http://firstmonday.org/issues/issue7_11/bocij/index.html.

Boden, D. and Molotch, H. 1994 'The Compulsion to Proximity' in Friedland, R. and Boden, D. (eds) *Now/Here. Time, Space and Modernity*. Berkeley: University of California Press.

Bodisch, R. 2002 'Cyber Warfare: The Perfect Terrorist Weapon', *Close Up*, 8 (4), Texas Commission on Law Enforcement.

Bogard, W. 1996 *The Simulation of Surveillance: Hyper Control in Telematic Societies*, New York: Cambridge University Press.

—— 2006 'Welcome to the Society of Control: The Simulation of Surveillance Revisited' in Haggerty, K. and Ericson, R. (eds) *The New Politics of Surveillance and Visibility*, pp. 55–78.

Böhle, K., Rader, M. and Riehm, U. 1999 *Electronic Payment Systems in European Countries: Country Synthesis Report*, Institute for Technology Assessment and Systems Analysis, Karlsruhe (September), at http://www.itas.fzk.de/deu/projekt/pez/emuis.htm.

Bollag, B. 2004 'Don't Steal This Book', *Chronicle of Higher Education* 02/04/04, see: http://chronicle.com/free/v50/i30/30a03801.htm.

Bolter, J. and Grusin, R. 1999 *Remediation*, Cambridge, MA: MIT Press, pp. 230–265, reprinted as 'The Remediated Self' in Bell, D. *Cybercultures: Critical Concepts in Media and Cultural Studies* (2006).

Bonabeau, E., Dorigo, M. and Theraulaz, G. 1999 *Swarm Intelligence: From Natural to Artificial Systems*, New York: Oxford University Press.

Bone, J. 2006 'Body Parts Thieves Cut Off Alistair Cooke's Legs', *Times* 26/03/06, see: http://www.timesonline.co.uk/tol/news/world/us_and_americas/article737888.ece.

Boneva, B. and Kraut, R. 2002 'Email, Gender and Personal Relations' in Wellman, B. and Haythornthwaite, C. (eds) *The Internet in Everyday Life*, Blackwell.

Borgmann, A. 2001 'Information, Nearness, and Farness' in Goldman, K. (ed.) *Robot in the Garden: Telerobotics and Telepistemology in the Age of the Internet*, Cambridge, MA: MIT Press, pp. 90–107.

Boston Phoenix 2000 'Murder.Com', 10/08/00, available at: http://72.166.46.24//archive/features/00/08/10/MURDER.html.

Bosworth, M. 2005 'Loyalty Cards: Reward or Threat?', *Consumer Affairs* 27/07/05, see: http://www.consumeraffairs.com/news04/2005/loyalty_cards.html.

Boulter, J. and Grusin, R. 2006 'The Remediated Self' in Bell, D. *Cybercultures: Critical Concepts in Media and Cultural Studies*, 3–29. Reprinted from their *Remediation*, Cambridge, MA: MIT Press (1999).

Bourdieu, P. 1977 *Outline of a Theory of Practice*, Cambridge: Cambridge University Press.

—— 1984 *Distinction: A Social Critique of the Judgement of Taste*, Cambridge, MA: Harvard University Press.

—— 1990 *The Logic of Practice*, Cambridge: Polity Press.

—— 1998 *Practical Reason: On the Theory of Action*, Cambridge: Polity Press.

Bowling, B. and Weber, L. 2004 'Policing Migration: A Framework for Investigating the Regulation of Global Mobility', *Policing and Society*, 14 (3) 195–212.

Boyd, A. 2003 'Email & the Internet Rewires the U.S. Social Change Movement', *The Nation* 04/08/03, available at: http://www.organicconsumers.org/corp/internet_social_change.cfm.

Boyd, D. 2003 'Reflections on Friendster, Trust and Intimacy', see: http://www.danah.org/papers/Ubicomp2003WorkshopApp2.pdf.

—— 2006 'Identity Production in a Networked Culture: Why Youth Heart MySpace', at http://www.danah.org/papers/AAAS2006.html.

Boyle, J. 1997 'Foucault in Cyberspace; Surveillance, Sovereignty and Hard-wired Censors', *University of Cincinnati Law Review*, 66, 177–205.

Brand, S. 1988 *The Media Lab: Inventing the Future at M.I.T.*, Penguin Books.

Brandeis, L. 1928 'Dissenting Opinion in Olmstead vs. United States', 277 U.S. 438.

Brandon, D. 2004 *Stand and Deliver!: A History of Highway Robbery*, Sutton.

Brantingham, P.J. and Brantingham, P.L. 1978 'A Topological Technique for Regionalization', *Environment and Behavior*, 10, 335–353.

Brantingham, P.J. and Brantingham, P.L. 1991 *Environmental Criminology*, Prospect Heights, IL: Waveland Press.

Braudel, F. 1981 *Civilization and Capitalism 15th–18th Century*. Volume I. *The Structures of Everyday Life*, trans. Sian Reynolds, New York: Harper and Row.

Braverman, H. 1999 *Labor and Monopoly Capital*, New York: Monthly Review.

Breining-Kaufman, C. 2007 *Globalization And Labour Rights*, Hart Books.

Brenner, S. 2001 'State Cybercrime Legislation in the United States of America: A Survey', *Richmond Journal of Law & Technology*, 7 (28), see: http://law.richmond.edu/jolt/v7i3/article2.html.

—— 2004 'Towards a Criminal Law for Cyberspace – Distributed Security', *Boston University Journal of Science and Technology Law*, 10 (2).

—— 2007 'Cybercrime: Re-thinking Crime Control Strategies' in Jewkes, Y. (ed.) *Crime Online*, Willan, pp. 12–28.

Breslow, H. 1997 'Civil Society, Political Economy and the Internet' in Jones, S. G. (ed.) *Virtual Culture: Identity and Communication in Cybersociety*, London: Sage, pp. 236–257.

Breslow, M. 1995 'Crimes of Fashion: Those Who Suffer to Bring You Gap T-Shirts'. *Dollars and Sense*, November/December.

Briggs, A. and Burke, P. 2002 *A Social History of the Media*, Oxford: Polity Press.

BCS 2003/4 'Crime in England and Wales 2003/2004': British Crime Survey, Supplementary Volume 1: Homicide and Gun Crime, HOSB 14/04.

Brodeur, J.P. 1983 'High Policing and Low Policing; Remarks about the Policing of Political Activities', *Social Problems*, 30 (5), 507–520.

—— 2000 'Cops and Spooks', *Police Research and Practice*, 1 (3), 229–321.

Brodeur, J.P. and Leman-Langlois, S. 2006 'Surveillance Fiction or Higher Policing' in Haggerty and Ericson (eds) *Surveillance and Visibility*, pp. 171–198.

Broersma, M. 2005 'Security Experts Criticize Malware List', *Techworld.com* 08/12/05, see: http://seclists.org/isn/2005/Dec/0061.html.

Brooke, J. 1985 'A Suicide Spurs Town To Debate Nature Of Game', *New York Times*, 22 August.

Brown, J. and Duguid, P. 2002 'Local Knowledge: Innovation in the Networked Age', available at: http://www.johnseelybrown.com/LocalKnowledge(6_02).pdf.

Brown, M. *et al.* 1997 'Epidemiology of Suicide Pacts in England and Wales, 1988–92', *British Medical Journal*, 315, 286–287.

Brown, R. 1968 *History of Accounting and Accountants*, London: Frank Cass & Co.

Brown, S. 2006 'The Criminology of Hybrids: Rethinking Crime and Law in Technosocial Networks', *Theoretical Criminology*, 10 (2), 223–244.

Bruce, R.V. 1990 *Alexander Graham Bell and the Conquest of Solitude*, Ithaca, NY: Cornell University Press.

Bruckman, A. 1996 'Gender Swapping on the Internet' in Ludlow, P. (ed.) *High Noon on the Electronic Frontier: Conceptual Issues in Cyberspace*, Cambridge, MA: MIT Press, pp. 317–325.

Buckley, M. 2004 'Do Loyalty Cards Invade Our Privacy?', BBC 19/11/04.

Budd, T. 2001 'Burglary: Practice Notes from the British Crime Survey', *Home Office Briefing Note* 5/01, available at: http://www.homeoffice.gov.uk/rds/prgpdfs/ brf501.pdf#search=%22uk%20burglaries%20main%20access%20points%22.

Burke, J. 1991 'Communication in the Middle Ages' in Crowley, D. and Heyer, P. *Communication in History*, Longman, pp. 67–76.

Burns, S. 1998 *A Morning's Work: Medical Photographs from the Burns Archive & Collection, 1843–1939*, Twin Palms Publishers.

Burroughs, W. 1959 *Naked Lunch*, Grove Press; Reissue edition (January 1992).

Burrus, V. 2003 'Macrina's Tattoo', *Journal of Medieval and Early Modern Studies*, 33 (3) 403–417.

Bush, V. 1945 'As We May Think', *The Atlantic Monthly*, July, see: http://www.ps. uni-sb.de/~duchier/pub/vbush/vbush-all.shtml.

Button, J. 2006 'How Lucy's Email Became an Inbox Hit', *The Age*, 01/09/2006, http:// www.theage.com.au/news/web/how-lucys-email-became-an-inbox-hit/2006/09/01/ 1156817083656.html?page=fullpage.

Byassee, W. 1995 'Jurisdiction of Cyberspace: Applying Real World Precedent to the Virtual Community', *Wake Forest Law Review*, 30, 197–220.

Cabinet Office 2002 'Identity Fraud: A Study', July.

Cahlink, G. 2004 'War of the Machines', *Government Executive*, 11/0704, see: http:// www.govexec.com/features/0704–15/0704–15s5.htm.

Cairncross, F. 1997 *The Death of Distance: How the Communications Revolution Will Change Our Lives*, Boston, MA: Harvard Business School Press.

CALEA 1994 'Communications Assistance for Law Enforcement Act', see: http:// www.askcalea.net/calea/.

Calhoun, C. (ed) 1992a *Habermas and the Public Sphere*, Cambridge MA: MIT Press.

—— 1992b 'Infrastructure of Modernity: Indirect Relationships. Information Technology, and Social Integration' in Hafercamp, H. and Smelser, N. *Social Change & Modernity*, Berkeley: University of California Press, pp. 205–236.

—— 1994 *Social Theory and the Politics of Identity*, Oxford: Blackwell.

Calliau, R., Gillies, J. *et al.*, 2000 *How the Web was Born: The Story of the World Wide Web*, Oxford University Press.

Campanella, T. 2001 'Eden by Wire: Webcameras and the Telepresent Landscape' in Goldman, K. (ed.) *Robot in the Garden: Telerobotics and Telepistemology in the Age of the Internet*, Cambridge, MA: MIT Press, pp. 22–47.

Campbell, A. 2006 'Playing The Clash Made Me a Terror Suspect', *Daily Mail* 06/04/06, see: http://www.dailymail.co.uk/pages/live/articles/news/news.html?in_ article_ id= 382039.

Campbell, D. 1999 'Interception Capabilities 2000', Report to the Director General for Research of the European Parliament, available at: http://www.cyber-rights.org/ interception/stoa/interception_capabilities_2000.htm.

—— 2000 'Signals Intelligence and Human Rights: The ECHELON Report', EPIC, see: http://cryptome.org/sigint-hr-dc.htm.

—— 2007 'Are You Being Bugged?', *Guardian* 21/02/07, see: http://www.guardian. co.uk/g2/story/0,,2017615,00.html.

Campbell, J. 2004 *Getting It on Online: Cyberspace, Gay Male Sexuality, and Embodied Identity*, Haworth Press.

Campbell, S. 2006 'Indian Call Center Agents Suffering Health Problems Due to Caller Abuse', TMCNet 14/04/06, see http://www.tmcnet.com/news/2006/04/19/1587334.htm.

Cannataci, J. and Bonnici, J. 2003 'Can Self-regulation Satisfy the Transnational Requisite of Successful Internet Regulation?', *International Review of Law, Computers & Technology*, 17, 1, 51–61.

Canny, J. and Paulos, E. 2001 'Tele-embodiment and Shattered Presence: Reconstructing the Body for Online Interaction' in K. Goldberg (ed.) *Robot in the Garden: Telerobotics & Telepistemology in the Age of the Internet*, Cambridge, MA: MIT Press.

Canter, D. 1977 *The Psychology of Place*, New York: St Martin's Press.

Capeller, W. 2001 'Not Such a Neat Net: Some Comments on Virtual Criminality', *Social and Legal Studies*, 10 (2), 229–242. Reprinted in Wall, D. (ed.) *Cyberspace Crime*, Aldershot: Ashgate.

Caplan, J. and Torpey, J.C. 2001 *Documenting Individual Identity: The Development of State Practices in the Modern World*, Princeton University Press.

Cardwatch, 2007 'Types of Card Fraud, APACS', see: http://www.cardwatch.org.uk/default.asp?sectionid=5&pageid=124&Title=Types_Of_Card_Fraud.

Carey, J. 1989 *Communication as Culture*, London: Routledge.

Carlos, A. M. and Nicholas, S. 1996 'Theory and History: Seventeenth Century Joint-Stock Trading Companies, *Journal of Economic History*, 56 (4), 916–924.

Carnoy, M. 2002 *Sustaining the New Economy: Work, Family, and Community in the Information Age*, Cambridge, MA: Harvard University Press.

Carroll, J. and Rossen, M.B. 1996, 'Developing the Blacksburg Electronic Village', *Communications of the ACM*, 39 (12), 69–74.

Carvel, J., Carter, H. and Campbell, D. 2001 'Blair Demands Law on Internet Baby Trade', *Guardian*, 18/01/01, see: http://society.guardian.co.uk/intercountry adoption/story/0,,427348,00.html.

Casey, E. 2000 *Digital Evidence and Computer Crime*, London: Academic Press.

Casimir, M.J. and Rao, A. (eds) 1992 *Mobility and Territoriality: Social and Spatial Boundaries Among Foragers, Fishers, Pastoralists and Peripatetics*, Oxford: Berg.

Caslon 2006 '419 Advance Fee Scam', *Caslon Analytics Note*, see: http://www.caslon.com.au/419scamnote.htm.

CASPIAN 2005 'Is There a Tag in Your Bag'?, Boycott Tesco website, see: http://www.boycotttesco.com/spychips.html.

Cassidy, J. 2006 'Me Media', *New Yorker*, 82, 3, 0–59.

Casson, H. 1910 *History of the Telephone* (Select Bibliographies Reprint), Ayer Co Pub; Facsimile edition, online edition available at: http://www.worldwideschool.org/library/books/tech/engineering/TheHistoryoftheTelephone/toc.html.

Castells, M. 1996 *The Rise of the Network Society*, Volume I, *The Information Age: Economy, Society and Culture*, Oxford: Blackwell.

—— 1997 *The Power of Identity*, Vol II, *The Information Age*.

—— 2001 *End of Millennium*, Vol III, *The Information Age*.

Castranova, E. 2003 'On Virtual Economies', *Game Studies*, 3, 2, available at: http://www.gamestudies.org/0302/castronova/.

—— 2005 *Synthetic Worlds: The Business and Culture of Online Games*, Chicago, IL: University Of Chicago Press.

Castree, N. *et al.* 2003 *Spaces of Work: Global Capitalism and Geographies of Labour*, London: Sage.

Cate, F. 2005 'Information Security Breaches and the Threat to Consumers', downloadable at http://www.hunton.com/files/tbl_s47Details/FileUpload265/1280/InformationSecurity_Breaches.pdf.

CBS 15/08/06 'Is Owning 1,000 Cell Phones Terrorism?', see: http://www.cbsnews.com/stories/2006/08/14/national/main1890470.shtml.

CCMW 2007 'Cybercriminals Most Wanted', homepage, see: http://www.ccmostwanted.com/.

CDT 2003 'Ghosts in Our Machines: Background and Policy Proposals on the "Spyware" Problem', Center for Democracy and Technology, November, available at: http://www.ftc.gov/os/comments/spyware/040305centerfordemocandtech.pdf.

Census 2001 See: www.statistics.gov.uk/census2001.

Cere, R. 2007 'Digital Undergrounds: Alternative Politics and Civil Society' in Jewkes, Y. (ed.) *Crime Online*, Willan, pp. 144–159.

Ceruzzi, P. 2000 *A History of Modern Computing*, Cambridge, MA: MIT Press.

CFCA 2006 'Global Telecom Revenues Increase 12% and Fraud Increases 52% from 2003–2005', Survey for Communications Fraud Control Association, see: http://www.cfca.org/Documents/fraudloss_press_release.pdf.

CFW 2007 'Computer Forensics World', homepage, see: http://www.computerforensicsworld.com/index.php.

Chainey, S. P. and Ratcliffe, J.H. 2005 *GIS and Crime Mapping*, London: Wiley & Sons.

Chambliss, W. and Seidman, R. 1971 *Law, Order, and Power*, Reading, MA: Addison-Wesley.

Chandler, D. 1964 *The Campaigns of Napoleon*, London: Macmillan.

Channel 4 05/10/06 'The Data Theft Scandal', see: http://www.channel4.com/news/dispatches/article.jsp?id=473.

Chaudhuri, K.N. 1965 *The English East India Company: The Study of an Early Joint-stock Company 1600–1640*, London: Frank Cass.

Cheney, A. 2006 *Body Brokers: Inside America's Underground Trade in Human Remains*, Broadway.

Cheung, C. 2006 'A Home on the Web: Presentations of Self on Personal Homepages' in Bell, D. (ed.) *Cybercultures; Critical Concepts*, IV, pp. 30–41.

Children's Society 2007 'The Good Childhood Inquiry', see: http://www.childrenssociety.org.uk/what+we+do/The+good+childhood+inquiry/.

Chimni 2004 'International Institutions Today: An Imperial Global State in the Making', *European Journal of International Law*, 15(1), 1–37.

China Daily 20/10/05 'Internet "Baby Sale" Sparks Investigation', see: http://english.peopledaily.com.cn/200510/20/eng20051020_215519.html.

Choate, P. 2005 *Hot Property: The Stealing of Ideas in an Age of Globalisation*, New York: Knopf.

Cho, C.H. and Choen, J. 2005 'Children's Exposure to Negative Internet Content: Effects of Family Context', *Journal of Broadcasting & Electronic Media*, 49(4), 488–509, available at: http://www.leaonline.com/doi/pdf/10.1207/s15506878jobem4904_8?cookieSet=1.

ChoicePoint 2005a Annual Report.

ChoicePoint 2005b 'Response to 5/3 Article in The Wall Street Journal', available at: http://www.choicepoint.com/news/statement_050405_1.html.

Christie, N. 1981 *Limits to Pain*, Oxford: Martin Robertson. online version at: http://www.prisonpolicy.org/scans/limits_to_pain/index.html.

—— 2004 *A Suitable Amount of Crime*, London: Routledge.

Chubb 2005 Security Report on Identity Theft, *Chubb Insurance Company*, February.

Church, A. 1941 *The Calculi of Lambda-Conversion*, Princeton: Princeton University Press.

Cieraad, I. (ed.) 1999 *At Home: An Anthropology of Domestic Space*, Syracuse University Press.

Cieslak, M. 2006 'Rise of the Web's Social Network', BBC 30/09/2006, http://news.bbc.co.uk/1/hi/programmes/click_online/5391258.stm.

CIFAS 2004 'Deceased Fraud' in Identity Fraud: How Serious is the Problem? CIFAS see: http://www.cifas.org.uk/identity_fraud_is_theft_serious.asp.

—— 2005 Bin Raiding – see: http://www.cifas.org.uk/identity_fraud_how_fraudsters_work.asp#binraiding.

Cigno, A., Rosati, F. and Guarcello, L. 2002 'Does Globalisation Increase Child Labour?' *World Development*, 10 (9), 1579–1589.

CIPD 2005 'Survey on Employee Internet Use', available at: http://www.clearlybusiness.com/cb/articles/nf_1087782759711616.jsp (viewed March 2005).

Clarke, G. 1999 *Hot Products: Understanding, Anticipating and Reducing the Demand for Stolen Goods*, Police Research Series Paper 98, London: Home Office.

Clarke, R. 1988 'Information Technology and Dataveillance', Communications of the ACM, 31 (5), 498–512.

—— 2004 'Resources: Workplace Privacy', see: http://www.anu.edu.au/people/Roger.Clarke/DV/Workplace.html (viewed March 2004).

Clodfelter, M. 2002 *Warfare and Armed Conflicts: A Statistical Reference to Casualty and Other Figures*, 1500–2000, McFarland & Company.

CNN 01/05/98 'Father Arraigned, Held after Internet Confession', available at: http://edition.cnn.com/US/9805/01/online.confession.update/.

CNN 29/12/03 'Cyber Blackmail Targets Office Workers', see: http://www.cnn.com/2003/TECH/internet/12/29/cyber.blackmail.reut/index.html.

CNN 11/02/05 'Man Held Over Alleged Internet Suicide Plot', see: http://www.cnn.com/2005/US/02/10/valentine.suicide/index.html.

CNN 26/01/06 'Google to Censor Itself in China', see: http://edition.cnn.com/2006/BUSINESS/01/25/google.china/.

CNN 23/5/06 'FBI Seeks Stolen Personal Data on 26 Million Vets', see: http://www.cnn.com/2006/US/05/22/vets.data/index.html.

CNN 19/09/06 'Whitehouse Uploads Anti-drug Videos to Youtube'.

COE 2001 'Convention on Cybercrime', Council of Europe, see: http://conventions.coe.int/Treaty/EN/Treaties/Html/185.htm.

Cobain, I. and Luck, A. 2005 'The Beauty Products from the Skin of Executed Chinese Prisoners', *Guardian* 13/09/05, see: http://www.guardian.co.uk/china/story/0,7369,1568622,00.html.

Coe, L. 1995 *The Telephone and Its Several Inventors: A History*, North Carolina: McFarland.

Cohen, B.J. 2001 Electronic Money: New Day or False Dawn? *Review of International Political Economy*, 8 (2), 197–225.

—— 2003 *The Future of Money*, Princeton: Princeton University Press.

Cohen, F. 1984 'Computer Viruses – Theory and Experiments', seminar presentation, available at: http://all.net/books/virus/index.html.

Cohen, L.E. and Felson, M. 1979 'Social Change and Crime Rate Trends: A Routine Activity Approach', *American Sociological Review*, 4, 588–608.

Cohen, N. 2007 'Google Halts "Miserable Failure" Link to President Bush', *New York Times* 29/01/07.

Cohen, R. and Rai, S. (eds) 2000 *Global Social Movements*, London: The Athlone Press.

Cohen, S. 1985 *Visions of Social Control*, London: Polity Press.

—— 2002 'Human Rights and Crimes of the State: The Culture of Denial' in McLaughlin, E. *et al.* (eds) *Criminological Perspectives*, 2nd edition, London: Sage.

Cole, W. 1958 'Trends in 18th Century Smuggling', *Economic History Review*, 395–409.

Collin, B. 1996 'The Future of CyberTerrorism', *Proceedings of 11th Annual International Symposium on Criminal Justice Issues*, The University of Illinois at Chicago, see: http://afgen.com/terrorism1.html.

Collins, M. 1992 'Flaming: The Relationship Between Social Context Cues and Uninhibited Verbal Behavior in Computer-mediated Communication', available at: http://emoderators.com/papers/flames.html (viewed March 2007).

Collins, V. 1993 *Recreation and the Law*, London: Routledge.

Competition Commission 2007 Groceries Market Inquiry, see: http://www.competition-commission.org.uk/inquiries/ref2006/grocery/index.htm.

Compton, J. 2003 'Taking the Sting out of Mobile Data Theft', *Computing*, 22/09/03, see: http://www.computing.co.uk/computing/features/2072312/taking-sting-mobile-theft.

Computer Weekly 27/10/06 'Fraudsters Infiltrate Glasgow Call Centres'.

Context 2006 'The Mobiles: Social Evolution in a Wireless Society', *Context Research Group*, see: http://www.contextresearch.com/context/study.cfm (viewed March 2007).

Conway, M. 2002 'What is Cyberterrrorism?', *Current History*, December, 436–442, see: http://209.85.129.104/search?q=cache:pnv_LdDDzNIJ:www.currenthistory.com/org_pdf_files/101/659/101_659_436.pdf+inter+global+communications+hack+attack+spanish+protesters&hl=en&ct=clnk&cd=9&client=firefox-a.

Cook, P. and Ludwig, J. 2000 *Gun Violence : The Real Costs*, Oxford University Press.

Cooley, C.H. 1909 *Social Organisation: A Study of the Larger Mind*, New York: Charles Scribner's Sons.

Coopersmith, J. 1998 'Pornography, Technology and Progress', *ICON*, 4, 94–125.

Cordes, C. and Miller, E. 2000 'Fool's Gold: A Critical Look at Computers in Childhood', retrieved 10 March, 2004 from http://www.allianceforchildhood.net/projects/computers/computers_reports_fools_gold_contents.htm.

Cornerspyshop 2006 http://www.cornerspyshop.com/sterling/frmain.htm (viewed October 2006).

Couch, C., Fraser, C. and Percy, S. (eds) 2003 *Urban Regeneration in Europe*, Oxford: Blackwell.

Coupland, D. 1995 *Microserfs*, London: Flamingo.

Cowan, R. 2006 'Internet Rape Paedophile Jailed', *Guardian* 09/11/06, see: http://www.guardian.co.uk/crime/article/0,,1943793,00.html.

CPJ 2006 'Iraq: Journalists in Danger', *Campaign to Protect Journalists*, Statistical Profile, see: http://www.cpj.org/Briefings/Iraq/Iraq_danger.html.

CPTech 2005 'Page on Hague Convention', see: http://www.cptech.org/ecom/jurisdiction/hague.html#cptdocs.

Creasey, G.L., and Myers, B.J. 1986 'Video Games and Children: Effects on Leisure Activities, Schoolwork, and Peer Involvement'. *Merrill–Palmer Quarterly*, 32, 251–262.

Cross, M. 2007 'Address Database Plan Finally Abandoned', *Guardian* 07/06/07, see: http://technology.guardian.co.uk/weekly/story/0,,2096639,00.html.

Crowley, J. and Adrian, L. 1992 'Women Misdemeanants in the Allegheny County Jail 1892–1923', *Journal of Criminal Justice*, 20, 311–331.

CSTB 1991 'Computers at Risk: Safe Computing in the Information Age', *Computer Science and Telecommunications Board*, National Academies Press, available at: http://www.nap.edu/books/0309043883/html/index.html.

CSTS 2007 'Convergence', *Center For the Study of Technology and Society*, see: http://www.tecsoc.org/convergence/convergence.htm.

CSP 2005 Report on RSI, Chartered Society of Physiotherapy, September, see http://www.out-law.com/page-6108 (viewed March 2006).

Cubitt, S. 1998 *Digital Aesthetics*, London: Sage.

Cummins, R. 1989 *Meaning and Mental Representation*, Cambridge, MA: MIT Press.

Curtin, P. 1984 *Cross-cultural Trade in World History*, Cambridge University Press.

Curtin, S.L. 2004 'Japan: Suicide Also Rises in Land of Rising Sun', *Asia Times* 28/07/04, see: http://www.atimes.com/atimes/Japan/FG28Dh01.html.

Cutler, R. 1995 'Distributed Presence and Community in Cyberspace', *Interpersonal Computing and Technology*, 3 (2), 12–32, see: http://www.helsinki.fi/science/optek/1995/n2/cutler.txt.

CyberAngels 2007 Homepage, see: http://www.cyberangels.org/.

Cyberpunk Project 2007 'Phreaks', at: http://project.cyberpunk.ru/idb/phreaks.html.

Daily Mail 20/10/06 'Video Website YouTube Faces Violence Purge', see: http://www.dailymail.co.uk/pages/live/articles/news/.
news.html?in_article_id=411543&in_page_id=1770.

Daponte, B. 1993 'A Case Study in Estimating Casualties from War and Its Aftermath: The 1991 Persian Gulf War', available at: http://www.ippnw.org/MGS/PSRQV3N2Daponte.html.

Davey, B. and Priestley, H. 2002 *Introduction to Lattices and Order*, 2nd edn, Cambridge University Press.

David, L. 2005 'Flash Dance as Mob Takes Over Liverpool Street', Evening Standard 03/06/05, see: http://www.findarticles.com/p/articles/mi_qn4153/is_20050603/ai_n14653327.

Davidson, R. 1981 *Crime and Environment*, London : Croom Helm.

Davies, G. 1996 *A History of Money: From Ancient Times to the Present Day*, Cardiff : University of Wales Press.

Davies, R. 1998 *Main Street Blues: The Decline of Small-town America*, University of Ohio Press.

Davis, H. and McLeod, S.L. 2003 'Why Humans Value Sensational News: An Evolutionary Perspective', *Evolution and Human Behavior*, 24, 208–216.

Davis, M. *et al.* 2006 'E-dating, Identity and HIV Prevention: Theorising Sexualities, Risk and Network Society', *Sociology of Health & Illness*, 28 (4), 457ff.

Davis, T. 2006 'Gore Says Bush Wiretapping Could Be Impeachable Offense', *ABC* 16/01/06, see: http://abcnews.go.com/US/story?id=1511599.

De Certeau, M. 1984 *The Practice of Everyday Life*, Berkeley: University of California Press.

Dean, G. and Gottshalk, P. 2007 *Knowledge Management in Policing and Law Enforcement Foundations, Structures and Applications*, Oxford University Press.

Dear, W. 1984 *Dungeon Master: The Disappearance of James Dallas Egbert III*, New York: Houghton Mifflin.

Death Penalty Information Center 2006 Homepage, see: http://www.deathpenaltyinfo.org/ (viewed March 2007).

Debord, G. 1994 *Society of the Spectacle*, Zone Books. Digital version available at: http://www.bopsecrets.org/SI/debord/.

Defencetech 2004 'Armed Drones Rolling to Iraq', 1/12/04, see http://www.defensetech.org/archives/001246.html.

Deflem, M. 2002 'Technology and the Internationalization of Policing: A Comparative-Historical Perspective', *Justice Quarterly*, 19(3), 453–475.

Deleuze, G. 1988 *Foucault*, trans. S. Hand, University of Minnesota Press.

—— 1990 'Control and Becoming': Gilles Deleuze in Conversation with Antonio Negri in *Futur Anterieur* trans. Martin Joughin, http://www.generation-online.org/p/fpdeleuze3.htm.

—— 1992 'Postscript on the Societies of Control', *October*, 59, pp. 3–7, all page references cited from online version at: http://www.n5m.org/n5m2/media/texts/deleuze.htm.

Deleuze, G. and Guattari, F. 1972 *Anti-Oedipus: Capitalism and Schizophrenia*, trans. Robert Hurley, Mark Seem and Helen Lane, New York: Viking Press.

—— 1977 'Balance Sheet-program for Desiring-Machines', *Semiotexte*, II, 3.

—— 1983 *Anti Oedipus: Capitalism and Schizophrenia*, University of Minnesota Press; reprint edn.

—— 1988 *A Thousand Plateaus: Capitalism and Schizophrenia*, trans. Brian Massumi, London: Athlone.

Delio, M. 2001 'Cyberwar? More Like Hot Air', *Wired News* 04/05/01, see: http://www.wired.com/news/politics/0,1283,43520,00.html.

Dempsey, J. 1997 'Communications Privacy in the Digital Age: Revitalizing the Federal Wiretap Laws to Enhance Privacy', *Albany Law Journal of Science & Technology*, 8 (1), see: http://www.cdt.org/publications/lawreview/1997albany.shtml.

Denning, D. 2002 'Is Cyber-terrorism Coming?', available at: http://www.marshall.org/pdf/materials/58.pdf.

Denning, P. 2001 *The Invisible Future: The Seamless Integration Of Technology Into Everyday Life*, New York: McGraw-Hill.

Der Derian, J. 2002 'Cyberspace as Battlespace' in Armitage, J. and Roberts, J. (eds) *Living with Cyberspace*, New York: Continuum, pp. 61–71.

Derrida, J. 1978 *Writing and Difference*, trans. Alan Bass, London: Routledge & Kegan Paul.

Derry, T. K. and Williams, T.I. 1960 *A Short History of Technology*, Oxford: Clarendon.

Descartes, R. 1984 'The Passions of the Soul' in Cottingham, J., Stoothoff, R. and Murdoch, D. *The Philosophical Writings of Descartes*, 2 vols, Cambridge.

Deutsche Presse-Agentur 14/10/99 'Cambodia Up in Arms Over Bondage Pornography Internet Site'.

Devlin, P. 1965 *The Enforcement of Morals*, Oxford University Press.

DeVoss, D. 2002 'Women's Porn Sites – Spaces of Fissure and Eruption or "I'm a Little Bit of Everything" ', *Sexuality and Culture*, 6 (3), 75–94.

Dewey, J. 1944 *Democracy and Education*, New York: Free Press, online version available at: http://www.ilt.columbia.edu/Publications/dewey.html.

DeYoung, K. 2007 'Terror Database Has Quadrupled In Four Years', *Washington Post* 25/03/07, see: http://www.washingtonpost.com/wp-dyn/content/article/2007/03/24/AR2007032400944.html.

DHS 2003 'National Strategy to Secure Cyberspace', *Department of Homeland Security*, see: http://www.dhs.gov/xlibrary/assets/National_Cyberspace_ Strategy.pdf.

—— 2006 'Secure Border Initiative', *Department of Homeland Security*, see: http://www.dhs.gov/ximgtn/programs/editorial_0868.shtm.

Dibbell, J. 1993 'A Rape in Cyberspace', *Village Voice*.

—— 1996 'Viruses are Good for You', *Wired 3.02*, available at: http://www.epidemic.ws/wired.html (viewed January 2007).

—— 2002 'In Gold we Trust', *Wired* 01/10/02, see: http://www.wired.com/wired/archive/10.01/egold.html.

Diffie, W. and Landau, S. 1998 *Privacy on the Line: The Politics of Wiretapping and Encryption*. Cambridge University Press.

Direct Marketing Today 2001 'Profits Forecast, 2005'.

Dirlik, A. 1996 'The Global in the Local' in Wilson, R and Dissanayake, W (eds) *Global/Local: Cultural Production and the Transnational Imaginary*, Duke University Press, pp. 21–45.

Dixon, N.F. 1971 *Subliminal Perception: The Nature of a Controversy*, New York: McGraw-Hill.

Docherty, A. 2004 'Anatomy of an Internet Porn Panic', Internet Freedom 15/10/04, see: http://www.netfreedom.org/news.asp?item=213.

Dodge, M. and Kitchin, R. 2001 *Mapping Cyberspace*, London: Routledge.

Doh, J. 2005 'Offshore Outsourcing: Implications for International Business and Strategic Management Theory and Practice', *Journal of Management Studies* 42 (3), 695–704.

Doherty, B. 2003 'Great Firewall of China: War on cybercafé society', *Reason Online*, February, see: http://www.reason.com/news/show/28653.html.

Dohoney-Farina, S. 1999 *The Wired Neighborhood*, New Haven, CT: Yale University Press.

DOL 1997 *Genetic Information and the Workplace*, U.S. Department of Labor Report, 20/01/97.

Dolu 2004 'Credit Card Fraud: The Nature of the Crime, How Credit Card Fraud Occurs, Prevention Methods – Experiences of Turkish National Police', Conference presentation, ASC Nashville.

Donaldson, G.H. 1988 'Signalling Communications and the Roman Imperial Army', *Britannia*, 19, 349–356.

Donaldson, T. 1982 *Corporations and Morality*, Englewood Cliffs, NJ: Prentice Hall.

Donath, J. 1998 'Identity and Deception in the Virtual Community' in Smith, M. and Kollock, P. (eds), *Communities in Cyberspace*, London: Routledge. References cited from PDF document available at: http://smg.media.mit.edu/papers/Donath/IdentityDeception/IdentityDeception.pdf.

Donnelly, John (ed.) 1990 *Suicide: Right or Wrong?* Buffalo: Prometheus.

Dorling, D. 2005 'Prime Suspect: Murder in Britain' 23–38 in Hillyard, P. *et al.* (eds) *Criminal Obsessions: Why Harm Matters More than Crime*, Crime and Society Foundation, pp. 23–38.

Downes, D. and Rock, P. 2003 *Understanding Deviance*, Oxford University Press.

Downing, J. 2001 *Radical Media: Rebellious Communication and Social Movements*, Thousand Oaks, CA: Sage.

Draper, J. 2003 'Captain Crunch', homepage at: http://www.webcrunchers.com/crunch/.

Dretkste, F.I. 1981 *Knowledge & the Flow of Information*, Oxford: Blackwell.

Dreyfus, H. 2001 'Telepistemology: Descartes Last Stand' in Goldberg, K. (ed.) *Robert in the Garden*, Cambridge, MA: MIT Press, pp. 48–63.

—— 2005 'Overcoming the Myth of the Mental: How Philosophers Can Profit from the Phenomenology of Everyday Expertise', *APA Pacific Division Presidential Address*, available at: http://socrates.berkeley.edu/~hdreyfus/pdf/Dreyfus%20APA%20Address%20%2010.22.05%20.pdf.

Drucker, S. and Gumpert, G. 1999 *Real Law at Virtual Space: Communication Regulation in Cyberspace*, Hampton Press.

DTI 2006 Information Security Breaches Survey, with Price Waterhouse, see: http://www.dti.gov.uk/sectors/infosec/infosecdownloads/page9935.html.

Dummett, M. 1959 'Wittgenstein's Philosophy of Mathematics', *The Philosophical Review*, 68, 324–348.

Dunbar, R. I. M. 2004 'Gossip in an Evolutionary Perspective', *Review of General Psychology*, 8, 100–110.

Duncan, P. and Thomas, S. 2000 'Neighbourhood Regeneration: Resourcing Community Involvement', *Joseph Rowntree Foundation/The Policy Press*, see: http://www.jrf.org.uk/Knowledge/findings/housing/320.asp.

Dunn, M. 2006 'Banned for a George Bush T-shirt', *Herald Sun* 14/12/06, see: http://www.news.com.au/story/0,23599,20925632-38200,00.html.

Dupont, B. D. 2004 'Security in the age of networks', *Policing & Society*, 14 (1), 76–91.

Durkheim, E. 1933 *The Division of Labour in Society*, trans. George Simpson, New York: The Free Press.

—— 1952 *Suicide: A Study in Sociology*, trans. J.A. Spaulding and G. Simpson, London: Routledge & Kegan Paul.

DVLA 2005 Homepage, see: http://www.dvla.gov.uk/?sc_lang=en.

Dvornik, F. 1974 *Origins of Intelligence Services*, New Brunswick: Rutgers University Press.

Dworkin, G. (ed.) 1994 *Morality, Harm and the Law*, Boulder, CO: Westview Press.

Dwyer, S. 2006 'Enter Here – At Your Own Risk: The Moral Dangers of Cyberporn' in Spinello, R. (ed.) *The Impact of the Internet on Our Moral Lives*, Albany, NY: State University of New York Press, pp. 69–94.

East Anglian Daily Times 8/04/05 'Family Fed up at Noise from Store'.

Ebay 2006 http://cgi.ebay.co.uk/ws/eBayISAPI.dll?ViewItem&item=290015948187 (viewed 20 October 2006).

EC 2002 'Data Protection at Work: Commission Proposes New EU Framework to European Social Partners', European Commission see: http://europa.eu.int/comm/employment_social/news/2002/nov/181_en.html.

Eco, U. 1996 'From Internet to Gutenberg', Lecture presented at The Italian Academy for Advanced Studies in America, 12/11/96, see: www.italianacademy.columbia.edu/pdfs/lectures/eco_internet_gutenberg.pdf.

Edwards, S., Edwards, T. and Fields, C. (eds) 1996 *Environmental Crime and Criminality: Theoretical and Practical Issues*, New York: Garland.

EFF 1995 Electronic Frontier Foundation, 'Summary of Stratton-Oakmont & Porush v. Prodigy', *Electronic Freedom Foundation Legal Summary*, see: http://www.eff.org/legal/cases/Stratton_Oakmont_Porush_v_Prodigy/.

—— 2005 Electronic Freedom Foundation, homepage http://www.eff.org/about/ (viewed November 2005).

—— 2006 ' "The World's Worst Internet Laws Sneaking Through the Senate" ', see: http://www.eff.org/deeplinks/archives/cat_misc.php.

—— 2007a 'Sony BMG Litigation Info, Update', Electronic Frontier Foundation, see: http://www.eff.org/IP/DRM/Sony-BMG/.

—— 2007b 'EFF's Class-action Lawsuit Against AT&T for Collaboration with Illegal Domestic Spying Program', see: http://www.eff.org/legal/cases/att/.

E-Gold 2006 See: http://www.e-gold.com/.

E-Gold 2007 Home page for E-Gold, see: http://www.e-gold.com/.

EFA 2007 'Internet Content and Filtering', *Electronic Frontiers Australia*, see: http://www.efa.org.au/Issues/Censor/cens2.html.

Einstein, A. 1920 *Relativity: The Special and General Theory*, London: Methuen & Co.

Eisenstein, E. 1979 *The Printing Press as an Agent of Change*, Cambridge University Press.

Ekblom, P. 2000 'Future Crime Prevention – A Mindset – A Way of Thinking Systematically about Causes of Crime and Solutions to Crime Problems' in *Foresight Turning the Corner*, London: Department of Trade and Industry, Crime Prevention Panel.

Ellens, J.H. (ed.) 2003 *The Destructive Power of Religion: Violence in Judaism, Christianity, and Islam*, Praeger.

Ellison, L. 2001 'Tackling Harassment on the Internet' in Wall, D. (ed.) *Crime and the Internet*, London: Routledge, pp. 141–151.

Ellison, L. and Akdeniz, Y. 1998 'Cyberstalking: The Regulation of Harassment on the Internet', *Criminal Law Review*, Special Edition: Crime, Criminal Justice and the Internet.

Ellsworth, C. 2005 'Website "Swapped War Photos for Porn" ', *Daily Telegraph* 11/10/05, see: http://www.telegraph.co.uk/news/main.jhtml?xml=/news/2005/10/11/website11.xml&sSheet=/news/2005/10/11/ixworld.html.

Elmer, G. 2004 *Profiling Machines*, Cambridge, MA: MIT Press.

Emsley, C. 1996 'Albion's Felonious Attractions: Reflections Upon the History of Crime in England' in Emsley, C. and Knafla, L. *Crime History and Histories of Crime: Studies in the Historiography of Crime and Criminal Justice in Modern History*, Greenwood Press, pp. 67–85.

EPIC 2003 'The Amy Boyer Case', available at:: http://www.epic.org/privacy/boyer/#history.

—— 2004 'Privacy and Consumer Profiling', Electronic Privacy Information Center available at http://www.epic.org/privacy/profiling/.

—— 2005a 'Letter to Choicepoint', available at: http://www.epic.org/privacy/choicepoint/cpltr2.18.05.html.

—— 2005b ' "Terrorism" Information Awareness (TIA)', see: http://www.epic.org/privacy/profiling/tia/.

—— 2006 US-VISIT page, see: http://www.epic.org/privacy/us-visit/.

—— 2007 'Caller ID', see: http://www.epic.org/privacy/caller_id/.

Ericson, R. 2007 *Crime in an Insecure World*, Cambridge: Polity Press.

Ericson, R.V. and Haggerty, K.D. 1997 *Policing the Risk Society*, Toronto: University of Toronto Press.

Espiner, T. 2006a 'Red Hat Disputes CERT Vulnerability Figures', *ZdNet* 06/01/06, see http://news.zdnet.co.uk/software/0,1000000121,39245889,00.htm?user_rating=1.

—— 2006b 'Crime Surge Sparks Calls for Internet Interpol', *ZdNet* 12/12/06 see: http://news.zdnet.co.uk/security/0,1000000189,39285121,00.htm.

ES-UK 2005 'Personal Stories and Symptoms', Electrosensitivity-UK, see: http://www.electrosensitivity.org.uk/personal%20stories.htm.

Etzioni, A. 1995 *Rights and the Common Good*, New York: St Martin's Press.

EU 2006 European Union: Legislative History of 2002/0047/COD, available at: http://ec.europa.eu/prelex/detail_dossier_real.cfm?CL=en&DosId=172020.

EU Kids 2007 Homepage, see: http://www.eukidsonline.net/.

Evans, C. 2002 'Dictatorship of the Net Censors', *Internet Freedom* 05/11/02, see: http://www.n+etfreedom.org/news.asp?item=192 (viewed March 2002).

Evenson, E.A. 2000 *The Telephone Patent Conspiracy of 1876: The Elisha Gray–Alexander Bell Controversy*, North Carolina: McFarland.

Evers, J. 2005 'Bots May Get Cloak of Encryption', *CNET News*, 14/11/05, see: http://news.com.com/Bots+may+get+cloak+of+encryption/2100-7349_3-5952102.html.

Exxon-Mobil 2004 Summary Statement of Income, *Annual Report 2004*, available at: http://www2.exxonmobil.com/corporate/files/corporate/AR_2004_statementincome.pdf.

—— 2005 ' "Stop Esso" Campaign', see: http://www.exxonmobil.co.uk/UK-English/Newsroom/UK_NR_VP_Viewpoint_StopEsso.asp.

Fagan, M. 1991 'August is a Wicked Month for Fraud', *Independent* 16/09/91.

Family Watchdog 2007 Homepage, see: http://www.familywatchdog.us/ (viewed March 2007).

FBI 2001 *Crime in the USA*, Section II – *Crime Index Offenses Reported*.

—— 2003 Cybersweep Operation, see: http://www.fbi.gov/cyber/cysweep/cysweep1.htm.

—— 2004 Congressional Testimony by Steven M. Martinez, Deputy Assistant Director (FBI) before the House Government Reform Committee's Subcommittee on Technology, Information Policy, Intergovernmental Relations and the Census, 22 September 2004, available at: http://www.fbi.gov/congress/congress04/martinez092204.htm.

FCC 2006 Federal Communications Commission website, at http://www.fcc.gov.

FDC 2005 'Death Row FactSheet', *Florida Department of Corrections*, see: http://www.dc.state.fl.us/oth/deathrow/ (viewed November 2005).

Featherstone, M. 1996 'Localism, Globalism and Cultural Identity' in Wilson, R. and Dissanayake, W. (eds) *Global/Local: Cultural Production and the Transnational Imaginary*, Duke University Press, pp. 46–77.

Featherstone, M. and Burrows, R. (eds) 1995 *Cyberspace/Cyberbodies/Cyberpunk: Cultures of Technological Embodiment*, London: Sage.

FEB 2006 Homepage: *The Swedish Association for the ElectroSensitive*, see: http://www.feb.se/index_int.htm.

Feinberg, J. 1968 'Collective Responsibility', *Journal of Philosophy*, 65: 674–688.

—— 1984 *Harm to Self*, Oxford University Press.

—— 1986 *Harm to Others*, Oxford University Press.

—— 1988 *Harmless Wrongdoing*, New York: Oxford University Press.

Felson, M. 2000 'The Routine Activity Approach as a General Crime Theory' in Simpson, S. (ed.) *Of Crime and Criminality*, Thousand Oaks, CA: Pine Forge Press, reprinted in McLaughlin *et al. Criminological Perspectives*, Sage, 2003, pp. 160–166.

Fensel, D. Sycara, K. and Mylopoulos, J. (eds) 2003 *The Semantic Web*, Springer.

Fenwick, H. 2002 'The Anti-terrorism, Crime and Security Act 2001: A Proportionate Response to 11 September?' *Modern Law Review*, 65 (5), 724–762.

Ferguson, K. 2004 'Caller ID – Whose Privacy Is It, Anyway?' *Journal of Business Ethics*, 29 (3), 227–237.

Ferrell, J. 2005 *Crimes Of Style: Urban Graffiti and the Politics of Criminality*, University Press of New England.

Ferrell, J. and Hamm, M. S. (eds) 1998 *Ethnography at the Edge*, Boston, MA: Northeastern University Press.

Ferrier, J.L. *et al.* 1988 *Art of Our Century, The Chronicle of Western Art, from 1900 to the Present*, New York: Prentice Hall.

Fildes, J. 2006 'Taking Control of your Digital ID', BBC 01/11/06, see: http://news.bbc.co.uk/1/hi/technology/6102694.stm.

Finch, E. 2007 'The Problem of Stolen Identity and the Internet' in Jewkes, Y. (ed.) *Crime Online*, Willan, pp. 29–43.

Findlaw 2002 Homeland Security Bill, available at: news.findlaw.com/hdocs/docs/terrorism/hsa2002.pdf.

Findlay, M. 1999 *The Globalisation of Crime: Understanding Transnational Relationships in Context*, Cambridge University Press.

Findlay, P. and McKinlay, A. 2003 'Surveillance, Electronic Communications Technologies and Regulation', *Industrial Relations Journal*, 34 (4), 305–318.

Fine, G. 2002 *Shared Fantasy: Role Playing Games as Social Worlds*, University of Chicago Press.

Finnis, J. 1998 *Aquinas: Moral, Political, and Legal Theory*, Oxford University Press.

First Data 2005 'New Identity Theft Survey Reveals Latest Count of Victims', Press Release 17/05/05, see: http://ir.firstdatacorp.com/news/releasedetail.cfm?ReleaseID=163659.

Firth, A. (ed.) 1997 *The Prehistory and Development of Intellectual Property Systems*, London: Sweet & Maxwell.

Fischer, C.S. 1982 *To Dwell among Friends: Personal Networks in Town and City*, University of Chicago Press.

—— 1997 'The Telephone Industry Discovers Sociability' in Cutliffe, S.H. and Reynolds, T.S. (eds) *Technology and American History*, University of Chicago Press, pp 271–300.

Fletcher, C. 1974 *Beneath the Surface: An Account of Three Styles of Sociological Research*, London: Routledge & Kegan Paul.

Flohr, U. 1995 'Bank Robbers Go Electronic', *Byte*, November, see: http://www.byte.com/art/9511/sec3/art11.htm (viewed March 2007).

Flynn, J. 2004 'Communicative Power in Habermas' Theory of Democracy.', *European Journal of Political Theory*, 3 (4), 433–454.

Flynn, N. 2006 *Blog Rules: A Business Guide to Managing Policy, Public Relations, And Legal Issues*, Amacom.

FOE 2005 'Good Neighbours? Community Impact of Supermarkets', *Friends of the Earth, Briefing Paper*, available at: http://www.foe.co.uk/resource/briefings/good_neighbours_community.pdf. *Community Development Journal*, 2005 40(3), 265–274; doi:10.1093/cdj/bsi017.

Foley, S. 2006 'US Taxman Targets Virtual World Booming on the Internet' *Independent* 20/10/06, see: http://news.independent.co.uk/business/news/article1905009.ece.

Ford Motors 2006 'Fusion Flash Concerts Aim to Bring Younger Buyers to New Sedan', Press/Communications Release, see http://media.ford.com/newsroom/feature_display.cfm?release=21172.

Forst, B. 2000 'The Privatization and Civilianization of Policing' in *Criminal Justice 2000*, Vol 2, *Boundary Changes in Criminal Justice Organizations*, pp. 19–79, National Institute of Justice, Washington, DC.

Foucault, M. 1977 *Discipline and Punish: The Birth of the Prison*, New York: Pantheon.

—— 1977 'Nietzsche, Genealogy, History' in Bouchard, D. (ed.) *Language, Counter-memory Practice: Selected Essays and Interviews*, Ithaca: Cornell University Press.

—— 1980 'Questions on Geography' in *Power/Knowledge: Selected Interviews & Other Writings*, ed Gordon, C., New York: Pantheon Books, pp. 63–77.

—— 1990 *The History of Sexuality* (Volume I), New York: Random House.

Fox, H.R. 1998 *English Newspapers: Chapters in the History of Journalism*, London: Routledge: Thoemmes Press (1887).

France, M. 1984 'Sadomasochism and Feminism', *Feminist Review*, 16, 35–42.

Frege, G. 1967 'Begriffsschrift, a Formula Language, Modeled upon that of Arithmetic, for Pure Thought' in *From Frege to Gödel*, ed. J. van Heijenoort, Cambridge, MA: Harvard University Press.

—— 1980 'On Sense and Reference' in Geach, P. and Black, M. (eds) *Translations from the Philosophical Writings of Gottlob Frege*, 3d edn, Oxford: Blackwell, pp. 56–78.

Fremeaux, I. 2005 'New Labour's Appropriation of the Concept of Community: A Critique', *Community Development Journal*, 40(3), 265–274.

French, P. A. 1984 *Collective and Corporate Responsibility*, New York: Columbia University Press.

Freud, S. 1916 'Introductory Lectures on Psycho-analysis' in Strachey, J. (ed.) *The Standard Edition of the Complete Psychological Works of Sigmund Freud*, London: Hogarth, 1953–1974, pp. 15–16.

—— 1991 'The Ego and the Id' in *The Essentials of Psycho-Analysis: The Definitive Collection of Sigmund Freud's Writing*, trans. James Strachey, ed. Anna Freud, London: Penguin Books.

Frisby, D. 1985 *Fragments of Modernity*, Cambridge: Polity Press.

Froehling, O. 1999 'Internauts and Guerilleros: The Zapatista Rebellion in Chiapas Mexico and its Extension into Cyberspace' in Crang *et al.* (eds) *Virtual Geographies*, London: Routledge, pp. 164–177.

Frohmann, B. 2000 'Cyber-ethics: Bodies or Bytes?' *International Information and Library Review*, 32, 423–435.

Froomkin, A.M. 2000 'Wrong Turn in Cyberspace: Using ICANN to Route Around the APA and the Constitution', 50 *Duke Law Journal*, 17.

FTC 2003 'FTC Charges Internet Mall Is a Pyramid Scam', Federal Trade Commission Press Release, FTC File No. 012-3153, available at: http://www.ftc.gov/opa/2003/07/nexgen.htm.

Fukuyama, F. 2004 'An Antidote to Empire', Review of Hardt & Negri's Multitude, *New York Times* 25/07/04, see: http://query.nytimes.com/gst/fullpage.html?res=9F0DE6D7173AF936A15754C0A9629C8B63.

Furnell, S. 2002 *Cybercrime: Vandalising the Information Society*, London: Addison Wesley.

Gann, G. 2003 *First Globalization: The Eurasian Exchange, 1500–1800*, Lanham, MD: Rowman & Littlefield.

Garafoli, J. 2005 'Wal-Mart Hit Twice: Critical Film, Activism', *San Francisco Chronicle* 30/05/05, see: http://www.sfgate.com/cgi-.bin/article.cgi?file=/c/a/2005/10/30/MNG4QFGE3H1.DTL.

Garcelon, M. 2006 'The "Indymedia" Experiment: The Internet as Movement Facilitator Against Institutional Control', *Convergence: The International Journal of Research into New Media Technologies*, 12(1), 55–82, available at: http://con.sagepub.com/cgi/reprint/12/1/55.pdf.

Gardner, S. 1999 *Kant and the Critique of Pure Reason*, London: Routledge.

Garfinkel, H. 1967 *Studies in Ethnomethodology*, Englewood Cliffs, NJ: Prentice Hall.

Garland, D. 1996 'The Limits of the Sovereign State: Strategies of Crime Control in Contemporary Society', *British Journal of Criminology*, 36(4), 445–471.

Garland, D. 2001 *The Culture of Control: Crime and Social Order in Contemporary Society*, Oxford University Press.

Garton, L. and Wellman, B. 1995 'Social Impacts of Electronic Mail in Organisations', *Communication Yearbook*, 18, 434–453.

Geddes, A. 2000 *Immigration and European Integration: Towards Fortress Europe*, Manchester University Press.

Gentile, C. 2000 'Palestinian Crackers Share Bugs', *Wired News*, 02/12/00, see: http://www.wired.com/news/politics/0,1283,40449,00.html.

George, R. 1992 *Natural Law Theory: Contemporary Essays*, Oxford: Clarendon Press.

—— 1996 'Natural Law and Positive Law,' in George, R. (ed.) *The Autonomy of Law: Essays on Legal Positivism*, Oxford: Oxford University Press, pp. 321–334.

Gershuny, J. 1978 *After Industrial Society: The Emerging Self-service Economy*, New Jersey: Humanities Press.

Geser, H. 2004 'Towards a Sociological Theory of the Mobile Phone', University of Zurich, see : http://socio.ch/mobile/t_geser1.pdf (viewed March 2007).

Gibb, F. 2006 'Law Lords to Rule on Internet Defamation', Times Online 26/06/06, see: http://www.timesonline.co.uk/article/0,,200-2243300,00.html.

Gibbons, T. 1998 *Regulating the Media*, London: Sweet & Maxwell.

Gibson, W. 1984 *Neuromancer*, Ace Books.

Giddens, A. 1990 *The Consequences of Modernity*, Cambridge: Polity Press.

—— 1991 *Modernity and Self-identity. Self and Society in the Late Modern Age*, Cambridge: Polity Press.

Gieryn, T. 2000 'A Space for Place in Sociology', *Annual Review of Sociology*, 26, 463–496.

Gillan, A. 2005 'Shocking Images Revealed at Britain's "Abu Ghraib Trial" ', *Guardian* 19/01/05, see: http://www.guardian.co.uk/Iraq/Story/0,2763,1393637,00.html.

Gilligan, A. 2005 'Revealed: How Blair is Playing the Fear Card', *Evening Standard* 20/06/05, available at: http://p10.hostingprod.com/@spyblog.org.uk/blog/2005/06/evening_standard_andrew_gillig.html.

Gilling, D. 2001 'Community Safety and Social Policy', *European Journal on Criminal Policy and Research*, 9 (4), 381–400.

Glanz, J. 2006 'U.S. is Said to Fail in Tracking Arms Shipped to Iraqis', *New York Times* 30/10/06.

Glanz, S. 2000 'The truth about big tobacco in its own words', *British Medical Journal*, 321, 313–314, available at: http://www.bmj.com/cgi/reprint/321/7257/313.pdf.

Glass, J. 1993 *Shattered Selves: Multiple Personality in a Postmodern World*, Cornell University Press.

Gluck, C. 2002 'South Korea's Gaming Addicts', BBC 27/11/02, see: http://news.bbc.co.uk/1/hi/world/asia-pacific/2499957.stm.

Godwin, M. 1998 *Cyber Rights: Defending Free Speech in the Digital Age*, Crown Business.

—— 2005 'Cybermurder.com: Bound for Death', *Web Mystery Magazine*, III, I, available at: http://lifeloom.com/III1Godwin.htm (viewed December 2006).

Goetzman, W. and Rouwenhorst, G. 2005 *The Origins of Value*, Oxford University Press.

Goff, S. 2006 'TfL drops Proposal to Expand Oyster Card Use', Financial Times, 01/05/06, see: http://www.ft.com/cms/s/296a2200-d8ae-11da-9715-0000779e2340.html.

Goffman, E. 1959 *The Presentation of Self in Everyday Life*, New York: Doubleday.

—— 1963 *Behavior in Public Places*, New York: The Free Press.

Goldberg, K. 2001 *Robot in the Garden: Telerobotics & Telepistemology in the Age of the Internet*, Cambridge, MA: MIT Press.

Goldsmith, J. and Wu, T. 2006 *Who Controls the Internet?: Illusions of a Borderless World*, Oxford University Press.

Goodchild, P. 1996 *Deleuze and Guattari: An Introduction to the Politics of Desire*, London, California: Sage.

Goodman, N. 1976 *Languages of Art*, Hackett.

Goodnough, A. and Drew, C. 2007 'Florida Shifting to Voting System With Paper Trail', *New York Times* 02/02/07, see: http://www.nytimes.com/2007/02/02/us/02voting.html?hp&ex=1170478800&en=9f5342a78ef82375&ei=5094&partner=homepage.

Goody, J., and Watt, I. 1968 'The Consequences of Literacy' in Goody, J. (ed.) *Literacy in Traditional Societies*: Cambridge University Press, pp. 53–84.

Gordon, G., Willox, N. and Regan, T. 2003 'Identity Fraud: A Critical National and Global Threat', *Lexisnexis & Utica Economic Crime Institute Joint Report*, October, see: www.lexisnexis.com/presscenter/hottopics/ECIReportFINAL.pdf.

Gordon, S. and Ford, R. 2003 'Cyberterrorism?', *Symantec Security Response White Paper*, available at: http://www.symantec.com/avcenter/reference/cyberterrorism.pdf.

Gordon, Z. 1999 'Miles of Aisles – A Supermarket Pricing Survey', *Amador*, see: http://www.amadorbooks.com/nocardsi.htm.

Gore, A. 2006 'Restoring the Rule of Law', EPIC, available at: http://epic.org/privacy/terrorism/fisa/gorespeech0106.pdf.

Gospel, H. and Wood, S. 2003 *Representing Workers: Trade Union Recognition and Membership in Britain*, London: Routledge.

Goss, J. 1995 'We Know Who You Are and We Know Where You Live', *Economic Geography*, 71 (2), 171–198.

Gow, D. and Wray, R. 2006 'US Loosens Grip on Running of Internet', Guardian 03/10/06, see http://business.guardian.co.uk/story/0,,1886022,00.html.

Grabosky, P. 2001 'Virtual Criminality: Old Wine in New Bottles?', *Social and Legal Studies*, 10 (2), 243–249.

Grabosky, P. and Smith, R. 2001 'Telecommunication Fraud in the Digital Age' in Wall, D. (ed.) *Crime and the Internet*, London: Routledge, pp. 28–43.

Grabosky, P., Smith, R.G. and Dempsey, G. 2002 *Electronic Theft: Unlawful Acquisition in Cyberspace*, Cambridge University Press.

Graham, E. 2002 *Representations of the Post/Human: Monsters Aliens and Others in Popular Culture*, Manchester University Press.

Graham, S. and Marvin, S. 1996 *Telecommunications and the City: Electronic Spaces, Urban Places*, New York: Routledge.

Gramsci, A. 1988 *A Gramsci Reader*, ed. David Forgacs, London: Lawrence and Wishart.

Greeley, A.W. 2002 'The Military Telegraph Service' in *The Photographic History of the Civil War*, Vol. IV Originally published 1911, article available at: http://www.civilwarhome.com/telegraph.htm.

Green, J. 2002 'The Myth of Cyberterrorism', Washington Monthly, November, see: http://www.washingtonmonthly.com/features/2001/0211.green.html.

Greenberg, S. 1997 'Threats, Harassment and Hate Online: Recent Developments', *Boston Public Interest Journal*, 6, 673–696.

Greene, T. 2000 'Net "privacy" bill rewards data marketers', *Register* 25/10/00, available at http://www.theregister.co.uk/2000/10/25/net_privacy_bill_rewards_data/.

Greenfield, L. 1997 'Sex Offences and Offenders: An Analysis of Date Rape and Sexual Assault', *US Department of Justice Bureau of Justice Statistics*, NCJ-163392.

Greenland, S., Sheppard, A.R., Kaune, W.T., Poole, C. and Kelsh, M.A. 2000 'A Pooled Analysis of Magnetic Fields, Wire Codes and Childhood Leukaemia', *Epidemiology*, 11, 624–634.

Greenleaf, G. 1998 'An Endnote on Regulating Cyberspace: Architecture vs. Law?', *University of New South Wales Law Journal*, 21(2) (reproduced in D.S. Wall (ed.) *Cyberspace Crime*, Aldershot, UK: Ashgate/Dartmouth, 2003, pp. 89–120).

Grenville, M. 2006 'Text Message Injury Affects Millions', *160 Characters*, see: http://www.160characters.org/news.php?action=view&nid=1949.

Grimes, J. and Wharf, B. 1997 'Counter-hegemonic Discourses and the Internet', *Geographical Review*, 87(2), 279–274.

Grinsven, L. 2007 'Visa, Nokia Turn Mobile Phones into Mobile Wallets', Yahoo 09/01/07, see: http://news.yahoo.com/s/nm/20070109/tc_nm/electronics_show_visa_dc.

Gross, G. 2006 'Senate Approves Cybercrime Treaty', Computerworld 04/08/06, see: http://www.computerworld.com/action/article.do?command=viewArticleBasic& articleId=9002214.

Gross, S. 2007 'Drag Race, Face Jail Time? Florida Lawmakers Look To Curb Souped-up Car Street Racing', *CBS* 21/01/07, see: http://www.cbsnews.com/stories/ 2005/05/04/politics/main693027.shtml?CMP=ILC-SearchStories.

Grossman, D. 1999 *Stop Teaching Our Kids to Kill*, New York: Random House.

Grossman, W. 2002 'Watching the Internet Watchers', *The Inquirer* 15/02/02, see: http://www.theinquirer.net/default.aspx?article=2574.

Grosz, E. 1998 'Bodies-cities' in Pile, S. and Nast, H. (eds) *Places Through the Body*, London: Routledge.

Guardian 28/12/77 Charlie Chaplin: Obituary.

Guardian 01/02/05 'British Soldier "Threatened Naked Iraqi Prisoners with Metal Pole" ', see http://www.guardian.co.uk/Iraq/Story/0,,1403392,00.html.

Guardian 15/02/05 'China Closes Cybercafes'.

Guardian 04/11/05 'Electrical Fields Harmless', see http://www.guardian.co.uk/ science/2005/nov/04/uknews.

Guardian 28/01/06 'Nuisance Calls'.

Guardian 01/04/06 'Fraud in Yorkshire Credit Card Centres'.

Guerry, A.M. 1833 *Essai Sur la Statistique Moral de la France Avec Cartes*, Paris: Crochard.

Haack, S. 1996 *Deviant Logic, Fuzzy Logic: Beyond the Formalism*, University of Chicago Press.

Habermas, J. 1987 *The Theory of Communicative Action (Vol. 2) The Lifeworld and System*, Cambridge: Polity Press.

—— 1996 *Between Facts and Norms: Contributions to a Discourse Theory of Law and Democracy*, trans. William Rehg, Cambridge, MA: MIT Press.

Hacking, I. 1975 'The Identity of Indiscernibles', *Journal of Philosophy*, 72(9), 249– 256.

Hafner, K. 2006 'Laptop Slides Into Bed in Love Triangle', *New York Times* 24/08/06.

Haggerty, K. 2003 'From Risk to Precaution: The Rationalities of Personal Crime Prevention' in Ericson, R. and Doyle, A. (eds) *Risk and Morality*, University of Toronto Press, pp. 193–214.

—— 2006 'Visible War: Surveillance, Speed and Information War' in Haggerty and Ericsson (ed.) *The New Politics of Surveillance and Visibility*, University of Toronto Press, pp. 250–279.

—— and Ericson, R. 2000 'The Surveillant Assemblage', *British Journal of Sociology*, 51, 605–622.

—— and —— (eds) 2006a *The New Politics of Surveillance and Visibility*, University of Toronto Press.

—— and —— (eds) 2006b 'Introduction' in *The New Politics of Surveillance and Visibility*, University of Toronto Press.

Haines, L. 2004a 'Internet Rape Fantasy "Game" Goes Horribly Wrong', *The Regis- ter*, 05/04/04, see: http://www.theregister.co.uk/2004/04/05/internet_rape_fantasy_ game_goes/Hall.

—— 2004b 'Seven Dead in Net Suicide Pact', *The Register* 12/10//04, see: http:// www.theregister.co.uk/2004/10/12/net_suicide_pact/.

—— 2004c 'Feds Slap Cuffs on US College eBay Blaggers', *The Register* 15/07/04, see: http://www.theregister.co.uk/2004/07/15/college_ebay_blaggers/.

—— 2006 'Men Removed from Jet for "Speaking Arabic" ', *The Register* 21/08/06, see: http://www.theregister.co.uk/2006/08/21/arab_speakers_grounded/.

Halberstam, S. 1999 'Defamation and the Internet', Sprecher Grier Halberstam & Co Advisory Note, see: http://www.weblaw.co.uk/art190499.php.

Hale, B. 2002 'Companies Learn to Live with Online Fury', BBC 19/02/02, see: http://news.bbc.co.uk/1/hi/business/1826964.stm.

Hall, E. 1966 *The Hidden Dimension*, New York: Anchor Books and Doubleday.

—— 1973 'Proxemics' reprinted in Low, S.M. and Lawrence-Zuniga, D (eds) *The Anthropology of Space & Place*, Oxford: Blackwell (2003).

—— 1976 *Beyond Culture*, New York: Doubleday.

Hallsworth, S. 1996 'Punishment and Pleasure', Conference Paper, *European Group for the Study of Deviance and Social Control*, Kasmiercz.

—— 2002 'The Case for a Postmodern Penality', *Theoretical Criminology*, 6 (2), 145–163.

—— 2005 *Street Robbery*, Willan.

—— 2006 'Cruelty and Popular Culture', unpublished paper.

Hallsworth, S. and McGuire, M. 2003 Stop and Search Practice in the City of London.

—— 2005 Stop and Search in the Kent Constabulary.

Halpin, T. 2007 'Putin Accused of Launching Cyber War', Times 18/05/07, see: http://www.timesonline.co.uk/tol/news/world/europe/article1805636.ece.

Halsey, M. 2004 'Against Green Criminology', *The British Journal of Criminology*, 44, 833–853.

Hamel, P., Lustiger-Thaler, H., Pieterse, J.N. and Roseneil, S. (eds) 2001 *Globalisation and Social Movements*. London: Palgrave.

Hamelink, C. 2000 *The Ethics of Cyberspace*, London: Sage.

Hamilton, B. and Whalley, J. 1984 'Efficiency and Distributional Implications of Global Restrictions on Labor Mobility', 14 *Journal of Developmental Economics* 61, 74.

Hammersley, B. 2004 'Put the Tab on my Mobile', Guardian 27/05/04, see: http://technology.guardian.co.uk/online/story/0,3605,1225058,00.html.

Hampson, R. 2006 'Fear "As Bad as After 9/11" ', *USA Today* 13/12/06, see: http://www.usatoday.com/educate/college/polisci/articles/20061217.htm.

Hanna, F.D. 1927 'Automobiles as a Factor in Crime'. *Journal of the American Institute of Criminal Law and Criminology*, 18, 116–120.

Hannaford, B. 2001 'Feeling is Believing: A History of Telerobotics' in Goldberg, K. (ed.) *The Robot in the Garden: Telerobotics and Telepistemology in the Age of the Internet*, Cambridge, MA: MIT Press.

Hannigan, W.J. 1999 *New York Noir: Crime Photos from the Daily News Archive*, Rizzoli.

Hansen, F. 2002 'Opting for Work/Life Imbalance', *Workforce Management*, December, available at: http://www.workforce.com/section/02/feature/23/36/99/233701.html.

Haraway, D. 1991 'A Cyborg Manifesto: Science, Technology, and Socialist-feminism in the Late Twentieth Century' in *Simians, Cyborgs and Women: The Reinvention of Nature*, New York: Routledge, pp. 149–181.

Hardt, M. 1995 The Withering of Civil Society, *Social Text*, 27–44.

Hardt, M. and Negri, P. 2001 *Empire*, Harvard University Press.

—— 2004 *Multitude: War and Democracy in the Age of Empire*, New York: Penguin Press.

Harfield, C. 2006 'Soca: A Paradigm Shift in British Policing', *British Journal of Criminology*, 46 (4), 743–761.

Harmon, A. 1999 'Auction for a Kidney Pops Up on Ebay's Site', New York Times 03/09/99, see: http://query.nytimes.com/gst/fullpage.html?sec=health&res=9B01EED9153AF930A3575AC0A96F958260.

Harries, K. 1982 'Building and the Terror of Time', *Perspecta*, 19, 58–69.

—— 1999 *Mapping Crime: Principles and Practice*, Washington, DC: National Institute of Justice.

Harrison, T. 1999 'Globalization and the Trade in Human Body Parts', *The Canadian Review of Sociology and Anthropology*, (36) 1, 21ff.

Hartman, L. P. 2001 'Technology and Ethics: Privacy in the Workplace', *Business and Society Review*, 106 (1), 1–27.

Hartmann, S. 1996 'The World as a Process: Simulations in the Natural and Social Sciences' in Hegselmann, R. *et al.* (eds) *Modelling and Simulation in the Social Sciences from the Philosophy of Science Point of View*, Theory and Decision Library, Dordrecht: Kluwer, pp. 77–100.

Harvey, D. 1989 *The Condition of Postmodernity*, Oxford: Blackwell.

—— 1999 *The Limits to Capital*, London: Verso.

—— 2001 *Spaces of Capital: Towards a Critical Geography*, University of Edinburgh Press.

Hatcher, M. *et al.* 1999 'Computer Crimes', *American Criminal Law Review*, 36, 397–410.

Haugeland, J. 1981 'Analog and Analog', *Philosophical Topics*, 12, 213–226.

Havelock, E. A. 1963 *Preface to Plato*, Cambridge, MA: Harvard University Press.

Havick, J. (ed.) 1983 *Communications Policy and the Political Process*, Westport, CT: Greenwood Press.

Hayek, F. 1976 *Denationalisation of Money: An Analysis of the Theory and Practice of Concurrent Currencies*, London: Institute of Economic Affairs.

Hayles, N.K. 1991 *Chaos and Order: Complex Dynamics in Literature and Science*, University of Chicago Press.

—— 1995 'Embodied Virtuality, or How to Put Bodies Back into the Picture' in Argaitis, D. *et al.* (eds) *Immersed in Technology: Art & Virtual Environments*, Cambridge MA: MIT Press.

—— 1999a 'Simulating Narratives: What Virtual Creatures Can Teach Us', *Critical Inquiry*, 26 (1), 1–26.

—— 1999b *How We Became Posthuman*, University of Chicago Press.

Hayward, K. 2004 *City Limits: Crime Culture and the Urban Experience*, Glasshouse Press.

Heffernan, V. and Zeller, T. 2006 'Lonely Girl' (and Friends) Just Wanted Movie Deal', *New York Times* 12/09/06, see: http://www.nytimes.com/2006/09/12/technology/12cnd-lonely.html?ex=1315713600&en=abf28fc073b3c6e9&ei=5088&partner=rssnyt&emc=rss (viewed November 2006).

Heidegger, M. 1927 *Sein und Zeit (Being and Time)*, Halle a.d.S.: M. Niemeyer.

—— 1971 'Building Dwelling Thinking' in *Poetry, Language, Thought*, trans. Hofstadter, D., Harper Colophon Books. Citations from online version available at: http://pratt.edu/~arch543p/readings/Heidegger.html.

Heim, M. 1993 *The Metaphysics of Virtual Reality*, New York: Oxford University Press.

Held, D. 2002 *Governing Globalization: Power, Authority and Global Governance*, Cambridge: Polity Press.

Held, D., McGrew, A., Goldblatt, D. and Perraton, J. 1999 *Global Transformations: Politics, Economics and Culture*, Cambridge: Polity Press.

Hermida, A. 2002 'Behind China's Internet Red Firewall', BBC 03/09/02, see: http://news.bbc.co.uk/1/hi/technology/2234154.stm.

Herodotus 1924 *The Famous History of Herodotus*, trans. B. Rich, London: Constable.

Herschmann, T. 2001 'Israel's First Internet Murder', *Wired* 19/01/01, available at: http://www.wired.com/news/politics/0,1283,41300,00.html.

Herz, J.C. 1997 *Joystick Nation: How Videogames Ate Our Quarters, Won Our Hearts, and Rewired Our Minds*, Boston, MA: Little, Brown.

HGC 2005 'Profiling the Newborn: A Prospective Gene technology?', *Human Genetics Commission*, March 2005 report, see: http://www.hgc.gov.uk/UploadDocs/Contents/Documents/Final%20Draft%20of%20Profiling%20Newborn%20Report%2003%2005.pdf.

Highfield, R. 2007 'Scientists Develop Remote-controlled Pigeon', *Telegraph* 02/03/07, see: http://www.telegraph.co.uk/news/main.jhtml?xml=/news/2007/02/27/wpigeon127.xml.

Higney, F. 2006 'Interview with Robert Schifreen', LITF bulletin, 1, available at: http://www.legalitforum.com/ipi/legalitforumv2/index.jsp?pageid=litf_bulletin_015.

Hill, R.B. 1953 'The Early Years of the Strowger System', March 1953, *Bell Laboratories Record*, XXXI, 3.

Hilliard, R. 1991 *The Federal Communications Commission: A Primer*, Boston, MA: Focal Press.

Hillyard, P., Pantazis, C., Tombs, S. and Gordon, D. (eds) 2004 *Beyond Criminology. Taking Harm Seriously*, London: Pluto.

Himanen, P. 2001 *The Hacker Ethic and the Spirit of the Information Age*, London: Vintage.

Hobbes, T. 1950 *Leviathan*, Everyman's Library, New York: E.P. Dutton.

Hobsbawm, E. J. 1990 *Nations and Nationalism Since 1780: Programme, Myth, Reality*, Cambridge University Press.

HOC Home Affairs Committee 2004 'Identity Cards', *House of Commons*, HC130-I, available at: http://news.bbc.co.uk/nol/shared/bsp/hi/pdfs/29_07_04_idcards.pdf.

Hodson, R. (ed.) 1998 *The Globalization of Work*, Elsevier.

Holidays Uncovered 2007 Homepage; see: http://www.holidays_uncovered.co.uk.

Holmwood, J. 2005 'Functionalism and its Critics' in Harrington, A. (ed.) *Modern Social Theory: an introduction*, Oxford University Press, pp. 87–109.

Home Office 2004a *Violent Crime in Britain*.

—— 2004b 'Identity Theft: Don't Become a Victim', *Home Office Identity Fraud Steering Committee*, available at: http://www.identity-theft.org.uk/.

—— 2004c 'Defining and Measuring Anti-social Behaviour', Home Office Development and Practice Report, *Research, Development and Statistics Directorate. HO*, available at: www.together.gov.uk/cagetfile.asp?rid=468.

—— 2004d 'Computer Misuse Act', http://www.homeoffice.gov.uk/crime/ internetcrime/compmisuse.htm (no longer extant).

—— 2006a 'Why Do we Need the National Identity Scheme?', see: http:// www.identitycards.gov.uk/scheme-why.asp.

—— 2006b 'Updated Estimate of the Cost of Identity Fraud to the UK Economy', 02/02/06, accessible from 'Identity Theft: Don't Become a Victim', *Home Office Identity Fraud Steering Committee*, at: http://www.identitytheft.org.uk/ ID%20fraud%20table.pdf.

HOP 1997 'Judgments – Regina v. Burstow, Regina v. Ireland', Houses of Parliament Publications, House of Lords Judgement Index, see: http:// www.publications.parliament.uk/pa/ld199798/ldjudgmt/jd970724/irland01.htm.

Hopkins, T. 2005 ' "Cyber-rape" Outlawed: N.J. Cracks Down on Computer-aided Crime', *Computer Crime Research Center* 19/01/05, see: http://www.crime-research.org/news/19.01.2005/910/.

Hopper, I. and Stenger, R. 1999 'Large-scale Phone Invasion Goes Unnoticed by all but FBI', *CNN* 14/12/99, see: http://archives.cnn.com/1999/TECH/computing/12/ 14/phone.hacking/index.html.

Horgan, T. and Tienson, J. 1989 'Representations without Rules', *Philosophical Topics*, 17, 147–174.

Horstmann, R.P. 1976 'Space as Intuition and Geometry', *Ratio*, 18, 17–30.

Hosein, I., Tsiavos, P. and Whitley, E. 2002 'Regulating Architecture and Architectures of Regulation: Contributions from Information Systems', *International Review of Law, Computers and Technology*, 17 (1), 85.

Hott, J.R. 1983 'The Telephone Rape: Crisis Intervention for an Obscene Phone Call', *Issues Health Care Women*, 4 (2–3), 107–113.

House of Lords 1997 'Judgments – Regina v. Burstow, Regina v. Ireland', HOP, Judgement Index, see: http://www.publications.parliament.uk/pa/ld199798/ ldjudgmt/jd970724/irland01.htm.

Howe, M. 2007 'Men Jailed for Internet Plot to Rape Schoolgirls', *Independent* 06/02/07, see: http://news.independent.co.uk/uk/crime/article2241464.ece.

HPA 2005 'Definition, Epidemiology and Management of Electrical Sensitivity Report for the Radiation Protection Division of the Health Protection Agency', *Health Protection Authority*, HPA-RPD-010.

HSE 2004 'Psychosocial Risk Factors in Call Centres: An Evaluation of Work Design and Well-being', *HSE report 169*, HMSO, see: http://www.hse.gov.uk/research/ rrpdf/rr169.pdf.

—— 2007 'Health and Safety in the Entertainment and Leisure Industry', *Health and Safety Executive*, see: http://213.212.77.20/entertainment/index.htm.

Huber, P. 1997 *Law and Disorder in Cyberspace: Abolish the FCC and Let Common Law Rule the Telcosm*, Oxford University Press.

Hudson, B. 2003 *Justice in the Risk Society: Challenging and Re-affirming 'Justice' in Late Modernity*, London: Sage.

Hughes, D. 2000 ' "Welcome to the Rape Camp": Sexual Exploitation and the Internet in Cambodia', *Journal of Sexual Aggression*, available at: http://www.uri.edu/ artsci/wms/hughes/rapecamp.htm.

—— 2003 'Final Report, Group of Specialists on the Impact of the Use of New Information Technologies on the Trafficking in Human Beings for the Purpose of

Sexual Exploitation', *Council of Europe*, February 2003, available at: http://www.uri.edu/artsci/wms/hughes/hughes.htm.

Hugill, P. 1999 *Global Communications since 1844: Geopolitics and Technology*, Maryland: Johns Hopkins University Press.

Humane Society of USA 2006 'The Latest Fad in Internet Animal Cruelty: Pay-per View Hunting', available at: http://www.hsus.org/wildlife/wildlife_news/pay_per_view_slaughter.html (viewed October 2006).

Hunter, D. 2003 'Cyberspace as Place, and the Tragedy of the Digital Anticommons', *California Law Review*, 91, 439.

Huurdeman, A. 2003 *The Worldwide History of Telecommunications*, London: Wiley.

Huus, K. 2003 'Japan's Chilling Internet Suicide Pacts', MSNBC 10/06/03, see: http://www.msnbc.msn.com/id/3340456/.

Hyslop, J. 2002 'General Motors Stops the Trollies', *Stay Free*, 19, available at: http://www.stayfreemagazine.org/archives/19/generalmotors.html.

ICANN 2007 Internet Corporation for Assigned Names and Numbers (ICANN), homepage, see: http://www.icann.org/index.html.

Icannwatch 2007 Homepage at: http://www.icannwatch.org/.

ICC 1998 'Statute of the International Criminal Court', available at: http://www.un.org/law/icc/statute/romefra.htm.

ICO 2006 'Monitoring at Work: Guidance for Small Businesses', *Information Comissioner's Office*, available at: http://www.ico.gov.uk/.

IFAW 2005 'Caught in the Web: Wildlife Trade on the Internet', *International Fund for Animal Welfare Report*, available at: http://www.caughtintheweb.co.uk/atf/cf/%7b9fde63d6-73ca-4d8c-bb39-d60bccc83e28%7d/internet%20trade%20report%20final.pdf.

iFilm 2007 'Happy Slapping' (enter the term in 'search' to view footage), see: http://www.ifilm.com/.

IFR 2007 Internet Filter Review, see: http://internet-filter-review.toptenreviews.com/.

IKA 2007 Imperial Klans of America, homepage, see http://www.kkkk.net/ (viewed February, 2007).

ILPF 2007 'Bibliography of Internet Self Regulation', *Internet Law and Policy Forum*, see http://www.ilpf.org/groups/bib4_15.htm.

IMC 2007 Independent Media Center, see: http://www.indymedia.org/en/index.shtml.

Innis, H.A. 1950 *Empire and Communication*, University of Toronto Press (reprinted 1971).

—— 1962 *The Bias of Communication*, University of Toronto Press.

—— 1991 'Media in Ancient Empires' in Crowley, D. and Heyer, P. *Communication in History: Technology, Culture, Society*, Longman.

Interpol 2007 'Information Technology Crime', see: http://www.interpol.int/Public/TechnologyCrime/default.asp.

IPPR 2004 'A Responsibility Shared? Finding Solutions to Protect Children Online', Ippr Manifesto for a Digital Britain, available at: http://www.ippr.org.uk/uploadedFiles/research/projects/Digital_Society/child_safety_seminar.pdf.

ITF 2001 'Internet Task Force for Child Protection on the Internet', Home Office, http://police.homeoffice.gov.uk/operational-policing/crime-disorder/child-protection-taskforce.

ITN 13/10/06 'Terry Lloyd "Unlawfully Killed by US Forces" ', see: http://itn.co.uk/news/headlines_abd145ba72e04bb02c6a8be56da3b5c2.html.

ITRC 2004 Identity Theft Resource Centre, see: http://www.idtheftcenter.org/index.shtml (viewed November 2005).

IWF 2005 Internet Watch Foundation, see: http://www.iwf.org.uk/.

JA 2007 Just Adventure, see: http://www.justadventure.com/SUR_Index.shtm.

Jackson, T. 2005 'Survey on Staff Email Use', Loughborough University, see: http://www.lboro.ac.uk/service/publicity/news-releases/2005/49_email.html.

Jacobs, J. B. and Potter, K. 1998 *Hate Crimes: Criminal Law and Identity Politics*, Oxford and New York: Oxford University Press.

Jacobson, J. 2004 'A Liberal Professor Fights a Label', *Chronicle of Higher Education* 26/11/04, see: http://chronicle.com/errors.dir/noauthorization.php3?page=/weekly/v51/i14/14a00801.htm.

Jacques, R. 2007 'Poor Wi-Fi Security Leaves Users at Serious Risk', *Vnunet* 03/04/07, see: http://www.vnunet.com/vnunet/news/2187063/quarter-uk-surfers-face-serious.

James, B. 1991 'From Nigeria, a Business Proposition You Ought to Refuse', *International Herald Tribune* 24/09/91, see: http://www.iht.com/articles/1991/09/24/lago.php (viewed March 2007).

James, C. 2002 'Selling Organs: The Answer to the Burgeoning Organ Deficit', *Food & Drug Law*, winter.

James, W. 1890/1950 *The Principles of Psychology* 1890, Reprint edn New York: Dover.

Jameson, F. 1991 *Postmodernism, Or, The Cultural Logic of Late Capitalism*, Durham, NC: Duke University Press.

Jaspers, K. 1961 *The Question of German Guilt*, trans. E.B. Ashton, New York: Capricorn.

Javelin 2006 'Mitigating New Account Fraud: Reduce Risk and Expand Customer Base with Evolving Authentication Solutions', Javelin Syndicated Report, October 2006, see: H http://www.javelinstrategy.com/uploads/622.R_NewAccountFraud_Brochure.pdf.

Jeeves, P. 2005 'Sex-trade Children Flown to Region', *Yorkshire Post* 10/11/05, see: http://www.yorkshiretoday.co.uk/
ViewArticle2.aspx?SectionID=55&ArticleID=1249308.

Jefferies, D. 1998 'The Body as Commodity: The Use of Markets to Cure the Organ Deficit', *International Journal of Global Legal Studies*, 5 (2), 621–623.

Jenkins, E. 2005 'Happy Attack at 2am: Clubber Beaten', *Sun* 25/06/06.

Jenkins, J. 2007 'A. Frederick Collins . . . Genius or Fraud?', *Spark Museum*, available at: http://www.sparkmuseum.com/COLLINS.HTM.

Jenks, C. 2003 *Transgression*, London: Routledge.

Jennings, R. *et al.* 2006 'European Music Download Forecast: 2006 To 2011', *Forrester Research*, see: http://www.forrester.com/Research/Document/Excerpt/0,7211,38733,00.html.

Jessop, B. 2003 'Informational Capitalism and Empire: The Post-Marxist Celebration of US Hegemony in a New World Order', *Language and Capitalism*, see: http://www.languageandcapitalism.info/lnc/papers/.

—— 2005 'Gramsci as a Spatial Theorist', *Critical Review of International Social and Political Philosophy*, 8 (4), 421–437.

Jewkes, Y. (ed.) 2002 *Dot.cons: Crime, Deviance and Identity on the Internet*, Willan.

—— (ed.) 2006a *Crime Online*, Willan.

—— 2006b ' "Killed by the Internet": Cyber Homicides, Cyber Suicides and Cyber Sex Crimes' in Jewkes, Y. (ed.) *Crime Online*, Willan, pp. 1–11.

Jha, A. 2003 'Tesco Tests Spy Chip Technology', *Guardian* 19/07/03, see: http://www.guardian.co.uk/uk_news/story/0%2c3604%2c1001211%2c00.html.

Johnson, B. 2006 'German Gamers Face Jail for Acts of Virtual Violence', *Guardian* 12/12/06, see: http://www.guardian.co.uk/germany/article/0,,1969920,00.html.

—— 2007 'Apple and Sony under Threat after Microsoft is Fined \$1.5bn', *Guardian* 24/02/07, see: http://business.guardian.co.uk/story/0,,2020362,00.html.

Johnson, D and Post. D. 1996 'Law And Borders: The Rise of Law in Cyberspace', 48 *Stanford Law Review*, 1367.

—— 1997 'And How Shall the Net Be Governed? A Meditation on the Relative Virtues of Decentralized, Emergent Law' in Kahin, B. and Keller, B. (eds) *Coordinating the Internet*, Cambridge, MA: MIT Press.

Johnson, S. 2004 'The (Evil) Genius of Comment Spammers', *Wired* 12/03/04, see: http://www.wired.com/wired/archive/12.03/google.html?pg=7.

Johnston, L. and Shearing, C. 2003 *Governing Security: Explorations in Policing and Justice*, London: Routledge.

Joinson, A. 2003 *Understanding the Psychology of Internet Behaviour: Virtual Worlds, Real Lives*, Basingstoke: Palgrave Macmillan.

Jones, G. 2006 'Nationality and Multinationals in Historical Perspective', Harvard: Business School Working Paper, HBS 06–052.

Jones, J. 2003 'Cyberstalking: An International Perspective' in Jewkes, Y. (ed.) *Dot.Cons* Willan, 105–125.

Jones, J. *et al.* 2006 'Self-reported Work-related Illness' in 2005/05, *Health and Safety Executive*, available at: http://www.hse.gov.uk/statistics/causdis/musc.htm.

Jones, M. (ed.) 1990 *Fake?: The Art of Deception*, University of California Press.

Jones, T. and Newburn, T. 2002 'The Transformation of Policing. Understanding Current Trends in Policing Systems', *British Journal of Criminology*, 42, 129–146.

Jordan, T. 1999 *Cyberpower: The Culture and Politics of Cyberspace and the Internet*, London: Routledge.

Joyce, P. (ed.) 1987 *The Historical Meanings of Work*, Cambridge University Press.

Judson, K. 2000 *Computer Crime: Phreaks, Spies and Salami Slicers*, Berkeley Heights, NJ: Enslow Publishers.

Kalouche, F. 2005 'Social Imaginary, Multiple Self, and Globalization', *International Studies in Philosophy* 37 (1), 19–35.

Kant, I. 2003 *Critique of Pure Reason*, trans Kemp-Smith, N., Basingstoke: Palgrave Macmillan.

Katsh, M.E. 1989 *The Electronic Media and the Transformation of Law*, Oxford University Press.

Katz, J. 1999 *Connections: Social and Cultural Studies of the Telephone in American Life*, New Brunswick (USA) and London: Transaction Publishers.

Katz, J. *et al.* 2004 'Personal Mediated Communication and the Concept of Community in Theory and Practice', *Communication Yearbook*, 28 (1), 315–371.

Keating, D. 2004 'Electronic Voting Raises New Issues', *Washington Post* 25/10/04, see: http://www.washingtonpost.com/wp-dyn/articles/A59554-2004Oct24.html.

Keizer, G. 2005 'EBay Yanks Auction Of Avian Flu Vaccine', *Information Week* 18/10/05, see: http://www.informationweek.com/story/showArticle.jhtml?articleID=172302134.

Keller, J. 2005 *In Focus: Weegee Photographs from the J. Paul Getty Museum*, Oxford University Press.

Kellner, D. 1997 'Intellectuals, the New Public Spheres, and Technopolitics', *New Political Science*, 41–42, 169–188.

Kelly, G. 2000 'Employment and Concepts of Work in the New Global Economy', *International Labour Review*, 139 (1), 5–32.

Kelly, L. *et al.* 2005 'A Gap or a Chasm? Attrition in Reported Rape Cases', *Home Office Research Study* 293, available at: http://www.homeoffice.gov.uk/rds/pdfs05/hors293.pdf.

Kern, S. 1983 *The Culture of Time and Space 1880–1918*, Cambridge, MA: Harvard University Press.

Khazanov, A. M. 1984 *Nomads of the Outside World*, Cambridge University Press.

Kieve, J. 1973 *The Electric Telegraph: A Social and Economic History*, Exeter: David & Charles.

Killias, M. 2006 'The Opening and Closing of Breaches: A Theory on Crime Waves, Law Creation and Crime Prevention', *European Journal of Criminology*, 3 (1), 11–31.

Killoran, J. B. 2003 'The Gnome in the Front Yard and Other Public Figurations: Genres of Self-presentation on Personal Home Pages', *Biography*, 26 (1), 66–83.

Kim J. (ed.) 1993 *Supervenience and Mind: Selected Philosophical Essays*, Cambridge University Press.

Kim, W. 2005 'On Digital Convergence and Challenges', *Journal of Object Technology*, 4 (4), 67–71, see: http://www.jot.fm/issues/issue_2005_05/column5.

Kinshott, G. 2001 'Vehicle Related Thefts: Practice Messages from the British Crime Survey', *Home Office Briefing Note* 6/01, available as download at: http://www.homeoffice.gov.uk/rds/prgpdfs/brf601.pdf.

Kinzelbach, A. 2006 'Infection, Contagion, and Public Health in Late Medieval and Early Modern German Imperial Towns' *Journal of the History of Medicine and Allied Sciences*, 61 (3), 369–389.

Kleeman, J. 2007 'Wiki Wars', *Observer* 25/02/07, see: http://media.guardian.co.uk/newmedia/story/0,,2042423,00.html.

Klein, N. 2007 *The Shock Doctrine: The Rise of Disaster Capitalism*, London: Picador.

Klugman, C. 2001 'From Cyborg Fiction to Medical Reality', *Literature and Medicine*, 20 (1), 39–54.

Knapp, L (ed.) 2001 *The Abortion Controversy*, San Diego CA: Greenhaven Press.

Kochanek, K.D., Murphy, S.L., Anderson, R.N. and Scott, C. 2004 'Deaths: Final Data for 2002', *National Vital Statistics Reports,* 53 (5), Hyattsville, MD: National Center for Health Statistics. DHHS Publication No. (PHS) 2005–1120.

Koepsell, D. 2000 *The Ontology of Cyberspace: Philosophy, Law, and the Future of Intellectual Property*, Chicago, IL.: Open Court.

Kollock, P. and Smith, M. (eds) 1999 *Communities in Cyberspace*, London: Routledge.

Koppell, J. 2000 'Why Cyberspace isn't Anyplace', *Atlantic*, August, pp. 16–18.

Korenman, J. and Wyatt, N. 1996 'Group Dynamics in an E-mail Forum' in Herring, S. C. (ed.) *Computer-mediated Communication: Linguistic, Social and Cross-cultural Perspectives*, Philadelphia: John Benjamins, pp. 225–242.

Kornblum. J. 2003 ' "Flash Mobs" Activated by E-mails', *USA Today* 17/08/03, see: http://www.usatoday.com/news/nation/2003-08-17-flash-mob-usat_x.htm.

Kortmann, J. 2001 'Liability for Nonfeasance; A Comparative Study', Oxford University Comparative Law Forum 1, see: http://ouclf.iuscomp.org/articles/kortmann.shtml.

Koslowski, R. 2006 'Immigration Reforms and Border Security Technologies', Border Battles: The US Immigration Debates, SSRC, see: http://borderbattles.ssrc.org/Koslowski/.

Krause, K. 1995 Arms and the State: Patterns of Military Production and Trade, Cambridge University Press.

Kraut, R., Brynin, M. and Kiesler, S. (eds) 2006 Computers, Phones, and the Internet: The Social Impact of Information Technology, Oxford University Press.

Krepinevich, A., Watts, B. and Work, R. 2003 'Meeting the Anti-access and Area-denial Challenge', Center for Strategic and Budgetary Assessments see: http://www.csbaonline.org/4Publications/Archive/R.20030520.Meeting_the_Anti-A/R.20030520.Meeting_the_Anti-A.pdf.

Krim, J. 2004a 'Report Faults Cyber-security', Washington Post, 23/07/2004, see: http://www.washingtonpost.com/ac2/wp-dyn/A7192-2004Jul22?language=printer.

—— 2004b 'Suspected File-sharing "Hubs" Raided', Washington Post 26/9/04 available   at: http://www.washingtonpost.com/wp-dyn/articles/A33959-2004Aug25.html.

—— 2005 'Angry BellSouth Withdrew Donation, New Orleans Says', Washington Post 03/12/05, see: http://www.washingtonpost.com/wp-dyn/content/article/2005/12/02/AR2005120201853_pf.html.

Kroker, A. and M. 1987 'Body Digest. Theses on the Disappearing Body in The Hyper-modern Condition', 'Body Digest. Fashion, Skin & Technology', Canadian Journal of Political and Social Theory, v.XI, nos 1–2.

Krueger, M. 2005 'Offshore E-money Issuers and Monetary Policy', First Monday, 6, 10 (updated version of October 2001), available at: http://www.firstmonday.org/issues/issue6_10/krueger/index.html.

Kruks, S. 2000 Retrieving Experience: Subjectivity and Recognition in Feminist Politics, Ithaca, NY: Cornell University Press.

Labour Party 2006 'Blogs', see: http://www.labour.org.uk/blogs.

Lacan, J. 1994 'Notebooks of Jacques Lacan' in Critical Art Ensemble, New York: Autonomedia.

Lacey, N. and Zedner, L. 1995 'Discourses of Community in Criminal Justice', Journal of Law and Society, 22 (3), September.

Lake, M. 2005 'Is Municipal Wi-Fi doomed in the United States?', CNET 18/01/05, see: http://reviews.cnet.com/4520-6028_7-5621367-1.html.

Lakoff, G. 2006 Whose Freedom?: The Battle Over America's Most Important Idea, New York: Farrar, Straus & Giroux.

Lamanna, M. 2001 Emile Durkheim on the Family, London: Sage.

Landow, G. 2006 Hypertext 3.0: Critical Theory and New Media in an Era of Globalization (Parallax: Re-visions of Culture and Society), Baltimore, MD: Johns Hopkins University Press.

Lapham, C. 1997 'The Internet is "Mission Critical" for Business', Computer-mediated Communication, 4 (2), available at: http://www.december.com/cmc/mag/1997/feb/lapham.html.

Larson, E. and Amundson, D. 1998 A Different Death: Euthanasia and the Christian Tradition, Downers Grove, IL: InterVarsity Press.

Lascia, J.D. 2005 *Darknet: Hollywood's War Against the Digital Generation*, New York: John Wiley & Sons.

Lash, S. 2002 *Critique of Information*, London: Sage.

Latour, B. 1993 *We Have Never been Modern*, Cambridge, MA: Harvard University Press.

Law, J. 1991 *A Sociology of Monsters: Essays on Power Technology and Domination*, London: Routledge.

Law, J. and Hassard, J. (eds) 1999 *Actor Network Theory and After*, Oxford and Keele: Blackwell and the Sociological Review.

Lea, J. 2002 *Crime and Modernity: Continuities in Left Realist Criminology*, London: Sage.

Lean, G. 2006 'UK Ministers Back "Terminator" GM Crops', *Independent* 05/03/06, see: http://news.independent.co.uk/environment/article349331.ece.

Lebkowsky, J. 1997 'Nodal Politics', *Mindjack Magazine*, see http://www.mindjack.com/feature/nodal.html.

Lechner, F. 2000 'Review of Findlay 1999', The Globalisation Website, see: http://www.sociology.emory.edu/globalization/reviews/findlay.html.

Lee, E. 1997 'Globalization and Labour Standards: A Review of Issues', *International Labour Review*, 136.

Lee, R. and DeVore, I. (eds) 1968 *Man the Hunter*, Aldine de Gruyter.

Leets, L. 2001 'Responses to Internet Hate Sites: Is Speech Too Free in Cyberspace?', *Community Leadership & Policy, 6*, 287–317.

Lefebvre, H. 1976–78 *De L'Etat* (Vols 1–4), Union Generale d'Editions.

—— 1991 *The Production of Space*, London: Blackwell.

Leibniz, G. 1965 *Monadology and Other Philosophical Essays*, trans. and ed. Schrecker, P. and Schrecker, A., New York: Bobbs-Merrill Co.

Leinbach, T.R. and Brunn, S.D. (eds) 2001 *Worlds of E-commerce: Economic, Geographical and Social Dimensions*, New York: Wiley & Sons.

Lemos, R. 2003 'A Twenty Year Plague', *CNET* 25/11/03, see: http://news.com.com/2009-7349-5111410.html.

—— 2004 'U.S. Cybersecurity Chief Resigns', *CNET*, 01/10/2004, http://news.com.com/U.S.+cybersecurity+chief+resigns/2100-7348_3-5392501.html.

—— 2005 'Arrests Unlikely to Impact Bot Net Threat, Say Experts', *Security Focus* 12/10/05, see http://www.securityfocus.com/news/11344.

—— 2006 'Survey: Identity Theft Hits 3 Percent', *Security Focus* 03/04/06, see: http://www.securityfocus.com/brief/177.

Lersch, K.M. 2004 *Space, Time, and Crime*, Carolina University Press.

Lessig, L. 1999 *Code and Other Laws of Cyberspace*, New York: Basic Books., Uri Dekel.

Lettice, J. 2001 'Smart Tagging in Office XP – What Melissa did Next?', *Register* 06/08/01.

—— 2003 'Al Jazeera and the Net – Free Speech, But Don't Say *That*', *Register* 7/04/03, see: http://www.theregister.co.uk/2003/04/07/al_jazeera_and_the_net/.

—— 2006 'SOCA Saves UK High-tech Crime Unit – Offline', *The Register* 26/05/05, see: http://www.theregister.co.uk/2006/05/26/soca_saves_nhtcu_site/.

Levesley, T *et al.* 2004 'Emerging Methods of Car Theft – Theft of Keys', *Crime Reduction Series*: Findings 239, available at: http://www.crimereduction.gov.uk/vehiclecrime44.htm.

Levey, R. 2003 'Nectar Feeds Sainsbury's Segmentation Efforts', *Direct* 01/04/03, see: http://directmag.com/mag/marketing_nectar_feeds_sainsburys.

Levy, P. 1997 *Becoming Virtual: Reality in the Digital Age*, trans. Bononno, R., New York: Plenum Trade.

—— 2000 *Collective Intelligence: Mankind's Emerging World in Cyberspace*, trans. Bonnono, R., Perseus Books.

Levy, S. 1984 *Hackers: Heroes of the Computer Revolution*, New York: Penguin Books.

Lewis, D. 1971 'Analog and Digital', *Noûs*, 5, 321–328.

Lewis, H.D. 1948 'Collective Responsibility', *Philosophy*, 24, 3–18.

Lewis, P. 2006 'Teenage Networking Websites Face Anti-paedophile Investigation', *Guardian* 03/07/2006, see: http://www.guardian.co.uk/uk_news/story/0,,1811159,00.html.

LexisNexis 2005 Press Release, available at: http://www.lexisnexis.com/about/releases/0790.asp.

—— 2007 National Fraud Center, see: http://www.lexisnexis.com/fraudcenter/.

Leyden, J. 2002 'Mobile Phone Theft is Far Worse Than We Thought', *Register* 20/02/02, see: http://www.theregister.co.uk/2002/02/20/mobile_phone_theft_is_far/.

—— 2003 'NatWest Customers Targeted in "Phishing" Scam', *Register* 24/10/03, see http://www.theregister.co.uk/2003/10/24/natwest_customers_targeted_in_phishing/.

—— 2005a 'Cyber Cops Foil £220m Sumitomo Bank Raid', *Channel Register* 25/03/05, see http://www.channelregister.co.uk/2005/03/17/sumitomo_cyber-heist_foiled/.

—— 2005b 'Fake Tsunami Appeal Website Terminated', *The Register* 04/02/05, see: http://www.theregister.co.uk/2005/02/04/fake_dec_site_pulled/.

—— 2006a 'Web Suicide Pacts Sweep Japan', *The Register* 10/02/06, see: http://www.theregister.co.uk/2006/02/10/japanese_suicide_pact_surge/.

—— 2006b 'UK Workers Abuse Net Access', *The Register* 27/03/06, see http://www.theregister.co.uk/2006/03/27/net_misuse_dti_survey/.

LibertyCentral 2006 'Briefing Notes – Police and Justice Bill, Sections 33–36', see http://www.libertycentral.org.uk/content/view/406/34/.

Library Journal 28/07/07 'DOPA Passes House by Wide Margin; ALA Dismayed', see: http://www.libraryjournal.com/article/CA6357145.html.

Lichtblau, E. and Zernike, K. 2006 'Panel in Senate Backs Bush Plan for Monitoring', *New York Times* 14/09/06, see http://select.nytimes.com/gst/abstract.html?res=FA0F17FC39550C778DDDA00894DE404482.

Liebowitz, S. and Margolis, S. 2004 'Network Externalities (Effects)', online article available at: http://www.utdallas.edu/~liebowit/palgrave/network.html.

Lindblom, C. 1977 *Politics and Markets: The World's Political-economic Systems*, New York: Basic Books.

Linklater, A. 2006 'The Harm Principle and Global Ethics', *Global Society*, 20 (3), 329–343.

Linux Security 2001 'Cyberwar Or Just Plain Vandalism?', *IT World* 15/05/01, see: http://www.itworld.com/nl/lnx_sec/05152001/.

Lippens, R. 2001 'Rethinking Organizational Crime and Organizational Criminology', *Crime, Law and Social Change*, 35 (4), 319–331.

Littler, C. 1982 *The Development of the Labour Process in Capitalist Societies*, London: Heinemann.

Lloyd, I. and Mellor, D. 2003 *Telecommunications Law*, LexisNexis.

Lloyd-Roberts, S. 2001 'How Big Business Bankrolls the Sick Trade in Human Body Parts', *Independent*, 07/07/01 see: http://news.independent.co.uk/europe/article232827.ece.

Loader, B. (ed.) 1997 *The Governance of Cyberspace: Politics, Technology and Global Restructuring*, London: Routledge.

Loader, I. 2000 'Plural Policing and Democratic Governance', *Social & Legal Studies*, 9 (3), 323–345.

Logsden, J. 2006 'Just Say Wait to Space Power', *Issues in Science and Technology*, see: http://www.issues.org/17.3/p_logsdon.htm.

Lomas, J. 2005 'New Jersey's Adult Internet Luring Statute: An Appropriate Next Step?', *Duke Law & Technology Review*, 16.

Loney, M. 2002 'Industry Lambasts Snooping Law Costs', *ZdNet* 30/04/02, see: http://news.zdnet.co.uk/itmanagement/0,1000000308,2109430,00.htm.

Lopes, P. 2005 'Signifying Deviance and Transgression: Jazz in the Popular Imagination', *American Behavioral Scientist*, 48 (11), 1468–1481.

Lucas, G. 2005 'Sutter County: Students Kept Under Surveillance at School', *San Francisco Chronicle* 10/02/05 see http://www.sfgate.com/cgi-bin/article.cgi?f=/c/a/2005/02/10/BAGG0B8I4D1.DTL.

Lucas, J. 1973 A *Treatise on Time and Space*, London: Methuen.

Lupton, D. 1995 'The Embodied Computer/User' in Featherstone, M. and Burrows, R. (eds) *Cyberspace, Cyberbodies, Cyberpunk: Cultures of Technological Embodiment*, Thousand Oaks, CA: Sage, pp. 97–112.

Lutterbeck, B., Ishii, K. and Gehring, R. 2000 'Governing Legal Identities, Lessons from the History of Seals and Signatures', presentation given at the Information Security Solutions Europe Conference (ISSE) 2000 in Barcelona on 28 September, available at: ig.cs.tu-berlin.de/oldstatic/ap/rg/2000-09/ISSE_Paper_Gehring_etal.pdf.

Lyon, D. 1994 *The Electronic Eye: The Rise of the Surveillance Society*: Cambridge: Polity Press.

—— 2001 *Surveillance Society: Monitoring Everyday Life*, Open University Press.

—— 2002 'Cyberspace: Beyond the Information Society?' in Armitage, J. and Roberts, J. (eds) *Living With Cyberspace*, London: Continuum.

—— 2006 '9/11, Synopticon and Scopophilia: Watching and Being Watched' in Haggerty, K. and Ericson, R. *The New Politics of Surveillance and Visibility*, pp. 35–54.

Lyotard, J.F. 1991 *The Inhuman: Reflections on Time*, Cambridge: Polity Press.

Macalister, T. 2007 'Private Equity Boss Rounds on "Enemy Within" ', *Guardian* 18/06/07, see: http://business.guardian.co.uk/story/0,,2105349,00.html.

MacCall, A. 1979 *The Medieval Underworld*, New York: Barnes and Noble.

MacCartney, J. 2006 'Dissident Jailed After Yahoo Handed Evidence to Police', *Times* 10/02/06, see: http://www.timesonline.co.uk/tol/news/world/asia/article729210.ece.

MacCormack, H. 2006 'Record-breaking Flashmobbers Come Dancing', *Independent* 2/10/06, see: http://news.independent.co.uk/uk/this_britain/article2032714.ece.

MacDonald, J. and Carpenter, E. 2006 'Web Ad Leads to Illegal Fireworks', *Orange County Register* 30/06/06, see: http://www.ocregister.com/ocregister/news/atoz/article_1197449.php.

MacIntosh, M. 1971 'Changes in the Organisation of Thieving' in Cohen, S. (ed.) *Images of Deviance*, London: Penguin.

MacIntyre, A. 1999 *Dependent Rational Animals: Why Human Beings Need the Virtues* (The Paul Carus Lecture Series, no. 20), Chicago, IL: Open Court.

Mack, A. (ed.) 1993 *Home: A Place in the World*, New York: New York University Press.

MacKinnon, R. 1997 'Punishing the Persona: Correctional Strategies for the Virtual Offender' in Jones, S. (ed.) *Virtual Culture*, London: Sage, pp. 206–235.

Macpherson, W. 1999 *The Stephen Lawrence Inquiry*, London: The Stationery Office, February.

Malik, A. 2005 'Federal Police Crack Down on Melbourne Teenager', Music & Media, 457 31/05/05, see: http://www.themusic.com.au/im_m/display.php?s= guest&id=38.

Malpas, J. 2001 'Acting at a Distance and Knowing from Afar: Agency and Knowledge on the Internet' in Goldberg, K. (ed.) *The Robot in the Garden: Telerobotics and Telepistemology in the Age of the Internet*, Cambridge, MA: MIT Press.

Mandeville, B. 1970 *The Fable of the Bees*, ed. Harth, P., Harmondsworth: Penguin.

Maney, K. 2003 'If U.S. Launches Cyberattack, it Could Change Nature of War', *USA Today* 11/2/03, see http://www.usatoday.com/tech/columnist/kevinmaney/ 2003-02-11-cyberattack_x.htm.

Manning, P. K. 1992 'Policing and Technology' in Morris, N. and Tonry, M. (eds). *Modern Policing*, University of Chicago Press, pp. 349–398.

Manning, S. 2006 'Psy-Ops Countered By Islamic Digital Propaganda', *Scoop* 1/06/06, see: http://www.scoop.co.nz/stories/HL0606/S00016.htm.

Margatts, H. 2003 'Electronic Government: Method or Madness', *UCL School of Public Policy Working Paper Series*: ISSN 1479–9472.

Margolis, J. 1995 'Beyond Postmodernism: Logic as Rhetoric', *Argumentation*, 9 (1). 21–31.

Mark, R. 2005 'Bush's Cyber Security Force Loses Another One', *Internet News* 12/01/05, see: http://www.internetnews.com/bus-news/article.php/3458241.

Markoff, J. 2006 'Adding On to the House of Google', *New York Times* 10/10/06, see: http://www.nytimes.com/2006/10/10/technology/10google.html?ex=1318132800 &en=91027e8fd41514b6&ei=5088&partner=rssnyt&emc=rss (viewed January 2007).

Marshall, K.P. 1999 'Has Technology Introduced New Ethical Problems?', *Journal of Business Ethics*, 19 (1), 81–90 (10).

Martin, H.J. 2001 'Printing' in Williams, R. (ed.) *Contact: Human Communications and its History*, London: Thames and Hudson, pp. 128–150.

Marx, G.T. 1988 *Undercover Police Surveillance in America*, Berkeley: University of California Press.

—— 1999 'Measuring Everything That Moves: The New Surveillance at Work' in Simpson, I. and R. (eds) *The Workplace and Deviance*, JAI series on Research in the Sociology of Work.

—— 2001 'Identity and Anonymity, Some Conceptual Distinctions and Issues Research' in Caplan, J. and Torpey, J. (eds) *Documenting Individual Identity*, Princeton, NJ: Princeton University Press.

—— 2006 'Varieties of Personal Information as Influences on Attitudes Toward

Surveillance' in Haggerty, K.D and Ericson, R.V (eds) *The New Politics of Surveillance and Visibility*, University of Toronto Press, pp. 79–110.

Marx, K. 1964 *Karl Marx: Early Writings*, trans. and ed. T. B. Bottomore, New York: McGraw-Hill.

—— 1976 *Value, Price and Profit*, New York: International Publishers.

Massey, D. 1993 'Power-Geometry and a Progressive Sense of Place' in Bird, J. *et al.* (eds) *Mapping the Futures: Local Cultures, Global Change*, New York and London: Routledge, pp. 59–69.

Mathiesen, T. 1992 'The Viewer Society', *Theoretical Criminology*, 1 (2), 215–234.

Mattelart, A. 1996 *The Invention of Communication*, University of Minneapolis Press.

Mayhew, P. *et al.* 1976 *Crime as Opportunity*, Home Office Research Unit, London: HSMO.

McAfee 2006 Virtual Criminology Report, July 2006, available at: http://www.softmart.com/mcafee/docs/McAfee%20NA%20Virtual%20Criminology%20Report.pdf.

McCarthy, K. 2001a 'IT Consultant Denies £25m Web Site Blackmail', *The Register* 17/05/2001, see: http://www.theregister.co.uk/2001/05/17/it_consultant_denies_163_25m/.

—— 2001b 'Murderer Confesses on Anandtech Forum', *The Register* 18/05/01, see: http://www.theregister.co.uk/2001/05/18/murderer_confesses_on_anandtech_forum/.

McCleneghan, J. S. 2002 ' "Reality Violence" on TV News: It Began with Vietnam', *Social Science Journal*, 9 (4), 593–598.

McClellan, J. 1994 'Netsurfers', *Observer* 13/11/94.

McCloud, S. 2000 *Reinventing Comics*, New York: HarperCollins.

McCormick, A. 2001 *The Pony Express in American History*, Enslow Publishers.

McCullagh, D. and Broache, A. 2006 'US Government Web Tracking under Scrutiny', *ZDNet* 05/01/06, http://news.zdnet.co.uk/internet/0,1000000097,39245724-1,00.htm.

McCullagh, D. and Kawamoto, D. 2004 'Microsoft not out of Legal Woods Yet', CNet 11/10/05, see: http://news.com.com/Microsoft+not+out+of+legal+woods+yet/2100-1030_3-5893349.html.

McCurry, J. 2004 'Koreans Made Online Suicide Pact', *Guardian* 24/03/04, see: http://www.guardian.co.uk/korea/article/0,2763,1176482,00.html.

McDowell, M. 2004 'Understanding Denial-of-Service Attacks', US-CERT Security tip ST04-015, see http://www.us-cert.gov/cas/tips/ST04-015.html.

McGruff 2006 'McGruff Crime Dog Safety and Crime Prevention Products', see: http://www.mcgruff-safe-kids.com/ (viewed March 2006).

McGuire, D. 2005 'Security Concerns Boosted VeriSign's Dot-Net Bid', *Washington Post* 18/04/05, see: http://www.washingtonpost.com/wp-dyn/articles/A62302-2005Apr18.html (viewed March 2005).

McGuire, M. 2006 'Analysis of Suicide Websites', unpublished research.

McGurk, B.J., McEwan, A.W. and Graham, F. 1981 'Personality Types and Recidivism among Young Delinquents', *British Journal of Criminology*, 21 (2), 159–165.

McKenna, K. Y. A. and Bargh, J. A. 2000 'Plan 9 from Cyberspace: The Implications of the Internet for Personality and Social Psychology', *Personality and Social Psychology Review*, 4 (1), 57–75.

McKenzie, R.D 1924 'The Ecological Approach to the Study of the Human Community', *American Journal of Sociology*, 287–301.

McLuhan, M. 1962 *The Gutenburg Galaxy: The Making of Typographic Man*, 1st edn, University of Toronto Press; reissued by Routledge & Keagan Paul.

—— 1964 *Understanding Media – The Extensions of Man*, London: Routledge.

McLuhan, M. and Fiore, Q. 1967 *The Medium is the Massage: An Inventory of Effects*, San Francisco, CA: Hardwired.

—— 1997 *War and Peace in the Global Village*, Gingko Press.

McLynn, F. 1989 *Crime and Punishment in Eighteenth Century England*, London: Routledge.

McMahon, J. 2002 *The Ethics of Killing: Problems at the Margins of Life*, Oxford University Press.

McMillan, R. 2005 'Phony E-mail Tricks eBay', *PC World* 06/12/05, see: http://www.pcworld.com/article/id,123842-page,1/article.html.

McMullin, E. 1968 'What Do Physical Models Tell Us?' in van Rootselaar, B. and Staal, J.F. (eds) *Logic, Methodology and Science III*, Amsterdam: North Holland, pp. 385–396.

McNeill, J. and McNeill, W. 2003 *The Human Web: A Birds Eye View of World History*, New York: W.W. Norton.

McWilliams, B. 2003 'Blackmailed by Pop-up Advertising', *Wired* 22/09/03, see http://www.wired.com/news/business/0,1367,60509,00.html.

Mead, G.H. 1934 *Mind, Self and Society*, University of Chicago Press.

Mehta, A.K. and Shepherd, A. (eds) 2006 *Chronic Poverty and Development Policy in India*, London: Sage.

Meinong, A. 1904 'The Theory of Objects' in Meinong (ed.) *Untersuchungen zur Gegenstandtheorie und Psychologie*, Barth: Leipzig.

Melnick, A. 1973 *Kant's Analysis of Experience*, University of Chicago Press.

Merleau-Ponty, M. 1962 *Phenomenology of Perception*, trans. C. Smith, London: Routledge & Kegan Paul.

—— 1964 *The Primacy of Perception*, Northwestern University Press.

Messmer 1999 'Kosovo Cyber-war Intensifies: Chinese Hackers Targeting U.S. Sites, Government Says', CNN 12/05/99, see: http://www.cnn.com/TECH/computing/9905/12/cyberwar.idg/.

Metropolitan Police 2006a 'Internet Auction Fraud', see: http://www.met.police.uk/fraudalert/internet_auction.htm.

—— 2006b 'Computer Crime Unit Homepage', see: http://www.met.police.uk/computercrime/.

Meyrowitz, J. and Maguire, J. 1993 'Media, Place and Multiculturalism', *Society*, 30 (5), 41–48.

Michael, M. 1998 'Co(a)gency and the Car: Attributing Agency in the Case of the "Road Rage"' in Brenna, B., Law, J. and Moser, I. (eds) *Machines, Agency and Desire*, Oslo: TMV Skriftserie.

Mickelson, K. D. 1997 'Seeking Social Support: Parents in Electronic Support Groups' in Kiesler, S. (ed.) *Culture of the Internet*, Mahawah, NJ: Lawrence Erlbaum Associates, pp. 157–178.

Mikkelson, D. and Mikkelson, P. 2003 'Nigerian Scam', see http://www.snopes.com/crime/fraud/nigeria.asp.

—— 2005 'Ketchup Trousers', see: http://www.snopes.com/embarrass/email/ketchup.asp.

Mill, J. S. 1869 *On Liberty*, London: Longman Roberts & Green.

Mills, M. 2004 'The Security-Industrial Complex', Forbes.com available at http://www.forbes.com/business/forbes/2004/1129/044.html.

MIM 2006 Morality in Media (Inc), homepage, see: http://www.moralityinmedia.org/.

Mimoso, M. 2005 'ISP Liability II: Does the Bot Stop Here?', *Information Security News* 15/09/06, see: http://searchsecurity.techtarget.com/originalContent/0,289142,sid14_gci1124707,00.html?track=spyware.

Minois, G. 2001 *History of Suicide: Voluntary Death in Western Culture*, Baltimore, MD: Johns Hopkins University Press.

Minsky, M. 1980 'Telepresence', *Omni* (June), pp. 45–51.

Mirkovic, J., Dietrich, S., Dittrich, D. and Reiher, P. 2005 *Internet Denial of Service: Attack and Defense Mechanisms*, New York: Prentice Hall.

Mirzoeff, N. 2005 *Watching Babylon: The War in Iraq and Global Visual Culture*, London: Routledge.

Mitchell, J. 2002 *Concepts in Programming Languages*, Cambridge University Press.

Mitchell, W. 1995 *City of Bits*, Cambridge, MA: MIT Press.

Mnookin, J. 1996 'Virtual(ly) Law: The Emergence of Law in LamdaMOO', *Journal of Computer Mediated Communication*, 2 (1).

Mobile Life Youth Report 2006 'The Impact of the Mobile Phone on the Lives of Young People', Yougov published with Carphone Warehouse, available at http://www.yougov.com/archives/pdf/CPW060101004_2.pdf.

Monto, M. 2004 'Female Prostitution, Customers, and Violence', *Violence Against Women*, 10 (2), 160–188.

Moore, W. J. 1992 'Taming Cyberspace', *National Journal*, 24 (13), 745–749.

Moores, S. 2006 'Rising eCrime a National Threat – MP', *Netcrime Report*, see: http://netcrime.itproportal.com/?p=586.

Moravec, H. 2000 *Robot: Mere Machine to Transcendent Mind*, Oxford University Press.

Morgan Report 1991 *Safer Communities*, London: HMSO.

Morris, W. 1888 *A Dream of John Ball*, London: Reeves & Turner, reprint edition 2004, Kessinger Publishing.

Morley, D. 2000 *Home Territories: Media, Mobility and Identity*, London: Routledge.

Moschovitis, C. *et al.* 1999 *History of the Internet – 1843 to the Present*, Santa Barbara, CA: ABC-Clio Inc.

Mosco, V. 2004 *The Digital Sublime: Myth, Power & Cyberspace*, Cambridge, MA: MIT Press.

MPS 2007 'Police Boxes', *Metropolitan Police*, see http://www.met.police.uk/history/policebox.htm.

MSN 2006 'MSN Cyberbullying Report', available at: http://www.msn.co.uk/img/specials/portal/cyberbullying/cyberbullying_tall_revised3.pdf.

MSNBC 21/11/06 'Six Muslim Imams Removed from U.S. Airliner', see: http://www.msnbc.msn.com/id/15824096/.

Muir, H. 2005 'Far Right and Football Gangs Plot "Revenge" ', *Guardian* 15/07/05, see: http://www.guardian.co.uk/uk_news/story/0,3604,1529009,00.html.

Mulgan, G.J. 1991 *Communication and Control*, Cambridge: Polity Press.

Muncie, J. 2000 'Decriminalising Criminology', The British Criminology Conference: Selected Proceedings, Volume 3.

Murdoch, J. 1995 'Actor-networks and the Evolution of Economic Forms: Combining Description and Explanation in Theories of Regulation, Flexible Specialization, and Networks', *Environment and Planning A*, 27(5), 731–757.

Murphy, K. 1994 'Wharf TV Has Airtime For the BBC', *International Herald Tribune* 30/03/94, see: http://www.iht.com/articles/1994/03/30/wharf_1.php.

Murray, D. 2000 'Changing Technologies, Changing Literacy Communities', *Language Learning & Technology*, 4 (2), 43–58.

Musgrove, M. 2004 'Phishing' Keeps Luring Victims', *Washington Post* 21/10/05, available at: http://www.washingtonpost.com/wp-dyn/content/article/2005/10/21/AR2005102102113.html.

Myhill, A. and Allen, J. 2002 'Rape and Sexual Assault of Women: The Extent and Nature of the Problem – Findings from the British Crime Survey', Home Office Research Study 237, London: Home Office.

NAC 2007 Network Abuse Clearinghouse, homepage, see: http://www.abuse.net/.

Nakamura, L. 2002 *Cybertypes: Race, Ethnicity, and Identity on the Internet*, London: Routledge.

Nakashima 2007 'Harsh Words Die Hard on the Web', *Washington Post* 07/03/07, see: http://www.washingtonpost.com/wpdyn/content/article/2007/03/06/AR2007030602705.html.

Nanaveti, S., Thieme, M. and Nanavati, R. 2002 *Biometrics: Identity Verification in a Networked World*, New York: John Wiley.

NAS 2001 'Musculoskeletal Disorders and the Workplace', National Academy of Science, January 2001. see www.nationalacademies.org.

Nasar, J. and Fisher, B. 1993 ' "Hot Spots" of Fear and Crime: A Multi-method Investigation', *Journal of Environmental Psychology*, 13 (3), 187–206.

Naughton, P. 2006 'German Cannibal Jailed for Life after Retrial', Times Online 09/05/06, available at: http://www.timesonline.co.uk/article/0,,13509–2172012,00.html.

NCPCF, 2006 US National Coalition for the Protection of Children and Families, homepage, see: http://www.nationalcoalition.org/.

Neff, S.C. 2005 *War and the Law of Nations: A General History*, Cambridge University Press.

Negroni, C. 2004 'Fired Flight Attendant find Blogs can Backfire', *New York Times* 16/11/04, available at http://select.nytimes.com/gst/abstract.html?res=FA0716FD3E5B0C758DDDA80994DC404482.

Nelken, D. (ed.) 1994 *The Futures of Criminology*, London: Sage.

Nelson, T. 2007 Ted Nelson homepage, see: http://xanadu.com.au/ted/.

Neuman, J. 1997 'Live, from the Persian Gulf War', *Media Studies Journal*, pp. 27–130.

Newburn, T. 2003 'The Future of Policing' in Newburn, T. (ed.) *Handbook of Policing*, Cullompton, Devon: Willan, pp. 707–721.

Newman, G. (ed.) 1999 *Global Report on Crime and Justice*, Oxford University Press.

Newman, G. and Clarke, R. 2003 *Superhighway Robbery: Preventing E-commerce Crime*, Collumpton, Devon: Willan.

Newman, O. 1972 *Defensible Space: Crime Prevention Through Urban Design*, New York: Macmillan.

Newton, A. 2004 'Crime on Public Transport : "Static" and "Non-Static" (Moving) Crime Events', *Western Criminology Review*, 5 (3), 25–42.

New York Times 20/10/1862 'Brady's Photographs: Pictures of the Dead at Antietam'.

New York Times 31/08/06 'Laptop Slides Into Bed in Love Triangle', Correction.

Nicholson, J. 2005 'Flash! Mobs in the Age of Mobile Connectivity', *FibreCulture* 6, available at: http://journal.fibreculture.org/issue6/issue6_nicholson.html.

Niditch, S. 1993 *War in the Hebrew Bible: A Study in the Ethics of Violence*, Oxford and New York: Oxford University Press.

Nie, N., Hillygus, S. and Erbring, L. 2002 'Internet Use, Interpersonal Relations and Sociability: Findings from a Detailed Time Diary Study' in Wellman, B. (ed.) *The Internet in Everyday Life*, London: Blackwell.

NIEHS 1999 National Institute of Environmental Health Sciences: Report on Heath Effects from Exposure to Power-line Frequency Electric and Magnetic fields. *NIH Publication* No. 99–4493, P. O. Box 12233, Research Triangle Park, NC 27709.

Nietzsche, F. 1979 'On Truth and Lies in a Nonmoral Sense' in Breazeale, D. (ed.) *Philosophy and Truth: Selections from Nietzsche's Notebooks of the Early 1870's*, Humanities Press.

Nilson 2005 'Credit Card Fraud in the U.S.', *Nilson Report*, 830, March, see: http://nilsonreport.com/issues/2005/830.htm.

NISCC 2006 National Infrastructure Security Co-ordination Centre homepage, see http://www.uniras.gov.uk/niscc/index-en.html.

NNC 1818 New Newgate Calendar.

Norrgard, J. and Norrgard, M. 1998 *Consumer Fraud: A Reference Handbook*, ABC-Clio Inc.

Norris, C. and Armstrong, G. 1999 *The Maximum Surveillance Society: The Rise of CCTV*, Oxford and New York: Berg.

North Country Gazette 11/10/05 'AG, eBay Agree To Block Sale of Weapons to New Yorkers', see: http://www.northcountrygazette.org/articles/101105EbayWeapons.html.

Novak, M. 1992 'Liquid Architectures in Cyberspace' in Benedikt, M. (ed.) *Cyberspace, First Steps*, Cambridge, MA: MIT Press.

NSF 2000 *National Science and Engineering Indicators*, available at: http://www.nsf.gov/statistics/seind00/ *Cyberspace: First Steps*, MIT Press.

NSPS 2006 National Suicide Prevention Strategy, *Institute for Mental Health*, available at: http://kc.nimhe.org.uk/upload/suicide.pdf (viewed March 2007).

Nyberg, A. 1998 *Seal of Approval: The History of the Comics Code*, Jackson: University Press of Mississippi.

Oakeshott, M. 1990 *On Human Conduct*, Oxford University Press, Clarendon Press Paperbacks.

Observer 27/04/03 'Two-thirds of Organisations do not Report Computer Attacks'.

Observer 10/9/06 'How US Merchants of Fear Sparked a $130bn Bonanza'.

O'Donnell, T. 2005 'Executioners, Bystanders and Victims: Collective Guilt, the Legacy of Denazification and the Birth of Twentieth-century Transitional Justice', *Legal Studies*, 25 (4), 627–667.

Ofcom 2006 Company website at http://www.ofcom.org.uk.

Ogilvie, E. 2000 'Cyberstalking', *Trends and Issues in Criminal Justice*, No. 166, Camberra: Australian Institute of Criminology.

Ogrish 2005 Website discontinued. Archive content accessible at: http://web.archive.org/web/20060427143834/www.ogrish.com/index2.html.

Ohmae, K. 1995 *The End of The Nation State*, New York: The Free Press.

Ollmann, G. 2005 'The Phishing Guide: Understanding and Preventing Phishing Attacks', *Technical Info.*

Olsen, S. 2003 'Government Forms Cybersecurity Unit', *CNET* 06/06/03, see http://news.com.com/2100–1028_3–1014067.html.

Olzak, T. 2006 'Workplace Privacy Versus Computer Abuse Prevention: Which Prevails?', *Tech Republic*, see: http://articles.techrepublic.com.com/5100–10878–6144095.html.

O'Malley, P. (ed.) 1998 *Crime and the Risk Society*, Aldershot: Ashgate.

O'Neill, G. 1995 'The Social Construction of Economic Regeneration: An Examination of the Case of Derry', *Community Development Journal*, 30, 182–188.

O'Neil, M. 2003 'Establishing the Cost of Spam', CIO 13/10/03, see: http://www2.cio.com/analyst/report1840.html.

ONS 2003 'Value of E-trading by Non-financial Sector UK Businesses', *Survey of Business*, UK Office of National Statistics, available at: http://www.statistics.gov.uk/statbase/product.asp?vlnk=6645.

—— 2005a 'Labour Market Trends', October.

—— 2005b 'Labour Market Trends', 113, 10, October 2005, available at: http://www.statistics.gov.uk/downloads/theme_labour/LMT_Oct05.pdf.

—— 2006a 'Cancer Trends in England and Wales 1950–1999', see: http://www.statistics.gov.uk/StatBase/Product.asp?vlnk=4822.

—— 2006b 'Transport', Chapter 12, Social Trends, 236, available at: http://www.statistics.gov.uk/socialtrends36/.

Opennet Initiative 2004a 'Internet Filtering', see: http://www.opennetinitiative.org/modules.php?op=modload&name=Archive&file=index&req=viewarticle&artid=5 (viewed March 2007).

—— 2004b Internet Filtering Map, see: http://www.opennet.net/map/.

Orlowski, A. 2006 'SF Wi-Fi a "Dinosaur Deal" for the Poor', *The Register* 08/04/06, see: http://www.theregister.co.uk/2006/04/08/google_sf_muni_wifi/.

Owen, J. 2006 'Teens Die after Logging into "Suicide Chat Rooms" ', *Independent* 10/12/06, see: http://news.independent.co.uk/uk/this_britain/article1433393.ece.

Pahl, R. E. (ed.) 1988 *On Work: Historical, Comparative and Theoretical Approaches*, Oxford: Blackwell.

Painter, M. 2001 'Supervised Release and Probation Restrictions in Hacker Cases', Bulletin, *Computer Crime and Intellectual Property Section*, see: http://www.usdoj.gov/criminal/cybercrime/usamarch2001_7.htm.

Palast, G. 2002 *The Best Democracy Money Can Buy*, London: Pluto Press.

—— 2006 'Mexico and Florida Have More in Common Than Heat', *Guardian* 08/07/06, available at: http://www.guardian.co.uk/comment/story/0,,1815601,00.html.

Palen, R. 2003 *The Offshore World: Sovereign Markets, Virtual Places, and Nomad Millionaires*, New York: Cornell University Press.

Palti, L. 2005 'Measuring Hate', *Foreign Policy*, January/February, see: http://www.foreignpolicy.com/story/cms.php?story_id=2767.

Parameswaran, S. 2003 *Futures Markets, Theory and Practice*, New Delhi: Tata McGraw-Hill.

Park, R. and Burgess, E. 1921 *Introduction to the Science of Sociology*, University of Chicago Press.

Park, R., Burgess, E. and McKenzie, R. 1925 *The City: Suggestions for Investigation of Human Behavior in the Urban Environment*, University of Chicago Press (1967).

Park, W.K. 2005 'Mobile Phone Addiction' in Ling, R. and Pedersen, P. (eds) *Mobile Communications, Re-negotiation of the Social Sphere*, Springer, pp. 253–272.

Parker, D. 1976 *Crime By Computer*, New York: Charles Scribner's Sons.

Parry, E, and Bertillon, A. 2000 *Crime Album Stories: Paris 1886–1902*, Scalo.

Parsons, T. 1951 *The Social System*, New York: Free Press.

Paternoster, R. and Tittle, C. R. 1988 'Geographic Mobility and Criminal Behavior', *Journal of Research in Crime and Delinquency*, 25 (3), 301–343.

Pearlstein, D. 2004 'FCC Gives Seats to AT&T', *Washington Post*.

Peirce, C.S. 1933, *Collected Papers*, Cambridge, MA: Harvard University Press.

Perrons, D. *et al.* 2006 *Gender Divisions and Working Time in the New Economy*, Edward Elgar Publishing.

Pew Internet Project 2006 'Internet Activities', Pew Internet & American Life Project, December 2006 Survey, see: http://www.pewinternet.org/trends/Internet_Activities_1.11.07.htm.

PFIR 2000 'PFIR Statement on Internet Policies, Regulations, and Control', *People For Internet Responsibility*, see: http://www.pfir.org/statements/policies.

Phillips, B. 2005 *The Complete Book of Locks and Locksmithing*, New York: McGraw Hill.

PI 2004 'Threats to Privacy', *Privacy International*, PHR2004, available at: http://www.privacyinternational.org/article.shtml?cmd[347]=x-347–82586&als [theme]=Privacy%20and%20Human%20Rights&headline=PHR2004#_Toc497888016.

Pickering, S. and Weber, L. (eds) 2006 *Borders, Mobility and Technologies of Control*, Springer.

PID 2000 'Penndot Reaches Agreement with Information-services Provider', Commonwealth of Pennysylvania Insurance Department News Release, see http://www.ins.state.pa.us/ins/cwp/view.asp?A=11&Q=525493.

Pike, L. 1873–76 *A History of Crime in England*, Vols 1–3, London: Smith Elder & Co.

Pilger, J. 1999 'Blood on Our Hands', *Guardian* 21/01/99, see: http://www.guardian.co.uk/ethical/article/0,,191992,00.html.

Pinkerton, J. 1995 *What Comes Next: The End of Big Government – and the New Paradigm Ahead*, Hyperion Books.

Pinsent-Masons 2005 'The Laws Relating to Monitoring your Employees', Out-Law.com, see: http://www.out-law.com/page-449.

Pitts, V. 2003 *In the Flesh: The Cultural Politics of Body Modification*, Basingstoke: Palgrave.

Pitzke, M. 2005 'War Against Walmart: The Battle of the Compañeros', *Speigel* 16/11/05, see: http://www.spiegel.de/international/0,1518,385295,00.html.

Plato 1998 *Republic*, trans. Benjamin Jowett, Project Gutenberg Ebook, available at http://www.gutenberg.org/etext/1497.

Plunkett, J. 2005 'Bush Claim Revives Al-Jazeera Bombing Fears', *Guardian* 23/11/05, see: http://www.guardian.co.uk/Iraq/Story/0,2763,1648988,00.html.

Pollitt, M. 2007 'Getting the Blog Spammers to Hang Up their Affiliations', *Guardian*, 25/01/07, see: http://technology.guardian.co.uk/online/insideit/story/0,,1997650,00.html.

Polybius 1925 *Histories*, trans. W.R. Patton, Cambridge, MA: Harvard University Press.

Pool, I. 1983 *Forecasting the Telephone: A Retrospective Technology Assessment*, Ablex Publishing.

Popenoe, D. 1993 'American Family Decline, 1960–1990: A Review and Appraisal', *Journal of Marriage and the Family*, 55 (3), 527–542.

Poplin, D. E. 1979 *Communities: A Survey of Theories and Methods of Research*, New York.

Postman, N. 1985 *Amusing Ourselves to Death: Public Discourse in the Age of Show Business*, New York: Penguin.

Poster, M. 1995 *The Second Media Age*, Oxford: Blackwell.

—— 2001 *What's the Matter With the Internet?*, University of Minnesota Press.

Poulantzas, N. 1969 'The Problem of the Capitalist State', *New Left Review*, 58, 67–78.

—— 1978 *State, Power, Socialism*, Verso.

Poulsen, K. 2002 'Lawyers fear misuse of cyber murder law', *The Register* 25/11/02, see: http://www.theregister.co.uk/2002/11/25/lawyers_fear_misuse_of_ cyber/.

—— 2005a 'T-Mobile Hacker Pleads Guilty', *The Register* 17/02/05, see: http://www.theregister.co.uk/2005/02/17/t-mobile_hacker_pleads_guilty/.

—— 2005b 'Net Dust Storm Blows Into Tunis', *Wired* 15/11/05, see: http://www.wired.com/news/politics/1,69586-0.html.

Povey, D. (ed.) 2005 *Crime in Britain and Wales: Supp. Volume: Homicide and Gun Crime*, available at http://www.homeoffice.gov.uk/rds/pdfs05/hosb0205.pdf (viewed March 2007).

Powerwatch 2005 'Mobile Phones May Increase Brain Cancer', see: http://www.powerwatch.org.uk/news/20050901_neuroma.asp.

Pratley, N. 2005 'Tesco Faces Questions Over True Value of its Computer Vouchers' *Guardian* 07/03/05, see http://business.guardian.co.uk/story/0,,1431888,00.html.

Preece, J. 2000 *Online Communities: Supporting Sociability, Designing Usability*, Chichester: John Wiley & Sons.

Prescott, G. 1860 *History, Theory, and Practice of the Electric Telegraph*, Ticknor and Fields.

Presdee, M. 2000 *Cultural Criminology and the Carnival of Crime*, London: Routledge.

Price, M.E. and Verhulst, S. 2000 'In Search of the Self: Charting the Course of Self-regulation on the Internet in a Global Environment' in Marsden, C. (ed.) *Regulating the Global Information Society*. London: Routledge.

Prigogine, I. 1984 *Order Out of Chaos*, Bantam.

Pro-death Penalty 2006 Homepage, see: http://www.prodeathpenalty.com/ (viewed March 2006).

Provenzo, E. 1991 *Video Kids: Making Sense of Nintendo*, Harvard, MA: Cambridge University Press.

PRC 2006 'Employee Monitoring: Is There Privacy in the Workplace?, *Privacy Rights Clearinghouse Factsheet 7*, see: http://www.privacyrights.org/fs/fs7-work.htm.

—— 2007 'A Chronology of Data Breaches', *Privacy Rights Clearinghouse* (list updated twice weekly), see: http://www.privacyrights.org/ar/ChronDataBreaches.htm.

Punday, D. 2000 'Derrida in the World: Space and Post-deconstructive Textual Analysis', *Postmodern Culture*, 11, 1.

Putnam, R. 1996 'The Strange Disappearance of Civic America', *The American*

Prospect, vol. 7 no. 24, 1 December 1996. Online edition available at: http://www.prospect.org/print/V7/24/putnam-r.html.

—— 2000 *Bowling Alone: The Collapse and Revival of American Community*, New York: Simon & Schuster.

Quetelet, M.A. 1842 *A Treatise On Man*, Edinburgh: William and Robert Chambers.

Quine, W.V.O. 1960 *Word and Object*, Cambridge, MA: MIT Press.

—— 1969a 'Speaking of Objects' in *Ontological Relativity and Other Essays*, New York: Columbia University Press.

—— 1969b 'Natural Kinds' in *Ontological Relativity*, New York: Columbia University Press.

—— 1978 *The Web of Belief*, New York: Random House.

Radcliff, D. 2000 'A Case of Cyberstalking', CNN 31/05/00, see: http://archives.cnn.com/2000/TECH/computing/05/31/cyberstalking.idg/.

Radford, T. 2005 'Fraudsters Show How to Beat Chip and Pin', *Guardian* 05/09/05, see: http://www.guardian.co.uk/crime/article/0,2763,1562681,00.html.

Rawls, J. 1971 *A Theory of Justice*, Cambridge, MA: Harvard University Press.

Rawson, R.W. 1839 'An Inquiry into the Statistics of Crime in England and Wales', *Journal of the Statistical Society of London*, 2, 316–344.

Read, J. 2002 'A Fugitive Thread: The Production of Subjectivity in Marx', *The Warwick Journal of Philosophy*. 13, 126–144.

—— 2005 'From the Proletariat to the Multitude: Multitude and Political Subjectivity', *Postmodern Culture*, 15, 2.

Reclaim the Streets 1999/2003 Website: http://www.reclaimthestreets.net (no longer extant).

Redhead, S. 1995 *Unpopular Cultures: The Birth of Law and Popular Culture*, Manchester University Press.

Redwatch 2006 'Redwatch The Site the Traitors Love to Hate', see: http://www.redwatch.org.uk/index2.html.

Regan, T. 2005 'Iraq is Becoming "Free Fraud" Zone', *Common Dreams Newscenter*, see: http://www.commondreams.org/cgi-bin/print.cgi?file=/headlines05/0408-09.htm.

Register 5/11/03 'Bluetooth Boom Spawns "Bluejacking"', available at: http://www.theregister.co.uk/2003/11/05/bluetooth_boom_spawns_bluejacking/.

Register 18/08/06 'Cowboy DNA Testers Face Prison Terms'.

Reich, R. 1990 *The Work of Nations: Preparing Ourselves for 21 Century Capitalism*, New York: Knopf, New York.

Reid, T. 2007 'Internet Porn Pop-Ups Cost this Teacher her Job and her Freedom', *Times* 03/03/07.

Reno, J. 1997 'Keynote Address on High-tech and Computer Crime', *P8 Senior Experts' Group on Transnational Organized Crime* 21/01/97, Chantilly, Virginia, available at: http://www.cybercrime.gov/agfranc.htm.

—— 2000 'Statement before the United States Senate Committee', available at: http://www.usdoj.gov/archive/ag/testimony/2000/reno22900.htm.

Reuter Library Report 1991 'Nigeria Syas Millions of Dollars Extorted from Foreigners', 05/09/91.

Reuters 2003 'Cyber Blackmail Targets Office Workers', December.

Rheingold, H. 1993 *The Virtual Community*, Reading, MA: Addison Wesley.

—— 2002 *Smart Mobs: The Next Social Revolution*, Cambridge, MA: Perseus.

—— 2006 'Rethinking Virtual Communities' in Bell, D. (ed.) *Cybercultures: Cultural Concepts in Media & Cultural Studies*, London: Routledge, pp. 3–66.

Rice, X. 2007 'Kenya Sets World First with Money Transfers by Mobile', *Guardian* 20/03/07, see: http://www.guardian.co.uk/international/story/0,,2037930,00.html.

Richardson, T. 2001 'Ebone Warns of Euro Broadband Bottleneck', *The Register* 03/05/01, see: http://www.theregister.co.uk/2001/05/03/ebone_warns_of_euro_broadband/.

—— 2004 'ISPA Seeks Analysis of BT's "Cleanfeed" Stats', *The Register* 21/07/04, see: http://www.theregister.co.uk/2004/07/21/ispa_bt_cleanfeed/.

—— 2005 'Brits Fall Prey to Phishing', *The Register* 03/05/05, http://www.theregister.co.uk/2005/05/03/aol_phishing/ (viewed March 2007).

—— 2006 'Cleanfeed Working Overtime, Says BT', *The Register* 07/02/06, see: http://www.theregister.co.uk/2006/02/07/bt_cleanfeed_iwf/.

Ridings, C. and Gefen, D. 2004 'Virtual Community Attraction: Why People Hang Out Online', *Journal of Computer Mediated Communication*, 10 (1), Article 4, available at: http://jcmc.indiana.edu/vol10/issue1/ridings_gefen.html.

Rifkin, J. 1996 *The End of Work*, Tarcher/Putnam.

Robertson, R. 1992 *Globalisation: Social Theory and Global Culture*. London: Sage.

—— 2003 *The Three Waves of Globalization: A History of a Developing Global Consciousness*, London: Zed Books.

—— 2006 'NHTCU Disappears into SOCA', *Outlaw.com/The Register* 05/04/06, see: http://www.theregister.co.uk/2006/04/05/soca_launched/.

Robins, K. and Webster, F. 1986 *Information Technology: A Luddite Analysis*, Norwood, NJ: Ablex.

—— 1999 *Times of the Technoculture*, London: Routledge.

Rodrick, V. 'Government "Loses" 34,000 Passports', *Scotsman* 02/05/06, see: http://news.scotsman.com/topics.cfm?tid=428&id=653762006.

Rojas, R. and Hashagen, U. (eds) 2000 *The First Computers: History and Architectures*, Cambridge, MA: MIT Press.

Rojek, C. 2000 *Leisure and Culture*, Basingstoke: Palgrave.

Rolfe, B. 2005 'Building an Electronic Repertoire of Contention', *Social Movement Studies*, 4 (1), 65–74.

Ronson, J. 2005 'Who Killed Richard Cullen?', *Guardian* 16/07/05, see: http://money.guardian.co.uk/creditanddebt/creditcards/story/0,1456,1529921,00.html.

Rorty, R. 1979 *Philosophy and the Mirror of Nature*, Princeton, NJ: Princeton University Press.

Rose, N. 2000 'Genetic Risk and the Birth of the Somatic Individual', *Economy and Society*, 29 (4), 484–513.

Rosenberg, T. 2005 'The Great Firewall of China', *International Herald Tribune* 18/08/05, http://www.iht.com/articles/2005/09/18/opinion/edtina.php.

Rosenblaum 1971 'Secrets of the Little Blue Box', *Esquire*, October, available at: http://www.lospadres.info/thorg/lbb.html#journal.

Rosenbush, S. 2005 'The Birth of Murdoch.Com', *Business Week*, 16/08/05, see: http://www.businessweek.com/technology/content/aug2005/tc20050816_5029_tc024.htm.

Ross, A. 2006 'Jobs in Cyberspace' in Bell, D. (ed.) *Cyberspace Cultures*, London: Routledge, 377–400. Excerpt from his *Real Love*, London: Routledge, 1998.

Ross, I. and Ross, C. 1979 'Body Snatching in Nineteenth Century Britain: From Exhumation to Murder', *British Journal of Law and Society*, 6 (1), 108–118.

RSF 2006 Internet Annual Report, see: http://www.rsf.org/article.php3?id_article=17177&Valider=OK.

Ruggiero, V. 2004 'Organized and Corporate Crime in Europe: Offers that Can't Be Refused', *Crime, Law and Social Change*, 31 (2), 159–161.

Rusch, J. 2005 'The Rising Tide of Internet Fraud', *US Attorneys Bulletin*, Computer Crime & Intellectual Property Section, United States Department of Justice, see: http://www.usdoj.gov/criminal/cybercrime/usamay2001_1.htm.

Rushkoff, D. 1994 *Cyberia: Life in the Trenches of Hyperspace*, New York: Harper-collins.

Russell, R.V. 1996 *Pastimes – The Concept of Contemporary Leisure*. Dubuque, IA: Brown and Benchmark.

Ryan, M. 2003 'Internet Spawns "Flash Mobs" ', *Knight Ridder Tribune Business News* 11/07/03.

Ryle, S. 1999 'Insurers Balk at Risks of Phones', *Observer*, 11/04/99.

Sachdave, K. 2006 'Warning Over "Realistic" Fake Cash Machines', *Daily Mail* 14/03/06, see: http://www.dailymail.co.uk/pages/live/articles/news/news.html?in_article_id=379857&in_ page_id=1770&t=5&expand=true.

SafeSurf 2007 Homepage, see: http://www.safesurf.com/.

Safire, W. 2002 'You Are a Suspect', *New York Times*, 14/11/02, see: http://select.nytimes.com/gst/abstract.html?res=F00617F63D540C778DDDA80994DA404482.

Sahadi 2005 'Your Identity . . . For Sale', *CNN Money*, 09/05/05, see: http://money.cnn.com/2005/05/09/pf/security_info_profit/.

St Petersburg Times 31/05/05 'City Hall "Ignoring Rights" ', see: http://www.sptimesrussia.com/index.php?action_id=2&story_id=3681.

Sale, K. 1995 *Rebels Against the Future: The Luddites and Their War on The Industrial Revolution, Lessons for the Computer Age*, Reading, MA: Addison Wesley.

Sameer, H. 2004 'Perceptions of Local and State Law Enforcement Concerning the Role of Computer Crime Investigative Teams', *Policing*, 3: 341–357.

Sanders, D. 1991 'Collective Rights', *Human Rights Quarterly*, 13 (3), 368–386.

Sanders, T. 2006 'Extortionists Behind Million Dollar DoS Attack', *IT Week* 19/06/06, see: http://www.itweek.co.uk/vnunet/news/2148849/cyber-criminals-target-pixel.

Sandoval, G. 2006 'MPAA Accused of Hiring a Hacker', *CNet* 24/05/06, see: http://news.com.com/2100–1030_36076665.html?part=rss&tag=6076665&subj=news.

Sang-Hun, C. 2007 'Tracking an Online Trend and a Route to Suicide', *New York Times* 23/05/07, see: http://www.nytimes.com/2007/05/23/world/asia/23korea.html?ex=1180843200&en=de4cf6975a753328&ei=5070.

Sassen, S. 2001 *The Global City*, 2 edn, Princeton, NJ: Princeton University Press.

Saunders, R. 2005 'Happy Slapping: Transatlantic Contagion or Home-grown, Mass-mediated Nihilism?', *Static*, 01, available at: http://static.londonconsortium.com/issue01/saunders_happyslapping.pdf.

Saussure, F. 1983 *Course in General Linguistics*, trans. Harris, R., London: Duckworth.

Schaeffer, K.H. and Sclar, E. 1980 *Access for All: Transportation and Urban Growth*, Columbia University Press.

Schaefer, S. 2000 'Mobile Phones to Carry Government Health Warning',

Independent 27/11/2000, see: http://news.independent.co.uk/uk/health_medical/article151446.ece.

Schall, B.H. *et al.* 2002 *The Hacking of America*, Quorum Books.

Schaum, M. and Parrish, K. 1995 *Stalked: Breaking the Silence on the Crime of Stalking in America*, New York: Simon & Schuster.

Schecter, R. and Thomas, J. 2003 *Intellectual Property: The Law of Copyrights, Patents and Trademarks*, West Publishing Company.

Schelp, R.K. 1981 *Beyond Industrialisation: Ascendancy of the Global Service Economy*, New York: Praeger.

Schiavetta, S. and Komaitis, K. 2003 'ICANN's Role in Controlling Information on the Internet', Presentation, BILETA Conference: *Controlling Information in the Online Environment*, April, London, see: http://www.bileta.ac.uk/Document%20Library/1/ICANN%E2%80%99s%20Role%20in%20Controlling%20Information%20on%20the%20Internet.pdf (viewed February, 2006).

Schinkel, W. 2004 'The Will to Violence'. *Theoretical Criminology*, 8, 15–31.

Schlage's History of Locks 2007 see http://www.locks.ru/germ/informat/schlagehistory.htm.

Schmidt, C. and Darby, T. 2001 'The What, Why, and How of the 1988 Internet Worm', available at: http://snowplow.org/tom/worm/worm.html.

Schneier, B. 1996 *Applied Cryptography*, 2nd edn, New York: Wiley.

—— 1999 'Biometrics: Uses and Abuses', *Inside Risks* 110, *CACM*, 42, August, available at: http://www.schneier.com/essay-019.pdf.

—— 2003 *Beyond Fear: Thinking Sensibly About Security in an Uncertain World*, Copernicus.

—— 2004 'What's Wrong with Electronic Voting Machines?', *OpenDemocracy* 11/09/04.

—— 2006 'How Bot Those Nets?', *Wired* 27/07/06, see: http://www.wired.com/news/technology/0,71471-0.html.

Schoemaker, M. J. *et al.* 2005 'Mobile Phone Use and Risk of Acoustic Neuroma: Results of the Interphone Case-control Study in Five North European Countries', *British Journal of Cancer*, September, available from: http://www.nature.com/bjc/journal/v93/n7/abs/6602764a.html.

Schopenhauer, A. 1892 *Studies in Pessimism: A Series of Essays*, Sanders, T.B. (ed and trans), London: Swan Sonnenschein & Co. Pages cited from online version available at: http://www.uncharted.org/frownland/books/Schopenhauer/sip.html.

Schor, J. 1991 *The Overworked American*, New York: Basic Books.

Schrag, C. 1998 'The Self After Postmodernity', *Human Studies*, 21 (2), 197–206.

Schuler, D. 1996 *New Community Networks: Wired for Change*, New York: ACM Press.

Schultz, E. 2005 *Body Snatching: The Robbing of Graves for the Education of Physicians in Early Nineteenth Century America*, McFarland & Company.

Schwartz, E. 1996 *NetActivism: How Citizens Use the Internet*, Cambridge, MA: O'Reilly Media, Inc.

Schwartz, J. 2004 'Always on the Job, Employees Pay With Health', *New York Times* 05/09/04, available at: http://www.nytimes.com/2004/09/05/health/05stress.html?pagewanted=1&ei=5090&en=efbfdc03e549544d&ex=1252036800&adxnnl=1&partner=rssuserland&adxnnlx=1167484044-aIOCoZGPoPUshz0VK++/Vg.

SCIP 2006 Society of Competitive Intelligence Professionals Ethical Code, see: http://www.scip.org/2_ethicis.php (viewed January 2007).

Sclar, E. and Schaefer, K. 1980 *Access for All: Transportation and Urban Growth*, Columbia University Press.

Scoble, R. 2006 *Naked Conversations: How Blogs are Changing the Way Businesses Talk with Customers*, New York: Wiley.

Scott, J. 2000 *Social Network Analysis: A Handbook, Second Edition*, London: Sage.

Second Life 2007a 'Community: Fan Site Regulations', see: http://secondlife.com/community/fansites_regs.php.

—— 2007b 'Terms of Service', see: http://secure-web11.secondlife.com/corporate/tos.php.

Secure Computing 2007 Smartfilter Database, see: http://www.securecomputing.com/index.cfm?skey=86.

Sen, A. 1987 *The Standard of Living*, Cambridge University Press.

Sennett, R. 1988 *The Uses of Disorder*, New York: Random House.

—— 1989 'The Civitas of Seeing', *Places*, 5, 4.

—— 2000 *The Corrosion of Character: Personal Consequences of Work in the New Capitalism*, New York: W. W. Norton.

—— 2004 *Respect in a World of Inequality*, New York: W. W. Norton.

Seron, C. and Ferris, K. 1995 'Negotiating Professionalism: The Gendered Social Capital of Flexible Time', *Work and Occupations*, 22 (1), 22–47.

Seser, H. 2004 'Towards a Sociological Theory of the Mobile Phone', University of Zurich, Online Publications, see: http://socio.ch/mobile/t_geser1.htm.

Setright, L. 2004 *Drive On!: A Social History of the Motor Car*, Granta Books.

Shannon, C.E. and Weaver, W. 1949 *The Mathematical Theory of Communication*, London: University of Illinois Press, pp. 8–9.

Shapiro, A.L. 1999 *The Control Revolution: How the Internet is Putting Individuals in Charge and Changing the World We Know*, New York: PublicAffairs.

Shaw, C.R. and McKay, H.D. 1942 *Juvenile Delinquency in Urban Areas*, University of Chicago Press.

Shaw, D. 1997 'Gay Men and Computer Communication: A Discourse of Sex and Identity in Cyberspace' in Jones, S. (ed.) *Virtual Culture*, London: Sage, pp. 133–146.

Shaw, M. 2000 *Theory of the Global State: Globality as an Unfinished Revolution*, Cambridge University Press.

Shea D. A. 2003 'Critical Infrastructure: Control Systems and the Terrorist Threat,' *Congressional Research Service*, 1–14.

Sheeres, J. 2001 'The Condemned and Their Websites', *Wired* 12/06/00, see: http://www.wired.com/news/business/0,1367,44439,00.html.

Sheriff, L. 2000 'Wanted: One Contract Killer', *The Register* 1/12/00, available at: http://www.theregister.co.uk/2000/12/01/wanted_one_contract_killer/.

Sherman, L. 1998 'Policing; Evidence Based Policing', *Police Foundation*, July, available at: www.policefoundation.org/pdf/Sherman.pdf.

Sherman, L.W., Gartin, P.R. and Buerger, M.E. 1989 'Hot Spots of Predatory Crime: Routine Activities and the Criminology of Place', *Criminology*, 27, 27–55.

Shermer, M. 1995 'Exorcising Laplace's Demon: Chaos and Antichaos, History and Metahistory', *History and Theory*, 34 (1), 59–83.

Shifrin, T. 2006 'Westminster Plans Service Boost with Wi-Fi Network', *Computer*

Weekly, 1/12/06, see: http://www.computerweekly.com/Articles/2006/12/01/220304/westminster-plans-service-boost-with-wi-fi-network.htm.

Siddle, J. 2001 'Global Demand Fuels Human Organ Trade', BBC 28/06/01, see: http://news.bbc.co.uk/1/hi/world/asia-pacific/1412348.stm.

Silver, B. 2007 *Forces of Labor, Workers' Movements and Globalization Since 1870*, Cambridge University Press.

Simester, A. and Smith, A. T. H. 1996 *Harm and Culpability*, Oxford: Clarendon Press.

Simmel, G. 1902 'The Number of Members as Determining the Sociological Form of the Group', *American Journal of Sociology*, 8, 1–46, 158–96.

—— 1971 *On Individuality and Social Forms*, trans. Levine, D.N., University of Chicago Press.

—— 1978 *The Philosophy of Money*, trans. Bottomore, T. and Frisby, D., London: Routledge & Kegan Paul.

—— 1997 'The Sociology of Space' reprinted in Frisby, D. and Featherstone, M. (eds) *Simmel on Culture: Selected Writings*, London: Sage, pp. 137–170.

Simon, B. 2005 'The Return of Panopticism: Supervision, Subjection and the New Surveillance', *Surveillance & Society*, 3(1), 1–20.

Simonetti, E. 2007 'Diary of a (Fired) Flight Attendant', Ellen Simonetti blog, see: http://queenofsky.journalspace.com/.

Simpson, B. 2005 'Identity Manipulation in Cyberspace as a Leisure Option: Play and the Exploration of Self', *Information & Communications Technology Law*, 14 (2), 115–131.

Singel, R. 2003 'Pentagon Defends Data Search Plan', *Wired* 21/05/03, see: http://www.wired.com/news/privacy/0,1848,58936,00.html (viewed March 2007).

Singer, P. 1996 *Rethinking Life & Death: The Collapse of our Traditional Ethics*, New York: St Martin's Press.

Singh, S. 2000 *The Code Book: The Science of Secrecy from Ancient Egypt to Quantum Cryptography*, Anchor.

Sismondo, S. *et al.* (eds) 1999 *Modeling and Simulation*. Special Issue of *Science in Context*, 12.

Situ, Y. and Emmons, D. 1999 *Environmental Crime: The Criminal Justice System's Role in Protecting the Environment*, London: Sage.

Sklair, L. 2001 *The Transnational Capitalist Class*, Oxford: Blackwell.

Sklar, L. 1974 *Space, Time and Spacetime*, Berkeley: University of California Press.

Slapper, G.J. and Tombs, S. 1999 *Corporate Crime*, London: Addison Wesley Longman.

Slater, D. 1997 *Consumer Culture and Modernity*, Cambridge: Polity Press.

Slaughter, M.J. 2007 'Globalization and Declining Unionization in the United States', *Industrial Relations: A Journal of Economy and Society*, 46 (2), 329–346.

Slevin, J. 2000 *The Internet & Society*, Cambridge: Polity Press.

Smith, A. *et al.* 2005 'The Validity of Food Miles as an Indicator of Sustainable Development', DEFRA, ED50254, Issue 7, available at: http://statistics.defra.gov.uk/esg/reports/foodmiles/execsumm.pdf.

Smith, M. P. 2001 *Transnational Urbanism: Locating Globalization*, Oxford: Blackwell.

Smith, M. 2004 'Microsoft Settles Sendo "Tech Theft" Lawsuit', *The Register* 13/09/04, see: http://www.theregister.co.uk/2004/09/13/sendo_ms_settle/.

Smith, P. *et al.* 2006 'An Investigation into Cyberbullying, its Forms, Awareness and

Impact, and the Relationship Between Age and Gender in Cyberbullying', Anti Bullying Alliance, available at: http://www.anti-bullyingalliance.org.uk/down loads/pdf/cyberbullyingreportfinal230106_000.pdf.

Smith, R. 2004 'Criminal Forfeiture and Restriction-of-use Orders in Sentencing High Tech Offenders', *Trends & Issues in Crime and Criminal Justice*, 286, Australian Institute of Criminology, see: http://www.aic.gov.au/publications/tandi2/tandi286t.html.

—— 2007 'Biometric Solutions to Identity Related Cybercrime' in Jewkes, Y. (ed.) *Crime Online*, Collumpton: Willan, pp. 44–59.

Smith, R., Holmes, M. and Kaufmann, P. 1999 'Nigerian Advance Fee Fraud', *AIC Trends and Issues in Crime and Criminal Justice*, 121, Canberra: AIT.

Smith, R.G., Grabosky, P. and Urbas, G. 2004 *Cybercriminals on Trial*, Cambridge University Press.

Smith, S.J. 1986 *Crime Space and Society*, Cambridge University Press.

Smithers, L. 2001 'Vouchers for School Aid Under Attack', *Guardian* 06/12/01, see: http://education.guardian.co.uk/schools/story/0,,614090,00.html.

Sokoloff, W. 2001 'Politics and Anxiety in Thomas Hobbes's Leviathan', *Theory & Event*, 5, 1.

Solomon, E. 1997 *Virtual Money: Understanding The Power & Risks Of Money's High-speed Journey Into Electronic Space*, New York: Oxford University Press.

Solymar, L. 1999 *Getting the Message: A History of Telecommunications*, Oxford University Press.

Sontag, S. 2004 'Regarding the Torture of Others', *New York Times* 23/05/04, see: http://www.nytimes.com/2004/05/23/magazine/23PRISONS.html?pagewanted=1&ei=5007&en=a2cb6ea6bd297c8f&ex=1400644800&partner=USERLAND.

Sorokin, P. 1957 *Social and Cultural Dynamics: A Study of Change in Major Systems of Art, Truth, Ethics, Law and Social Relationships* (reprinted 1970), Boston, MA: Extending Horizons Books.

Sparks, R., Genn, H. and Dodd, D. 1977 *Surveying Victims*, New York: John Wiley.

Spinello, R. 2003 *Cyberethics: Morality and Law in Cyberspace*, Sudbury, MA: Jones and Barlett.

Spraggs, G. 2001 *Outlaws and Highwaymen: The Cult of the Robber in England from the Middle Ages to the Nineteenth Century*, Pimlico.

Spyblog 2006 'Cumulative Effect of the Computer Misuse Act Amendments in the Police and Justice Bill 2006, the Identity Cards Bill 2005 and the Terrorism Bill 2005', see: http://www.spy.org.uk/spyblog/2006/02/cumulative_effect_pajb_icb_tb.html#more.

Squires, P. 1999 'Criminology and the "Community Safety" Paradigm: Safety, Power and Success and the Limits of the Local', *The British Criminology Conferences: Selected Proceedings*, Volume 2. Editor: Mike Brogden.

Stalnaker, R. 1996 'Varieties of Supervenience', *Philosophical Perspectives*, 10, 221–241.

Standage, T. 1998 *The Victorian Internet*, Walker.

Starr, B. 2005 Website: U.S. Troops Traded Iraq Photos for Porn Access, CNN 28/09/05, see: http://www.cnn.com/2005/US/09/28/web.photos/index.html.

Steiner, G. 1975 *After Babel. Aspects of Language and Translation*, Oxford University Press.

Steiner, I. 2003 'MIT Student Sentenced for Selling Stolen Goods on eBay', *Auctionbytes* 06/01/03, see: http://www.auctionbytes.com/cab/abn/y03/m01/i06/s02.

Sterling, B. 1994 *The Hacker Crackdown: Law and Disorder on the Electronic Frontier*, New York: Bantam.

Stern, C. 2006 'The Coming Tug of War Over the Internet', *Washington Post* 22/01/06, see: http://www.washingtonpost.com/wp-dyn/content/article/2006/01/21/AR2006012100094.html.

Stevens, A. 2004 'The Treatment/Punishment Hybrid: Selection and Experimentation', paper presented at European Society of Criminology, 2004, available at: http://www.kent.ac.uk/eiss/Documents/pdf_docs/Alex%20Stevens%20Amsterdam%20paper.pdf.

Stewart, H. 2002 'Harms, Wrongs, and Set-Backs' in Feinberg, J. 'Moral Limits of the Criminal Law', *Buffalo Criminal Law Review*, 5, 47–67.

Stewart, I. 1929 'The International Telegraph Conference of Brussels and the Problem of Code Language', *The American Journal of International Law*, 23 (2), 292–306.

Stoker, C. 1993 'Telepresence in the Human Exploration of Mars: Field Studies in Analog Environments', NASA. Lewis Research Center, Vision 21: *Interdisciplinary Science and Engineering in the Era of Cyberspace*, pp. 23–34.

Stoll, C. 1995 *Silicon Snake Oil: Second Thoughts on the Information Highway*, New York: Doubleday.

Stop the War 2007 Stop the War Coalition, homepage, see: http://www.stopwar.org.uk/.

StopText Bully.com 2007 Homepage, see: http://www.stoptextbully.com/.

Stormfront 2006 See; http://www.stormfront.org/forum/.

Strasburger, V. C. and Donnerstein, E. 1999 'Children, Adolescents, and the Media: Issues and Solutions', *Pediatrics*, 103, 129–13.

Strawson, P. 1959 *Individuals*, London: Methuen.

Stroessen, N. 1995 *Defending Pornography: Free Speech, Sex and the Fight for Women's Rights*, New York: Scribner.

Sturgeon, T.J. 2002 'Modular Production Networks: A New American Model of Industrial Organization'. *Industrial and Corporate Change*, 11, 451–496.

Suárez-Orozco, M. and Qin-Hilliard, D.B. 2004 *Globalisation: Culture and Education in the New Millennium*, University of California Press.

Suler, J. 2004 'The Online Disinhibition Effect', *Cyber Psychology and Behaviour*, 7, 321–326.

Sullivan, L. 2004 'Legoland Uses Wireless And RFID For Child Security', *Information Week*, 28/04/04, see: http://www.informationweek.com/showArticle.jhtml?articleID=19202099.

Sunday Mirror 30/04/06 'SOCA Own Goal'.

Sunday Times 11/9/05 'Electrical Fields Can Make You Sick'.

Sunday Times 1/12/06 ' "NatWest Shuns ID Fraud" victims', see: http://business.timesonline.co.uk/article/0,,9558-2449436,00.html.

Sunstein, C. 2004 *Risk and Reason: Safety, Law, and the Environment*, Cambridge University Press.

Susskind, C. 1995 *Heinrich Hertz: A Short Life*, San Francisco, CA: San Francisco Press.

Sutherland, E. 2007 'Rivals Say Vista Still Violates EU', Ruling, *Internet News* 27/01/07, see: http://www.internetnews.com/bus-news/article.php/3656326.

Sutherland, E. and Cressey, D. 1960 *Principles of Criminology*, Philadelphia: J. B. Lippincott.

Sutherland, S. 1959 *Gold*, London: Thames and Hudson.

Sutter, G. 2003 'Penny Dreadfuls and Perverse Domains: Victorian and Modern Moral Panics' in Rowbotham, J. and Stevenson, K. (eds) *Behaving Badly*, Aldershot: Ashgate.

Sutton, M., Schneider, J. and Hetherington, S. 2001 'Tackling Theft with the Market Reduction Approach', *Crime Reduction Research Series* Paper 8, London: HMSO.

Sveningson, M. 2002 'Cyberlove: Creating Romantic Relationships in the Net' in Fornas, J. *et al.* (eds) *Digital Borderlands: Cultural Studies of Identity and Inter-activity on the Net*, New York: Peter Lang.

Symantec 2006 'Symantec Internet Security Threat Report', Volume X: September 2006, available at: http://www.symantec.com/enterprise/threatreport/index.jsp.

Szasz, T. 1999 *Fatal Freedom: The Ethics & Politics of Suicide*, Praeger Trade.

Tabb, W. 2000 'After Seattle, Understanding the Politics of Globalisation', *Monthly Review*, 51, 10, see: http://www.monthlyreview.org/300tabb.htm.

Tanner, B. 2006 'London to Install City-wide Wi-fi Network', DMEurope, 20/02/06, see: http://www.dmeurope.com/default.asp?ArticleID=13546.

Tarde, G. 1999 *Oeuvres de Gabriel Tarde*, Paris: Collections Les Empecheurs de Penser en Rond.

Taylor, C. 1992 *Sources of the Self: The Making of the Modern Identity*, Cambridge, MA: Harvard University Press.

Taylor, M. 2000 'Maintaining Community Involvement in Renegeration: What are the Issues?', *Local Economy*, 15, 251- 255.

Taylor, P. 1999 *Hackers: Crime in the Digital Sublime*, London: Routledge.

—— 2000 'Hackers – Cyberpunks or Microserfs? in Thomas, D. and Loader, B. *Cybercrime*, London: Routledge, pp. 35–55.

Taylor, P. and Jordan, T. 2004 *Hacktivism & Cyberwars; Rebels With a Cause?*, London: Routledge.

Taylor, T. 1999 'Life in Virtual Worlds: Plural Existence, Multimodalities, and Other Online Research Challenges', *American Behavioral Scientist*, 43, 3, November/ December, 436–449.

TDCJ 2007 'Death-Row Homepage', Texas Department of Criminal Justice, see: http://www.tdcj.state.tx.us/stat/deathrow.htm (viewed March 2007).

Telephony 1907 'The Burglar and the Telephone', 14 August (2), 921.

Tesco 2006 'Tesco Clubcards', see: http://www.tesco.com/clubcard/clubcard.

—— 2007 'Talking Tesco', see: http://www.tesco.com/talkingtesco/retailing/.

Thale, C. 2004 'Telegraph', *The Encyclopedia of Chicago*, The Newberry Library. see: http://www.encyclopedia.chicagohistory.org/pages/1235.html.

Thomas, D. 2002 'Cybercrime and the Politics of Hacking', in *Criminology, A Reader*, London: Sage, pp. 387ff.

Thomas, D. and Loader, B. (eds) 2000 *Cybercrime: Law Enforcement, Security and Surveillance in the Information Age*, London: Routledge.

Thomas, K. 1964 'Work and Leisure in Pre-industrial Society', *Past and Present*, 29, 50–62.

Thomas, M. 2005 'Selling Torture in London's Docklands', *New Statesman* 26/09/05, see: http://www.newstatesman.com/200509260018.

Thompson, B. 2003 'How Spammers are Targeting Blogs', BBC 24/10/03, see: http://news.bbc.co.uk/1/hi/technology/3210623.stm.
—— 2004 'Doubts over Web Filtering Plans', BBC 11/06/04, http://news.bbc.co.uk/1/hi/technology/3797563.stm.
—— 2006 'How to legislate Against Hackers', BBC 13/03/06, see: http://news.bbc.co.uk/1/hi/technology/4799338.stm.
Thompson, C. 2006 'Internet Experts Testify About Illegal Drug Sales', ASHP (American Society of Health-System Pharmacists), see: http://www.ashp.org/s_ashp/sec_news_article.asp?CID=167&DID=2024&id=13736.
Thompson, I. 2005 'Identity Theft – The Facts', *VNUnet*, 17/06/05, see: http://www.vnunet.com/computeractive/features/2138242/identity-theft-facts?page=2.
—— 2007 'Singapore Judge Sentences Teen for Wi-Fi Hack', *IT Week* 13/01/07, see: http://www.itweek.co.uk/vnunet/news/2172846/teen-gets-months-wi-hijack.
Thompson, S. 1999 'The Internet and its Potential Influence on Suicide', *Psychiatric Bulletin*, 23, 449–451.
Thornton, S. 1996 *Club Cultures: Music, Media and Subcultural Capital*, Middletown, CT: Wesleyan University Press.
Thrift, N. 1996 *Spatial Formations*, London: Sage.
Tifft, L. 1995 'Social Harm Definitions of Crime', *The Critical Criminologist*, 7 (1).
Time 25/03/91 'Rodney King Story'.
Times 01/03/06 'Credit Card debt in the UK'.
Times 11/07/06 'Passports in Circulation'.
Tiryakian, E. (ed.) 1994 'The 100th Anniversary of Sociology's First Classic: Durkheim's Division of Labour in Society', *Sociological Forum*, 9 (1).
Todd, B. 2000 'Distributed Denial of Service Attacks', Linuxsecurity note, available at: http://www.linuxsecurity.com/resource_files/intrusion_detection/ddos-whitepaper.html.
Todorov, T. 1975 *The Fantastic: A Structural Approach to a Literary Genre*, trans Howard, R., Ithaca, NY: Cornell University Press.
Tomlinson, J. 2000 'Proximity Politics', *Information, Communication & Society*, 3 (3), 402–414.
Tonnies, F. 1955 *Community and Association (Gemeinschaft und Gessellschaft)*, London: Routledge Kegan Paul (trans C.P. Loomis).
Toretti, 1978 *Philosophy of Geometry from Riemann to Poincare*, Kluwer.
Torpey, J. 2000 *The Invention of the Passport: Surveillance, Citizenship and the State*, Cambridge University Press.
Townsend, E. 2002 'E-Activism Connects Protest Groups', Hartford Courant 2/12/02, see: http://www.commondreams.org/headlines02/1204-01.htm.
Toynbee, P. 2001 'The Future is Tactical', *Guardian* 25/05/01, see: http://www.guardian.co.uk/comment/story/0,,496316,00.html.
Traynor, I. 2007 'Watchdog Attacks US Swoop for Bank Secrets', *Guardian* 2/02/07, see: http://www.guardian.co.uk/international/story/0,,2004128,00.html.
Trendle, G. 2002 'Internet Warfare in the Middle East: Cyberwar', *The World Today*, 58 (4), 7–8.
Troll Kingdom 2007 Forum, see: http://www.trollkingdom.net/forum/.
TUC 2000 'Surveillance at Work: Sensible Solutions', November, see: www.fipr.org/rip/SurveillanceAtWorkTUC.doc.
Turing, A.M. 1936 'On Computable Numbers, with an Application to the Entschei-

dungsproblem', *Proceedings of the London Mathematical Society*, series 2, 42 (1936–37), 230–265.

Turkle, S. 1995 *Life on the Screen: Identity in the Age of the Internet*, New York: Simon & Shuster.

—— 1997a 'The Myth of "Computer Addiction" ', Lecture, Cambridge Hospital Department of Psychiatry Grand Rounds.

—— 1997b 'Computational Technologies and Image of Self', *Social Research*, 64, 1093–1110.

Turow, J. 2006 'Cracking the Consumer Code: Advertisers, Anxiety and Surveillance in the Digital Age' in Haggerty, K. and Ericson R. (eds) *The New Politics of Surveillance and Visibility*, University of Toronto Press, pp. 279–307.

Twist, J. 2005 'Global Blogger Action Day Called', BBC 22/02/05, see: http://news.bbc.co.uk/1/hi/technology/4278241.stm.

UAF 2006 'Unites against Fascism' website, see: http://www.uaf.org.uk/US Congress 1955–56, 'Comic Books and Juvenile Delinquency', Senate Report, Senate Committee on the Judiciary.

UFPJ 2007 'United for Peace and Justice', homepage, see: http://www.unitedforpeace.org/index.php.

Underhill, G., Bieler, A. and Higgott R. 2000 *Non-state Actors and Authority in the Global System*, London: Routledge.

UNFPA 2006 'Selling Hope and Stealing Dreams: Trafficking in Women and the Exploitation of Domestic Workers', *State of World Population Report*, United Nations Population Fund, see: http://www.unfpa.org/swp/2006/english/chapter_3/.

UNISON 2004 'Bargaining on Privacy', Guidance Note, available at: http://www.unison.org.uk/resources/doc_view.asp?did=144 (viewed December 2006).

Urban Dictionary 2007 'Happyslap', see: http://www.urbandictionary.com/define.php?term=happy+slap&page=3, (viewed December 2006).

Urry, J. 1999 'Automobility, Car Culture and Weightless Travel: A Discussion Paper', *Lancaster University*, available at: http://www.comp.lancs.ac.uk/sociology/papers/Urry-Automobility.pdf.

—— 2001 'Globalising the Tourist Gaze', Paper Presentation, *Cityscapes Conference*, Graz, November.

USA Bureau of Statistics 1975 *Historical Statistics of the USA*, Washington, DC.

USA Today 28/04/06 'Sales in Body Parts top $6million'.

USA Today 02/05/07 'Study: Rising Number of Kids Exposed to Online Porn, and Most Say it Turns them Off', see: http://www.usatoday.com/tech/news/2007-02-05-kids-onlineporn_x.htm.

US Bureau of Census 1975 *Historical Statistics of the USA*.

—— 2004 *Annual Retail Trade Survey*, available at: http://www.census.gov/svsd/www.artstbl.html.

US-CERT 2005 'Cyber Security Bulletin SB2005: Summary', see: http://www.us-cert.gov/cas/bulletins/SB2005.html.

—— 2006 United States Computer Emergency Readiness Team homepage, see: http://www.us-cert.gov/aboutus.html.

US Congress 1955–56 'Comic Books and Juvenile Delinquency', Interim Report, see: http://www.geocities.com/Athens/8580/kefauver.html.

US Department of Justice 1998 'Incarceration Sentence Length', Bureau of Justice Statistics, available at: http://www.ojp.usdoj.gov/bjs/pub/html/cjusew96/isl.htm.

USDOJ 1998 Cross-national Studies in Crime and Justice, *US Department of Justice, Bureau of Statistics*, available at http://www.ojp.usdoj.gov/bjs/abstract/cnscj.htm.

USDOJ 1999 'Cyberstalking: A New Challenge for Law Enforcement and Industry – A Report from the U.S. Attorney General to the Vice President', US Department of Justice, see: http://www.usdoj.gov/criminal/cybercrime/cyberstalking.htm.

USDOJ 2004 'Homicide Trends in US', US Department of Justice, Bureau of Justice Statistics, available at: http://www.ojp.usdoj.gov/bjs/homicide/hmrt.htm.

—— 2007a 'Fraud Section', US Department of Justice, see: http://www.usdoj.gov/criminal/fraud.html.

—— 2007b 'Hate Crime: The Violence of Intolerance', http://www.usdoj.gov/crs/pubs/htecrm.htm.

USDOT 2004 Fatality Analysis Reporting System, US Department of Transport, *National Center for Statistics and Analysis*, see http://www-fars.nhtsa.dot.gov/.

USJFCOM 2006 'Command and Control of Space, Information Operations, Computer Network Operations Group', see http://www.jfcom.mil/about/experiments/mc02/concepts/c2space.htm.

USNPS 2006 'U.S. National Space Policy', Unclassified document superceding Presidential Decision Directive/NSC-49/NSTC-8, National Space Policy, available at: http://www.ostp.gov/html/US%20National%20Space%20Policy.pdf.

Vale, E. 1967 *The Mail Coach Men of the late Eighteenth Century*, Newton Abbot: David & Charles.

Valente, K. 2004 'Transgression and Transcendence: Flatland as a Response to A New Philosophy', *Nineteenth-Century Contexts*, 26 (1), 61–77.

Vanderlippe, J. 2002 'Everyday High Prices: A Comparison of Standard Supermarket Prices', CASPIAN, see: http://www.nocards.org/savings/regular_price_study.shtml.

van Creveld, M. 1991 *The Transformation of War*, New York: Free Press.

van der Meulen, N. 2006 'The Challenge of Countering Identity Theft: Recent Developments in the United States, the United Kingdom, and the European Union', International Victimology Institute Tilburg (INTERVICT), Commissioned by National Infrastructure Cyber Crime program (NICC), available at: http://www.tilburguniversity.nl/intervict/publications/NicolevanderMeulen.pdf.

van Dijk, J. 2005 *The Deepening Divide, Inequality in the Information Society*, London: Sage.

—— 2006 *The Network Society*, London: Sage.

Van Hove, L. 2000 'Electronic Purses: (Which) Way To Go?', First Monday, 5, 7, see: http://www.firstmonday.org/issues/issue5_7/hove/.

Van Schendel, W. and Abraham, I. (eds) 2005 *Illicit Flows And Criminal Things: States, Borders, And the Other Side of Globalization (Tracking Globalization)*, Indiana University Press.

van Swaaningen, R. 1999 'Reclaiming Critical Criminology: Social Justice and the European Tradition', *Theoretical Criminology*, 3 (1).

Varady, L., Beirne, P. and South, N. 2007 *Issues in Green Criminology: Confronting Harms Against Environments, Other Animals and Humanity*, Collumpton: Willan.

Vargas, J.A. 2006 'Virtual Reality Prepares Soldiers for Real War', *Washington Post* 14/02/06, see: http://www.washingtonpost.com/wp-dyn/content/article/2006/02/13/AR2006021302437.html.

Vasagar J. and Topham, G. 2000 'Cyber Sweet Nothing Goes Public via Loose Lips in City', *Guardian* 16/12/00, see: http://www.guardian.co.uk/uk_news/story/0,3604,412140,00.html.

VDC 2006 Virginia Department of Corrections, see: http://www.vadoc.state.va.us/ (viewed March 2006).

Verisign, 2005 'Versign Security Review', December, available at: http://www.verisign.com/Resources/Security_Services_Newsletters/The_VeriSign_Security_Review/page_dev036206.html.

Verma, A. and Lodha, S.K. 2002 'A Topological Representation of the Criminal Event', *Western Criminology Review*, 3(2).

Vermilya, I. 1917 'Amateur Number One', *QST*, February, 8–12, see: http://earlyradiohistory.us/1917tg.htm.

Verton, D. 2003 *Black Ice: The Invisible Threat of Cyber-terrorism*, Osborne/McGraw-Hill, U.S.

VGT 2007 'Virtual Global Taskforce Homepage', see: http://www.virtualglobaltaskforce.com/what_we_do.asp.

Vijayan, J. 2007 'Cambridge University Researchers Hack Chip-and-PIN Payment Terminals', *Computer World* 07/01/07, see: http://www.computerworld.com/action/article.do?command=viewArticleBasic&articleId=9007498.

Villeneuve, N. 2006 'The Filtering Matrix: Integrated Mechanisms of Information Control and the Demarcation of Borders in Cyberspace', *First Monday*, 11, 1, see: http://firstmonday.org/issues/issue11_1/villeneuve/index.html.

Violence Policy Center 2002 *When Men Murder Women: An Analysis of 2000 Homicide Data*, available at http://www.vpc.org/studies/dv5cont.htm.

Virilio, P. 1986 *Speed and Politics, An Essay on Dromology*, New York: Semiotext(e).

—— 1997 *Open Sky*, trans Rose, J., London: Verso.

—— 2002 *Crepuscular Dawn*, New York: Semiotext(e).

Virilio, P. and Lotringer, S. (1997 [1983]) *Pure War* (revised edition), New York: Semiotext(e).

Virilio, P. and Petit, P. 1999 *Politics Of The Very Worst*, New York: Semiotext(e).

Vise, D. 2005 'Microsoft Acts on Antitrust Ruling', *Washington Post* 25/01/05, see: http://www.washingtonpost.com/wp-dyn/articles/A34058-2005Jan24.html.

Visser, G. 2003 'Wireless Email Use Increases Corporate Productivity', *Smartmobs*, October, see: http://www.smartmobs.com/archive/2003/10/17/wireless_email_.html.

Vold, G.B. 1946 'Postwar Aviation and Crime', *Journal of Criminal Law and Criminology*, 35 (5), 297–310.

Volkmer, I. 1999 *News in the Global Sphere. A Study of CNN and Its Impact on Global Communication*, Luton, UK: University of Luton Press.

—— 2007 'Governing the "Spatial Reach"? Spheres of Influence and Challenges to Global Media Policy', *International Journal of Communication*, 1, 56–73, available at: http://ijoc.org/ojs/index.php/ijoc/article/viewFile/17/18.

Von Hirsch, A. 1987 'Guiding Principles for Sentencing: The Proposed Swedish Law', *Criminal Law Review*, 746.

Von Hirsch, A. and Jareborg, N. 1991 'Gauging Criminal Harm; A Living-standard Analysis', *Oxford Journal of Legal Studies*, II (1), 1–38.

Wakefield. J. 2002 'UK Snooping Laws in Disarray', BBC 18/01/01, see: http://news.bbc.co.uk/1/hi/sci/tech/1761974.stm.

—— 2005 'Wireless Hijacking under Scrutiny', *BBC* 28/07/05, see: http://news.bbc.co.uk/1/hi/technology/4721723.stm.

Walby, S. and Allen, J. 2004 'Domestic Violence, Sexual Assault and Stalking', *Findings from the British Crime Survey*, Home Office Research Study 276, London: Home Office, available at: http://www.homeoffice.gov.uk/rds/pdfs04/hors276.pdf.

Walker, L. 1989 'Psychology and Violence Against Women', *American Psychology*, 44 (4), 695–702.

——— 2006 'New Trends in Online Traffic', *Washington Post* 2006/03/04, available at: http://www.washingtonpost.com/wp-dyn/content/article/2006/04/03/AR20060 40301692.html.

Wall, D. 2001a *Crime and the Internet*, London: Routledge.

——— 2001b 'Cybercrimes and the Internet' in Wall, D. (ed.) *Crime and the Internet*, London: Routledge.

——— (ed.) 2003 *Cyberspace Crime*, Aldershot: Ashgate.

——— 2005 'Digital Realism and the Governance of Spam as Cybercrime', *European Journal on Criminal Policy and Research*, 10 (4), 309–335.

——— 2006 'Surveillant Internet Technologies and the Growth in Information Capitalism' in Haggerty, K. and Ericsson, R. (eds) *The New Politics of Surveillance and Visibility*, University of Toronto Press, pp. 340–362.

——— 2007 *Cybercrime: The Transformation of Crime In an Information Age*, Cambridge: Polity Press.

Wallace, P. 1999 *The Psychology of the Internet*, Cambridge University Press.

Wallach, L. and Sforza. M. 1999 *Whose Trade Organization? Corporate Globalization and the Erosion of Democracy*, Washington, DC: Public Citizen.

Wallman, S. (ed.) 1979 *Social Anthropology of Work*, London: Academic Press.

Wall Street Journal 03/05/05 'Choicepoint Breach'.

Walmsley, T. and Winters, A. 2002 'Relaxing the Restrictions on the Temporary Movement of Natural Persons: A Simulation Analysis', *Centre for Economic Policy Research Discussion Paper* No. 3719, available at: http://www.gtap.agecon.purdue.edu/events/Board_Meetings/2003/docs/Walmsley_Mobility .pdf (viewed September 2006).

Walters, R. 2005 'Eco-crime' in Muncie, J. and McLaughlin, E. (eds) *The Sage Dictionary of Criminology*, 2nd edn, London: Sage, pp. 146–148.

——— 2006 'Crime, Bio-agriculture and the Exploitation of Hunger', *British Journal of Criminology*; 46, 26–45.

——— 2007 'Food Crime, Regulation and the Biotech Harvest', *European Journal of Criminology*, 4 (2), 217–235.

Walton, G. 2001 'China's Golden Shield', *International Centre for Human Rights and Democratic Development*, available at: http://www.dd- rd.ca/site/_PDF/publications/globalization/CGS_ENG.PDF.

Wang, G., Hsinchun, C. and Atabakhsh, H. 2004 'Criminal Identity Deception and Deception Detection in Law Enforcement', *Group Decision and Negotiation*, 13, 111–127.

Ward, M. 2001a 'The Medium, the Message and the Money', BBC 08/01/01, see: http://news.bbc.co.uk/1/hi/sci/tech/1106700.stm.

——— 2001b 'US and Chinese Hackers Trade Blows', BBC 01/05/01, see: http://news.bbc.co.uk/1/hi/sci/tech/1306591.stm.

——— 2001c 'Tackling Computer Crime', BBC 19/04/01, see: http://news.bbc.co.uk/1/hi/sci/tech/1283866.stm.

—— 2005 'Sony BMG Repents over CD Debacle', BBC 09/12/05, see: http://news.bbc.co.uk/1/hi/technology/4514678.stm.

Warf, B. and Purcell, D. 2001 'The Currency of Currency: Speed, Sovereignty, and Electronic Finance' in Brunn, S. and Leinbach, T. (eds) *Worlds of Electronic Commerce: Economic, Geographical and Social Dimensions*, London: Wiley. pp. 223–240.

Warner, B. 2006 'Net Neutrality: A Tale of Two Internets', *Times Online* 12/07/06, see: http://technology.timesonline.co.uk/article/0,,20411-2267110,00.html.

Washington Post 20/07/04 'Web Child Porn Widespread in Britain', see: http://washingtontimes.com/upi-breaking/20040720–100609–2108r.htm (viewed October 2004).

Washington Post 2002–2005 'US v Microsoft 2001 Ruling', US v Microsoft Archive, see: http://www.washingtonpost.com/wp-dyn/business/specials/microsofttrial/.

Washington Times 05/04/04 'TV "Rewires" Developing Brains, Researchers Fear'.

Wasik, B. 2006 'My Crowd, Pt I', *Harpers*, March, except viewable at: http://harpers.org/MyCrowd_01.html   see: http://www.washtimes.com/national/20040405–120940–2602r.htm.

Waters, M. 1995 *Globalization*, London: Routledge.

Waters, R. 2006 'US Group Implants Electronic Tags in Workers', *Financial Times* 12/02/06, see: http://www.ft.com/cms/s/ec414700-9bf4-11da-8baa-0000779e2340.html.

Watts, J. 2005 'China's Secret Internet Police Target Critics with Web of Propaganda', *Guardian* 14/06/05, see: http://technology.guardian.co.uk/online/news/0,12597,1505988,00.html.

Waxman, H. 2006 'Evaluation of Halliburton's Performance under RIO2', *Committee of Oversight and Government Reform*, available at:.

Wearden, G. 2004 'ISPs Want More E-crime Protection', *ZdNet* 13/03/04, see: http://news.zdnet.co.uk/security/0,1000000189,39150624,00.htm
http://www. democrats.reform.house.gov/story.asp?ID=1032.

Webroot 2005 *Annual Report into Spyware*, February, see www.webroot.com.

Websense 23/05/05 'Coding Fraud Reported'.

Weegee 2000 *Weegee's New York Photographs, 1935–1960*, Te Neues Publishing Company.

Weimann, G. 2004 'Cyberterrorism: How Real is the Threat?', *United States Institute of Peace*, Special report, 119, available at: http://www.usip.org/pubs/specialreports/sr119.html.

—— 2006 *Terror on the Internet*, USIP Press Books.

Wellmann, B. 1988 *Social Structures: A Network Approach*, Cambridge University Press.

—— (ed.) 1999 *Networks in the Global Village: Life (in?/and) Contemporary Community*, Boulder, Co: Westview Press.

Wellman, B. and Gulia, M. 1999 'Virtual Communities as Communities: Netsurfers Don't Ride Alone' in Smith, M. and Kollock, P. (eds) *Communities in Cyberspace*, London: Routledge, pp. 167–194.

Wells, C. 2001 *Corporations and Criminal Responsibility* (2nd edn), Oxford University Press.

Wertham, F. 1954 *Seduction of the Innocent*, Toronto: Clarke, Irwin & Company.

Whimster, S. 2007 *Understanding Weber*, London: Routledge.

Whitaker 2006 'A Faustian Bargain? America and the Dream of Total Information Awareness' in Haggerty, K. and Ericson, R. (eds) *The New Politics of Surveillance and Visibility*, University of Toronto Press.

White, H., Boorman, S. and Breiger, R. 1976 'Social Structure From Multiple Networks: Blockmodels of Roles and Positions', *American Journal of Sociology*, 8, 1730–1779.

White, M. 2005 'Wars, Massacres and Atrocities of the Twentieth Century', see: http://users.erols.com/mwhite28/war-1900.htm.

Whitehead, P. and Gray, P. 1998 'Pulling the Plug on Computer Theft', *Police Research Series Paper 101*, Home Office Policing and Reducing Crime Unit.

White House 2006 'Fact Sheet: The President's Identity Theft Task Force', see: http://www.whitehouse.gov/news/releases/2006/05/20060510-6.html.

Whitehouse, P. 2005 'Internet Link to Suicide of Manager, 32', *Yorkshire Post* 9/11/05, see: http://www.yorkshiretoday.co.uk/ViewArticle2.aspx?SectionID=3593&ArticleID=1247967.

WHOA 2006 Online Harassment/Cyberstalking statistics, available at: http://www.haltabuse.org/resources/stats/index.shtml.

Wiener, N. 1954 *The Human Use of Human Beings: Cybernetics and Society*, New York: Doubleday Anchor.

Williams, D.J. 2006 'Different (Painful¡) Strokes for Different Folks: A General Overview of Sexual Sadomasochism (SM) and its Diversity', *Sexual Addiction & Compulsivity: The Journal of Treatment and Prevention*, 13 (4), 333–346.

Williams, M. 2001 'The Language of Cybercrime' in Wall, D. (ed.) *Crime & the Internet*, London: Routledge, pp. 152–166.

—— 2004 'Understanding King Punisher and his Order', *Internet Journal of Criminology*, see: http://www.cybercrimeresearch.com/Williams%20-%20Understanding%20King%20Punisher%20and%20his%20Order.pdf.

—— 2006 *Virtually Criminal*, London: Routledge.

Williams, R. 1981 'Communications Technologies and Social Institutions' in *Contact: Human Communications and its History*, ed Williams, R., Thames and Hudson.

Wilson, C. 2003 'Computer Attack and Cyber Terrorism: Vulnerabilities and Policy Issues for Congress', CRS Report for Congress, available at: http://www.fas.org/irp/crs/RL32114.pdf.

Wilson, P. 1988 *The Domestication of the Human Species*, New Haven, CT: Yale University Press.

Wilson, R. and Dissanayake, W. (eds) 1996 *Global/Local: Cultural Production and the Transnational Imaginary*, Duke University Press.

Winch, P. 1958 *The Idea of a Social Science*, London: Routledge & Kegan Paul.

Winn, M. 2002 *The Plug-In Drug: Television, Computers, and Family Life* (updated edition), London: Penguin.

Winsberg, E. 2003 'Simulated Experiments: Methodology for a Virtual World', *Philosophy of Science*, 70, 105–125.

Winseck, D. 2002 'Netscapes of Power', *Media Culture and Society*, 24 (6), 795–819.

Winston, B. 1998 *Media Technology and Society: A History from the Telegraph to the Internet*, London: Routledge.

Wired 15/02/06 'Tech's China Policy a "Disgrace" ', see: http://www.wired.com/politics/law/news/2006/02/70224 (viewed March 2007).

Wired Safety 2006 Homepage, see: http://www.wiredsafety.org/resources/biographies/parry/index.html (viewed December 2005).

Wise, J.M. 2000 'Home: Territory and Identity', *Cultural Studies*, 14 (2), 295–310.

Wiseman, T.P. 1970 'Roman Republican Road-Building', *PBSR*, 38, 122–152.

Wisemarketer 2006 Loyalty Marketing Feature Articles, see: http://www.thewisemarketer.com/features/index.asp.

Wittgenstein, L. 1953 *Philosophical Investigations (PI)*, Anscombe, G.E.M. and Rhees, R. (eds) Anscombe, G.E.M. (trans), Oxford: Blackwell.

—— 1972 *On Certainty*, Anscombe, G.E.M. and von Wright, G.H. (eds) Harper Perennial.

Wolf, G. 1995 'The Curse of Xanadu', *Wired* 3.06, see: http://www.wired.com/wired/archive/3.06/xanadu_pr.html.

—— 2004 'How the Internet Invented Howard Dean', *Wired*, 12.01, see: http://www.wired.com/wired/archive/12.01/dean.html.

—— 1994 'The (Second Phase of the) Revolution Has Begun', *Wired*, 2.10, see: http://www.wired.com/wired/archive/2.10/mosaic.html.

Wood, S. 2007 'Automated Behavior-based Interaction Customization for Military Command and Control', *Army Research Institute*, available at: http://www.research.ibm.com/iui-workshop/papers/wood-wiui04.pdf.

Woods, S. 2005 'Tesco Delivers Pledge to Cut Noise', *Richmond and Twickenham Times*, 04/02/05, see: http://www.richmondandtwickenhamtimes.co.uk/search/display.var.567363.0.tesco_delivers_pledge_to_cut_noise.php.

Woolf, B. 2001 *Loyalty Marketing: The Second Act*, Teal Books.

Wright, C. 1984 'Wittgenstein on the Foundations of Mathematics', *The Journal of Symbolic Logic*, 49 (4), 1415–1417.

Wright, C. and Jagger, G. (eds) 1999 *Changing Family Values: Difference, Diversity and the Decline of Male Order*, London: Routledge.

Wright, E. 2004 *Generation Kill*, Putnam Adult.

Wynn, E. and Katz, J. 1997 'Hyperbole over Cyberspace: Self presentation & Social Boundaries in Internet Home pages and Discourse', *The Information Society*, 13 (4), 297–328.

Yar, M. 2005 'The Novelty of "Cybercrime": An Assessment in the Light of Routine Activity Theory', *European Journal of Criminology*, 2 (4), 407–427.

—— 2006 *Cybercrime and Society*, London: Sage.

—— 2007 'Teenage Kicks or Virtual Villainy? Internet Piracy, Moral Entrepreneurship and the Social Construction of a Crime Problem' in Jewkes, Y. (ed.) *Crime Online*, Collumpton: Willan, pp. 95–108.

Young, G. 2004 'From Broadcasting to Narrowcasting to "Mycasting": A Newfound Celebrity in Queer Internet Communities', *Journal of Media & Cultural Studies*, 18 (1), 43–62.

Young, J. 1971 *The Drugtakers: The Social Meaning of Drug Use*, London: Paladin, p. 1.

—— 1999 *The Exclusive Society*, London: Sage.

—— 2007 *The Vertigo of Late Modernity*, London: Sage.

Zelizer, V. 1997 *The Social Meaning of Money*, Princeton, NY: Princeton University Press.

Zeller, T. 2006 'A New Campaign Tactic: Manipulating Google Data', *New York Times* 26/10/06, see: http://www.nytimes.com/2006/10/26/us/politics/

26googlebomb.html?ei=5090&en=cf9c1ba8c49c62b2&ex=1319515200&partner&pagewanted=print.

Zetter, K. 2004 'Germans Protest Radio-ID Plans', *Wired* 28/02/04, see: http://www.wired.com/techbiz/media/news/2004/02/62472.

—— 2005 'How Humble BBS Begat Wired World', *Wired* 08/06/05, see: http://www.wired.com/news/culture/0,67776-0.html?tw=wn_story_page_prev2.

Zizek, S. 1991 *For They Know Not What They Do*, London: Verso.

—— 2007 'Robespierre or the "Divine Violence" of Terror', *Lacan dot com*, available at: http://www.lacan.com/zizrobes.htm.

Znaniecki, F. 1925 *The Laws of Social Psychology*, University of Chicago Press.

Zone, H. 2007 'Digital Attacks Archive', see: http://old.zone-h.org/en/defacements.

Zoroya, G. 2003 'Return of U.S. War Dead Kept Solemn, Secret', *USA Today* 30/12/03, see: http://www.usatoday.com/news/nation/2003-12-31-casket-usat_x.htm.

Zuboff, S. 1988 *In the Age of the Smart Machine: The Future of Work and Power*, New York: Basic Books.

Zukin, S. 1995 *The Culture of Cities*, Oxford: Blackwell.

NOTE: All websites were last viewed between December 2006 and May 2007, unless otherwise stated.

Index